BRITISH THEATRE

*

VOLUME 2
1660 to 1895

Volume 2 of *The Cambridge History of British Theatre* begins in 1660 with the restoration of King Charles II to the throne and the re-establishment of the professional theatre, interdicted since 1642, and follows the far-reaching development of the form over two centuries and more to 1895. Descriptions of the theatres, actors and actresses, acting companies, dramatists and dramatic gen-res over the period are augmented by accounts of the audiences, politics and morality, scenography, provincial theatre, theatrical legislation, the long-drawn-out competition of major and minor theatres, and the ultimate revocation of the theatrical monopoly of Drury Lane and Covent Garden, initiating a new era. Chapters on two representative years, 1776 and 1895, are complemented by chapters on two phenomenal productions, *The Beggar's Opera* and *The Bells*, as well as by studies of popular theatre, including music hall, sexuality on the Victorian stage and other social and cultural contexts, and the appearance of new departures in dramatic art and the first glimmerings of modernism.

JOSEPH DONOHUE is Professor of English at the University of Mass-achusetts, Amherst. He is the author of books and articles on the British and Irish theatre and drama, including *Dramatic Character in the English Romantic Age* (1970), *Theatre in the Age of Kean* (1975), 'The London Theatre at the End of the Eighteenth Century' (1980), and 'Distance, Death and Desire in *Salome*' (1997). He is the editor, with Ruth Berggren, of *Oscar Wilde's* The Importance of Being Earnest: *A Reconstructive Critical Edition of the Text of the First Production, St James's Theatre, London, 1895* (1995).

THE CAMBRIDGE HISTORY OF
BRITISH THEATRE

General Editor
PETER THOMSON, *University of Exeter*

The Cambridge History of British Theatre provides a uniquely authoritative account of the turbulent and often troublesome public life of performance in Britain. Whilst making full use of new research in a subject that is at the centre of current concern, the essays are designed for the general reader as well as for the specialist. Each volume is fully illustrated. Together, they offer a comprehensive and comprehensible history of theatre, of which plays are a part but by no means the whole.

The Cambridge History of British Theatre, Volume 1: Origins to 1660
EDITED BY JANE MILLING AND PETER THOMSON

The Cambridge History of British Theatre, Volume 2: 1660 to 1895
EDITED BY JOSEPH DONOHUE

The Cambridge History of British Theatre, Volume 3: Since 1895
EDITED BY BAZ KERSHAW

THE CAMBRIDGE
HISTORY OF
BRITISH THEATRE

*

VOLUME 2
1660 to 1895

*

Edited by

JOSEPH DONOHUE

CAMBRIDGE
UNIVERSITY PRESS

PUBLISHED BY THE PRESS SYNDICATE OF THE UNIVERSITY OF CAMBRIDGE
The Pitt Building, Trumpington Street, Cambridge, United Kingdom

CAMBRIDGE UNIVERSITY PRESS
The Edinburgh Building, Cambridge, CB2 2RU, UK
40 West 20th Street, New York, NY 10011–4211, USA
477 Williamstown Road, Port Melbourne, VIC 3207, Australia
Ruiz de Alarcón 13, 28014 Madrid, Spain
Dock House, The Waterfront, Cape Town 8001, South Africa

http://www.cambridge.org

First published 2004

Printed in the United Kingdom at the University Press, Cambridge

Typeface DanteMT 10.5/13 pt.   System LaTeX 2$_\varepsilon$ [TB]

A catalogue record for this book is available from the British Library

ISBN 0 521 65068 2 hardback

Volume 1: Origins to 1660
ISBN 0 521 65040 2

Volume 3: Since 1895
ISBN 0 521 65132 8

Three-volume set:
ISBN 0 521 82790 6

Contents

Contents

Contents

Illustrations

Notes on contributors

The editor

JOSEPH DONOHUE is Professor of English at the University of Massachusetts Amherst, where he has taught dramatic literature since 1971. He is the author of books and articles on the British and Irish theatre and drama, including *Dramatic Character in the English Romantic Age* (1970), *Theatre in the Age of Kean* (1975), 'The London theatre at the end of the eighteenth century' (1980), and 'Distance, death and desire in *Salome*' (1997). He is the editor, with Ruth Berggren, of *Oscar Wilde's* The Importance of Being Earnest: *A Reconstructive Critical Edition of the Text of the First Production, St James's Theatre, London, 1895* (1995), which won the first Modern Language Association of America prize for a distinguished scholarly edition and the Barnard Hewitt Award of the American Society for Theatre Research for a distinguished work of scholarship. For a decade he was the editor of the Greenwood Press *Contributions in Drama and Theatre Studies* and, again for a decade, editor of the journal *Nineteenth Century Theatre*. His long-term research programme, *The London Stage 1800–1900: A Documentary Record and Calendar of Performances*, has published *English Drama of the Nineteenth Century: An Index and Finding Guide* (1985), edited by James Ellis, and has overseen the publication in print and microfiche and later as an Internet website of *The Sans Pareil Theatre and Adelphi Theatre (1806–1900)*, a daily calendar of performances compiled by a team of contributors and edited by Alfred L. Nelson and Gilbert B. Cross. His chapter 'Actors and Acting' appears in the *Cambridge Companion to Victorian and Edwardian Theatre* (2003).

The recipient of fellowships and awards from the National Endowment for the Humanities, the American Council of Learned Societies, the Folger Shakespeare Library, the William Andrews Clark Library, the Bibliographical Society of America, the American Society for Theatre Research and the University of Massachusetts Amherst, he is past president of the American Society for Theatre Research. He is editing a volume of plays for the Oxford English Texts edition of the complete works of Oscar Wilde and is at work on a book-length study of Wilde and the theatre. *Fantasies of Empire*, a study of the licensing controversy of 1894 surrounding the Empire Theatre of Varieties, Leicester Square, is forthcoming in 2004 from the University of Iowa Press.

The contributors

MARK S. AUBURN is Professor of English, Professor of Theatre and Dean of the College of Fine and Applied Arts at the University of Akron. His books include *Sheridan's Comedies*,

Drama through Performance and the Regents Restoration Drama edition of Dryden's *Marriage à la Mode.*

CHRISTOPHER BAUGH is Professor of Drama at the University of Kent, where he teaches scenography and scenographic history. He has published on the relationship between director and designer in *Garrick and Loutherbourg* and curated an exhibition on Edward Gordon Craig at the Victoria & Albert Theatre Museum. He reconstructed Clarkson Stanfield's 1831 Drury Lane diorama of Venice. He has written on more recent scenography and on Caspar Neher and Brecht in *The Cambridge Companion to Brecht.*

JIM DAVIS is Professor and Chair of Theatre Studies at the University of Warwick. Formerly he was Head of the School of Theatre, Film and Dance at the University of New South Wales. He has published widely on nineteenth-century British theatre, is the author of books on John Liston and on the Britannia Theatre, and is the co-author (with Victor Emeljanow) of *Reflecting the Audience: London Theatregoing, 1840–1880* (2001).

GÖREL GARLICK is a theatre and architectural historian specializing in theatre design. After a teaching career in the further education sector she is now an independent researcher and has contributed articles on theatre architecture and the English provincial theatre to various journals. She has recently completed an architectural biography of the nineteenth-century theatre designer Samuel Beazley.

DEREK HUGHES is Professor of English and Comparative Literary Studies at the University of Warwick. His many publications on Restoration drama include *Dryden's Heroic Plays* (1981), *English Drama, 1660–1700* (1996) and *The Theatre of Aphra Behn* (2001). He has also published on German Romantic opera and acted as general editor of *Eighteenth-Century Women Dramatists* (2001). He is currently preparing a study of representations of human sacrifice in western literature and opera.

ROBERT D. HUME is Evan Pugh Professor of English Literature at the Pennsylvania State University. He is author, co-author or editor of fourteen books, including *Dryden's Criticism* (1970), *The Development of English Drama in the Late Seventeenth Century* (1976), *Producible Interpretation* (1985), *Henry Fielding and the London Theatre, 1728–1737* (1988), *A Register of English Theatrical Documents, 1660–1737* (2 vols., 1991), *Reconstructing Contexts: The Aims and Principles of Archaeo-Historicism* (1999) and *Italian Opera in Late Eighteenth-Century London* (2 vols., 1995, 2001).

JOEL KAPLAN is Professor of Drama and Theatre Arts at the University of Birmingham. His publications include *Theatre and Fashion: Oscar Wilde to the Suffragettes* and *Look Back in Pleasure: Noel Coward Reconsidered* (both with Sheila Stowell) and *The Edwardian Theatre: Essays on Performance and the Stage* (with Michael R. Booth). He is presently at work on a stage history of *The Importance of Being Earnest* for Cambridge University Press and a critical edition of Wilde's society dramas for the Oxford University Press complete works of Oscar Wilde.

JOANNE LAFLER received her Ph.D. in dramatic art at the University of California, Berkeley. Currently affiliated with the Institute for Historical Study (San Francisco) and the National

Coalition of Independent Scholars, she has taught at the Davis and Santa Cruz campuses of the University of California. Her publications include *The Celebrated Mrs Oldfield: The Life and Art of an Augustan Actress* (1989), articles about theatrical performance at the Bohemian Grove and women's autobiography, and numerous reviews. She lives in Oakland, California.

EDWARD A. LANGHANS received degrees from Rochester, Hawaii and Yale. He is the author of *Restoration Promptbooks* (1981), co-author of *A Biographical Dictionary of Actors . . . 1660–1800* (16 vols., 1973–93), co-editor of *An International Dictionary of Theatre Language* (1985) and contributor to the *New Grove Dictionary of Opera* (1992) and the *Cambridge Companion to English Restoration Theatre* (2000). He was Chairman of Drama and Theatre at the University of Hawaii and is now Professor Emeritus.

DAVID MAYER studies nineteenth- and early twentieth-century British and American popular entertainment, especially melodrama and pantomime, and is the author of *Playing out the Empire: 'Ben-Hur' and Other Toga Plays and Films, 1888–1903* (1994) and other books and essays on these topics. He also investigates links between the Victorian and Edwardian stage and early (pre-1928) motion pictures. Co-editor of the journal *Nineteenth-Century Theatre and Film*, he is Emeritus Professor and Research Professor at the University of Manchester.

JUDITH MILHOUS is Distinguished Professor in the Ph.D. Program in Theatre at the Graduate Center of the City University of New York. Her interests include the finances of post-1660s theatre companies and the use of music and dance in the English theatre. Her most recent book, written with Gabriella Dideriksen and Robert D. Hume, is volume II of *Italian Opera in Late Eighteenth-Century London* (2001).

JANE MOODY is a lecturer in the Department of English and Related Literature at the University of York. She is the author of a monograph, *Illegitimate Theatre in London, 1770–1840* (2000). She has also contributed essays to a number of collections including *Women and Playwriting in Nineteenth-Century Britain*, edited by Tracy C. Davis and Ellen Donkin (1999), *Women in British Romantic Theatre*, edited by Catherine Burroughs (2000) and *The Cambridge Companion to Shakespeare on Stage*, edited by Stanley Wells and Sarah Stanton (2001).

KERRY POWELL is Professor of English at Miami University, Oxford, Ohio. His books include *Oscar Wilde and the Theatre of the 1890s* (1990) and *Women and Victorian Theatre* (1997). He is the editor of *The Cambridge Companion to Victorian and Edwardian Theatre* (2003). He is a contributor to *The Cambridge Companion to Oscar Wilde* and *The Cambridge Companion to George Bernard Shaw*, as well as to a collection of essays on the Salome legend forthcoming from the University of Chicago Press. He is currently working on a book on performativity, feminism and Oscar Wilde.

DAVE RUSSELL is Reader in the History of Popular Culture at the University of Central Lancashire. He is especially interested in the histories of popular music and sport and is the author of *Popular Music in England, 1840–1914: A Social History* (second edition, 1997) and *Football and the English* (1997). He is currently working on a book investigating the idea of the 'North' in the English national imagination from 1850 to the present.

RICHARD W. SCHOCH is Reader in Drama and Theatre History at Queen Mary, University of London. He is the author of *Shakespeare's Victorian Stage* (1998), *Not Shakespeare* (2002), *Victorian Theatrical Burlesques* (2003) and *Queen Victoria and the Theatre of her Age* (2004). He has received fellowships from the Folger Shakespeare Library, the Leverhulme Trust and the Stanford Humanities Center. His works have been shortlisted for the Barnard Hewitt Award and the Theatre Book Prize.

PETER THOMSON is Emeritus Professor of Drama at the University of Exeter and the general editor of the Cambridge History of British Theatre. His books include *Shakespeare's Theatre* (1984 and 1992), *Shakespeare's Professional Career* (1992), *On Actors and Acting* (2000) and three on Bertolt Brecht. He is an editor of the journal *Studies in Theatre and Performance* and of *Plays by Dion Boucicault* (1984) and an associate editor of the *New Dictionary of National Biography*.

CALHOUN WINTON is a native of Nashville, Tennessee, and received his bachelor's degree at Sewanee (the University of the South), a master's at Vanderbilt and the doctorate at Princeton. He has taught at Dartmouth College and the universities of Virginia, Delaware, South Carolina and, since 1975, Maryland, where he is now Professor Emeritus. His publications include a two-volume biography of Richard Steele and *John Gay and the London Theatre* (1993).

General preface

It is not the aim of the three-volume *Cambridge History of British Theatre* to construct theatrical history as a seamless narrative, not least because such seamlessness would be a distortion of the stop/start/try-again, often opportunistic, truth. Chronology has guided, but not bullied, us. The editorial privilege has been to assemble a team of international scholars able to speak with authority on their assigned (or sometimes chosen) topics. The binding subject is theatre, to which drama is a major, but not the only, contributor.

Each of the volumes includes some essays which are broad surveys, some which treat specific themes or episodes, some which are socio-theatrical 'snapshots' of single years and some which offer case studies of particular performance events. There is, of course, an underlying assertion: that a nation's theatre is necessarily and importantly expressive of, even when resistant to, the values that predominate at the time, but the choice of what to emphasise and what, however regretfully, to omit has rested with the volume's editor or editors. The aim has been to provide a comprehensive 'history' that makes no vain pretence to all-inclusiveness. The character of the volumes is the character of their contributors, and those contributors have been more often asked to use a searchlight than a floodlight in order to illuminate the past.

It is in the nature of 'histories' to be superseded. These volumes, though, may hope to stand as a millennial record of scholarship on a cultural enterprise – the British theatre – whose uniqueness is still valued. They are addressed to a readership that ranges from students to sheer enthusiasts. A 'history' is not the place for scholars to talk in secret to other scholars. If we have ever erred in that direction, it has been without the sanction of Victoria Cooper, who has shepherded these volumes through to publication with the generosity that is well known to all the authors who have worked with her.

Peter Thomson

Acknowledgments

Over the course of a long period of organizing, researching, writing and editing a volume covering 235 years of theatrical and dramatic activity, a number of debts and obligations have inevitably been incurred. It is a pleasure to thank here the many persons and institutions that have contributed in one way or another to the preparation and completion of this volume of the *Cambridge History of British Theatre*.

First and foremost thanks are due to the seventeen contributors whose chapters make up the majority of this volume of the *History*: Mark S. Auburn, Christopher Baugh, Jim Davis, Görel Garlick, Derek Hughes, Robert D. Hume, Joel Kaplan, Joanne Lafler, Edward A. Langhans, David Mayer, Judith Milhous, Jane Moody, Kerry Powell, Dave Russell, Richard W. Schoch, Peter Thomson and Calhoun Winton. Peter Thomson, in addition to providing a much needed chapter on the drama and theatre of the late Victorian period, as general editor of the *History* read and advised on every chapter in the book, including my own two introductions, and on the historical and theatrical chronologies as well, much to their benefit. I am deeply appreciative of the great collective knowledge of these contributors and grateful for their ability to distil it into a coherent series of chapters covering so many important aspects of this vast, unwieldy and challenging subject. I thank them also for their timeliness in responding to editorial queries and for their flexibility in adapting their vision of the topic at hand to the requirements of a work that had to be at once comprehensive and of reasonable length. Their own acknowledgments are not recorded here except by way of a general and cordial tribute, which I offer on their behalf, to libraries and individuals around the world that played a part in the making of this book.

I also wish to thank the staffs of the University of Massachusetts Amherst Library and Photographic Services; of Smith College Library, especially the Josten Library of Performing Arts; of Amherst College Library; of the Folger Shakespeare Library, especially Georgianna Ziegler, Head of Reference; of the

British Library; and of the Library of Congress. A special debt is owed the Harvard Theatre Collection, in particular its curator, F. Woodbridge Wilson; Annette Fern, Research and Reference Librarian; and Kathleen Coleman, Curatorial Assistant. This volume would be much the poorer without the research assistance they provided and without the presence of images, some never before published, gleaned from the holdings of this treasured resource.

At Cambridge University Press, Victoria L. Cooper, Commissioning Editor, and Paul Watt, Production Editor, piloted this work through to completion with expert knowledge, cheerfulness and aplomb. Hilary Hammond brought a sharp eye to the rigorous task of copy-editing, catching errors, omissions and inconsistencies that might otherwise have been perpetuated in print.

To this list I happily add a wide community of personal and profes-sional benefactors: my many colleagues in the American Society for Theatre Research, most especially Don B. Wilmeth and Thomas Postlewait; my col-leagues and friends in Valley Light Opera, particularly Bill Venman, with whom I have had the pleasure of performing almost all the musical works of Gilbert and Sullivan, an experience that has enlarged and enriched my love of the theatre; and uncounted students, graduate and undergraduate, taught since 1971 in courses in British and Irish drama at the University of Massachusetts Amherst, who have contributed in so many ways to my understanding and appreciation of the endlessly engrossing subject of British theatre.

Chronology

	Theatrical events	Political events
1642	Closing of the theatres in London.	
1649–60		The Commonwealth.
1653–8		The Protectorate under Oliver Cromwell.
1656	William Davenant produces *The Siege of Rhodes* at Rutland House, employing changeable scenery designed by John Webb, a pupil of Inigo Jones.	
1658	Davenant's *The Cruelty of the Spaniards in Peru* is produced at the Cockpit.	
1658–9	*The Siege of Rhodes* transfers to the Cockpit.	
1659		Birth of Henry Purcell, composer (d. 1695).
1660	Charles II agrees to bestow royal patents on Davenant and Thomas Killigrew permitting the establishment of two public playhouses and two acting companies and forbidding all competition; although the effect of the creation of theatrical monopoly is felt mainly in London, the act sets up the fundamental circumstances for	Restoration of Charles II to the English throne. Samuel Pepys begins diary (last entry 1669).

	theatrical production in England for almost the next two centuries, until the Theatre Regulation Act of 1843 abolishes patent rights.	
1661	Davenant's company, the Duke's Men, move to their new playhouse, the former Lisle's Tennis Court.	Coronation of King Charles II.
1662	The Smock Alley Theatre opens in Dublin; its patentee, John Ogilby, had in 1660 been reappointed to his old, pre-Interregnum post as Irish Master of the Revels.	Founding of the Royal Society.
1663	Killigrew's King's Company moves from the renovated Gibbons's Tennis Court, in Lincoln's Inn Fields, to the first theatre royal, in Bridges Street, Drury Lane. Katherine Philips's *Pompey*, a translation of Corneille's *La Mort de Pompée*, is brought out at Smock Alley, Dublin, the first play by an Englishwoman to be performed in public.	
1664	George Etherege's *The Comical Revenge; or, Love in a Tub*, appears at Lincoln's Inn Fields. Richard Flecknoe publishes *A Short Discourse of the English Stage*. Molière's *Tartuffe* is presented at Versailles and promptly banned.	
1665	King Charles employs John Webb to build a house in Whitehall for ballets, masques and plays.	

1666	Aphra Behn serves as an English spy in Antwerp; beginning in 1670 she will commence her career as a writer, the first to make a living as a professional woman of letters.	Great Fire of London. The plague.
1667		Birth of Jonathan Swift (d. 1745).
1670	Birth of William Congreve, dramatist (d. 1729).	
1671	Under Davenant family control (Davenant had died in 1668), a new theatre, costing some £9,000, opens in Dorset Garden. George Villiers, Duke of Buckingham, *The Rehearsal* (Theatre Royal in Bridges Street). Birth of Colley Cibber, actor, dramatist and manager (d. 1757). John Dryden, *Marriage A-la-Mode* (Lincoln's Inn Fields).	
1672	*25 January*: the theatre in Drury Lane burns. Thomas Shadwell, *Epsom Wells* (Dorset Garden). Birth of Joseph Addison, essayist and dramatist (d. 1719).	
1673	Elkanah Settle, *The Empress of Morocco* (Dorset Garden).	
1674	*March*: the new Drury Lane Theatre, built at a cost of £4,000, opens.	
1675	Elizabeth Barry begins her 35-year career as the most admired and highly paid actress of her age, with a wide range from comedy to tragedy but especially successful in the	Christopher Wren begins rebuilding St Paul's Cathedral (completed 1710).

latter, from ingenue to villainess.
Dryden, *Aureng-Zebe* (Drury Lane).
Thomas Shadwell, *The Libertine* (Dorset Garden).
William Wycherley, *The Country Wife* (Drury Lane).

1676   Sir George Etherege, *The Man of Mode; or, Sir Fopling Flutter* (Dorset Garden).
Wycherley, *The Plain Dealer* (Drury Lane).
Twelve of Aphra Behn's twenty plays will be produced beginning in this year and up through 1682.

1677   Aphra Behn, *The Rover: or, The Banish't Cavaliers* (Dorset Garden).   Marriage of Princess Mary, daughter of the Duke of York, with William of Orange, afterwards William III.
Dryden, *All for Love; or, The World Well Lost*, a rescension of Shakespeare's *Antony and Cleopatra* (Drury Lane).
Nathaniel Lee, *The Rival Queens; or, The Death of Alexander the Great* (Drury Lane).

1678   The Popish Plot, which began with information given by Titus Oates concerning an alleged plot for the murder of Charles and establishment of Roman Catholicism in England.

1679	Thomas Otway's *The History and Fall of Caius Marius* (Dorset Garden), one of numerous adaptations of Shakespeare in the Restoration period and one of many reflecting issues of contemporary politics, transposes the story of Romeo and Juliet to the first century BC and the civil war between Marius and Sulla, depicting Rome in the grip of two warring factions.	The Exclusion Crisis, occurring in the wake of the Popish Plot, centred on attempts by Protestant nobles to exclude the Catholic James, Duke of York, King Charles's brother, from the succession, in favour of Charles's bastard son James, Duke of Monmouth, a Protestant, and creating great unrest lasting until 1681.
1680	Thomas Otway, *The Orphan; or, The Unhappy Marriage* (Dorset Garden).	
1681	Nahum Tate's *The History of King Lear* (Dorset Garden) imposes a happy ending on Shakespeare's bleak tragedy: the Fool is eliminated altogether, Lear is restored to his throne, and Edgar and Cordelia marry at the end. Tate's *The Ingratitude of a Common-Wealth* (Drury Lane), a sensationalized treatment of Shakespeare's *Coriolanus*.	
1682	*November*: the United Company, formed from two separate companies, begins performing at Drury Lane. Thomas Otway, *Venice Preserv'd; or, A Plot Discover'd* (Dorset Garden).	

1683		Henry Purcell becomes court composer to Charles II. Discovery of Rye House Plot to assassinate Charles II and his brother.
1684	Joseph Ashbury, a member of the original Smock Alley company, becomes manager and patentee of the theatre, holding the post for some thirty-six years, until his death in 1720.	
1685		Death of Charles II; accession of James II. Duke of Monmouth's rebellion.
1687		Publication of Isaac Newton's *Principia mathematica philosophiae naturalis*.
1688		The Glorious Revolution brings William III to the English throne. King William III and Queen Mary (until 1694).
1689		Toleration Act grants freedom of worship to dissenters.
1690	Dryden's *Amphitryon*, staged at Drury Lane, is one of the few successful sex comedies of the 1690s, an indication that tastes and mores are changing in advance of Jeremy Collier's epochal diatribe against them, to be published eight years later.	John Locke's *Essay Concerning Human Understanding*. James II's invasion of Ireland thwarted at the Battle of the Boyne. Outbreak of War of Spanish Succession (ended 1713). Death of the exiled James II.
1694	Thomas Southerne's *The Fatal Marriage; or, The Innocent Adultery* (Drury Lane) and another of his tragedies, *Oroonoko*, produced in 1695 and	

based on a fiction by Aphra
Behn, among the best of the
period, will hold the stage for a
century or more, aided by a
succession of accomplished
tragediennes beginning with
Elizabeth Barry and also by
Garrick's canny adaptation of
the play in 1757 as *Isabella; or, The
Fatal Marriage*, whose title
character will become one of
Sarah Siddons's most
distinguished roles.

1694–5   During this season Betterton
and other principal players
withdraw from the United
Company, forming their own
shareholding enterprise and
undertaking a remodelling of
Lisle's Tennis Court in Lincoln's
Inn Fields; the new theatre
opens propitiously in April with
the première of Congreve's *Love
for Love*.

1696   Colley Cibber, *Love's Last Shift*
(Drury Lane).
Mary Pix's tragedy *Ibrahim,
Thirteenth Emperor of the Turks*
and her comedy *The Spanish
Wives*, both mounted at Drury
Lane, are the first of her six
tragedies and six comedies to be
produced over a decade of
remarkable accomplishment.
Delariviere Manley, *The Royal
Mischief* (Lincoln's Inn Fields).
Sir John Vanbrugh, *The Relapse;
or, Virtue in Danger* (Drury Lane).

1697	Congreve, *The Mourning Bride* (Lincoln's Inn Fields). Vanbrugh, *The Provok'd Wife* (Lincoln's Inn Fields).
1698	Jeremy Collier publishes *A Short View of the Immorality, and Profaneness of the English Stage*, a frontal assault on the unbridled sexual licentiousness which, in the view of Collier and, increasingly, of other observers as well, singles out contemporary dramatic comedy for opprobrium, even as the trend for writing this type of play is already noticeably waning. Mary Pix, *Queen Catharine; or, The Ruines of Love* (Lincoln's Inn Fields).
1699	Colley Cibber's redaction of Shakespeare's *King Richard III*, first performed this year, at Drury Lane, will become one of the sturdiest of star acting vehicles, lasting into the twentieth century.
1700	Congreve, *The Way of the World* (Lincoln's Inn Fields). Death of Dryden (b. 1631).
1702	Death of William III; succeeded by Queen Anne.
1703	Nicholas Rowe, *The Fair Penitent* (Lincoln's Inn Fields).
1704	Duke of Marlborough's victory at the Battle of Blenheim.

1705	Vanbrugh completes the new Queen's Theatre in the Haymarket, called the King's from 1714, when George I succeeds Anne, until 1837, when it becomes Her Majesty's Theatre on the accession of Victoria.
1706	George Farquhar, *The Recruiting Officer* (Drury Lane).
1707	Farquhar, *The Beaux' Stratagem* (Queen's).
1708	By this date Vanbrugh's Queen's Theatre has become exclusively an opera house.
1709	The triumvirate of Colley Cibber, Robert Wilkes and Thomas Doggett (Barton Booth from 1713) take over as principal actors and managers of Drury Lane, until 1732; they are joined in 1715 by Richard Steele, a valuable ally because of his court connections.
	Susanna Centlivre's *The Busie Body*, produced at Drury Lane, along with *The Wonder! A Woman Keeps a Secret* (1714) and *A Bold Stroke for a Wife* (1717), proves to be among the most successful and long-lasting of her seventeen plays.
	Nicholas Rowe publishes his edition, *The Works of Mr William Shakespeare*, in nine volumes.
1710	Death of Thomas Betterton, tragedian (b. 1635).

Act of Union unites Scotland with England. *(beside 1707)*

1709–12		Addison and Steele publish essays in the *Tatler* and the *Spectator*.
1710	Norwich magistrates, having continued to license visiting players, allow a six-week winter season presented by a troupe called the Duke of Norfolk's Servants – one of the early signs of a developing provincial theatre in England.	Birth of Thomas Arne, composer (d. 1778).
1711	George Frederick Handel's first London opera, *Rinaldo*, is performed at the Queen's.	Anthony Ashley Cooper, Third Earl of Shaftesbury, publishes *Characteristics of Men, Manners, Opinions and Times*.
1712	Ambrose Philips, *The Distrest Mother* (Drury Lane).	Birth of Jean Jacques Rousseau (d. 1778).
1713	Addison's *Cato*, long delayed in reaching the stage, receives a triumphant response at Drury Lane from Whig and Tory alike.	Treaty of Utrecht ends War of Spanish Succession. Birth of Denis Diderot (d. 1784).
1714	John Rich, son of Christopher Rich, manages a company performing in the third Lincoln's Inn Fields, rehabilitated by Christopher; it would not be until the next decade, when John Rich realizes the potential of pantomimes, that the theatre will begin to flourish. Susanna Centlivre, *The Wonder: A Woman Keeps a Secret* (Drury Lane). Rowe, *The Tragedy of Jane Shore* (Drury Lane).	Death of Queen Anne. George, Elector of Hanover, becomes George I of England.
1715		Death of Louis XIV, King of France. First Jacobite uprising on behalf of the 'Old Pretender',

		James Stuart, son of James II. Inauguration of the reading of the Riot Act at sites of public disorder.
1716		Birth of Lancelot 'Capability' Brown, landscape designer (d. 1783).
1717	John Gay, Alexander Pope and John Arbuthnot, *Three Hours After Marriage* (Drury Lane). Around this date John Rich begins introducing pantomimes at Lincoln's Inn Fields.	Handel's *Water Music* first played on the Thames.
1718	Centlivre, *A Bold Stroke for a Wife* (Lincoln's Inn Fields).	London Society of Antiquaries founded.
1719		Danie Defoe publishes *Robinson Crusoe*. Thomas D'Urfey publishes *Wit and Mirth; or, Pills to Purge Melancholy*. Handel becomes musical director of the Royal Academy of Music. Westminster Hospital founded in London.
1720	Another, smaller theatre in the Haymarket opens, called the Little Theatre. Steele's theatre criticism published in the *Theatre*, largely devoted to stating his case for patent rights at Drury Lane.	Birth of Charles Edward Stuart, the 'Young Pretender' (d. 1788). Bursting of the South Sea Bubble causes financial panic. Act grants British Parliament the right to legislate for Ireland.
1721	Edward Young, *The Revenge* (Drury Lane).	J. S. Bach composes the Brandenburg concertos.
1721–42		Administration of Sir Robert Walpole as English prime minister.

1722	Steele's *The Conscious Lovers*, intended by the author for the reformation of comedy by endorsing the role of sentiment in human relations and inspiring a 'joy too exquisite for laughter', appears at Drury Lane, to great applause, and goes on to become a staple of the comic repertory throughout the century.	Bach publishes first volume of *The Well-Tempered Clavier*. Thomas Guy, a London bookseller, promises £300,000 to found Guy's Hospital.
1723		Birth of Joshua Reynolds, English portrait painter (d. 1792).
1724		Captured again after four spectacular escapes from prison, the notorious highwayman Jack Sheppard is executed before a crowd reputedly numbering 200,000.
1725		Alexander Pope publishes his translation of *The Odyssey* and his edition of Shakespeare. Jonathan Swift publishes *Gulliver's Travels*.
1727		George II accedes to the English throne. Birth of Thomas Gainsborough, English painter (d. 1788).
1728	*10 January*: Cibber's *The Provok'd Husband*, altered from Vanbrugh, a critical failure but a popular success, runs at Drury Lane for a then unprecedented twenty-eight nights; during the Garrick period, 1747–76, the play would amass a total of 189	

performances at Covent Garden and Drury Lane.

29 January: John Gay's ballad opera *The Beggar's Opera*, an enormous hit and a telling satirical blast at Sir Robert Walpole, the prime minister, and the political establishment, begins a run at Lincoln's Inn Fields, lasting sixty-two nights in the first season.

1729	Thomas Odell opens a theatre in Ayliff Street, Goodman's Fields, Whitechapel. Gay's *Polly*, a sequel to *The Beggar's Opera*, fails to reach the stage, interdicted by the Lord Chamberlain.	
1730	Henry Fielding, *Tom Thumb: A Tragedy* (Little Haymarket).	Colley Cibber created Poet Laureate, to the disgust of Alexander Pope (and others).
1731	George Lillo's *The London Merchant; or, The History of George Barnwell* (Drury Lane), one of the sturdiest of perennial presences on the London stage, begins teaching its object lesson in honesty and resistance to temptation to entire generations of apprentices.	Hogarth's *The Harlot's Progress*. Birth of Erasmus Darwin, English scientist and poet (d. 1802).
1732	The first Covent Garden Theatre opens, designed by Edward Shephard; John Rich moves his company there from Lincoln's Inn Fields. Shephard is also the designer of a new theatre in Ayliff Street, Goodman's Fields, undertaken by Henry Giffard and his touring company.	Birth of Warren Hastings, English governor-general of India (d. 1818). Birth of Franz Joseph Haydn, Austrian composer (d. 1809).

1733		Pope's *Essay on Man*.
		Voltaire's *Lettres sur les anglais*.
		Birth of Johann Zoffany,
		German-English painter
		(d. 1810).
		Birth of Franz Anton Mesmer,
		Austrian physician (d. 1815).
1734	Francis Elrington, new manager	Birth of George Romney,
	of Smock Alley, had persuaded	English painter (d. 1802).
	Ireland's leading architect, Sir	Hogarth's *The Rake's Progress*.
	Edward Lovett Pearce, to design	
	a new theatre to be situated in	
	Aungier Street; it opens this	
	year with a production of	
	Farquhar's *The Recruiting Officer*.	
1734–5	In this season the young Peg	
	Woffington, daughter of a	
	Dublin bricklayer, began an	
	apprenticeship as an actress at	
	the Aungier Street Theatre,	
	soon graduating to central	
	comic roles.	
1735	Louis Duval erects a new theatre	
	on the old Smock Alley site,	
	competing with the Aungier	
	Street house for an audience	
	less broad than he had hoped.	
1736	Fielding's *Pasquin: A Dramatick*	Butler's *Analogy of Religion*.
	Satire on the Times produced at	Birth of James MacPherson,
	the Little Haymarket,	Scottish poet (d. 1796).
	becoming, along with *The*	Gin Act sparks off popular riots
	Historical Register, for the Year	in defence of cheap liquor.
	1736 (Little Haymarket, 1737),	Captain Porteous lynched by
	one of this author's sharpest	Edinburgh mob.
	attacks on Walpole; wildly	
	successful, it plays for over sixty	
	nights.	
	Aaron Hill's theatrical criticism	
	published as the *Prompter*.	

1737	Henry Carey's *The Dragon of Wantley*, a burlesque of Italian opera, is performed at the Little Haymarket. Passage of the Licensing Act (10 Geo. II, cap. xxviii), provoked by Fielding's dramatic satire and other barbs and led by Walpole, institutes extensive and long-lasting changes in theatrical and dramatic life by imposing a rigorous censorship on the performance of dramatic texts and even on prologues and epilogues, a power effectively exercised by a newly created Examiner of Plays in the office of the Lord Chamberlain, who may levy a fine of £50 for any unlicensed performance.	Death of Queen Caroline, Walpole's patron.
1738	Milton's masque *Comus* (Drury Lane), with music by Thomas Arne.	
1739		Handel's oratorios *Saul* and *Israel in Egypt* first sung, at the King's Theatre.
1740	*Lethe; or, Aesop in the Shades*, performed at Drury Lane for Giffard's benefit, establishes the young David Garrick as a master of afterpiece dramaturgy. Peg Woffington, having persuaded John Rich to hire her for Covent Garden at £9 per week, makes her début in November in the breeches role of Silvia in *The Recruiting Officer*. Colley Cibber publishes his memoir, *Apology for the Life of*	Samuel Richardson publishes his novel *Pamela; or, Virtue Rewarded*. Thomas Arne's masque *Alfred*, containing the chorus 'Rule, Britannia', is performed.

Colley Cibber, Comedian, and Late Patentee of the Theatre Royal, one of the most delightful and informative of all theatrical autobiographies.

1741	*19 October*: 'Mr Lydall' (David Garrick) performs Richard III at Goodman's Fields Theatre, London, under the subterfuge of 'A Concert of Vocal & instrumental Music'. *28 November*: Garrick's name appears in the Goodman's Fields bills for the first time. Garrick's afterpiece *The Lying Valet* (Goodman's Fields).	Jonathan Edwards's sermon 'Sinners in the Hands of an Angry God' at Enfield, Connecticut. Birth of Henry Fuseli, Swiss painter (d. 1825). Birth of Angelica Kauffmann, Swiss painter (d. 1807).
1742	Garrick signs articles of association to appear at Drury Lane beginning in the autumn season. Garrick and Peg Woffington travel to Dublin for the summer and appear in various roles at Smock Alley.	Handel's *Messiah* first performed in Dublin. Fall of Walpole.
1743	Garrick and Macklin lead a rebellion against Fleetwood's management at Drury Lane, reaching an uneasy truce in December that excludes Macklin.	Henry Fielding's picaresque novel *Jonathan Wild the Great*. Hogarth's *Marriage à la Mode*. George II leads the British Army to victory over the French at the Battle of Dettingen during the War of the Austrian Succession.
1744	Garrick mounts a new production of *Macbeth*.	
1745	The two debt-ridden Dublin companies agree to merge, under the managership of the Dublin-born actor Thomas	The Pretender, Charles Edward ('Bonny Prince Charlie'), lands in Scotland. Samuel Johnson's

	Sheridan; Smock Alley becomes the sole venue for drama.	'Observations on the Tragedy of *Macbeth*'.
1746		Battle of Culloden; defeat of the Pretender and his escape to France.
1747	*15 September*: Garrick, now manager of Drury Lane, having purchased a half-share and assumed control of day-to-day operations, reopens the theatre for the season, speaking a prologue written for the occasion by his friend and former teacher Samuel Johnson in which he famously explains, in a terse couplet, the essence of the player–audience relationship: 'The drama's laws, the drama's patrons give; / For we that live to please, must please to live.' In Edinburgh the actress Sarah Ward, supported by wealthy townspeople, succeeds in opening a theatre in the Canongate, officially dubbed Canongate Concert Hall, interspersing plays with concerts in order to circumvent the provision of the 1737 Licensing Act that any theatre in the kingdom must have either a royal patent or a licence from the Lord Chamberlain.	Samuel Johnson publishes his plan for a dictionary of the English language.
1748	Garrick's adaptation of *Romeo and Juliet* appears.	David Hume begins publication of his *Philosophical Essays Concerning Human Understanding* (completed in 1753).

1748–9		Treaty of Aix-la-Chapelle ends War of Austrian Succession. Bach's Mass in B minor (full version).
1749	Repaying a debt of friendship, Garrick mounts Samuel Johnson's sole tragedy, *Irene*, at Drury Lane, keeping it up for nine performances and so insuring Johnson the income from three author's nights (the third, sixth and ninth).	David Hartley publishes his *Observations on Man*. Handel's *Music for the Royal Fireworks*.
1750	The Bath brewer and chandler John Palmer's efforts to raise a subscription for a new theatre result in the opening of an unlicensed, unpatented theatre in Orchard Street; Palmer's son John will succeed in obtaining a patent for the theatre in 1768. Catherine Clive's *The Rehearsal; or, Bays in Petticoats*.	Thomas Gray's 'Elegy Written in a Country Church Yard'. The first Westminster Bridge completed in London.
1750–72		Diderot and D'Alembert's *Encyclopédie*.
1751	Birth of Richard Brinsley Sheridan (d. 1816).	By Act of Parliament the British calendar is altered, making 1 January the beginning of the new year.
1751–2	Peg Woffington is engaged by Thomas Sheridan to perform through the season at Smock Alley at a salary of £400, which then is doubled in the following two seasons.	
1752	A group of Birmingham businessmen build a theatre for the comedian Richard Yates, who has been performing with a	Adoption of the reformed (Gregorian) calendar.

company there during the
summer since the 1740s.

1753   The British Museum is granted
a royal foundation charter.

1755   Garrick engages Jean-Georges
Noverre, a Swiss ballet-master,
and his company on a one-year
contract; a riot breaks out at
Drury Lane on the fifth night of
the company's performance of
Noverre's ballet *The Chinese
Festival*, fomented by
irrepressible Francophobe
sentiment in the audience.
*A Narrative of the Life of
Mrs Charlotte Charke*, by Colley
Cibber's daughter, one of only a
few autobiographical accounts
of the lives of actresses in this
age, describes her career as an
actress-playwright-manager and
strolling player.

Samuel Johnson begins
publication of his *Dictionary
of the English Language*
(completed in 1773).
Birth of Marie Antoinette, later
Queen of France (d. 1793).

1756   After acting in London and
Dublin, Sarah Ward returns to
Edinburgh to perform Lady
Randolph, the tragic heroine of
a new play, *Douglas*, by the Revd
John Home (who in defying
Church of Scotland prohibitions
against writing for the theatre
foments a pamphlet war); it
scores a great success in
Edinburgh and, the next year, in
London, where Woffington and
Spranger Barry triumph in the
two main roles – which go on to
become staples of the tragic
actress's and actor's repertoire
into the nineteenth century.

Edmund Burke's *Origin of Our
Ideas of the Sublime and
Beautiful*.
Birth of Thomas Rowlandson,
English caricaturist (d. 1827).
Birth of Wolfgang Amadeus
Mozart (d. 1791).
Outbreak of Seven Years' War
(1756–63).

Garrick's *Catherine and Petruchio*, a redaction of *The Taming of the Shrew* as a three-act afterpiece, virtually eclipses Shakespeare's play for the rest of the century and well into the next.

1757   Birth of James Gillray, English caricaturist (d. 1815).

1758   Dublin-born actor and Covent Garden manager Spranger Barry opens a second theatre in Dublin, in Crow Street, competing once again for an audience of insufficient size.

1759   The British Museum is opened, at Montagu House.
Adam Smith publishes his *Theory of Moral Sentiments*.
Haydn completes his first symphony, in D major.
Capture of Quebec by General James Wolfe.

1760   Death of George II, succeeded by his grandson George III.
James MacPherson, writing as 'Ossian', commits one of the most famous forgeries in literary history by pretending to have discovered *Fragments of Ancient Poetry, Collected in the Highlands*.
Laurence Sterne publishes his charming, eccentric novel *Tristram Shandy*.
First exhibition of contemporary art, at the Royal Society of Arts, London.
The botanical gardens at Kew are opened.

1761	Revd Charles Churchill's theatrical verse satire *The Rosciad*.
1761–2	

Rousseau's *Emile* and *Nouvelle Héloise*.

1762	Thomas Arne, *Artaxerxes: An English Opera* (Covent Garden). Kane O'Hara, *Midas: An English Burletta* (Crow Street, Dublin; Covent Garden, 1764), often identified as the fountainhead of English burletta, a seemingly harmless *jeu d'esprit* which eventually provides a sure-fire means of circumventing the law forbidding performance of the legitimate drama, the province of the 'major' or patent theatres, at 'minor' houses.

Rousseau's *Social Contract*. Death of Beau Nash, dandy and master of ceremonies at Bath (b. 1674).

1763	Uprisings at both Covent Garden and Drury Lane over managements' attempts to abolish the practice of half-price admission; both managements soon capitulate to the non-negotiable demands of 'the drama's patrons'. In the *Public Advertiser* for 21 February Garrick, noting complaints of interruptions to the stage action, announces his intention of excluding self-privileging 'bucks' and all other persons from behind the scenes, that is, from the stage itself, compensating for the potential loss in revenue by increasing the seating capacity of Drury Lane Theatre; Covent

Peace of Paris concludes Seven Years' War, but its terms are widely criticized, most vehemently by John Wilkes in the notorious no. 45 of the *North Briton*.
Resignation of George III's favourite minister, the Earl of Bute.

	Garden follows suit almost immediately, and Garrick never has to retreat from this controversial policy.	
1764		Wilkes expelled from the House of Commons.
1765	A stone building is erected on the site of an older wooden structure dating from 1683, called Sadler's Wells, in Finsbury, where, for a long period beginning in the 1840s, soon after the Theatre Regulation Act of 1843, it becomes the home of well-produced Shakespearean drama under the artistic leadership of Samuel Phelps; reconstructed in 1879 by C. J. Phipps, it has lasted up to the present time.	Horace Walpole publishes a 'Gothic novel', *The Castle of Otranto*. Thomas Percy and William Shenstone publish a collection of ballads, *Reliques of Ancient English Poetry*.
1766	A royal patent granted to the actor Samuel Foote, in compensation for an unfortunate accident, establishes the Little Theatre in the Haymarket as the summer home of legitimate theatre. A theatre in King Street, Bristol, opens under the aegis of a group of local merchants. George Colman the elder and Garrick, *The Clandestine Marriage* (Drury Lane).	Oliver Goldsmith's novel *The Vicar of Wakefield*. Lessing publishes his *Laokoön*, countering Winckelmann's theories of art.
1767	The first patent for an Edinburgh theatre is granted to the proprietors of the Canongate, who promptly sell it	Rousseau settles in England and receives a pension from King George. Joseph Priestley publishes *The*

to the London actor David Ross, who proposes to build a new theatre.

History and Present State of Electricity.

1767–9 Lessing's *Hamburgische Dramaturgie.*

1768 Thomas Ivory, a wealthy builder and merchant, who eleven years earlier had built a theatre in Norwich, obtains a royal patent for it, and simultaneously buys up the Norwich Company of Comedians, along with their scenery and wardrobe and rights to the East Anglian touring circuit; the underwriting of this theatrical enterprise by a prosperous businessman instead of by theatrical managers sets an important precedent for similar ventures in other provincial cities.

Samuel Foote, *The Devil upon Two Sticks* (Little Haymarket). Horace Walpole, Earl of Orford, *The Mysterious Mother* (octavo, Strawberry Hill press), an unproduced, or 'closet', drama which sets an important precedent for the large wave of Gothic drama that will draw theatre audiences for the rest of the century and into the next.

Founding of the Royal Academy, London, Joshua Reynolds its first president. The first of the weekly numbers of the *Encyclopaedia Britannica* are published. Captain James Cook's first voyage.

1769 The Stratford Shakespeare Jubilee, Garrick's ambitious project to celebrate the bicentenary of the Elizabethan dramatist's birth, finally occurs

James Watt patents the steam engine. Richard Arkwright invents the water-powered spinning frame.

some five years late and is a costly failure because of torrential rain.

David Ross's Theatre Royal opens in Edinburgh.

The actor and provincial manager Tate Wilkinson obtains two royal patents for theatres, in York and Hull, and proceeds to build two theatres, in Hull and in Leeds, at the same time expanding his touring company's already considerable circuits.

The Adam brothers build the Adelphi in London.

Josiah Wedgwood founds a pottery works at 'Etruria', near Hanley, Staffordshire.

Old Blackfriars Bridge, London (destroyed 1860).

1770

James Hargreaves patents his spinning jenny.

1771   Richard Cumberland, *The West Indian* (Drury Lane), one of a series of plays in which Cumberland will pursue his programmatic intention of rescuing from disdain and disapproval certain fringe elements of society, of which *The Jew* (1794) is one of the more prominent and influential examples.

Benjamin West's painting *The Death of General Wolfe*.

First edition of the *Encyclopaedia Britannica*.

Warren Hastings appointed governor of Bengal.

1772   Arthur Murphy, *The Grecian Daughter* (Drury Lane), a late-century addition to the lengthy repertoire of plays with tearful, sorrowful heroines which emerged a century before.

Garrick brings out his production, extensively revised, of *Hamlet*, 'rescued', Garrick proudly claimed, 'from all the rubbish of the fifth act'.

Captain Cook's second voyage.

Financial crash.

The New Rooms in Tottenham Street, St Pancras, opens as a place of entertainment, principally concerts; by the early nineteenth century it is functioning as a theatre, continuing through a series of changes of name – Regency, West London, Queen's and Fitzroy – and in 1839 achieving the doubtful distinction of being known as the 'Dust Hole'; it is this unpromising venue which at length will be taken over by the Bancrofts, rehabilitated and renamed the Prince of Wales's Theatre and in which a series of plays with one-word titles by T. W. Robertson will breathe some new life into English drama; renamed once again as the Scala and then New Scala, the theatre will continue into the twentieth century until its demolition in 1969.

1773 Goldsmith's comedy *She Stoops to Conquer; or, The Mistakes of a Night* appears at Covent Garden. In the 1773–74 season Garrick hires the Alsatian painter Philippe Jacques de Loutherbourg, at a salary of £500, to design new kinds of scenery and take charge of stage decoration and machinery.

The Boston Tea Party, Massachusetts colonists' protest against duty on tea.

1774 A new theatre in Birmingham, in New Street, replaces the one built earlier for Richard Yates; it opens with Yates's excellent

Louis XVI becomes king of France.
Goethe's *The Sorrows of Young Werther*.

performance of Touchstone in
As You Like It.
Charles Dibdin, *The Waterman;
or, The First of August* (Little
Haymarket).
Hugh Kelly, *The School for Wives*
(Drury Lane).
William Richardson's
psychological study *Philosophical
Analysis and Illustration of Some of
Shakespeare's Remarkable
Characters* appears, an important
contribution to a growing shelf
of character criticism of
Shakespeare.

1775	Robert Adam undertakes a large-scale renovation of Drury Lane.	Birth of J. M. W. Turner, English painter (d. 1851). James Watt perfects his invention of the steam engine.

The amphitheatre of Astley's
Theatre, in Westminster Bridge
Road, Lambeth, is partially
covered over and furnished with
seating in this year; in 1782 the
ring is covered.
The first Manchester Theatre
Royal opens, under the
leadership of the managers of
the Liverpool Theatre Royal,
George Mattocks and Joseph
Younger.
Richard Brinsley Sheridan, *The
Rivals* (Covent Garden).
Sheridan, *The Duenna; or, The
Double Elopement* (Covent
Garden).

1775–83		War of Independence of British colonies in America.
1776	1o *June*: after reprising, over several weeks, the most	Adam Smith's *The Wealth of Nations.*

prominent roles of his career, including the exhausting but unavoidable Richard III, Garrick makes his farewell performance before the Drury Lane audience as Don Felix in Centlivre's *The Wonder*.

Sheridan and a coalition of investors acquire control of Drury Lane, and Sheridan becomes manager.

American Declaration of Independence.
Edward Gibbon begins publishing *The Decline and Fall of the Roman Empire* (completed in 1788).
Birth of John Constable, English painter and watercolourist (d. 1837).
Captain Cook's third voyage.

1777   Sheridan, *The School for Scandal* (Drury Lane).
Maurice Morgann publishes his *Essay on Sir John Falstaff*, extrapolating a coherent life of the character, almost as if he were a human being with a personality and a history, from the three Shakespeare plays in which his character figures.

After a victory at Ticonderoga, General John Burgoyne, having led an expedition from Canada into New York State, surrenders at Saratoga.

1778   William Larpent begins his long tenure as Examiner of Plays in the Lord Chamberlain's office.

France intervenes in the American War of Independence.

1779   In Sheridan's third season of management at Drury Lane, Loutherbourg stages a harlequinade, *The Wonders of Derbyshire*, a spectacular travelogue based on sketches he made the previous summer and notable for the accuracy of its depiction of the landscape of the Peak section of Derbyshire and, also, for its influence on the early development of pictorial realism.

Sheridan, *The Critic; or, A Tragedy Rehearsed* (Drury Lane). Death of Garrick.

1780	Hannah Cowley, *The Belle's Strategem* (Covent Garden).	Dunning's motion carried in the House of Commons: 'the influence of the crown has increased, is increasing and ought to be diminished'. Anti-Catholic Gordon Riots in London.
1781	After continual difficulties, David Ross sells both his Edinburgh theatre and its patent to John Jackson, who erects a theatre in Glasgow and divides his company's activities between the two cities. Loutherbourg opens his panoramic model theatre the *Eidophusikon* (literally translatable as 'same as nature machine'); exhibited in various rooms in the 1780s, it features in small scale a display of five scenes interspersed with transparencies, including Milton's Hell and a sunrise at Greenwich, which undergo frequent, unpredictable changes of light, making advantageous use of the brilliance of the newly invented Argand lamp, used at Drury Lane beginning in 1785. Charles Macklin, *The Man of the World* (Covent Garden). Schiller, *Die Raüber* (*The Robbers*), the most well known of the plays of the German *Sturm und Drang* (storm and stress) school.	Kant's *Critique of Pure Reason*. British Army surrenders at Yorktown.

1782   *10 October*: after a disappointing failure at Drury Lane in 1775–76, Sarah Siddons returns there in the title role of Garrick's redaction of Southerne, *Isabella; or, The Fatal Marriage*, registering the first of many triumphs as a tragic actress. The Royal Circus opens in Blackfriars Road, Lambeth, is burned and rebuilt twice, in 1799 and 1805, and after 1810, the amphitheatre and stables being removed, becomes known as the Royal Surrey Theatre, enjoying the distinction of the transpontine home of nautical melodrama, its single most memorable example of the form being Douglas Jerrold's *Black Eyed Susan*, produced in 1829; after a third fire in 1865 it emerges again, becoming for some time a music hall in the early twentieth century. Michael Novosielski reconstructs the King's Theatre in the Haymarket.

1783   John Philip Kemble scores a brilliant success as an unconventionally steady Hamlet at Drury Lane, subsequently proceeding to join his sister, Mrs Siddons, in a number of famous pairings of roles over the next three decades. Beaumarchais's *The Marriage of Figaro*.

    Peace of Versailles: peace treaty between the United States and Britain.

1784	Philip Astley constructs the first completely covered amphitheatre with a stage, on the site of the previous Astley's Theatre; it burns ten years later; a third theatre, opened in 1795, is destroyed by fire in 1803; still another fire in 1830 destroys the fourth theatre, which had opened in 1804; its replacement is in turn destroyed by fire in 1841; the sixth building on the site opens a year later and, defying the odds against conflagration, lasts through two reconstructions before being declared unsafe and demolished in 1893 – a textbook case for the indomitable optimism of theatrical entrepreneurs. Beaumarchais's comedy *The Marriage of Figaro*. Sir Joshua Reynolds paints Mrs Siddons as 'The Tragic Muse'.	The Brighton Pavilion, built for the Prince Regent, partly by John Nash.
1785	Loutherbourg collaborates with John O'Keeffe to create *Omai; or, A Trip Round the World*. Thomas Whately's posthumous *Remarks on Some of the Characters of Shakespeare*, another important contemporary contribution to Shakespearean character criticism.	The *Daily Universal Register* begins publication, becoming the *Times* in 1788.
1786	Richard Daly, granted an exclusive patent by the Irish Parliament, closes Smock Alley and makes Crow Street the Theatre Royal.	

Lt. Gen. John Burgoyne's *The Heiress* (Drury Lane), the best-known play of 'Gentleman Johnnie' Burgoyne, forced to surrender at Saratoga in 1777, who in later years pursued a second career as the author of a romantic melodrama, *Richard Coeur de Lion*, also produced at Drury Lane this year, as well as two comic operas and a comedy. Mozart's opera *The Marriage of Figaro* performed in Vienna.

1787   The actor John Palmer attempts to open a rival legitimate theatre, the Royalty, in Wellclose Square, but the managements of Drury Lane and Covent Garden thwart his efforts and he is forced to make it into a house for burletta and musical theatre. George Colman the younger's *Inkle and Yarico: An Opera*, with music by Samuel Arnold, opens at the Little Haymarket, bravely addressing the evils of the slave trade.
Elizabeth Inchbald's *Such Things Are* is produced at Covent Garden, one of several comedies of her making that stretch the limits of generic convention, reflecting a thoughtful independent-mindedness and determination that will distinguish her career as a dramatist, novelist and editor. Mozart's opera *Don Giovanni*

	receives its first performance in Prague.	
1788		Birth of George Gordon, Lord Byron, English poet and dramatist (d. 1824). Protracted trial of Warren Hastings opens.
1789	The King's Theatre burns and is replaced temporarily by the converted Pantheon, which itself burns down in January 1792 and is succeeded by the new and enlarged King's Theatre, Haymarket.	*14 July*: Attack on the Bastille in Paris; the French Revolution begins; Declaration of the Rights of Man. Mutiny on Captain Bligh's HMS *Bounty*. George Washington inaugurated as first president of the United States. Charles Burney completes his *History of Music*.
1790	The architect George Saunders publishes his landmark study *A Treatise on Theatres*, advocating the design of theatre auditoriums based on acoustical principles.	Edmund Burke's *Reflections on the Revolution in France*. Goethe's *Faust: A Fragment*.
1791	Charles Dibdin opens his small theatre, the Sans Souci, in the Strand, near Southampton Street, with the partly spoken, partly sung one-man entertainment by Dibdin, *Private Theatricals; or, Nature in Nubibus*. John O'Keeffe, *Wild Oats; or, The Strolling Gentleman* (Covent Garden). Boswell publishes his life of Johnson. Goethe is named director of the Weimar Court Theatre, a post he holds until 1817.	James Boswell publishes his *Life of Samuel Johnson*.

1

	Mozart's opera *The Magic Flute* is performed in Vienna.	
1791–4	Drury Lane is enlarged, to a design by Henry Holland, to a maximum auditorium capacity of over 3,600, its stage now measuring 83 feet wide, 92 feet long and 108 feet high.	
1792	Covent Garden is enlarged, also based on designs by Holland, to an auditorium capacity of 3,013, making it of even greater size than in its previous enlargement, in 1782, to a capacity of 2,170. Thomas Holcroft, *The Road to Ruin* (Covent Garden).	Abolition of the French monarchy; France declared a republic. Mary Wollstonecraft publishes *Vindication of the Rights of Women*. Birth of Percy Bysshe Shelley, English poet (d. 1822).
1793	Inchbald's comedy *Every One Has His Fault* is performed at Covent Garden.	Execution of Louis XVI; the Reign of Terror begins; Marat is murdered by Charlotte Corday; Queen Marie Antoinette is executed. William Godwin publishes his *Inquiry Concerning Political Justice*. Eli Whitney invents the cotton gin.
1794	James C. Cross, *The Purse; or, Benevolent Tar* (Little Haymarket). John Philip Kemble, *Lodoiska: An Opera* (Drury Lane).	Godwin publishes his radical novel *Things as They Are; or, The Adventures of Caleb Williams*. Habeas Corpus Act suspended in Britain (until 1804). Erasmus Darwin, *Zoonomia; or, The Laws of Organic Life*. Thomas Paine, *The Age of Reason*.
1795	Cumberland, *The Wheel of Fortune* (Drury Lane).	Warren Hastings is acquitted of high treason.

1796	Charles Dibdin closes the first Sans Souci in March and, transferring the entire interior of the theatre, opens its namesake in October in Leicester Place, Leicester Square.	
	Colman the younger, *The Iron Chest* (Drury Lane), based on Godwin's radical novel of 1794, *Things as They Are; or, The Adventures of Caleb Williams*.	
1797	Matthew Gregory Lewis, *The Castle Spectre* (Drury Lane), one of the most successful and sensational of English Gothic dramas.	
	August Wilhelm von Schlegel begins his translations of Shakespeare.	
1798	Kemble and Mrs Siddons join forces in a production of Benjamin Thompson's translation of a play by August von Kotzebue as *The Stranger*, Kemble in the title character and Mrs Siddons as the wayward, repentant wife Mrs Haller.	Horatio Nelson destroys the French fleet at Abukir Bay. T. R. Malthus's *An Essay on the Principle of Population*. Wordsworth's and Coleridge's *Lyrical Ballads*.
1799	Anne Plumptre publishes her translation *The Virgin of the Sun*, from an original by Kotzebue. *Pizarro*, Sheridan's adaptation of Kotzebue's *Die Spanier in Peru oder Rollas Tod*, is produced to great fanfare at Drury Lane and attains an extraordinary success both theatrically and politically.	The Rosetta Stone found near Rosetta, Egypt, making possible the deciphering of hieroglyphics.
1800	Joanna Baillie's tragedy *De Monfort*, produced at Drury Lane, the first to reach a theatre	

audience of her 'plays on the passions' – a systematic approach to the writing of tragedy and comedy, focusing on one predominant emotion at a time.

Thomas Morton, *Speed the Plough* (Covent Garden), in which, for the first time, a reference to 'Mrs Grundy' appears.

John Fawcett's *Obi; or, Three Finger'd Jack* (Haymarket), a play about the vengeance of a wronged slave, is one of several plays of the period raising the issue of the morality of slavery.

1801	Charles Isaac Mungo Dibdin, *The Great Devil; or, The Robber of Genoa* (Sadler's Wells; remounted at the Coburg in 1828).	The population of Britain reaches 10.4 million; of London, 864,000. The Union Jack becomes the official flag of the United Kingdom of Great Britain and Ireland.
1802	*13 November*: Holcroft's afterpiece, *A Tale of Mystery*, based on Pixérécourt's *Coeline; ou, L'Enfant du mystère*, appears at Covent Garden, the first play on the English stage to be advertised as a melodrama in the playbill. Having quarrelled with Sheridan, Kemble and his sister Mrs Siddons abandon Drury Lane for Covent Garden, in which Kemble purchases a sizable share, to be paid for over time from his earnings as manager and chief tragedian.	John Debrett publishes his *Peerage*, followed in 1808 by *Baronetage*.

1803	Colman the younger, *John Bull; or, The Englishman's Fireside* (Covent Garden). Cross, *Louisa of Lombardi; or, The Secret Nuptials* (Royal Circus). Frederick Winsor sets up an apparatus on the stage of the Lyceum in order to promote a new type of lighting, fuelled by gas.	The United States obtains from France a large tract of land stretching from the Gulf of Mexico to the north-west, including Louisiana, a transaction known as the 'Louisiana Purchase'.
1804		Napoleon proclaimed emperor of France. Beethoven's 'Eroica' Symphony. Alexander Hamilton, American revolutionary and statesman, is killed in a duel with Aaron Burr.
1805	Beethoven's opera *Fidelio* is performed in Vienna.	
1806	John Scott, a wealthy merchant, establishes the Sans Pareil Theatre in the Strand for his daughter, the enterprising actress, singer and dramatist Jane Scott; a great success, it changes hands in 1819, becoming the Adelphi Theatre. Philip Astley opens the Olympic Pavilion, in Newcastle Street and Wych Street, the Strand, as a venue for horsemanship and pantomime; undergoing frequent changes of name (Pavilion Theatre, Olympic Saloon, Astley's Middlesex Amphitheatre, Little Drury Lane Theatre), it will become the Olympic Theatre in 1813	Birth of John Stuart Mill, English philosopher (d. 1873).

(sometimes the Olympic New Theatre and the Royal Olympic Theatre) and the home of delightful extravaganzas by James Robinson Planché, performed by Eliza Vestris and her husband and leading man, Charles James Mathews; in 1849 a new theatre built on the site appears and lasts for forty years, to 1889, then making way for a third theatre, the New Olympic, under Wilson Barrett's management, which opens in 1890 but is forced to close in 1899 and is demolished in 1905 to make way for the Aldwych and Kingsway development scheme.

1807	Thomas John Dibdin, *Harlequin in his Element; or, Fire, Water, Earth and Air* (Covent Garden). Charles and Mary Lamb's *Tales from Shakespear Designed for the Use of Young Persons* is published.	Britain abolishes the slave trade. Streets in London begin to be lighted by gas.
1808	*20 September*: Covent Garden Theatre, built in 1732 and greatly enlarged in 1792, is destroyed by fire.	Slave trade ends in America. Birth of Honoré Daumier, French painter (d. 1879).
1809	*24 February*: Drury Lane, built in 1674 and rehabilitated and much enlarged in 1791–4, is destroyed by fire. The new Covent Garden Theatre, designed by Robert Smirke and rapidly constructed, opens, prompting the O. P. Riots, which go on for	

	sixty-seven nights, eventually forcing the theatre management to return to former prices for the pit, though not for the boxes.	
1811		George III insane, the Prince of Wales is appointed regent. Luddites destroy industrial machinery in the north of England.
1812	The new Drury Lane, designed by Benjamin Dean Wyatt, opens. Mrs Siddons retires from the stage in the character of Lady Macbeth, one of her most successful and deeply realized roles, in which she introduced startling innovations including new line readings and the setting down of her candle in the sleepwalking scene, the better to mime the washing of her hands.	United States declares war on Britain. Birth of Charles Dickens (d. 1870). Assassination of prime minister, Spencer Percival, in the House of Commons. Elgin Marbles are brought to England.
1811–13		Luddite risings in Britain.
1813	Samuel Taylor Coleridge, *Remorse* (Drury Lane). Isaac Pocock, *The Miller and his Men* (Covent Garden).	Westminster Bridge is illuminated by gas lighting. Jane Austen publishes *Pride and Prejudice*. Birth of Richard Wagner (d. 1883).
1812–14		War between United States and Britain.
1814	*26 January*: Edmund Kean makes his Drury Lane début as Shylock, to tremendous acclaim, making an instant convert of William Hazlitt, a reviewer of the event. The occupants of the fictional Mansfield Park, in Jane Austen's	

novel of that name, published
this year, attempt an amateur
production of Kotzebue's *Lovers'
Vows*.

1814–15		Congress of Vienna.
1815	At His Majesty's in the Haymarket, eight rows of 'stalls', individually upholstered seats, are introduced at the front of the pit, traditionally comprised of backless benches set out in rows.	Battle of Waterloo, in which the Duke of Wellington scores his most famous victory; Napoleon abdicates.

On opening night, 11 September,
at Covent Garden, the playbill
announces that 'The Exterior,
with the Grand Hall and
Staircase will be illuminated by
Gas.'

1816	William Charles Macready makes his London début, going on to become an indifferent manager first of one patent theatre and then the other, but in the process proving himself one of the great tragedians of the century, bringing deep, authentic feeling and a common touch to the traditional roles of the repertory and to the new characters written for his dark, brooding style by such eminent dramatists of the time as Edward Lytton Bulwer and James Sheridan Knowles.	Regular transatlantic service in sailing ships between Liverpool and New York. The Elgin Marbles are bought and ultimately placed in the British Museum. *Blackwood's Magazine* founded in Edinburgh.
1817	*Giovanni in London*, W. T. Moncrieff's burlesque of Mozart's opera, appears at the Olympic.	Opening of Waterloo Bridge, London.

John Philip Kemble retires from the stage in the role of Coriolanus.

The first recorded use of gas lighting on an actual stage occurs at the Lyceum, on 6 August, 'introduced over the whole Stage', the playbill announces; within a month the new technology has come into use at Drury Lane, where, the *Times* reported the next day, gas lights were employed 'on the sides of the stage, on which there are twelve perpendicular lines of lamps, each containing 18, and before the proscenium a row of 80', conferring much greater flexibility in intensity of illumination than the oil and candles in use up to this time, as well as eliminating the adverse effect of smoke and odour on the audience.

| 1818 | Hazlitt publishes *A View of the English Stage*, a collection of his reviews written over the period 1814–18 for the *Morning Chronicle*, the *Champion*, the *Examiner* and the *Times*. | The *Savannah* is the first steamship to cross the Atlantic, making the passage in twenty-six days. |

The Royal Coburg Theatre opens in the Cut, Lambeth, near the foot of Waterloo Bridge; in 1833 it is renamed the Royal Victoria and subsequently the Victoria; despite additional changes of name, its identity has long been fixed as the 'Old Vic'; having passed through several

The Peterloo 'Massacre' in Manchester.

incarnations, as a theatre, a temperance tavern, a variety house, and again a theatre, it will become for a period in the late twentieth century the temporary home of the National Theatre, surviving to this day as one of the longest lived of all London theatre buildings.

1819   The Sans Pareil is sold to Willis Jones and James T. G. Rodwell, who rename it the Adelphi. Walter Scott publishes his 'Essay on the Drama', in which he identifies three factors of central concern in the current malaise: the exorbitant size of theatre buildings, conditions hostile to both performers and dramatists, and the systematic toleration of prostitutes.

Birth of John Ruskin, English art critic (d. 1900).
Burlington Arcade opens in Piccadilly, London.

1820   Eliza Vestris makes her Drury Lane début singing the role of Lilla in James Cobb's 1791 comic opera *The Siege of Belgrade* and goes on to become one of the most delightful and influential singers and actresses of the time, known especially for her breeches roles, as well as an important entrepreneur admired for her beautiful mountings of burletta and extravaganza at the Olympic. James Sheridan Knowles's domestic tragedy *Virginius; or, The Liberation of Rome*, produced

Death of King George III, succeeded by the Prince Regent as George IV.
Birth of Florence Nightingale, English nurse (d. 1910).
Walter Scott publishes *Ivanhoe*.

originally in Glasgow in this year, is mounted at Covent Garden with Macready in the title role.

William Thomas Moncrieff, *The Lear of Private Life; or, Father and Daughter* (Coburg), a significant example of the domestication of classical character and theme occurring in the drama of the day, at major and minor theatres, as Knowles's *Virginius* additionally demonstrates.

After the period of mourning for the death of King George III is over, rival productions of Shakespeare's *King Lear*, withheld from the stage during the monarch's long insanity, are mounted at Drury Lane and Covent Garden.

1821 W. T. Moncrieff's dramatization of Pierce Egan's 'flash' novel *Life in London* as *Tom and Jerry; or, Life in London* runs at the Adelphi for ninety-four performances, a stunning achievement in its time.

The second theatre called the Haymarket (formerly the Little Haymarket) is built, immediately to the south of the first theatre, which had opened its doors in 1720 and become a theatre royal in 1766; the reason for the shift in orientation is explained as a desire to capture the vista into St James's Square; reconstructed in 1879 by C. J.

Britain adopts the gold standard.
Death of Napoleon.
Manchester Guardian begins as a weekly, becomes a daily in 1855.
The population of Great Britain reaches 20.8 million.

Phipps and again in 1904, it exists to this day as one of the pillars of West End theatre.

1822		Royal Academy of Music, London, founded. The world's first iron railway bridge built, for the Stockton–Darlington line. Suicide of British foreign minister, Viscount Castlereagh.
1823	James Robinson Planché publishes his designs for *King John*, produced at Covent Garden in this year, in his *Costumes of Shakespeare's Historical Tragedy of 'King John'*, a reflection of Planché's abiding interest in things antiquarian and a harbinger of the enormous efforts expended by Charles Kean at the Princess's at mid-century to reconstruct historically accurate scenes for his Shakespearean productions.	Sir Robert Smirke designs a permanent home for the British Museum, London. Birth of Ernest Renan, French historian (d. 1892). First issue of the British medical journal, the *Lancet*. George IV presents the library of his father, George III, henceforth called the 'King's Library', to the British Museum.
1824		Death of Byron in Greece during Greece's struggle for independence from Turkey.
1825		John Nash designs Buckingham Palace.
1826	John Baldwin Buckstone, *Luke the Labourer; or, The Lost Son* (Adelphi), one of the most telling melodramas of Buckstone's prolific career.	
1827	Victor Hugo's preface to *Cromwell*, one of the most notable manifestos of the Romantic movement.	

	Edward Fitzball, *The Flying Dutchman; or, The Phantom Ship* (Adelphi).	
1828	Birth of Henrik Ibsen (d. 1906).	
1829	Douglas Jerrold, *Black Eyed Susan; or, All in the Downs* (Surrey), one of the most famous and best written of all nautical melodramas.	George Stephenson perfects the steam locomotive. The omnibus comes into use in London public transport.
	Fanny Kemble, daughter of Charles and niece of John Philip, makes a reluctant début as Shakespeare's Juliet at Covent Garden, thereby rescuing her father's foundering enterprise and launching an all-too-brief career as one of the most emotive actresses of the century.	
1830	Douglas Jerrold's *The Mutiny at the Nore* (Pavilion).	Death of George IV; his brother succeeds as William IV. Berlioz's *Symphonie fantastique*.
1830–33		Charles Lyell's *Principles of Geology*.
1831	Planché, *Olympic Revels; or, Prometheus and Pandora* (Olympic).	Charles Darwin sails as a naturalist to South America, New Zealand and Australia on the HMS *Beagle*.
	Cremorne Gardens, initially a stadium for sports, sited on twelve acres west of Battersea Bridge, becomes a pleasure gardens in the 1840s under Renton Nicholson, featuring a circus, theatres (including the Marionette Theatre and the Ballet Theatre) and sideshows; it will be closed in 1877 after protests by the Chelsea Vestry.	

A theatre called the Garrick opens in Leman Street, Whitechapel; a second building on the site, opened in 1854, closes around 1881.

1831–4

Revolutions in Poland, Spain and Italy.
Nat Turner leads a rebellion of slaves in Virginia.

1832   The Select Committee formed by Parliament to inquire into the decline of the drama, chaired by Edward Lytton Bulwer, newly elected member for St Ives and soon to become a famous novelist and dramatist, publishes its findings in *Report from the Select Committee on Dramatic Literature*; the recommendations of the committee will take some eleven years for final enactment into law.

After a near revolution, the First Reform Act is passed by the House of Lords, increasing the cohort of voters from 500,000 to 1,000,000.
Abolition of slavery throughout the British Empire.
Greek independence declared at Conference of London.

1833   The Dramatic Copyright Act, informally known as 'Bulwer-Lytton's Act', gives the author of 'any tragedy, comedy, play, opera, farce or other dramatic entertainment' the sole right to perform it or authorize its performance, but only for a limited period.
The translation of Shakespeare into German begun by August Wilhelm von Schlegel in 1794 is completed by Schlegel and collaborators.

1833–9

Invention of photography.

1834	The Lyceum Theatre, in which Henry Irving will rise to fame, built this year in Wellington Street, the Strand, is the fifth building on the site, the earliest having opened in 1765 as an exhibition hall; subsequent venues, used as theatres for music and dancing, appear in 1790, 1809, when S. J. Arnold completes a theatre for the English Opera, and 1812, the last being destroyed by fire in 1830; Irving will hold the Lord Chamberlain's licence from 1878 to 1899, during which period the theatre will be redecorated at least three times, in 1882, 1885 and 1893, a measure of its increasing cachet, established by the actor who would, in 1895, become the first such person to be knighted. Fanny Elssler, Austrian ballerina, makes her début at the Paris Opéra.	Bulwer-Lytton publishes his novel *The Last Days of Pompeii*. Charles Babbage, English mathematician, invents in principle the 'analytical engine', the basis of the modern computer. The British Houses of Parliament suffer a disastrous fire.
1835	The St James's Theatre opens in King Street, St James's; after a chequered history and an interior reconstruction and redecoration in 1879, and then further reconstruction and enlargement, it reopens in 1890 under the management of George Alexander and soon reaches pre-eminent status, along with the Haymarket, as one of the two most fashionable London theatres in the period	David Straus's *Life of Jesus*. Alexis de Tocqueville's *Democracy in America*, vol. i; vol. ii appears in 1840.

before the Great War; in February 1895 it becomes the venue for the première of Oscar Wilde's *The Importance of Being Earnest*.
Buckstone, *The Dream at Sea* (Adelphi).
John Thomas Haines, *My Poll and My Partner Joe* (Surrey).

1836	Charles Dickens, *The Village Coquettes* (St James's).	Birth of Lawrence Alma-Tadema, Dutch-English artist (d. 1912).
1837	The likely first use of limelight (an extremely intense light casting sharp shadows, produced by heating a stick of calcium oxide, or quicklime, to incandescence) on stage, in Balfe's opera *Joan of Arc* at Drury Lane.	Victoria becomes Queen of Great Britain. Birth of Mary Elizabeth Braddon, English sensation novelist (d. 1915).
1838	Edward Bulwer-Lytton, *The Lady of Lyons; or, Love and Pride* (Covent Garden). The *Era*, the single most important theatrical journal of the century, begins publication in this year and continues for an entire century. Henry Brodribb, born this year into a rural Methodist family, eventually becomes an actor and in 1856 adopts the name Henry Irving.	
1839–42		First Opium War against China.
1839	Bulwer-Lytton's perfervid blank verse tragedy *Richelieu; or, The Conspiracy*, written as a vehicle	

for the singular talents of Macready, is brought out at Covent Garden.

Van Amburgh's lions attract the young, enthusiastic theatre-goer Queen Victoria to the Drury Lane pantomime seven times in six weeks.

1840   Built on the site of the Queen's Bazaar, an exhibition hall in Oxford Street, Marylebone, the Princess's Theatre opens this year, its goal of drawing an affluent clientèle reflected in its four tiers of boxes; from late 1851 until 1859 Charles Kean, the Eton-schooled son of the fiery tragedian Edmund, will continue as sole manager, as he and his wife Ellen Tree proceed to produce and act in a series of sumptuously mounted, historically 'accurate' plays by Shakespeare, along with plays by contemporary dramatists such as Boucicault, who for a time serves as Kean's house dramatist; a second theatre will be built on the site in 1869, and a third in 1880, but neither achieves the cachet attained by Kean, who could count Queen Victoria herself among his faithful audience.

The Royalty Theatre in Dean Street, Soho, opens as one of the last theatres to appear before the two-decades-long drought in new theatre building sets in, but

Queen Victoria marries Prince Albert of Saxe-Coburg-Gotha. Nelson's Column erected in Trafalgar Square. Death of Beau Brummell (George Bryan Brummell), English dandy (b. 1778). Penny postage established in Great Britain. Birth of Edward, Victoria's eldest son, the future King Edward VII (d. 1910).

it lasts only five days before vibrations caused by elaborate stage machinery close it down; it takes a decade for the theatre to reopen, after which it undergoes two more reconstructions, in 1861 and 1883, the latter to designs by the prominent theatre architect Thomas Verity, with a capacity finally of only 657.

1841   The very young Dion Boucicault's *London Assurance* appears at Covent Garden, as the work of the pseudonymous 'Lee Moreton', the first success of a dramatist whose career under his own name will epitomize the all-around man of the theatre – playwright, actor, producer, manager and technical innovator – in the Victorian age.

The Britannia Saloon is built at the back of a tavern in High Street, Hoxton, and by 1858, in a genuine reincarnation, it has become the Britannia Theatre; by 1872 Sara Lane has become its manager, writing a number of melodramas for performance here and staging the works of a half-dozen other women dramatists as well, over the years becoming a virtual East End institution.

1842   Macready's spectacular production of Shakespeare's *King John* at Drury Lane.

As manager of Drury Lane, Macready limits access to the theatre for women of the town, allowing them only in the gallery and requiring them to gain admission at a separate pay box and enter through a dismantled lobby.

The Literary Copyright Act reconciles the law as it relates to dramatic, literary and musical property, combining within a single statute the two distinct rights of multiplying copies (copyright) and representation (performing right); dramatization of a non-dramatic work is not covered, however, and consequently the author of a work of fiction needs to dramatize it himself or herself and secure separate copyright in that text; the act also institutes the confusing practice of 'copyright performance', since it indicates, if ambiguously, that publishing a play before it is performed will result in loss of performance rights; authors such as Bernard Shaw were, therefore, at pains to ensure that a 'performance' – however hasty or rudimentary, and often no more than a staged reading – takes place before a play is allowed to appear in print.

| 1843 | The Theatre Regulation Act, a tardy outcome from the | John Ruskin publishes the first volume of *Modern Painters*, to |

recommendations of the 1832 Select Committee of Parliament, officially does away with theatrical monopoly, legalizing a *de facto* condition of some years' standing.

be completed in five volumes in 1860.

The weekly financial paper the *Economist* founded in London by Sir James Wilson.

1844 Samuel Phelps takes over the management of Sadler's Wells Theatre in Islington and makes it the unlikely but popular home of a long series of distinctive and spectacular revivals of Shakespeare, including an important production of *A Midsummer Night's Dream*, in which Phelps plays a 'dreamy, dogged, and dogmatical' Bottom.

1845

Friedrich Engels's *The Condition of the Working Class in England in 1844*.

1846

Britain repeals the Corn Laws. The 'Great Hunger' in Ireland begins.

c. 1847 About this time the number of music halls, pleasure gardens and other places of popular resort in operation in London grows to be approximately equal, at something like twenty-five, with the number of theatres and opera houses; the number of music halls and other popular resorts will reach a high point of nearly one hundred by 1870 and then decline, in the closing years of the century, falling again approximately equal with a now more than

	twice as large contingent of theatres and opera houses, numbering about fifty-five by 1895.	
1847	J. Sterling Coyne, *How to Settle Accounts with Your Laundress* (Adelphi), one of the funniest farces of the century by an author whose name itself constitutes a kind of verbal farce. John Maddison Morton, *Box and Cox* (Lyceum), another such farce and an hilarious send-up of countless fictions since the time of the ancient Romans about long-lost brothers reunited through telltale birthmarks.	Birth of Millicent Garrett Fawcett, British suffragist (d. 1929).
1848		Chartism threatening in England. Marx and Engels's *Communist Manifesto*. Revolt in Paris, followed by Louis Philippe's abdication; Louis Napoleon Bonaparte proclaimed president of the French Republic. Revolutions in Vienna, Venice, Berlin, Milan, Parma, Rome, Czechoslovakia. Alexandre Dumas *fils* publishes his novel *La Dame aux camélias*. J. S. Mill publishes *Principles of Political Economy*. John Everett Millais's painting *Ophelia*. Holman Hunt, Millais and Dante Gabriel Rossetti found the Pre-Raphaelite Brotherhood.

1849	Queen Victoria and Prince Albert begin a series of private theatricals at Windsor Castle that will last for twelve years, their object to 'revive and elevate the English drama'.	
1850–9	Charles Kean and Ellen Tree's seasons at the Princess's Theatre, during which they will mount a combination of Shakespearean and contemporary plays notable for the sumptuous scenic surround in which they are produced and for their unprecedented degree of attempted historical accuracy, expounded on at length in Kean's double-broadside playbills.	
1851	On the site of a place of public entertainment active since Elizabethan times, in Drury Lane, Holborn, where the Mogul Saloon was operating from 1847, the Middlesex Music Hall opens and begins its sixty-year history, until 1911, when for a time it becomes the Middlesex Theatre of Varieties and then, in 1919, the Winter Garden Theatre.	The Great Exhibition opens at the iron-and-glass Crystal Palace in Hyde Park, London. The population of Great Britain reaches 20.8 million.
1851–2	Mary Cowden Clarke's *The Girlhood of Shakespeare's Heroines* is published in three volumes.	
1852	Dion Boucicault's drama *The Corsican Brothers* is a great success at the Princess's, with Charles Kean doubling one brother and the ghost of his	Second French Empire.

murdered sibling, who makes an eerie appearance by way of a gliding trapdoor especially designed for this spellbinding moment by Boucicault; the device becomes known as a 'Corsican trap'; the *Theatrical Journal* scolds the Queen for attending 'this vulgar Victorian trash' four times in only two months.

1853   Francis Talfourd's *Macbeth Somewhat Removed from the Text of Shakespeare*, at the Olympic, with Frederick Robson in the starring role, suceeds as a direct parody of Charles Kean's production of *Macbeth*, which has just opened at the Princess's; Talford's burlesque is one of six Shakespearean travesties performed in London this year, an indication of how popular and widespread the form is becoming.

Marriage Act secures wives' limited control over their own property.

1853–6   Crimean War.

1854   The Panopticon of Science and Art opens in Leicester Square; from 1858 it is known as the Alhambra Palace, then, over succeeding years, as the Royal Alhambra Palace, the Royal Alhambra Theatre and Alhambra Theatre of Varieties; in 1860 the addition of a stage will make it viable as a music hall; burned in 1882 and immediately rebuilt, it reopens the next year and remains one of

the grandest and most
capacious theatres of variety in
Britain, rivalled only by its
competitor at the top of the
square, the Empire Theatre of
Varieties, both theatres
featuring spectacular ballet as
well as music hall acts – and
both notorious for the presence
of high-class prostitutes in their
promenades.
Birth of Oscar Wilde (d. 1900).

1856   Covent Garden, consumed once
again by fire, is rebuilt yet again,
opening in 1858 as the opera
house it had already become
after alterations carried out in
1847; the building is still in use
today, for opera and ballet.
Birth of George Bernard Shaw
(d. 1950).

1857   Charles Kean is elected to the
Society of Antiquaries.
Beginning life as the Seven
Tankards and Punch Bowl
Public House, in High Holborn,
this venue becomes, in turn,
Weston's Music Hall, the Royal
Holborn Empire and, in 1892,
the Royal Holborn Theatre of
Varieties.

National Portrait Gallery
opens.
Victoria and Albert Museum
opens in London, as Museum
of Ornamental Art (until 1899).
Baudelaire, *Les Fleurs du mal*.
Divorce Act passed.

1858   Act for the Better Government
of India.

1859   Vauxhall Gardens, the long-lived
pleasure gardens opened in the
course of the seventeenth
century and, along with
Cremorne Gardens, one of the

Darwin's *On the Origin of
Species by Natural Selection*.
J. S. Mill, *Essay on Liberty*.

	two most popular resorts of their kind in London, closes.	
1860	Birth of Anton Chekhov (d. 1904).	
1861	The London Pavilion opens on a site that had previously seen a hall built in the stable yard of the Black Horse Inn, used as an exhibition place for waxworks and as a skating rink and, in 1859, as a 'sing-song' saloon; it was demolished in 1885. The Oxford Music Hall, in Oxford Street, Marylebone, opens its doors; a second building on the site, opened in 1869, lasts only three years before being replaced by a third, in 1873, which in turn is replaced in 1893.	Abraham Lincoln inaugurated as sixteenth president of the United States. Outbreak of the American Civil War with the Confederates taking Fort Sumter, South Carolina. Mrs Henry Wood's novel *East Lynne* published, spawning over two dozen dramatized versions. Isabella Beeton publishes *The Book of Household Management*. Death of Albert, Prince Consort.
1862	After a nearly complete drought lasting two decades, the Gaiety Theatre, built in the Strand (and later demolished and reconstructed in 1903 on a nearby site as part of the formation of Aldwych), becomes the first (over something like two decades) of a long series of new theatre buildings in London, some two dozen in the West End and additional theatres in other, sometimes more outlying, districts, transforming the theatrical landscape of the city in the last third of the century. Sarah Bernhardt makes her début at the Comédie Française in Racine's *Iphigénie en Aulide*.	Herbert Spencer publishes *First Principles*.

1863	Tom Taylor's *The Ticket-of-Leave Man* (Olympic), distinctive for its detailed realistic overlay on a melodramatic plot and for its introduction of the memorable, ultimately archetypal detective Hawkshaw.	J. S. Mill publishes *Utilitarianism*. President Lincoln issues the Emancipation Proclamation, freeing all slaves held in rebel territory. Beginning of construction of the London Underground.
1864		Over a five-year period Tolstoy publishes *War and Peace*.
1865	Squire Bancroft and Marie Bancroft take over the old Queen's Theatre in Charlotte Street, St Pancras, and transform it into the fashionable Prince of Wales's Theatre, where, among other attractive offerings, a series of plays by the ambitious realist T. W. Robertson is performed, including *Society* (1865), *Ours* (1866), *Caste* (1867), *Play* (1868), *School* (1869) and *The MP* (1870).	*9 April*: the Confederate States of America formally surrender at Appomatox; five days later, Lincoln is assassinated in a Washington, DC theatre by the actor John Wilkes Booth. The Thirteenth Amendment to the United States Constitution abolishes slavery. William Booth founds the Christian Revival Association in London, renamed the Salvation Army, in 1878. The Queensberry Rules of boxing are first proposed. Alfred Nobel invents dynamite.
1866	A parliamentary committee inquiring into the state of the theatre publishes its findings as *Report from the Select Committee on Theatrical Licences and Regulations*.	
1866–73		David Livingstone's search for the source of the Nile.
1867		Marx's first volume of *Capital* appears, the second and third following posthumously in 1884 and 1894.

		Second Reform Act in Britain. Quelling of Fenian uprising in Ireland. British North America Act creates the Dominion of Canada.
1869	In this year the Polygraphic Hall, opened in 1854 in a building used earlier as a cigar divan and a chapel, is converted into the Charing Cross Theatre, renamed the Folly in 1876 and, after an enlargement in 1881, Toole's, presided over (from 1879) by the prominent comedian J. L. Toole until 1895, when it is demolished to make way for an extension to the Charing Cross Hospital, meanwhile having added to the remarkable density of theatres in the West End, and particularly in the vicinity of the district between Cambridge Circus, Piccadilly Circus and Trafalgar Square, as the century nears its end.	Opening of the Suez Canal. The transcontinental railway across the United States is completed. W. S. Gilbert publishes the 'Bab' Ballads. J. S. Mill, *On the Subjection of Women*.
1870	W. S. Gilbert's delightful bagatelle *Our Island Home* is performed at Mr and Mrs German Reed's Gallery of Illustration in Regent Street; Gilbert will serve a self-imposed apprenticeship in comic opera by contributing five such works to the Reeds' socially respectable alternative to a theatre still considered risqué by many of London's potential audience.	Married Women's Property Act (further strengthened in 1874 and 1920).

The Opera Comique opens in
the Strand; with a capacity of
862, it is part of a trend towards
smaller specialty theatres;
intermittently housing foreign
theatre companies, it
participates in the
popularization of burlesque and,
beginning in 1878, under the
management of Richard D'Oyly
Carte, becomes the home of
early Gilbert and Sullivan
operas – *The Sorcerer* (1877),
HMS Pinafore (1878), *The Pirates
of Penzance* (1880) and *Patience*
(1881) – the last work
transferring to D'Oyly Carte's
new theatre, the Savoy, that
same year; like other theatres in
this part of the Strand, it will
close in 1899 to make way
for the Aldwych development.
Still another theatre, the
Vaudeville, designed by that
budding master theatre architect
C. J. Phipps (responsible for the
Queen's in 1867 and for
numerous additional theatres
into the 1890s), opens in the
Strand, where in ensuing
decades a theatre can be found
at almost every turning; its
capacity of 1,000 is reduced in
1891, in a reconstruction also
designed by Phipps, to 740.
The New Chelsea Theatre
opens in Lower George Street,
Chelsea, converting for dramatic
use what had been a dissenting

chapel constructed in 1818; two subsequent renamings, the Belgravia and Royal Court, see it through its most well-known period, beginning under the management of Mr and Mrs Kendall and John Hare, for four years from 1875; in 1879 the Polish tragedienne Helena Modjeska makes her London début here under Wilson Barrett's management; and then, in 1885, the famous series of farces by Arthur Wing Pinero begins with *The Magistrate* and continues with *The Schoolmistress* and *Dandy Dick*, all of them long runs; the life of the theatre then comes to a premature end as a result of improvements in Sloane Square which require its demolition; it is rebuilt on a new site, as the Royal Court Theatre, opening in 1888 (q.v.).

1871   As the Franco-Prussian War ends, London theatre managers can once more raid the Parisian theatre for likely plays to adapt, among them the Théâtre Cluny's popular *Le Juif polonais* by Emile Erckmann and Pierre-Alexandre Chatrian; H. L. Bateman, lessee of the Lyceum Theatre in London, commissions a translation from Leopold Lewis, and *The Bells* opens there in November of this year, with Henry Irving in the

Paris Commune.
Franco-Prussian War ends.
Darwin's *The Descent of Man*.

central role of Mathias, upstanding family man, public official – and secret, guilt-stricken murderer; it becomes one of Irving's most powerful, successful and characteristic roles.

P. T. Barnum opens his circus, 'The Greatest Show on Earth', in Brooklyn, New York.

1872   *Babil and Bijou*, an elaborate Covent Garden spectacle and James Robinson Planché's last work for the stage, in a collaboration with Boucicault, caps Planché's long career of writing and designing scenes and costumes for the theatre, begun as early as 1818 and notable for his many successful collaborations with Madame Vestris at the Olympic and elsewhere.

Eleonora Duse makes her début at age 14 in Verona, as Juliet.

1873   Walter Pater, *Studies in the History of the Renaissance.*
J. S. Mill publishes his autobiography.
Herbert Spencer, *The Study of Sociology.*
Irish Home Rule League founded.

1874   The Criterion Theatre is built in the basements of the Criterion Restaurant in Piccadilly Circus, to a design by Thomas Verity, and extensively reconstructed in 1884; by 1892 its original

	capacity of 675 has increased to 1,000.	
1875	George Henry Lewes publishes *On Actors and the Art of Acting*, one of the most intelligent and well-realized commentaries on English acting.	
	H. J. Byron's *Our Boys* (Vaudeville), produced this year, will hold the record of 1,362 performances for a long-running play until eclipsed by Brandon Thomas's *Charley's Aunt* in the 1890s.	
1876	The former captain of the London Fire Brigade, Eyre Shaw, publishes his cautionary book *Fires in Theatres*.	Invention of the telephone. Queen Victoria named Empress of India.
1877		Charles Stuart Parnell elected president of Irish Home Rule Confederation.
1878	Henry Irving takes over the management of the Lyceum, with Ellen Terry as his leading lady; he becomes equally famous for productions of Shakespearean and contemporary drama, to all of which he will bring his unique, eccentric style of acting.	James McNeill Whistler sues John Ruskin for libel after Ruskin in a review of Whistler's exhibit at the new Grosvenor Gallery accuses him of 'flinging a pot of paint in the public's face'; Whistler wins, but is awarded only one farthing in damages and is bankrupted.
		George Grove launches his *Dictionary of Music and Musicians*, completed in 1889.
1879	Augustus 'Druriolanus' Harris becomes manager of Drury Lane and sets in motion the spectacular pantomime for	

which the theatre will become
famous.

1880   Squire Bancroft and Marie
Bancroft take over management
of the Haymarket and construct
an elaborate gold picture-frame
border around the proscenium
arch; they also eliminate the pit
entirely, in favour of stalls, a
decision which provokes a riot.
15 December: a play by Ibsen in
English, in a translation by
William Archer, is presented for
the first time on the London
stage, appearing as a matinée at
the Gaiety: the title, newly
invented for the occasion and
pressed on a reluctant Archer, is
Quicksands, the more faithful
original being added only
as a subtitle, *The Pillars of Society*.

Parnell elected leader of the
Irish party in the House of
Commons.

1881   Henry Irving and the American
tragedian Edwin Booth act
Othello and Iago alternately at
the Lyceum.
D'Oyly Carte's Savoy Theatre,
in the Strand, the first theatre
lighted entirely by electricity,
opens with a transfer from the
Opera Comique of Gilbert and
Sullivan's *Patience*.
The Meiningen Company,
formed in the 1860s by the
serious theatrical amateur
George II, Duke of
Saxe-Meiningen, visit London,
performing Shakespeare in
German but nonetheless
making a noteworthy

Natural History Museum in
South Kensington, London, is
opened.
Czar Alexander II assassinated.
Death of Benjamin Disraeli
(b. 1804).

impression, in part because of the sure control of atmospherics and the brilliant, focused manipulation of crowds.

The Comedy Theatre, designed by the prominent theatre architect Thomas Verity (designer of the Criterion in Piccadilly Circus and the Empire Theatre of Varieties in Leicester Square), opens, its capacity just over 1,000 persons.

1882   Henry Arthur Jones and H. A. Herman's *The Silver King* opens at the Princess's and becomes a great hit, testifying to the perennial appeal of melodrama in up-to-date garb.

1883   Fabian Society founded in London.
Death of Karl Marx (b. 1818).

1884   Ibsen's *A Doll's House*, badly translated and disfigured with a 'happy' ending by Henry Arthur Jones and Henry Herman, is presented as *Breaking a Butterfly* at the Prince's Theatre.

Third Reform Act in Britain. James Murray's *New English Dictionary*, later called the *Oxford English Dictionary*, begins to appear (begun 1879, completed 1928).

Built on the site of the old Saville House, destroyed by fire in 1865, the lavishly appointed Empire Theatre of Varieties opens its doors; after protracted difficulties, under the managerial consortium headed by George Edwardes it develops the perfect combination of music hall acts, spectacular romantic ballet, and up-to-date *ballet divertissement*.

1885	George Edwardes and John Hollingshead form a partnership at the Gaiety. Gilbert and Sullivan's *The Mikado; or, The Town of Titipu* (Savoy). Irving's *Faust* (Lyceum). George Moore's *A Mummer's Wife* appears, one of a large cohort of theatrical novels published in the course of the nineteenth century.	Criminal Law Amendment Act.
1886	Percy Bysshe Shelley's *The Cenci*, written in 1819, is privately produced by the Shelley Society at the Grant Theatre, Islington. George Edwardes becomes manager of the Gaiety, the first major stepping-stone in the professional career of an entrepreneurial genius who will transform the marketing of commercially viable plays and entertainments, contribute to the rapid emergence of the long run and change the overall face of popular theatre as the virtual inventor of musical comedy.	Gladstone introduces the First Home Rule Bill in Parliament, its defeat splitting the Liberal Party. The Berne Convention on copyright establishes the International Copyright Union. Robert Louis Stevenson publishes his novel *The Strange Case of Dr Jekyll and Mr Hyde*.
1887	Herbert Beerbohm Tree takes over the management of the Haymarket. The worst recorded theatre fire, in respect of loss of life (127), occurs in the burning of the Theatre Royal Exeter. André Antoine founds the Théâtre Libre in Paris.	

1888	The Royal Court Theatre opens in Sloane Square, Chelsea, as a rebuilding of the earlier Court Theatre in Lower George Street, opened 1870 (q.v.); it will achieve renown as the venue, from 1904 to 1907, of the John Vedrenne–Harley Granville Barker management, dominated by productions of plays by Bernard Shaw; later in the century, it will earn another reputation, beginning in 1956, as the home of the English Stage Company. The architect J. G. Buckle brings out his comprehensive technical handbook *Theatre Construction and Maintenance*, advocating a principle of theatre design based on safety. Gilbert and Sullivan's *The Yeomen of the Guard; or, The Merryman and His Maid* (Savoy).	Jack the Ripper kills six women in London. Wilhelm II ('Kaiser Bill'), grandson of Queen Victoria, succeeds his father as King of Prussia and Emperor of Germany.
1889	Antoine's Théâtre Libre visits London, performing at the Royalty. The first coherent English production of Ibsen's *A Doll's House*, in a translation by William Archer and largely directed by Archer, and featuring Janet Achurch and her husband Charles Charrington, opens at the Novelty Theatre; it serves as a corrective to the abortive misrepresentation of the play as *Breaking a Butterfly*, produced in 1884. A second theatre called the	Parnell named as co-respondent in divorce case; Irish cause crucially weakened.

Garrick (the first, in Whitechapel, having closed in 1881) opens in Charing Cross Road, built by two of the foremost theatre architects of the day, Walter Emden and C. J. Phipps.

| 1890 | George Alexander becomes the lessee and manager of the St James's Theatre in King Street, St James's. | William James publishes *The Principles of Psychology*. Wilhelm II secures Bismarck's resignation and inaugurates policy of German expansion. |

| 1891 | Richard D'Oyly Carte's grand scheme to build a new home for English opera is seemingly realized in January of this year in the opening of a monumental theatre in Cambridge Circus with Arthur Sullivan's *Ivanhoe*, but the plan is unsuccessful, and in 1892 Augustus Harris takes over, reorienting its purpose and changing its name to the Palace Theatre of Varieties, offering formidable competition to its sister venues, the Alhambra and the Empire, a short walk to the south in Leicester Square. J. T. Grein founds the Independent Theatre Society, modelled on Antoine's Théâtre Libre, produces Ibsen's *Ghosts* and is lambasted by the conservative critic for the *Daily Telegraph* and *Illustrated London News*, Clement Scott, who condemns the play as 'a dirty act done publicly'. | George Du Maurier's novel *Trilby*, written and illustrated by him. Oscar Wilde publishes his novel *The Picture of Dorian Gray*. |

The American actress Elizabeth Robins and her American collaborator Marion Lea, dissatisfied with the small opportunities for serious drama in London and having founded what they called the 'Joint Management', produce the first English-language production of Ibsen's *Hedda Gabler*, translated by Edmund Gosse and William Archer, at the Vaudeville Theatre for a single matinée performance.

Shaw publishes the first edition of *The Quintessence of Ibsenism* and takes on the hostile Clement Scott as virtually his personal *bête noir*.

1892   Wilde's *Lady Windermere's Fan* opens at the St James's, the play written in response to Alexander's request to him for a 'comedy of modern life'.

June: Wilde's symbolist play *Salome*, written in French and in rehearsal at a London theatre with the acclaimed French tragedienne Sarah Bernhardt in the title role, is denied a licence by the Examiner of Plays, citing the long-standing prohibition of biblical characters from representation on the English stage.

J. T. Grein's Independent Theatre Society produces Shaw's *Widowers' Houses* in two

Edgar Degas's portrait of addiction, *L'Absinthe*, is exhibited in London, inspiring shock in the public and abusive language from reviewers.

matinées at the Royalty Theatre.
Brandon Thomas's *Charley's
Aunt* opens at the Royalty and
subsequently transfers to the
Globe; when it closes there, on
3 April 1896, it has set a new
long-run record of 1,466
performances.

A committee of Parliament
appointed to 'inquire into the
operation of Acts of Parliament
relating to the Licensing and
Regulation of Theatres and
Places of Public Entertainment'
and to make recommendations
for appropriate alteration
publishes its 592-page report.

The Trafalgar Square Theatre,
known by 1894 as the Trafalgar
Theatre and henceforth as the
Duke of York's, opens in
St Martin's Lane.

1893	Wilde's *A Woman of No Importance* opens at the Haymarket, with Tree as Lord Illingworth and Julia Neilson as Hester Worsley.	Second Home Rule Bill is passed by the Commons but rejected by the Lords.

Wilde's *A Woman of No
Importance* opens at the
Haymarket, with Tree as Lord
Illingworth and Julia Neilson as
Hester Worsley.

Pinero's *The Second Mrs
Tanqueray*, with Mrs Patrick
Campbell as Paula, opens at the
St James's.

After a commercial production
proves impossible, Elizabeth
Robins persuades Grein to
produce *Alan's Wife*, a play
co-authored by Robins and
Florence Bell about the killing
of a gravely ill child by its

Second Home Rule Bill is
passed by the Commons but
rejected by the Lords.
W. B. Yeats publishes *The Celtic
Twilight*.

sympathetic working-class mother; it lasts only for two matinée performances.

Henry Pettitt and Augustus Harris, *A Life of Pleasure*, is staged at Drury Lane.

Augustin Daly, American dramatist and manager, opens a new theatre, Daly's, in Cranbourne Street, Leicester Square.

1894   William Poel founds the Elizabethan Stage Society and produces *Twelfth Night* and *The Comedy of Errors* according to the principles, as he has reconstructed them, of Elizabethan stage management, which feature a platform stage in lieu of a pictorial, proscenium theatre.

Shaw's *Arms and the Man* opens and succeeds at the Avenue Theatre, with Florence Farr in the role of Louka, the rebellious servant, Farr's attempts to promote a theatrical season in London being financed by a secret source who turns out to be Annie Horniman, a tea heiress, who will later finance the Abbey Theatre in Dublin and the Gaiety in Manchester; the first of Shaw's 'Pleasant Plays', it marks a conscious turn on Shaw's part away from his commercially unsuccessful 'Unpleasant Plays' ('bluebook plays', he called them), of which only *Widowers' Houses* has seen production, in two matinée performances in 1892.

The Case of Rebellious Susan, Henry Arthur Jones's study of contemporary mores as they relate to a possibly adulterous wife, in rebellion against an undoubtedly adulterous husband, appears at the Criterion.

Grein's Independent Theatre Society produces Ibsen's *The Wild Duck*.

The Empire Theatre of Varieties becomes the focus of a huge controversy, its relicensing challenged by a group of reformers headed by the formidable social purity activist Laura Ormiston Chant; their opposition ultimately fails, but not before Edwardes and the Empire are embroiled in issues reaching widely out into the cultural and moral matrices of contemporary society, issues aired for weeks on end during the autumn in letters to the editor of the *Daily Telegraph*.

Oscar Wilde's *Salome*, first written in French, is published in English translation with drawings by Aubrey Beardsley.

1895 *January*: George Bernard Shaw becomes dramatic critic for Frank Harris's weekly *Saturday Review*.

3 January: Wilde's *An Ideal*

Grant Allen publishes his shocking novel *The Woman Who Did*.

London School of Economics and Political Science founded.

Husband opens at the Haymarket, but closes prematurely on 27 April in the face of the broadening scandal generated by Wilde's suit against the Marquess of Queensberry for criminal libel.

5 January: Henry James's last play for the stage, *Guy Domville*, opens and fails at the St James's; Alexander keeps it up for a month while readying a new play by Wilde.

14 February: Wilde's *The Importance of Being Earnest* opens at the St James's; in a desperate attempt to keep the play going Alexander takes Wilde's name off the programmes and posters, but is forced to close on 8 May. Pinero's contribution to a burgeoning audience interest in rebellious women, *The Notorious Mrs Ebbsmith*, opens at the Garrick, with Mrs Patrick Campbell in the title role. Queen Victoria confers a knighthood on Henry Irving. George Redford becomes Examiner of Plays. Eleonora Duse and Sarah Bernhardt act in London, competing in one instance in the performance of the same role (Magda, in Sudermann's *Heimat*), reviewed by Shaw in the *Saturday Review* for 15 June. Aurélien Lugné-Poe's Théâtre de l'Oeuvre, sponsored by

With Josef Breuer, Sigmund Freud publishes *Studien über Hysterie* (*Studies in Hysteria*), marking the beginnings of psychoanalysis.

5 April: Oscar Wilde's suit for criminal libel against the Marquess of Queensberry is withdrawn after telling evidence is revealed; on 26 April the trial of Regina *vs.* Wilde and Taylor commences; on 25 May, after the trial ends in a hung jury, a new trial is ordered, and Wilde is at length convicted of 'gross indecency' under the terms of the 1885 act and sentenced to two years with hard labour; many contemporaries view it as the end of an era.

Grein's Independent Theatre,
visits London and performs
Ibsen and Maeterlinck (both in
French) at the Opera Comique;
in 1896 Lugné will produce, for
one performance, Wilde's
Salome, the only performance
during his lifetime.

Grein's Independent Theatre,
fallen on financial hard times,
cancels its 1895 season, including
planned productions of Ibsen's
The Lady from the Sea and of a
new play by Shaw, and
reorganizes as a limited liability
company; Shaw criticizes the
organization for having
effectively lost its independence
and become respectable.

PART I

*

1660 TO 1800

Introduction
The theatre from 1660 to 1800

JOSEPH DONOHUE

Approaching the Restoration theatre

Paradoxically, the theatre of the English post-Restoration seems more remote to us than the theatre of Shakespeare, Jonson and Webster. The Elizabethan and Jacobean theatre has been fully assimilated by modern and post-modern stagecraft, but the theatre of the Restoration, Georgian and Victorian years – from Dryden, Wycherley and Aphra Behn through Goldsmith and Sheridan to the dawn of the modern day – largely remains encapsulated in its historical and theatrical milieu. *The Importance of Being Earnest* scintillates in 1930s finery, but *The Beaux' Strategem* is almost never mounted in late Victorian lounge suits or Congreve as if contemporary to Coward. In recent times *'Tis Pity She's a Whore* has been set in a romantic *faux* Regency surround and *The Merchant of Venice* in a fascist, anti-Semitic Italy; by the same token, the Elizabethan-Jacobean repertory has been cloaked in the modernist panoply of Gordon Craig or Granville Barker. But Boucicault's comedies and Pinero's farces still walk unmediated in the costume of their day. We simply do not treat post-Restoration plays metaphorically, whether historically or stylistically. True classics of the theatre are timeless, we think, and may be redressed in the habits of any amenable time, but plays from the days of Charles II to the near end of the nineteenth century have yet to become classics *in the theatre*, though some have done as literary art. A greater leap of historical imagination is therefore required to understand the post-Restoration theatre for what it is and to measure its considerable aesthetic and cultural distance back from our own time.

An additional issue emerges. The essentially bare Elizabethan stage holds a remarkable likeness to the metonymous unitary set of the post-realist modern theatre; but the long tradition of changeable representational scenery, established in the public theatre in 1660 and continued for over two centuries, constituted a wholesale departure from the early seventeenth-century theatre's non-representational scene. That departure, in the direction of ever greater 'realism', reached its apogee in the mid-nineteenth century on the picture-perfect stage of Charles Kean's Princess's Theatre. It was against this impulse to mount a three-dimensional illusion of actual life, historical or contemporary, that modernist English and European producers and designers rebelled. Their radical new aesthetic effectively mothballed the long history of the British theatre from Dryden to Shaw and the history of performance from Betterton and Bracegirdle to Irving and Terry. Only recently, as the second theatres of the Royal Shakespeare Company, the Stratford, Ontario Shakespeare Festival and numerous other multi-stage companies began adapting Wycherley's *The Country Wife* (1675), Gay, Pope and Arbuthnot's *Three Hours after Marriage* (1717) and other 'lost' plays to the modest reaches of the Swan, the Young Vic and other small-scale venues, has the gulf separating audiences of our day from the pleasures of *Marriage à la Mode* (1672), *The Clandestine Marriage* (1766) and hundreds of other neglected but still stageworthy works begun to be bridged.

This development promises significant new insights into an entire theatrical and dramatic culture, along with deeper understanding of its connection to its own day and to ours. Meanwhile, these are the present circumstances in which the history of the British theatre from 1660 to 1895 must necessarily be written.

Renewed beginnings, 1660 to 1700

In less than three months after King Charles II had landed triumphantly at Dover, on 29 May 1660, restoring the monarchy to Britain, his courtiers William Davenant and Thomas Killigrew came into possession of a joint warrant granted by the King for the exclusive representation of plays – a remarkable triumph of their own. For eighteen years, since the closing of the theatres in 1642 by agents of the Commonwealth, no theatrical performance had been officially tolerated. Perhaps with the Puritans' bias against stage plays in mind, Charles enjoined Killigrew and Davenant to avoid works containing 'profanation and scurrility', choosing instead entertainments which 'might serve as moral instructions in human life' and provide 'innocent and harmless divertissement'. Banning all others from performing plays in the cities of London and Westminster, Charles entitled Davenant and Killigrew to form two companies and build two theatres 'for the representation of tragedies, comedies, plays, operas, and all other entertainments of that nature'. Left unmentioned, but articulated in subsequent patents, was Charles's instruction that all women's parts be 'performed by women'.[1]

Anticipating the King's return, more than one group of actors had re-emerged or been freshly constituted. A group of older players, survivors of pre-Commonwealth theatre companies, offered plays by Fletcher and Shakespeare at the Red Bull and Gibbons's Tennis Court. A younger troupe including Thomas Betterton and other actors destined for distinction were performing at the old Cockpit in Drury Lane. William Beeston had evidently taken over Salisbury Court on a licence from Sir Henry Herbert, Master of the Revels, who still insisted on regulating theatrical entertainments.[2] During the closing years of the Interregnum the canny Davenant circumvented the official ban by producing 'opera'. First at his residence, Rutland House, and then at the Cockpit, Davenant mounted *The Siege of Rhodes* (1656) and *The Cruelty of the Spaniards in Peru* (1658), entertainments whose extensive musical content legitimized a fictional action presented on stage, before an audience.[3] These and other events combined to establish the framework within which legally countenanced theatrical performance would occur for the better part of the next two centuries.

Although Charles's patent permitted the erection of two theatres, a combination of renovation, adaptation and new construction ensued. After functioning briefly as the home of Davenant and Killigrew's temporarily united company, the old Phoenix, or Cockpit, in Drury Lane disappeared from view. Still another old theatre, the Salisbury Court, similar in design to the Cockpit and Blackfriars and renovated by Beeston in 1659, was occupied briefly by Davenant over the winter of 1660–61 before moving to his new playhouse, the former Lisle's Tennis Court, the following summer. Like so many other buildings, it perished in the Great Fire of 1666. The renovated Gibbons's Tennis Court, in Lincoln's Inn Fields, served Killigrew and his company, under Charles's patronage, as the first theatre royal until May 1663, when a permanent theatre opened in Bridges Street, Drury Lane. And, even while performances of Davenant's company, styled 'the Duke's Men' after their patron, the Duke of York, continued at Salisbury Court, he converted and enlarged Lisle's to accommodate both a goodly audience and the changeable scenery introduced at Rutland House. Davenant's troupe remained at Lisle's, even after Davenant's death in

---

[1] Thomas and Hare, eds., *Restoration and Georgian England*, 11–12, 18.
[2] Nicoll, *History of English Drama*, I: 287–92.
[3] The title of Davenant's opera as first published is instructive: *The Siege of Rhodes: Made a representation by the art of prospective in scenes and the story sung in recitative music.* See Thomas and Hare, eds., *Restoration and Georgian England*, 86–91.

Plate 1. Duke's Theatre, Dorset Garden. Opened in 1671 as the permanent home of the Duke's Company and built to designs supposedly by Christopher Wren, the theatre fronted on the Thames at Dorset Stairs. Thomas Betterton, acting manager and 'keeper' of the playhouse, occupied an upper apartment (Leacroft, *Development of the English Playhouse*, 86).

1668, until November 1671, when an entirely new and sizable theatre finally opened in Dorset Garden, under Davenant family control.

Meanwhile, Killigrew's new theatre in Drury Lane had begun performances as early as May 1663. Surviving receipts suggest that a £100 house represented about 1,000 persons, while a greater crowd could generate as much as £140.[4] The nearly circular auditorium and steeply sloped pit, surrounded by tiers of boxes and augmented by a higher, undivided gallery, defined the physical circumstances. Provision had been made, following Davenant's precedent, for scenes and machines, now the *sine qua non* for spectacle. Unfortunately short-lived, the theatre burned on 25 January 1672 – the first in a long series of conflagrations punctuating the history of theatre building in Britain over the next two centuries and beyond. Temporarily based in the old Lincoln's Inn Fields tennis court, Killigrew set about constructing the second Drury Lane, of

[4] Avery and Scouten, *London Stage 1660–1700*, xlii–xliii.

a size with its predecessor and so smaller than Dorset Garden, but augmented by a 28-foot scene house, reaffirming the irresistible trend towards spectacle. By March 1674 the theatre had opened. The King's Company remained there until 1682, when it came to be occupied by the United Company, formed from both troupes under the pressure of hard times. The company continued to offer dramatic works there, using Dorset Garden principally for spectacle, until the 1694–95 season, when Betterton, along with Elizabeth Barry, Anne Bracegirdle and others, complaining of oppressive treatment by the patentees, withdrew from the United Company and, forming their own shareholding enterprise, undertook a hasty remodelling of Lisle's Tennis Court. Supported by a sympathetic Lord Chamberlain, the Earl of Dorset, the New Theatre in Lincoln's Inn Fields opened with Congreve's *Love for Love* in April 1695, an auspicious beginning for them and for a play which became a mainstay of the comic repertoire.

And so, encouraged by a powerful, pleasure-loving monarch, the theatre had again asserted its perennial vitality. Not content with regulating theatres and companies, Charles had caused lists to be drawn up of plays allotted exclusively to Davenant or to Killigrew. Documents dating from 1660 and 1668 identify scores of plays from the Elizabethan, Jacobean and Caroline repertory awarded to one or the other (mostly to Killigrew).[5] Davenant proposed to reform 'some of the most ancient Playes . . . playd at Blackfriers',[6] and the idea of adaptation caught on. Charles, as *de facto* Master of the Revels, ended up replicating the conditions of the Elizabethan repertory system, in which companies jealously guarded the plays written for them, exhibiting them by turn and interspersing a smaller number of new plays which, if successful, joined the rotation. Evolving over the years, this system would enhance the strengths and minimize the limitations of the acting company, creating the conditions under which companies could flourish simultaneously.

The chasm opened during the Interregnum in the previously unbroken continuity of performance was, however, not easy to bridge. A new, smaller audience required cultivation; only gradually did daily performance become the norm, as a wider range of the public began to attend. In 1668 the indefatigable diarist Samuel Pepys, attending a play at the Duke of York's and noticing 'a mighty company of citizens, prentices and others', realized he could not remember seeing so many 'ordinary prentices and mean people in the pit', where the admission price was 2s 6d. Pepys and his wife were more likely to

---

[5] Nicoll, *History of English Drama*, 1: 352–54.
[6] Lord Chamberlain's document, quoted ibid., 1: 352.

sit in the gallery, for a more modest 1s 6d. Once, when a crowded house drove them into an upper box 'at 4s a piece', it was a novelty dearly bought.[7]

The character of this new audience derived partly from the unprecedented connection with the court; never had a monarch been associated so closely with the public theatre. Surviving warrants for expenses of performing plays before royalty, at the two public theatres and in private at Whitehall, contain lengthy lists of titles.[8] Charles and his entourage attended the Duke of York's Theatre some twenty-three times between November 1668 and June 1670.[9] Numerous courtiers, including George Villiers, Duke of Buckingham, John Wilmot, Earl of Rochester, and the Duke and Duchess of York were to be seen, along with the dramatist Sir George Etherege, the poet Edmund Waller and the pre-eminent poet, satirist and dramatist, John Dryden. Pepys identifies a broad range of persons in attendance, including royalty, aristocracy, the socially prominent and the well-to-do.[10] Charles invested heavily in private theatricals, notwithstanding his meagre purse. By 1665 he had built a house in Whitehall for ballets, masques and plays. The construction, supervised by John Webb (pupil of the great Inigo Jones), articulated the King's expansive interest in scenic display.[11] Other court venues for plays emerged at St James's Palace and Windsor Castle. A measure of Charles's fascination with things theatrical, nurtured during a long continental exile, appears in the warrant awarded to Davenant and Killigrew allowing for entrance prices reflecting 'the great expences of scenes'.[12] In *A Short Discourse of the English Stage* (1664), Richard Flecknoe contrasted the 'plain and simple' theatres of former times, having 'no other scenes nor decorations of the stage,' with 'ours', which 'for cost and ornament are arrived to the height of magnificence'.[13]

The reconfiguration of Restoration performance space resulted in the situating of the action predominantly on a forestage thrust well out in front of scenes standing symmetrically on the stage proper, behind the proscenium arch. The actor would enter the 'scene' (literally, the stage) through a door in the proscenium arch and proceed down the forestage, quickly becoming the focal point of attention. Once the prologue was spoken and the curtain drawn, the audience would experience the action of the play by means of

---

[7] Thomas and Hare, eds., *Restoration and Georgian England*, 176–7.
[8] Lord Chamberlain's documents transcribed in Nicoll, *History of English Drama*, 1: 345–50.
[9] Schedule of plays in the Harvard Theatre Collection, illustrated in Avery and Scouten, *London Stage 1660–1700*, after lxxviii.
[10] Ibid., clxiv–clxv.
[11] Boswell, *Restoration Court Stage*, 22ff.
[12] Thomas and Hare, eds., *Restoration and Georgian England*, 12.
[13] (London: R. Wood, 1664), excerpted ibid., 93.

changes of scene. Sets of flats running in parallel grooves in the stage floor, left and right, were arranged on diagonal lines receding upstage towards a vanishing point. The scene would be changed in full view of the audience by a stage hand stationed at each set of flats who, on signal, would pull one flat off and push another on. By closing flats completely the scene could be made as shallow or as deep as required. Frequent stage directions at the ends and beginnings of scenes – 'the scene closes', 'the scene opens' – attest to the rhythmic movement of changeable scenery. 'Discovery' scenes were accomplished by pulling a pair of flats open to reveal characters already in place. Selective use of proscenium doors could convey a change of location as well.[14] Although the represented locations – a chamber, a hall, a park, a grove, a marketplace, a coffee house, a throne room, a prison cell – were necessarily generalized, the dramatic action was conducted by moving from one locale to some other, contrasting one. Through these means the dramatic art of the Restoration emulated the Elizabethan dramaturgical convention of movement from one location to another, taking the audience on a repetitive, metonymic tour of the world, until the scene changed to a place where the action could resolve. It may be said that a Restoration play is over when it is no longer dramatically necessary to change the scene again, so closely are the settings linked with the development and resolution of the intrigue.

The impact of this ingenious new system of changeable scenery on the theatre and drama of post-Restoration Britain cannot be overestimated.[15] Two plays produced within two years of one another in the 1670s exemplify the new way. In William Wycherley's *The Country Wife*, first performed by the King's Company at Drury Lane in 1675, five different locations are represented, two of them public, three private; and two – Horner's lodging and the jealous husband Pinchwife's house – become the double lodestones for an action pitting Horner's ingenuity as a cuckolder against the vain efforts of Pinchwife to protect his wife.[16] Clearly, Wycherley is manipulating a well-established convention to his own comic and satiric ends. In a more sombre vein, Elkanah Settle's drama *The Empress of Morocco* (1673), the only Restoration play whose published text illustrates the scenic particulars of its mounting on the Dorset Garden stage, features five deep, elaborate scenes: a dungeon, a seascape, a scene of state, a masque scene and a discovered tableau of figures impaled on spikes against a wall, graphically demonstrating 'the reward of treason'.[17]

[14] Southern, *Changeable Scenery*, 126.
[15] Holland, *Ornament of Action*, chap. 2.
[16] Shepherd and Womack, *English Drama*, 130.
[17] Thomas and Hare, eds., *Restoration and Georgian England*, 95–9.

Whereas the tragedies and heroic dramas of the age occur in exotic climes, comedy represented the world inhabited by play-goers. A contemporary English locale proved the exception, not the rule, in earlier comedy, but after the Restoration a different norm prevailed: the streets, parks, marketplaces, drawing-rooms and coffee houses of London remain the almost invariable settings, and the action of the play moves back and forth among them. Sometimes actual coffee houses are set. As in the Exchange and St James's Park, the hustle and bustle of the city itself become part of the interest. In contrast, interiors are usually domestic establishments where only those who live, serve or are invited may appear. Of course, interlopers abound, like the worried suitor Mirabell in Lady Wishfort's house, in Congreve's *The Way of the World*. Decades would pass before a play like George Farquhar's *The Beaux' Strategem* (1707), whose action abandons the city for the country, could succeed, so intensely preoccupied with London life was the comedy of the age – and its audience.

It would be some years before the scenes and scenic effects which drew so many to the theatre would be memorialized in the bill of the play. For a century and more after play-going recommenced, in 1660, the playbill remained mostly a listing of titles, actors' names and roles, preceded by the name of the theatre, the date, and the play's status as new or revived. The repertory system, with its constant changes, required the publication of bills for each performance, made available to audiences and posted outside the theatre and elsewhere, this information augmented by the 'giving out' of the next day's play at the close of each performance. Repetition of an unusually successful mainpiece or farce might occur, and once pantomimes, introduced around 1717 by John Rich at Lincoln's Inn Fields, became popular and audiences were substantial enough to support longer runs, extended repetition might ensue. The fact would appear in the daily bills. As a result, no single source provides more information about the Restoration theatre or frames its character more perspicuously. Rare indeed was a bill supplying the name of the dramatist; dramatic authorship was considered a literary, not a theatrical, phenomenon, and the Restoration theatre was an actor's, not a playwright's, theatre. In the early years only principal actors might be named, in order of the prominence of their role or the size of their reputations, male actors' names always preceding female names. At the bottom of the bill, given sufficient space, offerings on the next night might be advertised. Overall, the size of the bill and the amount of information it provided resulted in a document that implied as much about its intended audience as it stated about the fare it promised. Ultimately, it was playbills, as much as actors and actresses themselves, which proved to be the abstract and brief chronicles of the time.

The printing of playbills was always a last-minute affair, except for benefit bills, printed in advance at actors' expense and used by them to drum up audiences on whose patronage their livelihood so greatly depended. A sparsely populated house could result in catastrophic loss; if the proceeds fell short of house charges, the beneficiary would owe the management money. Much to be envied was an actor awarded a 'clear' benefit, free of charges. Benefit bills provide more detailed information about performers' specialties and preferences of role and play, but they also document a humiliating practice persisting over generations.[18] They nevertheless reflect the solidarity of acting companies, whose members regularly performed in fellow-members' benefits. Authors' benefits followed a different principle: the net proceeds of the third night (and, if it occurred, the sixth) were the main reward, aside from whatever could be gleaned from a willing publisher's efforts.

The social coherence of the acting company, despite large egos, inevitable squabbles and claims of prior right, underlay its viability, which in turn was tied to the nature of the repertory system itself. Once successful, plays passed into the rotation, to be alternated one with another over the season and perhaps beyond. Meanwhile, new plays, always in a minority, had their chance. The notion of favourites revisited became the basis of performance, year after year, each play given one or more times during the season or revived after a lapse. Classics from a previous age often held pride of place, sometimes adapted to changed circumstances and new audiences. *Macbeth* in Davenant's hands became a spectacular masque 'With all the Alterations, Amendments, Additions, and New Songs', as the title page of the 1673 edition boasted. Dryden and Davenant joined forces in 1667 on *The Tempest; or, The Enchanted Island*, a comedy which in turn gave way to Thomas Shadwell's operatic version of 1674. Fletcher's *The Chances* was rewritten by Buckingham in 1666, and another Fletcher play, *The Wild Goose Chase*, became Farquhar's *The Inconstant; or, The Way to Win Him* (1703). Colley Cibber's redaction of Shakespeare's much longer *King Richard III* (1699) into a sleek acting vehicle proved one of the sturdiest warhorses of the repertory, still performed into the early twentieth century. Otway's *Venice Preserv'd; or, A Plot Discover'd* (1682) became over time an analogical glass through which successive audiences could scrutinize the current political climate.[19] As new plays survived the test of time – Aphra Behn's *The Rover; or, The Banish't Cavaliers* (1677), Thomas Southerne's *The Fatal Marriage; or, The Innocent Adultery* (1694), Susanna Centlivre's *The Wonder: A*

---

[18] Troubridge, *Benefit System in the British Theatre.*
[19] Taylor, *Next to Shakespeare.*

Woman Keeps a Secret (1714), to name a few – they were assimilated into this constantly shifting repertory, creating a profoundly conservative culture of repetition and continuity.

The composition of the repertory company must therefore be understood in the context of its scheme of daily offerings. A tragedy without a hero and a villain, or a comedy without a heroine and a blocking character or antagonist, would have had no chance of success, doomed to rejection by a management whose actors specialized in the 'lines of business' of hero, villain, heroine and so on. A viable dramatic script was consequently one which, depending on its genre, featured a role for each of the prominent members of the company and additional roles for supporting players, under conditions where doubling seldom or never occurred.[20]

The four comedies and one tragedy of William Congreve acted between 1693 and 1700 – *The Old Batchelour*, *The Double-Dealer*, *Love for Love*, *The Mourning Bride* and *The Way of the World* – offer a revealing example. In analyzing their casts we quickly discover how Betterton's predilection for tragic heroes, such as Osmyn in Congreve's sole tragedy *The Mourning Bride*, is countered, in the comedies, by his enactment of villainous or blocking characters, as in the eponymous old bachelor and in Fainall, the thwarted villain of *The Way of the World*. Yet Betterton plays the besieged romantic hero Valentine in *Love for Love*, perhaps because the antagonist, Valentine's father, Sir Sampson Legend, played by Cave Underhill, a specialist in such heavy or character roles as a pimp in *The Old Batchelour* and Sir Wilfull Witwoud in *The Way of the World*, is insufficiently prominent. Broad comedy was the province of Thomas Doggett, who wore 'a Farce in his Face'[21] and who excelled in dim-witted and eccentric characters such as the banker Fondlewife in *The Old Batchelour*, the foolish old knight Sir Paul Plyant in *The Double-Dealer* and the comical sailor Ben, Valentine's younger brother, in *Love for Love*.

Congreve was especially happy in the actresses for his plays, particularly Elizabeth Barry, the first great English actress, who had found fame as Monimia in Otway's tragedy *The Orphan*. An affecting, magnetic personality on and off the stage, Mrs Barry performed in all five of Congreve's plays, and her range was considerable. Her Laetitia, the wife of Fondlewife, was followed by Lady Touchwood, married but in love with a handsome young man, in *The Double-Dealer*; Mrs Frail, a woman of the town, in *Love for Love*; the captive Queen Zara in *The Mourning Bride*; and Mrs Marwood in *The Way of the World*,

---

[20] Van Lennep *et al.*, *London Stage 1660–1800*.
[21] Highfill, *et al.*, *Biographical Dictionary*, IV: 450.

caught between her friendship with Fainall and her liking for Millamant's suitor, Mirabell. Opposite Mrs Barry in all five plays, and the perfect foil to her characters, appeared the charming Anne Bracegirdle, a romantic comedienne with whom half the town was in love (and the occasion, in 1692, of the sensational murder of the actor-dramatist William Mountfort by the infatuated Lord Mohun and Captain Hill[22]). The cool, consummate attractiveness of Millamant, brilliantly tailored to Bracegirdle's talents by Congreve, had counterparts in the previous four plays. The supporting role of the coquette in Congreve's plays found a vibrant performer in Susanna Mountfort, whose name falls out of the bills at a point and is replaced by the precocious Elizabeth Boman (or Bowman), who apparently at age 16 played Vainlove's forsaken mistress Sylvia in *The Old Batchelour*, along with heavier roles in *Love for Love*, *The Mourning Bride* and *The Way of the World*.[23] The brisk economy of the repertory company shines out in this eight-year sequence. Low comedians and such utility players as the 'walking gentleman' would exhibit even greater range, often call for forty characters or more. Such were the challenges of this long-lived system in which various entertainments were mounted day after day and, as dinner hours advanced from early afternoon to early evening, night after night.

In extreme circumstances the integrity of acting companies could suffer unexpected trials, however, as in the defection from the United Company in early 1695 of Betterton, along with some fifteen fellow-actors, 'the very beauty and vigour of the Stage', tyrannized over by the ambitious lawyer and manager Christopher Rich. Their goal a reorganized, less oppressive enterprise, they left behind a company hard pressed to find enough actors for all the characters in a play.[24] The United Company had begun performing, at Drury Lane, in November 1682, already the worse for some key retirements. Charles II's death in February 1685 had closed the theatre for a time (the first since the plague of 1665). Charles's younger brother, James II, a Catholic, had continued Charles's patronage of the theatre and, in January 1688, had reconstituted the United Company.[25] James's brief reign was followed, however, by the advent of William and Mary in 1689, beginning a period in which theatre and court enjoyed only vestiges of the intimacy that had characterized the quarter-century of Charles's monarchy. By 1695 the renewed presence of two

---

[22] See the accounts in the lives of Mrs Bracegirdle and William Mountfort in Highfill, *et al.*, *Biographical Dictionary*, II: 271–2 and X: 357–9.
[23] Ibid., II: 201.
[24] *A Comparison between the Two Stages*, 7, quoted in Nicoll, *History of English Drama*, I: 336.
[25] Nicoll, *History of English Drama*, I: 332.

rival London companies made for continued hard times, now exacerbated by a troubled economy. The status quo by the close of the century has been aptly decribed as 'a state of unrest and of uncertainty in theatrical affairs, a tyrannical government at the Drury Lane and Dorset Garden houses, a mixed republic at Lincoln's Inn Fields'.[26] The reformer Jeremy Collier's *Short View of the Immorality and Profaneness of the English Stage* (1698), attacking the alleged immorality of stage comedy, served notice that the age was changing. In 1697 the Lord Chamberlain had anticipated Collier's critique in decreeing that all plays must be licensed by the Master of the Revels, eliminating 'all Obsenityes & other Scandalous matters' offensive 'against ye Lawes of God'.[27] The royal and aristocratic licence under which dramatic comedy had flourished was under siege by a more upright, well-to-do citizenry, many of them merchants making fortunes in trade and favouring greater stability in public life. The professional theatre, vitiated by power struggles between management and actors, carried on at a less than stalwart pace. Actors, though entitled to wear royal livery protecting them from arrest except on the Lord Chamberlain's warrant, could assert their rights and claim their privileges, and yet, turned away from their company, like the veteran Michael Mohun in 1682, they had nowhere to go if not to the shelter of a sympathetic monarch's protection.[28]

New theatres, burgeoning audiences, 1700 to 1741

Thanks to a multitude of surviving documents, the course of theatre building in the early decades of the new century may be precisely tracked. The theatres in London devoted to 'legitimate drama' open at the century's end numbered only three in all, and were occupied by only two companies: the United Company, performing at Drury Lane and Dorset Garden (until the demise of the latter in 1709), and the breakaway company headed by the long-lived Betterton at Lincoln's Inn Fields. Four additional structures were to rise in just a few more years, extensively altering the theatrical landscape. In 1705, John Vanbrugh, architect and dramatist, completed the splendid new Queen's Theatre (called 'The King's' after the accession of George I in 1714) in the Haymarket, a new sector of London west of Drury Lane; Betterton's company repaired to that grander theatre. Lincoln's Inn Fields fell into disuse until the enterprising Christopher Rich laid plans in 1714 to exploit the old tennis court. Meanwhile,

---

[26] Ibid., 1: 340.
[27] PRO LC 7/1 and 7/3, Quoted in Nicoll, *History of English Drama*, 1: 341n.
[28] Ibid., 1: 331, 365–6.

by 1700 Rich had modified the Drury Lane auditorium, enlarging its boxes and pit and, to accommodate the increase, shortening the forestage. The continued abbreviation of the forestage over the new century and beyond would prove an inexorable development, altering extensively the circumstances in which an audience would view the performance.[29] The correlative enlargement of the auditorium would result, by the end of the eighteenth century, in cavernous spaces accessible only to actors of stentorian range. The poor acoustics of the spacious Queen's, more suitable for the singing voice than the spoken, were a harbinger of this trend. It soon became exclusively an opera house, flourishing under the tremendous vogue for Italian opera.[30]

By 1720, in the Haymarket, just opposite the opera house, a theatre protected by the patronage of the Duke of Montague was allowed to be built and to open. The Little Theatre in the Haymarket, the name distinguishing it from its more imposing neighbour, depended at first on imports from France and Italy or on amateur groups closer to home.[31] A venue for unlicensed but tolerated theatre, for seven years beginning in 1730 it drew attention with such pieces as Henry Fielding's burlesque *Tom Thumb*, providing a home for satire of the political establishment. By 1766, by virtue of a royal patent granted to the actor Samuel Foote, the Little Haymarket would become a welcome summer home for actors when the two major theatres were dark and the patentees could tolerate a rival presence.

Still another theatre, even more important than the Queen's, opened in December 1732 at the north-east corner of Covent Garden Piazza, in Bow Street just by the market, around the corner from Drury Lane. Covent Garden Theatre was the brainchild of John Rich, who moved his company there from Lincoln's Inn Fields. Covent Garden shared with earlier venues what had become a standard design: a deep, raked stage with several sets of wings and an upstage extension penetrating the back wall to accommodate a vanishing point; the stage extending into the house, beyond the proscenium arch with its built-in doors, to the edge of the orchestra; facing it, a horseshoe-shaped auditorium comprising a wide, raked pit with backless benches and, above it, two (later, three) tiers of boxes, including some at the sides of the stage below the proscenium arch, and galleries (normally two) above the boxes. In sum, 'pit, box and gallery', a configuration and a term epitomizing the eighteenth-century theatre and the society that comprised its audience. Until

---

[29] *Survey of London*, xxxv, *passim*. For more detailed discussions of London theatres over the period of coverage, see the introductions to the five parts of *The London Stage 1660–1800*.
[30] Nalbach, *King's Theatre 1704–1867*.
[31] Mander and Mitchenson, *Theatres of London*, 96.

the early nineteenth century, by which time the forestage had disappeared and stage boxes were only a memory, there must have been a great sense of intimacy for occupants of the nearer boxes and pit. From the actors' point of view, the same sense of closeness may have prevailed, despite the distancing of the action effected by a dwindling forestage. Such intimacy would not have been entirely incompatible with the estimated capacity, some 1,400 persons, of Rich's theatre.[32]

Meanwhile, well to the east of the theatre district, in Whitechapel, a theatre had opened in Ayliffe Street, Goodman's Fields, in October 1729. Despite strong opposition, Thomas Odell, who had obtained 'Letters Patent' to erect a theatre funded by subscriptions, made a success of the venture. Giving notice of serious intent by opening with Farquhar's *The Recruiting Officer* – the very comedy mounted by John Rich on reopening Lincoln's Inn Fields in 1714 – Odell swiftly built an audience. Goodman's Fields Theatre had only a single gallery and modest admission prices, but its daily expenses were also lower than the £40 overhead at the major houses. Opposition continued, however, and in two years Odell turned the theatre over to the competent, experienced manager Henry Giffard and his touring company.[33]

Giffard soon undertook the construction of a superior theatre in Ayliffe Street, designed by the busy architect of Covent Garden, Edward Shepherd; it opened in October 1732. Like Odell before him, Giffard challenged the West End theatres at their own game with Shakespeare's *Henry IV, Part 1*, further tempting the theatrical Fates by installing over the heads of pit-dwellers a painting of an heroic George I surrounded by theatrical immortals.[34] Giffard enjoyed mixed success in subsequent years with this theatre, half the size of Shepherd's more imposing edifice. After the Licensing Act of 1737 extensively altered the theatrical landscape, the demoralized Giffard put Goodman's Fields up for sale, but then returned in 1740 and in the next season introduced a young, unknown actor called 'Mr Lydall', who would soon reveal his actual name, David Garrick.[35]

Complementing these developments in theatre construction were important advances in dramatic art. In certain plays which instantly capture the imaginations of their audiences one may read the temper of the times. Such is the case with Richard Steele's *The Conscious Lovers* (1722) and Joseph Addison's

---

[32] *Survey of London*, xxxv: 75.
[33] Scouten, *London Stage 1729–1747*, 21–2.
[34] Ibid., xxiii–xxiv. For an account of the surviving plans and other specific documentation, see ibid., xxiii–xxvii.
[35] Ibid., xxvi–xxvii.

Cato. The latter play, about the life and death, by suicide, of the famous Roman orator, had been circulating widely in manuscript. Spurred by favourable critical interest and astute estimates of likely audience response, Addison gave the completed drama to Drury Lane, where it finally appeared in April 1713, to adulation from all quarters. Already an arbiter of taste and opinion as contributor or co-editor with his friend Richard Steele of essays in the *Tatler* and the *Spectator* from 1709 to 1712, with this consciously classical tragedy Addison established himself as one of the foremost men of letters of his age. Just as unusual was the political unification (for the moment) of the Whig and Tory parties effected by the sumptuous Drury Lane production, each party outdoing the other in approbation of Cato's sententious speeches on liberty and the fall of state. Addison had kept enough ambiguity in the fable to encourage interpreters on either side. The play went through eight editions that year and, partly owing to the splendid performances of Barton Booth as the Stoic hero, Anne Oldfield as Cato's selfless daughter Marcia and Robert Wilks as the romantic Numidian prince Juba, ran for twenty continuous performances at a time when six proclaimed a success.[36]

Cibber attributed that success to its appeal to patriots compelled to assent to 'the Conduct of a suffering Virtue'.[37] The notion of virtue in distress, along with the representation of exemplary selfless behaviour, would eventually link Addison's tragedy thematically with Steele's comedy. Cibber himself had paved the way for a more reformative drama with his first comedy, *Love's Last Shift* (1696), which treats a moral problem seriously and presents a rake who, as the epilogue observes, has been 'lew'd for above four Acts' but who reforms at the end. Not the first dramatist to traffic in fifth-act repentance, Cibber appears to have anticipated Collier's withering attack, three years later, against the immorality of the stage. The twenty-seven years separating Cibber's play from Steele's comprise a period of pervasive change in both the drama and society. Vanbrugh's playful answer to Cibber, *The Relapse; or, Virtue in Danger* (1696), in which Cibber's Sir Novelty Fashion is created Lord Foppington, was, like its predecessor, immensely popular but could not stem the tide of moralising sentiment arising in the wake of Collier's strictures. Collier protested that nowhere in contemporary comedies could he discover 'a pattern to be imitated' except for a hero or a gentleman who was an 'accomplished debauchee'.[38] By Steele's time a society and a theatrical audience were

---

[36] Lafler, *Celebrated Mrs Oldfield*, 106–11; Nicoll, *History of English Drama*, II: 87–9, 294.
[37] Cibber, *Apology*, ed. Lowe, II: 27.
[38] *A letter to a lady concerning the new playhouse* (1706), excerpted in Thomas and Hare, eds., *Restoration and Georgian England*, 191.

Plate 2. Colley Cibber as Lord Foppington in John Vanbrugh's *The Relapse; or, Virtue in Danger* (Drury Lane, 26 December 1696), a comedy written as a riposte to Cibber's *Love's Last Shift; or, The Fool in Fashion* (Drury Lane, January 1696), in which Cibber played the reformed rake Sir Novelty Fashion and, in Vanbrugh's play, the same character advanced to the peerage.

developing which increasingly looked to plays to set examples of refined, morally upright conduct. As effectively the first theatre critic England had produced, in essays beginning in 1709 in the *Tatler* and the *Spectator* Steele insisted that a play in performance 'must raise very proper incitements to good behaviour'. Etherege's hero Dorimant in *The Man of Mode* (1676) is a fine gentleman who nonetheless 'trample[s] upon all order and decency', Steele argued, and the play is built on 'the ruin of virtue and innocence'.[39]

The Conscious Lovers carries out to a fault Steele's programme for the reformation of society through the reform of dramatic comedy. The distressed heroine Indiana (feelingly performed by Anne Oldfield), an ostensible orphan, is loved by the hero Bevil Junior (Barton Booth's role), whose restraint actually increases Indiana's misery. But Bevil Junior's admirable selflessness in preferring the penniless Indiana to the heiress Lucinda, with whom he has been matched by his father Sir John Bevil, a member of the landed gentry, and Lucinda's wealthy merchant father Mr Sealand, eventually reaps its just reward: discovering the bracelet left to Indiana by her dead mother, Sealand recognizes her as his long-lost daughter by his first wife. This latest in a series of providential turns in Bevil Junior's favour endorses his conscious virtue and, simultaneously, bestows the politically crucial double blessing of the gentry and the merchant class on the compact of love, inspiring in the audience (as Steele explains in his preface) 'a Joy too exquisite for Laughter'.[40] And so the political unification of Whig and Tory effected by the grandiose libertarian sentiments of Addison's *Cato* was replicated a decade later, in *The Conscious Lovers*, through the conjoining of traditionally genteel and emergent mercantile powers in a reoriented Georgian society. Steele's play accomplishes a timely social *détente* while imparting a timeless moral lesson for lovers. The time was, arguably, ripe for it. In his *Discourse Upon Comedy* (1702) George Farquhar had described contemporary comedy as 'a well-framed tale handsomely told as an agreeable vehicle for counsel or reproof'. Although the comedy of this age is far from reducible to the staging of exemplary patterns of behaviour and the material rewards of virtue, Steele's phenomenal influence on comedy would persist through Goldsmith and Sheridan's time on down to the age of Pinero and Wilde.

The theatrical context of Steele's innovations invites additional scrutiny. The role of Indiana proved a noteworthy departure from the often amoral, high-spirited young women constituting Mrs Oldfield's usual line in comedy, as in Millamant in *The Way of the World* (revived at Drury Lane as recently as 1718) and Mrs Sullen in Farquhar's *The Beaux' Stratagem*. In playing Indiana, however, she had to draw on talents for such tragic heroines as Andromache in Ambrose Philips's *The Distrest Mother* and Calista in Rowe's *The Fair Penitent*.[41] 'What have I to do but sigh, and weep', Indiana laments, 'to rave, run wild,

---

[39] Thomas and Hare, eds., *Restoration and Georgian England*, 196–8.
[40] Steele, *Plays of Steele*, ed. Kenny, 299.
[41] Lafler, *Celebrated Mrs Oldfield*, 140–2.

a Lunatick in Chains, or hid in Darkness, mutter in distracted Starts and broken Accents, my strange, strange Story!'[42] The tone is indistinguishable from the lachrymose wailings of heroines of earlier 'she-tragedies' by Otway and other late Restoration dramatists. Equally new, to Steele's audience, was the benevolent paternalism of Bevil Junior, tender lover but also solicitous protector. These sober characters were a far cry from the gay couple of Restoration comedy who, like Congreve's Mirabell and Millamant, craft their own contract for connubial bliss.[43] Seen in the light of actors' lines of business and the ethos of dramatic comedy they entail, *The Conscious Lovers* proves not only a sign of the times but also a harbinger of times to come. In one example, working with the materials of Restoration comedy, Steele created a new kind of country bumpkin in Humphry Gubbin in *The Tender Husband; or, The Accomplish'd Fools* (1705), setting an example for Goldsmith's immortal Tony Lumpkin in *She Stoops to Conquer*. In another case of parallel profiles, Steele's Biddy Tipkin (an Oldfield role) in the same play stands behind Sheridan's Lydia Languish in *The Rivals*.[44] In countless instances of this kind, the remarkable homogeneity of the acting company and the repertory system, season after season, remains evident.

The triumvirate of actor-managers at Drury Lane, principally Cibber and Robert Wilks (and Booth, for a period), which took over the management of Drury Lane in 1710 initiated a period of upwards of thirty years of increasing efficiency and prosperity, solidified in 1715 by the advent of Steele, with his influential connections at court, as joint patentee.[45] By the 1730s brilliant and spectacular performance of comedy, tragedy, farce and opera was available at no fewer than six venues: Drury Lane, Covent Garden, the King's, Lincoln's Inn Fields and Goodman's Fields, along with the summer fare available at the little theatre in the Haymarket. In these theatres music and theatre were almost constant companions. Italian opera, predominantly *opera seria* (the triumph of *opera buffa* would come later), had taken London by storm shortly after the new century began, its popularity only heightened by light-hearted mockery in the *Spectator*. By 1708 Vanbrugh's Queen's Theatre, which had opened in April 1705, had become exclusively an opera house, offering two performances a week. Over the next few decades opera became a heavily subscribed fixture of the London theatre world, not only at the King's but also at other theatres, which competed by mounting opera themselves. Between masques, pantomimes, ballad operas, so-called English operas (sung lyrics combined with spoken

---

[42] Steele, *Plays of Steele*, ed. Kenny, 5.3, p. 375.
[43] Lafler, *Celebrated Mrs Oldfield*, 41–2; Smith, *Gay Couple in Restoration Comedy*.
[44] Steele, *Plays of Steele*, ed. Kenny, 199–201.
[45] Loftis, *Steele at Drury Lane*, 46.

Plate 3. Theatre Royal Richmond, built 1764, opened May 1765, a hand-coloured print
showing separate entrances for box, pit and gallery. James Winston, who includes the
plate in his extensive survey of provincial theatres, *The Theatric Tourist* (1805), explains that
this was the third theatre in Richmond and comments on its 'picturesque appearance',
but adds: 'The front is certainly mean; and having to gain the Pit by a descent of several
steps, it is not only extremely dangerous on crowded nights . . . but furnishes a receptacle
in wet weather for mud and filth' (209).

dialogue), burlesques and pastorals (Milton's *Comus*, with music by Thomas
Arne, appeared at Drury Lane in 1738), music in some form was well nigh
inescapable for contemporary audiences.[46]

The vitality of the theatre of the age derived not only from a variety of
theatrical genres (including entr'acte entertainment, especially dancing) but a
wide range of alternatives, theatrical or quasi-theatrical, to the dramatic and
operatic art on view at the major theatres. Dramatic performance now flourished in numerous locations. Over three seasons beginning in 1709 William
Penkethman was attracting audiences willing to go down-river to Greenwich
in the summer. Starting in 1718, subscribers followed the enterprising Penkethman to Richmond, where he built a second theatre in 1719 and where summer
performance flourished, if inconsistently, until his death in 1725. Meanwhile, a

[46] Fiske, *English Theatre Music*, 31ff., *passim*, and, for later decades, Woodfield, *Opera and
Drama*.

theatre for royalty was created at Hampton Court, where performances began in the summer of 1718. Dramatic performance could also be found in booths at the various fairs in and around London: May Fair, Bartholomew Fair, Welsh Fair, and fairs in Tottenham Court Road and Southwark. In addition to singing and dancing, entertainment consisted of shorter, farcical pieces called drolls, often performed by first-rank players out of season. Other houses also captivated Londoners in search of concerts, puppet shows and other, miscellaneous entertainments. One of the oldest, at a spa in Islington, Sadler's Wells, was functioning by 1733 as a house for pantomime.[47]

Signs of vibrant theatrical life were nearly ubiquitous, and major theatres thriving in such an atmosphere of varied choice and salutary competition might have been thought to serve everyone's turn; but the facts were otherwise. Despite long-term official suppression of the scurrilous, the blasphemous and the politically libellous, and despite assaults on the licentious launched by moralists such as Collier, a great latitude of utterance persisted on the public stage. Two figures emerge in the growing controversy over how much freedom of speech might be safely allowed, Sir Robert Walpole, a canny Whig politician and leading minister under George I and George II from 1721 onwards, and Henry Fielding, later a novelist and judge but, beginning around 1730, a thorn in the side of the establishment as the author of a series of highly potent dramatic burlesques and satires. The most brilliant, *Pasquin*, subtitled *A Dramatic Satire on the Times*, produced in 1736 at the little Haymarket, and *The Historical Register, For the Year 1736*, produced there in 1737, identified Walpole obliquely but effectively, revealing beneath the cloak of fiction a corrupt, egotistical figure not exactly unrelated to Macheath, the other 'Great Man' of the age, the highwayman hero of John Gay's popular satirical ballad opera *The Beggar's Opera* (1728). *Pasquin*, wildly successful, played for over sixty nights and drew a glittering crowd of highly placed, influential persons. The battle was on.

The history of the great reassertion of theatrical regulation and censorship in the ensuing Licensing Act of 1737 cannot be told, however, simply in terms of the clash of two strong personalities.[48] Various persons at court, in Parliament

---

[47] Avery, *London Stage 1700–1729*, xxii–xxxix, and Scouten, *London Stage 1729–1747*, xix–xliii. For records of daily activities by these numerous venues see Van Lennep *et al.*, *London Stage 1660–1800*, parts 2 and 3.

[48] For the history and aftermath of the Act, see especially Nicholson, *Struggle for a Free Stage*; Crean, 'Stage Licensing Act of 1737'; Ganzel, 'Patent wrongs and patent theatres'; Loftis, *Politics of Augustan Drama*, 128–53; Scouten, *London Stage 1729–1747*, xlviii–lx; Conolly, *Censorship of English Drama*; Winton, 'Dramatic censorship'; Thomas and Hare, eds., *Restoration and Georgian England*, 205–19.

and in the theatrical establishment itself were troubled over an unruly and potentially dangerous situation in the conduct of theatrical affairs. There was wide support in this age, even in theatrical circles, for stricter control. In 1735 Walpole introduced a bill in Parliament intended to throttle satirical voices. It did not succeed, but then, in March 1737, a vicious attack on Walpole and his followers appeared in print as *The Vision of the Golden Rump*. A dramatization of the work was sent to Henry Giffard at Goodman's Fields, who instead of producing the play passed it on to Walpole, perhaps to curry favour. Walpole, who is said to have read out portions of the flagrantly scurrilous text to fellow MPs, pushed forward a bill to curb the hostile voices of Fielding, Gay and others foolhardy enough to impugn governmental authority. The principled opposition of Lord Chesterfield, who feared the bill would open the door to censorship of the press and thence lead to the loss of liberty overall, went for nought. In his autobiography Cibber, long-term member of the Drury Lane triumvirate, argued effectively for the law and against Chesterfield's view, observing that wit in print never fomented rebellion, but wit on the stage, heightened by the actor's skill, might 'unite and warm a whole body of the malicious or ignorant', leaving reason defenceless.[49]

As a result of the passage of the Licensing Act (10 Geo. II, cap. xxviii), the activities of dramatic production, theatrical management and acting companies were all materially and in some ways radically altered. Walpole's bill provided for strict control of theatre companies and the plays they might be allowed to mount, limited the King's patent-granting authority to the city of Westminster, and restricted dramatic performance to the two patent theatres, Drury Lane and Covent Garden.[50] To effect the censorship of plays the bill established an Examiner of Plays in the office of the Lord Chamberlain. All new plays, additions to old plays and even prologues and epilogues were to be submitted by the theatre manager for licensing at least fifteen days before performance; violation of the requirement subjected the offender to a fine of £50. Walpole had cleverly divided his enemy: theatre management and dramatic authorship were thrown much at odds by his assault upon them. Fielding, silenced as a dramatic author, turned to writing novels and, somewhat ironically, another career as a magistrate. Before long, at least two plays were denied a licence, setting a chilling tone which would prevail, with varying severity, for over 230 years, until the repeal of the law in 1968.

---

[49] Quoted in Thomas and Hare, eds., *Restoration and Georgian England*, 215.
[50] See the discussion of the patents in *Survey of London*, xxxv: 1–8.

The age of Garrick, 1741 to 1776

Not untypically of non-patent-theatre managers, Giffard divided his time between managing and acting in the metropolis and the provinces, in Dublin and Edinburgh, but by 1739 he was back in London, acting at Drury Lane.[51] There, for his benefit on 15 April 1740, he played Aesop in the first performance of an afterpiece entitled *Lethe: or, Aesop in the Shades*, its author an aspiring young dramatist and actor, David Garrick. Notwithstanding the terms of the Licensing Act, an appeal to the Lord Chamberlain restored Giffard as manager of the theatre in Goodman's Fields for the 1740–1 season, where Giffard invoked the subterfuge of selling tickets to 'A Concert of Vocal & instrumental Music', inserting in the middle a play offered without charge. The ruse succeeded, and in the next season, on 19 October 1741, he introduced 'A Gentleman (*who never appear'd* on any Stage)' – a goodly stretch of the truth – in the role of King Richard the Third.[52]

The 'Gentleman', Garrick, had come up to London from Lichfield in 1737 in the company of his friend and teacher Samuel Johnson. For a while he worked as a wholesale wine merchant in partnership with his brother Peter, but early success as an amateur actor fired enthusiasm for another calling. He came to know the great and problematic Charles Macklin and other actors, whom he met on business in the inns and taverns in Covent Garden and Drury Lane; perhaps he met Giffard in the same way. In any event, it is said that in the winter of 1740–1 Garrick stepped in at short notice as Harlequin, for two or three scenes, for the ailing Richard Yates in the Goodman's Fields pantomime. That summer Garrick had led a divided life, pursuing a clandestine vocation as an actor at the Tankard Street Theatre in Ipswich with Giffard's travelling company. Performing as 'Mr Lyddall', he took on a number of roles, some of which would become standards of his repertoire, all in a period of about two months.

It proved to be one of the briefest theatrical apprenticeships on record. For the next eight nights of October at Goodman's Fields, Garrick played the part of the villainous Richard to universal admiration, his text, inevitably, Cibber's redaction of Shakespeare. By the end of the month Garrick had become the best-known actor in London before almost anyone knew his name, and Giffard's theatre had turned into an easterly magnet for theatre-goers captivated by the prodigious talent and unorthodox style of the suddenly famous young actor (he was 24 years old). Garrick remained cloaked in

---

[51] For Giffard and Garrick, see Highfill *et al.*, *Biographical Dictionary*, VI.
[52] Facsimile playbill, Folger Shakespeare Library.

pseudonymity until the night of 28 November, when his name appeared in the bills for the first time. Continuing through the winter and into the spring, he presented additional new characters (new to him, but mainstays of the repertory) along with previously performed roles, which quickly became audience favourites: Lothario in *The Fair Penitent*, Fondlewife in *The Old Batchelour* and Bayes in Buckingham's hilarious Restoration burlesque of theatrical excess, *The Rehearsal*, among others. In March he essayed King Lear for the first time (in Nahum Tate's 1681 reduction of Shakespeare's tragedy to the stricter mores and hopeful biases of a later age), reducing his audience to tears. As wonderful in comedy as in tragedy, he treated theatre-goers four days later to his consummate Lord Foppington. A new level of actorly excellence had been established, in a most unlikely place. It was only a question of time before the managements of Drury Lane and Covent Garden began to exert pressure to close down Giffard's illegal playhouse; by the following May they had succeeded. Pursuing a time-tested strategy of co-opting a resourceful enemy, they engaged in behind-the-scenes competition for the exclusive services of an actor who could name his own price. Drury Lane won the contest. On 26 May, Garrick signed articles to join the company there the next season. His long association with that theatre, broken only briefly early on and lasting almost thirty-five years until his retirement in 1776, was begun.

The nature of Garrick's remarkable innovation seemed as easily described as it was marvellous to behold. In 1716 at Drury Lane an observer of a performance of *Tamerlane* had found the 'manner of speaking' in tragedy noticeably 'theatrical', that is, 'stiff and affected'.[53] Garrick's much more natural manner ran clean against precedent. Traditional declamation, the bookseller and sometime actor Thomas Davies explained, called for actors to make 'points' by raising and then suddenly lowering their voices, whereas Garrick's style was 'easy and familiar, yet forcible'.[54] Modulating language and flowing facial expression combined in a continuous presentation of character in action. Such apparently effortless power commanded the assent of his audience – and fellow-players. Far from isolating or eclipsing them, he drew them into the circle of his dominance, influencing their own characterization and delivery for the better and so creating a more mellifluous ensemble.

By these means, Garrick made the best of what had become, as a result of the Licensing Act, a much more straitened situation for professional actors. Actors still travelled a good deal, using the summer to venture to Ireland and

---

[53] *Diary of Dudley Ryder*, quoted in Avery, *London Stage 1700–1729*, cxxv.
[54] Quoted in Burnim, 'Garrick, David', in Highfill *et al.*, *Biographical Dictionary*, vi: 7.

Scotland as well as to the provinces. Now, in the diminished post-Licensing Act world, because of the effective restriction of opportunities to Covent Garden and Drury Lane and the heavy penalties levied on players who previously could move about more freely, a much less salubrious atmosphere prevailed. As the number of theatres increased, in the first three decades of the century and after, a much enlarged corps of performers – actors, singers and dancers – became the norm. By 1737 as many as 300 names can be discovered in seasonal bills and advertisements; at Drury Lane alone the number remained constant at just below seventy-five.[55] And so, ten years later, when Garrick purchased a half-interest in Drury Lane from its current patentee, James Lacy, for £8,000 and took over the management of the theatre, a much altered situation existed. Ironically, the reining in and regularizing of actors' careers after 1737 allowed Garrick to establish unprecedented coherence and continuity of artistic achievement, despite the large number of performers under his control.[56]

Garrick's entry into management at Drury Lane followed a theatre season of almost unprecedented excellence and variety. Garrick had had his troubles at Drury Lane, and in May 1746 signed articles of agreement with Rich to act at Covent Garden for the 1746–7 season. Beginning the following November, he was paired in a series of plays with one of the greatest actors of the century, James Quin, in a succession of roles which drew royalty and thousands of other Londoners to witness that rare sight. One of the century's greatest theatrical events began on 14 November, when for ten nearly consecutive performances Garrick played Lothario opposite Quin as Horatio in Rowe's pathetic tragedy *The Fair Penitent*, with Mrs Cibber in the title role. At the same time, Drury Lane was featuring its new leading man, the handsome, sensitive tragedian Spranger Barry. Meanwhile, a company at Lincoln's Inn Fields would offer fully one hundred nights of plays through the winter. So commanding was the presence of good acting in mainpieces at all three theatres that pantomimes were in scarce supply and, for many nights, no afterpieces were included in the bill.[57] In later years, brisk competition between Drury Lane and Covent Garden would occasionally result in even more direct rivalry.

Though obedient to 'the Drama's Laws', sometimes tyrannically enforced by 'the Drama's Patrons', as Dr Johnson identified the theatre audience in his prologue written for Garrick's opening night, 15 September 1747, the new half-owner and manager of Drury Lane displayed remarkable initiative, foresight

---

[55] Scouten, *London Stage 1729–1747*, cxxv.
[56] Statistics gathered in Stone and Kahrl, *David Garrick*, 661–2.
[57] Scouten, *London Stage 1729–1747*, cliii.

Act V. THE ORPHAN. *Scene 6.*

Publish'd for Bells British Theatre Sept 7. 1776.

M.ᵣˢ *CIBBER, in the Character of* MONIMIA.

Read'st thou not something in my Face, that speaks
wonderful Change and Horror from within me?

Plate 4. Susanna Maria Cibber (née Arne) as Monimia in Thomas Otway's *The Orphan; or,*
The Unhappy Marriage. Aaron Hill praised the indescribable 'manner in which Mrs Cibber
engages our affection, our tears, in the character of Monimia' (*The Actor*, 1750).

and tact over the length of his career. The precedents set by actor-managers in the past had established a proactive style of management, which Garrick carried to even greater lengths. A telling instance lies in his decision not to perform on that opening night, ceding the honours instead to the strong-willed, long-lived actor and dramatist Charles Macklin, once his mentor, with whom Garrick had patched up a serious quarrel. Macklin appeared in his most famous role, Shylock, an incomparable portrayal fixed in the slow, deliberate articulation of his first words, 'Three thousand ducats'.[58] Garrick waited until 15 October to delight audiences with his first role as actor-manager, Archer in *The Beaux' Stratagem*.

An autocrat of quicksilver mental powers, in the years of his dominance over the English-speaking theatre Garrick functioned brilliantly as actor, manager, dramatist, man of the theatre, friend and frequent guest of the aristocracy and pre-eminent representative of the English theatre. One measure, among many, of his contribution to the art and culture of his age was his introduction of estimable actors to the London theatre scene and his enhancement of promising careers: Peg Woffington, Hannah Pritchard, William Powell, Kitty Clive, Spranger Barry, Anne Street Dancer (who would become Mrs Barry), among others. And the competitive presence of the Drury Lane company encouraged Covent Garden to mount plays supported by some of the best actors of the day: Mrs Barrington, Mrs Bellamy, Mrs Bland, Bensley, Quick, Shuter and Woodward, along with the perennial favourites Macklin, Quin, Thomas Sheridan and Mrs Woffington (a migrant from Drury Lane) and, later on, Barry and Mrs Barry, who left Garrick's company in 1774.

Often envied where not admired, Garrick inevitably rubbed some up the wrong way. Thirteen surviving letters document his efforts to placate the unhappy Mrs Abingdon.[59] Nor could the aspiring dramatist avoid Garrick's unrelenting critical eye, even if he was Professor of Poetry at Oxford. After five failed attempts, the Revd William Hawkins threatened to take his case to the public. 'I have ye same right to reject a Play, which I think a bad one', Garrick replied, 'as You have to compose it'. Many aggrieved individuals developed great powers of tact and patience under his inadvertent tutelage, and numerous persons dependent on him for their livelihoods were respectful 'from fear of his power', Dr Johnson observed, 'and hopes of his favour, and admiration of his talents'.[60] Less respectful was the critical establishment, some of whose

---

[58] Appleton, *Charles Macklin*, 50.
[59] Garrick, *Letters*, ed. Little and Kahrl.
[60] Boswell, quoted in Burnim, 'Garrick, David', in Highfill *et al.*, *Biographical Dictionary*, VI: 77.

Plate 5. Charles Macklin as Shylock: 'Most Learned Judge!' The German visitor Georg C. Lichtenberg recalled, of Macklin's Drury Lane début in the role on 14 February 1741, that his first words, 'Three thousand ducats', were 'slowly and impressively spoken', and observed: 'Three such words uttered thus at the outset give the keynote of the whole character'.

members were happy to instruct him, in personal letters or in print, in the salient truths about the characters he portrayed. Garrick's was the first age of theatrical criticism, which came into its heady youth even as he made his bid for actorly fame. It was sometimes difficult to distinguish between criticism and satire in matters theatrical. Perhaps their most notable combination occurred in the Revd Charles Churchill's *The Rosciad* (1761), full of critical complaints about actors but complimentary to Garrick himself. Goldsmith complained, 'On the stage he was natural, simple, affecting, / 'Twas only that, when he was off, he was acting.'[61] Theatre criticism in Garrick's time ran the gamut from scurrilous condemnation and pique to incisive observation and insight – a reflection of the centrality and fascination of the theatre in this age. Beyond the early precedent set by Steele in the *Theatre* (1720) and Aaron Hill in the *Prompter* (1734–6), no critics match the reputations achieved in a later day by William Hazlitt, Leigh Hunt and Charles Lamb. All the same, a remarkable flourishing of critical pens, encouraged by Garrick's own success, occurred, both in newspapers and the more specialized journals and periodicals devoted to the theatre and its social surround.[62]

Garrick's engagement with Shakespeare was one of the most important, and typical, aspects of his career, for it enabled him to combine broad abilities as an actor, dramatist, producer and even book collector with his admiration for Shakespeare's plays and their limitlessly actable characters.[63] Of the ninety-six roles he played over the length of his career, sixteen were Shakespearean, and his performance often embraced the restoration of lines unheard in theatres since the Restoration.[64] Prominent among new productions by Garrick were his remountings (based on extensively revised texts) of *Macbeth* (1744), *Romeo and Juliet* (1748) and, much later, *Hamlet* (1772). Garrick's prompt-books, still extant, record in detail his handling of these and other plays, revealing his approach to Shakespeare as his own entirely.[65] Its results on the stage speak of both his own tastes and interests and those of his age. He declined to set aside the Tate adaptation of *King Lear* and to restore the Fool and the rest of Shakespeare's original play, including the tragic ending which his friend Samuel Johnson could not bear to read, let alone see acted. And, having played Hamlet for years in a text not far removed from the Davenant version, in 1772 Garrick

[61] *Retaliation*, quoted in Burnim, 'Garrick, David', in Highfill *et al.*, *Biographical Dictionary*, VI: 77–8.
[62] Stratman, *Britain's Theatrical Periodicals 1720–1967*; Gray, *Theatrical Criticism*.
[63] Stone and Kahrl, *David Garrick*, chap. 6.
[64] Ibid., 656–8.
[65] Shattuck, *Shakespeare Promptbooks*; Burnim, *David Garrick: Director*; for Garrick's own plays and adaptations, Garrick, *Plays of David Garrick*, ed. Pedicord and Bergmann.

mounted a new version of the play 'rescued', he asserted, 'from all the rubbish of the fifth act'. Despite its familiar characters, the action of this last act is barely recognizable; in James Boaden's opinion it 'sullied the page of Shakespeare'. The production nonetheless 'merited the great Applause', as the prompter William Hopkins noted, of the Drury Lane audience.[66]

The most original 'Shakespearean' production of Garrick's entire career depended only incidentally on Shakespeare's plays and much more on the reputation of the dramatist himself, who by the mid-eighteenth century was becoming a cultural divinity without compare.[67] No clearer instance occurs of Garrick's own veneration for this secular saint than the Shakespeare Jubilee of 1769, which belatedly took place at Stratford some five years after the more appropriate date of 1764. Enormous thought and planning by Garrick, who wrote an ode and song lyrics and devised processions and other events, and by the Stratford city fathers, went into the celebration, arousing mixed reactions but generating great excitement as the date of the opening, on 6 September, approached. After a promising start, however, torrential rains caused the cancellation of a procession of Shakespeare's characters and other scheduled events. Although Garrick was able to recite his *Ode upon Dedicating a Building and Erecting a Statue to Shakespeare* 'amidst admiring multitudes',[68] accompanied by music composed by Thomas Arne, the jubilee proved a sad failure, incurring a deficit of £2,000. Garrick made the best of it by assuming the debt himself and by mounting a series of processions and related festive shows on the Drury Lane stage, featuring a work called *The Jubilee*, consisting mostly of songs written for the Stratford event. Long after memories of the soggy disaster had faded, *The Jubilee* was still to be seen on the Drury Lane stage into the nineteenth century.[69] So godlike had the Bard of Avon become in this period, perhaps principally owing to Garrick's efforts in the theatre and at the jubilee, that Garrick himself enjoyed an apotheosis of sorts. In a print now in the British Library, he is depicted as a reclining figure being borne aloft to Mount Olympus by winged figures of comedy and tragedy, while a host of Drury Lane actors, dressed as their favourite Shakespearean characters, pay him obeisance. To the partial observer, Garrick would seem to be standing (or sitting) in for Shakespeare himself.[70]

---

[66] Burnim, *David Garrick: Director*, 152–5.

[67] Hogan, *Shakespeare in the Theatre, 1701–1800*.

[68] Comment by Garrick's chief rival at Covent Garden, William 'Gentleman' Smith, quoted in Stone and Kahrl, *David Garrick*, 581.

[69] Burnim, 'Garrick, David', in Highfill et al., *Biographical Dictionary*, VI: 46–8, and Deelman, *Great Shakespeare Jubilee*.

[70] Reproduced in Burnim, 'Garrick, David', in Highfill, et al., *Biographical Dictionary*, VI: 66.

Although Garrick is sometimes presented as bestriding the world like a pint-sized colossus, crowd-pleasing entertainments of myriad kinds were a staple of theatrical and extra-theatrical performance since the Restoration. When the pantomimes, a significant element of Christmas celebrations, were on in the winter at Covent Garden and Drury Lane, they often drew the fullest crowds of the year, sometimes spelling the difference between net gain and loss over a season.[71] Pantomime, from its English origins in the early eighteenth century, remained an increasingly seasonal entertainment, characterized by ever greater spectacle. Most characteristic of these eye-pleasing features was the culminating transformation scene, which took on even greater importance in Regency and Victorian pantomime, overshadowing the harlequinade, the latter a major attraction in the days of Rich at Lincoln's Inn Fields and Covent Garden in the 1720s. A detailed description, published in the *Gentleman's Magazine*, of the favourite Covent Garden pantomime *Harlequin a Sorcerer*, first performed in 1725 and revived in 1752, captures the ripe flavour of the form. In the final transformation scene 'the stage is extended to a prodigious depth, closing with a prospect of fine gardens and a temple', followed by a 'grand chorus' and 'lastly, a low bow from the performers'.[72] Audiences thronging to see these effects were sometimes perennial consumers of major theatre fare, for once able to take their families to an entertainment which would not bring blushes to the cheeks of young persons; others were part of a much wider segment of the populace hungry for a variety of non-intellectual entertainment.

To be sure, the performances traditionally available on patent theatre stages themselves covered a wide range, harking back to offerings available from the end of the Interregnum. Incidental, entr'acte entertainment, a prominent feature of the Elizabethan and Jacobean theatre, survived intact on the Restoration stage: dancers, singers, rope-dancers and jugglers shared backstage space with dark-visaged tragedians and tearful heroines and their sprightlier counterparts in comedy. The patentees were permitted to perform virtually anything viable on the stage of a playhouse, while no others were allowed the performance of anything that smacked of dramatic art. All the same, human ingenuity and a talent for evasion, coupled with an expanding metropolitan population and the authorities' preoccupation with other matters, had resulted, by the third quarter of the century, in a situation far different from the one in which Davenant and Killigrew first exercised their joint monopoly. By this time, even as Garrick

---

[71] Donohue, *Dramatic Character*, 84–5n.
[72] *Gentleman's Magazine* 23 (1752): 52–3, quoted in Price, *Theatre in the Age of Garrick*, 71–3.

reigned over what was coming to be called the legitimate theatre, the amusements available on either side of the Thames and for miles beyond were extraordinarily various.

The English love for music and song, along with delight in show and a taste for tea, fostered and characterized the amusements of the people, in London as elsewhere throughout the kingdom. Attractions included spas, circus rings, taverns, pleasure gardens, exhibition halls and other venues which filled idle hours and tempted many from their work. Masquerades, perennially popular, could be found at pleasure gardens, in public rooms and even on the stages of patent theatres. Elsewhere, concerts and fireworks were the rule nightly, and tea gardens had sprung up throughout the metropolis, offering far more than tea to patrons thirsty for novelty.[73] Music and song were ubiquitous and dancing widespread. Out of the pleasure gardens grew the circus, where equestrian feats alternated with monkeys and acrobats and where, towards the end of the century, dramatic presentations went so far as to offer Shakespeare – without words. Astley's Amphitheatre, masterminded by Philip Astley, a showman capable of stunning feats of horsemanship,[74] and the Royal Circus, backed by the ambitious but uneasy partnership of Charles Hughes and Charles Dibdin and offering pantomime, ballet and spectacle on a par with Astley's, were in fierce competition. Although puppet-shows were not born in the ring, they thrived there and elsewhere, in domestic settings and even on the stages of major theatres.[75] Solo entertainers such as the gifted mimic Samuel Foote had emerged before mid-century. And, as the century drew to a close, the burletta, originally a brief, sprightly musical entertainment imported from Italy, combining arias and recitative, became popular and took on ever greater significance with respect to the character and legal standing of theatrical and quasi-theatrical entertainment.[76]

Amidst this rich, complex theatrical environment, when it came time for Garrick, his health increasingly unsatisfactory, to retire, he planned a long goodbye in the form of a series of performances of the characters by whom audiences knew him the best. His farewell appearance, as Don Felix in Centlivre's *The Wonder*, on 10 June 1776, was preceded by a series of still masterful characterizations: Lusignan in *Zara*, Abel Drugger, based on *The Alchemist*, Kitely in *Every Man in His Humour*, Hamlet, Sir John Brute in *The Provok'd Wife*, King Lear, Ranger in *The Suspicious Husband* and, of necessity,

---

[73] Wroth, *London Pleasure Gardens*, 4–7.
[74] Saxon, *Enter Foot and Horse*.
[75] Speaight, *English Puppet Theatre*.
[76] Donohue, 'London theatre at the end of the eighteenth century'.

though requiring great effort, Richard III. He was 59 years of age, Already, on 19 January, Garrick had concluded the sale of his share of Drury Lane to an elite group of investors spearheaded by the young Richard Brinsley Sheridan.[77] On his retirement the following June, Garrick left behind him a theatre, a company and an art greatly improved by his efforts. Never one to defy his audience's tastes or biases, he had nevertheless led them to experience the best and the worst of what they understood to be human, and had entertained them mightily well in the process. At the same time, he had bettered the circumstances for viewing plays, banishing forever from the stage the nuisance of aristocratic audience members ranged almost cheek-by-jowl with performers. His efforts at technical improvement had resulted in a more elegantly costumed corps and a better lighted, scenically improved *mise-en-scène*. The efforts of the brilliant European scene designer Philippe Jacques de Loutherbourg, whom Garrick had recruited, had taken the theatre in new, romantic and Gothic directions. Efficient managerial practices had established remarkable regularity and stability in the seasonal round of rehearsals, performances and benefits, along with more equitable pay scales, favourable assignment of roles and humane conditions in which actors might pursue their craft. Large-scale renovation of the theatre building in 1775 by one of the premier architects of the day, Robert Adam, had resulted in a more decorous, beautifully ornamented architectural surround.[78] All in all, the theatre seemed well poised for continued success.

Unfortunately, as Garrick himself would find before he died in 1779, the case would prove otherwise.

Sheridan and the post-Garrick age, 1776 to 1800

The mid-1770s mark not only Garrick's retirement but the appearance of a brilliant new writer of stage comedy, the young Irish wit, ambitious political genius and sometime theatrical manager Richard Brinsley Sheridan. Sheridan's mother was the dramatist and successful novelist Frances Sheridan. Sheridan's father Thomas had enjoyed a long career in the theatre as an actor in Dublin and London and as manager of the Crow Street Theatre, Dublin, beginning in 1745, though his greater influence lay in the field of elocution, in which he was an important innovator and tutor.[79] The elder Sheridans' talents do not explain their son's brilliance, but surely they contributed to his extraordinary verbal facility. Well before he established a reputation as a spellbinding political

---

[77] Stone and Kahrl, *David Garrick*, 605.
[78] *Survey of London*, xxxv: 45–8.
[79] Sheldon, *Thomas Sheridan of Smock-Alley*.

orator, within the single year of 1775 three works in comical and musical veins by the precocious 24-year-old appeared on the stage of Covent Garden Theatre: the extravagant comedy *The Rivals* (17 January), set in Bath; *St Patrick's Day; or, The Scheming Lieutenant* (2 May), a charming farce with an Irish hero; and *The Duenna; or, The Double Elopement* (21 November), an intricately plotted comic opera. By early 1777, having acquired the managerial reins of Drury Lane from Garrick in the previous year, Sheridan had mounted there still another comedy, *A Trip to Scarborough* (24 February), an alteration of Vanbrugh's *The Relapse*, along with his crowning achievement as a comic dramatist, *The School for Scandal* (8 May). Unfortunately, by the time he produced *The Camp*, a slight entertainment performed as an afterpiece, in October 1778, he had only one more major comic work before him: *The Critic; or, A Tragedy Rehearsed* (30 October 1779), a burlesque of authorial, critical and theatrical excesses in the tradition of Buckingham's *The Rehearsal*, lampooning an attempt at high drama by an aspiring critic and revealing a masterful grasp of the theatre and drama of his day. In a much changed world two decades later, as author of the spectacular pot-boiler *Pizarro; or, The Conquest of Peru* (24 May 1799), Sheridan would engage in the same sort of self-indulgent display for which he had mocked his egotistical critic Puff. The production of *Pizarro* accomplished Sheridan's royalist political ends but remained a far cry from the two comic masterpieces of 1775 and 1777 and *The Duenna*, an enormously successful piece of musical theatre.[80]

Sheridan's complex latter-day reputation thus depends on the memorable comic writing of his early manhood, his lifelong record (he died in 1816) as an unsinkable survivor of political vicissitudes and his chronic mismanagement, for more than three decades, of the theatre he had hoped would make his fortune but which became a noose around his neck.[81] With the sole exception of *She Stoops to Conquer*, the only dramatic works of the 1770s still performed today are Sheridan's. Exploring his characters' disruptive, self-serving desires, these comedies and comic operas develop conflicts that throw society into disorder but then reverse course to effect its rescue. Authenticity is their hallmark; their invariable product, the laughter of knowing assent. Their impact on contemporary audiences resulted from Sheridan's knack for setting conservative processes in clandestine motion; identifying the qualities that make for happy community, he invented actions which called those elements into question but which ended up endorsing them. To draw an example from *The Rivals*,

---

[80] Loftis, *Sheridan and the Drama of Georgian England*.
[81] O'Toole, *Traitor's Kiss*.

early in the play the circulating library on which the heroine Lydia Languish depends for her sentimental novels is condemned by the curmudgeonly Sir Anthony Absolute as 'an evergreen tree of diabolical knowledge!' Implicating the powerful influence of print culture on the age, Sir Anthony's comment invites reflection on the disparity between romantic ideals and real experience, a conflict thoroughly explored in the subsequent action of the comedy.

The social coherence of these plays may also be discovered in the architectural features of the venues in which they were mounted. An engraving illustrating the interior design by Robert Adam of his reconstructed Drury Lane Theatre of 1775 (a fine example of neoclassical scale and balance) recapitulates the character of the theatre of Garrick as he prepared to quit its precincts.[82] The view, unusually, is of the empty theatre auditorium from the stage. Below the proscenium door on either side is a stage box, contiguous with additional boxes along the sides of the auditorium above the pit. An ornate metal barrier has replaced the more dangerous-looking spikes shown in earlier illustrations of the Drury Lane forestage. A group of three actors at centre stage is oriented towards the audience. From this perspective the broad, raked expanse of backless benches has the feel of a real 'pit', the boxes and galleries standing at eye level or higher. A palpable sense emerges of a full, varied surround, a virtual cohort of audience and players much aware of one another, engaged in a common enterprise: here are over 2,000 virtual participants in the on-going action on stage, an assembly clearly visible under the continuous illumination of stage and auditorium. Descriptions of such an audience must reflect the complex conditions – economic, demographic, political and otherwise – of a rapidly growing metropolis. The contentious elements of this society comprise a sometimes rowdy, opinionated and demanding auditory, yet on most nights audiences remained attentive and appreciative, well aware of themselves and insistent on a high standard of performance from actors, each of whom they had already seen in numerous roles, on many a night.

The celebrated screen scene in Act 4 of *The School for Scandal* provides a vantage point on the audience Sheridan inherited from Garrick. In the spirit of fun Charles Surface pulls the screen down; it falls forward, on a stage raked steeply enough for the entire house from pit to gallery to view the moment clearly. Because the audience knows she is hiding there, the sudden revelation of Lady Teazle's presence in the house of her would-be seducer, Joseph Surface, is extremely funny, but comic also in a deeper sense. The dialogue that

---

[82] *Works in Architecture of Robert and James Adam*, pl. 93 (exterior) and pl. 94 (interior). See *Survey of London*, xxxv, pl. 8 and 9a.

ensues when the screen falls to the floor – Charles's exclamation 'Lady Teazle! by all that's wonderfull!' and her outraged husband's 'Lady Teazle! by all that's Horrible!' – sums up the conflict and precipitates the resolution in a single brilliant moment. The wayward young wife, whose foolhardiness by implication threatens the whole of society, appeals for forgiveness from a now wiser husband and is taken back into society's supportive embrace – poised though it is on the brink of momentous change. The date of the play, 1777, marks a time when political revolution, already under way in America, is undermining the traditional sanctions of a privileged, hierarchical society. No revolution will occur in Britain, but revolution outside its boundaries will profoundly affect what goes on within them. Even by the 1780s alterations in the make-up of British society and concomitant changes in the generic attributes of comedy will set the theatre of Garrick and Sheridan on a new and perilous course.

The years following Garrick's retirement are often viewed as a regrettable decline, but reassessment is in order. To be sure, Garrick's remarkable dominance proves all the more striking in the context of subsequent history. As the American Revolution began, indications of an insurgent mentality were surfacing in various quarters in Britain itself, in the arts as well as in politics and society. A world-altering transition would occur in the theatre, the drama and society at large. The age of Sheridan (as it might, from our perspective, be called), extending by a good decade into the next century, proved one of the most tumultuous periods of British theatre, as forces for change grappled with increasingly conservative, even reactionary, counter-powers.

In forming a coalition to purchase the Drury Lane patent from Garrick and Lacy, Sheridan's intention was to make a double-fortune, as both patentee and manager of the theatre – an irresistible prospect for someone with his talents and energies. Surely, few more attractive opportunities for investment were available in London in the 1770s than the theatre Garrick had raised to such a pinnacle of achievement. Within just a few years, however, the profitable enterprise in Bridges Street, Drury Lane, had developed severe financial problems. A decades-long history of bad management and debt would ensue. The near half-century after 1776 was also a time when demography became a crucial factor affecting matters theatrical. The phenomenal increase in population over this period, witnessed most alarmingly in London, was reflected obliquely in the enlargement of major theatres and an influx of a more boisterous and unlettered audience, inspiring much anxiety in theatre managers, shareholders and players.

Riots in the theatre provide the most vivid examples of such disorder. The uprisings over the attempted abolition of half price in 1763 at both major

Plate 6. Fitzgiggio riots of 1763 at Covent Garden Theatre. The caption reads: 'Riot at CG Theatre in 1763 in consequence of the Managers refusing to admit half-price in the Opera of Artaxerxes'.

theatres and the so-called 'O. P.' ('Old Price') riots of 1809 are among the most telling instances.[83] Riots do more than characterize the unruly society of the long Georgian age and its high-profile counterpart, the theatre audience, however; they indicate what power and magnetism the theatre could exert. Fears of a large cohort of society sent out of control by a displeasing stage performance, an insufficiently self-abasing actor, or some other affront to its sensibilities are understandable. As the Licensing Act of 1737 acknowledged, such fears lay behind the censorship of the theatre, for it was widely believed that theatrical representations could arouse human 'passions' beyond the limits of self-restraint. In his discussion of Shakespearean drama, Samuel Johnson had insisted that 'a play read affects the mind like a play acted',[84] but the solitary act of reading rarely conduced to violent public display. Censorship of books (novels, for instance) was relatively unobtrusive, where it existed at all, but the potential reactions of theatrical audiences were a different matter entirely.[85]

---

[83] Lynch, *Box Pit and Gallery*; Pedicord, *Theatrical Public in the Time of Garrick*; Hughes, *Drama's Patrons*; and Baer, *Theatre and Disorder in Late Georgian London*.

[84] *The Plays of William Shakespeare*, ed. Samuel Johnson (1765), preface, in *Samuel Johnson on Shakespeare*, ed. Wimsatt, 40.

[85] Altick, *English Common Reader*; Peters, *Congreve*.

William Godwin's radical novel of 1794, *Things as They Are; or, The Adventures of Caleb Williams*, provides an illuminating case in point. Godwin's intention was to expose the tyrannical power of the privileged over society's less fortunate, yet the novel was published without official opposition. Two years later a dramatic adaptation, as *The Iron Chest*, by the younger George Colman, reached the Drury Lane stage and, after initial failure, became a perennial favourite up through the age of Irving. As in the case of all other plays, however, it had needed prior approval by William Larpent, since 1778 Examiner of Plays in the Lord Chamberlain's office, from whose decisions no appeal was possible. Colman's new title and different names for the chief characters, coupled with a facile melodramatic dramaturgy and muting of the novel's radical energies, distanced the play from Godwin's reputation. Colman's sympathetic rendering of the guilt-stricken murderer, Sir Edward Mortimer, played by the saturnine John Philip Kemble, nonetheless parallels Godwin's psychologically subtle treatment of his agonized villain, Falkland. The timeliness of *Caleb Williams*, its insistence on the rights of a powerless underclass and its surprising survival of the licensing process in Colman's *The Iron Chest*[86] reflect the pressure of forces for change from which patent theatre proprietors were not exempt.

After a brief flirtation with the idea of a third patent theatre, in the 1790s both Covent Garden and Drury Lane were transformed by the construction of larger auditoriums and wider and deeper stages. Faced with the need to entertain a larger audience and nursing a desire for greater profits, the managerial powers of Covent Garden and Drury Lane theatres made a decision of epochal magnitude, abandoning their felicitous, well-proportioned houses, yet bowing only ambiguously to the imperative imposed by a growing population and a troubled economy. By 1794 these two theatres, reconstructed by the architect Henry Holland, boasted maximum capacity figures of slightly more than 3,000 and 3,600 respectively; yet, instead of enlarging the gallery to include a greater if less cultivated audience, that space was reduced in favour of a more generous accommodation of boxes (a pattern repeated in the succeeding century).[87] Such factors qualify in crucial ways the enormous effort expended to rehabilitate both patent theatres.

The proprietary mentality of the patentees was already on record in their earlier response, in 1787, to one of the most significant attempts at insurgency in eighteenth-century theatrical history: the attempt by the actor John Palmer to establish an alternative theatre, the Royalty, in Wellclose Square. This district, one of the liberties of the Tower, situated in the midst of a large potential

---

[86] Loftis, 'Political and social thought in the drama', 281–2.
[87] Donohue, 'London theatre at the end of the century', 365–7.

INTERIOR OF THE LATE THEATRE ROYAL DRURY LANE *BUILT BY HENRY HOLLAND ESQ. R.A.*
OPENED WITH A SELECTION OF SACRED MUSIC 12TH MARCH 1794, DESTROYED BY FIRE, 24TH FEBRUARY 1809

Plate 7. The greatly enlarged interior of Drury Lane after the renovation by Holland in 1791–4. Included in an extra-illustrated edition of James Boaden's *Life of Mrs Jordan* (1831), II: opp. 251.

audience, presented a striking alternative to Covent Garden and Drury Lane. The audience to which Palmer hoped to appeal is evident in the very configuration of the Royalty auditorium: some 60 per cent of an overall capacity of nearly 2,600 persons was devoted to galleries, a far higher proportion than in the rehabilitated Drury Lane and Covent Garden of half a decade later. Unfortunately for Palmer, despite the apparent gravity of his threat to the hegemony of the majors, the enterprise hung on the slender thread of permission from the Lord Lieutenant Governor of the Tower to build within Tower jurisdiction and a licence from the Tower Hamlets magistrates.

The crush of the crowd on opening night, 20 June, was immense, but by that time Palmer's venture had already been marked for failure. Harris and Sheridan and their patent theatre colleagues threatened legal redress if he persisted, and Palmer was frightened badly enough to declare the first performance a benefit for the London Hospital. 'Tumblers and Dancing Dogs' would have excited no interest, he complained to his audience, but mounting 'a moral play' (*As You Like It*, plus Garrick's perennial afterpiece *Miss in Her Teens*) invoked the wrath of malevolent West End demigods. The Royalty remained a venue for dogs, dancers and other miscellaneous entertainment, predominantly musical and undignified by the interdicted spoken word. The sad defeat of Palmer's ambitious but naïve attempt to carry dramatic art to a non-traditional audience reinforced the supremacy of mainstream theatrical forces. Wresting control of the drama from the patentees would require many more years, and the participation of many 'minor' theatres, to accomplish.

Ironically, the less sophisticated audience to which Palmer had hoped to appeal was calling for types of performance not represented by his opening bill. This sign of the times was writ large in the growing fragmentation and instability of the late eighteenth-century audience, many of whose members were clamouring ambiguously for something new and different yet reassuringly familiar. Their interests and needs are undoubtedly reflected in the gradual but significant mutation, beginning around this time, of the tried and true genres of comedy, tragedy and farce performed at the patent houses themselves. A comparison of the contemporary generic classifications assigned to plays in the extensive hand-lists of Allardyce Nicoll's *A History of English Drama* for the period up to Garrick's retirement and those assigned to offerings appearing in the next quarter-century reveals a significant tendency towards variation and subdivision.[88] Change of this kind is particularly noticeable in comedy, whose brief has always been one of engaging optimistically with common life as presently lived. As the period progressed, even where the basic generic designation of 'comedy' remains, study of the substance and tone of the play may reveal alteration in the ethos of the work.

Significant examples of changes of this kind may be discovered in the plays of Elizabeth Inchbald written and performed in the late 1780s and 1790s, especially such generically mixed works as *Such Things Are* (1787) and *Every One has His Fault* (1793) and her popular adaptation of a Kotzebue drama as *Lovers' Vows* (1798).[89] One of the most interesting, if atypical, writers of the period, Inchbald first came to notice in the London theatre as an actress but had greater aspirations as a playwright. Whilst still performing, she succeeded in having plays of her own produced. Early on, she learned how to navigate the treacherous shoals of dramatic authorship, including the perils presented by unscrupulous patent theatre managers unnerved by a woman attempting

---

[88] Nicoll, *History of English Drama 1660–1900*, vol. III, *Late Eighteenth-Century Drama 1750–1800*.

[89] Inchbald, *Plays of Elizabeth Inchbald*.

to break into a man's profession.[90] Ultimately, Inchbald became a novelist as well as a dramatist, and in addition edited two extensive collections of British plays and farces, rounding out a distinctive, unorthodox life in the theatre.

Among the factors affecting the changing theatre in which Inchbald and her fellow-professionals laboured, the legal context in which theatrical performance took place is of singular importance for understanding the form and format of minor theatre offerings and the strategies for survival employed by the major theatres. Legislation passed in the mid-eighteenth century, following on from the Licensing Act of 1737, regulating disorderly houses and the serving of intoxicating beverages forms the background for these developments.[91] In an age when actors and other performers were still legally classed, as in Elizabethan times, as 'vagabonds, rogues and sturdy beggars' and when the activities of the Lord Chamberlain's Examiner of Plays had become an ineluctable fact of life, the watchful eye of governmental regulation ranged far and wide. In their effort to bring wayward places of entertainment under stricter control, however, the authorities unintentionally ended up sanctioning what they could not suppress. As governmental overseers have always found, what calls for regulation must first be defined. In attempts to impose order on chaos, the authors of legislation enacted in 1755 as the Act of 28 George II opened a gaping loophole through which entertainments performed at unlicensed taverns and show places and even fly-by-night booths could creep to legal respectability.

The instrument of this remarkable development was that charming, quasi-operatic *jeu d'esprit*, the burletta. Historians have traced the English-language emergence of the form to an early burlesque of Italian opera by Henry Carey called *The Dragon of Wantley*, first performed (the coincidence is worth savouring) in 1737. The most influential instance of the 'new' English burletta was a Dublin-born musical interlude by the Irish wit Kane O'Hara called *Midas*, first played at the Crow Street Theatre in 1762 and staged two years later at Covent Garden. Identified variously as 'an English burletta' and 'a comic opera', *Midas* went through eight editions in fifteen years, became a staple of the afterpiece repertory, and enjoyed simultaneous revival as late as 1822 at Drury Lane and Covent Garden.[92]

That the English burletta form appeared first on a patent theatre stage and continued to succeed there was one of the trenchant ironies suffusing the

---

[90] Donkin, *Getting into the Act*, 110–31.
[91] Ganzel, 'Patent wrongs and patent theatres'.
[92] Playbills, Harvard Theatre Collection, and other sources cited in Donohue, 'Burletta and the early nineteenth-century English theatre'.

efforts of the patent theatres to prevent other, 'minor' theatres from performing the spoken drama. Eventually the designation *burletta* swelled into a portmanteau term covering anything the minor theatres chose to produce, even the spoken drama, the fiercely guarded property of Davenant and Killigrew and their heirs and assigns. Whatever generic characteristics it possessed, its popularity set a precedent for the phenomenal development of the form, over the rest of the century and into the next, as a transparent device for circumventing the law. By 1832, the year of a wide-ranging parliamentary enquiry into the wretched state of the London theatre, patent theatre proprietors had become helplessly unable to define a term which had come to mean whatever a theatrical entrepreneur might choose. Circumvention of the law had succeeded so well that the spoken drama had become ubiquitous on the stages of London theatres. Just over a decade later, in 1843, the official abolition of patent privilege served largely to acknowledge and endorse what had effectively been the unwritten law of the land for an entire generation.

In the context set by these extraordinary developments, the writings for the theatre of James C. Cross, produced both at the major theatres and at other venues in the 1790s and into the next century, comprise almost an index of prevailing conditions. Cross's range fell predominantly in the musical line, extending from ballet-pantomime and interlude to melodrama. One of the best examples of the encroachment of 'illegitimate' theatres on the prerogatives of the patent houses occurs in Cross's adaptation of *Macbeth*, as described on the title page of the 1809 edition: *The history, murders, life, and death of Macbeth: and a full description of the scenery, action, choruses, and characters of the Ballet of music and action, of that name: as performed . . . at the Royal Circus, St George's Fields, London.* In the same period, the record of Cross's activities as a writer for the patent theatres, detailed in calendar entries in *The London Stage 1660–1800*,[93] includes nine works of a generally musical nature, of which *A Divertissement*, which played twenty-two times at Covent Garden in the 1790–1 season and a further thirty-three times by the century's end, is a representative example. Similarly typical is his *Purse; or, Benevolent Tar*, a nautical melodrama prominent in the repertoire of afterpieces. Over the decade, to the bills of Drury Lane, Covent Garden and the Haymarket he contributed some eighteen pieces in various genres, amassing a total of 191 performances. Clearly, Cross had a foot planted in either camp, as in the case of his ballet-pantomime *Genoese Pirate; or, Black Beard*; its appearance on three occasions at Covent Garden in the 1798–9 season amounted to a sort of transfer from the Royal Circus,

---

[93] Van Lennep *et al.*, *London Stage 1660–1800*, part 5, 1776–1800, ed. Hogan.

where several performances are implied by a bill for 9 April 1798 reprinted by Cross in his memoirs. His burletta *The Village Doctor; or, Killing No Cure* has an evident generic affinity with O'Hara's *Midas* and its brethren: original lyrics written, in the manner of *The Beggar's Opera*, to be sung to familiar airs are interspersed with couplets intended for delivery in recitative – proof positive that the English burletta form, introduced some years before at the patent theatres, had become the staple format at a wide range of theatres where articulation of the spoken word could still result in fines and imprisonment.[94]

Cross's efforts should be seen as an attempt to respond to audiences that had no taste for or even comprehension of such standard fare as John Home's Scottish tragedy *Douglas* but which possessed a ravenous appetite for dramatic performances of almost any other kind, provided that music and song formed a prominent part of the mix. It was this irrepressible desire for the dramatic and the musical simultaneously, in broadening combinations, which inspired the proprietors of theatres north and south, east and west to develop and adapt burletta, that quintessentially malleable form. Whilst remaining within legal bounds but in practice becoming the instrument of blithe, universal circumvention of the law, burletta would prove to be the Trojan horse which, after a long siege, and virtually from within, would at last bring down the patent theatres' monopoly in smoking ruins.

The end of the century

In the long aftermath of revolutions in America and France, these developments characterize the world encountered in their first London triumphs in the 1780s by the ambitious young tragedian John Philip Kemble and his supremely talented elder sister Sarah Siddons, a world marked by wide-ranging turmoil, politically, socially and theatrically. Siddons had made a false start at Drury Lane in the 1775–6 season and had returned to Bath, pre-eminent among provincial theatres, to gain experience and hone her technique. When she appeared again at Drury Lane on 10 October 1782 in the title role of Southerne's *Isabella; or, The Fatal Marriage*, she met with universal acclaim.[95] Although Siddons had little aptitude for comedy, her portrayals of the tragedienne's standard characters – Calista in Rowe's *The Fair Penitent*, Jane Shore in Rowe's tragedy of that name, Belvidera in Otway's *Venice Preserv'd*, Zara in Congreve's *The Mourning Bride*, Euphrasia in Arthur Murphy's *The Grecian Daughter*, Lady Macbeth and

---

[94] Donohue, 'London theatre at the end of the eighteenth century', 355–6.
[95] See Highfill *et al.*, *Biographical Dictionary*, XIV: 8ff.

others – raised her to the pinnacle of English acting. When her younger brother John Kemble joined her at Drury Lane in 1783, appearing first, and triumphantly, as Hamlet, they together commanded the rapt admiration of audiences and even of carping critics, in such pairings of roles as Ophelia and Hamlet, Desdemona and Othello, Volumnia and Coriolanus, and Cardinal Wolsey and Queen Katharine.

Both Siddons and Kemble made their London débuts in the Adam Drury Lane of 1775. The reconstruction and enlargement of both patent theatres in the early 1790s, including the amplification of stage area, was to have a large impact on their acting styles, along with those of all their contemporaries, particularly on the pace and volume of delivery. Even Kemble, a possessor of formidable vocal reserves, though slightly asthmatic, had to strain sometimes in order to make his rounded tones understandable. A correlative change occurred in audiences. The yawning reaches of the new Drury Lane and Covent Garden stages and the better lighting of upstage areas (even in 1785 a critic described the new stage lights at Drury Lane as 'bright without dazzling, strong and vivid'[96]) exerted inevitable pressure for greater spectacle. Sheridan's Puff had already called for a fitting accompaniment to his new tragedy, *The Spanish Armada*: 'Now then for my magnificence! – my battle! – my noise! – and my procession!' (3.1). The actuality trailed close on the heels of its parody. The innovations of Loutherbourg in the 1760s away from symmetrical wing-and-shutter mounting towards three-dimensional depth and illumination were attaining ever fuller expression. In 1799, when Sheridan's adaptation of the prolific dramatist August von Kotzebue's play *Die Spanier in Peru*, as *Pizarro*, appeared at Drury Lane, scenic and lighting resources were grand enough to support a climactic scene far upstage, on a bridge poised over a waterfall, where Kemble as the Peruvian hero Rolla is fatally wounded by a Spanish bullet as he attempts to cross to the Peruvian camp.

The dramatic output of this post-reconstruction period tended ever more towards spectacular effect. Realization of the cataract of the Ganges would be merely a question of time.[97] One of the most notable exemplars of this development is Gothic drama, which exploited scenic resources more extensively than conventional tragedy had ever done. The Gothic has been frequently studied as an important aesthetic phenomenon, but not always identified as the symptom of social unrest and anxiety which it undoubtedly was. From what may be its first recognizable incarnation, in Horace Walpole's closet

---

[96] *Gazeteer and New Daily Advertiser*, 9 Feb. 1785.
[97] Moncrieff, *The Cataract of the Ganges! or, The Rajah's Daughter*. Drury Lane, 27 October 1823.

drama *The Mysterious Mother* (1768), Gothic drama over the next thirty years moves towards a ghostly apotheosis in the Drury Lane production of Matthew Gregory 'Monk' Lewis's *The Castle Spectre*, in 1797. In the oratory of the castle the shade of the murdered mother of the heroine, Angela, appears, her white robes spotted with blood, a large wound visible on her breast; she advances, casts a sad eye on the picture of Reginald, Angela's lover, the hero imprisoned by the villain Osmond, blesses her kneeling daughter, and as Angela rises and attempts to embrace her glides away with a farewell wave, as organ music rises to climax and the oratory doors close with a loud clap. Given such thrilling pleasures as these, the phenomenal popularity of the Gothic form is easily understood.

Gothic drama is noteworthy also as the first form to consistently portray a hero who, through imprisonment or some other stricture, is rendered ineffective for much of the play, leaving the heroine unprotected and open to the depraved desires of a villain. It was a dramaturgical formula appropriated and employed by melodrama from almost the beginning of its existence. The threatened chastity of the heroine may be interpreted in both cases as a figure for the embattled integrity of British life, culture and mores; such was the temper of the times. The common atmosphere of gloom and foreboding articulated by the *faux* medieval features of the plays – moated castles, ruined abbeys, haunted graveyards and other macabre locales – was frequently articulated in a picturesque landscape after the manner of Salvator Rosa and other painters who emulated the new sensibility for the irregular, the exotic and the menacing. Thomas Greenwood the elder, the antiquarian-minded William Capon and other English scene-painters of the period proved susceptible to these forces.[98] The intense, surprise-laden dramatic situations enacted in these scenes may reflect deep social anxiety over the threat of hostile, invasive forces both external and internal. At the same time, in more directly theatrical ways, they set the scene for the advent of melodrama, at the turn of the century, by objectifying the powers for good in the heroine, the hero and the comic servant and the threat of evil in the person of the villain. Seldom before had there been such rewarding roles for the 'heavy' in the acting company.[99] Well before the second decade of the new century, when Shelley was publishing his unactable Gothic play *The Cenci* (1819), the generic boundary lines between Gothic drama and melodrama had become difficult, and thankless, to draw. Both forms relied on an unvarying cast of characters – hero, heroine, villain,

[98] Rosenfeld, *Short History of Scene Design*, 87–110.
[99] Evans, *Gothic Drama*; Nicoll, *History of English Drama*, II: 98–100; Donohue, *Dramatic Character*, 86–8.

villain's henchman (sometimes a guilt-stricken, turncoat character), good old man, resourceful comic servant – and both conducted their actions in a fantasy world of ideal goodness pitted against seemingly insuperable evil. Additional testimony to its close kinship with Gothic drama occurs in the music composed to accompany the on-going action, characterize its chief figures and add emotional richness. Michael Kelly, who wrote the music for *The Castle Spectre*, Stephen Storace and Samuel Arnold were among the more prominent of composers who provided music for the theatre ranging across several genres.

Melodrama, far from having emerged overnight as an autonomous form, had thus been aborning for some time in theatres, major and otherwise, on either side of the English Channel. Notwithstanding its complex pedigree, most histories explain that melodrama took the English stage by storm just after the beginning of the new century, assigning its direct origins to a genre of music drama developing in the boulevard theatres of Paris. Thomas Holcroft, prominent author of the comedy *The Road to Ruin* (Covent Garden, 1792) and other dramatic works, mostly comedies, saw there an exemplar of the new form and persuaded Kemble, who had abandoned Drury Lane and Sheridan for the management of Covent Garden, to mount an adaptation of it as an afterpiece. The result was the appearance of the first melodrama on the English stage to be identified as such, *A Tale of Mystery*, described as a 'Melo-drame' on the playbill for its opening night. The French original which had captured Holcroft's eye was *Coelina; ou, L'Enfant du mystère*, by the prolific Guilbert de Pixérécourt ('the Corneille of the boulevards'), performed at the Ambigu in Paris in 1800 and, in Holcroft's adaptation as a two-act afterpiece, at Covent Garden on 13 November 1802. From this point on, melodrama would pursue a parallel course, at breakneck speed, in France and England, becoming urbanized over the course of the century in subjects, plots and locales but retaining its fantastic ethos of endangerment and near disaster finally issuing in vindication of the good, the true and the innocent.

And so, as the century reached its end, foreign influences appeared to be revivifying the theatre through the proliferation of a new, vital kind of drama which depended at least as much on music and pantomime as it did on the spoken word. Outside pressures viewed by many as seditious and condemned as 'Jacobin'-inspired were exerting their force on a native culture, resistant but susceptible, by introducing corrupt or morally ambivalent factors troubling to many play-goers. The twenty-six editions published in 1799 of Sheridan's *Pizarro* – a play derived from a foreign author of questionable moral bearing – indicate how widespread was the attraction, to some minds so dangerous, of foreign ways of thinking. As if he had taken centre stage

THEATRE ROYAL. COVENT GARDEN,
This present SATURDAY, November 13, 1802,
Will be presented (8th time) a NEW COMEDY, called

DELAYS and BLUNDERS.

With New Scenes and Dresses.
The Principal Characters by
Mr. L E W I S,
Mr. M U N D E N,
Mr. F A W C E T T,
Mr. M U R R A Y,
Mr. E M E R Y,
Mr. S I D D O N S,
Mr. DAVENPORT, Mr. SIMMONS, Mr. THOMPSON,
Mrs. L I T C H F I E L D,
Mrs. H. J O H N S T O N,
Mrs. H. S I D D O N S,
And Mrs. M A T T O C K S.
The PROLOGUE to be spoken by Mr. BRUNTON.
After which will be produced, for the First time, a New Melo-Drame in Two acts, consisting
of Speaking, Dancing & Pantomime, called

A TALE OF MYSTERY.

With New Music, Scenes, Dresses, & Decorations.
The OVERTURE and MUSIC composed by Dr. BUSBY.
The Principal Characters By
Mr. H. J O H N S T O N,
Mr. M U R R A Y,
Mr. B L A N C H A R D,
Mr. F A R L E Y,
Mr. B R U N T O N,
Mr. C O R Y, Mr. S I M M O N S,
Mr. CLAREMONT, Mr. BEVERLY,
Mr. CURTIES, Mr. ABBOT, Mr. TRUMAN,
Mrs. G I B B S,
And Mrs. M A T T O C K S.
The Dances by
Mr. BOLOGNA, Jun.
Mr. DUBOIS, Mr. KING,
Mess. Klanert, Blurton, Platt, Wilde, L. Bologna, Howell, Lewis, &c.
and Master BYRNE,
Mesdames Watts, Bologna, Norton, Bologna, Dibdin, Burnet,
And Mrs. W Y B R O W,
(Her First Appearance this Season)
From the uncommon great demand for Places for the MAN of the WORLD; Mr. COOKE will
appear in the Character of Sir Pertinax Macsycophent on Monday next——Lady Rodolpha
Lumbercourt by Mrs. H. JOHNSTON.
Ladies & Gentlemen who have Places for the succeeding nights of the popular New Comedy of
DELAYS & BLUNDERS, are respectfully informed the 9th, 10th & 11th representations
will be on Tuesday, Thursday and Saturday next Week.
In consequence of the extreme overflow from all parts of the Theatre Last night, at the Opera of
the CABINET, it will be repeated twice more this season, which will be on Wednesday & Friday
next——And the Week after will be produced a New Comic Opera in Three acts, called
FAMILY QUARRELS. With New Music, Scenes, Dresses & Decorations.
The Music entirely new, & composed by Mess. Reeve, Moorehead, Davy & Braham.
E. MACLEISH, Printer, 2, Bow-street, Covent-Garden.

Plate 8. Covent Garden playbill for Saturday, 13 November 1802, featuring *Delays and Blunders*, 'after which, for the first time, a New Melo-Drame in two acts, consisting of Speaking, Dancing, & Pantomime, called *A Tale of Mystery*'. This opening performance of Thomas Holcroft's play, adapted from Pixérécourt's *L'Enfant du mystère*, marks the first appearance of the term 'melodrama' on an English playbill.

in a melodrama writ large in the culture of the period, a single villain, a German migrant to the boulevards of Paris, suddenly became the material object of English mistrust and outright fear. Two examples of Kotzebue's considerable, problematic influence on the English theatre just before the turn of the century clarify the situation. The opposing moral qualities of misanthropy and repentance identified in the title of his drama *Menschenhass und Reue* were given an English habitation and a name in Benjamin Thompson's translation of the play as *The Stranger*, performed at Drury Lane in March 1798, with Kemble as the depressed, misanthropic figure of the title and Mrs Siddons as the guilt-ridden Mrs Haller, his long-estranged wife. The play centres on the private struggles of a husband betrayed by an unfaithful spouse whose sympathetic portrayal, by such an emotionally resonant actress as Siddons, is capped at the end by her husband's heartfelt forgiveness.

Kotzebue's drama reflects a significant change in the ethos of human relationships, in which a greater validity is accorded to personal feeling, in defiance of conventional morality. In January 1799 in a letter to King George, the Duchess of Würtemberg complained that Kotzebue 'tries to render vice plausible and virtue insignificant'.[100] The exculpating psychological richness of character in Godwin's *Caleb Williams* offers additional evidence of the trend. Behind it lie developments in the criticism of Shakespeare's characters and tendencies in characterization observable in such dramatists as Richard Cumberland, an advocate for characters often thought beyond the pale of sympathy. Cumberland's *The Jew* (1794) anticipates Edmund Kean's startlingly subjective portrayal of Shylock in his Drury Lane début two decades later. Earlier, in 1777, Maurice Morgann had based his *Essay on Sir John Falstaff* on the unconventional premise that Shakespearean character possesses an authentic life beyond the action of the play, an holistic profile recoverable by extrapolation from the text. William Richardson's study of Hamlet in his *Philosophical Analysis and Illustration of Some of Shakespeare's Remarkable Characters* (1774) and Thomas Whately's investigation of Macbeth in his posthumous *Remarks on Some of the Characters of Shakespeare* (1785) had offered comparable insights into the putative personality of the dramatic character.[101] This kind of rethinking of the relationship between dramatic character and human personality constitutes a fascinating discovery by literary and dramatic criticism of the notion of an ideal, fully rounded dramatic entity, only some coherent fragments of which are displayed in the performed play or in the script on which performance is based.

[100] Quoted in O'Toole, *Traitor's Kiss*, 345.
[101] Donohue, *Dramatic Character*, chap. 8.

Plate 9. John Philip Kemble in the title role of *The Stranger*, by Benjamin Thompson, altered from August von Kotzebue's *Menschenhass und Reue*. With Mrs Siddons also in the cast, the play opened at Drury Lane on 24 March 1798 for the first of twenty-six performances that season.

Indicative of a swelling sea-change in notions of human nature, these ideas were seemingly countered by the threat of depersonalization implied in the nightmarish vision presented by Thomas Malthus in *An Essay on the Principle of Population* (1798), an alarming study of the dangers of allegedly excessive numbers and the unrestrained breeding of still more, especially among the lower classes and unlettered migrants from Ireland to England and country to city. Complex strands of social connection and the tension these developments created were observable in the congested markets of Covent Garden and Smithfield by day, in the nightly crush of audiences in Covent Garden, in Drury Lane, and in a host of theatrical and other venues in and around the city and across the river, as well as in the incessant influx of individuals and families seeking work and shelter in metropolitan London and its environs. The enlargement of the two patent theatres in the early 1790s becomes more perspicuous when set in these larger contexts of social life, thought and feeling, reflected obliquely on the stages of the theatres themselves. The greatly expanded stage and auditorium of Drury Lane might have been construed as a graceful bow by the management to undeniable demographics, an opening of arms to a new audience, were it not for their systematic exclusion of what came to be called the 'lower orders'. To be sure, the expansion of the theatres at this time reflects, on the part of the patentees, concessions viewed as economically necessary, but overall the reconfiguration and enlargement of auditoriums tell quite a different story. Despite the increase of an economically disadvantaged populace in search of entertainment, the proportion of gallery space allotted, relative to that given to pit and boxes, was significantly reduced, while the number of higher-priced places was raised, increasing potential income even more than the total number of added seats might imply. Crass economic concerns underlying larger cultural conditions thus created a poignant irony: the admission of foreign, 'democratic' elements, in the form of hugely successful plays by Kotzebue, onto the stages of the patent theatres was accompanied by a redoubled effort, on the part of the patentees, to exclude analogous elements, in the shape of a mushrooming, unlettered or ill-educated population, from the auditorium. The larger analogy between those potential English audiences and the revolutionary hordes which had stormed the Bastille and brought down the monarchy in France, sharpened by fears of Britain being invaded by those same barbarous elements, must have been felt by theatre managements and by occupants of pit and box as well.

As in other times of political unrest, the drawing of analogies constituted an important mode of perception and understanding in the theatres of the 1790s. The long life on the English stage of Otway's play about failed revolution, *Venice Preserv'd*, is attributable only partly to the sympathetic portrayal of its heroine, Belvidera, by actresses as varied as Elizabeth Barry, Anne Oldfield, Susanna Maria Cibber, Sarah Siddons and Eliza O'Neill, the toast of London in 1814. The subject matter itself had a deeply troubling contemporary point. No less pointed a case occurred with Sheridan's *Pizarro*, in which the conflict between the Inca's loyal followers and the dreaded Spanish interlopers from across the sea, led by the villainous Pizarro (accompanied by his guilt-ridden mistress Elvira, played with her customary pathos and panache by Mrs Siddons), held easily perceived parallels with current unrest and anxieties. On the night of 5 June 1799, when King George III attended a performance, a critical moment drew tumultuous expressions of loyalty throughout the dangerously overcrowded Drury Lane auditorium. The audience's reaction came when Kemble as Rolla delivered a stirring patriotic speech in which he cried: 'We serve a Monarch whom we love – a God whom we adore.' The ultimate defeat of Peruvian forces on their home ground by Spanish *conquistadores* encoded in no uncertain terms widespread British fears of catastrophic destruction by foreign forces of the time-honoured traditions, beliefs and values associated with an hereditary monarchy.

Thus, the remarkable unrest and anxiety troubling a conservative English polity and culture at the turn of the century. Not for everyone was the feeling of the time what it was for William Wordsworth, who in retrospect declared it a moment when it was bliss to be alive and heaven to be young. The publication in 1798 of Wordsworth and Coleridge's *Lyrical Ballads*, invoking the fresh tones of a 'language such as men do use', was an epochal event – but best viewed in the elongated perspective set by forces already at work in the society for a quarter-century or more, which would continue to exert their power well into the new century. By 1800, the phenomenal developments in theatre, drama and society over the years after Garrick retired from the stage had produced a theatrical situation and climate that Garrick would never have recognized.

2

Theatres and repertory

ROBERT D. HUME

An historian of English drama in the period 1660–1776 needs to start by admitting that sequential analysis of new plays by themselves can only yield a very partial picture. We may legitimately characterize the new plays and trace generic changes, but we must reckon with the fact that these plays were the product of a theatre system that emphasized the appeal of favourite actors and relied heavily on stock repertory. New plays occupied few nights in most seasons and they do not really have a separate history of their own.

The period we are considering is tidily bounded at the outset by the restoration of the theatres by Charles II when he returned from exile in 1660. No satisfying *terminus ad quem* exists: there is no sharp break in the drama between the revival of playwriting in the 1750s (following the lull caused by the Licensing Act of 1737) and the 1820s, when 'illegitimate' competitors put the patent theatres on the skids. The year 1776 makes a convenient stopping point: Garrick retired from acting and management at Drury Lane that year (selling out to a partnership headed by Richard Brinsley Sheridan), and Thomas Harris was just beginning his long reign as manager at Covent Garden. In drama, though there is no abrupt change, the social comedies and fancy musicals ('English operas') of the eighties and nineties reflect norms significantly different from those of the sixties and seventies.

The future of English drama was profoundly affected by the terms of its relegitimation in 1660. Four points are fundamental. These are the duopoly created by the patent grants of 1662 and 1663, the introduction of actresses on the public stage, the construction of changeable scenery theatres, and the radically unequal division of rights to old plays between the two companies that jointly shared a monopoly on dramatic entertainment in London.

As early as August 1660 Charles II agreed to grant patents governing the right to perform plays in London.[1] He appears to have had nothing in mind

---

[1] British Library Add. MS 19,256, fol. 47 (21 August 1660). Printed in Bawcutt, *Control and Censorship of Caroline Drama*, 226–8.

beyond giving a virtually cost-free reward to a pair of Cavalier loyalists, but the result was to shape the whole history of the London theatre for nearly two centuries. The courtiers, Thomas Killigrew (King's Company) and Sir William Davenant (Duke's Company), had to wage an aggressive campaign of subversion and intimidation to enforce their monopoly, but by 1667 they had eradicated all competition. The patents were perpetual (the Royal Opera House in Covent Garden still operates under one of them); they were also divisible and transferable by purchase, which meant that they could be sold in whole or part to any buyer – putting English drama in the power of whatever commercial speculator was willing to outbid his competitors. The disastrous histories of such owner-managers of Drury Lane as Christopher Rich (1693–1709), Charles Fleetwood (1734–44) and R. B. Sheridan (1776–1809) are gruesome testimony to the effects of drama's dependence on the whims of owners whose enjoyment of a monopoly made them almost impossible to dislodge.

The importance of competition to the writing and staging of new plays can hardly be overemphasized. When two companies competed vigorously, quite a lot of new plays got staged each year. When they entered a formal or informal cartel, competition virtually vanished (as happened in the 1720s), and little money was risked on mounting new work. When the two companies merged into one, there was even less reason to bother with new plays. Thus in four years from 1675 through 1678 two companies put on 68 new plays (17 per annum); in the first five seasons of the United Company (1682–7) just 19 were done (not quite 4 per annum). In the whole history of the United Company (1682–94) the average number of new plays was just 5.75. The near blank in new mainpieces in the first decade after the Licensing Act of 1737 reiterates this lesson.

The impact of actresses and changeable scenery on the nature of new drama (and on the staging and theatrical impact of pre-1642 plays) has been much studied.[2] The inequality of the division of rights to old plays has long been known, but its importance has been little understood. In the autumn of 1660 the King's Company successfully laid claim to virtually all extant English plays. Davenant had to petition for the right to mount his own plays, and for a few others regarded as essentially obsolete and not especially valuable (a group that included *Hamlet*, *The Tempest*, *Romeo and Juliet*, *King Lear*, *Macbeth* and *The Duchess of Malfi*). The result was a dire need for new plays on the part of the Duke's Company. Davenant competed with music, changeable scenery and

---

[2] See particularly Howe, *First English Actresses*; Southern, *Changeable Scenery*; Langhans, 'Staging practices in the Restoration theatres'.

(of necessity) new scripts; his success forced the King's Company to build a new theatre (Bridges Street, opened in May 1663) and reply in kind.[3] Had the Duke's Company enjoyed rights to something like half the old plays, or had both companies been allowed to stage any pre-1642 play, far fewer new ones would have been mounted in the 1660s and 1670s, and generic change would almost undoubtedly have been much slower.

Theatres, audiences and performers

When the King's Company reopened for business in the autumn of 1660, it did so at the Vere Street Theatre, formerly Gibbons's Tennis Court. The dimensions were tiny: probably around 25 feet by 70 feet; the capacity was probably no more than 400 to 500.[4] It was an indoor theatre (lit by candles), without scenic capacity – in short, a reconstruction of a standard kind of 1630s playhouse. The 'first' Lincoln's Inn Fields theatre – built by Davenant for the Duke's Company – was nearly identical in size and capacity, and likewise contrived from a tennis court (Lisle's), but differed radically in being a scenic theatre. Limited and simple as its machinery was, the theatre possessed wing, shutter and valance changeable scenery such that painted flats provided sharply differentiated interior and exterior settings that could be shifted (in full view) in a matter of seconds. They could also expose action in progress and cut it off without clearing the stage. Going up against a vastly more experienced troupe of actors who had rights to virtually all English plays, Davenant needed a competitive edge, and scenery provided it. He had long wished to operate a public theatre in London that would capitalize on the sorts of scenery and machinery employed in court masques of the 1620s and 1630s (he had obtained a patent for such a theatre in 1639). By comparison with either the masques of Charles I or the offerings of the Dorset Garden Theatre in the 1670s, Lincoln's Inn Fields' technical capacities were terribly limited, but they clearly dazzled the theatre-going public in late June 1661, when Davenant mounted the first part of *The Siege of Rhodes*. A few days later, Pepys went to Vere Street and commented, 'strange to see this house, that use to be so thronged, now empty since the opera begun – and so will continue for a while I believe' (4 July). By

---

[3] The limited grant of plays to Davenant is PRO LC 5/137, pp. 343–4. On the importance of rights to plays, see Hume, 'Securing a Repertory'. In 1668 the Duke's Company managed to lay claim to twenty-three rather tatty old plays (PRO LC 5/139, p. 375); the King's Company responded by getting the Lord Chamberlain to confirm its rights to one hundred and eight old plays, many of them far more theatrically viable (PRO LC 5/12, pp. 212–13).

[4] For statistics on theatre buildings, see Langhans, 'Theatres', especially 61–5.

December the King's Company sharers had been forced to bite the bullet and finance construction of their own scenic theatre.

Davenant did not live to build the sort of theatre he had dreamt of a generation earlier, but following his death in 1668 his successors in management at the Duke's Company did so. Dorset Garden cost a stunning £9,000 to build and gave the company enormous technical capacity. What it could do with scenes and machines is best understood by comparing the stage directions of the 1667 adaptation of *The Tempest* by Dryden and Davenant with the 1674 operatic version (probably by Thomas Shadwell) or by looking at the scene descriptions and stage directions (contributed by Betterton) for *Albion and Albanius*, an all-sung allegorical opera by Dryden and Grabu (1685). When the King's Company's Bridges Street Theatre burnt down in 1672, they replaced it with Drury Lane, a 'Plain Built House' (as Dryden's prologue for the opening terms it) that cost only £4,000 and was not designed for opera or splashy displays of scenery and machinery. Drury Lane ultimately proved the more satisfactory theatre for ordinary plays, but Dorset Garden established technical expectations that were to become the norm in eighteenth-century London.

From the outset of the period, the theatres' auditorium arrangements and price structure established a strong sense of hierarchy in the audience. Two or more levels of boxes ringed a gently raked pit with benches; normally two galleries occupied upper levels at the furthest distance from the stage. A place in a box cost 4s; the pit was 2s 6d; the first (lower) gallery 1s 6d and the upper gallery 1s.[5] The gentry (including most women) occupied boxes; men (and prostitutes patrolling for business) patronized the pit; those interested in economy went to the first gallery, and the lower orders went to the upper one. By comparison with a public theatre like the Globe at the beginning of the century, the Restoration theatres were extremely pricey, but as Pepys noted with distaste (1 January 1668), even apprentices could afford to attend if they really wanted to. People tended to wander in and out of all parts of the theatre: until well after 1700 a patron could see one act for free and leave without paying. The audience talked and bought refreshments; by no means did it arrive early and sit in worshipful silence from start to finish. Historians have made much of riots, but these were in fact few and far between. As at sporting events today, the audience was unquestionably noisy, erratically attentive, and inclined to walk about, chat and eat. People used theatres as social centres. The silence that a great actor such as Betterton could command was spoken of with

---

[5] An extra shilling was charged for premières and 'operas'. These prices stayed surprisingly stable. After the firm establishment of the mainpiece/afterpiece system in the 1720s the 'raised' scale became standard – 5s, 3s, 2s, 1s – and remained customary until the 1790s.

awe by contemporaries precisely because it was not common. Nonetheless, a high proportion of the audience went frequently to the theatre and was knowledgeable about it.

Early twentieth-century historians assumed that the Restoration audience consisted of a coterie of courtiers, government officials, their families and prostitutes. This cliché was long ago demolished. References in Pepys and many other sources make clear that the audience was highly diverse in age, class and occupation. A lot of respectable women attended, often unescorted, and they brought their children.[6] No substantial evidence has ever been found to suggest that the two theatres pursued a 'niche strategy' or attracted significantly different audiences. Drury Lane and Lincoln's Inn Fields (from 1732 Covent Garden) offered similar repertory to much the same audience pool. The Queen's (later King's) Theatre in the Haymarket, opened by Vanbrugh as a replacement for Lincoln's Inn Fields in 1705, quickly became an Italian opera house and catered to an élite audience at more than double the regular theatre prices: pit and boxes 10s 6d, gallery 5s. In the 1730s the Little Haymarket functioned largely as an experimental, fringe theatre (especially when Fielding occupied the building), while Goodman's Fields offered modern classic repertory to an audience that lived closer to the City than the West End. But after the Licensing Act of 1737, Drury Lane and Covent Garden held sway, with summer fare at the Little Haymarket (under Samuel Foote from 1760) for variety.

The audience of the time of Charles II that supported the sex comedy boom of the 1670s was dying off by 1688, when Shadwell said in a prologue, 'Our Poet found your gentle Fathers kind.' Charles and James II attended a lot of public performances and commanded performances in the court theatre. Actors were, technically, liveried servants of the monarch, and not liable to prosecution for debt without the permission of the Lord Chamberlain of the royal household. This happy state of affairs began to change with the accession of William in 1688, a monarch with no interest in the drama, though Queen Mary did attend the theatre. Following her death in 1694, English drama was never again to be seriously patronized by a monarch in this period. Changes at court, a new generation and the moral assault on the theatre that culminated in Jeremy Collier's *A Short View of the Immorality, and Profaneness of the English Stage* (1698) probably all contributed to the shaky state of the theatres in the years *circa* 1697 to 1705. Audiences were thin; the two companies were nearly forced to amalgamate; and many good new plays failed dismally, though they were

---

[6] See particularly Avery, 'Restoration audience'; Love, 'Who were the Restoration audience?'; Botica, 'Audience, playhouse and play'.

later revived and became repertory staples.[7] Only gradually did the theatres build a new audience base with a more bourgeois and mercantile character. As London grew, so of course did the potential theatre-going audience. The 'third' Lincoln's Inn Fields (1714) held about 1,400 people with extreme crowding. Gradual expansion of both patent theatres brought both of them up to around 2,000 by the 1770s. Extant account books, however, show that they were rarely more than about two-thirds full.

A major part of what attracted audiences to the theatre was favourite performers. There was some turnover: actresses got pregnant or married or went into keeping; men joined the army or turned stroller or went off to Dublin (and, later, to America). The key players in any company, however, tended not only to go on for decades but also to be on display several nights every week. Until well into the eighteenth century, most performers acted regularly in both comedy and tragedy, and principals took substantial roles in most repertory staples. Charles Hart, Michael Mohun and Edward Kynaston for the King's Company; Thomas Betterton for the Duke's and United Companies; Elizabeth Barry and Anne Bracegirdle from the 1680s until 1707; Robert Wilks, Colley Cibber and Thomas Doggett (the last replaced by Barton Booth in 1713) as principal actors and triumvirate managers of Drury Lane from 1709 to 1732; the great Anne Oldfield at Drury Lane for the first three decades of the eighteenth century; the comedienne Kitty Clive from the 1730s until 1769; David Garrick as perennial star and co-manager at Drury Lane from 1747 to 1776 – to a degree now difficult to conceive, these people *were* what a theatre-goer experienced in London, and what he or she went to see. Daily performance records are radically incomplete until *circa* 1705 (when both companies realized the advantages of printing a playbill in the newly founded daily newspapers), but early eighteenth-century statistics show that principal performers regularly took major roles four or more nights a week – often all different roles. In the week of 6 November 1710, Wilks was Carlos in *Love Makes a Man* on Monday; Lorenzo in *The Spanish Fryar* on Tuesday; Col. Careless in *The Committee* on Wednesday; Valentine in *Love for Love* on Thursday; Pedro in *The Pilgrim* on Friday; and Hamlet on Saturday. He was also, to be sure, co-manager of the company, charged with the responsibility for superintending rehearsals and mounting

---

[7] See Scouten and Hume, 'Restoration comedy and its audiences'. Among the plays that initially failed to succeed as expected were Congreve's *The Way of the World*, Cibber's adaptation of *Richard III*, and Rowe's *The Fair Penitent*. On the effects of stormy competition at the turn of the century, see Milhous, *Thomas Betterton and the Management of Lincoln's Inn Fields*. For very different first-hand accounts of the theatre at this time, see the anonymous *A Comparison Between the Two Stages* and Cibber's *Apology*.

revivals, as well as overseeing accounts with Cibber and Doggett – but this workload was normal for an actor in his position.

Anyone who went to the theatre, even a few times a year, quickly became familiar with the same group of performers in a wide array of roles. Basically, a performer 'owned' a role as long as he or she was with the company: aging actors did eventually change their 'line' in new plays, and sometimes gradually ceded roles to younger colleagues, but a lot of the casting was decidedly mature. Some performers became deeply identified with particular roles: Wilks as Sir Harry Wildair; Cibber as Foppington; Doggett as Sailor Ben in *Love for Love* – a part he was paid astonishing sums to perform a few times as a guest when he was not a member of the company. Because company membership was quite stable, playwrights generally wrote with particular performers in mind from the start. Writing a piece for the Barry–Bracegirdle tandem greatly increased the chance of acceptance by their company. Major actors often wound up involved in management (if male), and several of them became workmanlike playwrights (or at least play doctors), notably Betterton, Cibber and Garrick. What they wrote or adapted was naturally more performer vehicle than work of literature.

What theatre companies advertised on their great bills (and later in their newspaper bills) was title (and title of afterpiece, when those became common after 1714), often the performers' names and perhaps roles, and added entertainments (song, dance, entr'actes of various sorts). Dryden reports disapprovingly in a letter of 1699, apropos of seeing his friend Congreve's name in a playbill for a revival of *The Double-Dealer*, 'the printing an Authours name, in a Play bill, is a new manner of proceeding, at least in England'.[8] Plays were only gradually becoming 'literature', and not until the 1740s were even Shakespeare's plays systematically advertised with his name attached. A play was an entity in its own right, and many of the stock pieces had been heavily adapted and sometimes readapted. A large number of audience members went to the theatre on the basis of title – and to enjoy seeing favourite performers.

New plays and old ones

Any attempt to characterize the plays of the period 1660–1776 faces a quantitative obstacle: we are trying to talk about something of the order of 1,100 mainpieces and 800 afterpieces. Of these, fewer than forty are commonly read and only about twenty-five have received more than cursory critical

---

[8] Dryden, *Letters*, no. 59.

attention.[9] Most historians, critics and anthologists have subscribed to a trio of dichotomies. 'Restoration comedy' has been contrasted to the 'rhymed heroic drama', the one presenting gritty cuckolding actions and harsh satire, the other devoted to love-and-honour rants and grandiose rhetoric. Few serious plays after 1682 have received much notice, leaving critics to contrast 'Restoration comedy' (dominant in the late seventeenth century) with the 'sentimental comedy' that allegedly flooded the stage after 1700. The third dichotomy, 'laughing versus sentimental comedy', has often been used to glorify the plays of Goldsmith and Sheridan, viewing them as a noble attempt to return to satiric comedy and reject the pathetic sentiment found in the work of such writers as Hugh Kelly and Richard Cumberland. Unfortunately, all three of these long-dominant characterizations seriously distort the reality one can discover by looking at more than a handful of selected plays. The new plays are enormously varied in type and tone throughout the 116 years at issue; generic norms change quite rapidly from decade to decade; and any attempt to characterize theatrical taste must reckon with the old plays that dominated the repertory at all times.

Scholars have long debated the degree to which there is continuity or discontinuity in play types between 1642 and 1660. Given that Davenant and Killigrew had been prominent Caroline playwrights, and the unavoidable preponderance of old plays in the repertory in the first seasons after 1660, a high degree of carry-over could hardly have been avoided. Alfred Harbage has traced play types (considering all surviving plays) from 1626 through 1669, concluding that there is virtually no generic break at all on account of the Interregnum, and that throughout this period there was a 'natural progression' from pre-Restoration types towards 'Drydenesque heroic tragedy and Etheregean social comedy'.[10] Surprise has been expressed that the comedies of James Shirley do not make a more conspicuous appearance after the Restoration: more than any others, they seem to anticipate the London-set wit comedy that reached its high points in Etherege, Wycherley and Congreve. The heart of the repertory during the Carolean period, however, consisted of the plays of 'Beaumont and

---

[9] Allardyce Nicoll supplies brief, uncritical accounts of most plays in the whole period, categorized in procrustean generic ways, in his *History of English Drama, 1660–1900*. Vol. v of *The Revels History of Drama in English* is patchy, but has perceptive accounts of selected plays by A. H. Scouten. For surveys of virtually all extant, performed plays from 1660 to 1700, see Hume, *Development of English Drama in the Late Seventeenth Century*, and Hughes, *English Drama 1660–1700*, taking generic and intellectual history approaches respectively. Detailed accounts of eighteenth-century plays are largely lacking. The best account of mid-century work is Bevis, *The Laughing Tradition: Stage Comedy in Garrick's Day*.

[10] Harbage, *Cavalier Drama*, especially 255.

Fletcher', much admired for their social and linguistic elevation.[11] Production norms naturally changed quickly after 1660, with even old plays affected by the presence of actresses and the use of scenery, but the high degree of continuity is undeniable. It stems in significant part from carry-over in performers: recently discovered lawsuit testimony proves that the members of the King's Company regarded it as the same troupe that its oldest members had joined in the 1620s, not as a new creation *ex nihilo* in 1660.[12]

The new plays of the 1660s are chaotically varied in type. Sir Robert Howard's *The Committee* (1662) is a satiric blast at the sequestration committee of evil memory, cast in the form of a lively Jacobean city comedy and contrasting noble cavaliers with thieving, hypocritical Puritans. Sir Samuel Tuke's *The Adventures of Five Hours* (1663), vastly admired by Pepys, is a 'Spanish romance' (based on Coello's *Los empeños de seis horas*) which turns on complex plotting and swordplay – and treats its love-and-honour conventions with the utmost seriousness. Multi-plot plays were popular. Most of them, like Dryden's *Secret Love* (1667), contrast near heroic tragi-comedy intrigue with a lower-level courtship plot (in varying degrees of farcicality or seriousness). Sir George Etherege's *The Comical Revenge; or, Love in a Tub* (1664) actually runs four plot levels in parallel, from rhymed heroics to plain farce. His second play, *She Wou'd if She Cou'd* (1668), has sometimes been held up as a key element in the evolution of the witty sex comedy of the next decade, but it was in fact not very successful. In the course of the decade English playwrights discovered Molière as a source, and a flock of translation/adaptations reached the stage, most of them decidedly farcical. The most popular was Edward Ravenscroft's *The Citizen Turn'd Gentleman* (1672), trashy but clearly effective in performance.

The vogue in serious drama was for rhymed heroics. The immediate precursor of the form was Davenant's *The Siege of Rhodes*, the first part of which was staged as an 'opera' in 1656 under the Puritan régime. Dryden and Howard mounted *The Indian Queen* in January 1664; the Earl of Orrery's *The Generall* and *Henry the Fifth* both appeared later that year. The form reached its apogee around the end of the decade with Dryden's two-part *The Conquest of Granada* (1670–1), whose superhuman hero, Almanzor, aspires to almost epic stature. How seriously such works were taken no doubt depended on the audience member. John Evelyn's wife was thrilled with admiration for the nobility and virtue exhibited; the Duke of Buckingham and his friends mounted a devastating satire of such plays in *The Rehearsal* (1671), savaging Dryden and many other

---

[11] See Sorelius, '*The Giant Race Before the Flood*'.
[12] PRO C10/62/8 and C10/80/55. For analysis, see Milhous and Hume, 'New light on English acting companies'.

playwrights. We should note, however, that this burlesque was mounted by the King's Company, in which Dryden was a sharing member and for which he wrote. Both *The Rehearsal* and some of its principal targets remained popular for decades.

The story of the 1670s is pre-eminently the rise of the cuckolding comedy, for which the Restoration was to remain permanently notorious. A large number of the new plays (the early works of Aphra Behn, for example) continued to be romantic tragi-comedies of a fairly sedate sort. The piquancy of the sex chase, however, was increasingly attractive to playwrights. During the 1660s Charles Hart and Nell Gwyn (of the King's Company) had helped popularize what John Harrington Smith unluckily dubbed 'the gay couple' – witty, emancipated lady and rake playing out a courtship game in the fashion of Beatrice and Benedick.[13] Adulterous or non-marital sex becomes an increasingly common centre to plays of the 1670s, whether consummated or abortive. Thomas Betterton's *The Amorous Widow* (1669?), a *mélange* of three French sources, is a successful early example; another is Dryden's *Marriage A-la-Mode* (1671), a split-plot play which comes right to the verge of wife-swapping but stops short of actual adultery.

The famous seventies sex comedies are Wycherley's *The Country Wife* (1675), in which Horner feigns impotence to identify women whose aversion signals their sexual desire, and Etherege's *The Man of Mode* (1676), in which Dorimant (a fictional version of the notorious Earl of Rochester) seduces and abandons two upper-class women before he falls in love with Harriett, a woman rich, beautiful and tough enough to force him to endure the prospect of matrimony if he is to have her. Far more brutal in their presentation of sex are the plays of spring 1678: Behn's *Sir Patient Fancy*, Otway's *Friendship in Fashion*, Dryden's *The Kind Keeper* and Shadwell's *A True Widow*. None of the last four plays succeeded; the audience was evidently tiring of smut. Aside from *The Country Wife* and *The Man of Mode*, the most enduringly popular sex comedies were two that used sex for farcical rather than smutty or satiric purposes, Durfey's *A Fond Husband* (1677) and Ravenscroft's raucous *The London Cuckolds* (1681). The latter, revived almost every year into the 1750s, presents the cuckolding of Wiseacre, Doodle and Dashwell, three contemptible wits whose wives console themselves with gentleman rakes. The libertine ethos is accepted in most of these plays, but by no means in all of them. Otway viciously satirizes it; Dryden and Shadwell are at best ambivalent. Parts of the audience unquestionably found sex comedy offputting.

[13] Smith, *Gay Couple in Restoration Comedy*.

In serious drama the seventies saw the flood of rhymed heroic plays dwindle into mediocrity, the craze terminating rather abruptly about 1677.[14] Nathaniel Lee's *The Rival Queens* (an Alexander the Great play), Dryden's *All for Love* (a rescension of the Antony and Cleopatra story), both in 1677, and Otway's *Venice Preserv'd* (1682) have been generally acknowledged as among the best of the serious plays of the period. They are in blank verse, they end tragically, and they present overwhelming emotion in convincing and largely positive ways. Otway's play is a clear if messy parallel to the politics of the Exclusion Crisis then playing out in England, but its searing personal passions kept it on the stage into the nineteenth century, more than a century after anyone had ceased to know or care about its political message. Like Otway's *The Orphan* (1680), this play has clear forward links to the pathetic 'she tragedies' produced by John Banks in the 1680s (*Vertue Betray'd; or, Anna Bullen*) and by Nicholas Rowe in the first two decades of the eighteenth century (*The Fair Penitent, Jane Shore*). These plays revel in the agony of their protagonists, inviting the spectator to empathize with suffering innocence.

A major generic development of the seventies was the 'semi-opera'. These works mixed spoken dialogue with music and song, and they were characterized by super-spectacular scenery and machinery. The cost of mounting the later, fancier ones was exorbitant, running up towards half the company's annual budget, which made such productions an occasional special treat.[15] The Dryden–Davenant–Shadwell(?) *Tempest* of 1674, Shadwell's *Psyche* (1675), Charles Davenant's *Circe* (1677) and the Dryden–Grabu *Albion and Albanius* (1685) are the famous early cases, predecessors to Henry Purcell's three great ventures in this genre, *The Prophetess* (1690), *King Arthur* (1691, with libretto by Dryden) and *The Fairy Queen* (1692) – the last two now regarded as important monuments in the history of opera.

The union of the King's and Duke's companies in 1682 drastically slowed generic experimentation. Magic and machinery farce was popular in the eighties. Dryden capitalized brilliantly on this form in *Amphitryon* (1690), a play whose cutting satire on libertinism is elegantly conveyed in what appears to be a sex comedy farce. By this time the audience was changing, and William's court was a world apart from those of Charles II and James II. Unsurprisingly, the new comedies of the nineties are different from those of the seventies.[16]

---

[14] See Cannan, 'New directions in serious drama'.

[15] See Milhous, 'Multimedia spectacular'.

[16] Obvious as this now seems, critics were long blind to the differences, lumping Congreve (b. 1670) with Wycherley and Etherege (whose careers both terminated in 1676). See Scouten, 'Notes toward a history of Restoration comedy'.

The later comedies are substantially darker in tone; they tend to focus on marital discord rather than rejoice in courtship; their view of sex is decidedly more ambivalent.

The two great writers of the nineties are Thomas Southerne and William Congreve. Southerne's *The Wives Excuse* (1691) is a bitter satire on libertinism and a protest against the treatment of women in contemporary society. Unsurprisingly, it died in a single night. Southerne's *The Fatal Marriage* (1694) concerns a woman who unintentionally commits bigamy; *Oroonoko* (1695) is a split-plot play that balances satire on sex comedy against the death of the noble slave king. Both have strong affinities with pathetic tragedy and were lastingly popular. Congreve's first play, *The Old Batchelour* (1693), is virtually a throwback to seventies comedy. His second, *The Double Dealer* (also 1693), is far more biting (and proved much less popular). *Love for Love* (1695) exhibits more sympathy for its better characters and proved a runaway success. Congreve's last comedy, *The Way of the World* (1700), is harsher, more in Southerne's disillusioned tone – an elaborately plotted, verbally elegant play with sadness at its core. Its initial reception was disappointing, but it was performed nearly three hundred times in London in the course of the eighteenth century. Both writers viewed their society with a cold eye, disliked what they found, and could imagine no viable alternatives.

How nineties comedy segues into its early eighteenth-century successor has been much debated over the last twenty-five years. Early twentieth-century critics presumed that the success of Colley Cibber's *Love's Last Shift* (1696) signalled an impending transition to 'sentimental' comedy, but this tidy theory does not stand up under serious scrutiny. Cibber's play revels in lewdness for 'above four acts' and then tacks on a wildly implausible reform of the rake and happy ending for his abandoned wife. Vanbrugh promptly satirized the ending in *The Relapse* (also 1696), but the satire was not unfriendly, and Cibber was delighted to star in the sequel. One can see the full spectrum of turn-of-the-century comedy in the works of George Farquhar. *Love and a Bottle* (1698) is an imitation of the seventies style; *The Constant Couple* (1699) presents a rake and a mild reform; *The Recruiting Officer* (1706) and *The Beaux' Stratagem* (1707) take us into a kinder world. The late plays admit the possibility of villainy or bad marriage, but they also celebrate the possibility of decency. Whether we should rejoice in the improbable happy ending of *The Beaux' Stratagem* (contrived by a flagrantly illegal 'divorce') or whether we should infer an ironic comment on the nature of the real world is hard to say. The ugly marital discord to be found in Vanbrugh's *The Provok'd Wife* (1697), Cibber's *The Careless Husband* (1704) and Susanna Centlivre's *The Gamester* (1705) is by no means wholly offset by the tidy plot solutions that critics have generally condemned as 'sentimental'. Virtually no plays in this period go very far towards the 'exemplary' concept of comedy championed by Richard Steele and embodied in his last play, *The Conscious Lovers* (1722). Rather, the plays of the turn of the century seem to fall in a middle mode somewhere between the harshly satiric and the exemplary or benevolist. Shirley Strum Kenny has termed this sort of work 'humane comedy', and that is a good name for it.[17]

The new theatrical union of January 1708 (ordered by the Lord Chamberlain at Vanbrugh's instigation) created a period of turmoil in the theatres and brought production of new plays down to a trickle. Even after a second company reopened under John Rich in 1714, managers on both sides relied heavily on stock plays. Renewed competition did lead to a boom in afterpieces, until then a rarity except as interpolated musical masques of the sort made popular by Peter Anthony Motteux and the composer John Eccles at Lincoln's Inn Fields between 1695 and 1704 (*The Loves of Mars and Venus, Acis and Galatea*). The majority of eighteenth-century afterpieces are cheerful little farces, fairly represented by such works as Thomas Doggett's *Hob* (1711) or Henry Fielding's *Tom Thumb* (1730), *The Mock Doctor* (1732) and *The Virgin Unmask'd* (1735). In March 1723, however, John Rich mounted *Jupiter and Europa*, the first of his long series of 'pantomimes'. These complex, expensive productions emphasized the fantasy elements of a high plot often drawn from classical myth and a mimed low plot with stock comic characters. Box office receipts show that music, dance and dazzling transformation scenes had enormous drawing power. Highbrows sneered, but Drury Lane hastened to reply in kind with *Harlequin Doctor Faustus* the following November. By mid-century the Christmas pantomime tradition was well established. The attraction of pantomime, however, proved no fad, and the famous exemplars retained year-round appeal for decades.

The peaceful coexistence and generic stodge of the 1720s came to an abrupt end in 1728 with the production of John Gay's *The Beggar's Opera*, which ran for a totally unprecedented sixty-two nights at Lincoln's Inn Fields in its first season. Partial precursors have been suggested, but Gay's venture into 'ballad opera' was a radical innovation. His social and political inversions were startling, equating Prime Minister Walpole with the highwayman Macheath. Gay mingled spoken dialogue with songs, employing tunes of all kinds lifted from sources ranging from street ballads to hymns and Handel. The text mocks the conventions of Italian opera, but most scholars no longer believe that the

---

[17] Kenny, 'Humane comedy'.

work was a serious attack on *opera seria*, then in its heyday, with Handel serving as principal composer to the Royal Academy of Music. Gay's satire is flippant, amusing and ultimately self-reflexive; far from taking a strong moral line, he concludes wryly that 'the World is all alike'.

The impact of *The Beggar's Opera* can hardly be overstated. It generated a flood of ballad opera imitations, but, even more important, its incredible run demonstrated that a growing London had developed a large, untapped potential audience. The same season *The Provok'd Husband*, Cibber's completion of an unfinished manuscript by Vanbrugh, enjoyed thirty-six nights at Drury Lane (twenty-eight straight): in the preceding thirty years hardly any new play had managed more than ten performances its first season. The result was a tremendous upsurge of theatrical activity in London. The Little Haymarket Theatre, built in 1720, had served as an occasional venue for French visitors, amateurs and variety shows: in the summer of 1728 it mounted a pirate production of Gay's ballad opera, and in the nine following seasons it offered quarters to a variety of pick-up troupes, most of which did new and experimental plays, many of them topical. A fourth theatre was hastily built in 1729 – Goodman's Fields, occupying a site much closer to the City of London. Rather than mounting new work, its managers generally preferred to offer modern classics, popular plays by Otway, Southerne, Centlivre, Banks, Rowe, Farquhar, Congreve and Cibber.

The abrupt upsurge in competition that resulted from the success of *The Beggar's Opera* generated quite a lot of new plays in the nine seasons before the imposition of the Licensing Act in 1737.[18] The most exciting and productive of the playwrights was Henry Fielding, who produced twenty-seven plays of five distinct types in the course of the decade. His traditional comedies are deservedly forgotten and his serious satires (*The Modern Husband*, 1732) now seem heavy-handed and contrived. The entertainments he wrote, mostly as vehicles for Kitty Clive, are utterly lightweight, but drew audiences for decades (*The Intriguing Chambermaid*, 1734). Fielding's genius lay in burlesque and topical satire. *Tom Thumb* (1730) and *The Author's Farce* (1730) exhibit a zany imagination that continues to delight readers: how many plays have their heroes eaten by a large, red cow, or feature the killing of a ghost? Fielding's last two major plays take him on to political and increasingly partisan ground. *Pasquin* (1736) is passably even-handed, but *The Historical Register for the Year 1736* (1737) slams Walpole with no pretence of generality or impartiality.[19]

---

[18] For an overview of theatrical affairs in this decade of frantic activity, see Hume, 'London theatre from *The Beggar's Opera* to the Licensing Act'.

[19] See Hume, *Henry Fielding and the London Theatre*.

Few plays of the thirties have stood up well in the estimation of literary critics. As in the 1660s, almost no experienced playwrights were alive and active, and about the time they might have learned their trade they were put out of business by the Licensing Act. George Lillo's *The London Merchant* (1731) goes over the edge of bathos at times, but is of considerable importance in establishing the possibility of bourgeois tragedy. Its protagonist, an apprentice tempted by a wicked woman into stealing from his master, is essentially unprecedented in English drama of this period: his repentance and execution produce a ringing moral still popular in the days of Dickens, who refers to the play in *Pickwick Papers*, *Martin Chuzzlewit*, *Barnaby Rudge* and *Great Expectations*. Lillo also wrote *Fatal Curiosity* (1736), a story of a son who returns home in disguise and is killed by his indigent and desperate parents. Contrived as it is, the piece has some genuine force, and it exerted significant influence on the beginnings of *Schicksalstragödie* in Germany.

After a very barren decade following the passage of the Licensing Act, English drama began a gradual revival partially attributable to David Garrick's becoming co-owner and manager at Drury Lane in 1747. Both patent theatres followed conservative repertory policies for the next generation. 'Roman tragedy' heavy on classical history and morality enjoyed critical warrant, and new exemplars were mounted with monotonous regularity – and almost always soon laid aside. The successful plays of the fifties and sixties were mostly 'laughing comedies' of a relatively mild sort, soft at the core – or musicals. Garrick scored a tremendous and lasting success as Ranger in Benjamin Hoadly's *The Suspicious Husband* (1747), which flaunts the elements of a sex comedy without consummation. Colman and Garrick's *The Clandestine Marriage* (1766) turns finally on good-hearted forgiveness by the blocking figures. The better plays of Arthur Murphy (*The Way to Keep Him*, 1761, in its five-act version) and the actor Charles Macklin (*Love à la Mode*, 1759) likewise contrive to acknowledge failures and defects in human nature while arranging satisfactory resolutions to their plots. The most individual writer of the age was the mimic and caricaturist Samuel Foote, much of whose work appeared during summers at the Little Haymarket. *The Minor* (1760) travesties the evangelist George Whitefield as Dr Squintum – outraging Methodists but not the government. *The Devil Upon Two Sticks* (1768) adapts Le Sage's *Diable boiteux*. *The Handsome Housemaid; or, Piety in Pattens* (1773; unpublished until 1973) is a caustic travesty of the *Pamela* story. The principal generic innovation of the sixties lay in musicals. The ballad opera boom was long gone, but it was succeeded by 'burlettas' (short pieces in that tradition, but with freshly composed music) and the precursors to the 'English operas' that were to flower in the eighties and nineties. The key figure was Isaac Bickerstaffe, who wrote a series of successful musicals, notably *Love in a Village* (1762), *The Maid of the Mill* (1765) and *The Padlock* (1768), before having to flee the country in 1772 when accused of sodomy.

The best-known plays of the sixties and seventies are those of Goldsmith and Sheridan. Goldsmith's *She Stoops to Conquer* (1773) is little more than a romp with a highly artificial happy ending, but much comic mileage is obtained from an old country house mistaken for an inn, an heiress mistaken for a serving maid, and so forth. Tony Lumpkin, the adolescent prankster who turns out to be of age, doted upon by his ghastly mother, is a splendid vehicle for the right actor. Sheridan's plays, notably *The Rivals* (1775) and *The School for Scandal* (1777), turn more on verbal wit and cheerful social satire of obvious butts. The 'screen scene' in the latter remains a brilliant *coup de théâtre*: the hypocritical Joseph Surface is unmasked and eventually foiled, while his scapegrace younger brother Charles wins fortune and gains his heiress out of sheer goodness of heart. The distance in dramatic elements and human values between Goldsmith and Sheridan (and such other 'laughing comedy' writers as Arthur Murphy and Garrick) and writers such as Hugh Kelly (*False Delicacy*, 1768) or Richard Cumberland (*The West Indian*, 1771) is far less than most early scholars of the drama claimed.[20]

Broadly surveying the plays written in this period, four observations seem to be in order. First, in the course of the later seventeenth century plays start to be taken more seriously as 'literature', partly because authors were allowed to publish them. Collaborative authorship was virtually unknown among professional dramatists in post-1660 London, and the gradual move towards advertising authors' names on playbills is another indication of the increasing prestige of playwrights as serious authors. Unacknowledged adaptation of old plays or other sources was increasingly frowned upon. The status of the best new plays was very high. *Circa* 1700 even so classically minded a critic as Charles Gildon could venerate Shakespeare, Jonson and Beaumont and Fletcher without rating their work above that of the best of contemporary playwrights.[21] For whatever reasons, the trend towards literary aspirations and originality was reversed in the eighteenth century. Lengthy periods of non-competition led to generic stasis, and, with the exception of actor-managers such as Cibber and Garrick, hardly any writer in England made a living solely from the theatre for any length of time after about 1710. Fielding came close

---

[20] On the underlying change in theory of humour, see Tave, *Amiable Humorist*.
[21] See Kewes, *Authorship and Appropriation*. On the reversal of this trend, see Kewes, ' "[A] Play, which I presume to call *original*" '.

to doing so in the thirties, and Isaac Bickerstaffe did so in the sixties, but virtually all other playwrights were lawyers or government employees or did literary hack-work or had family money or married money. Quite a lot might be made from a hit, but the theatre did not provide its writers anything like the possibility of a steady income.[22]

Second, prior to 1737 quite a lot of the new plays address topical and political issues and contain deeply embedded social ideology. Almost all such commentary, however, exists at an essentially commonplace level. Plays that seriously challenged the audience were rarely successful, as witness Southerne's *The Wives Excuse* and *The Maid's Last Prayer* (1693) or Farquhar's fiercely satiric, highly moral experiment in satire, *The Twin Rivals* (1702). Blatantly partisan plays sometimes flourished, as during the Exclusion Crisis.[23] Such instances as Dryden's *The Spanish Fryar* (1680) and Otway's *Venice Preserv'd*, however, held the stage for many years: clearly they had an appeal that transcended the political meaning they conveyed at the time of première. The bland socio-political content of eighteenth-century drama, except in the period 1728–37, we may ascribe to limited competition – and, after the Licensing Act, to censorship. Macklin's eleven-year struggle to get a licence for *The Man of the World* (hardly revolutionary in any way, but not staged until 1781) is testimony to the damping effect of the licenser.

Third, Shakespeare's growing eminence had a deleterious effect on the production of new plays. By 1700 a few of his plays were repertory staples (several in radically adapted versions) but many were not performed at all. The publication of the first 'modern' edition of the complete Shakespeare in 1709, edited by Nicholas Rowe, made less immediate difference to theatrical production than one might suppose.[24] Not until the 1730s, when a publishers' war brought the price as low as a penny per play, was Shakespeare truly available to any reader and the process of his deification intensified. Following the Licensing Act managers turned to Shakespeare as a source of free and highly respectable repertory variety, creating a flurry of productions of the comedies and other neglected parts of the canon in the early 1740s. The abrupt rise of Bardolatry is a phenomenon of the period 1730–70, and one might speculate that Shakespeare worship put mid-eighteenth-century playwrights at a hopeless psychological disadvantage in aiming to produce plays of great literary merit. Whatever the reasons, most of the really interesting and ambitious plays fall in the late

---

[22] See Milhous and Hume, 'Playwrights' remuneration in eighteenth-century London'.
[23] See Owen, *Restoration Theatre and Crisis*.
[24] See Hume, 'Before the Bard'. On the deification and influence of Shakespeare, see particularly Dobson, *Making of the National Poet*, and Bate, *Shakespearean Constitutions*.

seventeenth century and just beyond. What we find after the Licensing Act is mostly vehicles contrived for favourite performers, a state of affairs to which Shakespeare's status and prominence in the repertory contributed. Charles Beecher Hogan calculates that one performance in six featured Shakespeare in the first half of the eighteenth century (counting mainpieces only), the proportion rising sharply in the thirties and forties.[25]

Fourth, as a canon of English drama was formed, managers enjoying the comforts of duopoly felt ever less need to compete – or to take risks with the relatively few new plays they agreed to produce. Audiences seem to have been as much attracted by singers, dancers and flashy pantomimes as by plays. If variety was wanted, a great many proven, well-liked old plays were already available – and free. After 1695 all companies had the right to mount any play, even a new play staged by their competitors, though this was rarely done. Novelty was provided principally in lightweight afterpieces. New mainpieces did get written and staged, but most were formulaic vehicles for the actors. Many of these plays were expertly wrought; they rang skilful and imaginative changes upon the devices of their type; they provided what satisfied the audience. In purely theatrical terms, there are many wonderful plays written in the eighteenth century. One cannot claim, however, that in their depth, originality or literary quality they seek or achieve the heights of their late seventeenth-century predecessors, let alone Shakespeare. The audience did want a few new plays for variety, but a high proportion of what they went to see in any season consisted of modern classics (most of them twenty-five years or more old) and a smaller flock of pre-1642 favourites, including the increasingly revered and daunting works of Shakespeare.

[25] Hogan, *Shakespeare in the Theatre, 1701–1800*.

3

Theatre and the female presence

JOANNE LAFLER

In the autumn and winter of 1660–61, London play-goers witnessed a theatrical revolution. Women had begun performing in public playhouses, and before long they displaced the young men who had been trained, in the Elizabethan tradition, to play women's roles. Their impact would be far-reaching. In the winter of 1663–4, the first play by an Englishwoman to be performed publicly, Katherine Philips's translation of Corneille's *La Mort de Pompée*, was presented in Dublin. Other women followed Philips, though seldom in great numbers. Meeting resistance in ways that female performers did not, female playwrights never became a powerful presence, although a few women were signally successful.[1]

There had been female performers and playwrights in England in the early seventeenth century, but not in a public, commercial context. In the élite, protected environment of the court, female members of the royal family and court ladies appeared in elaborate entertainments known as masques and performed occasionally in plays. Whilst they enacted characters and spoke lines in plays, their function in masques was chiefly decorative and ceremonial: lavishly costumed, and displayed amid elaborate scenery, they joined in the dances that concluded these productions. Writing court masques in the 1630s, William Davenant learned how to display female performers and deploy stage spectacle – experience that he put to good use with his female performers in the Duke's Company in the 1660s.

Like the women who performed at court, early female dramatists were also amateurs functioning within an élite, protected environment. Plays by aristocratic women were likely read aloud, perhaps even given amateur performance, in private households. Plays by three women – Mary Herbert, Countess of Pembroke; Elizabeth Cary, Countess of Falkland; and Margaret

---

[1] For biographical information on performers, see Highfill, *et al.*, *Biographical Dictionary*; for playwrights, see Mann and Mann, eds., *Women Playwrights*.

Cavendish, Duchess of Newcastle – were published between 1599 and 1668.
There is no evidence that Aphra Behn and other women who began writing
professionally for the stage in the 1660s knew of Herbert and Cary or read
Cavendish's plays. They took as their models plays by men that had been
published and performed. The struggle of Behn, her contemporaries and successors for authorial legitimacy may be due in part to the fact that they did
not see themselves (and were not seen) as inheritors of an élite, 'respectable'
tradition of female playwriting.

Some acknowledgment should be made of the presence of female spectators. Scanty evidence for the Elizabethan period indicates that women of
all social classes attended public performances at the more élite indoor playhouses and the large outdoor theatres. Genteel Elizabeth Williams enjoyed
card-playing and going to the new Globe theatre in 1614. She would have felt at
home among female theatre-goers in the later seventeenth century. Women
identified by name in the 1660s include Elizabeth Pepys, who attended London
playhouses with and without her husband Samuel; the Duchess of Cleveland,
whose scandalous reputation made her presence in a box as compelling as the
scenes enacted on the stage; and poet and translator Katherine Philips, who
saw plays at the Red Bull, Lincoln's Inn Fields and Smock Alley, Dublin. 'Citizens' wives', domestic servants, prostitutes and other women not specifically
identified by contemporary observers completed the heterogeneous female
audience. The extent to which female spectators exerted influence on taste
has been the subject of scholarly research and debate, especially the notion of
genteel and aristocratic women as a monolithic, reform-minded faction at the
end of the seventeenth century.[2]

Our history is partial in several senses. In addition to the paucity of documentation for theatre in general, especially before the early eighteenth century, we
hear very little from women themselves. This is especially true for actresses,
who left few writings of their own. *A Narrative of the Life of Mrs Charlotte Charke*
(1755), by Colley Cibber's daughter, recounts at length the experiences of the
actress-playwright-manager as a strolling player and on the theatrical margins
in London. For the most part, however, actresses' voices must be teased out of
legal documents, such as complaints by Rebecca Marshall, in 1665, of harass-
ment by men who were pursuing her. In prefaces to their published plays
female playwrights often advert to problems with, and sometimes help from,
actors and managers, as well as to anti-female prejudice. Katherine Philips's
letters to Sir Charles Cotterell reveal various concerns about her work and

---

[2] See Roberts, *Ladies*.

ambivalence about its publication and public performance. More first-person accounts would enhance our understanding of the experiences of female performers and playwrights. We can, nevertheless, assess their impact.

Performers

There is no evidence of women in the acting companies that began performing in London in the spring and summer of 1660, nor are women mentioned in Charles II's grant of 21 August 1660, which gave exclusive authority to Thomas Killigrew and William Davenant to form acting companies. By the winter of 1660–1, however, female performers began to be noticed by spectators, one of whom wrote on 15 December: 'Upon our stages we have women actors, as beyond seas.'[3] The situation in which these women found themselves was unprecedented in theatre history. They were intruders in an all-male theatrical culture that had flourished for six decades, until the closing of the theatres in 1642. For a while – exactly how long is not certain – they shared the stage with young men who had been trained to play female roles, the most famous of whom was Edward Kynaston, who in his late teens 'made a Compleat Female Stage Beauty' and attracted a considerable following.[4] Unlike the young men, the first actresses did not have the training or protected status of apprentices, and there is evidence that they were not welcomed by their male colleagues.

The first reference of any kind to female performers appears in the context of a complaint. In a petition to Charles II on 13 October 1660, senior actors in the newly formed King's Company stated that their master Thomas Killigrew had, among other things, 'obliged' them to act with women. Whether the actors were opposed to the idea of female performers as such, or merely regarded the introduction of women as symptomatic of Killigrew's power over them, is not certain, but the inference is that the innovation was forced upon them.[5] If Killigrew's actors had been receptive to performing with women they might have recruited their wives, sisters and daughters. The surnames of the original female members of the King's Company indicate no such relationships. Unlike female performers in Italy, Spain and France, where acting companies were often extended families, the first English actresses lacked the protection – and control – of husbands and male relatives. As highly visible free agents

---

[3] Wilson, *All the King's Ladies*, 3.
[4] Downes, *Roscius Anglicanus*, 46.
[5] For actresses as an economic threat see Shapiro, 'Introduction of actresses in England', 185–6.

they constituted a disturbing presence. Their morality automatically suspect, they were commonly equated with prostitutes, an association which haunted female performers for generations to come.

Nothing is known about how the first female performers in the King's Company were recruited or trained. Samuel Pepys's observations suggest that they were raw beginners, flung before the public to fare as best they could. Pepys attended six productions of the King's Company between 20 November 1660 and 3 January 1661. On that January day he noted, without further comment: 'the first time that ever I saw Women come upon the stage'. His next mention of female performers was decidedly negative; a production of Middleton's *The Widow* on 8 January was 'wronged' by actresses who evidently forgot their lines and had to consult their scripts. A production of *The Scornful Lady* on 12 February occasioned his first words of praise. The leading role was 'now done by a woman, which makes the play appear much better than ever it did to me'. She may have been Anne Marshall, who is known to have played the role, but Pepys did not identify her, or any actresses in the King's Company, by name for several years. They remained 'a woman', or 'the women', remarkable for their gender rather than their personal accomplishments, until 1664 and 1665, when he first mentions by name the 'eldest Marshall' (Anne), her younger sister Rebecca, and 'pretty, witty' Nell Gwyn.

From the beginning William Davenant paid close attention to his actresses, as he did to all aspects of his theatrical enterprise. His contract with the Duke's Company actors on 14 November 1660 gave him seven shares for the maintenance of 'all ye Women that are to performe or represent Womens parts'.[6] As his personal charges, Hester Davenport, Mary Saunderson, Mary Davies and Jane Long boarded at his own house. Whilst his new playhouse was fitted out in Lincoln's Inn Fields he had time to prepare them for the grand opening production in June 1661, *The Siege of Rhodes*, which had been produced privately for limited audiences in 1656 and 1659.

For this spectacular two-part production Davenant used an expanded text that made excellent use of two of his female performers, and he employed changeable scenery to display them effectively. Stage directions for Act 4, scene 3 of the second part indicate a scene change whereby the stage is 'wholly fill'd with Roxalana's rich pavilion, wherein is discern'd at a distance, Ianthe asleep on a couch'. The use of a scenic 'discovery' for seductive female display thereafter became commonplace in Restoration drama. Katherine Philips, who undoubtedly saw this production, used a similar discovery for one of her

---

[6] Bawcutt, ed., *Control and Censorship of Caroline Drama*, 238.

scenic interludes in *Pompey*. The immense success of *The Siege of Rhodes* made its female performers instant stars. Diarist John Evelyn gossiped about the 'fair and famous comedian call'd Roxalana from the part she perform'd'. Pepys wrote of 'Ianthe' (Mary Saunderson) as well as 'Roxalana' (Hester Davenport).

Female performers were officially acknowledged in the patents issued to Killigrew and Davenant in 1662 and 1663, which specified that women's parts, having formerly been performed by men in female dress, would henceforth be played by women. By this time female performers were a *fait accompli*, but the wording of the patents suggests an underlying uneasiness. We are assured that what had once given offence – male impersonators of women – would now 'by such reformation be esteemed not only harmless delight, but useful and instructive representations of human life'. The reformation did not bar occasional performances by male comedians of bawdy or campy female characters.

Actresses had ceased being a novelty, but their bodies and their sexuality continued to claim attention.[7] The hedonistic culture of the restored Stuart court was partly responsible, but – as the critics of Elizabethan theatre who decried the sexual attractions of boy actors in female dress understood full well – theatre is a fundamentally eroticized enterprise. It is not surprising that actresses (most famously, Nell Gwyn) were sought after as mistresses by members of the royal family and the aristocracy, as well as by playwrights, fellow-actors and assorted gentlemen who came backstage to mingle with them. Although some actresses lived chastely, or at least unremarkably, few escaped the attention of gossipmongers and writers of scurrilous lampoons. Discretion, wealth and fame, far from offering protection, served to incite scandal. Circumspect in the conduct of her private life, Anne Bracegirdle was nevertheless the object of speculation about liaisons with actors and a secret marriage to playwright William Congreve. In the eighteenth century actresses became the subject of gossipy biographies.

Nowhere is the focus on the female body clearer than in the development of the 'breeches role' as a woman's specialty. Female characters in male dress, originally performed by boy actors, abounded in the Elizabethan–Jacobean plays that were the mainstays of the early Restoration repertory. In the 1660s the erotic potential of female performers in such roles was quickly discovered and exploited. On 28 October 1661, when Pepys saw an actress in breeches in *Argalaus and Parthenia*, his response was unambiguous: 'the best legs that

---

[7] For actresses as erotic objects see Howe, *First English Actresses*, chap. 2. Payne, in 'Reified object or emergent professional?', discusses actresses as more than objects of erotic interest.

ever I saw, and I was very well pleased with it'. New plays with female characters in male dress soon joined older stock pieces in the repertory. In *All the King's Ladies* John Harold Wilson estimated that eighty-nine new plays produced between 1660 and 1700 had one or more roles for a woman in male dress.

In the Elizabethan theatre, situations in which boy actors played female characters who don breeches provided opportunities for pointed sexual banter, heightened by hints at homoeroticism. The female performer in male dress, her legs and thighs clothed but still visible in breeches, constituted a different but equally dangerous erotic presence, complicated by a preoccupation with the sexuality of actresses and by cultural anxieties about female sexuality in general.

Breeches roles also provided scope for histrionic skill. Nell Gwyn, Anne Bracegirdle, Susannah Verbruggen and Peg Woffington were admired for their naturalness in such roles. Actresses took advantage of the freedom of male dress, the greater liveliness of female characters who donned breeches, and the opportunity to parody male behaviour. On some occasions they crossed gender lines altogether, playing male characters such as youths and effeminate men. Stock pieces were occasionally advertised as 'played all by women', evidently a titillating novelty. Charlotte Charke, who frequently cross-dressed off stage, was notorious for her performance of male roles – over forty altogether, including Macheath, George Barnwell, Lord Foppington (originally played by her father) and Lothario. Unfortunately, Charke's memoirs, which detail her real-life exploits in male dress, say little about her performance of male characters onstage.

If being female was the female performer's first important contribution, the skill and distinctive personalities of actresses had a long-term impact on adaptations of stock pieces, on character types and on the development of dramatic genres. Stock pieces from the Elizabethan repertory, whose female roles were neither large nor numerous, were adapted to accommodate female performers. For his version of *Macbeth* Davenant enlarged the role of Lady Macduff, providing a virtuous foil for Lady Macbeth and a meaty part for Jane Long. The Davenant–Dryden *Tempest* added the lovers Dorinda and Hippolito, the latter a breeches role for Long. Ben Jonson's *Epicoene*, popular throughout the Restoration and early eighteenth century, was performed after the mid-1660s with an actress as the title character, a boy disguised as a woman.

Despite the brevity of her career (1664–70) Nell Gwyn left her imprint on sprightly comic heroines such as Florimel (*Secret Love*) and the second Constantia (*The Chances*), and she and Charles Hart popularized the bantering

Plate 10. Margaret ('Peg') Woffington, speaking the epilogue 'The Female Volunteer' (1746). Woffington was especially admired for her performance of 'breeches' roles. Artist unknown.

lovers that became a staple of Restoration comedy. Katherine Corey originated a number of comical, sometimes bawdy, older female characters. Dark-haired Rebecca Marshall was famous for passionate, villainous 'tragedy queens' such as Nourmahal (*Aureng-Zebe*) and Roxana (*The Rival Queens*).

The popularity of *The Siege of Rhodes* highlighted the importance of theatrical music and song. Mary Davies, Jane Long, Charlotte Butler and Anne Bracegirdle were celebrated for their lovely voices. In addition to performing songs in regular comedy and tragedy, talented singer-actresses made possible the development of a distinctive new genre, dramatic opera, in the Restoration and the popular new genre, ballad opera, in the eighteenth century.

During a career of thirty-five years (1675–1710), Elizabeth Barry performed successfully in both comedy and tragedy, but she became, according to John Downes, 'famous Mrs Barry' – the most admired and highly paid Restoration actress – chiefly for her tragic portrayals. In his autobiography, Colley Cibber paid tribute to her emotional range: 'no Violence of Passion could be too much for her: And when Distress or Tenderness possess'd her, she subsided into the most affecting Melody and Softness.' She played a variety of tragic characters, from ingenues to Marshall-type villainesses, and she inspired playwrights to create the psychologically complex heroines who were the emotional and dramatic centre of so-called 'she tragedy'.[8] Barry's most famous roles – Monimia (*The Orphan*), Belvidera (*Venice Preserv'd*), Anna Bullen (*Virtue Betray'd*), Isabella (*The Fatal Marriage*), Zara (*The Mourning Bride*) and Calista (*The Fair Penitent*) – were greatly prized by later generations of actresses.

The drawing power of popular actresses did not translate into economic parity with actors.[9] In 1695 Elizabeth Barry was earning £2 10s a week (about £100 a year). At a time when a gentleman could subsist on £50 a year this was an impressive income for a woman, but it was half of Thomas Betterton's weekly salary and less than the salaries of four other men in the company. Perhaps as compensation, Barry was granted the sole privilege of an annual benefit performance yielding at least £70. In the eighteenth century annual benefits became the norm for all performers; actors' incomes were higher in general and salaries of leading performers increased greatly. The biggest disparities occurred between high-ranking performers of both sexes and those at the bottom of the hierarchy. In the 1760s Ned Shuter earned £287 a year and

---

[8] For discussion of Barry's influence as a tragic actress see Howe, *First English Actresses*, chap. 5.

[9] Information on salaries is scanty. See Milhous, *Thomas Betterton and the Management of Lincoln's Inn Fields*, 225–46; and Milhous, 'United Company finances, 1682–1692', 45ff. For salaries in the 1770s see the introduction to Van Lennep et al., *London Stage*, IV: lviii.

James Perry only £42; Georgeann Bellamy earned £272 a year and young Miss Helm only £35. With a few exceptions, male performers continued to earn more than females in each rank.

The privilege of sharing in company management and profits was denied to female performers except for the brief period of 1695–1705, when eight senior actors from the United Company, including Elizabeth Barry, Anne Bracegirdle and Elinor Leigh, established a rival company at Lincoln's Inn Fields, in which they shared managerial responsibilities and profits. When John Vanbrugh assumed control of the company in 1705 the sharing arrangement ended and all actors were paid salaries. No actress participated in the management of a major theatrical company for more than a century.[10]

In 1709, when Anne Oldfield was invited to become a sharer in a new company at the Queen's Theatre, Haymarket, the financial prospects were tempting. A 'fruitful' season in the early 1700s, according to Colley Cibber, yielded each actor-manager over £600 in profits. Oldfield's hopes were frustrated when co-manager Thomas Doggett objected to 'more than one Sex' in the management. Instead of pressing her claim to a share, she agreed to a thirteen-year contract that gave her the highest annual salary ever paid to a woman – £200 – and a 'clear benefit' (paying no house charge) early in each season. In 1745, when Susanna Arne Cibber (Colley's daughter-in-law) proposed a joint purchase of the Drury Lane patent to David Garrick, she was similarly frustrated. Fearing interference from her estranged husband Theophilus, Garrick never responded.[11]

Barred from exercising formal authority, actresses wielded power informally, perhaps especially in decisions about casting. Inevitably there were rumours of diva-ish backstage behaviour and gossip about actresses trading sexual favours for position and perquisites. Famous and popular performers could 'call in sick', refuse a role or threaten to quit, as Anne Oldfield successfully did in 1712, when she campaigned for the leading role in *The Distrest Mother*. Garrick's correspondence testifies to his fraught relationships with leading actresses Jane Pope, Mary Ann Yates and Frances Abington.[12] Actresses voiced complaints against other performers, managers and managerial policies in legal documents such as Mary Porter's petition to the Lord Chamberlain in

[10] See Milhous, *Betterton and the Management of Lincoln's Inn Fields*, for the managerial situation at Lincoln's Inn Fields, 1695–1705. Langhans, 'Tough actresses to follow', 5 discusses actress-managers of smaller companies and Mary Ann Yates's brief tenure as a co-manager of the opera house at the King's Theatre, Haymarket, in the 1770s.

[11] Nash, *Provoked Wife*, 217–18. For Anne Oldfield's exclusion from management in 1709 see Lafler, *Celebrated Mrs Oldfield*, 66.

[12] Garrick, *Letters*, vols. II and III, *passim*.

Plate 11. Anne Oldfield (1683–1730). A leading comedienne, Oldfield was also noted for dignity and grace in tragic roles. Engraved from a portrait by Jonathan Richardson.

1707, in which she protested that parts she had performed were given to women below her in rank. For the most part, however, female performers seemed satisfied with their professional circumstances. Elizabeth Barry's long career was by no means unusual. If she remained healthy and able to work, an actress in one of the patent companies might look forward to a tenure of thirty years or more. This was true not only for top-ranked performers but also for a 'journeywoman' such as Elizabeth Willis, whose career in supporting roles spanned nearly fifty years.[13]

Long hours at the theatre, rehearsing and performing six days a week, brought men and women together as partners, however unequal. Beginning with Mary Saunderson, who married Thomas Betterton in 1662, a number of actresses married actors. Elizabeth Willis, Elinor Leigh and the wives of Henry Norris and Martin Powell bore children who entered the profession, thereby creating the family networks so notably absent in 1660. Attracted to the theatre for a variety of reasons – financial need, a love of play-acting or adventure, or the desire to be visible at a time when women were generally effaced from public life – female performers made themselves indispensable in a remarkably short time. In the process, they changed theatrical culture.

Playwrights

In a space of seven years, from 1663 to 1670, two translations from Corneille by Katherine Philips were performed in Dublin and London, plays by Frances Boothby and Elizabeth Polwhele were produced in London, and Aphra Behn began her long, successful relationship with the Duke's Company. The future looked promising for female playwrights, but it proved otherwise. Philips died in 1664; Boothby wrote no more plays after the production of *Marcelia* in 1669; Polwhele married a clergyman and ceased writing plays. Behn, it is true, became one of the premier authors of the period, but her success did not open the floodgates for other women. From 1670 until 1695 – six years after Behn's death – no other woman had plays produced. At the turn of the century there was a flurry of new plays by women, but this activity halted abruptly after a dozen years.

Throughout the entire period of 1660 to 1776, female playwrights never gained a solid foothold, nor were their numbers great. Thirty-three women had their work produced in London playhouses; in the same period, 345 male

---

[13] Langhans, 'Tough actresses to follow', 4–5.

playwrights were active.[14] The women's output totalled 109 plays – mainpieces, afterpieces, ballad operas and 'musical entertainments'. Of these, forty-nine were the work of Aphra Behn, Susanna Centlivre and Mary Pix.

Unlike female performers, female playwrights were not a constant, familiar presence for theatre-goers. Plays by Behn and Centlivre were successful enough to become popular stock pieces, revived once or twice a season; the work of most other female playwrights did not outlast a single season. There were frequent long stretches when no new plays by women were produced – in one case, ten seasons in a row. These dry spells were sometimes the result of theatrical conditions that reduced the demand for new drama generally. Still, it is clear that something beyond market forces accounted for the small numbers and limited success of female playwrights. That 'something', most scholars agree, was the cultural prescriptions that regulated the participation of women in public life and excluded them from professions regarded as male.[15]

Entrenched assumptions about gender roles marked women as intruders in the masculine preserve of authorship. The anonymous dramatic dialogue *A Comparison Between the Two Stages* (1702) states the situation humorously. Decrying 'Petticoat-Authors', a character asserts: 'there's no Feminine for the Latin word [author], 'tis entirely of the Masculine Gender, and the Language won't bear such a thing as a She Author.' Female playwrights internalized such notions even in the process of transgressing them. In her preface to *The Luckey Chance* (1686), Aphra Behn speaks of 'my Masculine Part the poet in me' while objecting to the double standard by which her work was judged. From Frances Boothby in 1669 to Hannah Cowley in 1776, female playwrights attempted to forestall criticism of their authorial presumption. In prologues and epilogues they appealed to male chivalry and female solidarity, sometimes adopting a flirtatious or seductive manner. (Boothby's tragedy was offered as a 'woman's treat'.) When their earlier work was dismissed as 'women's stuff', female playwrights published their later work anonymously or disguised their gender. Writing well had its own dangers. If women were by nature deficient, their plays, if good, must surely be the work of men. Although male as well as female playwrights plundered the work of others

---

[14] Figures for women's plays throughout this chapter are drawn from Mann and Mann, eds., *Women Playwrights*, 337–402, and from Van Lennep *et al.*, *London Stage*. They do not include a handful of plays produced outside of commercial London venues, such as Centlivre's *Love at a Venture*, refused for production at Drury Lane but performed at Bath in 1706. Figures for men are based on the hand-lists of plays in Nicoll, *History of English Drama*, I–III.

[15] See Pearson, *Prostituted Muse*, and Donkin, *Getting into the Act*.

in varying degrees, women were disproportionately charged with outright plagiarism.[16]

Female playwrights violated prescriptive beliefs about women in positions of authority. Authors were expected to read their scripts to the actors, suggest casting, perhaps direct, and certainly attend, rehearsals – activities deemed more appropriate for men than women. In the anonymous farce *The Female Wits: or, The Triumvirate of Poets at Rehearsal* (1696) the female playwright Marsilia is ridiculed for her bustling self-importance during rehearsals. Backstage conditions were alien to the gently born Katherine Philips, who was clearly distressed by witnessing an actors' dispute during a rehearsal of *Pompey*. Tougher, less gently born Susanna Centlivre endured Robert Wilks's temper during a rehearsal of *The Busie Body*, when the actor flung down the script, proclaiming it 'a silly thing wrote by a woman' that no audience would tolerate.[17] Despite a less than full house on opening night the play became an undoubted hit, with an initial run of six performances. Whether Wilks, who had a fine role as Sir George Airy, apologized to Centlivre is not known.

It is surprising that more actresses, who clearly felt at home backstage, did not try their hand at playwriting, as actors such as Betterton, Cibber and Garrick did with considerable success. The few women who did combine playwriting with acting careers defined themselves primarily as performers and only secondarily as writers. Philippina Burton, Jane Egleton and Jane Pope wrote plays as vehicles for themselves, to be performed only once at their annual benefits. Susanna Cibber and Catherine Clive also wrote for their annual benefits, although Cibber's *The Oracle* (1752) and Clive's *The Rehearsal; or, Bays in Petticoats* (1750) were performed on other occasions in several succeeding seasons. Charlotte Charke played leading roles in her plays – *The Art of Management; or, Tragedy Expell'd*, which ran for three performances at the York Buildings, where the small company she managed relocated from the Haymarket in the fall of 1735, and *The Carnival; or, Harlequin Blunderer*, also performed that year. Eliza Haywood was unique in having her work produced by acting companies to which she did not belong (Lincoln's Inn Fields, Drury Lane) as well as by the company at the Haymarket in which she was a performer. *The Opera of Operas; or, Tom Thumb the Great* (1733), which she co-authored with William Hatchett and produced at the Haymarket, was a resounding success.

Success was measured by critical and popular acclaim and by financial gain. In her preface to *The Luckey Chance* Behn boasted: 'I am not content to write for

---

[16] See Rosenthal, *Playwrights and Plagiarists*, 38–41.
[17] Cotton, *Women Playwrights in England*, 138.

a Third day only. I value Fame as much as if I had been born a Hero.' Yet Behn, like most female playwrights, depended on the income from her writing. A well-attended author's benefit on the third night of a play's initial run yielded better returns than one could earn from non-dramatic writing. Mary Davys received three guineas for the sale of her first novel in 1700; she earned ten times as much – about £32 – from her author's benefit when *The Northern Heiress* was produced at Lincoln's Inn Fields in 1716. Established playwrights (chiefly male) earned much more, especially in the eighteenth century when initial runs were longer than in Behn's time and it became common to have authors' benefits on the sixth and ninth nights. Still, Davys's £32 equalled the annual income of a lower-ranked actress, and she would receive a small additional sum for the sale of her playscript.[18]

With a sense of the inducements that attracted women to write for the stage, and the cultural barriers they had to surmount, we can read the history of female playwrights through the careers of a few individuals. Katherine Philips, apostrophized during her lifetime and long afterward as the 'chaste, matchless Orinda', is something of a special case. Married at age 16 to a landed gentleman, she did not write out of financial need. Some have dismissed her as merely a translator of Corneille, and she has been described as a 'gifted amateur' in contrast to Behn, 'the commercial woman writer'.[19] Yet John Evelyn, who attended two performances of *Horace* 'by the virtuous Mrs Philips' in 1669, clearly regarded her as more than a translator; her correspondence with Sir Charles Cotterell shows her to be more than an amateur. Although she insisted that the Earl of Orrery 'importuned' her to complete the translation of *Pompey* and that he arranged for its production at the new Smock Alley Theatre in Dublin in February 1663, 'notwithstanding all my Intreaties to the contrary', she was pleased by Orrery's expenditure of £100 for authentic '*Roman* and *Egyptian* Habits'. She took pride in the exactness of her translation and her original entr'acte songs, set to music 'by the greatest Masters in ENGLAND', and kept an uneasy eye on a rival translation of Corneille's play, slated for production at Lincoln's Inn Fields. She died before completing her translation of *Horace*, which was finished by Sir John Denham and produced both at court and by the King's Company. We can therefore only speculate about whether, and how, she might have continued to occupy a position between amateur and

---

[18] For the sale of Davys's novel, see ibid., 157. I have calculated the amount of Davys's benefit from the day's receipts shown in Van Lennep *et al.*, *London Stage*, II: 400, deducting the standard 'house charge' of £40.

[19] Cotton, *Women Playwrights in England*, 194ff.

professional, as a number of male playwrights did throughout the Restoration and eighteenth century but no woman after Philips attempted.

Aphra Behn, the witty and manifestly unchaste 'Astrea', embraced – indeed, invented – the identity of the professional woman of letters. An English spy in Antwerp in 1666, apparently widowed and chronically short of funds, she was imprisoned briefly for debt on her return to London and began writing for the stage in 1670. Until her illness and death in 1689 she wrote tirelessly, publishing fiction, poetry and drama. Twelve of her twenty plays were produced between 1676 and 1682, including some of her finest work: *The Rover* (1677), *Sir Patient Fancy* (1678) and *The Feign'd Courtesans* (1679). Unlike Philips, Behn was neither modest nor deferential, nor did she shrink from strong political or sexual subject matter. For this she paid a price that later women writers, or coevals who might have been tempted to follow her lead, could hardly ignore. The support of male colleagues and highly placed patrons, including the Earl of Rochester, James II and playwrights Edward Ravenscroft and Thomas Otway, could not protect her from personal attacks: her writing was termed 'indecent', she was said to have traded sexual favours for professional assistance, and she would be haunted by charges of plagiarism.

After the success of *The Forc'd Marriage* in 1670 at the Duke's Company, Behn became in effect its house playwright, enjoying professional stability and the opportunity to create roles, season after season, for brilliant actors: Thomas and Mary Betterton, James Nokes, William Smith, Cave Underhill, Mary Lee, Elizabeth Barry and Anne Quin. Her most popular and highly regarded comedy, *The Rover* (1677), shows her as a skilled adaptor. Stung by charges that the play was essentially Thomas Killigrew's *Thomaso*, lightly 'alter'd', she insisted in a note to the published text that she had only 'stoln some hints'. Her debt to Killigrew's play was greater than that, but she shaped her source well for the requirements of the Duke's Company.[20] In the virtuous and resourceful Hellena (played by the young Elizabeth Barry), she created a memorable heroine who helped ensure the play's lasting popularity. Performed regularly through the mid-eighteenth century, *The Rover* perpetuated the fame of 'Astrea'.

Behn's fame, as I have shown, did not inspire other women to emulate her during her lifetime, and opportunities for the production of new drama were reduced with the merger of the two patent companies into the United Company in 1682. That situation changed with the establishment of a rival

---

[20] See, among many discussions of Behn's adaptation, Todd's introduction to *The Rover* in her edition of *The Works of Aphra Behn*, v: 46–9.

company at Lincoln's Inn Fields in the spring of 1695. In the following season Behn's *The Younger Brother* was produced posthumously and new female playwrights appeared on the scene: the pseudonymous 'Ariadne', Catherine Trotter, Delarivier Manley and Mary Pix. Women were responsible for seven of the twenty-six new plays in the 1695–6 season, with two each by Manley and Pix. During the next ten years Jane Wiseman and two 'young ladies' saw their work produced and Susanna Centlivre began her career. Of the nearly two hundred new plays staged between 1695 and 1707, women wrote thirty-one. Once again, prospects for female playwrights looked promising.

Encouraged by their initial success, Trotter, Manley and Pix published commendatory verses in which they proclaimed themselves the heirs of 'Orinda' and 'Astrea' and asserted their equality with male writers. Their pretensions were lampooned in the anonymous *Female Wits*, produced at Drury Lane in the fall of 1696, which featured Marsilia (Manley), 'a poetess that admires her own works, and a great lover of flattery', Calista (Trotter), 'a lady that pretends to the learned languages, and assumes to herself the name of critic' and Mrs Wellfed (Pix), 'a fat, female author' with a fondness for ale. In the next few years the three women would discover that although they could get their plays produced, they could not count on favourable reception of their work. Despite increased demand for drama, most new plays failed.[21] New plays by women seemed especially vulnerable; only Pix's *Ibrahim* and *The Spanish Wives*, and Centlivre's *The Beau's Duel*, *Love's Contrivance* and *The Gamester* – the latter a huge success – outlasted the seasons in which they were first performed. Other plays by women faded from sight after initial, often brief, runs.

Only 16 years of age when her tragedy *Agnes de Castro* (1695), based on a novella by Behn, was produced at Drury Lane, Trotter was pleased with its reception and encouraged to write two more tragedies. *The Fatal Friendship* (1698) and *The Unhappy Penitent* (1701) did not fare well, despite some effective pathetic touches in the former. Her only comedy, *Love at a Loss; or, The Most Votes Carry It* (1700), should have appealed to reformers who were inveighing against 'lewd and offensive' plays, but it, too, was not successful. After the failure of *The Revolution of Sweden* (1706) Trotter ceased writing for the stage and married a cleric, Patrick Cockburn.

Of her only comedy, *The Lost Lover* (1696), Delarivier Manley wrote: 'I am satisfied the bare Name of being a Woman's play damn'd it beyond its own want of Merit.' When the success of *The Royal Mischief*, handsomely produced at

---

[21] Milhous, in *Thomas Betterton and the Management of Lincoln's Inn Fields*, 113–88, discusses reasons for the failure of new drama after 1697.

Lincoln's Inn Fields in 1696, was tempered by objections to its sexual frankness, she observed bitterly – as Behn had done – that audiences accepted from men what they condemned in a woman. After her second tragedy, *Almyna*, failed in 1707 she turned to non-dramatic writing. Her fourth and final play, *Lucius, First Christian King of Britain*, eked out three performances (and one benefit) in the 1716/17 season and was performed once for her benefit in 1720, after which Manley retired permanently from theatrical writing.

Mary Pix's six tragedies and six comedies, produced over ten years, were a remarkable accomplishment by any standard. Her first two plays, *Ibrahim, Thirteenth Emperor of the Turks* (1696), a passionate, action-filled tragedy, and *The Spanish Wives* (1696), a comedy with a fine role for Susannah Verbruggen, were judged successful and revived in several subsequent seasons. Her next effort, *The Innocent Mistress* (1697), was damned as indecent in *A Comparison Between the Two Stages*. When *The Deceiver Deceiv'd* was produced at Lincoln's Inn Fields in the fall of 1697, trouble was in the air. The prologue asserted that the author had shown her play 'To some, who, like true Wits, stole't half away' and alluded to Drury Lane actor-playwright George Powell as the thief.[22] Her preface to the published text spoke of enemies who 'endeavour'd to discountenance this Play' and implied that Powell had accused her of plagiarizing his comedy, *The Imposture Defeated*, produced two months earlier at Drury Lane. Pix wrote eight more plays, none of which repeated the success of her earlier work. The last three were published anonymously, and the prologue of *The Conquest of Spain* (1705) identified the author as a man. After *The Adventures of Madrid* (1706) she drifted into obscurity. A performance of Centlivre's *Busie Bodie* on 28 May 1709 was held as a benefit for 'Mrs Pix's Executor'; the exact date of her death is unknown.

By 1707 a period of remarkable productivity for female playwrights had ended. Like Behn after 1670, Susanna Centlivre emerged as the dominant figure, if not quite to the exclusion of all other women. Between 1707 and 1723, when Centlivre died, only three plays by other women – Davys, Manley and Haywood – were produced. Like Behn, after an initial experiment with tragi-comedy Centlivre discovered her talent for lively, ingeniously plotted comedy. (A tragedy, *The Cruel Gift*, did not outlive the 1716–17 season.) Reflecting the reformed temper of her time, her plays are notable for less bawdry and satire, and a more circumscribed view of women, than Behn's. Instead of the active, determined Hellena in *The Rover*, who adopts numerous disguises in order to flout male authority and spy on Willmore, Centlivre's *A Bold Stroke for a Wife*

---

[22] Steeves discusses this incident in Pix, *Plays of Mary Pix*, xxiii–xxiv.

features a determined, resourceful hero who adopts numerous disguises in order to outwit the guardians of the woman he loves.

During her early years in London, Centlivre found male allies in a raffish circle of friends that included the successful new playwright George Farquhar. She also knew what it meant to be devalued as a woman and responded by publishing several early plays anonymously. Besides the high-handed Wilks, who denigrated *The Busie Body*, she had to deal with Colley Cibber, whose influence as a reader of new scripts (and later as co-manager of the Drury Lane company) was enormous. In 1706 Cibber rejected *Love at a Venture* for production, then paid Centlivre the dubious compliment of plagiarizing part of it for his own comedy, *The Double Gallant*.[23] Centlivre herself made good use of other people's work, borrowing plot elements from several Molière comedies and a play by John Lacy for her first successful piece, *Love's Contrivance* (1703), but Cibber's rejection and theft of her work was surely unforgivable.

With her marriage in 1707 to Joseph Centlivre, a royal cook, the former Susanna Carroll was no longer wholly dependent on an income from her writing. In the next fifteen years, under more settled theatrical conditions than the tumultuous period in which she made her début, she produced nine more plays, making a total of seventeen. *The Busie Body* (1709), *The Wonder: A Woman Keeps a Secret* (1714) and *A Bold Stroke for a Wife* (1718) were as successful as any work by male contemporaries. Along with *The Gamester* they were among the most popular stock pieces of the eighteenth century.

Centlivre achieved the legitimacy that great success bestows. After 1709 her work would not be dismissed as a woman's, but rather advertised as 'by the author of The Busie Body'. Success, however, was not transferable; after her death there was no flood of successors. For four decades – until the 1760s and 1770s, when a new generation of women that included Frances Sheridan, Elizabeth Griffith and Hannah Cowley began their careers – only ten female playwrights were active. Three were actresses writing for their annual benefits.

The Licensing Act of 1737 is sometimes cited as contributing to the dearth of plays by women in the 1740s and 1750s. This act, which strengthened the government's censorship powers and the monopolies of the two patent theatres, certainly reduced the market for new drama. Given the lesser participation by female playwrights overall, it is perhaps not surprising to find that between May 1736 and March 1747 there were no new plays by women. Still, it must be noted that female playwrights also made a poor showing during the five seasons before the Licensing Act, when as many as five theatres were operating in

---

[23] Lock discusses this incident in *Susanna Centlivre*, 55.

London and there was a great demand for new drama. In that period, women were responsible for only 8 of the 125 new plays produced in all London playhouses.[24] Even the prospect of greater profits, arising from additional authors' benefits for long-running plays, failed to attract female playwrights until much later in the eighteenth century. Theatrical vicissitudes do not explain the recurring pattern of appearances, disappearances, success and failure.

Surveying the entire period, it is possible to draw both positive and negative conclusions. It is remarkable that, despite ingrained gender bias, over thirty women managed to have their plays produced and a handful were successful. Yet their overall history was not one of growth and progress. The productivity of 1695–1706 was never equalled or even approached. Except for Susanna Centlivre, no woman writing during that period had a long-term impact. Successive generations of female playwrights, unable to build upon the achievement of their predecessors, struggled anew to claim authorial legitimacy. The situation was clearly different for female performers. After 1660 there would always be a demand for actresses. Female playwrights were never assimilated fully into their profession, nor were they welcomed as a uniquely valuable presence.

---

[24] See Hume, *Rakish Stage*, 302–11, for a discussion of the effects of the Licensing Act and p. 299 for figures on new plays from 1732–3 to 1736–7. Pearson, *Prostituted Muse*, 232, discusses the specific effects of the Licensing Act on the careers of Charlotte Charke and Eliza Haywood, who wrote and performed at non-patent theatres.

4

Theatre, politics and morality

DEREK HUGHES

In March 1660 the parliamentary general George Monck marched on London, restored to the Rump Parliament the members excluded in 1648, and thereby made possible the return of the King, in May. The fall of the Puritan régime restored not only the monarchy but legal, regular theatre, the right to perform plays being quickly restricted to two companies, the King's and the Duke's. Indeed Monck's intervention was celebrated on the stage as it was happening, in the first Carolean comedy, John Tatham's *The Rump*.[1] A year later, these events were redramatized in a more serious form in the Earl of Orrery's tragi-comedy *The Generall*, whose hero Clorimun unwillingly fights for a usurper, but eventually restores the true king.[2] Orrery's next play, *The History of Henry the Fifth*, also portrays the restoration of royal authority (the recovery of France), and so close was the relationship between theatre and politics that (not for the first time) Charles II loaned garments from his coronation, so that the final spectacle of the play is of stage royalty resplendent in the finery of the true.[3]

Yet the dramatist who thus made free with Charles's coronation apparel had not long before made free with his crown, for Orrery had served Cromwell throughout the 1650s, and in 1657 had taken a leading role in urging him to become king. After Cromwell's death, however, he had established links both with Monck and Charles II, and had indeed hoped to claim the role of restoring hero for himself. In his service of the usurper, Clorimun reflects Orrery's position in the 1650s; in his restoration of the true line, however, he performs an act of which Orrery was only an envious and frustrated onlooker.

---

[1] As is now usual, I use the term *Carolean* to refer to the period from 1660 to 1688. *Restoration drama* is too imprecise and confusing a term.
[2] It was first performed in Dublin in 1662, under the title of *Altemera*. The inefficient King's Company did not stage it in London until September 1664, a month after the rival Duke's Company had staged Orrery's *The History of Henry the Fifth*.
[3] The King's suit was worn by Owen Tudor and the Duke of York's by Henry V. Coronation apparel had also been used in Davenant's *Love and Honour* (1661). Downes, *Roscius Anglicanus*, 52, 61.

Simple and naïve as dramatic texts, Orrery's plays are nevertheless elaborate as falsifications.[4]

Though forgotten today, they set the pattern for early Carolean serious drama, the primary subject of which is reinstatement of the rightful king. Early adaptations of Shakespeare, for example, tend to be of plays topically concerned with restoration: *Measure for Measure* (as *The Law against Lovers*, 1662), *Macbeth* (1664), and *The Tempest* (1667).[5] The simplifications of these early political plays are gross. Civil conflict is exacerbated not by ship money, or forced loans, but by love: in *The Generall*, the usurper has seized the throne because he loves the heroine. Political relationships are reduced to ones of feudal dependance, sustained by respect for the moral power of language: for the oath, the vow, the sacred name of king. Although Orrery's characters constantly use the terminology of debt and payment, money does not exist for them: to repay a debt is to reciprocate an obligation, or to honour one's word. Such plays are at once highly contemporary, in that they allegorize recent events, and impossibly fantastic, in that they transpose them to a lost and idealized social order. It was, indeed, a long time before late seventeenth-century tragedians could adequately represent a contemporary commercial economy.

Like tragi-comedy, early Carolean comedy celebrates the re-emergence of a natural social hierarchy that has been unnaturally inverted: parvenus fall, and the gentry return. In *The Rump*, the Puritan upstarts become street vendors, and in one of the best early comedies, Sir Robert Howard's *The Committee* (1662), two impoverished Cavaliers recover their estates and their loved ones from the clutches of jumped-up Puritan ex-servants. Such plays are far removed from our usual conception of 'Restoration' comedies as witty plays about sex, and the movement towards such comedy was gradual. Nevertheless, by the mid-1660s comedies were appearing that were free in sexual sentiment, if not in sexual action. If *The Committee* idealizes an old hierarchical order, and shows a Cavalier hero reproved for wanting pre-marital sex, Etherege's immensely successful *The Comical Revenge* (1664), also set in the late Interregnum, celebrates the ending not only of Puritan rigidity but of Caroline formality and idealism, ushering in a culture of festive hedonism, personified in the play's comic hero, Sir Frederick Frollick. The chief vehicle of sexual daring was a comedy of

---

[4] See Staves, *Players' Scepters*, 15–24, 51–60.

[5] *The Tempest* was adapted by Dryden and Davenant, the others by Davenant alone. *The Law against Lovers* also incorporates the Beatrice and Benedick plot of *Much Ado about Nothing*. Non-political adaptations include John Lacy's farcical rewriting of *The Taming of the Shrew* as *Sauny the Scot* (1667) and, perhaps, James Howard's lost happy-ending version of *Romeo and Juliet*.

bantering courtship built around the talents of Charles Hart and Nell Gwyn at the King's Company.[6] The man's past could be very scapegrace – the comic hero of James Howard's *All Mistaken* (1665) is confronted on stage with no less than six of his infant bastards – but he is, as yet, denied solace in the play itself.

Tragi-comedies about the Restoration continued until the early 1670s, sometimes with comic and sexually adventurous subplots, but the court frivolity that energized comedy was more soberly treated in completely serious drama. The King's reputation quickly suffered from his extravagance and licentiousness, and the nation was afflicted by plague (1665), fire (1666) and military humiliation by the Dutch (1667). The Earl of Clarendon, who was Lord Chancellor and father-in-law of Charles's brother, James, Duke of York, was made a scapegoat for national humiliation and fled abroad to avoid impeachment for treason. In the early 1670s, when Charles allied himself with the Catholic Louis XIV for another war against the Protestant Dutch, and when James's Catholicism became public knowledge (rather than merely an open secret), fears of popery and arbitrary government took hold.

The King's changing reputation is reflected in serious drama. Despite the continuing appearance of plays about the Restoration, by the mid-1660s even some of his supporters were tactfully admonishing his sex life. Orrery wrote two plays – *Mustapha* (1665) and *The Black Prince* (1667) – about monarchs flawed by unwise love. Sir Robert Howard had collaborated with Dryden (his brother-in-law) on a fictitious play about Montezuma's youth, *The Indian Queen* (1664), portraying his restoration to the throne of Mexico. When, in order to reuse the lavish scenery and costumes, Dryden wrote a sequel, *The Indian Emperour* (1665), he showed the restored hero-king as being gravely weakened by imprudent love. Sir Robert went further. Though *The Committee* and *The Indian Queen* energetically celebrate the Restoration, he was by 1667 one of the parliamentary critics of Charles's administration, playing a leading role in the hounding of Clarendon. His dramatic output changed accordingly: in his *The Great Favourite* (1668), clearly aimed at Clarendon, the voice of factionalism is heard for the first time on the Carolean stage. After 1672, tragi-comedies of restoration yield to tragedies of problematic succession, often portraying kings as lustful tyrants (as in Nathaniel Lee's *The Tragedy of Nero*, 1674) and often diverting succession from the lineal heir (as even Dryden does in *Aureng-Zebe*). According to a hardy myth, Carolean tragedy and comedy showed a Jekyll-and-Hyde split between representation of the unrealistically heroic and the cynically rakish. Although there were both idealistic and cynical plays,

---

[6] See Smith, *Gay Couple in Restoration Comedy.*

however, they are not concurrent: post-Restoration euphoria had long gone when the first sex comedies appeared.

The unprecedented sexual daring of late Carolean comedy reflects a subculture of unprecedentedly vigorous opposition to revealed religion. As Orrery's brother, the scientist Robert Boyle, complained, men have always drunk and whored, but they formerly knew they were doing wrong: now men 'question the Truth, and despise the very Name of [Religion]'.[7] Particularly influential were a moral relativism, derived from Montaigne, and the materialism of Thomas Hobbes. Montaigne had argued that no moral principle is universally acknowledged, and that the moral systems which we take for global truths are like municipal bye-laws – a doctrine which encouraged the view that systems of sexual morality are arbitrary impositions upon healthy natural instinct. For Hobbes, the fundamental principle of existence was the movement of material particles: man was matter in motion, driven by bodily appetites and aversions, his reason a tool of his desires. Because of man's appetitive nature, his relationship to his fellows in the pre-social state of nature is that of war, for there is no institutional authority to define or enforce moral codes: all have right to all. In forming political societies, humanity erects defences against the horror of its own aggressive and anti-social nature, surrendering the natural rights exercised in the primal state of war in return for the protection of an absolute political authority.

Although Hobbes had feared, and sought to restrain, the anarchic power of appetite, some poets synthesized materialism and moral relativism, celebrating the triumph of the sex drive over the fictions of morality. Carolean sex comedy, however, recognizes that man's social nature is too complex and too dominant to permit the libertine dream to be realized: that sex invariably creates social and emotional complications, and that the life of free-ranging instinct, however beguiling as a goal, is not only practically but psychologically impossible. Exploring Hobbes's paradox that man is a social being *because* he is a savage, dramatists often portray characters as experimenting with dual identities in an attempt to separate the socially visible self from the personal pursuit of the instinctual drive. There are, for example, many bedroom tricks, wherein a lover enjoys the object of desire by impersonating a rival. The public self is erased in a regression to pure, pre-social instinct, during which all verbal or visual signs that might betray the impostor are banished; there must be silence and darkness, with copulation becoming an all-engulfing totality.

[7] [Boyl]E, *Some Considerations about the Reconcileableness of Reason and Religion*, ii.

But it cannot so remain, and many plays dwell on the moment when instinct confronts the renewed social consciousness of the perpetrator. Manly, the hero of Wycherley's *The Plain Dealer* (1676), is the most extreme primitivist in Carolean comedy, despising the effeminate verbiage and legalism of London and hankering for the honest savagery of the Indies. His supreme act of unrestrained manliness is to rape the villainess by means of a bedroom trick. But, as soon as his dark, voiceless copulation is over, he finds himself needing witnesses: craving the forms of law to finalize a rape. Deeply though he despises the tame, elaborate formality of London existence, he cannot separate himself from it. A tragic version of an almost identical situation occurs in Thomas Otway's once popular tragedy *The Orphan* (1680). One of the heroes, Polydore, shares Manly's nostalgia for the primitive, envying the unrestrained sexuality of the bull, who instantly satiates and escapes desire without impediment from restrictive custom. Through a bedroom deception, he sleeps with the woman his twin brother loves, not realizing that the couple has just married: that he has committed incest. Once the fact of incest becomes known, however, he is overwhelmed by guilt. The consciousness that distinguishes humanity from the brutes cannot escape the sexual codes it forges, and Polydore is driven to write the story, and then to commit suicide. *The Plain-Dealer* and *The Orphan* present comic and tragic versions of the same situation: the simultaneous inescapability and unattainability of the dream of pure instinct, unfettered by the claims of society. In doing so, they illustrate how closely linked Carolean comedy and tragedy can be.

As has been mentioned, comedy progressed only gradually from the daring banter of the 1660s to the portrayal of active sexual relationships involving the main characters; an intermediate stage is Shadwell's *Epsom Wells* (1672), in which adultery is achieved, but by foolish and socially marginal characters; both heroes are constantly interrupted at the critical moment (though one has a mistress and makes a cuckold, the relationship is not reconfirmed during the play).[8] The first social comedy to involve leading characters in sex was *The Mall* (1674), by the unidentifiable 'J. D.', which sank without trace. The first successful comedy to do so was Wycherley's *The Country Wife* (1675). Horner, the hero, pretends to have been emasculated in a botched treatment for syphilis. No longer (seemingly) a threat to husbands, he gains free access to the fashionable ladies, which he puts to good use. It is, however, far from clear that the play is a fantasy of total male dominance: there are far more male

---

[8] See Hume, *Development of English Drama*, 295–9 (though Hume believes that one of the heroes of Shadwell's *Epsom Wells* (1672) does consummate).

fools than female; in cases of near discovery, the women think of the way out while the men are nonplussed; and at the end of the play Horner, who started the play as the master-seducer, increasingly finds that he is the property of his seraglio, until finally he is a commodity in a time-share adultery scheme run by the women. This final arrangement demonstrates, again, that man can never be a purely instinctual and asocial being: adultery has its own social dimensions.

Along with Etherege's *The Man of Mode* (1676), with its portrayal of the coldly efficient seducer Dorimant, *The Country Wife* is often regarded as a 'typical' Carolean comedy. Yet each is very different from the other, and both are exceptional.[9] *The Country Wife* could only happen once. It continues the playful, insouciant attitudes of the comedies where free sex was contemplated but not achieved, but it moves from contemplation to action. If *The Country Wife* broke the taboos that had inhibited earlier comic portrayals of sexual conduct, however, it made it necessary to portray sex from an entirely different viewpoint; for, once characters actually engage in sex, there is a strong pressure to explore the real emotional and social complexities of deception and betrayal. This is what happens, equally for the first time, in *The Man of Mode*, which – while aesthetically detached from the events it portrays – is the first social comedy to portray the pain of sexual rejection, in Dorimant's ex-mistress Loveit:[10] a dramatically complex figure, despite the crudity of her name, veering between ludicrous self-abandon and a controlled and dignified authority. Unlike *The Country Wife*, *The Man of Mode* did directly and decisively influence the details of subsequent comedies. The carefree attitude to sex largely vanished, and was succeeded by a darker comedy of ruthless sexual predators. If *The Man of Mode* is morally inscrutable, succeeding plays – such as Otway's *Friendship in Fashion* (1678) and Durfey's *Trick for Trick* (1678) – clearly condemn the rake and side with his actual or intended victims. When Aphra Behn began her career, she was not confronting a man-created repertory that was entirely hostile to her outlook.

In the winter of 1663–4 Katherine Philips's translation of Corneille's *La Mort de Pompée* was staged in Dublin, and possibly London, and between 1668 and 1670 up to four women had plays staged in London,[11] though only Behn

---

[9] See Hume, '"Change in comedy"', 108–9.
[10] Aphra Behn had already done this in the more elevated genre of verse comedy, in *The Amorous Prince* (1671).
[11] Philips's translation of Corneille's *Horace*, completed after her death by Sir John Denham, was performed at court in 1668 and by the King's Company in 1669. Frances Boothby's *Marcelia* was also staged in 1669, and it is possible that Elizabeth Polwhele's *The Frolicks* and *The Faithfull Virgins* were also staged at this time. Behn reached the stage in 1670.

became a full-time professional. After Dryden and Shadwell, indeed, she was only the third professional dramatist to establish herself since 1660, appearing when Orrery and other gentleman amateurs were fading out. Although audience taste was, as always, capricious, Behn was often a prominent figure. For example, in the 1681–2 season,[12] when the demand for comedies revived after a lull caused by prolonged political crisis, half of the eight new comedies were by her.[13] She naturally provided a woman's-eye view of men's sexual dealings. For example, Willmore, the exiled and womanizing Cavalier who is the titular character of *The Rover* (1677), is a more bungling version of Dorimant: an engaging loose cannon, equally devoid of malice and feeling, too thoughtless to realize that rape is wrong, too incompetent to accomplish it. Yet Otway and Durfey create similar, or darker, figures: the man's-eye view was not always blind to the interests of the woman.

Indeed, men can treat the liberation of women with a utopian simplicity that Behn is too realistic to contemplate. In Shadwell's *The Woman Captain* (1679), for example, the unhappily married heroine does not, as we at first expect, cuckold her husband, but avenges herself with greater autonomy and dignity: she disguises herself as a recruiting officer, and in the few minutes necessary to don her uniform also acquires the linguistic habits and authority of a man, with which she terrorizes her husband into, seemingly, enlisting. Behn knew that the association between language and authority was more complex and indirect, and that the exercise of power through signs was secondary to a capacity for violence with which women could never compete. She also saw the patriarchal exchange of women as being fundamental to every known version of society, whether the pre-commercial, militaristic worlds of her earliest plays, the aristocratic hierarchies which she defended in times of crisis, or the unheroic bourgeois economies which she opposed to them. Her Tory play *The City Heiress* (1682), for example, creates a striking visual symmetry and causal relationship between the heroes' physical humiliation of the elderly Whig villain and their seduction of the vulnerable heroine: one interrupts his burglary of the villain's house in order to accomplish his seduction; the other gets drunk while forcing the villain to drink the King's health and, fired with this Dutch courage, browbeats her into sexual submission.

Generalization about Carolean sex comedy is rash, for its rapid changes did not cease with the impact of *The Man of Mode*. The theatre companies

---

[12] Theatrical seasons started in September.

[13] I accept the dating of Shadwell's *The Lancashire Witches* to the 1680–1 season. See Milhous and Hume, 'Dating Play Premières', 392; Danchin, *Prologues and Epilogues of the Restoration*, III: 289–90.

were jolted by the season of 1677–8: of the thirteen comedies premièred, eight contained sex (and a ninth portrayed a seducer ultimately marrying his victim). No comedy from this season is known to have succeeded, and the best sex comedies clearly failed, though probably for unrelated reasons.[14] In the following season only one comedy, Behn's *The Feign'd Curtizans*, was premièred: not a sex comedy, though it steered close to the wind. It too failed. At this point, politics intervened, transforming both the nature of drama and the fortunes of the theatres.

From late 1678 to 1682 Britain was racked by a political crisis, as fabricated disclosures about a planned Catholic coup magnified long-standing mistrust of James, and led to a prolonged but unsuccessful attempt to exclude him from the succession, in favour of the King's eldest illegitimate son, the Earl of Monmouth. During this crisis the terms *Whig* and *Tory* first entered politics, the Whigs supporting Exclusion and the Tories supporting the established order. There were fears of a return to civil war, and the tension inhibited the demand for comedy. Of the four comedies of 1679–80, only Otway's dark anti-Whig satire *The Souldiers Fortune* is a sex comedy. Shadwell, the only writer of Whig comedy, now avoids sex: the heroine's act of self-liberation in *The Woman Captain*, premièred in this season, is an allegory of the defeat of Stuart absolutism, and is chaste; a group of extravagant whoremasters and their women represent the alien, degenerate culture of the Stuarts, but there is no coition. Of the two comedies of the following season, one, the second part of Aphra Behn's *The Rover*, is a sex comedy, and again quite a dark one, placing the Royalist Willmore in a harsher light than in the original play; Shadwell's *The Lancashire Witches*, a celebration of English culture at the expense of Catholicism, is chaste.[15] As Tory victory became clear in 1681–2, however, eight comedies were staged, with two salient features. Three plays borrow from the political plays of the very early Restoration, so as to suggest that Charles II has re-enacted his triumph over the Puritan rebels. In *The Roundheads*, for example, Aphra Behn reworked *The Rump* and also drew on *The Committee*. Secondly, in six of the seven surviving plays, sex – often cheerful sex – makes a comeback. In contrast to the unpleasantness of recent sex

[14] Hume, *Development of English Drama*, 333. Behn's *Sir Patient Fancy* and Shadwell's *A True Widow* flopped, Otway's *Friendship in Fashion* seems not to have succeeded, and Dryden's *The Kind Keeper* was banned, for reasons now unknown: see Staves, 'Why was Dryden's *Mr Limberham* banned?'.

[15] Dryden's tragi-comedy *The Spanish Fryar* (1680) contains a comic subplot of fortunately frustrated sex between characters who turn out to be brother and sister. This parallels the averted usurpation in the main plot. We do not know when Nathaniel Lee's tragi-comedy *The Princess of Cleve* was premièred. Its elements of gross sexual comedy complement the tragically untameable desires that contaminate even the idealistic heroine.

comedy, three are festive comedies (of triumphant Tories cuckolding grasping, unattractive Whigs), with only Aphra Behn combining intense royalism with a sense that both sides oppressed women. The final play of triumphalist Whig-cuckolding was John Crowne's *City Politiques*, which was ready in June 1682 but banned until January 1683. This was popular, but then the bubble burst. In the fifteen years between *City Politiques* and Jeremy Collier's *A Short View of the Immorality, and Profaneness of the English Stage* (1698), only six sex comedies were clearly successful. The first of these, Thomas Southerne's *Sir Anthony Love*, did not appear until 1690. The real heyday of Carolean sex comedy lasted from just 1675 to 1683, with a gap in the middle, and many changes of character.

Exclusion Crisis tragedy is highly politicized though often opportunistic, with several dramatists changing tack as they struggled to interpret the shifting and obscure balance of power. Some, however (notably Shadwell), wrote out of principle, and there are also pessimistic portrayals of men and women trapped in cruel political conflicts that are beyond their comprehension or control. Like the political upheaval of the Restoration, that of the Exclusion Crisis stimulated adaptations (ten in all) of Shakespeare, chiefly as an interpreter of classical and British history. Between the first and second clutch of adaptations, in 1662–67 and 1678–82, and for the remainder of the century afterwards, Shakespeare was adapted only occasionally, chiefly as a source of opera. The first adaptation of this second wave was Shadwell's *The History of Timon of Athens* (1678), produced some months before the plot scare exploded, but when opposition to James was growing. Shadwell expands Shakespeare's portrayal of Athenian politics, staging a restoration of a kind very different from that celebrated in earlier Carolean plays: the reinstatement of democracy after the oligarchy of the Four Hundred Tyrants in 411 BC. It concludes with a public assembly of the people, and their cries of '*Liberty*'. Shadwell also includes attacks on the pride and corruption of the aristocracy, and he provides a remarkable rejection of patriarchal sexual morality by contrasting a vicious virgin with an exemplary fallen woman. This play provides the most radical attack on the old order to appear on the Carolean stage.

A sense of pessimistic entrapment is perhaps best seen in Thomas Otway's *The History and Fall of Caius Marius* (1679), which transposes the story of Romeo and Juliet to the civil war between Marius and Sulla in the first century BC, showing Rome in the grip of two factions that were equally bloody and equally contemptuous of individual life. By contrast, the time-serving suppleness of the jobbing dramatist is nicely illustrated by Nahum Tate, whose (non-Shakespearean) tragedy *The Loyal General* (1679) appears to be a pro-Monmouth allegory, but whose *The History of King Lear* of only a year later shows the triumph of legitimate order over a ruthlessly aspiring bastard, Edmund clearly standing for Monmouth. The notorious happy ending of this play is not, as is sometimes thought, typical of Carolean Shakespeare adaptations. More typically, the tendency is to add violence: for example, Durfey's adaptation of *Cymbeline, The Injured Princess* (1682), includes a blinding scene modelled on *King Lear* (which Tate had retained in his version). Incidents of attempted rape are added in the reworkings of *Lear, Cymbeline* and *Coriolanus*, again illustrating how closely sexual and political themes are linked. Planned or attempted rape had been a feature of the earliest Carolean drama: the usurper in *The Generall*, for example, plans to rape the heroine, his proposed sexual violence paralleling the violence by which he has already gained the kingdom. Some critics see the preoccupation with rape as a pornographic prostitution of the actress for the purposes of male titillation.[16] There is some truth in this (particularly in drama of the 1690s), but it is important to note that the appearance of actresses on the public stage pre-dates by more than a decade the first successful rape (in Dryden's *Amboyna*, 1672): the move towards tragic rape is almost as gradual as the move towards comic seduction, and it almost always makes a political point. If usurpers still plan and execute rapes, so now do legitimate rulers, and the rape victim is no longer a symbol of the kingdom but rather an individual menaced by cruel and indifferent authority. Indeed, one general feature of the Shakespeare adaptations is the increased priority of private experience. In adapting *Coriolanus* as *The Ingratitude of a Common-Wealth* (1681), Tate provided a new and very bloody ending, in which Virgilia commits suicide to avoid rape by Aufidius, Young Martius is tortured to death, and Volumnia goes mad with grandmaternal grief (hardly something we can imagine in Shakespeare's Volumnia). This is sensationalism, but it is also an exaltation of the private. The play no longer portrays fissures within a complex society that remains tied to the cult of the warrior; it is the family tragedy of a brave nobleman (James) with too overt a contempt for the mob.

The two best tragedies of the Exclusion Crisis are Nathaniel Lee's *Lucius Junius Brutus* (1680) and Thomas Otway's *Venice Preserv'd* (1682). Both portray individuals caught between opposing yet equally cruel systems of power (the Roman monarchy and the Republic which replaces it, and the Venetian Senate and the conspirators who plot to overthrow it), and in both the protagonist's involvement in the political conflict threatens to erase his personal (specifically his sexual) life: the son of the republican liberator, Brutus, becomes

---

[16] E.g., Pearson, *Prostituted Muse*, 95–9; Marsden, 'Rape, voyeurism, and the Restoration stage'.

impotent when he tries to consummate his secret wedding to the daughter of the deposed king, and Jaffeir, the hero of *Venice Preserv'd*, rebels against an oppressive plutocracy which makes his marriage financially unsustainable, only to join a conspiracy whose male bonding makes it psychologically impossible; for he can only bond with the other conspirators by surrendering his wife to them as a surety for good behaviour. In Orrery, the personal is easily subject to the social: though usurpers plan rapes, a right-thinking hero will willingly surrender the woman he loves to a friend who also loves her. Jaffeir's gesture recalls the self-sacrifice of the Orrery hero but also debases it: if the personal impedes social transactions, social transactions corrupt the personal.

In other ways, too, the outlook of Orrery has long gone. He had portrayed a feudal world unified by the inviolability of the word, in which money had no part. Although the Rome of *Lucius Junius Brutus* is controlled by language, the language is an unverifiable political rhetoric concerning people and events that are never seen: we do not directly see the hated royal dynasty that is deposed. If Orrery's protagonists honour the word, Lee's manipulate it, mastering the state by controlling the means of representation. Like so many other plays, *Lucius Junius Brutus* features a rape, of Lucretia, and this prompts the revolution. Yet, after her suicide, Lucretia becomes a mere rhetorical figment to be manipulated by Brutus in his political myth making. Again, the personal is consumed by the political. *Venice Preserv'd* travels still further from early Carolean models, since it is the first tragedy since the Restoration to portray the social and psychological power of money. For example, it treats prostitution, and particularly a prostitution of sexual domination and submission, as the fundamental constituent of all human relationships. There are two scenes in which a prostitute is paid to humiliate a masochistic, foot-fetishist politician named Antonio (possibly a partial caricature of the Whig leader, the Earl of Shaftesbury, whose first name was Anthony), but sexual transaction and sexual violence also pervade the higher levels of the play. It is in the brothel (significantly) that Jaffeir hands over his wife to the conspirators as a pledge for his good behaviour, to be stabbed to death if he defaults, and echoes of Antonio's submissive fantasies infiltrate the language even of those who would be heroic liberators. The dream of the libertine is for a primitive state of nature in which no artificial codes impede the gratification of desire, and this is what the conspirators wish to recover. Yet, even as desire induces such dreams, it undermines them with an addiction to slavery.

When *Venice Preserv'd* was staged in the aftermath of the Whig defeat, the court applauded the suppression of conspiracy and (perhaps) the mocking of Shaftesbury, but no one (not even Aphra Behn) had expressed loyalty with greater gloom. *The Country Wife* had comically shown that sexuality entangles man in complex social bonds, even as it drives him to overthrow all social prohibitions. *Venice Preserv'd* presents a tragic version of the same paradox: if social existence makes private sexuality impossible, sexuality carries cravings for servitude that nullify the dreams of the liberator and bind him to the very system he opposes. Man is not a naturally social animal; he is naturally a slave. Here is the sense of irremediably fissured civilization that Tate was busily editing out of Shakespeare. *Venice Preserv'd* is the best tragedy of the later seventeenth century.

If the Exclusion Crisis produced a resurgence in sex comedy, and brought out the best in Otway and Lee, its medium-term consequences for the theatre were damaging. The distractions of the period hit takings, and in 1682 the poorly managed King's Company merged with the Duke's. With no competitor, the United Company took the safe option of mounting tried favourites, and the demand for new plays dropped sharply, especially in the period from 1683 to 1688. (There was a revival in demand after the 1688 revolution, and a glut of new plays after the resumption of competition in 1695.) The mid-1680s were difficult times for playwrights (Otway died, perhaps of starvation): few tragedies were staged, and the three new sex comedies mounted in 1686–7 had a mixed or hostile reception. There was a new fashion for light farce, and the most successful heavyweight comedy of the period (indeed, of the late seventeenth century) was a comedy depicting the education and reform of a gentleman, Shadwell's *The Squire of Alsatia* (1688). Shadwell's hostility to sex comedy was of long standing, and reform comedies had appeared in the 1670s. *The Squire of Alsatia*, however, marks a clear advance in their importance.

It also marks a change in the political interpretation of sex and the family. Alsatia is an area of London that is beyond the law, a safe-haven for debtors and crooks. At the end of the play, it is to be subjected to the authority of law, and the taming of anarchy at the heart of the metropolis is closely paralleled by the hero's reform (his chief transgression had been to seduce the daughter of a *lawyer*): in perfect synchronicity, we see the maturing of a city and a citizen. The play uses the much adapted plot of Terence's *Adelphi* (*The Brothers*), in which two brothers are separately brought up, one by the strict natural father, the other by the father's kindly brother. Although kindly upbringing does not deliver perfection, its alternative is disastrous. Sir Charles Sedley and Aphra Behn had already used this plot to contrast Puritan repressiveness and Royalist exuberance,[17] but Shadwell reverses the application: the despotic

---

[17] In *The Mulberry Garden* (1668) and *The City Heiress* (1682).

father, deriving his authority from the act of generation, represents the absolute and hereditary monarchy of the Stuarts, whereas the kind stepfather, who realizes that authority must be earned, not merely inherited, represents an authority that is conditional, potentially contractual.

This was Shadwell's first play for seven years – in the dedication of his next, *Bury Fair* (1689), he claimed that he had been politically excluded from the stage – but now he was on the winning side. Having weathered the Exclusion Crisis, James II had become king in 1685; but in November 1688 he was deposed. He had alienated many natural supporters by his extension of royal power and confrontational advancement of his fellow-Catholics, and the birth of a male heir raised fears of a perpetual Catholic dynasty, prompting seven noblemen to invite William of Orange (husband of James's daughter, Mary) to intervene. In the Parliament which ratified the post-revolution settlement, the Commons (like Shadwell) held that James had broken his contract with the people, but the Lords opposed a contractual interpretation of kingship and adopted the fiction that James had abdicated. Many Tories accepted William, though as a *de facto* monarch, while the Whigs accepted him as a king *de jure*. Whereas Charles had prolonged, dissolved, called and done without Parliaments at will, William in 1694 had unwillingly – to accept an act stipulating that Parliaments should meet at least once every three years, and should last no more than three years.

Like early Carolean drama, the drama of William's reign frequently celebrates the newly established order, partly out of conviction, partly because the stage was kept under observant political control. Dryden's late plays, with their portrayal of exile and dispossession, do provide coded Jacobite statements, but his *Cleomenes* (1692), about an exiled king in a foreign court, was initially banned on the orders of Queen Mary. Colley Cibber's adaptation of *Richard III* (1700), which included the death of Henry VI, had to be cut lest Henry arouse sympathy for James. The control of the stage persisted throughout the reign of Queen Anne, though it was now controlled by political parties.[18] Despite its narrow range of class interests, Carolean drama had by the 1670s reflected in some detail the political discontents of the gentry and nobility. From Williamite drama, however, one would scarcely guess the extent of the King's initial unpopularity (partly caused by the unprecedentedly high taxes which financed his war against Louis XIV). Perhaps the frankest (though entirely supportive) play is Crowne's tragedy *Regulus* (1692), about the ingratitude of Carthage (Britain) to its foreign defender Xantippus. Celebratory drama flagged after mid-1692, as the war dragged on, but revived after the spring of 1696, when a plot to

---

[18] See Loftis, *Politics of Drama in Augustan England*.

assassinate William boosted his popularity and there were premature hopes of peace (eventually, if briefly, gratified by the Peace of Ryswick in 1697). It is noteworthy that, immediately after the revolution, tragedians tend to avoid portraying the deposition of a hereditary ruler (George Powell's *Alphonso King of Naples* of 1690 adopts the fiction of James's abdication). After the Assassination Plot, however, they eagerly portray the deposition and slaughter of legitimate but tyrannical rulers.

Much comedy also celebrates the revolution, by translating the defeat of absolutism to the domestic sphere: families are reconstituted after a tyrannical guardian or parent has been neutralized by expulsion or contractual constraint (as in Congreve's *Love for Love*, 1695, and *The Way of the World*, 1700). Here, on the stage, we see the contractual model of authority that had been rejected in the state; we also see resolutions of the tension between the individual and the social unit that had pervaded Carolean drama. The analogy between the contractual family and the contractual state did, however, throw up some problems. Guardians and parents might be disposed of, but spouses presented a thornier problem: as Lady Brute muses in Vanbrugh's *The Provok'd Wife* (1697), if a nation can depose an intolerable king, might a wife not rid herself of an intolerable husband? Why, wonders Mrs Sullen in *The Beaux' Stratagem* (1707), are British women subject to the absolutist tyranny that Queen Anne's generals are opposing on the battlefields of Blenheim and Ramillies?[19] One well-known development in post-revolution comedy of the 1690s is the increasing interest in unhappy marriages, from which there is often no satisfactory escape.[20] As part of the same tendency, dramatists often (as in Congreve's *Love for Love*) show women testing their prospective husbands, aware that marriage can turn a lover into a tyrant; the image is frequently of a judicial trial, again suggesting the containment of authority by law. After 1700, however, dramatists tend to find facile resolutions for sympathetic characters in unhappy marriages. Notoriously, Farquhar solves the marital problems of Mrs Sullen by sleight of hand, with an apparent, but legally impossible, divorce. Other dramatists are content that a jealous dotard married to a teenager should renounce his jealousy, like the titular character of Charles Johnson's *The Generous Husband* (1711).

After the revolution, the court was no longer favourable to sex comedy. James had liked *The Rover* and had accepted the dedication of its sequel, wherein Behn (astonishingly) claimed that he had been the model for Willmore. When

---

[19] 1.1.65–7, in Vanbrugh, *Vanbrugh: Four Comedies*; *The Beaux' Stratagem* 4.1.1–5, in Farquhar, *Works of George Farquhar*, vol. II.
[20] See Hume, 'Marital discord'; Cordner, 'Marriage comedy'.

The Rover was performed at court in 1690, however, Mary disapproved strongly of the play. Societies for the reformation of manners were founded, and in 1698 Jeremy Collier published his attack on the stage, initiating a bitter debate between playwrights and their enemies. In the same year, there were attempts to mount prosecutions, and in 1701 actors were successfully prosecuted for profanely using the name of God on the stage. Clearly, the theatre was under pressure, and the Collier controversy finally killed off sex comedy.

Yet, as already indicated, comedy writers had not been unregenerately turning out clones of *The Country Wife* for the previous quarter-century. Sex comedy was a sporadic, localized and mutable phenomenon, which had passed its peak before the ousting of James. Only six clearly succeeded after 1683: Southerne's *Sir Anthony Love* (1690), Dryden's *Amphitryon* (1690), William Mountfort's *Greenwich Park* (1691), Congreve's *The Old Batchelour* (1693) and *Love for Love* (1695), and Vanbrugh's *The Relapse* (1696). Except *Amphitryon*, all are predominantly festive and lightweight. Darker studies of sexuality, such as Congreve's *The Double Dealer* (1693), failed. The following comparison is very approximate, since the reception of plays is not always known, and the term *sex comedy* is imprecise (I use it, crudely, to mean comedy during which illicit sex is at some point known to be happening). Nevertheless, it may have some value. In the seasons from 1674–5 to 1682–3 and 1688–9 to 1697–8, comparable numbers of comedies were premièred (51 and 56). In the earlier period, over half were sex comedies, of which nearly half succeeded. In the later, a quarter were sex comedies; the six clear successes represent approximately one-tenth of the total. Of course, there are subtler differences than bed-counts: many Carolean comedies espouse sexual freedom without portraying it, for example. Conversely, comedies about reformed or exemplary characters recur throughout the post-revolution years;[21] Cibber's *Love's Last Shift* (1696) is the most famous, but by no means the first. Despite the changing pattern of new comedies, however, a taste for established sex comedies persisted well into the eighteenth century.[22]

As well as a change in sexual outlook, there are changes in the social emphasis of drama. Mountfort's *Greenwich Park* favourably portrays bourgeois characters (its witty, beautiful heroines are the daughters of a laundress), as do Mary Pix's *The Beau Defeated* (1700) and Farquhar's *The Twin Rivals* (1702). Such touches are sporadic, and Steele's *The Conscious Lovers* (1722, but conceived by 1710) remains a significantly polemic work in bringing the vindication of the bourgeois to the centre. Another change is the occasional setting of comedy in

---

[21] E.g., Shadwell's *Bury Fair* (1689) and *The Scowrers* (1690), and Durfey's *Love for Money* (1691).

[22] Scouten and Hume, '"Restoration comedy"'.

the provinces, an innovation often mistakenly attributed to the last comedies of George Farquhar.[23] A seminal play is Shadwell's *Bury Fair* (1689), which is one of many to re-enact the revolution within the space of a single family: a Francophile stepmother and her daughter are expelled, a natural daughter returns and a buffoonish but kindly father is free to indulge his love of native culture, of Shakespeare and Jonson. The liberation of native English culture reflects the belief that the revolution reinstated ancestral rights suppressed by Stuart absolutism, and the non-metropolitan setting (Suffolk) emphasizes a return to unspoilt Englishness. Interestingly, Shadwell had spent part of his childhood in Bury: the return to origins is personal as well as national.

There is also a subtler change, in that dramatists increasingly portray societies regulated by numerical systems rather than (as in Orrery) by the word, or by analogies between the distribution of social power and the hierarchic structure of the cosmos itself. The shift first appears in Otway and late Behn, and is really pronounced from the 1690s onwards, when dramatists were particularly responding to the growth of seemingly intangible forms of wealth, with no basis in land: in order to fund King William's war, the Bank of England was founded, covering the gap between assets and liabilities by paying investors in paper currency; there were lotteries; and trade in stocks flourished.

The encroachment of money upon older systems of order was portrayed in the two best tragedies of the 1690s, Southerne's *The Fatal Marriage* (1694) and *Oroonoko* (1695), both based on fiction by Aphra Behn. In possible allusion to the revolution (which Southerne had initially opposed), both show the power of money to dissolve the older obligations of oaths and kinship: an apparently widowed wife is forced by indigence to remarry, only to find that her first husband is still alive; an African prince is sold into slavery. The comedies which most ingeniously portray a society controlled by numbers are those which George Farquhar produced between 1698 and his early death in 1707. His heroes are obsessive and successful enumerators (of sexual conquests, wealth, time and space); his fools obsessive and inept enumerators of the same things.[24] Yet his heroes are always physically dislocated, in transit and normally without any landed property, until they gain it through a woman. Apart from his portrayal of an honest banker in *The Twin Rivals*, Farquhar concentrates on gentlemen; yet his gentlemen have to justify their roles and characters in a world whose rules have changed.

A recurrent Farquhar situation is one in which the bodies of inferior or victimized characters become subject to ritualized numerical control: in *The*

---

[23] Most recently in Bull, *Vanbrugh and Farquhar*, 110.
[24] Hughes, 'Who counts in Farquhar?'.

Recruiting Officer (1706), for instance, two raw recruits are sentenced to a spell of motionless clock-watching in a Shrewsbury street. Other dramatists also portray the social manipulation of the body and the social predominance of number. The undertaker in Steele's *The Funeral* (1701) slashes and embalms corpses so as to falsify the characters of the dead and the feelings of the survivors. Susanna Centlivre's *The Basset Table* (1705) parallels the reform of two women, one fascinated with manipulating the body, the other with counting: a scatty dissectionist and a compulsive gambler, who loves 'the Musick of [her] own Voice, crying Nine and Twenty, Threescore, better than the sweetest Poetry in the Universe'.[25] The numerically oppressed body is also the ruling conceit of Centlivre's most famous play, *A Bold Stroke for a Wife* (1717). Through an irrational phobia of posterity, the heroine's late father has devised a numerical trap to prevent her from reproducing, leaving her in the rotating quarterly control of four guardians so different in outlook that they will never agree on a suitable husband (one is a virtuoso, with an interest in embalming and dissecting bodies). The hero circumvents the ploy by adopting four different disguises, in the process encountering episodes of silly counting: a conversation about watches, and a scene of trading in South Sea stock. Counting is such an everyday activity that its occurrence, and its varieties, may not strike the eye. Yet, experienced as he was as a politician and landowner, Orrery gave a strikingly limited role to enumeration in his tragedies, showing a sharply declining interest in numbers as they rise beyond two; few numbers above six are mentioned at all. The reason for the prominence of *one* and *two* is that they are the numbers of love, friendship, rivalry and moral choice.

When one talks about the morality of Carolean comedies, one thinks of sex. After the great marital discord comedies of the 1690s, the resolution of sexual temptation or conflict tends to be facile, but there are other kinds of transgression. *The Basset Table* belongs to a wave of plays stressing the evils (and sometimes sexual dangers) of gambling,[26] and they in turn contribute to wider satire of waste, conspicuous consumption and luxury, reflecting the rapid growth of London as a residential and commercial centre. Although characters in Carolean comedy occasionally go shopping, their purchases are modest and quickly described: there is no equivalent to the aristocratic kleptomaniac in Southerne's *The Maid's Last Prayer* (1693), or to the brainless connoisseur in his *The Wives' Excuse* (1691), who (to the indifference of his guests) catalogues all his

---

[25] (London, 1706), II: 17.
[26] It is a follow-up to Centlivre's *The Gamester* (1705). Other such plays include Farquhar's *Sir Harry Wildair* (1701), Steele's *The Tender Husband* (1705) and Cibber's *The Lady's Last Stake* (1707). Gambling had been only sporadically and lightly satirized in Carolean drama.

brands of tea. The rapacious pseudo-hospitality of the gaming parties is a new development of an old theme: the decay of the hospitality once exercised by the mythical ideal gentleman. Generally including crooks disguised as gentlemen, the parties portray a society where old values have disappeared in the competitive circulation of coin and paper credit, with women in danger of paying otherwise unredeemable IOUs – papers inscribed with numbers – with their bodies.

The idealized bourgeois in *The Twin Rivals* displays his virtue by exercising hospitality while, for much of the play, the gentry are too impoverished or corrupt to follow suit. Although not a gentleman by birth, he proves himself by taking over the gentleman's role. By the second decade of the eighteenth century, however, there is a tentatively gathering positiveness in the portrayal of new forces: a conviction that, however suspect the pursuits of the specula-tor, the honest merchant can not only acquire the qualities of the gentleman but make a distinctive and necessary contribution of his own.[27] Cibber and Centlivre start to portray the merchant with some respect,[28] and in his ponder-ous, homiletic, but hugely successful *The Conscious Lovers* – trailed by an attack on Etherege's still popular *The Man of Mode* (*Spectator*, 65) – Steele contrasts the industry of the merchant with the gentleman's idle pride in ancestry, and vigorously denies that gentlemen have any right to a sexual double standard. Whereas many of his predecessors and contemporaries uphold morality by portraying the reform of a former rake, often paired with a man of sense, Steele insists on the wholly exemplary, and on the appropriateness of seri-ous subjects for comedy. It is even less 'typical' of its time than *The Country Wife*,[29] but it is a significant monument, as a play which systematically, and with discursive theoretical self-justification, purges itself of the last vestige of the Carolean ethos: not only sex comedy, which was long gone, but the right to a scapegrace past, to intolerant pride in genealogy and to contempt for industry.

[27] The point is, however, made when William Mountfort dedicated the anonymous *Henry the Second* (London, 1693), possibly by John Bancroft, to Sir Thomas Cooke, Alderman and Sheriff of London.

[28] See Loftis, *Comedy and Society from Congreve to Fielding*, 77–100.

[29] For the varieties of comic drama in the eighteenth century, see Bevis, *Laughing Tradition*, and Hume, 'Multifarious forms of eighteenth-century comedy'.

5

Theatre companies and regulation

JUDITH MILHOUS

The production of plays throughout this period was fundamentally affected by the duopoly established by royal command in 1660 and by the regulatory apparatus that controlled theatre companies and imposed censorship. The establishment of patent companies, shares of which could be sold to outside investors, tended to remove power from the hands of the actors. The patents also made the founding of additional companies almost impossible. Such companies did spring up between 1695 and 1705 and again after 1728, but for the most part they were suppressed by the Licensing Act of 1737. The passage of that act had dire consequences for British theatre not fully undone until the abolition of censorship in 1968. There is an enormous irony here. Theatres had been regulated by the Lord Chamberlain and all scripts censored by the Master of the Revels since back in the sixteenth century. Opposition to censorship was essentially non-existent: writers and actors alike accepted its propriety. The collapse of censorship early in the eighteenth century came about by accident, not because of a change in policy, and could not have been predicted. The ultimate result was reimposition of government control in much more drastic and damaging form in 1737.

The Carolean establishment

When the English monarchy was restored in 1660, concerted attempts were made in and around the court to return to the *status quo ante* as far as possible. Many such reinstatements were superficial and temporary, but theatre proved especially resilient, even though it too was 'the same, only different'. Scholars have made much of the contrast between the flourishing free enterprise theatre system under Elizabeth I and the narrow, exclusive design inscribed into law when Charles II, upon his return, granted a joint patent monopoly to Thomas Killigrew and Sir William Davenant. Yet the historian who looks backward from 1660 and measures by a professional lifetime will discover that, for at least five years before Parliament closed the theatres in 1642, just two companies were active enough to generate consistent records, while three others left only very intermittent traces.[1] Well before the official closure, theatre had lost its mass appeal, as all the actors who came back after the civil war knew from hard experience. If stability and the production of new plays are the criteria for judging the health of a theatre company, the joint monopoly after 1660 merely institutionalized a reduction that to all intents and purposes had already happened.

The patent duopoly was an inexpensive way for Charles II to repay the loyalty of two of his more enterprising Cavalier followers. Thomas Killigrew, his sometime companion in exile, was also named his court jester. After a short period of jockeying for control with the small group of actors who cared to resume interrupted careers, Killigrew became head of the King's Company, whose chief personnel made it the direct lineal descendant of the organization for which Shakespeare had worked. This mature, experienced troupe was already familiar with the pre-1642 repertory and eager to carry on as before. They would seem to have had every advantage, but quickly found themselves scrambling to keep up with a brilliantly managed and highly innovative younger company. Sir William Davenant had been knighted by Charles I for services on the field of battle and held an existing theatre patent, granted to him in 1639. Davenant was less close to the restored king than his rival, but Charles II was reluctant to invalidate or ignore a grant from his father. Davenant's plan before the civil war broke out had been to make the wonders of changeable scenery available to the public at large. In 1656 he fitted out Rutland House with a simple version of what he meant to supply, assembled a company and began to give private performances of 'entertainments' and 'operas'.

Relegitimized in 1660, his performers were recognized as the Duke's Company, 'patronized' by the Duke of York (who would become James II). Davenant immediately set out to construct a changeable scenery theatre. Having seen actresses on the Continent, he also made the bold choice of including women in his troupe from the beginning. Since Davenant trained most of his personnel from scratch, not only could he shape their emerging style, but he also wielded far more authority over them than Killigrew did over his.

Traces of these differences between the patentees continued to affect the theatre until the returning generation of actors retired *circa* 1682. The forward-looking Davenant and his successors ran a much more stable company than

---

[1] See Bentley, *Jacobean and Caroline Stage*, 1: chaps. 1, 6, 8, 10, and 11.

the oft-embattled Killigrew and his son Charles, who struggled to control a group of actors used to making their own decisions and reluctant to change the patterns in which they had been trained. The official patents were not issued until 1662 (King's Company) and 1663 (Duke's Company). Besides a number of standard provisions, they granted permission to increase ticket prices for the explicit purpose of paying for scenery, and they required that women play women's roles.[2] These provisions appear to have been included because the older actors resisted both scenery and actresses. Details of the developing competition survive only intermittently, but, early on, the King's Company went so far as to claim that the entire extant repertory belonged to them. In December 1660, Davenant actually had to petition the King for permission to perform a small selection of plays, including his own, because before the war he had written for what was now the rival company (RD, 50). (Their acute need for new plays made the Duke's Company more welcoming to new scripts, even scripts by women, than the King's Company.) However, so clear were Davenant and Killigrew on the benefits of limiting competition that they banded together to quash attempts, made most persistently by George Jolly, to challenge their duopoly (RD, 51, 179, 372).

Another carry-over from the past was the Master of the Revels, Sir Henry Herbert, who was among the first government officials reinstated. As soon as he was sworn in, on 20 June 1660, he set about enforcing and trying to expand the sphere of his authority.[3] (He licensed 'strollers' – companies playing outside London – as well as street performers of all kinds.) Though the patentees had to concede the survival of his office, they resisted his further encroachments, and his success at increasing his fees continued to rankle. He was able to claim £2 for each new play and £1 for each revived one, not inconsiderable sums.

Only a few exemplars of Herbert's censorship survive from the post-1660 period. The fullest instance is the manuscript of John Wilson's *The Cheats* (1663), over which there was considerable controversy.[4] In practice, Herbert's function was largely admonitory, another superficial 'restoration'. He rarely demanded major changes in plays after 1660, but his presence helped enforce self-censorship. To stifle any potential for difficulties from that quarter, Thomas Killigrew purchased the reversion of his office and succeeded Herbert when he died in 1673. Any conflict of interests that arose was likely to be settled in

---

[2] See Milhous and Hume, *Register of English Theatrical Documents, 1660–1737*, nos. 7, 19, 73, 131 and 186. Subsequent references will be given parenthetically as '*RD* [number]'.

[3] See Bawcutt, *Control and Censorship of Caroline Drama*; Milhous and Hume, 'New light on English acting companies'.

[4] See Wilson, *John Wilson's* The Cheats. The manuscript (now in the Folger Shakespeare Library) is reproduced in facsimile in Langhans, *Restoration Promptbooks*.

favour of theatre, and the transfer of power may have helped enable the spate of sex comedies in the later 1670s. Charles Killigrew took over from his father in 1677 and held office until 1725, but had scant interest in anything other than the collecting of fees. The toothlessness of the Master of the Revels would become an issue at the end of the century and early in the next.[5]

The patent grants made by Charles II established the basic structure of theatrical operations in London and, apart from brief challenges and periods of lax enforcement, the duopoly remained until it was toppled by long overdue parliamentary legislation in 1843. Names notwithstanding, there was no difference in status between the two companies: by another revived tradition, the senior actors of both were liveried servants of the King. The principal advantage was that they could not be sued for debt without permission first being obtained from the Lord Chamberlain. Charles II regularly attended performances by both companies in their public theatres and on occasion commanded performances in the court theatre.

Both companies maintained the old sharer–hireling arrangement in the production company. Senior actors were assigned or could sometimes buy parts of shares, which gave them a stake in the company and a percentage of profits as well as a salary. The patentees retained the largest block of shares, but from the outset both were forced to sell shares to 'adventurers' in order to raise capital for operating and for building.[6] Adventurers held most of the renters' shares in the buildings, because few actors could afford to buy in. The 'young company' or hirelings held no stake at either theatre and had little job security. Both houses had some difficulty retaining actresses, who held no shares, made less than their male colleagues and tended to get pregnant or go off into keeping. (Notable examples include Moll Davis and Nell Gwyn, who became mistresses to Charles II.) Dame Mary Davenant served as house mother to her husband's unmarried actresses, which perhaps accounts for a somewhat less dizzying turnover at the Duke's Company. During the early years Killigrew is rumoured to have kept a house prostitute for his younger actors (RD, 480).

The overall success of the two troupes reflects their proprietors. Davenant was closely involved in all day-to-day operations and interested in innovation of many kinds. Killigrew's chief concern soon became to squeeze money out of the theatre. From time to time he delegated responsibilities to his chief

---

[5] Much the fullest analysis of the theatrical functions of the Master of the Revels remains White, 'The office of revels and dramatic censorship'.

[6] For the best account of the business operations of the companies, see Hotson, *Commonwealth and Restoration Stage*.

actors, then reclaimed power, raising questions as to where authority lay. When Davenant died in 1668, he was succeeded by his wife until his son Charles was of age. Active management was carried out by two highly competent senior actors, Thomas Betterton and Henry Harris (the latter succeeded, after 1677, by William Smith). Killigrew so thoroughly mismanaged the King's Company that he was forced out: in settlement of a 1677 lawsuit against his father, Charles Killigrew was granted the patent, Thomas's remaining shares in the company and the Mastership of the Revels – though what he acquired was a theatre divided against itself (RD, 992, 994).

The fortunes of the two companies were also significantly affected by their theatres. The Duke's Company began to perform in a converted tennis court in Lincoln's Inn Fields that had been fitted up with rudimentary scene and machine capabilities. Davenant had long dreamt of constructing a really fancy stage, capable of the kind of display for which the Stuart court masques had been renowned. Three years after his death, his successors moved the company into the purpose-built Dorset Garden Theatre, which opened in November 1671. Just two months later the King's Company's theatre in Bridges Street burned to the ground, a financial setback from which they never altogether recovered (RD, 661). They opened Drury Lane, an excellent theatre, in 1674, but neither Killigrew was able to provide leadership. By this time, actors of the 'restored' generation were getting old, going out sick and starting to retire. Charles Killigrew proved no more effective a manager than his father. In 1678 John Dryden, principal playwright and a sharer in the King's Company, decamped to the opposition: a 'share' was of no value if there were no profits to divide. One faction in the company broke away and went to Scotland; performers stole costumes from the wardrobe and sold them. The theatre was dark from time to time on account of this dissension, and 'in or about 1680' the Lord Chamberlain informed Thomas Betterton that 'the King's will and Pleasure' was that the companies unite.[7] In May 1682 the remains of the King's Company were absorbed into a new entity called the United Company, managed by Betterton and Smith (RD, 1134, 1151). For all practical purposes, the King's Company had simply collapsed and been taken over by its rival. The principal gain to the Duke's Company was not the additional actors (most of whom were quickly pushed into retirement) or even lack of competition, but rather the right to perform the vast stock of pre-1642 King's Company plays, plus a few good new ones, such as those of Wycherley and Dryden. As the

---

[7] PRO C24/1197, no. 56, Betterton's deposition of 26 January 1697 in Kynaston v. Clayton.

old prompter, John Downes, observes, after the union 'The mixt Company then Reviv'd the several old and Modern Plays, that were the Propriety of Mr *Killigrew*'. Among others, he mentions such works as *Rule a Wife*, *The Plain Dealer*, *Bartholomew Fair* and *Othello*.[8]

Neither house had benefited from the swirl of political distractions around the Popish Plot crisis of 1678 and the ensuing Exclusion Crisis (1678–83). The country was severely destabilized by fears of a Catholic plot against the King and by subsequent attempts to remove the Duke of York, who was Catholic, from the succession in favour of the Duke of Monmouth, a Protestant bastard of Charles II (who had no legitimate heir). With the country seemingly on the verge of another civil war, the theatres ran lots of political plays, but attendance was sparse. The numerous propaganda plays were for the most part Tory rather than Whig (that is, pro Charles and James, not in favour of changing the succession), a bias hardly surprising in view of the prominence of the court in the theatre audience.[9] The authorities allowed quite a lot of blatantly anti-Whig plays, notably John Crowne's *The Misery of Civil War* (1680), Aphra Behn's *The Roundheads* (1681) and Thomas Southerne's *The Loyal Brother* (1682). Scholars differ in their interpretations of such allegory as Thomas Otway's *Venice Preserv'd* (1682) may possess, but its condemnation of 'plots' is clear. When political tension was at its height, the Lord Chamberlain prudently banned some of the most blatant anti-Whig satires, but allowed them once the Tories were clearly in the ascendant. Notable cases are John Dryden and Nathaniel Lee's vicious satire on the Duke of Monmouth, *The Duke of Guise* (1682), and Crowne's nasty but amusing satire, *City Politiques* (1683). Some implicitly Whig plays did get staged, among them Lee's *Lucius Junius Brutus* and Thomas Shadwell's *Lancashire Witches*. What the government was plainly most uncomfortable about was regicide, no matter how remote from current circumstances. Beaumont and Fletcher's *The Maid's Tragedy* was apparently forbidden, and Nahum Tate's adaptation of *Richard II* was halted by official order. When Killigrew tried it, with character names changed, under the title *The Sicilian Usurper*, the Lord Chamberlain angrily silenced the company. The lesson of the Exclusion Crisis was that the government had absolute power to censor scripts or to ban them outright, and a company that tried to sneak something onto the stage would simply be shut down until it had submitted to authority.

[8] Downes, *Roscius Anglicanus*, 82–3.
[9] For the fullest and best account of political drama at this time, see Owen, *Restoration Theatre and Crisis*.

Theatrical warfare at the turn of the century

The United Company weathered the succession of James II and the Glorious Revolution of 1688 with little damage, but these years mark the beginning of a more insidious threat to its success, which only gradually became apparent. In 1687 Charles Davenant sold the patents and his entire interest in the business to his brother Alexander, who made the purchase with borrowed money. Alexander replaced the experienced Betterton and Smith as managers with his 23-year-old brother, Thomas, and began to sell and trade shares recklessly. Between 1690 and 1692 the United Company invested ever larger sums in *The Prophetess, King Arthur* and *The Fairy Queen*, 'semi-operas' whose fantasy elements were realized in elaborate machine effects accompanied by Henry Purcell's charming scores. These productions, though ultimately successful, disrupted cash flow and left Alexander Davenant unable to pay his backers. In the spring of 1694 he absconded, leaving the company to the mercies of two entirely non-theatrical investors, the dilettante Sir Thomas Skipwith and Christopher Rich, a lawyer prepared endlessly to stall creditors and shareholders in the court of Chancery. The pre-1642 theatre had not been ravaged by generational transfers, in part because they happened gradually enough not to disrupt daily operations. However, the secret investors in the United Company owned a controlling interest, and Christopher Rich's first concern was to recoup his money. To that end he began to intervene in decision-making. He ruled out expensive productions and tried to reduce costs by favouring less expensive, younger actors and pressuring their seniors to retire. He violated company protocols on so many levels that by November of 1694 the offended actors delivered to the Lord Chamberlain a document known as the 'Petition of the Players' (*RD*, 1483). In it they complained of 'Arbitrary Acts' they summarized as 'treateing [the players] not as we were the Kings & Queenes servants but the Claimers slaves'. The patentees' 'Reply' was unyielding, so the senior actors walked out of the theatre, and in March the Lord Chamberlain, a long-time friend of Betterton, granted the rebels a licence 'at pleasure' to set up an alternative company (*RD*, 1486, 1499). The precedent set by this rebellion would produce several more challenges to patent authority, usually less successful.

This two-company competition was very different from that of 1660. Rich, Skipwith and Charles Killigrew among them held the two best theatres, Drury Lane and the rather run-down Dorset Garden, as well as both patents. Hence this troupe was known as the Patent Company. However, their performers were unseasoned and had no managerial experience. Promises of signing bonuses and generous profit-sharing came to naught, for want of profits. All Patent Company performers were reduced to the status of salaried employees, routinely short-paid. Only the inherent value of the patents encouraged their holders to keep performing despite the imbalance between the companies, while their actors learned and improved. The rebel actors at the antiquated Lincoln's Inn Fields Theatre got off to a good start with their first production, Congreve's *Love for Love*, drawing much sympathy from the public. In order to pool expertise, money and connections, they set up their company as a cooperative, though managerial responsibility soon devolved on Betterton, aided by Elizabeth Barry and Anne Bracegirdle. As holders of a non-transferable licence, they remained much more vulnerable than their rivals. Lords Chamberlain came and went; monarchs changed; 'at pleasure' made for a precarious existence. Lawsuits brought by Rich and others, some continuing for as long as a decade, harassed them as they squabbled and aged. The situation at Lincoln's Inn Fields degenerated to the point that the Lord Chamberlain had to step in and decree that Betterton, 'tak[ing] upon him the sole management', would have the right to spend up to 40 shillings (£2) on his own authority – quite a contrast with his days as United Company manager, when he had routinely spent hundreds and even thousands of pounds (*RD*, 1655).

Some of the Patent Company's fledgling actors, such as Robert Wilks, Colley Cibber and Anne Oldfield, gradually developed into the great performers of their generation, and William Bullock and William Pinkethman became the popular low comedians. Either company had a right to perform any play produced before 1695, but the senior actors naturally held the advantage in standard repertory. The patentees were fortunate in recognizing in their midst a talented playwright, Cibber, and in getting scripts from the young John Vanbrugh as well as a talented Irishman, George Farquhar. Rich was a brutally exploitative owner, but the company developed some attractive performers and mounted some fine new plays.

By 1698 both houses found themselves in trouble. The rebel company had failed to drive the patentees out of business; neither troupe was making money; competition hurt both parties, but no compromise between them was really conceivable. Lack of court patronage after the death of Queen Mary in 1694 hurt both, and the theatres found themselves with an aging audience that was not renewing itself as its older members died off. If ordinary plays failed to draw audiences, additional attractions would have to be tried: smutty epilogues delivered by barely pubescent girls; Shakespeare mini-seasons; guest appearances by the Irish comedian Thomas Doggett; performing dogs, acrobats and weightlifters as entr'actes, countered by French ballerinas and Italian castrato singers. Drury Lane even tried a monkey. In truth, neither theatre was offering a very appealing product, the unceasing animus between them grew tiresome, and the audience for both dwindled.[10]

In the midst of bitter competition and hard times, the theatres found themselves beset by moral reformers, many of whom simply wanted all public performances of plays suppressed. Jeremy Collier's diatribe, *A Short View of the Immorality, and Profaneness of the English Stage*, was published in April 1698 and immediately attracted a flood of frightened, angry responses from playwrights and theatre lovers.[11] Critics pitched in on both sides and created a great hullabaloo, which cannot have encouraged occasional play-goers to attend so disreputable an entertainment. Whilst not active patrons, neither King William nor his successor Queen Anne showed any disposition to shut down the theatres. As Cibber remarked, 'the last time they pull'd down the *Stage* in the City, they set up a *Scaffold* at Court'.[12] Stymied at the highest level, anti-theatricalists started attending performances, writing down objectionable phrases and laying information against the actors before the legal authorities. Ironically, the actors got off in almost all cases by arguing that the lines they spoke had been duly licensed by the Master of the Revels.

Collier certainly roused a furore, but how much impact he had in the long term may be questioned. Nineteenth-century critics believed that he 'caused' the shift to 'sentimental' comedy, but a careful look at generic trends long before Collier proves that this was simply not true.[13] Collier himself did not believe that he 'succeeded' in reforming the theatre: the people he had most bitterly denounced, Congreve and Vanbrugh, were given the Queen's licence to run a theatre company in 1704. The curious thing about the whole row is that, though the Lord Chamberlain piously issued orders to enforce strict licensing, no genuine effort was made to see that the lackadaisical Charles Killigrew did his job properly. Even playwrights agreed that abuses had been rife. Had Killigrew been replaced *circa* 1700, or a competent licenser appointed, then in all probability there would have been no Licensing Act of 1737, for censorship of the sort Walpole wanted would already have been in place.[14]

---

[10] For details see Milhous, *Betterton and the Management of Lincoln's Inn Fields*.

[11] For lists of contributions to this preface and pamphlet war, see Anthony, *Jeremy Collier Stage Controversy*, and Arnott and Robinson, *English Theatrical Literature, 1559–1900*, nos. 284–357.

[12] Dedication by Colley Cibber in *Love Makes a Man*.

[13] See Krutch, *Comedy and Conscience after the Restoration*.

[14] See Hume, 'Collier and the future of the London theater in 1698'.

Eighteenth-century developments and the impact of the Licensing Act

Through all this upheaval both companies somehow stayed in business. In 1703 John Vanbrugh, in his guise as architect, got the bright idea of constructing an elegant new theatre, calculating that he had the political connections to force a new union and combine the two companies under his management. His Queen's (later King's) Theatre in the Haymarket duly opened in 1705, but with no union in sight: basically it was occupied by the Lincoln's Inn Fields troupe, though Betterton and others began to ease towards retirement at this time. Vanbrugh had grandiose visions of hiring not only the best available actors but also a large contingent of specialist singers and dancers. He saw great possibilities in 'Italian opera', that is, all-sung opera of the sort by then a major craze throughout southern Europe.

When Rich refused all overtures for a union, Vanbrugh, with the connivance of a friendly Lord Chamberlain, simply took away most of the patent company's best performers, including Wilks, Cibber and Oldfield. In 1705 and 1706 Rich had stolen a march on Vanbrugh by mounting operas in translation, which had proved very popular. To still his protests over lost actors, he was allowed a monopoly on musical entertainments. In a dire miscalculation, Vanbrugh next decided that what he really wanted was opera. He persuaded the Lord Chamberlain to issue an order that united the actors under Rich at Drury Lane and created an opera monopoly for him at the Queen's Theatre (RD, 1927). The order took effect on 13 January 1708, and Vanbrugh was bankrupt in four months.[15]

All actors, meanwhile, found themselves back at Drury Lane under the rule of Christopher Rich, as though the rebellion of 1694 had never happened. When, predictably, he started cheating and abusing them, they plotted another revolution. The Lord Chamberlain agreed to entrap Rich by means of a decree forbidding him to appropriate for himself large portions of the actors' benefit proceeds. There was every reason to think Rich would violate this order, and he promptly did so. On 6 June 1709 the Lord Chamberlain silenced Drury Lane (RD, 2023). Such silencings had happened occasionally in the previous fifty years, but almost always for only a few days' duration. When Rich attempted to reopen in September, however, he was not permitted to do so, and the patentees discovered to their indignation that, patents or no patents, the Lord

---

[15] For details, see Milhous and Hume, eds., *Vice Chamberlain Coke's Theatrical Papers, 1706–1715*.

Chamberlain did not intend to let them reopen at all. The power of the Lord Chamberlain to regulate – or suppress – patent theatres could hardly have been more effectively demonstrated.[16] Formal protest to the Queen proved fruitless. Yet such was Rich's confidence in the patents that he bought the Lincoln's Inn Fields theatre and bided his time. Whilst official ire was focused on Rich, the Lord Chamberlain did not intend to starve the actors: under a series of licences held by gentlemen overseers, a single company was allowed to perform. For several years these nominal heads changed with politics by the season, but at the level of daily operations, Wilks, Cibber and Doggett controlled the company. (Membership for Anne Oldfield on this select committee had been bruited, despite reservations on Doggett's part, but she allowed herself to be bought off with a substantial monetary 'gift'. Thus for the rest of the century no woman replaced Elizabeth Barry in management.) The Wilks–Cibber–Doggett triumvirate kept most disagreements in house, with the exception of the outburst of 5 June 1710, when rioting actors unseated Aaron Hill as manager (*RD*, 2089). Having invited political interference, they were in no position to fend it off when, in 1713, the Lord Chamberlain ordered them to make room for the young actor Barton Booth in the management. The outraged Doggett refused to accept this invasion of property rights. He eventually sold his share of the business and retired. The modified triumvirate ran the Drury Lane company for the rest of their careers.

Christopher Rich rebuilt the Lincoln's Inn Fields theatre into its third form and, with the accession of George I in 1714, set about reviving his patents. A company led by his son, John, inaugurated the new theatre in December 1714. At first consisting largely of discards from Drury Lane and raw beginners, the company barely survived its first half-dozen seasons. When John Rich discovered his genius for pantomimes in the next decade, his organization began to flourish, and never again was London reduced to a single producing theatre. The accounts in 'Rich's Register' (preserved in the Folger Shakespeare Library) show just how marginal the early years of the new Lincoln's Inn Fields operation were, whereas recently discovered lawsuit evidence proves that Drury Lane was making substantial sums of money both before and after the revival of competition.[17]

The change of monarchs in 1714 also meant that Drury Lane needed a new licence and a new political figurehead. Richard Steele was invited to serve and used his Whig connections to arrange a limited royal patent, valid for his

---

[16] See Milhous and Hume, 'Silencing of Drury Lane in 1709'.
[17] See Milhous and Hume, 'Profits at Drury Lane, 1713–1716'.

lifetime plus three years. Granted in January 1715, this authority to perform made the company far more secure than a licence 'at pleasure'. It also provided an opportunity to defy the Master of the Revels. Steele and the triumvirate took the position that the patent 'made us sole Judges of what Plays might be proper for the Stage', as Cibber says gleefully when reporting his visit to Charles Killigrew to inform him that henceforward they would submit no scripts and pay no fees.[18] The patent actually conferred no such rights, but Killigrew's protest proved ineffectual. This total collapse of the long-established process of censorship may fairly be called astounding, but it seems to have passed virtually unnoticed until political satire in the 1730s brought the subject to the attention of Sir Robert Walpole.

What power did a patent confer? Steele's interpretation that he could circumvent the Lord Chamberlain was contrary to all historical precedent and in 1718 brought him into conflict with the incumbent, the Duke of Newcastle. A major public clash followed during the season of 1719–20. Newcastle denied the power of the 1715 patent, voided the licence of 1714, and issued another to the triumvirs only. Steele protested formally to the King and published a periodical called the *Theatre* from 2 January to 5 April 1720, largely devoted to laying his case before the public.[19] The gist of a complicated imbroglio is that Steele entirely failed to make his case about freedom from regulation, but was allowed to retain his share in the theatre's profits. Precedent on the Lord Chamberlain's side was strong – the patents of the 1660s had certainly not exempted companies from official control – but the ultimate legal basis came down to the actors being the monarch's servants. To underline the point Newcastle had them 'resworn', the last time this was ever done. The question of what power the Lord Chamberlain might have over a troupe that was not technically a part of the royal household did not come up, there being none at this time.

By 1722 the viability of the Lincoln's Inn Fields company was evident, and the two managements decided that cooperation would be more profitable than serious competition. They took to playing on alternate nights in slack periods, and in April 1722 the managers signed a formal if technically secret agreement that neither company would hire away a performer without the written permission of the other management.[20] This 'cartel', as the parties called it,

---

[18] Cibber, *Apology*, ed. Lowe, 1: 276–8.
[19] For the fullest account of the episode, see Loftis, *Steele at Drury Lane*, 121–82, and Steele, *Richard Steele's* The Theatre, ed. Loftis. For the principal primary documents, see *RD*, 2893, 2936, 2957–8, 2966–9, 2971–2, 2975–81, 2983, 2985, 2994, 2999, 3003, 3012, 3016–17, 3058–9, 3062.
[20] See Milhous and Hume, 'London theatre cartel of the 1720s'.

was a formidable barrier against salary demands: a performer unhappy with his or her salary could leave London, but had no other recourse. The stodgy condition of drama in the 1720s unquestionably reflects the complacency and collusion with which the two theatres were run. This state of affairs was disrupted by the explosive success of John Gay's *The Beggar's Opera* in 1728 and the burgeoning of often unlicensed theatrical activity that followed. A theatre in Goodman's Fields, run first by Thomas Odell and then by Henry Giffard, operated nearer the City than the West End; since 1720 the Little Theatre in the Haymarket had been a road house and temporary quarters for pick-up troupes, though never a repertory theatre. These venues did, however, considerably increase employment possibilities for actors, and a high proportion of the plays at the Little Haymarket were new and often topical, making it the fringe or off-Broadway of its day.

Vehement moral protests against Goodman's Fields led to a petition from the Lord Mayor and aldermen of London to the King, requesting its suppression.[21] The prime minister endorsed the petition; the King approved it; and on 28 April 1730 the Lord Chamberlain issued a formal order silencing the theatre (*RD*, 3503). Nevertheless, the company was back in business by 11 May. Exactly what happened is not recorded. We must presume that the government's legal advisors were able to find no basis in law by which the Lord Chamberlain could regulate or suppress a troupe that had no connection to the royal household.

Nor does any evidence suggest that the new theatres were submitting scripts to the Master of the Revels. The Little Haymarket got raided by constables in 1731 when it persisted in exhibiting *The Fall of Mortimer*, an anonymous 'parallel' play that was a seditious libel on Walpole. Henry Fielding's *The Welsh Opera* (1731) so riled the authorities with its allegorical mockery of the royal household and prime minister (who appears in the guise of butler) that the expanded version, *The Grub-Street Opera*, was in some fashion kept off the public stage. It was perhaps no more offensive than *The Beggar's Opera*, but that had found such public favour as to make suppression politically touchy, however irritating Walpole might find his semi-disguised representations, Macheath and Peachum. Gay wrote a much nastier sequel, *Polly* (1729), in which Macheath / Walpole gets hanged. That gesture went beyond a joke, and the play was stopped before performance on the direct order of the Lord Chamberlain, as Gay explains in his preface. The exact nature of the authority for the prohibition was not

---

[21] See *RD*, 3466–9, 3471, 3482, 3497–9, 3501–7.

stated, but even with the original patents behind him, Rich saw no future in disputing the issue.

The vagueness of both the actors' right to perform and the government's right to regulate their operations became glaringly apparent at the next generational shift, which centred on Drury Lane between 1732 and 1734. Booth retired for reasons of health in 1728. Steele died in 1729, Wilks in 1732. Cibber sold his share in 1733. The triumvirs had used friends in high places to wangle a 21-year patent, effective in 1732. However, when they variously died or retired, a young man about town named John Highmore bought a controlling interest in the theatre. He proved ignorant and inept, and in June 1733 most of his actors followed precedent and decamped to the Little Haymarket, led by Colley Cibber's talented if obnoxious son, Theophilus. A bitter struggle followed. The Lord Chamberlain declined to attempt to suppress the rebels; Highmore maintained a scratch company at Drury Lane while he tried to enforce his rights in court. The patentees of both companies joined in a suit designed to test the most recent revision of the law used in the Elizabethan era to control unauthorized acting.[22] They had one of the principal rebels, the popular John Harper, arrested as a vagrant, despite the fact that he was known to be a prosperous householder. As Robert D. Hume has pointed out, the issue they hoped to test was 'not the solvency or domicile of the actors, but whether performing without a licence made them, legally speaking, vagrants'. Meanwhile, the rebels struck a bargain with the owners of the Drury Lane building (who were different from the owners of the production company) and sued to evict Highmore. The vagrancy case never came to a decision. John Rich backed out early, and Highmore, beset at every turn, despaired and sold out at a huge loss to a speculator named Charles Fleetwood. The new owner caved in to the rebel actors' demands, and they returned to Drury Lane. By implication the acting of plays was not in itself an illegal thing, and the government had no basis in law for suppressing playhouses – but the matter could not be allowed to stand there.

Responding to what anti-theatricalists found a deplorable state of affairs, in 1735 Sir John Barnard introduced in Parliament a bill calling for the suppression of non-patent theatres and a ban on anything profane, obscene or offensive to piety and good manners, with enforcement to be handled by local justices of the peace. His bill might well have passed, if Walpole had not tried to add an

---

[22] The law was 12 Anne 2, ch. 23 (1714). For the fullest account of this rather confusing episode, see Hume, *Fielding and the London Theatre*, 155–64, 173–80. Subsequent quotation from p. 176.

amendment giving the Lord Chamberlain the power to censor plays. Barnard and many of his allies, no friends to the Walpole ministry, were loath to put additional power in their hands. On account of this impasse, the measure failed, but Walpole simply waited for a more opportune moment to try again.

In the spring of 1737 Walpole attached some theatre provisions to a revision of another vagrancy bill. At the same time, he denounced an outrageous satire on the King called *The Golden Rump* (probably concocted for the purpose) and cried up the need for censorship. The bill passed both houses of Parliament by lopsided votes and was instantly approved by the King.[23] It contained two key provisions. First, anyone who performed plays for money without a royal patent or a licence from the Lord Chamberlain should 'be deemed a Rogue and a Vagabond' and suffer the applicable penalties. Second, a 'true Copy' of anything spoken or sung on stage must be submitted to the Lord Chamberlain's office prior to performance, for licensing. Any company that failed to obey would be fined £50 and silenced. At a stroke, Walpole changed the whole history of the British theatre.

Censorship proved far less damaging than the restriction to two patent companies. Since censorship was what Walpole really wanted, one may wonder why he insisted on putting the unlicensed theatres out of business. The answer is probably just that this attracted votes from anti-theatricalists and effectively bought off objections from Covent Garden and Drury Lane. A bit of censorship, never onerous before, was a small price to pay for restoration of their profitable duopoly.[24] The effect of the restriction to two companies was that competition was permanently reduced to the vanishing point. The law squelched the possibility of 'niche' competition from a company devoted to new plays or musicals or any repertory aimed at a particular audience. The new arrangement also, incidentally, left actors at the mercy of vicious or incompetent owners: nothing had been learned from the series of actor rebellions going back before the turn of the century. Another negative effect of the Licensing Act that took time to appear was the elephantiasis it encouraged in the patent theatres. The capacity of 3,000 and up in the new versions of Covent Garden and Drury Lane erected in the 1790s discouraged the staging of

---

[23] For a detailed account of the bill and its passage, see Liesenfeld, *Licensing Act of 1737*.

[24] During the 1740s, theatres operated intermittently in Goodman's Fields and other venues despite the Licensing Act, but never established themselves for longer than a few seasons at a time. For a discussion of this contradiction between law and practice, see Kinservik, *Disciplining Satire*, 102–4. The law did not always languish: an attempt by 'Plausible Jack' Palmer to open the Royalty Theatre in Wellclose Square in June 1787 was swiftly quashed by the patent theatres. See discussion in the entry on Palmer in Highfill *et al.*, *Biographical Dictionary*, XI: 166–9.

plays in which complex or subtle dialogue needed to be heard. Huge theatres encouraged melodrama, musicals and scenic show.

The evils of the system created by the Licensing Act are evident in the dismal history of Drury Lane under Charles Fleetwood and the failed actors' rebellion of 1743. Fleetwood was a bankrupt gambler, and he milked the theatre for every penny he could squeeze out of it. Once again, an owner systematically short-paid his actors and cheated tradesmen and house servants. After mistreatment that grew worse for nearly a decade, the actors united behind David Garrick and Charles Macklin, walked out, and petitioned the Lord Chamberlain for protection or the right to rent the patent and run the theatre themselves. Documentation recently discovered in the Lord Chamberlain's registers shows that the theatre was thoroughly solvent: the problem was Fleetwood.[25] The result, after a pamphlet war and an ugly public fuss, was total failure. The Lord Chamberlain refused to lift a finger to see that employees were paid their contracted salaries, reportedly on the ground that star actors were over-compensated. Alternative theatres being illegal, the actors had no real option but to accept mistreatment and servitude. A few stars could command and usually collect large salaries, but over the course of the eighteenth century, lower salaries remained unchanged while those at the top of the scale soared.

How much impact did censorship have on playwrights? Most of the scripts submitted to the licenser employed in the Lord Chamberlain's office survive.[26] A very few plays were banned outright, and substantive objections were raised to a modest number, but the large majority of plays underwent only superficial changes in the course of licensing, most alterations being strictly verbal.[27] Writers and managers soon came to understand what the licenser would tolerate and what he would not, with the result that they sensibly refrained from getting themselves in difficulties. This self-censorship was very effective. In most respects the licensing was very similar to that carried out by Sir Henry Herbert, which is to say considerably more rigorous than in the *laissez-faire* days of Charles Killigrew. King, government and established church were off limits, and verbal decorum was insisted upon. However, if a playwright offered Roman history by way of example, and left the 'application' to the audience, the licenser was unlikely to object.

The course of theatre in the third quarter of the century was fundamentally altered by a change of management at Drury Lane in 1747. Fleetwood was

---

[25] See Milhous and Hume, 'Drury Lane actors' rebellion of 1743'.
[26] For manuscripts submitted from 1777 to 1824, see MacMillan, *Catalogue of the Larpent Plays in the Huntington Library*.
[27] See Conolly, *Censorship of English Drama*.

finally forced out in 1744, after an attempt to raise prices caused riots. The theatre fell into the hands of Norton and Amber, bankers, who themselves were about to go bankrupt. By 1746, under the management of James Lacy, it was on the verge of collapse. In these circumstances, Lacy in desperation arranged for the young David Garrick – the most popular actor in London – to buy a half-interest and assume responsibility for daily operations in 1747–8. Garrick was a prudent co-manager, socially adept, and a keen judge of scripts and public taste. The theatre immediately cleared huge profits, allowing him to pay off a £12,000 mortgage and large debts in just three seasons. Garrick's assumption of power at Drury Lane has almost always been treated as a matter of course, but in fact it was quite improbable. It came about because of Fleetwood's ruin and the theatre's falling into the hands of insolvent incompetents.[28]

Between 1747 and 1776, when Garrick retired, Drury Lane was stable, profitable and wholly predictable. In most respects, Garrick operated little differently from the triumvirate in the 1720s – or John Rich at Covent Garden, until his death in 1761, or his squabbling successors thereafter.[29] Garrick simply carried out daily business better than his rivals and predecessors. He was himself a tremendous drawing card, but he took few chances as actor or manager. The mainpiece repertory at both theatres consisted of about fifty old favourites from Shakespeare to *The Beggar's Opera*, with a substantial degree of overlap between the two theatres; occasional adaptations or revivals of other seventeenth- or early eighteenth-century English plays; and in most seasons three to six new ones. Garrick made every effort to run new plays nine nights so the authors could enjoy three benefits, but few of them lasted longer or were ever revived.[30] Both theatres ran afterpieces most nights, a high proportion of them farce or pantomime.

The evils of the Licensing Act are difficult to overstate. The stimulating competition introduced by fringe theatres in the 1730s was simply wiped out. With profits virtually assured, and competition from any other quarter against the law, Covent Garden and Drury Lane could afford to be lazy. They generally did not bother to operate in the summer, content to leave that to a pick-up troupe under Samuel Foote at the Little Haymarket. Both companies employed

---

[28] For details, see Milhous and Hume, 'Drury Lane account book for 1745–46', and Milhous and Hume, 'Receipts at Drury Lane: Richard Cross's diary for 1746–47'.

[29] After another brief interlude in which ownership and authority were shared, Thomas Harris, a soap manufacturer, won out. He managed Covent Garden, unadventurously but competently, from 1774/5 through to the end of the century and beyond.

[30] See Milhous and Hume, 'Playwrights' remuneration in eighteenth-century London', 16–17.

some splendid performers, but innovation was minimal in every realm. London was a rapidly growing city, and in the natural course of events more theatres should have sprung up to cater to different segments of the audience and offer different sorts of plays. The fundamental mediocrity of English drama after 1737 may be attributed directly to the suppression of competition and multiple venues imposed by the Licensing Act.

6

The Beggar's Opera
A case study

CALHOUN WINTON

Why a 'case study' of *The Beggar's Opera?* Because, first, the *Opera*'s astonishing opening run makes it a candidate for special attention in any historical account. Nothing like it, so far as the records demonstrate, had ever been seen on the London stage before then (nor seen there again, for a long time): thirty-two consecutive performances and a total run of sixty-two performances for the season, after the opening on 29 January 1728 at John Rich's theatre in Lincoln's Inn Fields (hereafter LIF).

As A. H. Scouten has noted, 'Heretofore, a run of nine nights had been considered excellent, one of twelve nights unusual'.[1] But sixty-two? A perception that something important was happening was almost immediate. By the third of February – in the first week of the run – the opposition newspaper the *Craftsman* gave first voice to the witticism that has become standard: the *Opera* 'has met with a general Applause, insomuch that the Waggs say it has made Rich very Gay, and probably will make Gay very Rich'. And so it turned out, with Gay transformed virtually overnight from an impoverished poet making do by living with his wealthy friends to the most prosperous dramatist of his time, and the saturnine Rich becoming, if not gay (i.e., merry), at least tranquil. In May 1728 the first imitation of *The Beggar's Opera* appeared at the Little Haymarket Theatre, Thomas Cooke and John Mottley's ballad opera *Penelope* – the *Odyssey* story set in Queen Anne's England – but ran only three nights. Gay's *Opera* continued serenely on at LIF through its sixty-second performance on 19 June.

The *Opera*'s initial success did not end with the London season. Five days after Rich darkened his theatre, on 24 June 1728, a new company at the Little Haymarket launched a production of its own with 'All the Songs and Dances set to Musick, as it is perform'd at the Theatre in Lincoln's-Inn-Fields', as if to guarantee its authenticity to prospective patrons. That same summer

---

[1] *The London Stage 1660–1800, Part 2: 1700–1729*, II: 931.

separate productions were offered at Southwark fair and in Bath, and in the autumn the new Little Haymarket company went head to head with the original cast at LIF, while the rival company at Drury Lane tried to stem the tide by presenting serious material such as *Othello* and *Henry IV*. *The Beggar's Opera* was securely established in the repertory of the English-speaking world. Through the century versions sprouted up here and there and everywhere: George Washington, an admirer, bought tickets for a production by the touring American Company at Williamsburg, Virginia, in 1761.

And the *Opera* may serve as a case study because, second, its success was not confined to the eighteenth century: in the twentieth century performances on stage and in film have appeared and are appearing all over the world. Variants, as will be seen, adapted to their times have been written and produced in the twentieth century by creative artists of the first rank, each reflecting the concerns of their times, as did Gay's original: Bertolt Brecht and Elisabeth Hauptmann depicting poverty and gender exploitation in Weimar Germany; Vaclav Havel satirizing political repression in Stalinist Czechoslovakia; Duke Ellington and John Latouche exposing economic injustice in mid-century America.

Not, of course, that the original *Opera* was bound to succeed. Its success was a mixed product of John Gay's own experience in writing for the theatre; of his association with Swift, Pope and the other satirists of the Scriblerus Club; of the acting companies' increasing professionalization; of an ever-growing interest in the musical theatre on the part of London audiences; and, finally, of the growth and developing sophistication of metropolitan London, which could look at itself in the *Opera* and laugh at what it saw.

Gay himself had acquired by 1728 a long experience in the working stage, though he did not make much of it publicly. The Scriblerians with whom he was associated – Pope, Swift, Arbuthnot – were inclined to view the professional theatre *de haut en bas*. But Gay had seen the London stage from the other perspective, as it were, from below, while serving as personal assistant to Aaron Hill. Hill was employed briefly as manager of Drury Lane and, after being ejected from the post by his actors, turned up as manager at the Queen's, Haymarket – Hill had important connections. At the Queen's (which of course was styled the King's in subsequent reigns), Hill, presumably with Gay's assistance, supervised the lavish production of Handel's first London opening: his *Rinaldo* (1711). Though satirized mercilessly by Addison and Steele in the *Spectator*, *Rinaldo* was to be Handel's most popular opera in his lifetime.

In 1712 Gay saw published but not produced his one-act farce, *The Mohocks*; the following year his comic adaptation of Chaucer, *The Wife of Bath*, was both produced at Drury Lane and published. His afterpiece *The What D'Ye Call It*, a farce burlesque, or, as its subtitle runs, echoing Polonius, *A Tragi-Comi-Pastoral Farce*, opened in 1715 to great success and stayed in the London repertory for more than half a century. *Three Hours after Marriage*, probably written with the assistance of fellow-Scriblerians Pope and Arbuthnot, was produced at Drury Lane in 1717 with a successful opening run, but evoked vehement criticism in the press, perhaps engineered by political anti-Scriblerians, on the grounds – undeniable – of its bawdry.[2]

About this time Gay renewed his acquaintanceship with Handel, which had presumably begun with the production of *Rinaldo*. He wrote the libretto for Handel's little gem of a pastoral masque or serenata, *Acis and Galatea*. Roger Fiske has judged that Gay 'provided Handel with the best dramatic libretto he ever set'.[3] Gay turned to the serious drama next for his pastoral tragedy, *Dione*, published but not produced, and his classical tragedy, *The Captives*, produced at Drury Lane in 1724 to little success. The drama's patrons were telling him to return to comedy. By this date he had acquired experience in every aspect of the London theatre world, including, most significantly, the musical theatre.

That theatre world was flourishing, as was London itself, when *The Beggar's Opera* received its initial production. This was the first complete season after the coronation of George II and Queen Charlotte in October 1727. John Rich's rivals at Drury Lane, the actor-managers Colley Cibber and his partners, had a remarkable hit of their own at the same time as the *Opera*. Vanbrugh's *The Provok'd Husband*, as altered and edited by Cibber, opened in January 1728 to the derision of critics but the applause of the audience and ran for a then unprecedented twenty-eight nights successively. Attendance no doubt was helped by theatre patrons who could not get admission to the *Opera*, which was selling out every night. These same Drury Lane managers had read the script for Gay's *Opera* but turned it down, after having produced four of his dramatic works. Young Henry Fielding was also preparing for his début on the London stage with *Love in Several Masques*, which opened and closed at Drury Lane after four performances in mid-February, in the very eye of the *Opera's* hurricane.

But that was after Gay's opening night. Before that glorious event there was the usual uncertainty when something new is on the way to the stage. This really was something new. As stated, the Drury Lane management had looked at it and officially said no, in their professional judgement. The verdict of Gay's friends was scarcely better: Pope later recalled that both he and Swift

---

[2] See Winton, *John Gay and the London Theatre*, 51–6.
[3] Fiske, *English Theatre Music in the Eighteenth Century*, 2nd edn, 95.

had read Gay's manuscript and 'neither of us thought it would succeed'. When they showed it to William Congreve, then the most renowned playwright in Britain, Congreve judged that it 'would either take greatly, or be damned confoundedly'.[4] Not the sort of opinion to make an author relax.

Swift had perhaps been involved in the creative process at the very beginning. Years earlier, in 1716, he had written to Pope about what Gay might do: 'what think you of a Newgate pastoral, among the whores and thieves there?'[5] – Newgate being the principal criminal, as distinguished from debtors, prison. Swift apparently had in mind a poem or series of poems such as Gay had published as *The Shepherd's Week* (1714), a pastoral burlesque where he had made extensive use of folklore, folk dialects and folk customs.

Gay was certainly capable of composing an urban pastoral poem if he had wished to do so, but his instinct was for the stage. Most importantly, he understood the musical stage. He had been writing ballads for stage performance over the years; two or three had already become popular 'standards', such as 'sweet William's Farewell to Black-Ey'd Susan', originally featured in Gay's *The Wife of Bath*. (The flower, by the way, takes its name from Gay's song rather than the other way around.)

In 1724 another ballad of his, 'Newgate's Garland', was sung in the pantomime *Harlequin Jack Sheppard*. Pantomimes, combining music and miming dance, were enjoying a vogue in the 1720s. This pantomime, written and performed by the principal Drury Lane dancer John Thurmond, concerns the last days of a real criminal, Jack Sheppard, who was turned in to the law – 'peached', for impeached, was the slang term – by his companion Jonathan Wild, for the reward offered. If this sounds like a prefiguring of the *Opera*, it was. Interestingly, some attempt was made to reproduce criminal argot in the pantomime, though not in Gay's ballad, with the result that the printed version required explanatory notes. It stands to reason that Gay saw his ballad performed in *Harlequin Jack Sheppard*, but if he did so he kept his mouth shut about it, probably because his friend Pope disapproved strenuously of pantomimes and satirized them in *The Dunciad*. Gay's ballad tells of the attempt by another criminal, Joseph Blake, to slit Wild's throat at the trial, with a penknife.

If ballads were widely sung and widely popular, the notion of a ballad opera was a fresh idea. Opera itself, in various forms and presented with either Italian or English libretti, had been flourishing, albeit with many financial problems, in London for decades. That same season of 1727–8 the Royal Academy of

---

[4] Spence, *Observations, Anecdotes, and Characters of Books and Men*, 107.
[5] Pope, *Correspondence*, I: 360.

Music was staging opera at the King's Theatre, Haymarket. *Opera seria*, in Italian, was in special demand, with the great Handel among others answering that demand. Gay was, as has been shown, familiar with Handel's world, probably from 1711 with *Rinaldo* and certainly from about 1717 with *Acis and Galatea*. Opera singers were the highest paid professionals in the London theatre world, imported from Italy and France, with artistic temperaments to match their salaries. At a performance in 1727 two leading Italian singers, Signora Faustina and Signora Cuzzoni, had aired their differences on stage, some said by scratching and hair-pulling, even as they were representing titled ladies. Opera in English, which had some success in the latter years of the preceding century but had then been eclipsed by the Italian, was making a comeback: Giovanni Bononcini's *Camilla*, with an English libretto, had a good run at LIF in 1727. But opera, whether presented in Italian or English, was ruinously expensive. The company at the King's was forced to cut short its season because it could not make ends meet, even with Handel writing the operas.

The Beggar's Opera, as its name implied, would not be a high-cost enterprise. The name was part of the joke: this is a beggar's, not a king's, kind of opera. As the Beggar (author) himself observes in the opening lines, 'IF Poverty be a Title to Poetry, I am sure No-body can dispute mine'.[6] It was planned for economy by Gay, who before the *Opera* had written four comic pieces for the stage and seen three of them produced, each employing music in one way or another. Gay himself was almost certainly a musician, playing the vertical flute or what we would call a recorder. He was surely a careful student of music and its effects, and with the *Opera* he presented a vehicle which was cheap and easy to perform. This has always been an aspect of its attractiveness: great singers and actors can produce memorable performances of the *Opera*, but ordinary singers and actors can also sound and look good in it. A part, no doubt, of Gay's plan. He realized that it would be produced by one of the two theatre companies, not by the Royal Academy opera company, and he tailored the music to fit the cast he could get.

Both Drury Lane and LIF had actors, male and female – the term 'actress' appeared later in the century – who could handle his limited vocal requirements and who could dance passably as well. For several decades, though to a lesser extent as the opera companies developed, it had been expected that an actor would be able either to sing or dance, some better than others. Both companies also had qualified instrumentalists on their payrolls: incidental and

---

[6] Gay, *Dramatic Works*, introduction, II: 1–2, hereafter cited parenthetically in the text.

entr'acte music had been part of the patent companies' offerings since the Restoration. Congreve, Steele, Farquhar and other dramatists, knowing the companies' capabilities, had included songs in their comedies, and had begun collaborating with composers such as John Eccles to supply the music for the songs. By the 1720s the musical magnet that was London was attracting composers of substantial ability to the theatres: Handel and Bononcini, as already noted, but also Henry Carey, Arcangelo Corelli and Francesco Geminiani. In the *Opera* or elsewhere in his works Gay employed the music of every one of these composers. The popular pantomimes, a staple at both houses, required both vocal and instrumental music and dancers. The musical director at LIF, Dr John Pepusch, was himself a composer and competent musical professional.

In the case of Gay's new ballad opera, John Rich would have to pay the actors and musicians, but the music came free. Gay simply plucked it from the air, as it were. The term *ballad opera* as applied to *The Beggar's Opera* is inevitable but somewhat misleading. Inevitable, because Gay's work was the first entry in what was to be a new genre, and by virtue of its amazing popularity widely copied, as will be seen. But the music that he used included but was by no means limited to ballads, in the sense of traditional folk songs. The first air in the *Opera*, 'An old Woman cloathed in Gray', was a Scottish folk ballad, and a rather dirty one at that. Popular songs, as distinguished from folk ballads and sometimes termed *street ballads*, were sold by pedlars in single-sheet broadside form and had been flourishing in London for a century and more. Many of these, in Gay's time, were first heard in the theatre. Gay himself had not only composed song lyrics for his plays, but also used traditional and popular music as their settings, as in his very first stage piece, *The Mohocks*. Folk music and popular music but also 'serious' music; musical boundaries were permeable in eighteenth-century London before the evolution of musical copyright, and certainly were so in John Gay's mind. We can imagine him humming to himself as he wrote, music being near the centre of his artistic creativity. Gay took what he wanted: Handel had provided the setting for Gay's song ''Twas when the Seas were roaring' in *The What D'Ye Call It*. This popular song was being reprinted as the *Opera* had its opening run, and Gay used Handel's tune again in the *Opera*. When Macheath's gang exit the tavern in Act 2, they leave to a march from Handel's *Rinaldo* which Gay may have helped stage.

Music from the folk, popular and 'serious' traditions, then, orchestrated, stitched together and given an overture by Pepusch: this was what the delighted crowd heard on opening night, a thoroughly professional performance. The actors were on the whole a competent if to that point undistinguished group. The managers of the rival company at Drury Lane could have gathered a much stronger cast if they had chosen to do the *Opera*, stronger both in terms of vocal and acting ability and also in audience recognition.

Lavinia Fenton, destined in this one role of Polly to become a superstar, had scarcely two years' experience on the LIF stage. Rich had cast her as Cherry in *The Beaux' Stratagem* during the previous season; she had also played Ophelia and appeared as an entr'acte singer and dancer. Someone right for the ingenue part of Cherry who could sing would be right for Polly as well. Thomas Walker, strictly a journeyman actor to this date, was chosen for the part of Macheath instead of the company's star lead, James Quin, who apparently declined the role. The rest of the cast were of a stature comparable to that of Fenton and Walker, that is, middling.

The first-night audience, like many another first-night audience, did not know at the opening curtain what to make of what they were seeing. This must have been especially galling to Gay, weighted with the gloomy predictions of his friends and of the Drury Lane managers. Benjamin Victor recalls it this way: 'On the first Night of Performance, its Fate was doubtful for some Time. The first Act was received with silent Attention, not a Hand moved; at the End of which they rose, and every Man seemed to compare Notes with his Neighbor, and the general Opinion was in its Favour.' But 'silent Attention' was not enough. Victor goes on: 'In the second Act they broke their Silence, by Marks of their Approbation, to the great Joy of the frighted Performers, as well as the Author; and the last Act was received with universal Applause.'[7] Act 2 opens with the great tavern scene, while Act 1 closes with the quiet love duet of Macheath and Polly. It is a notably understated act closing, one that does not draw much applause in modern productions. Victor's recollection accords with the dramatic logic of the *Opera* itself.

The Beggar's Opera contains elements of literary and artistic burlesque and of topical satire, but its driving force is comedy. Some have viewed it, with its contemporary publications *Gulliver's Travels* and *The Dunciad*, as the last flowering of the Scriblerus Club's satiric collaborations. Although, as we have seen, both Swift and Pope deprecated the *Opera* when they first read it, and made little or no direct contributions, there are some artistic interactions. Different as the *Opera* is from the other two works in almost every respect, it shares their comic gusto. As Yvonne Noble has put it, *The Beggar's Opera* 'exists in the comic mode . . . the satire, extensive and important as it is, alert as we

[7] Victor, *History of the Theatres of London and Dublin*, II: 154.

should be to its nuances, is throughout and finally encompassed by the values of comedy'.[8]

The comedy derives essentially from an inversion, and reinversion, of values – what Nietzsche termed 'transvaluation of values'. A criminal society is depicted, whose members however speak and act like aristocrats. If criminals resemble aristocrats, we are invited to ponder, then do aristocrats resemble criminals? The answer of course is yes. As the Beggar observes in his final speech, there is 'such a similitude of Manners in high and low Life, that it is difficult to determine whether (in the fashionable Vices) the fine Gentlemen imitate the Gentlemen of the Road, or the Gentlemen of the Road the fine Gentlemen' (3.16.19–22).

Throughout, Gay is careful to cast the dialogue in standard English; he elects not to attempt dialect or, with few exceptions, to employ criminal argot other than in the choice of names: Filch, Nimming Ned, Mrs Slammekin and so on. These are all accurately chosen: to nim is to steal, and a slammekin is 'a female sloven'. Filch, the apprentice pickpocket, is sent by Peachum to let their colleagues in jail know what is planned:

> FILCH: When a Gentleman is long kept in suspence, Penitence may break his Spirit ever after. Besides, Certainty gives a Man a good Air upon his Tryal, and makes him risque another without Fear or Scruple.
>
> (1.2.42–5)

Samuel Johnson could not have expressed the thought more elegantly, though he certainly would not have approved of the sentiment.

The transvaluation lends itself both to artistic and literary burlesque and to topical satire. The *Opera*, it goes almost without saying, burlesques conventions of opera as it was being performed at the time: the paired heroines; the happy ending; even, as the Beggar observes, the similes 'that are all in your celebrated Operas: The Swallow, the Moth, the Bee, the Ship, the Flower, &c.' They are all here: Polly in Act 2 sings of her plight, 'Thus when the Swallow, seeking Prey'. Lucy in Act 3 intones, 'I'm like a Skiff on the Ocean tost'. And so on, or as the Beggar put it, '&c.'

And so with topical, especially political, satire. A quest for political satire has preoccupied scholars for two and a half centuries and has certainly influenced the teaching of the *Opera*. Puzzled students all over the globe are informed that it is 'a satire on Sir Robert Walpole'. A moment's reflection will, however, convince one that George Washington would not have paid out good colonial

---

[8] Noble, '*The Beggar's Opera* in its own time', 12.

currency in 1761 to see a satire on the first minister of England, who had been dead for fifteen years. The *Opera* of course satirizes, among others, self-important politicians in any age. At the time of its opening there were many who thought, or were taught to think, that this particular shoe fitted Walpole. But both artistic burlesque and topical satire are enlisted in the cause of comedy.

Comedy, satire and burlesque are reinforced by Gay's lyric skills and by his adroit reuse of tunes that would have been familiar to his audiences. The Act I curtain song, for example, Macheath and Polly's duet of parting, is in the ballad stanza and is sung to a broadside ballad tune, 'The Broom', of enormous popularity (Johann Christian Bach and Haydn each later adapted it):

MACHEATH: The Miser thus a Shilling sees,
    Which he's oblig'd to pay,
   With Sighs resigns it by degrees,
    And fears 'tis gone for aye.
POLLY: The Boy, thus, when his Sparrow's flown,
    The Bird in Silence eyes;
   But soon as out of Sight 'tis gone,
    Whines, whimpers, sobs and cries.

                (1.13.70–7)

'The Broom' presents the lament of a milkmaid who has been betrayed by her lover, and so the tune would have an appropriate resonance in its own right for Polly, whose betrayal by Macheath is thus musically foreshadowed. This is the first-act curtain that did not gain applause on opening night: the bittersweet love duet is anything but a show-stopper.

Gay, however, once through that opening night, could sit back and watch money roll through the till. He had the usual author's benefit on the third, sixth and ninth nights, and on the fifteenth night – that is, the gross receipts less the house charge. By that fifteenth performance, 15 February, he had presumably worked out a different arrangement with Rich because he wrote Swift that 'I think I shall make an addition to my fortune of between six and seven hundred pounds', with the expectation that it would run another fortnight. Indeed, it ran through the end of the season in June. John Watts, the leading publisher of dramatic authors, began turning out editions of the *Opera* on 14 February, with the music added on copperplate engravings. There is no record of how much Gay was paid by Watts for the copyright, but Gay was in a position to bargain. It seems quite safe to assert that Gay made more from admissions and copyright than had any other dramatic author, at least in the English-speaking world, to that time.

The interjection of opposition politics just at this juncture simply provided more money for Gay, though in the long run it also stirred up trouble for him with the censors. It is not clear what part if any Gay played in the controversy over the *Opera*'s political content. The *Craftsman*, after its initial good-humoured comment about Rich and Gay on 3 February, waited until the opera was well established to publish on 17 February the richly ironic letter by 'Phil. Harmonicus' to the editor, 'Caleb D'Anvers'. 'Harmonicus' identifies *The Beggar's Opera* as 'the most venemous [*sic*] allegorical Libel against the G[overnmen]t that hath appeared for many Years past'. 'Harmonicus' demonstrates how to read the *Opera* for innuendo, of which he finds plenty.

In Ireland that spring, Swift was nudging the readers of the *Dublin Intelligencer* in the same direction, but by a different strategy. After a discussion of recent attacks on the morality of the *Opera*, Swift in his inimitable backhanded manner focuses attention on the transvaluation of values dramatized in the work:

> This Comedy contains likewise a Satyr, which without enquiring whether it affects the present Age, may possibly be useful in Times to come. I mean, where the Author takes the Occasion of comparing those common Robbers of the Publick, and their several Stratagems of betraying, undermining and hanging each other, to the several Arts of Politicians in Times of Corruption.[9]

Times of Corruption. Not these times, not the present Age, of course. It is the rhetorical device of praeteritio, saying by affecting not to say, one of Swift's favoured techniques. By the summer of 1728, then, the opposition press was using the *Opera* as one of its sticks with which to beat Walpole and his ministry. Although the charge is of dubious accuracy – there is no political allegory and not much topical political satire in the *Opera* – it was great box office. Everyone needed to go to LIF to judge for themselves.

London in 1728 was the place to be, in the theatre: the magnet. By far the largest city in the English-speaking world, it was also the most populous city of Europe. To many it was the Great Wen, sucking the life from the countryside like a cancer and poisoning earth and atmosphere. To others – to John Gay, Benjamin Franklin, Henry Fielding – London in the 1720s was the school, the place to learn. Either view could be easily and amply supported. Fielding

---

[9] Swift, *Irish Tracts, 1728–1733*, 36.

occupied his remaining years documenting the double view of London in his art – plays and novels – and in his life, as a working magistrate enforcing the laws. *The Beggar's Opera* is precisely located in the London of the 1720s, as the names of the characters remind us: Peachum, one who 'peaches'; Macheath, 'son of the heath', that is, a highwayman. But it is also, of course, a musical fantasy, a love story. London in the *Opera* is both villain and hero: will it all end with a hanging or a dance?

Everyone associated with the performances at LIF in 1728 was benefiting, some more than others. Vendors in the street and in the shops were soon selling mezzotint engravings of the stars, Lavinia Fenton as Polly and Thomas Walker as Macheath. Gay sent Swift, at Swift's request, a pair of these predecessors of publicity shots. The star system was developing. William Hogarth, a friend of John Rich, did a series of paintings that 'would inaugurate [Hogarth's] career as a painter'.[10] The paintings depict actors in the cast and also identifiable members of the audience, including Gay himself. To what extent the paintings represent realistic views of the LIF set continues to be a matter of lively debate among scholars, but one detail is without doubt realistic: the audience on stage. In an effort to squeeze every penny out of the performances that continued to sell out, night after night, Rich shoehorned audiences into every cranny, compressing, for example, an astounding ninety-eight spectators onto the stage for the performance of 23 March. Audiences had of course been on stage since Restoration times, but playing to some ninety-eight customers, many of them, doubtless, tipsy, must have provided special challenges for the cast.

One noble spectator was the Duke of Bolton, who attended a performance on 8 April when Gay also had a box seat there. The duke came to the next two performances and brought his duchess to the *Opera* on Saturday, 13 May. On 22 June the *Craftsman* reported: 'To the great Surprize of the Audience, the Part of Polly Peachum was performed by Miss WARREN, who was very much applauded; the first Performer being retired, as it is reported, from the Stage.' Retired indeed! 'The D[uke] of Bolton', Gay informed Swift, 'I hear hath run away with Polly Peachum, having settled £400 a year upon her during pleasure, & upon disagreement £200 a year.'[11] Lavinia Fenton, the superstar, had struck noble paydirt: eventually the widowed duke would make her his duchess. Lavinia, Duchess of Bolton. With Miss Warren, another star was born.

[10] Paulson, *Hogarth*, 180–2.
[11] Gay, *Letters*, 76.

The star system, evolving earlier with such performers as Robert Wilks, Barton Booth and Anne Oldfield, effectively came of age with the ascent, by virtue of her abilities, of Lavinia Fenton from entr'acte dancer to the nobility. Though the ducal union shocked and exasperated the aristocracy, there was nothing they could do about such levelling, and in the next generation David Garrick – actor, dramatist and manager – moved easily among his aristocratic friends in the Club and in society at large.

The Beggar's Opera may have made Gay rich and Rich gay, but it also strengthened the entire London stage, directly by giving sustained employment to the LIF actors and musicians, and indirectly by leading audiences to other theatrical venues and by adding to the number of those venues. The dominance of the two patent companies, at least temporarily, was being chipped away. For example, on the long weekend of Thursday through Monday (theatres were dark on Sundays), 7–11 March 1728, Londoners seeking entertainment would find Drury Lane offering Vanbrugh's *The Relapse* against LIF's *Opera* on Thursday (eighty paid spectators on the stage clogging business). Friday saw a pantomime called *The Rivals* at the Little Haymarket, and a concert at Sir Richard Steele's Great Room in York Buildings. On Saturday, Drury Lane ran a revival of Jonson's *The Alchemist* against the première of a comedy by James Carlisle at LIF, *The Fortune Hunters*, with Lavinia Fenton in the ingenue part of Nanny. Rich thus elected to interrupt the consecutive performances of the *Opera* with this new production. Its take was roughly two-thirds of what the *Opera* had been grossing, night after night. That same Saturday a performance of Handel's *Siroe* was offered at the King's, with the royal family in attendance. On Monday it was John Banks's tragic perennial, *The Unhappy Favourite*, at Drury Lane and back to the *Opera* at LIF, on the orders of John Rich, who could count. A total of seven different entertainments on three playing days. These were busy nights in the London theatre, more or less directly attributable to the *Opera*. Companies performing at the Little Haymarket were beginning to be commercially competitive with the patent companies.

One of the additional benefits of the London stage's new look was the increased opportunity for dramatists to see their works performed. Who could tell who might have another *Beggar's Opera* in his portfolio? Fielding, as we have seen, missed on his first attempt but would be back with more offerings. The Cooke–Mottley ballad opera *Penelope*, as also noted, did not succeed: perhaps it appeared too soon, during the *Opera*'s original run. The *Penelope* cast was competing, however: for the fourth, and as it turned out final, performance entr'acte dancing was advertised, as was 'an entire New Scene and several Songs'.

On 14 May of the following year, 1729, W. R. Chetwood, sometime prompter at Drury Lane, saw produced there as an afterpiece his one-acter *The Lover's Opera*, 'with above 40 Airs, made to Old Ballad Tunes and Country Dances'. Chetwood's attempt was decisively countered at the Little Haymarket by the première of Charles Coffey's *The Beggar's Wedding* on 29 May 1729. Coffey, a veteran of the Smock Alley Theatre in Dublin, had noted carefully what Gay did in *The Beggar's Opera* and attempted to reproduce the effect, using, as the newspaper advertisement had it, a 'Variety of English, Scotch, and Irish Ballads'. LIF was closing for the season and Coffey's ballad opera muscled on to the scene, running twice in May after the première, then had eighteen performances in June, ten in July, and four in August, when it was alternating at the Haymarket with a revival, already noted, of *The Beggar's Opera*. There was a production of *The Beggar's Wedding* at Southwark Fair in September. The genre of the ballad opera was on its way to a brief flowering in the wake of *The Beggar's Opera*'s success. The Cooke–Mottley *Penelope* and Coffey's work have already been noted. Coffey and Mottley collaborated to produce *The Devil to Pay* in 1730, which as an afterpiece had a long life on the London stage and which, translated to the Continent, became an early entrant in the genre of *Singspiel* and an ancestor, therefore, of *The Magic Flute*.[12] Henry Fielding, eager to make his way on the London stage, wrote and saw produced in 1731 *The Welsh Opera*, an audacious satire on the unhappy royal family, whose Welsh dialect is intended to remind the knowing public of the Hanoverians' awkwardness in spoken English.

There is evidence that Gay himself had a sequel in mind even when he was writing the *Opera*: in Act 3 Macheath, facing execution, advises Polly and Lucy to 'ship yourselves off for the West-Indies, where you'll have a fair chance of getting a Husband' (3.15.4). The West Indies becomes the setting for his next production, another ballad opera, *Polly*. But by 1729 Gay had become totally identified with Pope, Swift and the opposition to Walpole's government, by virtue of the brouhaha raised by the *Craftsman* in London and Swift's *Intelligencer* in Ireland. Although the *Opera* did not include much specific political satire, enough was made of what there was to insure that Gay's next production would enjoy the careful scrutiny of the ministry. One

---

[12] Noble, 'Charles Coffey and John Mottley: an odd couple in Grub Street', unpublished article graciously communicated to me by the author. It sets forth in greater detail information in articles by Noble on the two authors in the *Oxford Dictionary of National Biography*, forthcoming.

of the government hacks, Giles Jacob, attacked the *Opera* on moral grounds as a 'low and licentious dramatical Piece, design'd for the Encouragement of Gentlemen on the Highway, and their female Assistants [i.e., whores] in Drury-Lane'.[13] The government had good reason to suppose that Gay's next play would contain at least as much political satire as the *Opera*, if not more, and they possessed retaliatory powers they had not yet used.

Gay later asserted that he and Rich had agreed on terms for the production of *Polly* and that it was ready for rehearsal when the Lord Chamberlain, the Duke of Grafton, sent an order prohibiting rehearsal until the script had been examined. The Lord Chamberlain's office in theory retained the powers to regulate the theatre companies under the royal patent, but in practice had exercised those powers sparingly. Gay presented a copy of *Polly* to Grafton on 7 December 1728 and was told to await the judgement.

No one knows whether Grafton acted on his own initiative or whether Walpole ordered suppression himself; at any rate, Gay received the news on 12 December that his ballad opera would not be performed. (It did not see the stage until 1777, and then in altered form.) The opposition press gleefully used the suppression as an example of Walpole's tyrannical predispositions. Because of the commotion Gay stood to profit from the sales of the printed play: he decided to retain the copyright himself and have the play printed at his own expense. He ordered a huge printing, 10,500 copies, perhaps ten times the usual press run for a new play.

In spite of pirating by rival booksellers, Gay realized a large profit on his second ballad opera – but, from the point of view of the health of the British drama, at a high price. Pre-performance censorship, always a theoretical possibility, would soon become a practical reality. In the Licensing Act of 1737 this form of censorship was given statutory authority, which it possessed for more than two centuries. Even more serious than formal, statutory censorship was the resultant self-censorship which rendered theatre managers and authors increasingly timid. This was especially the case with anything judged to be morally dubious, and *The Beggar's Opera* had suffered from that allegation from the beginning: it was, after all, about the worst sort of people! In March 1728, Dr Thomas Herring, the chaplain at Lincoln's Inn and later Archbishop of Canterbury, preached a sermon criticizing the morality of the *Opera*, contending that the favourable presentation of criminals in the work would encourage crime. Daniel Defoe echoed this in a pamphlet: 'Every idle Fellow, weary of honest Labour, need but fancy himself a Macheath or Sheppard and there's

---

[13] Letter to John Dennis, in *Critical Works of John Dennis*, II: 373.

a Rogue made at once.'[14] Preposterous as they may seem, these allegations were taken seriously enough for Samuel Johnson to feel compelled to refute them in his 'Life of Gay' in the *Lives of the Poets*.

The *Opera*'s association with immorality perhaps damaged its popularity for a long time but, paradoxically, probably helped it in the disillusioned twentieth century. It is significant that the first great revival of modern times took place, appropriately, in London, shortly after the end of the First World War, which had transvalued many values. This production, directed by Nigel Playfair, with music by Frederick Austin, opened at the Lyric, Hammersmith, on 5 June 1920 and played for more than three years and 1,468 performances, another record run for the *Opera*. The role of Polly Peachum was performed by Angela Baddeley, known to television audiences fifty years later as Mrs Bridges, the faithful cook in *Upstairs Downstairs*. Playfair's production became a kind of benchmark in the London theatre world and, critics have argued, influenced British productions on stage and screen for decades.

It has been, however, Bertolt Brecht and Elisabeth Hauptmann's variant, *Die Dreigroschenoper* (*The Threepenny Opera*), with score by Kurt Weill, which has attracted most critical attention, no doubt because of the fame of its co-author Brecht and the sheer quality of its music. Although on the face of the matter discussion of *Die Dreigroschenoper* would seem to be part of the history of the German theatre – produced in Berlin as it was in 1928, during the Weimar Republic, with the Nazis, who detested it, figuratively waiting in the wings – in point of fact the work stems from the British theatre, beginning as a variant of Gay's *Opera* and returning to that theatre by the later production in New York and London of *The Threepenny Opera* in English. It represents an important event in the internationalization of theatre. The collaborators knew precisely what they were about: Brecht and Hauptmann worked from a translation of Gay's *Opera* which Hauptmann had prepared the previous year. They borrowed here and there as Gay had, adding songs based on Kipling's ballads and those of Villon, both poets admired by Brecht. Some of Gay's characters they eliminated, including Lockit and Mrs Coaxer, but others they retained: the two principal women, Lucy and Polly, Macheath as Mackie Messer (Mack the Knife), and most notably Jenny. Jenny was created by Lotte Lenya, Weill's wife, and her role is given increased importance, as it is in all of the twentieth-century variants of the *Opera*. Weill, who had done pioneering work in atonal music, realized the dimensions of his assignment here: 'The return to a primitive operatic form entailed a drastic simplification of musical language.

[14] *Second Thoughts are Best* (1729), quoted in Backscheider, *Defoe his Life*, 518.

It meant writing a kind of music that would be singable by actors, in other words by musical amateurs.'[15] This, as we have seen, had originally been Gay's insight as well.

Brecht and Hauptmann set *Die Dreigroschenoper* in Victorian rather than eighteenth-century London and made some effort to update it, adding for example a Scotland Yard sheriff named Tiger Brown to replace the character of Lockit. Peachum, exploiter of the London beggars, is portrayed as a religious hypocrite, given to quoting the Bible and plastering Christian quotations on the walls of his shop. As his name implies, Mack the Knife is intended to be a more threatening character than Gay's Macheath. The opening 'Ballad of Mack the Knife', added late almost as an afterthought, sets the general, cynical tone of the opera right up to the curtain scene, in which Macheath is pardoned from hanging and elevated, with a pension, to the hereditary peerage at Queen Victoria's command. Peachum comments: 'Which all means that injustice should be spared from persecution' (169).

The imagery of some of the songs, references to mutilated beggars and poverty, brings the focus back to Weimar Germany, where many of the mutilated beggars on the streets were in fact veteran soldiers from the First World War. The finale of Act 2 contains perhaps the most famous aphorism Brecht, or Brecht and Hauptmann, ever wrote: 'Erst kommt das Fressen, dann kommt die Moral', 'Food is the first thing. Morals follow on', or as it is in the Blitzstein adaptation of 1954, 'First feed the face; and then talk right and wrong.'[16]

As with Gay's *Opera*, the opening of the Brecht–Hauptmann–Weill production was attended by nervousness and uncertainty. And like its predecessor two centuries earlier, the 1928 Berlin audience withheld its applause at first, until the bitter, anti-war 'Cannon Song' in the second scene of Act 1. Then, as Brecht's recent editors note, 'the applause suddenly burst loose. Quite unexpectedly . . . management and collaborators found themselves with the greatest German hit of the 1920s on their hands' (xx).

Marc Blitzstein's adaptation, for the 1954 Off-Broadway production at the Theatre de Lys on Christopher Street, followed the original quite closely, except for some self-evident corrections. These include assigning Pirate Jenny's song to Jenny, memorably played by Lotte Lenya as in the original production, where the song had unaccountably been given to Polly. The imagery of the songs

---

[15] Quoted in Brecht, *Collected Plays: Two*, 319. Page references to the edition are cited parenthetically in the text. Much of my information on the German production is derived from this edition and from Fuegi, *Brecht and Company*.

[16] Brecht, 145. References to the Blitzstein *Threepenny Opera* are to the copyright copy of the libretto in the Library of Congress, shelfmark ML50/.W42D82/1954/Cage.

is noticeably lightened: the grainy 'Cannon Song' becomes a good-humoured 'Army Song', more in the spirit of Yip Yip Yaphank ('Let's all go barmy, live off the Army'). Still, the adaptation overall has an astringent tone, exemplified by Weill's 'Ballad of Mack the Knife'. Blitzstein uses this throughout as a *leitmotif*, to lyrics by the Street Singer, a character he has added. The curtain chorus, to this tune, is in the spirit of John Gay's original:

> Happy ending, nic[e] and tidy[,]
>> It's a rule I learned in school.
> Get your money every Friday,
>> Happy endings are the rule.
>
> So divide up those in darkness
>> From the ones who walk in light,
> Light 'em up, boys, there's your picture[,]
>> Drop the shadows out of sight.[17]

The removal of Lockit in both the German and English versions somewhat reduces the dramatic symbolism of official, as distinguished from individual, criminality. For interesting reasons the authors of both the other two twentieth-century variants on Gay's piece chose to retain the infamous jailer.

Vaclav Havel's *Beggar's Opera*, which had only one original performance, in Prague in 1975, before the secret police forbade a further, had its British première at the Orange Tree Theatre, Richmond, Surrey, in 2003, based on a translation by Paul Wilson.[18] Although set in eighteenth-century London, the *Opera* is transparently an allegory of life in Czechoslovakia under the repressive régime that followed the Soviet incursion there in 1968. In the allegory, Lockit, Chief of Police, has an enhanced role as representative of 'official' corruption, whereas Peachum is depicted as an 'unofficial' racketeer. In the final scene it is Lockit who induces Macheath to sign an agreement to become a police informer in return for personal safety; Filch, given the same choice, has elected execution and gone to his death crying 'Long live London's underworld'. Although a product of the Cold War, Havel's fine version of the *Opera* deserves further study and production as one of those dramas of the twentieth century, such as Arthur Miller's *The Crucible*, which deal with fidelity and betrayal, with repression and exploitation. As Filch's speech illustrates, it also utilizes precisely the transvaluation of values initially seen in Gay's original. In Havel's

---

[17] Copyright copy, Library of Congress. My emendations are in square brackets.
[18] Havel, *The Beggar's Opera*, trans. Wilson. For a fuller discussion, see Winton, 'Gay's *Beggar's Opera* and Vaclav Havel's'.

bleak depiction, the underworld is the only segment of society worthy of long life.

Havel wrote within the shadows, metaphorically speaking, of the political prison to which he would ultimately be condemned. The composer of the last twentieth-century variant to be considered here, Edward Kennedy 'Duke' Ellington, had to deal with shadows of his own. In the 1940s Ellington was attempting to alter his public image as only a Cotton Club performer, by making recordings and film appearances. The Cotton Club was one of those odd institutions which Americans today would prefer to forget: a Harlem nightclub owned and managed by white males from the underworld, entirely staffed by African-Americans – cooks, waiters, instrumentalists and singers – for the entertainment of a bejewelled, lily-white society audience. When Ellington undertook to compose a musical for Broadway he was, then, quite consciously, as his biographer observes, 'stretching himself beyond his "safe" boundaries'.[19]

Ellington demonstrated his prescience by selecting as his librettist John Treville Latouche, not yet 30 years old in 1946. Ten years later, at his death, Latouche was writing lyrics for *Candide* and had completed work on the libretto for Douglas Moore's *Ballad of Baby Doe*, which has become one of the most frequently performed modern operas in the repertory.

Latouche justified Ellington's confidence by presenting him with a well-constructed, and very funny, musical, entitled in its first version *Beggar's Opera* but finally *Beggar's Holiday*.[20] Latouche follows the general plot of Gay's *Opera* fairly closely, but sets the action in a city in the eastern United States, time contemporary, that is, immediate post-World War Two.

Hamilton Peachum, described as 'the crookedest ward-heeler who ever stuffed a ballot box', is the doting father of Polly, a sub-deb – a term from *Life* magazine exactly contemporaneous with the production. Peachum, played by the great comedian Zero Mostel, and Lockit, the Chief of Police, are white-collar criminals who plot to frame Macheath because the District Attorney needs a conviction before Election Day. Macheath was created by Alfred Drake, still enjoying acclaim for his triumphant run in *Oklahoma*. The virginal Polly and Lucy are contrasted, as in Gay's *Opera*, with Jenny, the prostitute with the heart of gold, who is given an important part and a swinging song in the first act: 'Take Love Easy'. Latouche introduces more dancing than had Gay, drawing on New York's bountiful supply of professional dancers (cf. *A Chorus*

---

[19] Hasse, *Beyond Category*, 292.
[20] Materials are scattered, because of the nature of their classification, in the Duke Ellington Collection, series 4, Scripts and Transcripts, Smithsonian Archives, Washington, DC.

Line) and Ellington's apparently unending melodic imagination. Macheath's fellow-prisoners, for example, form a conga line in Newgate just before his escape, to some peppy Ellington Latino sound.

Cast and stage crew were entirely desegregated; this seems to have been a Broadway first, presumably at Ellington's insistence, though there is no documentation to prove it. An African-American couple was added to the libretto and given important numbers: the legendary Harlem dancer Avon Long as Careless Love and Marie Bryant as his consort, the Cocoa Girl. Cocoa's song, 'On the Wrong Side of the Railroad Tracks', highlights the economic and social satire of *Holiday*: the rich men sneak away from their suburban wives to enjoy the company of women like Jenny and Cocoa on 'the wrong side', 'where the plumbing never plumbs / And the children shout'.[21] One of the most interesting borrowings is Lucy's song, a lament for her lost love. 'Brown Penny' is a poem by W. B. Yeats, one of his beggar poems, and Ellington and his musical alter ego Billy Strayhorn have provided it a memorable setting.

With a fine book by Latouche, the Ellington–Strayhorn score, and players like Drake, Mostel and Long, how could this production fail? And yet it did not succeed, disappointing its backers by closing after fourteen weeks. Competition could have been part of the problem: *Holiday* opened in a particularly strong Broadway season. Beyond this, the desegregated cast may have been too strong for audiences which expected racial separation.

At the least, however, *Beggar's Holiday* joins the other twentieth-century versions of *The Beggar's Opera* as testimony to the continuing intellectual and dramatic vitality of the work which in 1728 made 'Gay rich and Rich gay'. The drama's patrons have ensured the *Opera* its place in the history of the British theatre.

---

[21] Ellington Collection, series 4, box 3, folder 4. This is apparently Latouche's original typescript. For important new information, see Dugaw, *Deep Play*.

7

Garrick at Drury Lane, 1747–1776

MARK S. AUBURN

A shortlist of European plays before Ibsen and Shaw still regularly revived today by amateurs and professionals would include many of the works of Shakespeare, a number by Molière, one or two each by Racine, Wycherley, Congreve and Farquhar, and four other plays first produced in the eighteenth century: Gay's *The Beggar's Opera* (1728), Goldsmith's *She Stoops to Conquer* (1773), and Sheridan's *The Rivals* (1775) and *The School for Scandal* (1777). The greatest actor of the eighteenth century, the most pictured man in Europe in his time, arguably created the conditions whereby Shakespeare's works entered today's repertoire and Goldsmith and Sheridan conceived their three contributions.

David Garrick (1717–79) arrived in London from his native Lichfield in spring 1737 in the company of his teacher and lifelong friend, Dr Samuel Johnson (1709–84). Garrick registered as a law student at Lincoln's Inn Fields and soon was assisting his older brother Peter in the wine brokering business of their Huguenot forebears. But he also pursued his interest in theatre, begun even before his first remembered appearance as Sergeant Kite in Farquhar's *The Recruiting Officer* at age 12, on the grounds of the cathedral near where his family lived. It was one thing to perform in amateur theatricals as a boy, quite another to consider a trade like acting, so less genteel than the law or vintnery, a trade whose practitioners were still legally defined – like their Elizabethan predecessors – as vagabonds and sturdy beggars. Garrick only gingerly and gradually discussed his ambition in letters to his older brother. In London, he gained the notice of Henry Giffard, the manager of Goodman's Fields Theatre, which competed with Drury Lane and Covent Garden – the only two theatres in London since the Licensing Act of 1737 which could perform plays for paying customers – by the ruse of charging patrons for concerts during which free 'rehearsals' of plays might occur. For Giffard, Garrick acted under a billing as a 'young gentleman' in spring 1741 and at Ipswich that summer and then, on

Plate 12. David Garrick as Richard III awakening from his dream, before the Battle of Bosworth Field. Painted by William Hogarth, 1745.

19 October 1741, as Shakespeare's Richard III, this time billed as 'a Gentleman (*who has never appear'd on any Stage*)'.

The reception to Garrick's hunchback proved unprecedented, and crowds at Drury Lane and Covent Garden dwindled that autumn as patrons went to the more remote Goodman's Fields venue in Whitechapel to see Garrick perform. The actress Hannah Pritchard told him that 'You did more at your first appearing than ever anybody did with twenty years' practise'. Alexander Pope remarked, 'That young man never had his equal, and he never will have a rival'. Later, his contemporary, Tom Davies, wrote that Garrick was 'a theatrical Newton; he threw new light on elocution and action'. The playwright Richard Cumberland remembered about his first view of Garrick the actor (14 December 1746) that 'It seemed as if a whole century had been stepped over in the transition of a single scene'. Garrick exercised a sympathetic imagination in developing a fully rounded character in Richard III, a villain who was cool, calculating and hypocritical but also possessed of conscience, who showed hope overlaying guilt, who seemed lonely in his wretchedness: a particularized bloody king rather than a generalized, universal villain. And Garrick had not just introduced a new version of a favourite role by so doing; he had begun the process of creating a new way of acting.

Garrick's revolution in acting

According to the acting theory of Garrick's day, a performer seeks to transmit passions – such as joy, grief and anger, fear, pity and scorn, jealousy, hatred, wonder and love – to an auditor. In any time or place, the successful transmission depends not just upon the elements of dramatic occasion but also upon the expectations of the auditor. Between actor and auditor arise conventions as to what actions or behaviours should transmit, say, grief. Mourners wear black clothes. Mourners in the first throes of grief draw the head back and upward, avert their eyes from the object of grief, throw the right-hand palm outward upon the forehead, and howl or audibly stifle their howls. In other times and climes, the colour white may as easily symbolize death; a bowed head, staring eyes, silence and wringing of the hands, grief. We think natural in acting and other behaviour what is in fact conventional to our times and cultures.

To auditors of 1741, the conventions of rhetorical acting seemed natural. Specific and expected patterns of gesture conveyed each particular passion; declamation, enunciation, tonal range and changes signalled the desired effect, so that a spoken drama might encompass the frequent shifts of presentation which differentiate aria from recitative in grand opera. Commentators on Garrick's performances shared the conventional expectations of their times, and so when they admired Garrick's 'turns', his perceived ability to convey in a dramatic moment a range of particularized emotions, they were seeing a rhetorical demonstration of movement from one passion to another, a rapid series of changes from joy or grief to pity or fear or scorn, rather than the complex mixture of passions that animates most great dramatic characters. They saw a new perfection of a time-worn style rather than a new conception of means towards an end.

Garrick certainly knew the conventional rhetorical style of acting.[1] But he broke with the received traditions by focusing a sympathetic imagination upon characters as parts of whole dramas and as embodiments of behaviours observable in real life. Before Garrick and even during his years, actors of the old school were content to play their parts in isolation from other actors.

---

[1] See Stone and Kahrl, *Garrick*, especially 30–7, for discussion of acting theory from Cicero and Quintilian to Garrick's day.

Coming forward on stage without regard to on-going dialogue, addressing the audience directly, assuming postures and gestures and stentorian tones unlikely in conversation and ignoring near simultaneous or subsequent action by other players were behaviours so common as to go unreported in criticism at the beginning of the Garrick era; but they came to seem old-fashioned objects of disdain later in his career. Garrick's perception of characters as parts of whole dramas (and hence presented in concert with all other characters) led to an emphasis upon ensemble acting. One observer of Garrick in *Macbeth* at Drury Lane singled out for praise the theatre's weakest actors. At the banquet when the ghost of Banquo appears, their reactions were startlingly natural and, in the opinion of the critic, must have resulted from the effect of the great Garrick's passionate portrayal of Macbeth upon his lesser fellow-actors. This observer did not conceive that perhaps the lesser actors might have consciously performed their rapt and horrified attention on the new king, that it was as much their own art as the effect of Garrick's art upon them that resulted in the improved ensemble playing.

Once characters were conceived as constituents relating to other constituents in unique dramatic representations, it was no long reach for an actor of Garrick's sympathetic imagination to study the behaviour of particular human beings in life and to incorporate observed mannerisms into the representation of particular characters. Garrick himself was a great mimic, like his contemporaries Charles Macklin, Samuel Foote, Charles Bannister and Tate Wilkinson, but his mimicry went beyond the representation of specific individuals. Garrick's intense interest in the daily activities of persons from all walks of life was noted by his contemporaries: he studied shopkeepers to become tobacconist Abel Drugger in *The Alchemist* and menservants to create Sharp, the title character of his *The Lying Valet*. So, too, did his contemporaries remark the concentration he brought to creating his characters; peers were surprised by his preoccupation on days when he would perform and fellow-actors by his staying in character not just on stage but behind the scenes. The postures and tones of conventional rhetorical acting may have had their origins in observed human behaviour, but their practice began to seem remote as Garrick recreated the style and theory of acting through sympathetic imagination. When he was criticized by Theophilus Cibber for extravagant attitudes, twitches, jerks, hand gestures towards his breast or pockets or flourishes of his handkerchief, or for pausing in mid-sentence or neglecting the expected harmony of a noble sentiment by delivering it as a response, he was being faulted for not following the conventional rhetorical mode, for playing human behaviour as he saw it and enhanced it through his pantomimical ability.

In person, at 5 feet 4 inches, Garrick was somewhat below middle height, which is less a handicap for an actor than being greatly above middle stature. In musculature, he tended towards the dancer's long, flat strength more than the weightlifter's bulk. With age he became slightly paunchy but never corpulent, though he joked in a prologue after his return from a two-year Grand Tour in 1765 that he had become too fat to play romantic heroes. He was agile and fairly quick but more a wrestler than a gymnast, fit for dramatic roles rather than pantomimes. He studied dance, perhaps under the influence of his wife and life partner from 1749, Eva Marie Veigel, a dancer from Vienna; but his theatrical dancing was incidental. His eyes were dark and deeply set but sufficiently large and sparkling to catch and reflect the candle flames that illuminated his stage. His countenance was especially mobile; in a favourite parlour trick, he would entertain folks by standing behind a tall-backed chair so that only his head was visible, then silently use his facial muscles to display a suite of changing expressions running a wide emotional gamut. His vocal range was effective without being novel by itself; it could fill the 1,500-seat auditoriums of his day, even in a stage whisper, but it had neither the depths of *basso profundo* nor the heights of *contratenore*, and no one, least of all Garrick himself, pretended that he was a singer. It was personality and intelligence more than an extraordinary acting instrument, study and art and genius more than luck or occasion, that made him the greatest actor of his day.

Garrick's triumph as Richard III at age 24 permitted him to display at Goodman's Fields within the next month three other characters he had developed – Clodio in Colley Cibber's *Love Makes a Man*, Chamont in Otway's *The Orphan* and Jack Smatter in an adaptation of Richardson's *Pamela* – and within the season eight others, among them Bayes in Buckingham's *The Rehearsal* and Lear: young, old, tragic, comic, foppish, elegant. And he produced his farcical afterpiece (arguably his best comedy) *The Lying Valet* there. The previous spring at Goodman's Fields, the Irish actor Charles Macklin had introduced Shylock not as a universal villain but as a scheming and conniving man and father whose anger and grief at the loss of his daughter led him to seek revenge. That performance drew Pope's delighted praise, 'This is the Jew that Shakespeare drew!' Macklin's conception of character and his ideas about company development and ensemble acting impressed Garrick, and the influence of these ideas upon Garrick would be lifelong; Macklin's coaching for the part of Lear helped the young actor create a character three times his own age.

By the end of the season, Garrick had been hired by Drury Lane for £500 a year, the highest salary ever yet paid an actor and fully £200 more than he had privately imagined possible when he began to try to reconcile his family to his most important life choice. (An experienced actor capable of several dozen roles made between one and five pounds a week for thirty weeks, a leading actor somewhat more, and both journeymen and principals could expect to earn as much as their stated salary in their annual benefit nights in March or April.) He worked steadily at Drury Lane, with summer and winter trips to Dublin (his early patron, Giffard, had come from there), until in the 1746–7 season he went over to Covent Garden, his popularity and worth well established. Then came the tipping point in his career: with £12,000 of his own funds, in concert with James Lacy he purchased the letters patent for Drury Lane and became its manager beginning with the 1747–8 season. It was a conquest on which he had been working for several years. He would exercise his responsibilities as manager (and as most admired actor) there for nearly three decades, at last selling his share for £35,000 to Richard Brinsley Sheridan in 1776, by then London's most admired new playwright and not yet 26 years old.

Garrick's repertory

As manager of one of only two theatres in London licensed to present plays from September through May or to produce new plays at any time, Garrick had important responsibilities for people and for entertainment. Upwards of 12,000 Londoners a week came to the theatre, and hundreds of theatre workers and their families depended on ticket sales to support actors, dancers, singers; ticket collectors and property men; bill stickers and accountants; guards, scenemen, scene-painters and machinists; janitors of both genders; chief operating officers such as deputy acting managers, prompters, treasurers – all those who helped win the expenditure of perhaps one-quarter of the discretionary money spent for entertainment by London's 750,000 residents and its many visitors.

In Garrick's time a theatrical evening lasted for four to five hours and consisted of a five-act dramatic mainpiece or three-act musical followed by a two- or three-act farce, pantomime or burletta afterpiece, interspersed with prologues, epilogues and various entr'acte entertainments. The repertory presented by each of the two licensed winter houses consisted each year of fifty or so mainpieces cycled in and out of the regular offerings for 180 nights a year, accompanied by one of about twenty-five afterpieces. Of the mainpieces at Drury Lane, an average of sixteen were tragedies performed for about seventy nights in a season, thirty comedies (for one hundred nights a season) and four or five miscellaneous pieces such as ballad operas or history plays. Of Drury Lane's afterpieces, about one-third were pantomimes, two-fifths farces and the rest musicals and comedies. Those ratios held for most of Garrick's management. In those twenty-nine seasons, the top ten Drury Lane mainpieces were *Romeo and Juliet* (141 performances), *The Beggar's Opera* (128), *The Suspicious Husband* (127), *Hamlet* (114), *Much Ado About Nothing* (106), *Richard III* (100), *The Beaux' Stratagem* (97), *The Provok'd Wife* (97), *Cymbeline* (96) and *The Conscious Lovers* (93). Garrick appeared regularly as Romeo, Ranger, Hamlet, Benedick, Richard III, Archer and Sir John Brute, occasionally as Posthumus (twenty-three times), but not in Gay's ballad opera or Steele's sentimental comedy. The first four of the top ten afterpieces were pantomimes: Henry Woodward's *Queen Mab* (261), Woodward's *The Genii* (201), Garrick's *Harlequin's Invasion* (171) and Woodward's *Fortunatus* (156). Of the remaining, most were farces, with Edward Ravenscroft's *The Anatomist* (157), Garrick's *Lethe* (155), Garrick's Shakespeare pageant *The Jubilee* (152 in three years, with 90 in its first season, making it the longest continuous run of any play in the eighteenth century), Charles Coffey's *The Devil to Pay* (144), Isaac Bickerstaffe's burletta *The Padlock* (142) and James Townley's *High Life Below Stairs* (140) rounding out the list. Garrick walked on as Benedick in all 152 performances of *The Jubilee*, and he must have used his reputation to boost the box office for many of the performances of *Lethe*, since he appeared in five different roles: Lord Chalkstone (a new character in the 1757 version, 35 times), the Frenchman (10), the Poet (5), the Drunken Man (5) and a Fine Gentleman (3) (sometimes several parts in the same performance). For the most part, he did not act in afterpieces, Fribble (59) in his farce *Miss in Her Teens* being the exception.[2]

Since every night brought an afterpiece, comedy in some form appeared nearly every time the theatre was lit (except on Wednesdays and Fridays during Lent, when only oratorios were offered). Indeed, six of Garrick's ten most frequently performed mainpiece roles were of comic characters: Ranger (121), Benedick in the full version of *Much Ado About Nothing* (113), Sir John Brute (105), Archer (100), Bayes (91) and Kitely in *Every Man in His Humour* (81). The four major tragic roles were Hamlet (90), Lear (85), Richard III (83) and Lothario in *The Fair Penitent* (82). His next two most frequent roles were Abel Drugger in a cut-down version of *The Alchemist* (80) and Don Felix in Centlivre's comic intrigue *The Wonder* (70), the part he chose for his farewell to the stage on 10 June 1776. Of these twelve most frequently performed roles, only one was from a drama first produced during Garrick's own lifetime, Ranger in Benjamin Hoadley's *The Suspicious Husband*.

---

[2] Accounts of performances and Garrick's roles follow *The London Stage 1660–1800*, pt IV, *1747–1776*, ed. Stone, and Stone and Kahrl, *Garrick*.

Garrick's performing choices reflect the flavour and variety of the mainpiece repertory as a whole. In comedy, it was mostly a mixture of older plays from the early eighteenth century (Vanbrugh, Centlivre, Farquhar, Steele and Cibber) and the Elizabethan era (Shakespeare and Jonson, but Beaumont and Fletcher, too; *Rule a Wife and Have a Wife* was performed at both theatres, with Garrick as Leon for 35 performances at Drury Lane). In tragedy, it was predominantly Shakespeare, followed by Otway, Rowe and Congreve's *The Mourning Bride*. At Covent Garden, the top ten most popular mainpieces were *The Beggar's Opera* (255 performances from 1747 to 1776), *Romeo and Juliet* (188), Isaac Bickerstaffe's comic opera *Love in a Village* (183), *Richard III* (113), Centlivre's *The Busie Body* (111), Cibber's *The Provok'd Husband* (102), Milton's masque *Comus* (94), Bickerstaffe's comic opera *The Maid of the Mill* (94), *Jane Shore* (93) and *The Beaux' Stratagem* (87). The strength of Covent Garden's company, compared to Drury Lane's, lay in musical pieces and humours and intrigue comedies. Contemporaries saw Covent Garden as the home of 'low' comedy, Drury Lane of 'high' or 'genteel'.

Trends in Garrick's repertory: sentimentalism

Belief in the essential goodness of humankind, satisfaction in the benevolent actions of the fortunate towards the suffering and faith in a beneficent providence coexist in most eras with philosophical worldviews more bleakly materialistic or fatalistic, but the tide towards sentimentalism was waxing during Garrick's lifetime. Goldsmith tilted at no chimera when he propagandized in favour of his forthcoming new comedy in 'An Essay on the Theatre: or, a Comparison Between Laughing and Sentimental Comedy' (1772), since a dominant strain in the repertory (and especially in new 'genteel' comedies of the 1760s and 1770s) reflects a predilection for display of the virtues of private life and of the distresses rather than the faults of humankind, all resolved with a happy ending. Together, from 1747 through 1776, Drury Lane and Covent Garden offered 189 performances of *The Provok'd Husband*, Cibber's tale of Lord and Lady Townley's anxiety-producing marital misunderstanding, which is at last happily removed; 166 presentations of Steele's *The Conscious Lovers*, with its relief of 'pleasing anguish' and its 'joy too exquisite for laughter'; and 178 repetitions of *The Suspicious Husband*, woven of the same highly anxious plot and character complications and relieved by Garrick's display of a pale conscientious rake who seduces no one. Each of these had roughly the same number of performances that *The Beaux' Stratagem* managed at both houses (184) and slightly more than the 152 of *Every Man in His Humour*. It is hard to say if Farquhar's great laughing comedy, with its finessed crux about divorce, or Jonson's humours comedy came to be played with sentimental twists; but the evidence of some slight play-doctoring that Sheridan did to the Drury Lane version of *The Beggar's Opera* beginning 8 November 1777 suggests that even Gay's satiric work took on the softened patina of sentiment in later Georgian production.

If Garrick's audiences wanted pleasing anguish in their comedies, they also flocked to tragedies which dealt in the same currency but which banked on unfortunate conclusions. Six of the top ten tragedies at Drury Lane from 1747 through 1776 played for pathos rather than heroic, romantic or tragic downfall: *The Mourning Bride* (82), *The Orphan* (76), *The Fair Penitent* (72), *Venice Preserv'd* (64), Aaron Hill's translation of Voltaire's *Zara* (64) and *Jane Shore* (62). The most popular of Shakespeare's tragedies at both houses, *Romeo and Juliet*, must have been played for pathos. Garrick's version, which held the stage for a hundred years, follows Otway's redaction in omitting Romeo's love for Rosaline and having Juliet awaken before Romeo dies, and Garrick added sixty-two lines of his own before allowing Romeo to expire in Juliet's arms. Similarly, though Garrick restored much of *King Lear*, he retained the essence of Nahum Tate's 1681 adaptation, whose happy ending was standard well into the nineteenth century – the Fool eliminated from the story, Lear restored to his throne, Edgar and Cordelia marrying at the end. And while Garrick brought individualization (rival actor Spranger Barry 'was every inch a king, but Garrick was every inch King Lear' went a slogan of the day) to the part of the faulty monarch father stripped to bare essentials, his efforts pointed towards a recognition scene where love and understanding triumphed, just as they do in the world of sentimental comedy. Audiences loved this pathos, and even level-headed Dr Johnson could not bear to read Shakespeare's own, unfortunate ending for *King Lear*.

Trends in Garrick's repertory: Shakespeare

The rise of sentimentalism fairly characterizes the Garrick era, but so too does the recovery of Shakespeare, whose plays had been not so much lost as variously neglected, mined or adapted to transient tastes. In the prologue Dr Johnson wrote, at Garrick's request and with Garrick's discussion, for Garrick to speak on the opening night of his management, 15 September 1747, the very origin of the stage, the triumph of learning over barbarity, is attributed to Shakespeare in four heroic couplets. Speaking his own prologue at the opening of the 1750 season, and with the success of several Shakespeare revivals already behind him, Garrick calls for more when he declares 'Sacred to Shakespeare was this spot design'd'. Fully 20 per cent of the mainpieces at Drury Lane during his management were plays of Shakespeare. His versions of nine Shakespeare plays were published during his lifetime, and his twentieth-century editors found fit to reprint no fewer than twelve of Garrick's acting texts as examples worthy for future ages.[3]

Twenty-nine of Shakespeare's works had enjoyed revival or adaptation in the Restoration and early eighteenth century. Eleven were in the standard repertory when Garrick started out: a much-cut *Hamlet*; Tate's version of *King Lear*; Colley Cibber's arrangement of *Richard III* (Garrick's début performing text); Theobald's infrequently performed redaction of *Richard II*; *Julius Caesar*; *Henry VIII* (with masque-like emphasis on the procession); *Othello*; Davenant's *Macbeth*; Theophilus Cibber's Otway-based *Romeo and Juliet*; Shadwell's *Timon of Athens*; and the Dryden–Davenant–Shadwell opera of *The Tempest*.

By the end of his career, Garrick had touched, restored or improved current versions of at least twenty-two Shakespeare plays. Among them, his *Richard III* eventually produced a Cibber–Garrick acting script of about 2,050 lines that endured throughout the nineteenth century as the standard version. His famous Macbeth first walked the stage at Covent Garden on 7 January 1744, advertised as 'the Tragedy Reviv'd as Shakespeare Wrote it', though it followed Davenant. Garrick tried *Othello* at Drury Lane on 7 March 1745, acting the title role (three times) and later Iago (nine), with many small changes, notably restoration of Othello's jealous trance, but with not much success. His production of *Romeo and Juliet* with Spranger Barry and Susanna Cibber as the title characters on 29 November 1748 was the first ever at Drury Lane, and when Barry and Cibber crossed over to Covent Garden, Garrick took on Romeo himself (with George Anne Bellamy as Juliet) and made it one of his great tragic roles between 1750 and 1760. *Catherine and Petruchio*, his 1754 three-act, well-made farce based on *The Taming of the Shrew*, was the version by which most audiences knew the comedy for the rest of the century. He revived both an operatic (1755) and a full-length comic version (1763) of *A Midsummer Night's Dream*. Critics thought there was too much sheep-shearing in *Florizel and Perdita*, his three-act version of *The Winter's Tale* (1756), but it played well, occasionally paired with *Catherine and Petruchio* as an all-Shakespeare night. He revived *The Tempest* as opera unsuccessfully that same year, reverting to a dramatic form in 1757. Also in 1756, his version of Tate's rewriting of *King Lear*, noted by Drury Lane prompter Richard Cross in his diary for its 'Restorations

---

[3] See Garrick, *Plays of Garrick*, ed. Pedicord and Bergmann.

Plate 13. David Garrick standing with a bust of Shakespeare. Painted by Thomas Gainsborough, 1769.

from Shakespeare', reintroduced his most exhausting role. Despite an ambitious attempt to offer *Antony and Cleopatra* with himself as Antony for six performances beginning 3 January 1759, Dryden's *All for Love* remained the dramatic version of Plutarch's complicated story that endured into the next century. His Posthumus in *Cymbeline* (1761) represented not just revival but restoration. Even after his return to the stage in 1765 following the Grand Tour and his near death, when he vowed to take on no new roles, he produced in 1772 his controversial acting text of *Hamlet*, a part he had already played many times, in a version with no gravediggers, no Osric, no fencing match, no reported death of Ophelia and £3,426 in takings in his four remaining seasons. As actor and director, if not adapter or restorer, he brought *Much Ado About Nothing* to Drury Lane in 1749, after it had been played only eight times in London since the turn of the century, and he performed Benedick 113 times in the comedy (his most frequently performed Shakespearean character) and 152 times as a walk-on in *The Jubilee*. He was King Henry IV fifteen times in *2 Henry IV*, Hotspur six times in *1 Henry IV*, the Chorus five times in *Henry V*, Faulconbridge twelve times and the King nine in *King John*. In an age which saw the dawn of Shakespeare scholarship through the restoration and explication of his text, when poets such as Rowe and Pope and critics such as Johnson and Warburton devoted years to the study of Shakespeare's plays, when there were fifteen editors and fifty editions of Shakespeare's collected works from 1741 to 1779, the editor George Steevens paid what must be a scholar's most succinct compliment to Garrick's art as an actor in a letter of 27 December 1765: 'often when I have taken my pen in hand to try to illustrate a passage, I have thrown it down again with discontent when I remembered how able you were to clear that difficulty by a single look, or particular modulation of voice, which a long and laboured paraphrase was insufficient to explain half so well'.[4] And it was Garrick the manager who made Shakespeare the repertory's largest component.

Garrick and new plays

Garrick's contribution to lasting dramatic literature other than Shakespeare is important though indirect. Garrick produced 63 new mainpieces and 107 new afterpieces during his management, or an average of two new mainpieces and four new afterpieces a season. (At Covent Garden, only 51 new mainpieces and 47 new afterpieces appeared during this time.) Not one new play that Garrick

---

[4] Boaden, ed., *Private Correspondence of Garrick*, I: 217.

produced still regularly performs today, and only three produced during his lifetime still hold attention.

But Garrick worked hard to stimulate new drama. He received nearly ten scripts for every one he could produce, and so his rejections of 90 per cent of the supplicants earned him many more enemies than friends. It was, in fact, not a friendly time for new playwrights. The Licensing Act of 1737 reaffirmed exclusive rights to produce new plays to Drury Lane and Covent Garden; their fixed costs for wages and lighting militated against experimentation. Thus, playwrights had few outlets. The potential profit for a new writer who survived damnation was the receipt of the box office takings after expenses on the third, sixth and ninth nights (worth upwards of £300 to £600) and publication rights for £100 (plays outnumbered fiction ten to three in one 5,000-title circulating library catalogue of the time). In an age when a skilled craftsman earned about £1 a week, trying to write the one successful, produced play out of the ten submitted was not entirely a foolish enterprise, given the reward for even a nine-night wonder. Perhaps some great plays died aborning, for playwriting is so collaborative an art among writers, actors, directors and producers that one sees few lasting dramas from any period which did not have their origins in quality professional productions. But if there are great stillborn plays from England's eighteenth century, no one has yet discovered them.[5]

Probably, we could not expect tragedy from this age. Loyal, distracted maidens and wives and distressed mothers were more popular than conscience-pricked villains or rash, larger-than-life tragic heroes. Lady Randolph in Home's *Douglas*, Cleone in Dodsley's domestic tragedy of the same name and Mandane in Murphy's *The Orphan of China* were the new heroines. Garrick produced only one of these three new tragedies, for he rejected Home's popular play, which achieved great success when produced at Edinburgh and subsequently at Covent Garden, and he rejected Dodsley's. His lavish production of Johnson's *Irene*, a classical treatment of the distressed heroine motif, proved short-lived.

Perhaps more could have been expected from Thalia. Garrick was present for the conception or assisted the Comic Muse at the birth of a dozen or more good new full-length comedies. In three he created roles (all before 1763, when he ceased to add to his acting repertoire): Arthur Murphy's *The Way to Keep Him* (Garrick as Lovemore; 17 times); the elder George Colman's *The Jealous Wife* (Oakly; 35); and Frances Sheridan's *The Discovery* (Sir Anthony Branville; 23).

---

[5] For my discussion of new plays, and for many other matters, I am indebted to the single best narrative on Garrick's theatre, Price, *Theatre in the Age of Garrick*.

Plate 14. David Garrick and Hannah Pritchard as Ranger and Clarinda in Benjamin Hoadly's *The Suspicious Husband* (1747). Painted by Francis Hayman, 1747.

He was co-author with Colman of *The Clandestine Marriage*, which appeared for 120 performances in the fourteen seasons after its opening in 1766. He invested heavily in Hugh Kelly, producing his *False Delicacy* (1768), *A Word to the Wise* (1770) and *The School for Wives* (1773), and in Richard Cumberland, presenting *The West Indian* (1771), *The Fashionable Lover* (1772) and *The Choleric Man* (1774). Of these six comedies, only *The West Indian* became a hit.

None of these Garrick-produced comedies achieved success much beyond their generation, any more than did *The Suspicious Husband*, whose Ranger he played every season but three from 1747 until his retirement. Some of these comedies, such as *False Delicacy* and *The West Indian*, typify at least in part the objects of Goldsmith's attack in his 'Comparison between Laughing and Sentimental Comedy': their predominating anxiety-provoking plots dwell on the virtues and distresses of private life and provide comic characters and relief only incidentally. Still, most of these Drury Lane comedies maintain a laughing spirit and merit reading today, and perhaps *The Suspicious Husband* and *The Jealous Wife*, as well as *The Clandestine Marriage*, would repay the costs of a staged revival.

When Goldsmith came to write *The Good Natur'd Man* in 1768, he was able to find producers at Covent Garden, where they could see Drury Lane audiences accepting Garrick's productions of new laughing comedy in the first part of the programme, even though the 'genteel' *False Delicacy* would be Drury Lane's big new production of that season. Covent Garden bet on Goldsmith's somewhat 'low' comedy – more within the range of their actors than of Drury Lane's – and it succeeded to such an extent that when Goldsmith came back five years later with an even more frolicking 'low' story set in the country, Covent Garden put up many of the same regulars to play parts in *She Stoops to Conquer* and ignored criticism of its 'low mischief and mirth' while enjoying profits. (Garrick wrote the popular prologue for his fickle clubmate Goldsmith.) Impressed by audiences that flocked to this laughing comedy, Covent Garden sought another hit. If we are to believe Richard Brinsley Sheridan, while *She Stoops to Conquer* was still enjoying its initial success, Covent Garden manager Thomas Harris asked the 23-year-old son of a playwright mother and a player-manager father to write something, then cast five of the principals from *She Stoops to Conquer* in the resulting low country frolic with its sentimental subplot of falsely delicate lovers and opened *The Rivals* in January 1775. After an initial failure and a subsequent eleven days for rewriting and recasting (an unusual procedure that underscores Harris's part in commissioning it), it enjoyed such success that Harris took a Sheridan farce (*St Patrick's Day*) for the spring benefits, a Sheridan curtain-raising *Prelude to Opening Covent Garden* at the beginning of the 1775–76 season and an expensive Sheridan comic opera, *The Duenna*, as that season's first major new production. Harris played the last for fully seventy-five nights in 1775–76, in the eyes of some cynics driving Garrick into retirement as the season came to a close.

To be sure, Garrick's health was often problematic, especially from his middle thirties onwards. He suffered from gout and various urological disorders ('stone' and 'gravel'), and he had nearly died in 1764 of a wasting fever while on the Grand Tour. He had contemplated retirement many times and was fixed on retiring at the end of the 1775–76 season before *The Duenna* proved the single most popular new mainpiece of his era.

All the same, Garrick was the dominant theatrical force of the day. Ninety per cent of all public critical writings on theatrical management after 1747 were addressed to him. Goldsmith found success because there was a market for new laughing comedy that Garrick helped to create. Sheridan found initial success for the same reason. And when he assumed management at Drury Lane of the company that Garrick had mostly assembled and developed, Sheridan wrote a 'high' comedy for that company that ran for sixty-five nights in its first two seasons and which remains the finest English comedy between Shakespeare and Shaw. And it was Garrick who wrote the prologue that introduced *The School for Scandal*.

Garrick's contributions to the profession of acting

Garrick created a stability in the acting profession hardly ever seen before. A firm negotiator with his actors, he regularized compensation and other means of discipline so that, within only a few years, he had achieved a predictable expenditure side to the balance sheet. He enlarged the company to 100 actors, developed a system of scouting young talent in regional companies, applied Charles Macklin's lessons in encouraging the abilities and group cohesiveness of the newcomers he recruited, and he exercised remarkable skill in maintaining or boosting the morale necessary to hold together a company based upon ensemble acting, particularly in a time when rapidly increasing public press commentary meant countless morning meetings in the Green Room to assuage bruised egos.

Perhaps most important to the profession of acting, Garrick created the first guaranteed retirement fund. Thomas Hull, a Covent Garden actor, had floated the idea while Garrick was on the Grand Tour, and Garrick embraced it upon his return and started contributing. He used his prestige to win Parliament's approval for the guarantee (in March 1776) and added his talents by acting in annual benefit performances, including two in his last season. Thus did legal vagabonds and sturdy beggars win a security for themselves and their dependent heirs. The acting profession gained enough stability that temperamental actresses and actors could afford to bedevil Garrick with petty demands in the later years of his management.

Garrick had made the choice of a life of acting with much trepidation over his family's approval. By the time he retired, he was a very wealthy man. He owned a country estate and a town home. His library and his collection of art exceeded those of most great houses. He dined and visited in the highest circles. He was painted or drawn and etched more than public icons Alexander Pope or Voltaire. His friendships with the rich, powerful and talented were international, and he managed his business so well that he could take two years off to tour the Continent. Though children did not come for him and Eva, they were surrounded by loving nieces and nephews. His private virtues were such that he must have taken as much satisfaction in enhancing the profession of acting and in providing livelihoods for so many theatre workers as he did in his own financial and social success.

Garrick's innovations in theatrical representation

Garrick knew that the long-established tradition of permitting privileged folks to sit on the stage hindered ensemble portrayal and prevented potential scenic and lighting effects. His campaign to end the practice began in the winter of 1748, shortly after he assumed management, but took nearly fifteen years to complete. Part of the problem stemmed from the desire of actors to swell the audiences for their benefits by building seating on stage (which Garrick himself had done for his first benefit night at Goodman's Fields on 18 March 1742). When Garrick used the excuse of a newly enlarged auditorium to ban this practice in 1762, John Beard at Covent Garden followed suit, thus effectively ending the tradition. Problems with 'bucks' and others roaming behind the scenes must have continued, for Sheridan took occasion on beginning his management in 1776 to institute a ban on backstage visits, noted approvingly in the press.

Another battle fought to enhance the theatrical illusion focused on the auditorium and concerned the half-price discount, and this one Garrick did not win. Since early in the century, anyone coming after the third act of the mainpiece paid only half the five shillings for a box seat, 3s for the pit, 2s for the first gallery or 1s for the upper gallery; anyone leaving by the end of the mainpiece's third act could reclaim half the entrance fee. Whilst comings and goings and other disturbances occurred all the time, they particularly rankled the actors (and some auditors) during the second half of the theatrical evening. The managers tried citing additional expenses for scenery and effects in afterpieces as justification to charge full prices for the whole evening, and had some success when they offered a new pantomime or spectacle. But in 1763, when Garrick levied full prices for an author's sixth-night benefit (Benjamin Victor's modernization of *The Two Gentlemen of Verona*) without offering a new afterpiece, Thaddeus Fitzpatrick led the 'Half-Price Riots' that demolished the interior of Drury Lane. Garrick had learned a sad lesson through the anti-French riots that attended his hiring of Jean-Georges Noverre (a Swiss Protestant, though the distinction was too fine for the mob) to present the elaborate and expensive Chinese Festival in 1755, and he quickly backed off from any attempt to change the half-price tradition.

The period of Garrick's greatest innovations to support the theatrical illusion followed his return from the Grand Tour in 1765. Although he had quietly brought enhanced technology from the Comédie Française and other European venues after his trip in 1751, now he brought more. He introduced lighting effects which caused much public comment. Earlier he had substituted oil lamps for candles in some footlights and experimented with baffles to vary the illumination. In 1765, he achieved a better effect with reflectors in the footlights and tiered reflecting lamps in the wings, allowing him to eliminate the massive girandoles hanging above the stage. Whilst the footlights and the girandoles could be raised or lowered to achieve effects, actors had to come forward; with the new wing lights and baffling systems, the whole stage could benefit from variation in lighting intensity. He also added coloured glass filters to some lamps, achieving startling new effects. (His friend Sir Joshua Reynolds told him to tone down the colours; they were too bold for artificial conditions, Reynolds thought.) This basic technology and further refinements endured until the advent of gas lighting in the 1820s.

Garrick did not make much change to the basic technology of scenery. Flats at the wings and in the rear, held in place by tongue-and-groove battens below and above and changed as the audience watched, endured throughout his management. The perspective paintings on these flats depicted standard scenes: city walls and gates, temples, tombs, palaces, streets, forests, deserts, gardens, prisons, interiors and so on. They were treated as generic, and dialogue, costuming and perhaps some properties gave them whatever specificity a play demanded. Managers tended to use them over and over and repair them if they were damaged. But Garrick, always seeking for drama to communicate beyond the spoken word and the actor's movement, commissioned many more specific scenes – for Johnson's *Irene*, Aaron Hill's *Merope*, Murphy's *The Way to Keep Him* and his revival of *Antony and Cleopatra*, among other works. His greatest contribution to scene design, however, was employing the talented Alsatian painter Philippe Jacques de Loutherbourg, whom he hired in 1773–74 at a salary of £500, as much as he paid his leading actors, and to whom he gave wide authority for all aspects of stage decoration and machinery. Loutherbourg answered not just as a scene-painter but also as a designer who revolutionized stage effects in London over the next ten years. He introduced seemingly spontaneous scene changes, broken arch lines, differing levels, new perspectives, transparencies that permitted arresting colour changes, an array of effects which Sheridan not so much poked fun at as proudly displayed in the spectacular conclusion of *The Critic* (1779).

Nor was Garrick a revolutionary in costume. Although many of Drury Lane's advertisements would cite 'the characters new dressed in the habits of the times', and although Garrick possessed and studied expensive illustrated volumes on the history of costume, such historical authenticity as was known took second place to the actors' ease of movement and their comfort in unheated theatres. He laid out large sums for elegant contemporary

high-fashion dress and commissioned the construction of many more historically suggestive costumes for the stock. But mixtures of periods and generic
styles endured in the representation.

Garrick's legacy

Garrick changed how people saw drama. There was a seven-fold increase in
theatrical criticism and gossip in the public press during Garrick's professional
career. More profound than the growth in commentary was the shift in what
critics, and perhaps audiences, sought to experience from dramatic representation. Some part of this shift must have resulted from Garrick's revolution of
sympathetic imagination against the conventional rhetorical style of acting.
Before Garrick's techniques and emphases appeared and for quite some time
after, criticism of drama began with a judicial recounting of the story and an
assessment of the balance between the play's beauties and faults. This tem-
plate of universals, derived from seventeenth-century principles of dramatic
construction, endured to mid-century. The assumptions behind the questions
it asked did not reconcile with Shakespeare's unruly achievements, as the best
of the century's appreciations in Johnson's *Preface to Shakespeare* reveals. Johnson knew that individuated character differentiates a story from a tale, a plot
from a series of events. Like him, critics after mid-century began to approach
a theatrical experience by examining character, by assessing a play according
to the relationship of character to plot and the mimetic appropriateness of all
aspects. Whilst it would be three-quarters of a century before Ibsen would
create dramatic characters of individuated psychological depth, and while the
strain of Smollett and Dickens would coexist with Austen and George Eliot, it
just might be that one little man, exercising sympathetic imagination, breaking
with the rhetorical acting conventions of his time in his quest to realize character on stage, helped assure the dominance of the western mimetic tradition
from the eighteenth century onwards.

In the novel mimesis won centre stage, but not so in the British theatre for
nearly a century. Garrick made the stage so profitable and the profession so
stable that Covent Garden and Drury Lane embarked upon massive enlarge-
ments to their auditoriums, each reaching towards 3,000 seats by the 1790s.
The intimacy of the smaller houses in which Garrick had performed was lost;
stentorian tones and broad gestures reappeared in the generations of John
Philip Kemble, Sarah Siddons and Edmund Kean, and playwrights embraced
spectacular effects in the service of the pathetic strain of plot and character.
No new comedies in the same class as Sheridan's appeared before almost the

end of the nineteenth century, and no new tragedies of comparable quality until the twentieth. It took smaller theatres located in major cities on the Continent and the development of naturalistic drama to bring forth the director Konstantin Stanislavski, who taught his actors to approach their characters as parts of whole actions, to exercise a sympathetic imagination in discovering their characters' motivations and to concentrate on ensemble techniques in the representation. His was no rediscovery of Garrick's method: just as many cultures develop fermentation independently, based on the materials available, so Garrick for Shakespeare and Stanislavski for Chekhov found the process that released the spirit within.[6]

[6] In addition to the sources cited in the previous notes, I recommend for further study Highfill *et al.*, *Biographical Dictionary*, and Garrick, *Letters*, ed. Little and Kahrl.

8

Theatre outside London, 1660–1775

GÖREL GARLICK

Written records relating to the post-Restoration and early eighteenth-century development of theatre outside London are relatively scarce, but from the available source material a picture emerges of entrepreneurial London actors determined to bring the drama to an increasingly numerous and demanding provincial audience. Whilst theatre outside London thus maintained a strong link with the capital, the relationship was a complex one, not least because the political and social conditions under which provincial companies operated differed considerably between Ireland, Scotland and England. In order to highlight these important variations a separate section will be devoted to each.

Ireland

In Ireland the post-Restoration theatre operated under conditions similar to those of the London patent houses; that is, under the protection and control of a royal patent granted in 1661. The patentee was John Ogilby, who had been the Irish Master of the Revels at Dublin's vice-regal court before the Interregnum. In 1637 he had erected a small playhouse in Werburgh Street for the benefit of the vice-regal court and resident English government officials. When, in 1660, a new viceroy was established in Dublin, Ogilby lost no time in getting himself reappointed to his old post at the Irish Revels Office, taking care, at the same time, to obtain a royal patent which gave him the right not only to present plays and operas, but also to erect and license theatres anywhere in Ireland and to license other performers.[1] Ogilby began his second tenure by erecting a new theatre situated in Smock Alley, the Werburgh Street playhouse being, by now, too dilapidated for use. It was apparently similar in size to the 1674

[1] See Clark, *Early Irish Stage*, 26–31.

Drury Lane and, according to the London bookseller John Dunton, contained a 'Stage, pit, Boxes, two Galleries, Lettices [*sic*] and Musick Loft'.[2]

The Smock Alley playhouse was the first theatre royal outside London; it opened in October 1662. Among the original company was the actor Joseph Ashbury, who became the theatre's manager and patentee in 1684, a post he held until his death in 1720. Ashbury was considered to be not only a highly competent actor but also an excellent teacher, and during his tenure the Smock Alley established itself as a well-respected training ground for budding performers hoping for a career on the London stage. Records of the Smock Alley repertory during Ashbury's management are limited, but they indicate that, as on the London stage, Shakespearean tragedy (*Hamlet, Othello, Richard III*) and Restoration comedy dominated in the early years, while contemporary plays, including Farquhar's, became more prominent in the early part of the eighteenth century. By 1711, again following the London pattern, the mainpiece was followed by song and dance interludes, the evening often ending with a masque.[3] During the long winter season (October to June) the thirty-strong company gave around ninety performances of thirty to forty different plays. Dunton, on his visit to Dublin in 1698, found 'the actors in no way inferior . . . nor the Spectators . . . one degree less in Vanity and Foppery than those in another Place',[4] an observation which suggests that both Dublin performers and Dublin society were intent on emulating London in every way.

In 1720 Ashbury's son-in-law Thomas Elrington took over as actor-manager, while the patent passed into the hands of a government official. Elrington continued to run Smock Alley along the pattern established by Ashbury and in 1733 handed over the reins to his brother Francis. The brothers had long realized the need for a new and more up-to-date playhouse, and the same year Francis Elrington persuaded Ireland's leading architect, Sir Edward Lovett Pearce, not only to design a new theatre to be situated in Aungier Street, close to the fashionable St Stephen's Green, but also to raise a subscription to cover the cost. A year later the new playhouse, measuring 94 feet by 46 feet overall and equipped with a 54-feet-deep stage, opened with Farquhar's *The Recruiting Officer*.[5] Unfortunately, Pearce's classically ornamented auditorium, containing a pit, one complete box tier, a lower gallery flanked by side boxes and an upper gallery, was bedevilled by both poor acoustics and poor sightlines[6]

---

[2] Dunton, *Dublin Scuffle*, 339–40. Lettices, or lattices, were side boxes flanking the lower gallery.
[3] Clark, *Early Irish Stage*, 92–3, 204–6.
[4] Dunton, *Dublin Scuffle*, 339.
[5] Stockwell, *Dublin Theatres*, 50–3.
[6] Victor, *History of the Theatres of London and Dublin*, I: 16.

and was therefore less attractive to play-going Dubliners than Elrington had hoped.

The decision to build a new theatre may have been hastened by unexpected competition in the form of the Italian rope-dancer and tumbler Signora Violante, who erected a booth in Dame Street in 1730. Here she successfully presented plays and pantomimes performed by a company of children, which included the young Peg Woffington (c. 1718–60), the daughter of a Dublin bricklayer. In September 1732 Violante took her troupe to the Haymarket Theatre in London but failed to impress the metropolitan audience. Woffington, intent on a stage career, but too young and inexperienced to be taken on by a London company, returned to Dublin, where she joined the Theatre Royal company as an apprentice actor.[7] She first appeared on the Aungier Street stage as a dancer in the 1734–35 season before graduating to Rose in *The Recruiting Officer*. In February 1737 she acted Ophelia opposite John Ward's Hamlet with moderate success, but in the spring of 1740 the Dublin audience was finally won over completely by her performance in a series of breeches parts that included Silvia in *The Recruiting Officer*, the title role in Henry Brooke's *The Female Officer* and Sir Harry Wildair in Farquhar's *The Constant Couple*,[8] in which 'she appeared with the true spirit of a well-bred Rake of Quality'.[9] Flushed with success, she persuaded John Rich to engage her at Covent Garden for £9 a week, where she made a successful London début as the independent-spirited Silvia in November 1740.

By this time the Aungier Street theatre was facing competition from a new playhouse erected in 1735 on the old Smock Alley site by Louis Duval, who had taken over the remnants of Signora Violante's troupe after her departure. The enterprising Duval had secured not only a licence from the Irish Revels Office for his theatre but also financial support from Dublin merchants towards its construction.[10] His assumption that Dublin could support two theatres proved over-optimistic. Despite an estimated population of around 65,000, the audience base, as La Tourette Stockwell argued, was probably limited to the Anglo-Irish aristocracy, English government officials, members of Trinity College and Dublin merchants, with their respective servants filling the upper gallery.[11] The repertory of both theatres, as Greene and Clark have shown, was almost identical and closely followed that of the London stage. Restoration

---

[7] Dunbar, *Woffington*, 26–7.
[8] Greene and Clark, *Dublin Stage 1720–1745*, 25–6, 163, 173, 191, 210.
[9] Victor, *History of the Theatres of London and Dublin*, 1: 16.
[10] Greene and Clark, *Dublin Stage 1720–1745*, 30.
[11] Stockwell, *Dublin Theatres*, 174–96.

and eighteenth-century comedy plus Shakespeare were the most common offerings, alternating with a limited number of Restoration tragedies and a few new plays, though it seems that both playhouses took a cautious approach to the latest pieces that had been premièred in the capital, preferring instead more familiar work. As the companies were, in practice, chasing the same audience, they tended to perform on alternate days, thus giving the spectators an opportunity to compare alternative productions of the same play. However, watching the same pieces, albeit with different performers, proved too much for the Dublin audience, and both theatres soon faced severe problems.

To recoup their losses from the winter season the two companies spent the summer touring the smaller Irish towns, while actors from the London patent houses were brought over by both managers. The Smock Alley actors usually toured the north of the country, visiting Newry, Belfast and Londonderry, while the Aungier Street players went south to Limerick, Cork and Waterford. In the summer of 1742, Peg Woffington and David Garrick appeared at Smock Alley, where their natural acting style proved very successful. Aungier Street fared less well with Susanna Cibber and James Quin, whose traditional declamatory style no longer impressed the Dublin audience. In 1745 the two debt-ridden companies finally agreed to merge under the management of the Dublin-born actor Thomas Sheridan, and from now on plays were performed at Smock Alley, while Aungier Street was used for balls and assemblies.

Sheridan had been educated at Trinity College before turning to the stage. As a manager he made strenuous efforts not only to raise the standard of acting, which appears to have lapsed since Ashbury's days, but also to improve the behaviour of an increasingly rowdy audience. In 1747, after a lengthy court case, he finally succeeded in banning spectators from the stage and even managed to tame the unruly upper gallery, from which stones and apples often rained down into the pit and orchestra, by the simple expedient of doubling the price to two shillings for a short period.[12] As a result Smock Alley prospered and became, as the actor Robert Hitchcock observed, 'the fashionable resort of all ranks . . . [and] a source of entertainment and instruction'.[13]

In 1751 Woffington returned to Dublin, where she persuaded Sheridan to engage her for £400 for the 1751–52 season. Her legendary acting skills, carefully honed during eleven years on the London stage, coupled with her lively spirit and personal charisma, brought full houses to Smock Alley. Her salary was doubled for the following two seasons, and she continued to attract large

---

[12] Ibid., 88–119.
[13] Hitchcock, *Historical View*, I: 227.

audiences, often performing four times a week. This successful run came to an abrupt halt in March 1754, when Sheridan decided to stage Miller's adaptation of Voltaire's tragedy *Mahomet*, with himself as Zaphne and Mrs Woffington as Palmire. The theme of the play revolves around the right of man to live in a society free from the intolerance of tyrannical rulers, and it was probably an unwise choice at a time when Irish nationalism, fuelled by the King's decision to prorogue the Irish Parliament, was rapidly gaining ground in Dublin. Serious rioting broke out during the performance, begun, it seems, by Irish patriots who were critical of Sheridan and Woffington's apparent support of the ruling English aristocracy. The auditorium and part of the stage were destroyed, and Sheridan, furious with the Dublin audience, promptly departed for England, leaving Benjamin Victor, the company's treasurer, as his acting manager. Woffington remained, but returned to Covent Garden the following season, where she stayed until she was taken ill on stage in May 1757.

The overall success of the Smock Alley theatre in the early 1750s may have encouraged the Dublin-born actor and manager of Covent Garden, Spranger Barry, to believe that the city could successfully support an additional theatre. Despite vehement protests by the Smock Alley proprietors, Barry collected sufficient subscribers to fund the building of his playhouse on a site in Crow Street. Crow Street opened in 1758, but Barry's assessment of the size of the Dublin audience base proved to be wildly optimistic; after nine years, heavily in debt, he gave up the struggle and let the theatre to the manager of Smock Alley, Henry Mossop. Mossop, another graduate of Trinity College and a fine tragedian, tried to tempt a wider audience by putting on comedies and lighter entertainment at Smock Alley and tragedies at Crow Street. Still the spectators did not materialize in sufficient numbers, and in 1771 Mossop gave up and fled his creditors. Successive managers tried to keep both theatres going, with increasing difficulty, until November 1786, when the Irish Parliament intervened and granted an exclusive patent to Richard Daly, who closed Smock Alley and made Crow Street the Theatre Royal.

Scotland

In Scotland the political and social conditions after the Restoration were considerably less favourable for the theatre than in either Ireland or England. First, unlike Dublin, Edinburgh had no resident court that demanded theatrical entertainment. Second, the Church of Scotland, a powerful force in Scottish society, unhesitatingly denounced the theatre as the temple of the devil and threatened any potential spectators with dire consequences.[14] This unequivocal condemnation of the theatre by the Scottish church meant that any actors in Scotland, be they visiting English performers or resident players, found it hard to establish a firm foothold, even in Edinburgh, until the 1740s.

Despite consistent hostility towards the theatre on the part of the authorities, by the 1730s Edinburgh had a small resident company known as the Edinburgh Players. It was supported by the poet Allan Ramsay, but his attempt, in 1736, to establish the company in a small playhouse in Carruber's Close (originally used by rope-dancers and tumblers) was short-lived; on the passing of the Licensing Act of 1737, which rendered all theatres inside and outside London illegal unless they operated under a royal patent or licence from the Lord Chamberlain, the church compelled the city authorities to close the theatre.[15] Ramsay, however, persuaded his supporters among the Scottish nobility to petition Parliament for a royal patent in 1739. This was the first patent petition for a theatre outside London after the 1737 act, but the bill failed, mainly because of the combined opposition of the civil authorities and the university in Edinburgh. This setback did not prevent an English actor, Thomas Este, from bringing his company to Edinburgh in 1741, where he acted at the Taylor's Hall. The performances were announced as concerts with a play presented *gratis* in the intervals, a simple but generally effective way of avoiding the strictures of the Licensing Act.

Four years later the young York-based actress Sarah Ward (1727–71) joined the company, but she soon quarrelled with Este. Leading a breakaway group who wanted to erect a permanent theatre in Edinburgh, she managed to raise a subscription from wealthy Edinburgh citizens and secured the support of local tradesmen for a new theatre in the Canongate. The playhouse had a pit, one complete box tier and two galleries, the lower one flanked by side boxes. The upper one had no benches, and, as at the Dublin theatres, was designed for the servants of the box visitors.[16] It opened in November 1747 with *Hamlet*, interspersed with a concert. Initially, the Canongate Concert Hall, as it was officially known, was managed by Lacy Ryan (from Covent Garden), Sarah Ward and West Digges. The repertory, in common with Dublin, reflected the London stage and featured Shakespeare, notably *Hamlet*, *Richard III*, *Henry IV* and *Othello*, Otway and Congreve, together with Rowe, Steele, Cibber and

---

[14] Arnot, *History of Edinburgh*, 281.
[15] Scullion, 'Eighteenth century', 62–74, 87–90.
[16] Arnot, *History of Edinburgh*, 282.

Garrick, the evening often concluding with a pantomime or harlequinade.[17] After a year Sarah Ward left for London and Covent Garden before moving on to Drury Lane. In the summer of 1752 she returned to Edinburgh with the actor John Lee, who had fallen out with Garrick, and had taken on the management of the Canongate. The restless actress soon left Edinburgh again, this time for Smock Alley, where she stayed for three years, proving a popular performer with the Dublin audience. She returned to Edinburgh in December 1756 and acted Lady Randolph, perhaps her finest role, in the verse tragedy *Douglas*, a new play by John Home.

Home was an ordained minister in the Church of Scotland who, paradoxically, was also intent on making a career as a dramatist. He had previously offered *Douglas* to Garrick, who had rejected it because he found the story seriously flawed and lacking interesting characters or passions.[18] The play is set at the time of the Viking incursions in Scotland, and the plot revolves around the unexpected return of Douglas, the long-lost son of Lady Randolph conceived during a previous but clandestine marriage to Lord Douglas, of which her second husband is unaware. It is an improbable story, but the part of Lady Randolph, whose almost pathological grief, after her first husband together with her brother had been slain in battle, thus forcing her to abandon the infant to the care of an escaping servant, and the gradual transmutation of her emotions into an overwhelming and rapturous joy on finding Douglas alive, only for her happiness to be cruelly destroyed when the latter is murdered by her husband's cousin, offered great scope for a competent actress. Her ambivalent attitude to the perpetual male quest for honour in battle may also have struck a chord with the Scottish audience, for whom the bloody fighting during the 1745 rebellion was not yet forgotten history. West Digges was much admired as Douglas, and the Canongate spectators were moved to both tears and applause. The play ran for a week, an unusually long run at the time, and London could no longer dismiss Home's drama. The following March *Douglas* was performed with equal success at Covent Garden, with Peg Woffington as Lady Randolph and Spranger Barry as Douglas, and from then on the play entered the standard repertory of both the London and the provincial theatres.

The Church of Scotland, stung by one of its ministers not only writing a play but also by Home's total disregard for their views by then having it performed in a public theatre, counter-attacked by publishing an *Admonition*

---

[17] For a complete listing of performances see Armstrong, 'Edinburgh stage 1715–1820'.
[18] Garrick, *Letters*, ed. Little and Kahrl, 1: letter 166.

and Exhortation, in which its leaders inveighed against the theatre as a pedlar of folly and vice intent on seducing servants, apprentices and students away from their proper duties.[19] Furious pamphlets for and against the play flew back and forth, and clergy who attended the play were suspended, an extreme measure which gained little sympathy from the public. In the end the Church of Scotland had to concede defeat, at least in Edinburgh, and to allow anyone to attend the playhouse as they saw fit.

The Canongate, which still operated without a royal patent, continued to attract a regular audience for the next ten years, but, in January 1767, the management's refusal to reinstate the popular comedian George Stayley led to serious rioting and the destruction of most of the auditorium and stage. The proprietors, among whom were a number of senior Scottish judges, repaired their building, but now thought it prudent to legalize their operation by applying to Parliament for a patent as part of a bill to extend the city boundary northwards.[20]

A patent, the first to be issued since the 1737 act, was granted in June 1767. It was immediately sold by the proprietors to the Covent Garden actor David Ross, who proposed to build a theatre by the new North Bridge, just inside the fashionable New Town development. The London-born Ross had made his acting début at Smock Alley in 1749 before moving on to Drury Lane in 1751 and then to Covent Garden. During the 1760s Ross had toured northern Britain, including Edinburgh, with his own summer company, and had realized the need for a modern playhouse in the city. Ross's Theatre Royal measured *circa* 108 feet by 57 feet overall and contained an elegantly curved auditorium with pit, one complete box tier, an upper tier with side boxes and a centre gallery, plus an upper gallery. It opened in December 1769 with Steele's *The Conscious Lovers*, but Ross had seriously underestimated the building costs. The following summer, heavily in debt, he persuaded Samuel Foote, of the Haymarket Theatre, to lease the playhouse during the winter. Although Foote's company was well received, he soon sold the lease to West Digges, who rapidly ran into financial problems. His difficulties were compounded by the near impossibility of recouping any winter losses by taking his company on a summer tour outside Edinburgh, as many inhabitants of the smaller Scottish towns were still distrustful of the theatre. In 1781, after a succession of short lets to other managers, Ross sold both the patent and the theatre to John Jackson, who promptly erected a new playhouse in Glasgow and divided his company between the two cities.

[19] Home, *Douglas; Pamphlets*, 35.
[20] Jackson, *History of the Scottish Stage*, 66–7.

England

From 1660 to 1775 the provincial theatre in England developed from a somewhat haphazard enterprise by *ad hoc* groups of itinerant players, performing mainly at inns and local fairs, to a more firmly based operation run by London summer companies and local circuit companies playing in purpose-built theatres. This expansion of the English provincial theatre was gradual but steady, and it withstood both local Puritan objections and the restrictions imposed by the Licensing Act of 1737.

The restoration of the monarchy and the granting of royal patents for theatres in London to Davenant and Killigrew were accompanied by the restoration of the right to touring companies to operate outside London, providing they carried a licence from the Master of the Revels or a royal patent. In addition, they needed a licence from the local magistrates where they intended to perform.[21] A number of London-based actors, among them George Jolly, the patentee and manager of a training school or nursery for the capital's patent theatres, took advantage of this opportunity and regularly visited Norwich, then England's largest provincial city, where the magistrates were generally tolerant of the players, providing they did not stay too long. However, when Jolly stayed for three months in 1669 the city authorities complained to the King, arguing that his popularity among the cloth workers threatened the city's prosperous wool trade.[22]

Despite occasional misgivings and the publication of Jeremy Collier's *A Short View of the Immorality, and Profaneness of the English Stage* (1698), the Norwich magistrates continued to license visiting players, and by 1710 a regular six-week winter season was offered by a group of actors known as the Duke of Norfolk's Servants. They performed at local inns as well as at the duke's palace outside Norwich; their repertory, featuring predominantly plays by Shakespeare, Rowe, Centlivre and Farquhar, seems to have replicated that of the London stage. By 1726 the city had a permanent company, known as the Norwich Company of Comedians, who performed regularly from January to May at the White Swan Inn. For the rest of the year the company toured the smaller East Anglian towns, including Dereham, Ipswich, Beccles, Bury St Edmunds and Colchester, the dates arranged to coincide with local fairs and race meetings.[23] The Norwich company was one of the earliest locally

---

[21] Magistrates (Justices of the Peace) were given the power to license actors in 1572 (14 Eliz., ch. 5). See Liesenfeld, *Licensing Act*, 162.

[22] Rosenfeld, *Strolling Players*, 36–7, 43.

[23] Ibid., 48–56.

based circuit companies, which were to become the main providers of theatre outside London during the eighteenth century.

Collier's attack on what he perceived as the fundamentally immoral and evil nature of the theatre found more support in the port of Bristol, where the Puritan-minded authorities consistently repelled the advances of John Power's touring company during the 1690s and early 1700s. Power, however, met with a warmer welcome in Bath, a small but rapidly expanding spa resort only twelve miles from Bristol. In 1705 Bath's aristocratic visitors subscribed enough money for a small playhouse for Powers, where his company performed Centlivre's *Love at a Venture* the following year.[24]

There are few extant records of performances in Bath during the early eighteenth century, but it would be surprising if touring companies had not visited a town which harboured both a theatre and a potentially well-disposed audience among its wealthy tourists. Thus, in May 1728 a summer company of London actors under John Hippisley performed *The Beggar's Opera* in Bath with great success before moving on to the neighbouring small spa of Clifton Hotwells, just outside Bristol. Attitudes towards the theatre in the Bristol area had now changed, and the wealthy spa drinkers were so impressed by Hippisley's company that they subscribed £3,400 towards a theatre for him at Clifton. According to Mark Howell, the Jacob's Well theatre, as it was known, was probably only 62 feet by 37 feet overall, with a rectangular-shaped auditorium with one box tier, plus a second tier with front and side galleries and possibly an additional upper gallery.[25]

Hippisley's summer company became a firm favourite with the Bristol audience, and during the 1740s leading London actors such as Mrs Pritchard and Henry Woodward appeared at Clifton. The company operated on a profit-sharing basis plus benefit nights; as the income depended entirely on the popularity of a particular play, the repertory was often weighted in favour of reliable crowd pullers such as Cibber's *The Provok'd Husband*, Howard's *The Committee*, Shakespeare's tragedies and *As You Like It*.[26] Of these, *The Provok'd Husband*, which opens with the wilful Lady Townly, newly arrived in London from the country, setting off on a shopping spree against her husband's wishes and ends with her learning how to be a gentle wife, was one of the most popular and profitable benefit plays.

By the mid-1730s the gradual expansion of theatre outside London became a cause of concern to some members of Parliament, who, like the city fathers in

---

[24] Penley, *Bath Stage*, 17.
[25] Howell, '"Regular theatre" at Jacob's Well', 19–42.
[26] Rosenfeld, *Strolling Players*, 206–8.

Norwich forty years earlier, feared that theatre-going induced idleness among the workers, with a consequent damaging impact on the trade and manufacturing that underpinned the nation's prosperity. Thus, in 1735 Sir John Barnard attempted, but failed, to persuade Parliament to restrict the number of theatres in the whole country to the London patent houses only.[27]

However, two years later, in June 1737, Parliament delivered a more comprehensive attack on the drama by passing the Licensing Act,[28] brought forward by the Prime Minister, Sir Robert Walpole. Although the act was primarily concerned with the censorship of plays, decreeing that every new play must be submitted to the Lord Chamberlain for approval before it could be publicly performed, it also bore down on the actors. From now on, anyone who presented plays for profit in an unlicensed theatre in a town where they were not resident would be subject to the brutal punishments (whipping and/or imprisonment) for rogues or vagabonds as specified in the Vagrancy Act of 1714 (12 Anne 2, ch. 23). Actors who performed without a licence where they were legally domiciled could not, of course, be branded as vagrants, but they would be subject to a crippling £50 fine for each offence. The act did not specifically prohibit the building of playhouses outside London, but by stipulating that theatres could now only be licensed by petitioning Parliament and not the King, as before, it made the licensing process both costly and time-consuming, with no guarantee of success, as the petitioners behind the Edinburgh patent bill discovered in 1739.

In 1737 no theatre outside London except the Dublin Theatre Royal operated under a royal patent or a licence from the Lord Chamberlain; it was clearly the government's intention to severely restrict theatrical activity outside the capital, if not to curtail it altogether. However, those sections of the act regulating the licensing of theatres and players could only be enforced if a witness brought an action against the individuals concerned before the local magistrates. In practice, few people rushed to do so, and provincial touring companies continued to perform unhindered in unlicensed theatres, taking care to first obtain the permission of local magistrates. The latter, dismayed at having their right to license players effectively removed, and seeing no reason to deprive themselves and their families of occasional visits to the theatre in their own towns, were, in the main, happy to support visiting companies as long as they conducted themselves with decency and order.

[27] 'A bill for restraining the Number of Houses for Playing of Interludes'. See Liesenfeld, *Licensing Act*, 24–6, 54, 164–5.
[28] Reproduced ibid., 191–3.

One casualty of the new act, however, was the old Bath theatre, which was pulled down in 1737. The actors, nevertheless, continued to perform in converted assembly rooms and inns. In 1747, Hippisley, whose summer company at the Jacob's Well theatre had not been harassed by the new laws, boldly presented a *Proposal for a new Theatre in Bath addressed to the Nobility, Magistracy and Gentry of that City*, in which he emphasized the respectable nature of the theatre over other amusements: 'Theatrical performances, when conducted with decency and regularity have always been esteemed the most rational amusements by the polite and thinking part of mankind', he argued, further pointing out that a new theatre would be able to support a better company and provide greater comfort and social segregation in the auditorium.[29]

Upon Hippisley's death in 1748, the project was taken up by a wealthy local brewer and chandler, John Palmer, who raised £1,000 by subscription and erected a playhouse in Orchard Street. The new theatre, which had no patent or licence, opened in October 1750. It seems to have been similar in size, at 60 feet by 40 feet, to Jacob's Well, with prices set at 3s for the boxes, 2s for the pit, 1s 6d for the first gallery and 6d for the upper gallery. The company consisted of around fifteen actors and eight actresses, and the repertory was dominated by Shakespeare (*Macbeth, Hamlet, King Lear, Othello, Henry IV*), Centlivre (*The Busie Body, The Wonder*) and Cibber (*Love Makes a Man, The Provok'd Husband*). Among the most popular afterpieces were Fielding's *The Lottery*, Woodward's *Queen Mab* and Garrick's *Miss in Her Teens*.[30] With a repertory that tried hard to reflect the London stage, the Bath theatre gradually established itself as a nursery for young actors, gaining new respectability when its proprietor, John Palmer the younger, obtained a royal patent in 1768.

The same year a wealthy merchant and builder in Norwich, Thomas Ivory, also obtained a royal patent for his theatre, which he had erected eleven years earlier at the request of the city's leading citizens. Ivory's playhouse, on a site 103 feet by 60 feet and containing a box tier plus an upper tier with gallery and side boxes, was allegedly constructed 'after the model of one of the King's Theatres in London',[31] but there is no extant evidence to support this claim. To ensure full control over his originally unlicensed and therefore illegal venture, Ivory bought up the Norwich Company of Comedians, complete with scenery and wardrobe, and the rights to the East Anglian circuit, which now included Colchester, Ipswich, Great Yarmouth, Bury St Edmunds and Bungay. The developments in Norwich, whereby professional players became the hirelings

[29] Wood, *Description of Bath*, 443–6.
[30] Hare, ed., *Theatre Royal, Bath – Calendar of Performance*.
[31] Eshelman, *Committee Books 1768–1825*, 71–3.

of someone who was not an actor-manager but a local businessman and where the town's merchants and professional men, rather than the actors, were the driving force behind the erection of a purpose-built theatre, signal a form of interventionist support that was to prove crucial for the expansion of the provincial theatre in England. A brief look at the development of the drama in Bristol and Birmingham will further illustrate this point.

By the 1760s the port of Bristol had become a relatively wealthy city, owing to the profitable slave trade. Local merchants, feeling the Jacob's Well theatre was now outmoded and too far from the city centre, determined to construct a new playhouse in the more fashionable and easily accessible King Street. Interestingly, the businessmen did not think it necessary to apply for a patent or licence before the start of building in 1764. (A patent was granted in 1778.)[32] The King Street theatre, originally 115 feet by 48.5 feet internally, is still in use, though much altered. Unusually for a provincial theatre at the time, the lower box tier was elegantly curved, as was the upper tier, which contained the usual side boxes and a gallery. The auditorium, which held 935 spectators, was much admired in its day and set a standard for other provincial theatres to follow. The proprietors invited the London actor William Powell, who had been coached by Garrick before his début at Drury Lane in 1763, to run the theatre. In the first season, June to mid-September 1766, nineteen out of forty-two performances consisted of Shakespearean plays, while Restoration and eighteenth-century tragedies accounted for fifteen. The preponderance of tragedies, as Barker observes, was probably a reflection of Powell's fondness for playing tragic heroes rather than a direct response to audience demand.[33]

The rapidly expanding manufacturing town of Birmingham had been host to a London summer company under the comedian Richard Yates since the 1740s.[34] In 1772 a group of local businessmen decided to build a new and more comfortable playhouse than the one they had earlier built for Yates in 1752. However, they met with unexpected opposition from a group of manufacturers who argued, in time-honoured fashion, that the theatre 'promoted negligence . . . and corrupted the morals of the industrious' and threatened to invoke the 1737 act against the promoters of the new theatre. The attempt to derail the project met with a robust and definitive response, as the theatre's supporters asserted that no one had the right to 'deprive them of the most rational Amusement merely because he did not relish such amusement

[32] Barker, *Theatre Royal Bristol*, 8, 10–11.
[33] Ibid., 13–14, 19.
[34] Cunningham, *History of the Theatre Royal Birmingham*, 12–14.

himself'.[35] The opposition melted away, and the construction of the playhouse, situated in Birmingham's main thoroughfare, New Street, was completed in June 1774. The combined area of the auditorium and the stage was similar to that of the Bristol theatre, 112 feet by 48 feet, with Green Room, dressing rooms and scenery store in separate buildings adjoining.[36] It opened with *As You Like It*, in which Yates excelled as Touchstone, followed by *Miss in Her Teens*.

The willingness of the provincial business community to invest in local theatres is an indication of a growing prosperity among a rising merchant, manufacturing and professional class who had money and time to spend on leisure pursuits. Among the emerging middle class were many who liked to combine socializing with some form of rational amusement – that is, an entertainment – which had at its core a moral purpose. The concomitant growth of a drama, spearheaded by Cibber, Centlivre, Steele, Rowe and Lillo, in which virtue invariably triumphed over vice, undoubtedly helped to persuade the virtuous-minded middling classes of the theatre's didactic potential while, simultaneously, affording an opportunity for socializing. By taking on the role of theatre proprietors the local business community would, arguably, be able to ensure not only that the building met their standards of comfort and safety, but also that the performances did not altogether dispense with the didactic element. The fact that most provincial playhouses only presented plays for a few months each year did not necessarily deter would-be investors, as additional income could be generated by letting the building for concerts, lectures, public meetings and balls. Thus, the playhouse became something of a cultural centre, an emblem of enlightenment and prosperity in an expanding mercantile world.

Although the London summer companies were clearly an important factor in promoting the drama outside the capital, the locally based circuit companies were the main providers of theatre. By the 1750s most of the country, from Kent to Northumbria, was covered by at least one circuit company, if not two or three. In the north, the York company, which between 1767 and 1790 was first managed and from 1770 owned by Tate Wilkinson, became one of the most respected of this type. The city of York, an old administrative and commercial centre, had regularly welcomed visiting players since 1705 and had had a resident company since 1734, established by the actor Thomas Keregan.[37] When Keregan died his widow managed the company and in 1744 erected an unlicensed theatre on a site in Mint Yard leased from the York Corporation and

[35] *Aris's Gazette*, 31 May 1773.
[36] Garlick, 'George Saunders', 131–2.
[37] Rosenfeld, *Strolling Players*, 107–21.

close to the present Theatre Royal. Tate Wilkinson (1739–1803) was a competent comic actor who had been moderately successful on the London stage before venturing into provincial management. In York he prudently began by first obtaining a royal patent (1769) in his own name for both the York and Hull theatres before building a new, larger playhouse in Hull and one in Leeds at his own expense.[38] Equipped with two patents, he felt able to extend his circuit to include Wakefield (from 1774), Doncaster (from 1775) and Pontefract (from 1779).

A brief look at his first season as proprietor and manager (January–December 1771) reveals some of the 'ups and downs' of provincial theatre management. The season began at York with a newly decorated Theatre Royal and a variety of new scenes and costumes, expenditure that proved a good investment as 'The theatre was regularly and fashionably attended the like which has not been seen since', as Wilkinson later observed.[39] In March, the High Sheriff, the most pre-eminent member of York society and therefore the theatre's most valued and valuable patron, commanded Wilkinson to play Jaques in *As You Like It* and in return bought £40 worth of tickets (to distribute to his friends), a sum equivalent to the weekly salary bill for the whole company of sixteen men and eight women. A few weeks later Wilkinson tempted the York audience with a two-week guest appearance by the aging but still vigorous London comedian Henry Woodward, who brought full houses and excelled in his favourite parts of Bobadil (*Every Man in His Humour*), Ranger (*The Suspicious Husband*) and Razor, in Murphy's farce *The Upholsterer*.[40]

Although guest appearances by London actors were a profitable attraction, Wilkinson was fully aware that his permanent company must maintain a reasonable acting standard and to this end needed fresh blood from time to time. Thus, in the early summer of 1771 he engaged Mr and Mrs Henry King from the Edinburgh Theatre Royal and Mr and Mrs Robert Hitchcock from Norwich. Mrs King, who acted 'with a great deal of spirit', took the principal parts in both comedy and tragedy, while Sara Hitchcock's neat figure and liveliness made her an excellent Rosetta in Bickerstaffe's popular comic opera *Love in a Village*, despite her 'less proficient singing'.[41]

In August, after a successful season at York, Wilkinson's company departed for Leeds. Here an initial welcome was not sustained, as local Methodist preachers persuaded potential spectators to keep away from the pernicious

---

[38] Wilkinson, *Wandering Patentee*, I: 73, 101.
[39] Ibid., I: 80.
[40] Ibid., I: 81–3.
[41] Ibid., I: 86–7.

theatre. Even benefit performances did not cover costs. After a few miserable weeks the company left for Hull, where the fishermen, strong supporters of the drama, had returned from their summer fishing expeditions, as had the prosperous merchant families who deserted the port during the summer. For the Hull season Wilkinson had engaged three dancers-*cum*-acrobats from Sadler's Wells, who proved to be popular and profitable, and so the season ended on a satisfactory note.[42]

A much larger circuit taking in northern England, the Midlands and part of East Anglia was covered by James Whitley's company. Whitley had begun his career at Smock Alley in 1741, but had soon left for England and a successful career as a provincial manager. He ran a respectable company and, despite not having a patent, seems not to have run into difficulties with local magistrates. Indeed, such was his popularity that in many towns playhouses were built for him by local businessmen.[43] However, in Manchester, where Whitley's players had been performing regularly since 1760, he was outmanoeuvred by the managers of the Liverpool Theatre Royal, George Mattocks and Joseph Younger, who wanted to expand their operation and therefore applied, successfully, for a patent for a new playhouse in Manchester. The first Manchester Theatre Royal, situated on the corner of York Street and Spring Gardens, opened in June 1775 with the corpulent Younger in the title role of *Othello*. During the second season Mrs Siddons and her brother John Philip Kemble, who had received their early training as members of their father Roger Kemble's circuit company, joined the Manchester theatre. A year earlier Mrs Siddons had made an unsuccessful début at Drury Lane, after which she spent seven years on the provincial stage until her triumphant return to London in 1782. Kemble made his début at Manchester as Othello in January 1777 and a few weeks later played the title role in *Douglas* opposite his sister as Lady Randolph.

Whilst established circuit companies such as Wilkinson's and Whitley's travelled in relative comfort in coaches, the scenery carried in separate wagons, the humble strollers, who had no fixed base, usually walked carrying their costumes and props, sometimes pulling a cart with a couple of flats and a backdrop. They performed chiefly in so-called barn theatres, a simple timber structure often erected next to a local inn, or failing that a standard farmer's barn. The very basic and intimate audience and performance space that barn theatres provided is clearly illustrated in J. Wright's detailed engraving 'Macbeth in a Barn' (1788). In a slightly raked pit and rudimentary gallery

---

[42] Ibid., I: 116–19.
[43] Hodgkinson and Pogson, *Early Manchester Theatre*, 27, 45–52.

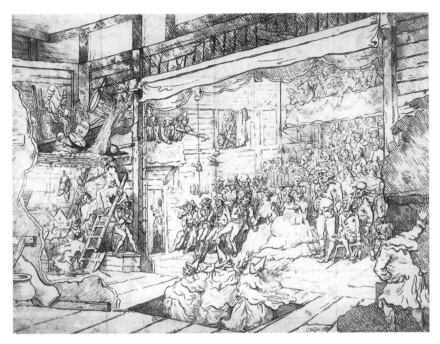

Plate 15. 'Macbeth in a Barn', engraving by J. Wright, 1788.

spectators of all classes and ages are squeezed together on chairs and benches eagerly anticipating the performance. The stage is level with the pit floor, thus creating a close intimacy between nervous, ill-equipped performers and gleeful spectators and inducing a powerful sense of shared space as well as of a shared event. The sense of a shared space that barn theatres provided is likely to have been replicated, to a large extent, in the purpose-built playhouses, though the lack of extant evidence relating to the physical structure of early theatre spaces outside London makes it almost impossible to assess the extent of the impact of the building itself on the theatre experience.

Similarly, the general shortage of surviving records before 1750 makes it difficult to form an accurate view of the gradual emergence and acceptance of theatre outside London in the early part of the period under discussion. However, it would seem that in England, if not in Scotland, Puritan opposition might have been less widespread than is sometimes assumed and that by 1737 the provincial theatre had been able to establish a strong enough foothold for it not to be displaced by the strictures of the Licensing Act. By the 1750s the concept of the theatre as a rational and therefore a more desirable entertainment than other, more popular but brutalizing amusements such as cockfighting and bear-baiting had taken firm root outside the capital, and the stipulations concerning the licensing of theatres in the 1737 act were largely ignored.

As locally based circuit companies expanded in England during the middle of the eighteenth century, they became an essential training ground for the London stage, rivalling the Dublin Theatre Royal, which had been regarded as such at least since the 1680s when Ashbury became manager. The provincial theatre also gave London-based performers a welcome opportunity to augment their income by appearing either as guest stars or with their own *ad hoc* company during the lean summer months, when the capital's patent theatres were closed. This competition no doubt helped to raise performance standards among the circuit-based actors, if not among the strollers.

From the point of view of the development of English drama the structure of theatre outside London ensured that the work of London-based playwrights was brought to a wider audience. It is arguable that the tendency of the provincial repertory to adhere to that of the London stage was at least partly due to the mutual interchange of performers between the provincial and London stages and between the provincial theatres themselves, as the players are likely to have preferred acting roles with which they were familiar rather than learn new and untried pieces. It is also probable that the more educated spectators outside London expected, indeed demanded, that their playhouses replicate the fare available in the London patent houses. In addition, the difficulties and expense of getting approval for new plays after 1737 must have been a strong disincentive to provincial managers to foster local dramatic talent. It is hardly surprising therefore that, on the whole, they chose to echo the London repertory and thus helped to establish, indeed reaffirm, a coherent body of English drama.

9

1776
A critical year in perspective

EDWARD A. LANGHANS

England was facing a revolt in the American colonies, and Horace Walpole feared the worst. To Sir Horace Mann on 27 May 1776 he wrote: 'Oh madness! To have squandered away such an empire! Now we tremble at France, which America enabled us to resist.'[1] The following 11 June in Philadelphia Thomas Jefferson and four others were elected to frame a Declaration of Independence. Meanwhile, George III, who had already shown signs of madness, was becoming a hands-on ruler and interfering with the running of England more than some of his government leaders liked. Captain Cook was on his ill-fated third Pacific voyage, Beaumarchais was working on *The Marriage of Figaro*, and the steam engine had just been perfected by James Watt. Goethe's Weimar years were beginning and Mozart's youthful works were being composed; Goya was finding himself as a painter while the portraitist Reynolds was completing his career. Voltaire had recently retired, Eli Whitney's life was just beginning, Byron, Shelley and Keats were not yet born. Gibbons's first volume of his examination of imperialism, *The Decline and Fall of the Roman Empire*, had just appeared; Adam Smith pleaded for a free economy in *The Wealth of Nations*; Tom Paine's *Common Sense* argued passionately for American liberty. The year 1776 was one of crises, doldrums, successes, failures, endings, beginnings; it was the best and the worst of years: one like no others, one like all the rest. The world, as always, was on the brink.

A stranger visiting London in June 1776, however, might have thought that the most serious threat to the even tenor of English ways was not some national or international confrontation, but rather the retirement of the century's greatest theatre personality. On the evening of the 10th at Drury Lane Theatre the actor-manager David Garrick played Don Felix in *The Wonder; or, A Woman Keeps a Secret*, a popular comedy by Susanna Centlivre. He was not

[1] Walpole, *Correspondence*, VIII: 213.

to appear in the afterpiece, the ballad opera *The Waterman* by Charles Dibdin, which was scheduled to complete the evening, so before it Garrick spoke to his play-goers. They were there to wish him farewell and to accept his last obeisance. The prompter William Hopkins told his diary that Garrick 'went forward and address'd the Audience in so pathetic a Manner as [to] draw Tears from the Audience and himself'. . .[2]

> *It has been customary* [he said] *with persons under my circumstances to address you in a farewell epilogue. I had the same intention, and turned my thoughts that way; but I found myself then as incapable of writing such an epilogue, as I should be now of speaking it. The jingle of rhyme and the language of fiction would but ill suit my present feelings. This is to me a very awful moment: it is no less than parting for ever with those, from whom I have received the greatest kindness, and upon the spot, where that kindness and your favours were enjoyed. (Here his voice failed him; he paused, till a gush of tears relieved him.)*[3]

Garrick stated his gratitude so deftly that his adoring spectators could take it all as a compliment to them, while his Drury Lane company would hear a final thanks not just to the audience but also to the hundreds with whom he had worked over the decades.

The actor had entertained London since 1741, when he astonished play-goers in Cibber's version of *Richard III*. His earliest biographer said that Garrick's 'easy and familiar yet forcible style' baffled critics who had been accustomed to 'an elevation of the voice, with a sudden mechanical depression of its tones'.[4] In his final season of 1775–76 Garrick acted some of the roles that during his career had pleased his followers most: jealous Kitely in Jonson's *Every Man in His Humour*, vivacious Benedick in *Much Ado About Nothing*, gentle Don Leon in Fletcher's *Rule a Wife and Have a Wife*, noble old Lusignan in Hill's *Zara*, foolish young Drugger in *The Alchemist*, anxious Hamlet, protean Sir John Brute in Vanbrugh's *The Provok'd Wife*, tormented Lear, rakish Ranger in Hoadly's *The Suspicious Husband*, intricate Richard III and volatile Don Felix in *The Wonder*. Between 9 May and 10 June he performed twelve times in six different characters to packed and appreciative houses, during which period he was also busy running the large Drury Lane troupe, arranging for an orderly transfer of management, writing prologues and epilogues to help

---

[2] Quoted in *The London Stage 1660–1800*, pt IV, *1747–1776*, ed. Stone, s.v. 10 June 1776. These essential volumes are the source of much of the basic information here on performances, finances and management.

[3] Murphy, *Life of Garrick*, I: 135–9. Quotations from Murphy's *Life* are set in italics throughout this chapter.

[4] Davies, *Memoirs of the Life of Garrick*, I: 40.

fellow-performers attract audiences to their spring benefit nights, preparing two characters he had not acted in years (Ranger and Richard III) and nurturing the Drury Lane Theatrical Fund, which he had established in 1766 to care for retired and disabled performers and to which he gave the income of his farewell night. Garrick was, incidentally, 59 years old and he had three years to live.

His farewell speech was an opportunity for him to review his considerable accomplishments in the thirty-four years he had been in the business. He could have boasted of his managerial success in reforming the theatre of his time – of getting rid of spectators sitting on the stage during performances, of improvements in stage lighting and scene design that led to more realism, of enlarging and beautifying old Drury Lane and of bringing a remarkable degree of social acceptance to his profession. He could have reviewed his successful career as an author (twenty-two mainpieces and afterpieces; twenty-seven adaptations, chiefly of Shakespeare; hundreds of prologues, epilogues, occasional verses and letters) and his encouragement and counselling of aspiring writers. He could have remarked on the ninety-six tragic and comic characters he had acted with aplomb and conviction during his career and his almost single-handed revolution of the acting style of his time from stately and declamatory to vivacious and intense. That, however, was not what his followers had come for, so he spoke instead, and only generally and fleetingly, of his audience, his theatre and those to whom he had sold his thriving enterprise.

Our purpose here is to take a look at what Garrick was leaving, how it worked and what the prospects were. Focusing on Garrick and Drury Lane does not mean that other theatres in London are of less interest. There were also many provincial theatres in such places as Bath, Belfast, Bristol, Edinburgh, Glasgow, Ipswich, Manchester, Norwich, York and, especially, Dublin. The strolling players of early in the century had evolved into more reliable and talented troupes touring on circuits that brought professional theatre with visiting London stars to towns large and small. But Drury Lane and its activity was the country's finest; it was also typical in its practices, well documented and thus ideal for this retrospective.

Garrick had done his job so well that there should have been no cause for alarm; through shrewd management and his own charisma he had made Drury Lane the premier theatre in England and the envy of Europe. But who could take his place? Though many of his roles had already been passed on to others, chiefly William Smith, Smith was no David Garrick, nor was anyone else; the management would be in the hands of the brilliant young playwright Richard Brinsley Sheridan, but he had no great expertise in management. One thing Garrick had not done – perhaps could not have done in view of the theatrical

talent available to him – was to groom successors in his own image. From
his point of view, perhaps, he thought he had done just that, for, confident of
his own skills, he had surrounded himself with the best talent available, as we
shall see. But there really was no one at that moment to fill his shoes, and he
and the audience knew it.

Within another ten years the old order would have changed; John Philip
Kemble and his sister Sarah Siddons would lead the way into a new theatrical
era. But the spectators of 1776 had only a slight taste of Mrs Siddons; she had
been cast by Garrick as Portia in *The Merchant of Venice* and had failed. Kemble
was still in the provinces, learning his trade and building his reputation. The
new Drury Lane season under Sheridan began in the autumn of 1776 with
false starts, bickering and managerial ineptitude. In the November following
Garrick's retirement, the *London Magazine* cried, 'It indeed may be said of the
stage, we hope with more truth, as our violent patriots have often said of the
nation, that it is on the *brink of ruin* if not *already* totally undone'.[5] Those who
had attended Garrick's farewell the previous June had good reason to mourn
their loss, and their worst fears would be borne out by Sheridan's first season.
In his adieu, what might Garrick have said to assuage those fears? Having
thanked them for their kindness and favours, he might have told his patrons
that bright new talent was waiting in the wings, but he knew it was not, not
yet at any rate, and so he skirted the matter. Garrick understood what his
audience family wanted: a sharing of emotion.

> *Whatever may be the changes of my future life, the deepest impression of your kindness
> will always remain here – here, in my heart, fixed, and unalterable.*

Too much sentiment? Probably not, not in 1776 and not for that audience.
They had come to have a good cry. They were apprehensive not only because
their theatre world would no longer be the same, safe place of illusion they had
known, but also because the real world was about to change as well. Anyone
who did not realize that was probably spending too much time at the theatre.

It is difficult now to determine just how much the average English family was concerned about the American problem. Theatre patrons certainly
seemed more agitated about Drury Lane matters than they were about international affairs. Few had yet been touched directly by the threat of war, and
few would be if all went well. The sound of the shot heard round the world
in April 1775 did not reach England for a month, and in January 1776 the government hired 18,000 German mercenaries to fight for Britannia. The turmoil

---

[5] Quoted in *The London Stage 1660–1800*, pt v, *1776–1800*, ed. Hogan, 1: 6.

was far, far away and in someone else's care, but the dramatic world of let's pretend was close at hand and accessible to all who had a shilling. The theatre in one way or another touched the lives of thousands of people who attended performances or worked for or near playhouses. And there were dozens of stages and performing companies large and small all over England, Scotland, Ireland and Wales.[6] The capital had two major playhouses, Drury Lane and Covent Garden; one opera house, the King's Theatre; and a secondary (mostly summer) theatre, the Haymarket. There was also an assortment of minor performing venues, including licensed suburban theatres for plays and spaces in taverns and halls for musical entertainments. In addition, pleasure gardens were popular attractions, especially those at Vauxhall, Ranelagh, Marylebone (though facing closure in 1776), Sadler's Wells, Islington Spa, Bagnigge Wells, Cuper's and Bermondsey. The gardens offered everything from musical concerts, masquerades and fireworks to rope-dancing, lectures, skits, boat races, burlettas, pantomimes and mazes, to say nothing of eating, drinking and gambolling on the grounds.

The theatre's place in the bustle and anxieties of the world has always been a paradox. Being concerned with fiction, it has served partly, sometimes largely, as a release from worldly cares, but its illusion is based on reality – it deals with people in desperate comic or tragic situations. Theatre is always in the thick of things, mirroring society and changing with it, yet it rarely shapes the real world. It usually simply reflects it, for better or for worse. The dramatic offerings in London in 1776 do not seem to have had much bearing on the impending conflict with America or on any other matters of great moment, for most play-goers did not want to confront reality, at least not in theatres, or not yet.

Managers of commercial theatres try not to give audiences what they don't want. However noble it might be to offer productions designed to enlighten an audience or improve its taste or make patrons more concerned about social problems, that is not a fiscally sensible way to run a business. Samuel Johnson in the Drury Lane prologue he wrote for his ex-student Garrick in 1747 declared: 'The drama's laws, the drama's patrons give, / For we that live to please, must please to live'.[7] That meant the production of a large body of mediocre dramatic literature, now forgotten and seldom studied. Sheridan's *The Rivals* and *The School for Scandal* and Goldsmith's *She Stoops to Conquer*, all from the 1770s and all first rate, should not be taken as typical. Most plays

---

[6] Thomas and Hare, eds., *Restoration and Georgian England, 1660–1788*, 4–5.
[7] Johnson, *Poems*, ed. Smith and McAdam, 109.

of the period were second or third rate or worse.[8] Typical, if one wants to study the real taste of the times, are the hundreds of pot-boilers that served their purpose and disappeared; some of these we will encounter in a moment, when we look at the Drury Lane schedule. Revived classic plays of merit – that is, by Shakespeare and other early birds – were regularly altered to make them more palatable to new audiences. Dramatic mediocrity has not killed theatre, however, because few people go to be intellectually or artistically stimulated; they seek entertainment, as much by the performers as by the play, and are usually unaware that they are settling for less. What seemed to work best in Garrick's day – and still does – was speed, spectacle, variety and histrionics.

If one side of the theatrical coin was entertainment, the other was business, the least visible part of the enterprise. Though audiences may not have been aware of it, theatres almost ran themselves. The organizational arrangements and operating procedures had become over the centuries so set and standardized that a change in leadership might bring fresh choices in repertoire that audiences could hiss or cheer but hardly any change in the way shows were brought before them. The routine for selecting plays, staging them, managing finances, selecting new employees, writing contracts, devising the production schedule, selling tickets, paying bills, keeping accounts, responding to audience disorders and demands, handling crowds and numberless other matters remained much the same. Thus the retirement or death of a performer may have been a loss to play-goers, but to performers it meant opportunities – roles opening up and chances for promotion. Though Garrick and his audience made an important occasion out of his farewell, Drury Lane did not fall apart; the company stumbled under the new management, but the fabulous invalid recovered and life in the theatre went on. Working at Drury Lane in 1776 was a company of over 175, almost all now forgotten. There were traditionally four salary ranks for performers, the fourth level consisting chiefly of supernumeraries. In addition, there were dozens of non-performing personnel employed backstage or in the (front of the) house: stage hands, scene-painters, box keepers, accountants, dressers, candle snuffers, cleaners, porters and the like. In 1776 the imperious Mary Ann Yates was the highest-paid performer in the Drury Lane organization at £26 10s weekly; William 'Gentleman' Smith received £14, versatile Elizabeth Younge £13, elegant Frances Abington and droll Thomas King £12 each, and the dancer Simon Slingsby £11 10s; they were

---

[8] Fiske, *English Theatre Music in the Eighteenth Century*, 581–2, makes the same point about music.

Garrick's top people – except, of course, for himself: he drew £500 annually.[9]
At the bottom of the salary scale were house-servants earning about a shilling
a week. For years Garrick shared the Drury Lane patent with James Lacy, who
concentrated chiefly on business matters; Tom King was the acting manager
(that is, manager of the actors); Davy's brother George was a valuable gofer;
and William Hopkins was the theatre's invaluable prompter. The strong personalities may have occasionally clashed, but Drury Lane had what must have
been the finest company in the business.

As play-goers knew, the early months of each London theatrical season were
given over to developing the season's repertoire, using as a basis many revivals
of productions from previous years. Whilst these were being performed, new
presentations were in rehearsal and joined the schedule as soon as they were
ready, alternating with the revivals. This was also a time when neophytes could
début and old-timers be tested in new parts. Drury Lane's schedule in the first
two weeks of 1775–6 shows what sorts of entertainments were offered:

Sat 23 Sept	Cumberland: *The Brothers* (revived comedy, mainpiece); Garrick: *The Theatrical Candidates* (new 'prelude'); and Dodsley: *The Miller of Mansfield* (revived comedy, afterpiece). Two actor firsts (one first time in a new character, one first time on this stage).
Mon 25 Sept	(dark – to give the troupe time to work on other productions)
Tue 26 Sept	Shakespeare: *As You Like It* (revived comedy); *Theatrical Candidates* (2nd time); Cumberland: *The Note of Hand* (revived farce); and dancing.
Wed 27 Sept	(dark)
Thu 28 Sept	Otway: *Venice Preserv'd* (revived tragedy); *Theatrical Candidates* (3rd time); and Foote: *The Lyar* (revived comedy). One first.
Fri 29 Sept	(dark)
Sat 30 Sept	Bickerstaffe: *Love in a Village* (revived comic opera); *Theatrical Candidates* (4th time); Whitehead: *A Trip to Scotland* (revived farce); and dancing. Two firsts.
Sun 1 Oct	(closed, always on Sunday)
Mon 2 Oct	(dark)
Tue 3 Oct	Shakespeare–Cibber: *Richard III* (revived tragedy); *Theatrical Candidates* (5th time); Garrick: *The Irish Widow* (revived comedy); and dancing. One first.
Wed 4 Oct	(dark)

[9] For the lives of performers see Highfill *et al.*, *Biographical Dictionary*. Anyone with a head for finances can find in *The London Stage 1660–1800*, s.v. September 1760, a richly detailed company roster and accounts for Covent Garden. See also Milhous, 'Company management'.

Thu 5 Oct	Jonson: *Every Man in His Humour* (revived comedy, replacing *Jane Shore*, revived tragedy, postponed on short notice); *Theatrical Candidates* (6th time); and Bickerstaffe: *The Padlock* (revived comic opera). One first.
Fri 6 Oct	(dark)
Sat 7 Oct	Congreve: *The Way of the World* (revived comedy); *Theatrical Candidates* (7th time); Dibdin: *The Deserter* (revived musical farce); and singing.

The mixed bag of worthy and worthless works would surely have pleased Polonius, whose dramatic tastes were about the same as most of Garrick's spectators. In these particular two weeks there appeared revivals of seven mainpieces and seven afterpieces, with the new, tuneful trifle *Theatrical Candidates* used to fill the bill until other works were ready. Drury Lane did not offer another brand new production until 28 October. By then the company was ready to perform six nights a week. The system was complicated and demanding, but it provided flexibility, splendid training for neophytes, great variety for audiences and a simple way to make quick changes so a show could always go on.

Within the constantly changing schedule there could be relatively long runs, such as *The Theatrical Candidates* (19 season performances) and *The Rival Candidates* (14). In 1775–6 at Covent Garden, Sheridan's comic opera *The Duenna* was given 75 times. That kind of success must have tempted managers to abandon the repertory idea and present one show at a time, allowing it to run as long as possible – the standard commercial arrangement today. If a work was successful, it could cover expenses in short order, bring a profit to investors and provide assured employment for participants. That approach puts all the eggs in one basket, however: if a show fails, almost everyone loses.

Company organization, management and recruiting practices were much the same everywhere in the land, linking one playhouse to another in common cause. Garrick wrote on 31 July 1775 to the playwright Henry Bate: 'If You pass by Cheltenham in Your Way to Worcester, I wish you would see an actress there, a *Mrs Siddon's* [sic], She has a desire I hear to try her Fortune with Us; if she seems in Your Eyes worthy of being transplanted, pray desire to know upon what conditions She would make ye Tryal, & I will write to her'.[10] Mrs Siddons came to Drury Lane and played Portia on 29 December, cited in the bills, typically, as 'a Young Lady (being her first appearance)'. She received poor reviews, and the production was shelved after two performances; she was tried

---

[10] Garrick, *Letters*, III: 1021.

in the title part in Jonson's *Epicoene* with no better success. The neophyte, just 21 years of age, was given other trials, but she needed further seasoning in the provinces before she would really be ready for London. When she returned in 1782, she triumphed and became the greatest actress of her time.

In the 1775–76 season Drury Lane presented, according to the *London Stage*, 189 performances of 100 works, consisting of 67 mainpieces and 32 afterpieces; new works were 1 mainpiece, 1 prelude and 5 afterpieces.[11] The list contained 27 tragedies, 42 comedies, 10 farces or burlesques, 8 pantomimes or musical farces, 9 comic or ballad operas and 4 preludes or interludes. Three works were from the sixteenth century, 26 from the seventeenth, and 71 from the eighteenth. The running times of mainpieces, recorded by the prompter John Brownsmith in *The Dramatic Time-Piece* (1767), show how common it was to shorten plays and how much the theatre of the time depended on the repetition of familiar pieces. Uncut, most would run two and a half hours or more, but he lists many plays at close to two hours or less (Farquhar's *The Recruiting Officer* 1:43; Rowe's *Jane Shore* 1:41; Jonson's *The Alchemist* 2:03; Shakespeare's *As You Like It* 1:49; *Much Ado* 1:52). Prompt-books provide further evidence of how freely the players altered texts. Garrick's annotated copy at the Folger Shakespeare Library of Vanbrugh's *The Provok'd Wife* is a good example. Many of the drastic cuts were designed to reduce everyone's role but Garrick's, but what was good for Garrick was usually what the audiences wanted and, thus, what was good for the theatre. The average running time of afterpieces was thirty minutes and of entr'acte entertainments seven minutes; typical performances lasted three to five hours, depending on delays and audience interruptions – of which, more anon.

Garrick and Shakespeare, as might be expected, were the most popular playwrights; others who had three or more works active this season were Bickerstaffe, Cumberland, Farquhar, Jonson and Rowe. But most of the journeyman authors who supplied many of the works given in 1775–76 are, like the performers who acted in their plays, strangers to us now: Andrews, Colman the elder, Charles Dibdin, Hill, Hull, Kelly, Murphy, Whitehead, Woodward. Women playwrights, a rarity in any age, sometimes found the audiences of the time responsive, but they, too, are little known today. Susanna Centlivre from the beginning of the century and Garrick's contemporaries Hannah Cowley, Elizabeth Griffith, Charlotte Lennox and Elizabeth Inchbald were among the

---

[11] Tallies like these are approximate, because playbills were inconsistent about citing genres and company records are incomplete, but the figures are close enough for our purposes. By comparison, the opera troupe at the King's Theatre in 1775–6 gave seventy performances of ten operas.

very few women who tried their hands at playwriting and who survived in a trade where many of their male counterparts failed. Cowley's first play, *The Runaway*, fared remarkably well in 1775–76, receiving seventeen performances. 'As we have lately been much afflicted with the melancholy fate of theatrical authors', wrote a critic in the *Westminster Magazine* in February 1776, 'we have a pleasure more than common in the great success of this piece.'[12] The comedy held the stage for eleven years. But it must have been discouraging for playwrights then to write for patrons so many of whom were more interested in performers and performing than in playwrights and plays and in afterpieces rather than mainpieces. A century earlier an evening's entertainment had normally consisted of just one play.

Serious theatre-goers in the 1770s might stay only for the main attraction; many others purposely arrived late, just to see the afterpiece and consequently pay a reduced charge (called half price). Garrick's *Jubilee* is fairly typical of the kind of frothy, showy second work that pleased eighteenth-century audiences so much. *The Jubilee* had been developed for presentation at the Shakespeare celebration in Stratford in 1769. When the event was rained off, Garrick salvaged the entertainment (as afterpieces were often called) by presenting it at Drury Lane with songs, dances, drums, cannons, bells, a spectacular transparency, new costumes and a colourful procession of the company's chief players, each dressed as a Shakespeare character. There 'never was an Entertainment produc'd that gave so much pleasure to all Degrees Boxes pit and Gallery', wrote the prompter.[13] The piece was laid aside after the 1770–71 season but was presented at Covent Garden in April 1775 and then revived in altered form at Drury Lane in 1775–76. The work was repeated throughout the 1780s; remarkable mileage for a piece of fluff, which tells us more than we may want to know about audience tastes in those days.

Patrons were never offered any Greek or Roman drama, but they traditionally received a fair sampling of *their* classics, works from the Elizabethan and Restoration eras. Prompt-books, however, show what the players and government censors did to the texts and are evidence that few productions were of the early works as we study them today. Only in modern times have we seen revivals of uncut old plays. *Hamlet* as played by Thomas Betterton in the late seventeenth century and Garrick a hundred years later was a lean play, swiftly moving, with depth diminished and characters missing (Garrick dropped the

---

[12] *The London Stage 1660–1800*, IV: s.v. 15 February 1776.
[13] Ibid., IV: s.v. 14 October 1769.

gravediggers, for instance). The actor-managers were not conducting classes in Elizabethan literature, they were running commercial theatres and had to make old plays work. Many dramatists from the licentious Restoration period were revived in the 1770s, albeit in doctored form. Dryden, Wycherley, Otway, Farquhar and Vanbrugh held the stage remarkably well in the eighteenth century. Of Garrick's contemporaries, only Goldsmith and Sheridan had comparable staying power in later periods.

Competition between theatres was common and therefore must have been profitable. Drury Lane offered twenty-nine pieces in 1775–76 that were also given at Covent Garden. A hundred years before, a theatre had more or less exclusive rights to a list of plays, but by Garrick's day one could frequently see a piece at Drury Lane and then, if the timing was right, walk over to the rival house and catch the same work with a different cast. The two patent theatres gave opposing productions of Rowe's *Tamerlane* on the same night each November from 1718 to 1780, and in the 1750s they ran rival versions of *Romeo and Juliet* starring the romantic Spranger Barry at Covent Garden and Garrick at Drury Lane. Garrick outlasted his rival but, according to most observers, lost the contest.

The benefit performance was an important part of theatre financing. In the 1770s the earliest benefits in the season, sometimes offered before Christmas, were usually for charities – to raise money for a hospital or church or for the troops (but, interestingly, there was no military support this season); such benefits helped earn the players respectability. Benefits for authors were a long-standing practice: playwrights usually, instead of being paid royalties or a flat fee by the theatres, received the profits (if any) from the third, sixth and ninth performances (if scheduled) of their new work. That meant a successful play could reap rewards, but a flop might leave the author bereft.

Employee benefits began about March, and the spring months saw many productions that were performed only once. First, the leading players were given solo benefits and, depending on their contractual arrangements, kept all or most of the takings for their evening plus any gifts they could lure from their patrons. The programme for each beneficiary, at least the major ones, was a personal choice. Some would appear in a role they did not usually play, or, conversely, would act in one of their popular showcases. Beneficiaries usually put together a mixed package just for the evening, hoping to attract as varied and generous a house as possible. It was an opportunity to boost their season income; so, demeaning as it may sometimes have been, they called personally upon patrons at their homes to sell tickets.

How the benefits worked and how well or poorly beneficiaries fared can be seen by looking at a typical week in 1776, when the second and third ranks of performers were having their nights.

Mon 22 Apr   Mrs Henry King's benefit: *The Fair Quaker* with Mrs King as Dorcas Zeal for the first time; also: *Bon Ton*, already in the active repertory, with Mrs King as Lady Minikin, which she had been playing all season. The profit for her came to a modest £10 13s 6d.

Tue 23 Apr   Mrs Sutton's benefit: *The Jealous Wife*, just revived in January, but she did not perform in it. Also: *The Elopement*, in which she had been playing Colombine this season; she danced with Froment and Slingsby between the acts. Her efforts won her only £3 15s 6d, because the evening's receipts came to £74 14s but house charges (the cost of giving the performance) were £70 18s 6d.

Wed 24 Apr   Jefferson's benefit: *The Roman Father* and *The Spleen* had been scheduled, but the actor Parsons was ill, so instead the audience saw *The Recruiting Officer*, in which Jefferson played Balance, and *The Man of Quality*, in which he did not appear. The attendance, perhaps because of the substitutions, was mediocre, and Jefferson lost £21 8s 6d.

Thu 25 Apr   No benefit: Garrick gave his last performance of Kitely in *Every Man in His Humour*. The receipts for Drury Lane came to over £250.

Fri 26 Apr   Hurst and Webb's shared benefit: *The School for Rakes* (not previously given this season) and *The Waterman* (done several times) lost the pair £33 15s.

Sat 27 Apr   This was to have been Baddeley's benefit night, but the management bought it from him for £60, keeping £20 on account for a debt he evidently owed them; Garrick played Hamlet and Baddeley Polonius. Also on the bill was *May Day*, which had been running all season but not with Baddeley in it.

By May, benefit evenings were granted to lesser performers and other employees, sometimes with several people sharing a benefit and the proceeds, if any. This May was special, of course, because Garrick, who had been appearing regularly all season in some of his favourite parts, began on 11 April to offer his final run of performances. These were not marked as benefits but as 'House' – that is, the profits were to go to the company and contribute to the season earnings. Hannah More wrote to Mrs Gwatkin that

> The eagerness of the people to see Garrick is beyond anything you can have an idea of. You will see half a dozen duchesses and countesses a night in the upper boxes; for the fear of not seeing him at all, has humbled those who used to go, not for the purpose of seeing but being seen; and they now courtsy to the ground for the worst places in the house.[14]

Employees with benefit nights in May did not profit from their leader's performances, however, for though the events kept many wealthy patrons in town through early June, they sought tickets mostly for Garrick's performances and skipped the benefits for minor players. The accounts show frequent deficits for the underlings.

Most of the time audiences were attentive and polite, often they were heartily responsive or amiably critical, but sometimes they ran amok. There was much ado over *The Blackamoor Wash'd White* on 1 February 1776 and subsequent performances. The *Westminster Magazine* that month considered the new comic opera a theatrical trifle unworthy of its author, Garrick's friend, the Reverend Henry Bate (later Sir Henry Bate Dudley), whose forgettable successes were still to come.[15] The opening night audience disliked the piece and cried 'no more, no more!' They particularly objected when an English character, Sir Oliver Oddfish, could not trust his servants and replaced them with 'foreign' blacks. When the work was announced for a repetition the next night (a common practice with a new work, to give the author a better chance to collect third-night profits), some spectators vowed vengeance. The second evening brought hisses, and the performers completed the work with difficulty. On 3 February, Bate's benefit, 'Wash'd White' was omitted from the title, but the audience complained anyway. Then one Captain Roper and a friend, both drunk, leaped from a stage box onto the stage. As the prompter Hopkins reported, 'Several of the Pit and Boxes follow'd and Some blows ensued and I thought they would have pull'd the House down'. At the performance on 5 February the acting manager, Tom King, tried to placate the spectators but failed. 'They Call'd for Mr Garrick he attended – but they would not hear him for a long time tho' [he] Attempted Several times to speak – at last Somebody said hear him! hear him! – Mr G. told them that he would wait their [*sic*] all Night with pleasure if they requir'd it – hear him! Again was bellow'd out'. Garrick said his 'Theatrical Life would be very Short and he should be glad to end it in peace – A man in the Pit said if you have a mind to die in Peace

---

[14] John Hampden's *Journal*, quoted ibid. IV: s.v. 13 May 1776.
[15] *The London Stage 1660–1800*, IV: s.v. 1, 3 and 5 February 1776.

don't let this Farce be play'd again'. So much for the audience's respect for their beloved actor-manager. The problem was finally settled when the author took the prompt copy away from Hopkins and left the theatre.

Audiences may have looked upon such occasional disruptions as their prerogative and part of the whole show, for the actors were, after all, their humble servants. Because there was no simple way of dimming the auditorium lights, audiences were well aware of themselves and their part in the theatrical experience. They may have been childlike, if not childish, in their behaviour, but they belonged to a long tradition of lively, participating spectators that nourished Shakespeare in England's great age of playwrights and now actors in her age of performers. Garrick spent his career sensing what would please audiences and giving it to them, even, perhaps, continuing to schedule such a work as *Blackamoor*, knowing it would create a hassle but give the protestors a chance to flex their critical muscles. He probably felt that, in this instance, all would end well, and it did.

As long as managers did nothing to alienate their customers, such as raise ticket prices, they could rest assured that if they built theatres and put on plays, their masters would come. Many, for fear of missing something, came night after night to their choice social gathering place, whether there was a change of bill or not. The *Blackamoor* hullabaloo was only the most exciting of the incidents occurring at Drury Lane in 1775–76: Hopkins recorded many hissings of plays or performers; during the season there were numerous firsts – new plays, costumes, scenery, music, songs, dances, performers and so on (for a period that was generally conservative, there was a relish for that kind of novelty); on 18 April an actor almost lost an eye in a supercharged stage fight; there were several instances of overcrowding and audience discombobulation during Garrick's final performances; on 9 May some scenery fell to the stage from above, luckily without harm to anyone. Disruptions were similar at Covent Garden: *Lloyd's Evening Post*, according to the *London Stage*, reported on 25 February 1776 that 'A fellow who sat on the sixth row of the Upper Gallery . . . threw a Keg (which he had brought full of liquor into the House) over the Gallery front. It fell upon a lady's head . . . but the Lady's hair being dress'd in high *ton*, the artificial mountain luckily prevented the mischief that otherwise might have been occasioned.'

Change was in the air in 1776, and it involved not just the changing of the guard at Drury Lane. Repertory as a system of stage production was being altered, as more and more theatrical works caught the fancy of audiences enough to be given longer and longer runs. At the same time, theatres were being renovated to accommodate the larger audiences that were needed to cover increased expenses. The larger the capacity, the bigger the acting style had to be to reach the furthest corners of the house. The new acting suited the growing popularity and cost of spectacle productions, with their scenic magnificence and special effects. Some of these interlocking changes had been taking place slowly over the years, and the trends would continue into the next century. Theatre capacities, however, which in London averaged about 2,000 in 1776, would reach a plateau in the 1790s; the completely new Drury Lane in 1794 seated 3,600 customers, a size we think of now as suitable only for grand opera.[16]

Larger theatres and a broader acting style would seem to be at cross purposes with increased realism in staging, but both trends were at work. Removing distracting stage spectators in 1763 was one of Garrick's steps towards making what was seen on stage more like life. The use of relatively authentic stage costumes instead of current fashions added another degree of realism, and by 1776 this trend was well under way, with bills sometimes advertising 'dresses of the period' to attract audiences. By the nineteenth century historical authenticity in stage costumes would become standard. Garrick's Alsatian scene designer, Jacques de Loutherbourg, developed lighting effects using colours and transparencies that created strikingly believable effects, and his scene designs show how exactly he tried to reproduce nature on stage. All this contributed to the slow but steady move towards realism that would triumph over the grandiose stage traditions of the Romantic theatre. By the 1880s playwrights would write plays about ordinary people in real situations speaking the language of everyday life and theatres for drama would become smaller and more intimate, just as they had been when our hero began his career.

Garrick's farewell speech would not have been complete without a small lie from the great pretender. He could not disparage Sheridan and the others who had purchased the Drury Lane patent from him and would now run the theatre, so he noted their arrival and tried to reassure the audience that all would be well, though he probably feared that it would not (and it was not):

> I will very readily agree to my successors having more skill and ability for their station than I have had; but I defy them all to take more uninterrupted pains in your favour, or to be more truely sensible of it, than is your grateful humble servant.

The successors were Sheridan, the musician Thomas Linley (Sheridan's father-in-law), the wealthy doctor James Ford and Willoughby Lacy, son of Garrick's

---

[16] The Metropolitan Opera House seats almost 4,000, La Scala 3,000, and the Bastille Opéra 2,700.

long-time co-patentee James. Sheridan was clearly a playwright of the first order, but he was just as clearly aiming for a life in politics, not theatre. Garrick, ever anxious to improve the lot of theatre people in the eyes of the general public and especially government authorities, had assiduously curried the favour of the upper classes and avoided upsetting officials; he had tried to please everyone. As an actor he was adored by the public, and as the leader of a successful company he won the respect of people of importance (though not enough to win him a knighthood). Sheridan, by contrast, was perfectly willing to upset anybody. He had an eye for what would further his career, and his choice of plays in 1776–77 and 1777–78, especially his own *School for Scandal* with its political overtones, was designed to sway patrons to his sympathy for the American colonists and for Irish Protestants.[17] The choice of plays at Drury Lane during the Garrick years had been safe. The change in 1776–77 to Sheridan's more volatile spirit must have been shattering to many old Drury patrons. The *London Stage* figures make it clear, too: Garrick brought Drury Lane a profit in 1775–76 of £4,463; Sheridan's profit in 1776–77 was £1,039 and in 1777–78 a mere £10. Could Garrick at his retirement possibly have imagined the financial pickle his theatre would be in within just two seasons?

After telling the audience the little lie about Sheridan and his fellows being better equipped to manage Drury Lane than he, Garrick gave thanks one last time and then, ever the actor,

> bowed respectfully, to all parts of the house, and in a slow pace, and much hesitation, withdrew forever from their presence . . . Every face in the theatre was clouded with grief.

The audience would not allow the afterpiece to be given, nor would the actors perform it. The evening was over, and so, with Garrick's final bow, was an era.

[17] O'Toole, *Traitor's Kiss*, 123–34.

10

The theatrical revolution, 1776–1843

JANE MOODY

The late eighteenth century witnessed a revolution both in dramatic genres and in theatrical institutions. In 1776, the year in which David Garrick retired from the stage, the patent theatres – Drury Lane and Covent Garden – still stood unchallenged as England's national theatres, the cultural Parliament of the nation. The stock dramatic repertoire performed each season at these houses represented a collection of plays which would have been utterly familiar to many of their leisured and aristocratic patrons: Shakespearean tragedies such as *Richard III* and *Macbeth*, John Gay's *The Beggar's Opera*, Susanna Centlivre's *A Bold Stroke for a Wife*, Goldsmith's comedy of class and mistaken identity, *She Stoops to Conquer*, and *Jane Shore*, Nicholas Rowe's pathetic tragedy of female suffering. By the middle of the nineteenth century, however, the monopoly over 'legitimate' plays enjoyed by Drury Lane and Covent Garden had been abolished; according to the provisions of the Theatre Regulation Act (1843), all theatres licensed for the public performance of plays were now permitted to stage any dramatic genre. The intervening period was an age of extraordinary institutional change that saw the commercial disintegration and ideological collapse of legitimate drama, the emergence of an influential cultural sphere – the so-called minor playhouses – and, most important of all for the history of British theatre, the irresistible rise of illegitimate dramatic forms such as extravaganza, burlesque and melodrama. This was an age, too, of sparkling dramatic celebrity. Newspapers, journals and grand dinner tables alike delighted in performers, playwrights and dramatic gossip. In John Philip Kemble's lofty, grandiloquent Coriolanus, Sarah Siddons's unforgettable representation of Lady Macbeth ('Power was seated on her brow', remembered William Hazlitt; 'she was tragedy personified'), and Edmund Kean's dignified Shylock or his playful, disconcertingly jocular Iago, critics and spectators acknowledged that they were witnessing a transformation in Shakespearean performance. But celebrity was by no means confined to the representation of Shakespeare. The dramatic stars of the age included comedians such as Joseph Munden, Dorothy Jordan, Charles Mathews and the cockney wit John Liston (a memorable Marplot, that insatiably curious star of Centlivre's *The Busie Body*), as well as Eliza Vestris – who captured the town's attention in a succession of delicately salacious breeches parts, most notably as Don Giovanni – not to mention Joseph Grimaldi, the lovable, criminal hero of Regency pantomime. To some extent, the late Georgian theatre is a period torn between the dull, increasingly anachronistic claims of legitimacy and the captivating, albeit vulgar vitality of illegitimate forms. Playwriting and performance, however, complicate these apparent oppositions in numerous and unexpected ways.

How did this revolution in performance and theatrical regulation come about? Let us begin with London's new playhouses. As we have seen, the Licensing Act of 1737 had confirmed in law the patent theatres' monopoly over the production of drama in London, as well as establishing a system for censoring the texts of all new plays to be performed at Drury Lane and Covent Garden. By this act, anyone convicted of acting 'for hire, gain or reward' in a theatrical performance not previously permitted by royal patent or licensed by the Lord Chamberlain now became liable to a fine of £50. Throughout the first half of the nineteenth century, the Licensing Act continued to cast a long shadow over metropolitan production. Managers became ingenious (though not always successfully ingenious) at circumventing the prohibition on acting for hire, gain or reward. When he opened the Royalty Theatre in 1787, John Palmer tried to escape prosecution by declaring that his production of *As You Like It* would be performed for the benefit of the London Hospital; certain unlicensed theatres made arrangements for spectators to buy tickets at nearby shops, which would then provide the purchaser with free entrance to the theatre.

The Licensing Act was intended to suppress all theatrical production in London beyond Drury Lane and Covent Garden. But an act of 1752 permitted magistrates to issue annual licences to places of entertainment in London and Westminster and within a twenty-mile radius. Sadler's Wells, then a rural place of entertainment reached from Westminster by crossing the fields, had presented singing, dancing, acrobatics and other entertainments since the late seventeenth century, and succeeded in obtaining a licence under this act for singing, dancing and similar entertainments. In the late 1770s Philip Astley, soon to become one of the nineteenth century's first cultural entrepreneurs, founded his Amphitheatre on a piece of waste land near Westminster Bridge, and similarly obtained permission, this time from the Surrey magistrates, to produce equestrian spectacles, pantomimes and, later, 'burlettas' (a notoriously capacious dramatic category, as we shall see). By 1843, over two dozen 'minor' theatres operated under this legislation, including the Tottenham Street play-house in Marylebone (later to become famous under the Bancrofts as the Prince of Wales's Theatre), the Surrey and Coburg theatres (the south bank of the Thames, of course, had a distinguished dramatic history stretching back to the Rose and Globe theatres of the Elizabethan period), the Britannia in Hoxton, and the Pavilion, located in Whitechapel Road amidst a poor arti-san and seafaring community. Beyond London, royal patents were also being granted to many provincial cities, including Bath, Bristol, Edinburgh, Norwich and York.

Within Westminster, the irrepressible comedian Samuel Foote had been granted a patent in 1766 for legitimate performances during the summer months at the Little Theatre in the Haymarket. The playhouse where Henry Fielding had produced his coruscating political satires on Walpole's ministry during the 1730s would be admired in the early nineteenth century, under the management of George Colman the younger, rather as the bastion of the British comic tradition: a theatre of old plays and old ways, as Hazlitt remarked with warm nostalgia. Many of London's leading comedians, including Charles Mathews and John Liston, made their début here; the theatre's fine sightlines, intimate atmosphere and loyalty to the stock comic repertoire provided a cher-ished contrast to the innovations at Drury Lane and Covent Garden. In the first decade of the new century, the Earl of Dartmouth, then Lord Chamberlain and therefore responsible for the regulation of theatre, also gave his quiet sup-port to the opening of minor theatres within Westminster. In 1806 John Scott, a colour merchant, established the Sans Pareil Theatre (later known as the Adelphi) in the Strand; the same year saw the opening of the Olympic Pavilion nearby in Wych Street, a theatre quickly improvised from the timbers of a disused French warship and fitted with a makeshift tin roof. Here the gruff, blunt Philip Astley produced a variety of circus and musical entertainments. Within a few decades, both playhouses would become celebrated places of metropolitan pleasure.

The geographical location of the minor theatres followed movements of population into the fast-growing neighbourhoods around the south bank and in the East End around Whitechapel, especially around the new docks. In many ways, playhouses such as the Pavilion, the Surrey and the Coburg were indeed neighbourhood theatres, gorgeous palaces of light, luxury and warmth, a fantastic refuge from the monotony of work and the cramped, dark conditions of modern urban life. For hundreds of artisans, sailors, dock workers and small shopkeepers, theatre-going now became a major form of leisure and also an important source of cultural knowledge. But though tongue-in-cheek reports of chimney-sweepers carrying the tools of their trade into the gallery, or accounts of costermongers delighting in murder, love and 'deep tragedies' might lead us to interpret the minor theatres as a vulgar, plebeian sphere, a broad selection of middle-class and aristocratic spectators also patronized the minor theatres, as, on occasion, did royalty. Princess Victoria even drew a sketch of *The Rape of the Lock*, a play she saw performed at the Olympic Theatre in 1837. Throughout this period, hit plays such as Moncrieff's burlesque of Mozart's opera, *Giovanni in London* (Olympic, 1817), or Fitzball's *Jonathan Bradford; or, The Murder at the Roadside Inn* (Surrey, 1833) – a melodrama featuring a box set in which the action unfolded simultaneously in four separate rooms of a roadside inn – brought a rapid influx of curious West End visitors eager to see the latest theatrical novelty for themselves.

The minor theatres transformed London's dramatic culture in a number of ways. Their programmes, each featuring from three to five separate plays (as well as entr'acte entertainments such as songs, slack rope performances and the exhibition of ethnic and quadruped 'curiosities'), created a large, virtually inexhaustible market for illegitimate forms such as burletta, melodrama and spectacle. Their geographical position, and cheap seats, also had the effect of transferring the balance of dramatic patronage in London from the aristocracy and the gentry to a much younger, poorer audience largely composed of artisans, shopkeepers, sailors and apprentices. In the eyes of many middle-class reviewers, playhouses like the Coburg therefore came to represent the frightening consequences of cultural democracy: a theatre of sensation ruled by the mob. Moreover, the minor theatres beyond Westminster constituted an institutional sphere beyond the regulation of the Lord Chamberlain, for no formal mechanism existed by which to censor the texts of the plays performed there. Several plays refused a licence by the Lord Chamberlain, including Mary Mitford's regicide drama, *Charles I* (1825), received their first performances at the minor houses. Then, in the summer of 1832, amidst the political crisis over parliamentary reform, the Coburg's audacious topical adaptation of Henry Fielding's satire, *Tom Thumb* (starring a King and Queen clearly designed to represent William IV and his consort) seemed to confirm the willingness of certain managers to risk staging forms of political drama, in bold defiance of convention. In a variety of ways, then, the minor theatres occupied an institutional position that disrupted and indeed helped to destroy the gentlemanly, decorous world of patent dramatic culture. For all these reasons, the audiences and performances at these minor houses troubled the dreams of legislators and critics alike.

In the late 1780s Jack Palmer, the famous comic actor known as 'Plausible Jack', decided to challenge the patent theatres' monopoly of legitimate drama. Palmer, for whom the part of Joseph in Sheridan's *The School for Scandal* was allegedly written, proceeded to open the Royalty Theatre, close to the Tower of London, without a licence. With still more bravado, he advertised for the opening night a performance of Shakespeare's *As You Like It*. Not surprisingly, the patent managers were quick to punish this upstart rival, and immediately began a prosecution against Palmer; when the Royalty reopened, its repertoire was confined to pantomime and other illegitimate entertainments.

In the wake of Palmer's transgression, Drury Lane and Covent Garden also attempted to redefine the nature of their dramatic monopoly. According to their arguments, the patents bestowed on the two theatres encompassed not only the traditional legitimate genres of tragedy and comedy but all forms of dramatic dialogue as well. By this definition, the minor theatres were only licensed to perform singing, dancing and dumbshow entertainments. Sadler's Wells and the Royal Circus therefore began to develop various ruses by which to perform dialogue and to convey plot and character without the aid of speech. The first of these was the scroll: a piece of linen mounted on two wooden poles and held aloft by the performer on which fragments of speech (often woefully misspelt) would be inscribed. Robert Elliston's dumbshow version of *Macbeth*, performed at the Surrey in 1809, for example, incorporated a series of banners which conveyed to the audience such information as 'Macbeth orders a banquet'; another banner gave Macduff the news that his wife and children had been murdered. Secondly, managers such as Philip Astley and Charles Dibdin realized that the genre of burletta – a form of musical theatre originating from Italy but assimilated into patent culture during the eighteenth century – might provide a convenient generic disguise behind which to stage dramatic dialogue. For by converting dialogue into rhyming verse, and interspersing five or six songs throughout a play, almost any legitimate drama, from *The Beggar's Opera* to *Richard III*, could be classified as a burletta. Within a few years, as George Colman wryly remembered, the process of subverting the category of burletta had begun in earnest. First, the minor theatres 'made their Recitative appear like Prose, by the actor running one line into another, and slurring over the rhyme; – soon after, a harpsichord was touch'd *now and then*, as an accompaniment to the actor; – sometimes once a minute; – then once in five minutes; – at last – not at all; – till, in the process of time, musical and rhyming dialogue has been abandoned'.[1] By the 1820s, then, even the vestiges

---

[1] Colman, *Random Records*, 1: 52–3.

of illegitimacy in performance were disappearing. Burletta had enabled the minor theatres to circumvent the ban on performing legitimate drama and to compete with the patent houses virtually on their own theatrical terms.

The French Revolution and Britain's war against Napoleon helped to establish minor theatres such as Sadler's Wells, the Royal Circus and Astley's Amphitheatre as the dramatic newsreels of the metropolis. Audiences from all over London came to watch spectacular documentary dramas such as *The Surrender of Condé* (Astley's, 1793) and *Naval Triumph; or, The Tars of Old England* (Sadler's Wells, 1794), featuring dastardly sans-culottes, tyrannical despots and courageous British tars. Sadler's Wells, which had recently installed a huge water tank flooded by water from the New River, thrilled spectators with its spectacular aquadrama, including the terrific sea battles represented in *The Siege of Gibraltar* (1804); Astley's was famous for quadruped plays featuring sagacious horses and glorious combats set amidst extensive military fortifications. Here, indeed, the economies of war and theatre had become intricately related: ship workers from the dockyards built the model ships seen in many a Sadler's Wells production, while sailors formed a large proportion of theatre audiences, especially in the East End and on the south bank. In a variety of ways, the dramatic representation of revolution and war laid the foundations for the physical aesthetic at the heart of illegitimate theatre, and that theatre's distinctive preoccupation with the heroism, loyalty and moral virtue of the common man.

In the decades that followed, the minor theatres challenged the dramatic supremacy of Drury Lane, Covent Garden and the Haymarket. Moncrieff's lively dramatization of Pierce Egan's ironic guide to metropolitan life, *Tom and Jerry; or, Life in London* (1821), drew huge crowds, and played for 100 consecutive performances; evangelical protestors placarded the theatre in vain to denounce the play's immorality. The Adelphi also cleverly exploited the vogue for supernatural sensation with productions such as Fitzball's *The Flying Dutchman; or, The Phantom Ship* (1827). Soon, 'Adelphi drama' would become a byword for melodramas skilfully combining pathos, laughter and remorse. In plays such as *Victorine*, *The Green Bushes* and *The Flowers of the Forest*, in which popular actresses like Elizabeth Yates and Fanny Fitzwilliam played leading roles, the Adelphi presented women facing conflicting loyalties and moral choices: melodrama began to dramatize a form of suffering femininity very different from the earlier stereotypes of loyal wife, beleaguered maiden and intrepid Amazonian.

At the Olympic, Eliza Vestris, arguably the first woman to manage a London theatre in her own right, shrewdly identified the demand for a theatre that epitomized luxury and gentility. During the 1830s Vestris and her leading authors (James Robinson Planché, Charles Dance and Bayle Bernard) produced a carefully judged repertoire of classical extravaganza (a genteel form of pantomime, starring mythological gods facing urban dilemmas) and elegant costume burlettas. The success of these Olympic productions can be traced to a variety of theatrical reforms: the abolition of 'puffing', shorter bills, studious rehearsal and immaculate *mise-en-scène*, from practicable doors and Axminster carpets to the King Charles spaniels which graced the Olympic's production of Planché's *The Court Beauties* (1835). Once a disreputable dive in a seedy neighbourhood, the Olympic Theatre under Vestris had become the favoured resort of fashionable theatre-goers.

Beyond Westminster, amidst the network of streets now cutting across St George's Fields, the comic actor Robert Elliston took over the management of the Royal Circus in 1809. The date marks a watershed in the history of illegitimate theatre. Elliston promptly converted the circus ring into a pit, renamed his theatre the Surrey and immediately revealed his determination to trespass on the legitimate drama by staging *Macbeth* as a *ballet d'action*, with music and dumbshow. Other stock plays soon followed, all performed in doggerel rhymed verse so as to fall within the official definition of burletta. Within a decade, Elliston would be the lessee of Drury Lane, a remarkable sign of the profits to be made from modern dramatic entrepreneurship and the now permeable boundaries between production at the minor and patent theatres. Later, under the management of the playwright Thomas Dibdin, audiences flocked to see the Surrey's highly praised dramatizations of *The Bride of Lammermoor* and other novels by Walter Scott. Within a decade, the Surrey had transformed itself from a circus house into perhaps the most respectable of the minor theatres.

In 1818 the Surrey acquired an important commercial rival in the shape of the Coburg Theatre, which opened close to the new Waterloo Bridge. Journalists soon began to refer to the theatre as the Blood Tub, for the Coburg rapidly gained notoriety for lurid and sensational melodramas such as *Trial by Battle; or, Heaven defend the Right* (1818), often based on recent crimes reported in broadsides and newspapers. This reputation for blood and sensation should not obscure the range of the Coburg repertoire, which featured a variety of historical plays, sometimes on classical themes, as well as spectacular oriental melodramas such as Barrymore's *El Hyder, the Chief of the Ghaut Mountains* (1818). Here, and in similar plays, spectators saw Britain's imperial ambitions dramatized as an heroic crusade for liberty against usurping tyrants and barbaric native customs. As the sailor Harry Clifton declares, 'We British lads espouse the cause of all who are oppressed . . . while a sword, a man, or guinea lasts, surrounding nations shall all allow that England is the first to combat in the cause of liberty'. In melodrama, empire was being reimagined as a spectacle starring the patriotic, dauntless British tar.

The minor theatres transformed London's cultural geography. Newspapers and dramatic periodicals soon began to review their productions; playbills for the Pavilion and the Adelphi jostled for space on walls and hoardings with those advertising productions at Drury Lane and Covent Garden. West End spectators could now collect tickets for a theatre such as the Surrey from box offices established at cigar divans and booksellers in Westminster; coaches, hackney carriages and Thames watermen competed to transport these audiences to the south bank. Meanwhile, high salaries for star performers and more flexible institutional structures encouraged leading performers such as John Liston and the versatile comedian Charles Mathews to migrate to the minor theatres. The minor theatres had also produced their own dramatic celebrities, notably T. P. Cooke, the sentimental hero of nautical melodramas such as Douglas Jerrold's *Black Ey'd Susan; or, All in the Downs* (Surrey, 1829) and, from Sadler's Wells, Joseph Grimaldi, Britain's most famous clown.

At the beginning of the century, the minor playhouses could justly be described as inhabiting the cultural margins of London theatre; by the early 1830s, the distinction between patent centre and minor periphery would no longer hold. Recent prosecutions of certain minor theatres by the patentees had been greeted with incredulity and ridicule. Playwrights, MPs and other public figures, as well as managers and spectators, began to campaign vigorously against the injustice of the dramatic monopoly; in 1832, a parliamentary select committee, chaired by the novelist, MP and playwright Edward Bulwer, took evidence from a variety of witnesses about the state of the drama. Only in 1843, however, was the patent monopoly finally abolished. Though all licensed theatres were now permitted to stage legitimate drama, the loophole by which those playhouses in London outside Westminster had formerly escaped censorship was decisively removed, for the Act granted the Lord Chamberlain and his Examiner of Plays the powers to scrutinize the texts of plays performed anywhere in London. Indeed, the Act removed the distinction between minor and patent theatres only to replace it with another kind of hierarchy, this time between a theatre (licensed for dramatic performance, but not for the consumption of alcohol within the auditorium) and what would become known as a music hall (licensed to purvey food and drink and to perform entertainments excluding plays). Nevertheless, the abolition of the monopoly was, above all, an important symbolic victory which finally dissolved the dramatic privileges enjoyed by the patent theatres for almost two hundred years.

The history of the patent theatres during the late Georgian period is a history of debt, bankruptcy and cultural ignominy. Throughout this period, Drury Lane and Covent Garden lurched from one financial crisis to the next, struggling under the burdens of high overheads and the expense of remunerating hundreds of dancers, singers and supernumeraries, not to mention the rising costs of engaging star performers. Prodigies such as Master Betty ('the Young Roscius'), who took Covent Garden by storm in 1804–5, or the celebrity of Edmund Kean at Drury Lane in roles such as Othello or the rapacious Sir Giles Overreach in Massinger's *A New Way to Pay Old Debts* (a performance so intense that Byron allegedly fell into a convulsive fit), provided only a temporary respite for the beleaguered patent finances. All too often, the receipts garnered from crowds who eagerly patronized the spectacular Christmas pantomimes such as *Harlequin and Padmanaba; or, The Golden Fish* (Covent Garden, 1811) merely helped to offset the costs of a half-empty pit and uninhabited boxes which greeted many a performance of the legitimate drama. Teetering on the edge of bankruptcy, especially during the economic depression of the early 1820s when prices for theatre seats were also falling, the patent houses had become unwieldy institutions, grossly inefficient in their management and clinging desperately to the shreds of their former glory as England's national theatres.

The patent managers of the day, from the playwright and leading Whig politician R. B. Sheridan at Drury Lane (1776–1809) to John Philip Kemble at Covent Garden (1796–1817) presided over a period of opulent, spectacular and ultimately ruinous expansion. The susceptibility of nineteenth-century theatres to damage by fire made reconstruction a physical necessity (Covent Garden burned to the ground in 1808, whilst Drury Lane was destroyed in a fire of 1809, watched by a stoical Sheridan from the Piazza Coffee House nearby). But by increasing the size and luxurious grandeur of their stages and auditoria, the patentees also hoped to lure the fashionable classes away from the rival attraction of Italian opera (the magnificent King's Theatre in the Haymarket had opened in 1791), as well as to head off the commercial threat of a third legitimate theatre in London.

Henry Holland's luxurious neoclassical playhouses, both completed in the early 1790s, each held over 3,000 spectators. As the playwright Richard Cumberland remarked, the new Covent Garden and Drury Lane had now become 'theatres for spectators rather than playhouses for hearers'.[2] The sociable intimacy of the old buildings had disappeared for ever; these vast, barnlike theatres also made it impossible for spectators to observe performers' nuances of expression and gesture. Moreover, the spiralling costs and salaries that were another by-product of theatrical expansion only served further to debilitate the already weak patent treasuries. But the new stages, now equipped with increased numbers of flats, flies and other modern facilities for machinery, did provide the technical infrastructure which made possible for the first time the production of spectacular Gothic plays such as George Colman's *Bluebeard* (Drury Lane, 1797) and Monk Lewis's ghostly drama, *The Castle Spectre* (Covent Garden, 1797). The vogue for Gothic plays also created leading roles for stage designers such as Thomas Greenwood the younger (who produced the sets for *Bluebeard*, including the fearful Blue Chamber, streaked with vivid streams of blood) and William Capon, who designed the Gothic chapel for Joanna Baillie's tragedy of cold and rivalrous hatred, *De Monfort* (Drury Lane, 1800). Indeed, the sophistication with which such designers and machinists produced the visual effects of suspense and dread ensured that these plays became the subjects of excited dramatic connoisseurship amongst many middle-class spectators.

The playhouses designed by Robert Smirke (Covent Garden) and Benjamin Wyatt (Drury Lane) in the following decade extended the practice of increasing the number of private boxes while reducing the space available for gallery spectators at the very top of the theatre. These attempts to convert the patent houses into still more exclusive establishments met with vociferous opposition. At the opening of the new Covent Garden Theatre (1809), noisy protests greeted the discovery of several innovations: new prices in the pit, the employment of Angelica Catalani, an Italian opera singer (xenophobia abounded in late Georgian theatre and spectators judged Catalani's fees to be exorbitant) and the increased number of private boxes. The Old Price Riots, which lasted for three months, became the longest-running and most colourful dispute between audience and management in British theatre history. Each night, audiences disrupted performances with their own carnivalesque OP songs, dances, catcalls and rousing speeches, until the beleaguered and increasingly desperate John Philip Kemble was compelled to concede to most of the rioters' demands. Even so, the memory of the Old Price Riots did not fade easily; on the contrary, the affair seemed to confirm the disdain of the patent managers about public opinion, and the patentees' willingness to sacrifice the stock repertoire

---

[2] Cumberland, *Supplement to the Memoirs of Cumberland*, 57.

(or 'national drama', as it was often defined) for more commercially profitable fare in the form of melodrama and spectacle. The Old Price Riots came to represent a huge nail in the coffin of patent monopoly; Covent Garden and Drury Lane alike began to be condemned by their critics as the cultural symbol of an unreformed Parliament: aristocratic, corrupt and unrepresentative of a modern nation.

The cultural status of the patent theatres, especially amongst the fashionable classes, was changing. Those once unquestioned social divisions between boxes, pit and gallery had begun to disintegrate. Italian opera, ballet and concerts of classical music offered competing, and more exclusive, forms of leisure. A climate of moral probity and evangelical fervour amongst the middle classes contributed towards increasing distaste for vulgar and bawdy humour. (The Bowdlers' *Family Shakespeare*, first published in 1818, builds on the meticulous, almost neurotic, expurgation of Congreve, Shakespeare and other stock dramatists in performance; stage censorship in the early nineteenth century was a ubiquitous institutional practice carried out by performers, managers and indeed by spectators, as well as being performed on behalf of the state by the Examiner of Plays.) The visibility of prostitutes in private boxes and around the saloons at Drury Lane and Covent Garden provided another focus for middle-class moral anxieties. Meanwhile, panoramas and exhibitions offered play-goers a genteel and spectacular alternative to theatre-going, while the rise of parlour entertainments (hit songs from popular dramas and toy theatre performances amongst them) represented another emerging form of respectable leisure. Moreover, the rise of the minor theatres had created a new kind of cultural market in London. Drury Lane and Covent Garden were now obliged to compete for spectators with a host of minor theatres, all quick to exploit the latest hyperbolic conventions of modern print advertising to promote their performances.

This transformation in the cultural and ideological status of Drury Lane and Covent Garden is closely related to a parallel transformation in dramatic forms. During the early nineteenth century, tragedy and comedy – the legitimate dramatic genres of eighteenth-century culture – began to be displaced by 'illegitimate' forms such as burletta, extravaganza, pantomime and melodrama. Not only were these the only dramatic forms legally producible at the minor houses, but – to the fury and despair of many reviewers and public figures – melodrama and spectacle also began to dominate the patent repertoire as well. The relationship between cause and effect in this process is difficult to determine: Sheridan and Kemble stubbornly insisted that plebeian audiences simply demanded sensation and spectacle; many of their critics, however, accused the patentees of a calculated and cynical determination to abandon Shakespeare and other stock dramatists for more profitable cultural goods. The critical reception accorded to Covent Garden's spectacular production of Monk Lewis's grand romantic melodrama, *Timour the Tartar* (1811), starring a troupe of horses hired from Astley's Amphitheatre, came to epitomize this controversy. Roundly condemned by reviewers and indeed in Parliament, hippodramas such as *Timour* (in which the hero and his horse plunge into a torrent of water in order to save Zorilda, his drowning mother) seemed to confirm the decadent sponsorship of illegitimate drama at Britain's national theatres.

As we have seen, by the 1820s the theatrical market for illegitimate forms far outweighed that for tragedy and comedy. Above all, however, such genres flourished because they succeeded in dramatizing most persuasively an age of extraordinary social mobility, technological innovation and colonial expansion. In panoramas of Alpine landscapes or of the icy wastes of the North Pole, for example, Regency pantomimes cleverly exploited the brilliant effects of contemporary visual technologies. The anarchic world of the harlequinade, in which an irate Pantaloon pursued Harlequin, Columbine and the Clown through a succession of London scenes, celebrated and simultaneously satirized the metropolis as a place of ceaseless change and whirlwind transformations. Melodrama, by contrast, was a genre preoccupied with the country as a place of lost innocence and virtue; the evolution of this dramatic form was inseparable from the traumatic experience of modern urbanization. Behind often stereotypical characters and formulaic plots, melodrama explored, often in deeply ambivalent ways, the nature of power, the integrity of the state and its institutions (notably the law) and the meaning of crime.

Turning to specific plays, the profusion and cross-fertilization of dramatic genres in this period is immediately striking. Though theatre historians often identify Holcroft's *A Tale of Mystery* (Covent Garden, 1802), translated from Guilbert de Pixérécourt's play *Coelina; ou, L'Enfant du mystère*, as the first English melodrama, the conventions and characters of this form were already present in a variety of plays produced during the 1790s. Indeed, the 1790s stands out as a decade during which, within a single play, dramatic genres seemed to intercut and clash against each other in unexpected and sometimes shocking ways. Many of the plays of George Colman the younger, Thomas Morton, Elizabeth Inchbald and Thomas Holcroft are hybrids, uneasy and occasionally controversial blends of sentimental comedy and social critique, farce and pathos.

Sheridan's dramatic career is best remembered by *The School for Scandal* (Drury Lane, 1777), a glittering, witty comedy powerfully indebted to the traditions of sentimental laughter. Yet in the malicious and hypocritical Joseph Surface, Sheridan introduces a character who can never be fully assimilated into the play's benevolent moral universe. Moreover, only two decades later, Sheridan would be celebrated (and, by others, maligned), for a play whose structure and ideological loyalties come, both literally and metaphorically, from a different world. *Pizarro* (Drury Lane, 1799), a dramatic allegory of British opposition to Napoleonic tyranny adapted from Kotzebue's drama about the Spanish colonization of Peru, is an operatic tragedy full of magnificent processions and spectacular stage effects. The play's climactic scenes, notably Rolla's perilous rescue of his lover's child from wild and rocky country, with a torrent falling down a steep and treacherous precipice, anticipate that recurring melodramatic trope in which moral jeopardy is presented in terms of physical peril. The interweaving of romance, pathos and colonial spectacle in *Pizarro* was certainly opportunist (Rolla's rousing speech to the Peruvian army – 'They follow an Adventurer whom they fear – and obey a power which they hate – *we* serve a Monarch whom we love – A God whom we adore' – was greeted with fervent and prolonged patriotic applause), but Sheridan also shrewdly anticipated the market for a drama which broke the generic boundaries of tragedy and comedy.

Many successful plays of this period seem to probe at the limits of sentimental comedy, exploring kinds of wrongdoing that call into question the integrity of a benevolent sentimental universe. Can Inkle, the brutish and mercurial man of commerce in George Colman the younger's *Inkle and Yarico* (Haymarket, 1787), who plans to sell his American Indian lover at the slave market, be reconciled with Inkle, the remorseful sentimental hero with whom the faithful Yarico is finally united? Inchbald's *Every One Has His Fault* (Covent Garden, 1793) also blends pathos, laughter and social criticism in disturbing ways: in the characters of Captain Irwin and Eleanor, Inchbald subtly dramatized poverty's indignity and indeed its susceptibility to exploitation – both social and sexual – by the wealthy. Several oriental plays, including Bickerstaffe's *The Sultan* (Drury Lane, 1775) and Inchbald's *Such Things Are* (Covent Garden, 1787) obliquely dramatize contemporary British debates about such issues as the subjection of women and the nature of arbitrary power. At a time when the Examiner of Plays was quick to strike out political allusions in the texts submitted to him for censorship, dramatists often relied on the quickness of many spectators to interpret oriental plays as allegories of topical conflicts at home.

The controversial humanitarian dramas of August von Kotzebue (1761–1819), many of which were produced by Sheridan at Drury Lane during the late 1790s, played an important role in the transformation of British theatrical

genres. Amidst fears in England about the spread of metropolitan radical-
ism, Kotzebue's plays attracted particular opprobrium because their piquant
situations, often featuring women who have transgressed society's codes of
behaviour, seemed to question conventional moral values. Kotzebue was an
important influence on leading British dramatists, notably Elizabeth Inchbald.
Lovers' Vows, the Kotzebue play rehearsed in Jane Austen's *Mansfield Park*, only
to be brusquely suppressed by Sir Thomas Bertram on his return, was one of
several dramas adapted by Inchbald for the London stage.

Sentimental comedy invariably ends with the reform of a wrongdoer who
is nonetheless essentially good: Belcour, the rakish Creole hero of Richard
Cumberland's *The West Indian*, first produced by Garrick in 1771, is a useful
and polemical example. In melodrama, the dramatic form in the ascendant
throughout most of the nineteenth century, the distinction between hero
and villain is more often stark and absolute. As Peter Brooks argues in *The
Melodramatic Imagination*, melodrama is a genre which strives for unequivocal moral clarity. Despotic tyrants, cruel landlords, oriental potentates, lustful
millers: these are the characters whose demise and destruction melodrama
rehearses. Whereas the world of sentimental comedy is one of conversation,
misrecognition and rhetorical debate, the melodramatic universe is characterized by physical conflict and providential intervention: explosions, conflagrations, shipwrecks, earthquakes and last-minute rescues.

The generic origins of melodrama are many and eclectic: sentimental
comedy, continental rescue opera, English pantomime and the robber dramas of Schiller, as well as Elizabethan and domestic tragedies like George
Lillo's *The London Merchant* (1731). Melodrama, indeed, becomes the meeting
point between a rich variety of British and continental dramatic traditions.
Some of the most compelling plays produced in the early nineteenth-century
British theatre also complicate conventional oppositions between good and
evil. Villainous characters such as Luke in John Buckstone's play *Luke the
Labourer* (Adelphi, 1826), or men justly punished for crimes against the state,
such as Richard Parker, the mutineer who goes to the scaffold in Jerrold's
The Mutiny at the Nore (Pavilion, 1830), are revealed also to be human beings
painfully wronged by others, individuals whose anger and insatiable desire for
revenge springs from long and bitter suffering. Such characters seem designed
to provoke conflicting, perhaps incommensurable, emotions of condemnation
and also of sympathy amongst the play's spectators; guilt and innocence can
no longer be confidently or unequivocally assigned.

To understand the emotional power of early melodrama, we need to imagine a form of musical theatre very close to opera, in which movement is highly

stylized and language, accompanied or interspersed by orchestral 'melos', is expressive of fear, doubt or joy, exclamatory and formulaic. To some extent, as the manager and dramatist Samuel Arnold pointed out, music in this form almost comes to supply the place of language. Dramatic action in this form characteristically alternates between periods of frenzied activity and climactic moments of stillness, when characters freeze into a stage tableau, often realizing a well-known image or picture from graphic artists such as Hogarth or Cruikshank. Melodrama represents emotion as an exterior, corporeal force; by the same token, perilous situations amidst rocks, cataracts, burning houses and dangerous precipices also render menacingly tangible the experience of moral danger. Though the familiarity (and near absurdity) of certain melodramatic characters and conventions (the long-lost child, the sudden reprieve of the innocent) provided burlesquers with an endless supply of material, these conventions also created a powerful framework of dramatic expectations that would be skilfully manipulated by playwrights such as Douglas Jerrold and, at the end of the century, by Shaw and Wilde.

Melodrama's foreign origins, plebeian characters and anti-aristocratic loyalties made the genre an easy target for conservative critics. According to many journalists, melodrama represented a dangerous dramatic virus, which was responsible for extravagant, hyperbolic acting styles, the usurpation of rhetoric by spectacle and sensation, the disintegration of dramatic authorship and, most dangerous of all, the death of tragedy. Yet many of the most successful stage tragedies of the day, notably *Virginius*, Sheridan Knowles's drama of Roman duty and domesticity, are also thoroughly melodramatic in mood and setting. *Bertram*, Charles Maturin's hit play (Drury Lane, 1816), is another hybrid, indebted in character and plot both to the conventions of tragedy and – especially in the wild and irrational extravagance of its eponymous hero, portrayed with a memorable mixture of pathos and passion by Edmund Kean – to those of Gothic melodrama. Similarly, popular comedies, including Thomas Morton's *Speed the Plough* (Covent Garden, 1800) and George Colman the younger's *John Bull; or, An Englishman's Fireside* (Covent Garden, 1803), also grafted on to comic structures those distinctly melodramatic values of hearth, home and the moral virtue of the common man.

Dramatic genres, then, are rarely pure or unadulterated in the early nineteenth-century theatre: romance, melodrama, spectacle, tragedy, comedy exist in bewildering varieties and unstable combinations. Melodrama, nonetheless, becomes the most profitable and ubiquitous theatrical form; its plots, characters and conventions also underpinned other kinds of contemporary discourse, most unforgettably the novels of Charles Dickens. To some extent, the triumph of melodrama can be attributed to its spectacular promise of a poetic justice which tragedy eschewed. As George Bernard Shaw later recognized, melodrama represented conduct 'as producing swiftly and certainly on the individual the results which in actual life it only produces on the race in the course of many centuries'. Melodrama's power lay in its capacity to encapsulate within a single form sharp and unreconcilable oppositions between laughter and pain, joy and sadness. Moreover, the perilous, physical world of melodrama also made it a form well suited to the dramatization of contemporary conflict, whether between classes or between nations. Game laws, the brutality of naval punishments and factory conditions were some of the controversial subjects represented in early melodrama; certain plays performed at the minor houses might well have been censored by the Examiner of Plays, had he possessed jurisdiction over the theatres in question. In dramas such as *Obi; or, Three Finger'd Jack* (Haymarket, 1800), John Fawcett's pantomimic play about the vengeance of a wronged slave, or William Moncrieff's *The Cataract of the Ganges* (Drury Lane, 1823), a spectacular piece about the British conquest of India (whose denouement took the form of a grand combat set amidst a burning forest in front of a huge waterfall), melodramatists also played an important and hitherto neglected part in shaping popular knowledge about slavery and empire.

The late Georgian period was an age of celebrated performers, but also one graced by talented and perceptive theatre critics. Essayists such as Charles Lamb, William Hazlitt and Leigh Hunt explored with fluid eloquence and verve the gestures, expression and characterization of particular performers: the sarcastic malignancy of George Frederick Cooke as Richard III, the solemn whimsy of Joseph Munden, the electric, colloquial, sometimes vulgar virtuosity of Edmund Kean. The scope of Romantic writing about theatrical performance is also notable, encompassing such varied and complex questions as the nature of stage illusion, the relationship between reading a play and seeing drama represented on stage (Lamb writes evocatively about the painful experience of watching *King Lear* compared to the play's sublime intensity in the closet) and the moral censorship of Restoration comedy imposed by anxious contemporary audiences. In addition, the generation of Hazlitt and Leigh Hunt defined for the first time the critical independence of the dramatic review (in the past, the patent theatres had paid for newspapers to print extravagant puffs, occasionally written by reviewers who had not even seen the production in question). Amidst a rapidly expanding print culture, dramatic criticism became an important forum for deeply political debates about Shakespeare's characters (Iago and Caliban in particular); Leigh Hunt and

Hazlitt also introduced dozens of mischievous parallels between the conduct of the patent theatres and the government of the Regency state.

Literary historians have often interpreted the late Georgian theatre through the eyes of disappointed Romantic playwrights such as Coleridge, Shelley and Byron. As Coleridge memorably lamented, 'What encouragement has a Man of Education and the feelings of a Gentleman to write either Comedy or Tragedy for Drury Lane?' The gaudy spectacle, often meretricious effects and obsessive vogue for realization on the contemporary stage (from 6-foot fairies in *A Midsummer Night's Dream* to the elephant from Pidcock's menagerie notoriously displayed in the Covent Garden pantomime of 1811) might indeed make dramatists and audiences alike long, as Byron did, for a 'mental theatre' that takes place in the silent oasis of the individual's imagination. Moreover, for a variety of often contingent reasons, a substantial number of plays by such distinguished writers as Joanna Baillie, Shelley, Keats and Byron were never performed on the early nineteenth-century stage. In the last decade, however, scholars have begun to recognize the intricate relationships between stage and closet in the late Georgian theatre. On the one hand, this is a period marked by the discernible (though often equivocal) alienation of certain leading poet-playwrights from the stage. On the other, the early nineteenth century is remarkable for a quiet revolution both in the organization of theatrical institutions and the production of dramatic genres. Amidst its transient and ephemeral wonders – Sarah Siddons as Lady Macbeth dismissing the guests in the banquet scene; Edmund Kean in the concluding scene of *Richard III*, fighting 'like one drunk with wounds' – we find also a fervent excitement surrounding the description and judgement of theatrical performance and the relationships between theatre and a modern society.

PART II

*

1800 TO 1895

11

Introduction
The theatre from 1800 to 1895

JOSEPH DONOHUE

1800 to 1843: tradition, innovation and regulation

Over the long period beginning with the restoration of King Charles II, the iron grip of the patent theatres on spoken-word performance, abetted by governmental oversight, had seriously impeded but not defeated the growth of theatres down through the late eighteenth century. Thanks in part to the vagueness of the laws related to burletta, as the new century began there were some ten theatres in operation in London, and by the end of the first decade fifteen.

The theatres in Drury Lane and Covent Garden were complemented by the opera house in the Haymarket, the King's, the smaller theatre across the street, traditionally known as the Little Theatre (largely a summer venue), the Lyceum (built in 1771, converted to a theatre in 1794) and the Royalty in Wellclose Square, intermittently called the East London Theatre, burned in 1826 but swiftly rebuilt. Charles Dibdin's hole-in-the-wall establishment, the Sans Souci, in the Strand near Southampton Street, lasted only from 1791 to 1796, but at his next venue, the New Sans Souci, in Leicester Square, he continued to charm audiences until 1804 with his idiosyncratic blend of songs and quasi-theatrical entertainment – meanwhile writing a five-volume history of the English stage.[1] Earlier on, he had composed ballad operas such as *The Padlock*, in which he created the role of Mungo, at Drury Lane in 1768. His one-man entertainment, *Private Theatricals; or, Nature in Nubibus,* which opened the first Sans Souci, offered such songs as 'The Sailor's Consolation', 'Roses and Lilies', and 'The Soldier's Last Retreat'. Dibdin's prolific output, amounting to hundreds of songs, contributed abundantly to popular pleasures of the time.

The two circus venues across the Thames in Surrey, Astley's and the Royal Circus, later the Royal Surrey Theatre, survived well into the new century. And in 1806 a theatre appeared in the Strand, beginning one of the longest

---

[1] Dibdin, *Complete History.*

tenures in the period. In that year Jane Scott, backed by her father's commercial success, opened a small house in the Strand called the Sans Pareil. Scott's irrepressible talents for singing, dancing and acting were enhanced by her facility in the writing of burlettas and skills for production and management.[2] The Sans Pareil prospered for well over a decade, changing hands in 1819 for 25,000 guineas. The new proprietors, Willis Jones and James T. G. Rodwell, rechristened their new venture the Adelphi, reflecting its proximity to Adelphi Terrace. The name persisted, as did the enterprise itself, becoming one of the most important and typical of middle-class London theatres, led by a succession of enterprising managers. At the Adelphi and elsewhere, adaptations of French plays abounded, along with native drama. W. T. Moncrieff's dramatization of Pierce Egan's 'flash' novel *Life in London* as *Tom and Jerry; or, Life in London* ran for ninety-four performances in 1821, solidifying an enduring Adelphi reputation for novelty. Ben Webster, who along with Madame Celeste managed the Adelphi through a brilliant period beginning in 1844, featured plays by the indefatigable John Baldwin Buckstone, acting in many of them himself. Buckstone, one of the most prolific playwrights, pursued a typical career. His early melodrama *Luke the Labourer; or, The Lost Son* opened in 1826 at the Adelphi, as did many of his melodramas, dramas, comedies, farces and burlettas. Despite enormous pressure on dramatists to turn out plays in days or even hours, some of Buckstone's works attain a distinctive freshness of dialogue and authenticity of character; the morose eponymous Luke displays a substance and depth comparable to the complexities of troubled Dickensian personages emergent on the Adelphi stage a decade later. The Adelphi remained at the forefront, offering its trademark sensation dramas, known, almost generically, as 'Adelphi dramas', and other crowd-pleasers.[3] Much later, in 1897, it became the setting for an even more sensational real-life crime, the murder of the matinée idol William Terris at the stage door.[4]

The Adelphi's success was echoed by various 'minor' or 'illegitimate' theatres in the period, surviving on the strength of the all-embracing burletta licence. Only in 1843 would Parliament finally terminate the hegemony of the patent theatres by endorsing, in the Theatre Regulation Act of this date, a *de facto* reality of years' standing. The background of this legislation requires particular scrutiny. By 1843 the number of theatres had risen to almost thirty-five, and houses specializing in some kind of theatrical entertainment had become

[2] Bratton, 'Jane Scott the writer-manager'.
[3] Nelson and Cross, eds., *Sans Pareil Theatre, Adelphi Theatre*; Howard, *London Theatres and Music Halls*.
[4] Rowell, *William Terris and Richard Prince*.

Plate 16. Playbill, Sans Pareil Theatre (1806), advertising the sort of varied offerings including burletta, expertly mounted at this theatre by Jane Scott, available at the 'minor' theatres in the opening years of the century.

a familiar fact of life. For all such 'minor' theatres, a licence for burletta proved the gateway for rival productions of works still categorized as 'legitimate drama' but now revamped with an overlay of music present throughout the performance.[5] Ironically, in offering theatrical fare with music, the burletta houses were only emulating the example of the major theatres themselves. An apt instance, the younger George Colman's charming opera *Inkle and Yarico*, with music by the prolific Samuel Arnold, set on a Caribbean island, bravely addressed the evils of the slave trade, succeeding at the little Haymarket in 1787 and quickly becoming part of the Drury Lane repertory. The airs, duets, trios and other ensembles were separately published for the delectation of a musically literate clientèle increasingly in evidence at alternative venues.[6]

By the end of the first decade of the new century, then, various theatres in London were offering some type of theatrical or quasi-theatrical entertainment replete with musical elements, in blithe defiance of patent theatre privilege. New theatres continued to emerge, and spates of theatre building would occur in these years and over the course of the century, in both London and the provinces, as well as in Scotland and Ireland. By the time of the first parliamentary inquiry, in June 1832, by the Select Committee on Dramatic Literature, convened to investigate the perceived decline of the drama, with Edward Lytton Bulwer, newly elected member from St Ives, in the chair, there were about twenty theatres operating in London, three of which – the Marylebone, the Strand and the short-lived Westminster Subscription Theatre – opened that same year. Typical of long available fare was a bill for Royalty Theatre entertainments on 27 October 1800, including a comic ballet, *The Hay-Makers*; a 'grand spectacle of action', *The Siege and Storming of Seringapatam*; a clutch of new songs; and *The Daemons Tribunal; or, Harlequin's Enterprises*, a 'Serio Comic Pantomime'.[7] The degree of impunity with which minor theatres conducted their affairs, offering the spoken drama with added music, was indicated in the inability of select committee witnesses to define the crucial term at issue. James Winston, stage manager of Drury Lane (and author of an important series of accounts of contemporary provincial theatres, *The Theatric Tourist*, 1805), reluctantly agreed with Bulwer's inference that even the Lord Chamberlain did not know what a *burletta* was. It was 'an entertainment of the stage', one expert witness abjectly explained.

---

[5] Moody, *Illegitimate Theatre in London*.
[6] Nicoll, *History of English Drama 1660–1900*, vol. III, *Late Eighteenth-Century Drama, 1750–1800*, 247; Fiske, *English Theatre Music in the Eighteenth Century*, 476.
[7] Royalty Theatre 1800–28, scrapbook of clippings, Harvard Theatre Collection.

Chief among the causes of alleged decline sufficient to spur a legislative inquiry was the stranglehold exercised by the patent theatres on the production of new plays. Those very theatres, Walter Scott had charged in his 'Essay on the Drama' published in 1819, were to blame for the sad debilitation of the art. Scott had identified three factors of central concern: the exorbitant size of theatre buildings, conditions hostile to both performers and dramatists and the systematic toleration of prostitutes, whose presence had driven away large segments of the potential audience.[8] Despite the recommendations of the 1832 report – most significantly, that all present theatres be allowed to exhibit 'the Legitimate Drama'[9] – no change would occur for eleven years, while flagrant violation of legal restrictions on spoken drama continued. Finally, by the time Parliament passed the Theatre Regulation Act of 1843 (6 & 7 Vict., c. 68), abolishing patent privilege, what the law now officially sanctioned was a manifest *fait accompli*.

Beset by competition and troubled by chronic mismanagement, from the beginning of the new century the patent theatres found solvency elusive. In this fraught situation, three profoundly formative events occurred within the space of two years. In the morning hours of 20 September 1808, Covent Garden Theatre, built in 1732 and greatly enlarged, to Henry Holland's designs, in 1792, was completely destroyed by fire. Five months later, on the night of 24 February 1809, Drury Lane was reduced to rubble by a conflagration which made quick work of Holland's rehabilitated theatre of 1791–4. Elaborate safety features then devised, including iron plates protecting the wooden shell, an iron fire curtain to separate stage and auditorium, and roof-top reservoirs of water, had all failed. The loss of a theatre that had lasted since 1674 was especially stunning in the context of the demise of its traditional competitor the year before. And still a third calamity lay just ahead.

The rebuilding of Drury Lane began in 1811, two years later, to designs by Benjamin Dean Wyatt; the new theatre opened its doors in October 1812.[10] Robert Smirke's new Covent Garden materialized more swiftly, almost exactly a year after the fire, in September 1809. Although no competition from the rival patent theatre, still in ruins, was to be feared, all was far from well at Covent Garden. Kemble, who with Mrs Siddons had been lured away from Drury Lane and chronic troubles with Sheridan, had become manager and part proprietor in 1803 by purchasing a one-sixth share from Thomas

---

[8] Cited in Donohue, 'London theatre at the end of the eighteenth century', 337; see also Donohue, 'Burletta and the early nineteenth-century English theatre'.

[9] *Report from the Select Committee on Dramatic Literature* (1832), 3–4.

[10] *Survey of London*, xxxv: chaps. 4–5.

Harris.[11] Kemble and the elderly Harris seem to have forgotten what had happened when the renovated Covent Garden reopened in 1792. An attempt had then been made, as part of a wholesale increase in admission prices, to eliminate the one-shilling gallery simply by charging a minimum price of two shillings for entrance. Exceedingly vocal opposition and general disorder on opening night, 17 September, carrying through the first two acts of the main-piece, forced the management to reverse itself on the spot. A promise issued from the stage to restore a gallery at the old price resolved the difficulty. The message sent to the proprietors on this occasion would seem to have been mislaid two decades later. On 18 September 1809, the night of the opening of the new Covent Garden with higher prices in effect, the cry in the audience for 'Old Prices!' was so great and continuous that the play, which went on any-way, could not be heard. Management dug in its heels, and a determined and well-organized opposition by 'OPs' carried out a riotous disturbance for sixty-seven nights. A report by an outside committee including the governor of the Bank of England and the Solicitor General concluded that the new prices were justified. The report fell on deaf ears. Riots continued nightly into December, forcing a humiliated management to capitulate. The old prices were restored (for the pit, though not the boxes), and the event went down in theatrical his-tory as the infamous Old Price Riots.[12] Despite the higher capacity of the new theatre, at 2,800 (excluding the private boxes) double that of its ancestor of 1732, Covent Garden limped along financially over the succeeding years, until in 1856 still another conflagration reduced it to ashes once again. From them a lyrical phoenix rose, in the shape of a new theatre devoted entirely to opera (still standing today, grander than ever after a late twentieth-century renovation).

And so the parallel march of the two patent theatres, begun in a frenzy of reconstruction in the 1790s, towards the mecca of increased capacity as a means to greater profits, had been routed at more than one juncture by 'the Drama's patrons'. It had been waylaid also by the inability of a succession of managements to cope with the demands of a growing populace eager for a variety of entertainments, fare which the minor theatres on either side of the Thames became evermore adept at supplying. In a tawdry irony, even as the patent theatres attempted to beat the minors at their own illegitimate game, they were rebuilding theatres with auditoriums configured in ways increasingly hostile to the accommodation of a more vocal, less well-educated cohort of theatre-goers. Private boxes were on the increase, shilling galleries

---

[11] Baker, *John Philip Kemble*, 273–4.
[12] *Survey of London*, xxxv: 78. See Boaden, *Memoirs of Kemble*, II: 493–516; and Baer, *Theatre and Disorder*.

Plate 17. Royal Opera House, Covent Garden (1858). Succeeding Sir Robert Smirke's Theatre Royal, built in 1809 in the early Greek Revival style and destroyed by fire on 5 March 1856, E. M. Barry's Royal Italian Opera House, completed in 1858, was smaller overall than its predecessor, but its stage was larger and its auditorium more accommodating.

in shorter supply and more likely to offer obstructed views. By the time the theatres of Smirke and Wyatt opened, the import of auditorium reconfiguration as a symbol of reified class division and antagonistic relations among various segments of theatre-goers had become unmistakably clear. Private boxes, installed at the third-tier level above two other tiers of boxes, walled off from one another and complemented by anterooms to which occupants could withdraw at will, were a distinguishing feature of Smirke's 1809 Covent Garden, reviled in many quarters. In this same theatre the one-shilling gallery, which almost entirely overhung the two-shilling gallery, offered only a limited view of the stage through a series of semicircular arches. The open boxes held some 1,200 persons (the private boxes, an undetermined additional number) and the pit 750, while the two galleries together accommodated only 850. Gallery seating therefore accounted for less than 30 per cent of total capacity. The contrast between these figures and those of the alteration of Covent Garden in 1782, where virtually 50 per cent of capacity was devoted to galleries, tells an all too patent tale of exclusionary motives and resultant social

Plate 18. 'A Minute and Correct View' of the interior of the new Covent Garden, February 1810, published by John Bell. The view, from the first-tier side boxes, capturing a moment during the tent scene of *Richard III*, encompasses the full auditorium, including the pit, three tiers of boxes and a fourth and fifth gallery, the latter rising behind arches creating obstructed views.

fragmentation. Inexperienced as a designer of theatres, Smirke nevertheless acted on instincts soundly consistent with theatre management's on how theatres ought to be built and patrons encouraged or discouraged. Control of the unruly and unsavoury by means of architectural revamping was evidently of even greater urgency than realizing a profit after costs. Fears of riot and disorder, implicit yet unmistakable in contemporary theatre design, became a self-fulfilling prophecy. By the time the Theatre Regulation Act of 1843 became the law of the land, the theatre world had changed irrevocably.

Ultimately, the resolution of the Old Prices crisis proved a victory for neither side. The 'drama's laws' had once again been tyrannically enforced by the *de facto* theatrical lawgivers of the nation. A chastened Kemble resumed the business of a nation's entertainment, but the mood had changed. A child of strolling players, Kemble had ridden a rising star of theatrical good fortune since his début as an unconventionally steady Hamlet at Drury Lane in 1783. He handily survived riots and other vicissitudes until his retirement in 1817. His celebrated elder sister had already left the stage in 1812. Despite their continued pre-eminence – Kemble bade his farewell in his acclaimed role of Coriolanus; Siddons, as the heartless but ultimately pathetic Lady Macbeth – the world of the theatre (like the world outside it) had become a different, even an alien place.

The departure of Siddons and Kemble brought to an end a long era of neoclassic acting, a carry-over from the previous century.[13] Meanwhile, in 1814 a fiery interloper, Edmund Kean, was gaining the ascendancy, encouraged by his critical champion, William Hazlitt, who had disliked Kemble's measured style enough to become his nemesis. He played the part 'like a man in armour', Hazlitt had said of Kemble's Hamlet, 'in one undeviating straight line'.[14] In stunning contrast appeared the impassioned, ostensibly undisciplined Kean. The début of this diminutive actor of unheroic profile as Shylock at Drury Lane on 26 January 1814 caused a huge sensation. Kean was borne on the crest of a tidal wave of adulation through the rest of the season, as Richard III, Hamlet, Othello and Iago, taking on additional roles, familiar and new, in subsequent seasons. In 1816 his performance as Sir Giles Overreach in the mad scene of Massinger's hardy favourite *A New Way to Pay Old Debts* affected Lord Byron so deeply that it was said he fell into a fit.[15]

---

[13] West, *Image of the Actor*; Downer, 'Nature to advantage dress'd'; and Downer, 'Players and painted stage'.
[14] *Complete Works of Hazlitt*, ed. Howe, v: 377.
[15] FitzSimons, *Edmund Kean*, 95; Hillebrand, *Edmund Kean*; Donohue, *Theatre in the Age of Kean*, 57ff.

Kean was inevitably compared to Kemble and also to a predecessor of another stamp, George Frederick Cooke, whose villains were imbued with a terrible energy and unrestrained passion. But Kean was irrepressible where Kemble was all control, and deeply grand and pathetic where Cooke was merely frenetic and caustic. Kean was incomparably the greatest actor George Henry Lewes had ever witnessed; one could not see his Othello, Shylock, Richard the Third or Sir Giles, Lewes insisted, 'without being strangely shaken by the terror, and the pathos, and the passion of a stormy spirit uttering itself in tones of irresistible power'.[16] In the short term Kean's astonishing success served to shore up the crumbling walls of the Drury Lane treasury, erasing the misgivings with which the Drury Lane committee had allowed him his début. Reaping an enormous bounty of publicity, Kean at once found himself championed by the recently appointed dramatic critic for the *Morning Chronicle*, the 35-year-old amateur philosopher and art critic Hazlitt, who for years had steeped himself in Shakespeare while reflecting on the origins of human motive and action.[17]

A major element contributing to the surprise and delight of audiences at the mercurial Kean's approach to the standard repertory was their detailed familiarity with how other actors had done it. The profound conservatism of theatrical tradition is evident in the relative paucity of new plays over a season, compared with the repetition of a number of familiar works, some on view since the Restoration or before. The early nineteenth century had inherited a substantial body of proven, actable plays of well-defined genre, featuring tailor-made roles for the nearly unvarying composition of the repertory company. These 'lines of business' included leading man, leading lady, juvenile, ingenue, soubrette, low comedian, high comedian, eccentric comedian (a late trans-mutation), heavy (sometimes the more specialized 'heavy father'), walking gentleman, walking lady, and a few others, all of them on view over the course of the season, though sometimes subject to variation, particularly on benefit nights. The attractions of theatre-going consequently included the pleasure of observing a well-known actor playing a series of well-known roles of a certain kind. A new role enacted by that player would have been immediately understood, generically and stylistically, because of the type of role that actor always took on; meanwhile, audiences would scrutinize the actor's performance for innovations introduced into the familiar profile. The history of acting from

[16] Lewes, *On Actors and the Art of Acting*, 14.
[17] Donohue, *Dramatic Character*, chap. 12.

Plate 19. Ticket for Mrs C. Sontley's benefit, signed by the actress and dated 1802.
Provenance unknown.

the age of Shakespeare well up into the nineteenth century is grounded in this
fundamental circumstance of repetition and variation.[18]

   The better actors would have placed their own recognizable stamp on any
role they assumed. Players brought to the task of performance a combination of competencies, along with a capacious, well-trained memory. Drawing
upon a large repertoire of artistic resources, the actor could be confident of
success. The low comedian, for instance, wielded a formidable set of entertaining tricks, including characteristic mannerisms, signature entrances and exits,

[18] Sprague, *Shakespeare and the Actors*; Sprague, *Shakespearian Players*.

eccentricities of delivery, pace and timing, and broadly rendered facial expressions, all of which worked to create an individualized yet gratifyingly familiar impersonation of a standard part. John Quick, creator of the role of Tony Lumpkin in Goldsmith's perennial *She Stoops to Conquer*, brought to his role an idiosyncratic approach common to such later actors as John Liston and the gifted mimic John Bannister; yet the combination of 'tall-boy airs, the mixed ignorance and cunning, and the mischievous perversity' Leigh Hunt identified in Bannister's Tony Lumpkin in 1815 was Bannister's alone.[19] (Over his career this actor would leave his impress on some 425 characters.[20]) Master tragedians or tragediennes would emblazon their own mark on a Shakespearean classic role in their singular way of delivering well-known passages and of enacting familiar pieces of business, as when Mrs Siddons's Lady Macbeth, in the sleep-walking scene in Act 5, set down her candle for the first time in the annals of the role, the better to wipe away the telltale tinct of blood from her hands.[21] True originality emerged from such careful departure from the practice of previous interpreters.

In the period after 1800, as before, actorly acknowledgment of the audience, in these ways, as patrons to be flattered and pleased remained a basic rhetorical component of acting style, as was the universally observed distinction between 'level' passages and passages of high emotion. The tragic actor's calculated differentiation between these two types of delivery conditioned audiences to anticipate the high points of the performance. They knew where those moments were and habitually compared the present actor's approach with that of every other actor of the role known to them. Performance of Shakespeare was widely subject to this phenomenon, but all plays in the traditional repertory were performed under the same conditions.

Broadly speaking, those conditions were inimical to nuance and subtlety, especially as the size of the stage and auditorium increased, the forestage receded and the need for vocal projection became more dire. Although the best actors could triumph over these limitations, clarity and boldness were the cardinal virtues of the workaday actor and actress, along with familiarity with a universal 'language of the passions'.[22] A coherent grammar of facial expression, gesture and attitude had been passed down from seventeenth- and eighteenth-century predecessors, and there were books codifying traditional gestures and poses. Two important examples occur in Gilbert Austin's *Chironomia* (1806)

---

[19] Hunt, *Hunt's Dramatic Criticism*, 99.
[20] Highfill et al., *Biographical Dictionary*, 1: 270.
[21] Sprague, *Shakespeare and the Actors*, 269–72.
[22] Roach, *Player's Passion*.

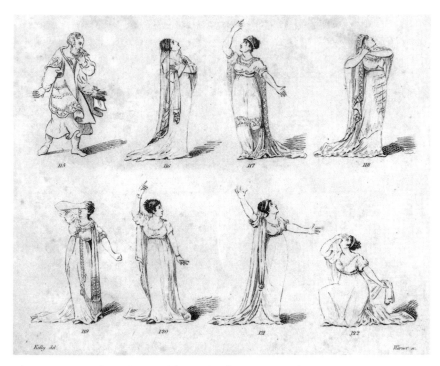

Plate 20. Excerpt from plate 11 of the Revd Gilbert Austin's *Chironomia; or, A Treatise on Rhetorical Delivery* (1806), including fig. 116, derived (as Austin acknowledges, p. 495) from Mary Hamilton's sketch for Calista – the first of seven sketches by Hamilton of Siddons in various characters reproduced in Austin's figs. 116–22. Austin describes the emotion depicted in fig. 116 as 'Resignation mixed with desperation[; she] stands erect and unmoved, the head thrown back, the eyes turned upward and fixed, the arms crossed' (p. 489).

and in a work published in 1807 by Mrs Siddons's eldest son, Henry Siddons, *Practical Illustrations of Rhetorical Gesture and Action*, demonstrating a systematic means of representing a character in situation. The task as Siddons frames it was, first, to acknowledge the teleological nature of dramatic character, which does not simply express sentiments and ideas momentarily but constantly launches itself into the future towards a 'determined mark'. In the reality of the present moment, Siddons explains, the sentiment of the character, conforming with the situation, shows itself as 'feeble or impetuous at its birth; imperious in its progress; mastered sometimes, or half extinguished; hid for a moment, to re-appear with greater force hereafter'. Siddons provides some sixty-eight illustrations of men and women under the impress of strong feeling in order to show how the clear representation of emotion in the heat

Plate 21. Mrs Siddons as Calista, in Act 5, scene 1 of Nicholas Rowe's *The Fair Penitent*, at the moment Sciolto describes her: 'See where she stands like Helen'. Watercolour by Mary Hamilton, dated 1 June 1802. Hamilton's sketch on which the watercolour is based, made from memory shortly after witnessing a performance, is included as figure 116 in Gilbert Austin's treatise *Chironomia* (1806).

of the moment provides the means of signifying and understanding human responsiveness.

An example of how this iconic vocabulary issues in memorable performance is provided by the eminent surgeon Charles Bell, who in 1806 had published his *Essays on the Anatomy of Expression in Painting*. Bell's description of the despair of Beverly, the hero of Edward Moore's tragedy *The Gamester* (1753) – 'he fixed his eyes upon the ground, and stood sometime with folded arms stupid and motionless: then snatching his sword . . . and with a look of fixed attention drew figures on the floor' – vividly anticipates Kean's business in Act 4 of *Richard III*, as recalled by Leigh Hunt, who described the 'reverie in which [Kean] stands drawing lines upon the ground with the point of his sword, and his sudden recovery of himself with a "Good night"'.[23] Kean's business succinctly illustrates the traditional approach to the enactment of character: the combination of a large vocabulary of conventional gesture and attitude with original touches revealing the individuality and genius of the actor and simultaneously enhancing the continuity of the moment.

Actors acquired these techniques not by attending academies of dramatic art (a much later innovation) but rather by observing other actors and, often, trying their wings as amateur performers before taking the considerable social and economic risk, amidst oppressive anti-theatrical prejudice, of turning professional.[24] Beginners hired on speculation by the hard-pressed manager of a touring company, as was Dorothea Jordan by Tate Wilkinson for his York circuit,[25] would often have to learn a new role several times a week, performing it for a single night and then passing on to another role the next night. Under these conditions, and even in the more secure circumstances of London patent houses and the established provincial theatres in Bath, Bristol, Birmingham, York, Edinburgh, Dublin and elsewhere, actors had to have prodigious memories as well as extensive techniques for memorization.

Learning the craft of acting thus involved learning how to play a certain kind of role. There were techniques and types of business which, once learned, were applicable to a range of characters in the same line. In low comedy, the actor who could play Tony Lumpkin could play the country squire Sullen in Farquhar's *The Beaux' Strategem*, Shakespeare's Sir Toby Belch in *Twelfth Night* and dozens of other such roles with comparatively little preparation. A truly 'quick study' could be ready in a day or even in a matter of hours, depending on the size of the role – traditionally measured in 'sides', the number of sheets

---

[23] Hunt, *Hunt's Dramatic Criticism*, 114.
[24] Barish, *Antitheatrical Prejudice*.
[25] Tomalin, *Mrs Jordan's Profession*, 24–6.

needed to write out the character's speeches and cues. In situations in which little time existed for rehearsal, much would depend on an actor's ability to fill out a familiar profile.

Everything, finally, was based on the constantly changing bill of the repertory theatre. As means of travel improved and opportunities multiplied for star actors in the provinces, resident companies became able to accommodate a visiting actor's schedule and preference of play. In a typical situation, a famous actor would arrive in a provincial city to play Othello. The local company would be ready for him: the leading man would be playing Iago opposite him and the rest of the company the remaining roles; the ingenue as Desdemona, the juvenile as Cassio, the leading lady as Emilia, the old man or 'heavy father' as Brabantio, the low comedy actor as Roderigo, the soubrette as Bianca, and various walking gentlemen as the Doge of Venice, Gratiano and Lodovico. The star actor would arrive, would 'walk' through his role, perhaps skipping from cue to cue or from one climactic moment or important sequence to another, passing over the level passages as unproblematic and informing the company of cuts in the script and where and how he would enter, move and exit. Actors as punctilious as Kean would count the number of steps to an exit. That would be the extent of a rehearsal, which only remotely resembled a full run-through. What enabled a perfunctory effort to issue in a successful performance was the wide range of tried and true techniques, the repertoire of gestures, actions and business and the basic assumptions shared by the visitor and the supporting company, including an understanding of how a role is to be acted and, just as important, how to avoid upstaging the star or otherwise 'stealing' from his centre-stage pre-eminence.

The English stage has always been a showplace for brilliant actors and a magnet for their audiences. Yet, even after the emergence of the minor theatres in London and the growth of the provincial stage, opportunities for professional acting remained relatively limited. Given the basic fact of theatrical life in London, where only two theatres (plus a third, in summer) were allowed the performance of 'legitimate' plays, actors' alternatives were few (aside from the ubiquitous burletta) and pressure to conserve the ways of their predecessors was great. The provincial theatres of Dublin, Edinburgh and a few other cities offered attractive possibilities, and touring companies became ever more the means for competent, seasoned actors to gain a livelihood and neophytes to get much-needed training and experience. Under these prevailing circumstances, 'Do what was done before' was the perennial wisdom of the workaday theatre. Tate Wilkinson, the distinguished, long-lived manager of a company based in York and Hull which toured Yorkshire and elsewhere for several decades in the late eighteenth century, understood and capitalized upon the practical realities of the theatre.[26] The pressures were unremitting, including the challenges offered by a demanding schedule and obstacles presented by the weather, inhospitable cities and towns and unsatisfactory, unsanitary venues. Provincial audiences were even more conservative than those of the London theatres. Adept at pleasing them, many such companies enjoyed a virtual monopoly over theatrical entertainment in their established circuit.

Notwithstanding these conditions, another sort of acting tradition developed quickly in the last years of the eighteenth century. As the forestage receded and techniques for lighting the stage, particularly its upper reaches, improved, actors had to abandon relative subtlety in favour of bolder, larger-scale effects. The emergence of melodrama in this period and its swift transplantation from French onto English stages appear, in retrospect, more than coincidental, as this extensively choreographed and musically accompanied dramatic form found a theatrical climate amenable to its defining features. Melodrama is rooted in a potent fantasy of the ultimate triumph of good over evil and the eventual happiness of a pure-hearted young man and woman whose only imperfection lies in their vulnerability. The abandonment of subtlety and nuance in favour of the bold effects required of actors performing in cavernous patent theatres and other venues almost as large transformed them into happy homes for melodramatic action. And so, despite a sturdy corpus of actorly ways defiant of alteration, a new development occurred: techniques and emphases perfected on patent theatre stages were carried by actors of melodrama into smaller houses, where this new form, an ingenious amalgam of under-music and bold, fast-paced action, came to be performed under the protective umbrella of a burletta licence.

By this time actors and the plays in which they performed were represented on increasingly large, more detailed and typographically varied playbills. The retirement in 1824 of the master-comedian Joseph Munden, on a night set aside for his benefit, attracted superabundant play-goers to Drury Lane, where, the playbill announced, the actor would attempt to take leave of his friends and the public. That public waited through three acts of Colman's *Poor Gentleman* to stop the action with shouts and applause on Munden's entrance as Sir Robert Bramble, as that matchless enthusiast Charles Lamb recorded the event. Long a devotee of Munden's acting, Lamb relished his extraordinary mobility of face and uncanny way of creating solid substance out of the make-believe of the

---

[26] Wilkinson, *Memoirs of his Own Life*; Wilkinson, *Wandering Patentee*; Rosenfeld, *Strolling Players and Drama in the Provinces*; Rosenfeld, *York Theatre*.

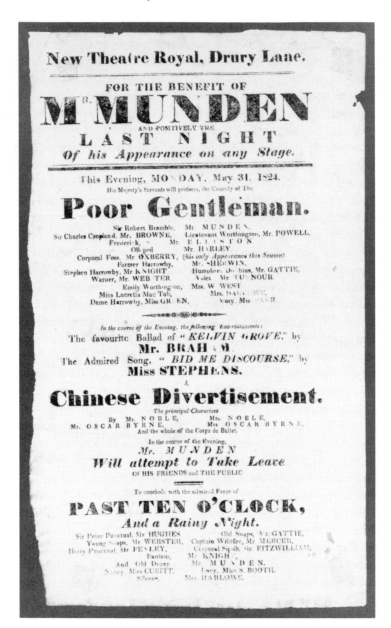

Plate 22. Benefit playbill for the pre-eminent comedian Joseph Munden, Drury Lane,
31 May 1824, Munden's retirement night, during which, the bill explains, 'Mr Munden Will
attempt to Take Leave of His Friends and The Public'. Munden played in both the
mainpiece and the farce.

theatre. In 'the grand grotesque of farce', Lamb asserted, Munden ennobled whatever he touched: 'a tub of butter, contemplated by him, amounts to a Platonic idea'.[27] Munden came on again in the afterpiece, Thomas Dibdin's popular farce *Past Ten O'Clock*, as the 'weather-beaten old pensioner' Old Dozey. In his 'determined attention to grog' he looked 'fireproof'. 'He *steers* at a table, and the tide of grog now and then bears him off the point', Lamb explained. The farce once over, and the 'farce of the long forty years' play' at an end, Munden became only the man himself, reading awkwardly from a prepared speech; but his audience forgave him and 'the people and Joe Munden parted like lovers'.[28]

The bill attracting audiences to Munden's farewell was a more informative document than its counterpart of the previous century, though still relatively brief. More typical is a Drury Lane bill for 13 January 1818, by which date the annual Christmas pantomime has been playing for over two weeks and is a constant feature. The mainpiece, the perennial favourite *John Bull; or, The Englishman's Fireside*, is given only brief space, for the main attraction is not Colman's play but the pantomime that follows, *Harlequin's Vision; or, the Feast of the Statue* (a burlesque of Mozart's *Don Giovanni*), offered for the tenth time and described as 'a New Splendid Pantomimick Romance'. Like most pantomimes, it had no author but, instead, an 'inventor', Lethbridge – probably J. W. Lethbridge, the acting manager, bent on exploiting the current mania for Mozart's opera by making a pantomimic spectacle out of it, replete with stage machinery Lethbridge himself had devised. It boasted direction by T. P. Cooke, the celebrated nautical actor, who also played Don Pedro and doubled as a singing Boatswain, along with important contributions by Thomas Ridgway, familiar to Sadler's Wells audiences, who managed the combats and dances and performed the Harlequin role of Don Juan. A cast list of over thirty personages is succeeded by an impressive list of scenes, credited to the master-artist Thomas Greenwood the younger, ranging widely over locations in this world and the next, from the 'Council Hall of Pluto' to 'A View of Pandemonium', the piece to conclude (blithely ignoring the ending of Mozart's opera) with a presentation of assembled gods in 'The Palace of Pleasure'.[29]

The playbill would continue its development in these directions, reaching an extreme of detail and verbosity in the bills devised by Charles Kean, Eton-educated son of the fiery tragedian, who took over the Princess's Theatre in

[27] Lamb, 'On the acting of Munden'.
[28] Lamb, 'Munden's farewell'.
[29] Mayer, *Harlequin in his Element*, 34, 62, 80.

Plate 23. Joseph Munden as Old Dozey in Thomas John Dibdin's farce *Past Ten O'Clock,
and a Rainy Night* (1815). Published 1 January 1823. Included in an extra-illustrated edition
of *Memoirs of Joseph Shepherd Munden, Comedian. By his Son* (London: Richard Bentley,
1844), opp. p. 291.

Oxford Street in 1850. Over the next years, through 1859, Kean produced a series
of Shakespeare's plays intended to realize historically accurate reconstructions
of the settings, from Venice, Athens and even Bohemia (translated to Bythinia)
to Scotland and elsewhere, augmented by interpolated spectacle. In the case of
Henry V, for example, Kean added a magnificent pageant dramatizing Henry's

return to London after the Battle of Agincourt – an episode described profusely in the bill.[30] Because such accounts would not fit on a single broadside, Kean employed sheets of double size, folded to the width of an ordinary bill.

Given the problems created by bulky playbills, a promising alternative emerged in booklets, or programmes, whose relatively small size made them more convenient to read and take away. The reduced scale required smaller type, affording a more efficient layout. Enterprising managers saw the programme as a means to additional profits from advertisements. Almost at the moment when Kean was beginning his forays into Shakespearean 'history', smaller bills, printed on one side and folded down the middle, had appeared at the Olympic Theatre. Drury Lane and other houses began to follow suit. Subsequent innovations in France and England, including bills for special occasions printed on silk and lace-bordered programmes supplied to the theatres on either side of the Channel in the 1860s by the perfumer Eugene Rimmel, advertising his products and impregnated with scent, reflected the ingenuity of the Victorian commercial establishment and the presence of audiences with substantial discretionary funds. Advertisements soon made their way on to entire pages of programmes as well as the margins of the titles, cast lists and settings printed in the middle pages. The booklet format proved a boon to theatres, accommodating more information not only about play, scenery, costumes and performers, but also about access to omnibuses and cabs and ending times. 'Carriages at eleven' became almost a proverbial phrase in the last decades of the century, capturing the pleasure and ambience of evening theatre-going for fashionable audiences, which were returning to the theatre after a decades-long absence.[31]

As the century advanced and season-long repertory companies gave way to companies hired for the duration of a run, theatrical entrepreneurs sought to avoid expense by offering patrons the same programme for a succession of nights, sometimes bearing only such vague indications as 'To-night and every night' and requiring reprinting only when one performer or more had been replaced or other elements of the performance had changed. During the run of the first production of Oscar Wilde's *The Importance of Being Earnest* (St James's Theatre, 14 February – 8 May 1895), Rose Leclercq as Lady Bracknell was replaced by Mrs Edward Saker, and Evelyn Millard as Cecily by Violet Lyster; new programmes were printed to reflect each change. Late in the run, when Alexander reduced the playing time of Wilde's farcical comedy, perhaps

---

[30] Schoch, *Shakespeare's Victorian Stage*; Meisel, *Realizations*; Booth, *Victorian Spectacular Theatre*, 52.

[31] Macqueen-Pope, *Carriages at Eleven*.

to render it as inoffensive as possible in the face of Wilde's trials for 'gross indecency', the St James's programme's 'Carriages at 11.00' became 'Carriages at 10.45'. Multi-coloured cardboard programmes featuring characters from the Gilbert and Sullivan operas became the rule at Richard D'Oyly Carte's Savoy Theatre in the Strand, opened in 1881 as the first theatre lighted entirely by electricity. At some time late in the century programmes printed on card stock or a small-format broadside, folded in thirds and featuring an ornate illustration of the theatre on the front flap and, inside, a title, the dramatis personae and descriptions of settings, became popular.

And so what had begun in the age of Betterton and Cibber as a small-format broadside providing a modicum of information had become, by the nineteenth century, a much larger, then much smaller but still complex document, broadly informative and responsive to audiences' requirements and preferences, amounting to a social history of the theatre in little.

One aspect of the importance of playbills and programmes is their documentation of the extraordinary impact of Shakespeare on the audience and culture of the time. By the turn of the century the name of Shakespeare had become a verbal talisman and 'Bardolatry' a widespread phenomenon. The early Restoration tendency to smooth over the perceived roughness and offensiveness of Shakespeare's language had achieved middle-class respectability in the sanitizing efforts of Thomas Bowdler, whose expurgated edition *The Family Shakespeare* appeared as early as 1807. Eighteenth-century character criticism lay behind such outcroppings as the retelling of Shakespeare's plays in Charles and Mary Lamb's two-volume *Tales from Shakespear Designed for the Use of Young Persons* (1807) and spawned such mid-Victorian writings as Mary Cowden Clarke's three-volume *The Girlhood of Shakespeare's Heroines* (1851–2). Although the plays of Shakespeare had become a sacrosanct literary artifact, they remained infinitely malleable and excerptible for generations of actors professional and amateur, declaimers, schoolboys, self-help enthusiasts, preachers, tutors and governesses and even working-class men in mechanics' institutes, who found Shakespeare a limitless artistic, social and moral resource.

Although the plays offered fewer opportunities for actresses, international stars such as Charlotte Cushman and, later, Sarah Bernhardt, essayed such roles as Romeo and Hamlet. Shakespeare was a perfect vehicle for the star system, embryonic in the age of Garrick but developing rapidly later. The Irish-born London actor Cooke commanded record audiences in New York in 1810, and Kean made his sensational début there a decade later.[32] Shakespeare

---

[32] Wilmeth, *George Frederick Cooke*, 259.

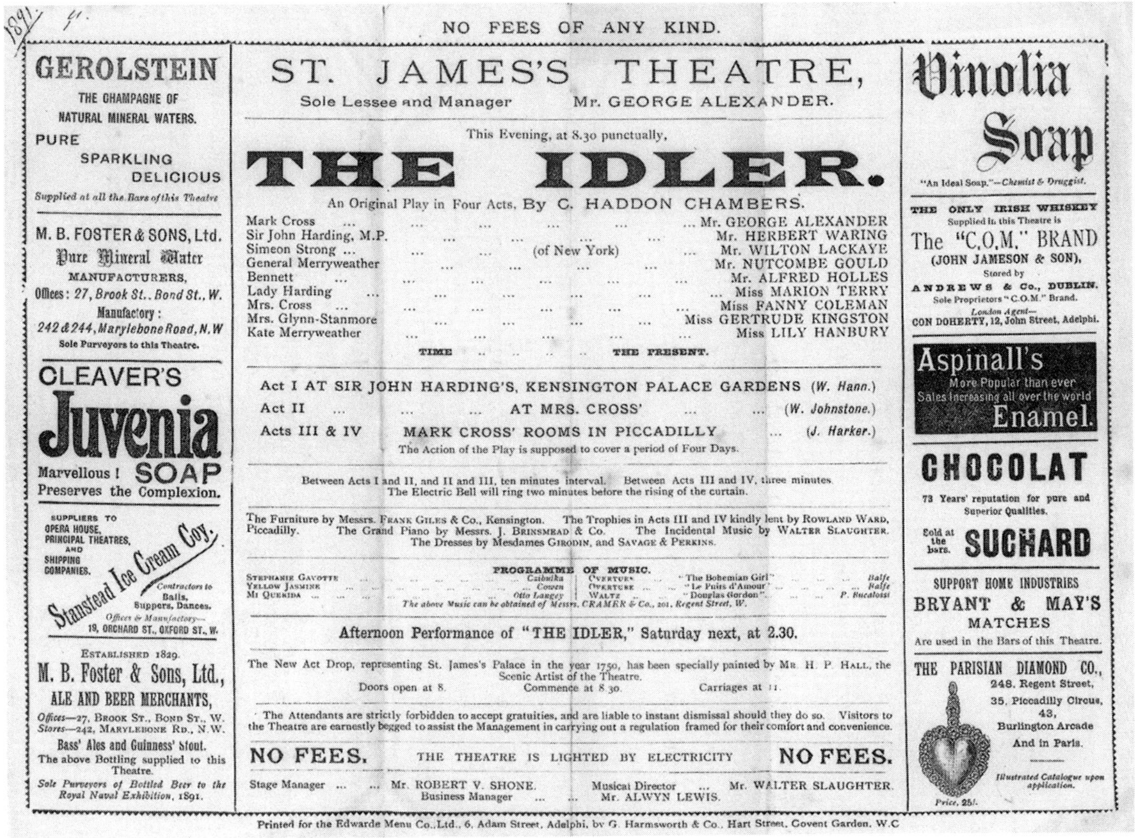

1891

NO FEES OF ANY KIND.

ST. JAMES'S THEATRE,

Sole Lessee and Manager Mr. GEORGE ALEXANDER.

This Evening, at 8.30 punctually,

THE IDLER.

An Original Play in Four Acts, By C. HADDON CHAMBERS.

Mark Cross	Mr. GEORGE ALEXANDER
Sir John Harding, M.P.	Mr. HERBERT WARING
Simeon Strong ... (of New York)	Mr. WILTON LACKAYE
General Merryweather	Mr. NUTCOMBE GOULD
Bennett	Mr. ALFRED HOLLES
Lady Harding	Miss MARION TERRY
Mrs. Cross	Miss FANNY COLEMAN
Mrs. Glynn-Stanmore	Miss GERTRUDE KINGSTON
Kate Merryweather	Miss LILY HANBURY

TIME .. .. THE PRESENT.

Act I AT SIR JOHN HARDING'S, KENSINGTON PALACE GARDENS (*W. Hann.*)

Act II ... ... AT MRS. CROSS' ... ... (*W. Johnstone.*)

Acts III & IV MARK CROSS' ROOMS IN PICCADILLY ... (*J. Harker.*)

The Action of the Play is supposed to cover a period of Four Days.

Between Acts I and II, and II and III, ten minutes interval. Between Acts III and IV, three minutes. The Electric Bell will ring two minutes before the rising of the curtain.

The Furniture by Messrs. FRANK GILES & Co., Kensington. The Trophies in Acts III and IV kindly lent by ROWLAND WARD, Piccadilly. The Grand Piano by Messrs. J. BRINSMEAD & Co. The Incidental Music by WALTER SLAUGHTER. The Dresses by Mesdames GIRODIN, and SAVAGE & PERKINS.

PROGRAMME OF MUSIC.

STEPHANIE GAVOTTE	*Czibulka*	OVERTURE	"The Bohemian Girl"	*Balfe*
YELLOW JASMINE	*Cowen*	OVERTURE	"Le Puits d'Amour"	*Balfe*
MI QUERIDA	*Otto Langey*	WALTZ	"Douglas Gordon"	*P. Bucalossi*

The above Music can be obtained of Messrs. CRAMER & Co., 201, Regent Street, W.

Afternoon Performance of "THE IDLER," Saturday next, at 2.30.

The New Act Drop, representing St. James's Palace in the year 1750, has been specially painted by MR. H. P. HALL, the Scenic Artist of the Theatre.

Doors open at 8. Commence at 8.30. Carriages at 11.

The Attendants are strictly forbidden to accept gratuities, and are liable to instant dismissal should they do so. Visitors to the Theatre are earnestly begged to assist the Management in carrying out a regulation framed for their comfort and convenience.

NO FEES. THE THEATRE IS LIGHTED BY ELECTRICITY NO FEES.

Stage Manager ... ... Mr. ROBERT V. SHONE. Musical Director ... Mr. WALTER SLAUGHTER.
Business Manager ... ... Mr. ALWYN LEWIS.

Printed for the Edwarde Menu Co., Ltd., 6, Adam Street, Adelphi, by G. Harmsworth & Co., Hart Street, Covent Garden, W.C.

Plate 24. Trifold programme, St James's Theatre, for C. Haddon Chambers's play *The Idler*, undated (the play ran for 176 performances beginning 26 February 1891), the text surrounded by a plethora of advertising, which continues on the obverse side.

was the mainstay of the repertory company, in London, the provincial cities of England, Scotland and Ireland, and the smaller urban centres favoured by touring companies, whose opportunities would expand enormously with the advent of the railway. English actors had been venturing across the Atlantic for decades; a troupe of players had arrived in colonial Williamsburg as early as 1752.[33] As steamship travel improved, English companies led by Henry Irving, George Alexander, Herbert Beerbohm Tree and others found lucrative opportunities in New York, Boston, Chicago and other American cities. Modern-day Burbages and Alleyns, from Kean, Macready, Phelps and Kean's son Charles to their end-of-century avatars Irving, Tree, Forbes Robertson and others, playing opposite female counterparts from Siddons, O'Neill, Fanny Kemble and Helen Faucit to Ellen Terry, Lillie Langtry (the 'Jersey Lily', sometime mistress of the future Edward VII) and Mary Moore drew continuous crowds, metropolitan and provincial. The complex development of Shakespearean production from Kemble to Irving framed the universal appeal of the plays to audiences, from disreputable booths at fairs to the summits of actorly excellence in London's West End. Nor was appreciation of the plays confined to the fashionable occupants of boxes or the stalls which, over the second half of the century, took over space once occupied by the pit. Shakespeare's plays were, of course, not the only attraction, but the pre-eminent status of actors who had won reputations performing in them proved the real measure of success. In one such example, Henry Irving's early triumph in the tortured character of the murderer Mathias, in Leopold Lewis's *The Bells* (1871), was instrumental in winning audiences for his eccentric yet affecting portrayal of such Shakespearean heroes and villains as Hamlet and Shylock.[34]

The texts of Shakespeare available to this great range of performers represented two distinct and separate traditions. Multi-volume literary editions swelled the shelves of actors from Garrick and Kemble onwards. When it came to preparing a text for production, however, an acting edition was a more likely choice, incorporating a time-tested version and sometimes memorializing a famous performance. In the case of Edmund Kean's Richard III, a convoluted textual history is preserved in a prompt-book made on an Oxberry acting edition of Colley Cibber's version of Shakespeare's play, which prints Kean's own redaction of Kemble's augmentation of Cibber's revision of his original 1700 version; the American actor James Henry Hackett then recorded Kean's performance in it, with a view towards re-enacting it. The resulting document

---

[33] Simon Williams, 'European actors and the star system'.
[34] Hughes, *Henry Irving*, 38–87, 230–40.

is one of the most dense and instructive theatrical relics of the century, demonstrating precisely how Kean tailored the play to his own strengths and needs.[35] In another instance, Macready's production of *King John* at Drury Lane in 1842 offers an elaborate example of Shakespearean spectacle.[36] These productions, and many others like them, reflect a Shakespeare who had become no less a myth than an institution, central to the life of the nation, a greater cultural landmark than the Crystal Palace.

1843 to 1865: theatres, actors, plays

The most visible result of the lapse of patent privilege following on from the Theatre Regulation Act of 1843 was that the status quo to which the act belatedly addressed itself simply became more firmly entrenched. Although Drury Lane and Covent Garden had cultivated a cachet to which other theatres could not pretend, both had invested heavily in melodrama, now the lingua franca of dramatic fare. Theatres other than the patent houses, including burletta houses and even saloons, were now legally free to perform the kinds of plays which for some time they had been circumventing the law in order to mount. Meanwhile, the late 1820s and 1830s saw the appearance of a good dozen new venues in the West End and beyond. In addition to those houses still standing in 1812, theatres emergent in the second, third and fourth decades of the century and still active well into the last third of the century included the Victoria, the Pavilion (Whitechapel), the Clarence, the Garrick (Whitechapel), the Marylebone, the Strand, the City of London, the East London, the St James's, the Theatre Royal Woolwich and the Standard. After 1840, however, when the Princess's Theatre and the Royalty in Soho opened their doors, a long dry spell in theatre building in central London set in, broken only by the Queen's Theatre in Long Acre, erected in 1850. As usual, the ironies attendant on theatrical regulation were not difficult to discover.

The drought, in the view of older historians, extended to the drama as well and had begun some years before. Traditionally, a pall has been perceived to have blighted the theatre of the long period before T. W. Robertson's supposed rescue of it at the Prince of Wales's Theatre with a more socially conscious, three-dimensional realism and, later, the reinvigoration of comedy and the addressing of emergent social issues in the 1890s by such dramatists as Oscar

---

[35] Downer, ed., *Oxberry's 1822 Edition of King Richard III*.
[36] Shattuck, ed., *William Charles Macready's King John*; Booth, *Victorian Spectacular Theatre*, 130, 127–60.

Wilde, Bernard Shaw, Arthur Pinero and Henry Arthur Jones. Such oversimplifications run at odds with the facts. Any theatre-goer leaving a stirring performance of James Sheridan Knowles's *Virginius; or, The Liberation of Rome*, mounted at Covent Garden in 1820 with William Charles Macready in the title role, or of J. R. Planché's charming *Beauty and the Beast*, produced there in 1841 with Madame Vestris as Beauty, or of Dion Boucicault's suspenseful *The Corsican Brothers* at the Princess's in 1852, with Charles Kean doubling as one brother and the ghost of his murdered sibling, might have been pardoned for believing that the Drama was alive and well and continuing to affect or delight audiences in great numbers, in London and far beyond. Queen Victoria seemed untroubled by the absence of literary value in the plays and operas she, and after her marriage her consort Prince Albert, regularly sought out at Drury Lane and Covent Garden, Her Majesty's (renamed in the Queen's favour in 1837), and the Haymarket, the Lyceum, the St James's, the Olympic and the Princess's – to say nothing of Andrew Ducrow's superb equestrian feats at Astley's Amphitheatre in 1833 or Van Amburgh's lions in the 1839 Drury Lane pantomime, which drew her back seven times in six weeks.[37] This age, like any other, had its peculiar delights and satisfactions.

The three decades and more which elapse up to the 1860s, when new theatre building again commenced, were a time when pre-eminent virtuosity, along with more broadly based genuine competence, distinguished the acting. As early as January 1820, when the theatres reopened after the death of King George III, London audiences were treated to the delightful singer and comic actress Eliza Vestris, who made her Drury Lane début in a perennially favourite comic opera, James Cobb's *The Siege of Belgrade*. In a career lasting into the 1850s Vestris combined revivals of classics by Shakespeare, Sheridan and Centlivre with new plays by Knowles, extravaganzas by Planché and other, more musically varied pieces in which her several talents might shine. Possessing legs so shapely that plaster replicas could command high prices, she was especially successful *en travestie* (in so-called 'breeches' roles), playing the title character in R. W. Elliston's Drury Lane production of W. T. Moncrieff's burlesque of Mozart's opera, *Giovanni in London*, in 1820 and, two decades later, Oberon in a sumptuous Covent Garden revival of *A Midsummer Night's Dream*. Opposite the actor who in 1835 would become her leading man and then her husband, Charles James Mathews, Vestris pursued a long career, succeeding particularly well at the Olympic, in Wych Street, off the Strand, which she leased in 1830 and where, under the legal largesse of a

---

[37] Rowell, *Queen Victoria Goes to the Theatre*, 24–5, 128ff.

burletta licence, she mounted a series of lively, quasi-musical pieces, some of them French in derivation. Among them was Planché's *Olympic Revels* (1831), in which Vestris as Jupiter's creation, the curious Pandora, opens a mysterious box from which emanate a cohort of fiends, but revealing Hope at the bottom.[38] Its great success spawned a sequel, Planché's exquisitely mounted *Olympic Devils* (1832), with Vestris in the *travestie* role of Orpheus. The younger Mathews, son of the famous comedian Charles Mathews, whose 'At Homes' had proved an irresistible showcase for his protean characterizations, had gained amateur experience in such traditional broad comedy parts as Tony Lumpkin in *She Stoops to Conquer*, Dogberry in *Much Ado*, and even Falstaff, before Vestris engaged him professionally for the 1835/6 Olympic season. Mathews's easy, gentlemanly style and all-around charm nicely complemented Vestris's light but precise touch and voluble musicality. As much as for her bravura performing, she is remembered for her managerial reforms, especially the advances in decor and polished realism of her *mise-en-scène*, realized at a time when traditional wing-and-shutter scenery was giving way to the box set.[39]

Yet, as far as sheer acting and attendant personality is concerned, Fanny Kemble is perhaps the most distinctive female presence of the early days of this period. Daughter of Charles Kemble, actor-manager and youngest brother of John Philip, she was a reluctant débutante at her father's financially troubled theatre, Covent Garden, in 1829, as Juliet, scored a great success with her lavishly emotive style and rescued the enterprise, going on to dominate the standard heroines of the repertory and creating the role of Julia in Sheridan Knowles's *The Hunchback* at its Covent Garden première in 1832. Acclaimed in two countries after an American tour, she left the stage in 1834 for an American marriage which proved unhappy. Her diaries are among the most interesting of the period.[40] Of comparable celebrity and talent was the American-born Charlotte Cushman, whose operatic début in Boston in 1835 was followed the next year, at the Bowery in New York, by a legitimate stage début as Lady Macbeth, a turn of career which proved to be permanent. Cast by temperament, body type and stentorian vocal qualities in roles once dominated by the legendary Siddons, Cushman went on to a London début in 1845 at the Princess's in the well-known role of the suffering heroine Bianca in Henry Hart Milman's *Fazio*. A standing ovation at the end of the trial scene signalled the

---

[38] Appleton, *Madame Vestris*, 57–9.
[39] Ibid., chaps. 4–5, *passim*.
[40] Kemble, *Fanny Kemble's Journals*. See, among various biographies, Furnas, *Fanny Kemble*; see also Williamson, *Charles Kemble*.

first of many triumphs, including her Queen Katharine, opposite Macready's Cardinal Wolsey, in 1847.[41] Born into a theatrical family, Helen Faucit, initially stricken by the stage fright that would perennially dog her steps, went on to a series of triumphant starring roles, chiefly in tragedy and melodrama, until 1851, when marriage to Theodore Martin decisively altered her theatrical career.[42] These were only the most illustrious of a burgeoning troupe of gifted female performers, complemented by the innumerable workaday sisters whose hard work gave pleasure to so many.[43] Among male performers, William Charles Macready, his protégé Samuel Phelps and the younger Kean stood out in serious roles, and in lighter roles actors such as the younger Mathews, whose delightful Dazzle in Boucicault's first success, *London Assurance*, in 1841, was followed by a distinguished line of fops and other boldly outlined comic roles. That there was no real heir, nor no real predecessor, to Joseph Grimaldi, the incomparable pantomime clown who died the year Victoria became queen, was not the fault of the age, which had not its Garrick either, nor, after 1816, its Dora Jordan.[44]

Macready, the son of a provincial actor-manager, enjoyed a distinguished career as an actor, first in the provinces and then, beginning in 1816, in London, with over two dozen Shakespearean roles and significant new characters to his credit. As sometime manager of both Covent Garden and Drury Lane, where he improved rehearsal practices and developed theories regarding harmony of tone and coherence in *mise-en-scène*, he made an even greater impress on the age.[45] Devoted to his actorly profession despite a low opinion of its social standing, Macready would act at full tilt in rehearsal and, before an entrance, build authentic rage by cursing under his breath and shaking a ladder fixed to a wall.[46] Thanks to the survival of Macready's private journals and reminiscences, much is known about his career as a man of the theatre and his concern for the legitimacy of the drama.[47] As manager of Covent Garden beginning in 1837, Macready's return to Shakespeare's text of *King Lear*, restoring the tragic ending and the long-lost character of the Fool (played, in a charming Victorian variation, by Priscilla Horton), is well known. An intense, gifted performer, his anxious quest for distinction characterized all he attempted, as actor, manager and man.

[41] Leach, *Bright Particular Star*.
[42] Carlisle, *Helen Faucit*.
[43] Tracy C. Davis, *Actresses as Working Women*.
[44] Tomalin, *Mrs Jordan's Profession*.
[45] Downer, *William Charles Macready*, 224–52.
[46] Lewes, *On Actors and the Art of Acting*, 44.
[47] Macready, *Reminiscences*.

Drawn and Engraved by J Condé

M^{RS} JORDAN.

Plate 25. Dorothy Jordan (who called herself Dora), one of the liveliest and most endearing comic actresses of her time, began her career around 1778, as Miss Lucy in Fielding's farce *The Virgin Unmasked*, and ended it a short time before her death in 1816. Print dating from 1794.

An irascible colleague, Macready nonetheless brought out the best in his company by drilling them unmercifully for five or six hours at a time, as Faucit wryly recalled. Already a well-established ingenue at Covent Garden under D. W. Osbaldiston's brief management, Faucit thrived under Macready's encouragement. Infatuated with a man twice her age, she trusted him enough to accept the small role of Virginia in his revival of *Virginius* and seized the additional opportunities he provided for deeply felt characterizations in Shakespeare and contemporary plays. Casting her, over the author's objections, as the long-suffering Pauline in Bulwer's new comedy-melodrama *The Lady of Lyons* in 1838, Macready, playing opposite her as the lowly Claude Melnotte, gave Faucit the chance to establish an enduring reputation.[48] Fifty-five performances of Miranda in *The Tempest* the next season were followed by thirty-seven of Julia, the Cardinal's orphaned ward, in Bulwer's *Richelieu; or, The Conspiracy*, its title role crafted expressly for Macready.[49] Macready's collaboration with Bulwer and its continued featuring of Faucit in ingenue roles survived Macready's abandonment of management at Covent Garden in 1839 in favour of an engagement at the Haymarket under Ben Webster. There, Webster brought out Bulwer's comedy *Money*, in which Faucit scored another resounding success as Clara Douglas, a role favouring her ability to depict passion beneath a frosty exterior; opposite her, once again, the saturnine Macready as the semi-misanthropic Alfred Evelyn. Together, the trio of actor, dramatist and actress comprises one of the most productive collaborations of the Victorian theatre.

A different sort of collaboration occurs in the case of Planché, antiquarian, costume and scene designer and prolific dramatist, a man of mobile imagination and a frequent partner with Vestris and Mathews at the Olympic. There, in the 1830s, and at various theatres major and minor from 1818 onwards, Planché wrote and produced hundreds of extravaganzas, burlesques, burlettas, vaudevilles and other fanciful works, along with farces, comedies, dramas and melodramas; his last work, the Covent Garden spectacle *Babil and Bijou* (with Boucicault), dates from 1872. Planché's consistent vision as a writer and designer, described in his memoirs, captured something quintessential of the English love of fun and make-believe.[50] In his initial collaboration with Vestris, *Olympic Revels*, in *Blue Beard* (Olympic, 1839) and in *Beauty and the Beast* (Covent Garden, 1841), as in numerous other witty works, Planché's efforts bore the rare stamp of the original and authentic. Audiences were attracted also by

---

[48] Carlisle, *Helen Faucit*, 59–63.
[49] Shattuck, ed., *Bulwer and Macready*, 79–131.
[50] Planché, *Recollections and Reflections*. The largest collection of Planché's works is *Extravaganzas of J. R. Planché*, ed. Croker and Tucker; see also Planché, *Plays*, ed. Roy.

his extensive innovations in historical stage costume, as in the triumphant designs for *King John* at Covent Garden, under Charles Kemble's management, in 1823, an important precedent for similar recreations by Macready, Phelps and Charles Kean. Still another, more technical innovation, the 'Vampire trap', is associated with Planché's *The Vampire; or, The Bride of the Isles* (English Opera House, 1820), through which the character of Ruthven suddenly disappears, to a *'terrific peal of thunder'*, at the end of the play.[51]

The bearer of comparable talents for pleasing the eye and ear, it was for his innovations as a Shakespearean producer and tragic actor that Phelps was most well known during his long lifetime; he was still performing in the year of his death, 1878, at age 74. The abolition of patent theatre privilege in 1843 gave Phelps the opportunity to distinguish himself. Taking over the management of Sadler's Wells Theatre, well off the beaten West End path, from 1844 Phelps made it the unlikely but congenial home of a series of productions of Shakespeare's plays that rivalled and even exceeded Macready's well-received innovations and attracted an unlikely, partly proletarian audience won over by the beauty of the illusion and the accessibility of well-spoken verse. By the time he retired from the 'Wells' in 1862, Phelps had mounted some thirty-one of the plays, succeeding particularly well with *Macbeth* in 1844, *Antony and Cleopatra* in 1849 and *A Midsummer Night's Dream* in 1853, in which he played a 'dreamy, dogged, and dogmatical' Bottom and in which a green gauze curtain, suspended across the proscenium arch by Phelps's scenic manager Frederick Fenton, revealed forest scenery gliding, illuminated by the gas lighting Fenton had installed for the purpose.[52]

Phelps's efforts at naturalistic illusion were a match for Charles Kean's at the Princess's, where for an entire decade the will-o'-the-wisp of historical accuracy, endorsed by an effulgent realism, was pursued.[53] Ten years old in 1850 when Kean acquired the lease, the Princess's was smaller than the Haymarket yet capable of a sumptuous illusionistic surround, including such thrilling features as the 'Corsican trap', a device invented by Boucicault (then Kean's house dramatist) for the production of his *The Corsican Brothers* in 1852, in which the ghost of the murdered brother of Louis dei Franchi appears by gliding up from the infernal regions at an angle on a platform attached to a belt moving on a hidden inclined plane.[54] Such effects enhanced the larger historical and

[51] Planché, *Plays*, ed. Roy, 4–5, 68.
[52] Gary Jay Williams, *Our Moonlight Revels*, 111–12; Richards, 'Phelps's production of *All's Well that Ends Well*'; see also Allen, *Phelps*.
[53] Schoch, *Shakespeare's Victorian Stage*.
[54] Booth, *Theatre in the Victorian Age*, 78.

atmospheric realities created at the Princess's by the foremost designers and painters of the day: Frederick Lloyds, William Gordon, J. Dayes, Thomas Grieve (one of a prominent family of designers) and William Telbin, who had worked for Macready.[55] Crowds of well-to-do and other spectators were lured to Kean's jewel of a theatre in Marylebone, filling its four tiers of boxes,[56] to see the gorgeous productions he mounted, performing often alongside his wife, the competent, versatile actress Ellen Tree. Audiences of the Princess's would have witnessed in 1856 the début of Ellen Terry at age 9 as Mamillius, the fated son of King Leontes, in Kean's mounting of *The Winter's Tale* (for 102 nights, Terry recalled in her memoirs[57]). Kean's high-minded motive to educate his audiences as well as to entertain them was extensively indulged, but at a heavy cost. Over their careers, Charles Kean and Ellen Tree earned large amounts of money, in keeping with their pre-eminent professional standing, not only in London and the provinces but also in Scotland and America. In contrast, the net profits for the first seven of Kean's nine seasons at the Princess's amounted to only £2,627 on an outlay of £243,859; he lost over £4,000 in his eighth season. Not surprisingly, the season of 1858–59 proved to be the Keans' farewell.[58] All the same, he had set an important precedent. Splendiferous mounting of plays on this scale, regardless of expense, along with a restless search for the ultimate in pictorial realism, would reach a kind of aesthetic apotheosis by 1880, when Squire Bancroft, veteran of repeated triumphs of Robertsonian realism at the Prince of Wales's, surrounded the stage picture at the Haymarket with a four-sided gilt frame 2 feet wide, whose base coincided with the front edge of the stage itself.[59]

Despite the nearly ubiquitous presence of Shakespeare, along with other familiar plays, in the repertory, new drama was an irresistible presence from the earliest years of the period, and extremely prolific dramatists were becoming a commonplace. Well before mid-century, the volume of plays being produced on London stages and in provincial venues had reached a phenomenal level, and the flow would not decrease over the remainder of the century. Dozens of playwrights such as William Thomas Moncrieff, Isaac Pocock, Charles Selby, Edward Stirling, William Brough, George Conquest, J. Stirling Coyne, W. S. Gilbert, C. H. Hazlewood, John Maddison Morton, Robert Reece and Tom Taylor wrote over fifty dramatic works apiece. Others, including

---

[55] Rosenfeld, *Short History of Scene Design*, 120–7.
[56] Howard, *London Theatres and Music Halls*, 186.
[57] Terry, *Terry's Memoirs*, 16.
[58] Accounts cited in Wilson, 'Career of Charles Kean', 44.
[59] Booth, *Victorian Spectacular Theatre*, 11.

Boucicault, Buckstone, Edward Fitzball, Douglas Jerrold (sometime editor of *Punch*), George Dibdin Pitt, Planché, Edward Leman Blanchard, F. C. Burnand (also an editor of *Punch*) and Henry James Byron, turned out one hundred, two hundred, or more. The three Dibdins are together credited with well over five hundred pantomimes, comic operas, melodramas, burlettas, spectacles, operatic farces, burlesques, interludes and musical entertainments. Countless hundreds of additional plays and other works have survived detached from their authors' names.[60] Recent scholarship has added to these familiar lists the names of a few significant and many other, more workaday women dramatists of the period, numbering close to two hundred and stretching back into the eighteenth century, some of whom, like Elizabeth Inchbald, were also actresses or theatre managers.[61]

One of the most colourful and characteristic of these authors was the Irish-born Boucicault, whose earliest success, *London Assurance*, produced at Covent Garden in 1841 under the pseudonym of 'Lee Moreton', led to a flood of successful comedies and dramas appearing not only in London and New York but also elsewhere in America and in Australia. An all-around man of the theatre, Boucicault was a virtuoso comic actor as well as an author, manager, producer and inventor of important improvements in theatre safety, who often starred in vehicles he wrote for himself, including a series of Irish plays, beginning in 1860 with *The Colleen Bawn* and followed by *Arrah-na-Pogue* (1864), *The O'Dowd* (1873) and *The Shaughraun* (1874), three of which had New York premières but were performed internationally. In each play Boucicault had promoted the familiar stage Irishman (played by himself) to a central figure whose jovial irresponsibility masks a resourceful saviour of the day. A brilliant exploiter of audience tastes and social trends, Boucicault was perhaps the most representative man of the theatre of the Victorian age.

A vivid glimpse of the popular audience may be found in Bulwer's *England and the English*, a study of people, politics and the arts, which proffers a sardonic picture of the male half of the English audience (the female half left unspecified). Appointed editor of the *New Monthly Magazine* in 1831 and elected MP for St Ives that same year, Bulwer, already a prominent novelist, headed up a select parliamentary committee into the state of dramatic literature whose

---

[60] See the hand-lists of known and unknown authors appended to Nicoll's *History of English Drama*, vols. IV (for 1800–50) and V (for 1850–1900); see also *English Drama of the Nineteenth Century*, ed. Ellis, especially appendix A. Women dramatists, 301–2.

[61] See Holder, 'The lady playwrights' and other articles in Tracy C. Davis and Donkin, *Women and Playwriting*; see also *English Drama of the Nineteenth Century*, ed. Ellis, appendix A.

eventual product was the act of 1843.[62] A decade before the act was passed, Bulwer devoted *England and the English* to an overview of contemporary institutions and the preoccupations and biases of public and private life which remained valid over time. His chapter delineating major types of English character identifies a cohort of representative men – Sir Harry Hargrave ('an excellent gentleman'), Tom Whitehead ('clever, sharp, shrewd', a profligate and liberal politician), William Muscle (an old school radical and John Bull epitome), Samuel Square (a new radical and Republican), Lord Mute (a dandy, notable only for the shine of his boots), Sir Paul Snarl (a vain, disagreeable coxcomb), Mr Warm ('a most respectable man' with '*a terror of descending*') and Mr Bluff ('a sensible, *practical* man' interested only in facts and thus 'always taken in')[63] – any of whom might be seen, of an evening, in the pit or a side box at Covent Garden. Sixty years later, the same assembly might be discovered at Irving's Lyceum, revelling in (or pooh-poohing) the magnificence of W. G. Wills's *Faust* or endorsing (or disputing) the painful psychological truths of Leopold Lewis's *The Bells*.[64]

The report of the 1832 Select Committee constitutes required reading for understanding the breadth and complexity of the social, political and aesthetic forces at work in the theatre and drama of the 1830s; its appendices provide valuable information about the history of theatrical licensing as well.[65] Three decades later another parliamentary committee revisited the subject of theatrical licensing, producing an equally informative report and appending materials including a concise summary of licensing since 1628, based on documents in the Lord Chamberlain's office.[66] The two reports usefully frame the present discussion. The 1866 report recommended placing the licensing of theatres and music halls under a single, highly placed authority (the Lord Chamberlain) whose jurisdiction extended to the entire country and whose ability to issue new licences would be retained, while local magistrates would be empowered to renew them. It was only in 1888, when the London County Council was created, and the year after, when its Theatres and Music Halls Committee became the effective licensing body for the City and Westminster (making recommendations to the council), that a coherent policy was committed to law. Meanwhile, recognizing the now nearly ubiquitous music hall, the 1866 report

---

[62] *Report from the Select Committee* (1832).
[63] Bulwer, *England and the English*, 69–79.
[64] Ibid., 307–12.
[65] Ganzel, 'Patent wrongs and patent theatres'.
[66] *Report from the Select Committee on Theatrical Licences and Regulations* (1866).

made a fundamental distinction between two kinds of licence, one covering music halls, where 'intoxicating drinks, refreshments, and tobacco may be consumed in the auditorium of the building', the other for theatres, where such consumption was prohibited.[67] As for censorship, despite the testimony of Boucicault and others favouring relaxation, the 1866 report endorsed the status quo and its extension to the country at large, reaffirming the required submission of scripts of all new plays in advance of performance and recommending the extension of the law to music halls. In this connection, the most important change recommended by the committee was to allow plays to be performed in music halls as well as theatres, a proposal vehemently opposed by theatre managements down through the end of the century and beyond.

Significantly, the 1866 report observed that all metropolitan theatres active in 1843 were still being relicensed in 1866, along with three new buildings – the Gallery of Illustration (1861), the Cabinet (1862) and the Alexandra (1865), producing a total number of twenty-four or twenty-five theatres currently licensed by the Lord Chamberlain.[68] Of the three newly licensed, the Gallery of Illustration and the Cabinet each held, respectively, only 362 and 300 persons, illustrating a trend towards smaller venues already noticeable in the New Royalty (722) and the Prince of Wales's (814).[69] One of the more noteworthy changes effected by the Theatre Regulation Act of 1843 was the licensing of saloons for the performance of stage plays, resulting, beginning in that year, in productions at the Britannia Saloon in Hoxton, the Grecian Saloon in Shoreditch (both rebuilt as theatres in 1858) and elsewhere. By 1866 no saloons remained, all having become either theatres or music halls. A table of capacities of concert halls, music halls, entertainment galleries and other venues shows a huge range, from the crowds of up to 100,000 daily thronging the Crystal Palace and the 20,000 at Agricultural Hall to the more modest capacities of the Westminster Music Hall in Pimlico (800), the Apollo in Bethnal Green (600) and Egyptian Hall (500).[70] Collectively these figures indicate the multiple opportunities for leisure activity in greater London and the formidable competition offered to the performance of stage plays. Overall, the two parliamentary reports demonstrate the vital part played by theatrical

---

[67] Ibid., iii.
[68] Ibid., 280. A separate count, covering perhaps a wider geographical area, produces a total of thirty-three (Donohue and Ellis, *Handbook for Compilers*, 'Chronological chart').
[69] Ibid., 295.
[70] Ibid., 313.

and quasi-theatrical entertainment in this age, in the lives of the British urban population.

1865 to 1895: a transformed theatrical landscape

The three most significant changes observable in the last three decades of the period down to 1895 are the demise of the old repertory company in the face of the long-running play, the return to the theatre of a more polite and affluent audience and another remarkable spate of theatre building.

After a fallow two decades, in the 1860s a new round of building began, with the Gaiety in 1862, the Duke's, in Holborn, in 1866, the Globe in 1868 and Toole's in 1869. Five more theatres appeared in the course of the 1870s: the Court (in Chelsea), the Opera Comique, the Vaudeville, the Criterion and the Imperial. By the 1880s a fair flood tide was rising, and by 1893 some fourteen additional houses were open in the West End or nearby: the Comedy, the Savoy, the Avenue, the Novelty, the Prince's (afterwards the Prince of Wales's, Piccadilly), the Court (Sloane Square), the Lyric Opera House (Hammersmith), the Lyric Theatre, the Shaftesbury, the Garrick in Charing Cross (the Garrick in Whitechapel, dating from 1831, having closed in 1881), the Royal English Opera House (after 1893 the Palace Theatre of Varieties), the Duke of York's and Daly's. Many of these theatres are still in use today, some under different names. It is no exaggeration to say that the theatrical scene in the West End was virtually transformed, over the last three or four decades of the century, by the increasing number of theatres open to the public; great continuity with them continues to this day. Additional theatres went up in outlying districts – in Elephant and Castle, Dalston, Hackney, Kilburn, Streatham, Battersea, Stratford East and elsewhere.

No small part of this transformation was caused by the rapidly increasing appearance, beginning as early as the second decade of the century, of scores of music halls and similar popular resorts that had overgrown tavern origins, places where music and dancing were universal and where smoking and drinking (forbidden or strictly curtailed in the theatres) were allowed. Among the most long-lived and well known were the Standard (1840) in Victoria, the Britannia Saloon (1841) in Hoxton, the Middlesex (1847) in Holborn, the Canterbury (1851), the Marylebone (1856), the Holborn Empire (1857), the Oxford (1861), the Cambridge (1864), Gatti's Palace of Varieties (1865), another Gatti's in Charing Cross (1867) and the Victoria (1867), almost all of which lasted into the twentieth century. An unfortunate additional fact is that no fewer than twenty-four theatres and music halls in greater London were destroyed by fire in the period 1866–91.[71]

The effect of these new theatres on acting style cannot be simply stated, but one prime indicator was physical size. Certain theatres, some of them a good deal older, could accommodate over two thousand persons (the City of London, Norton Folgate, 2,500; Sadler's Wells, 2,300) or even more than three thousand (Astley's, 3,780; the Britannia, Hoxton, 3,923; the Pavilion, Whitechapel, 3,500; Drury Lane, 3,800); but other, more recent buildings had often been constructed on a smaller scale. The Prince of Wales's held a mere 560, or perhaps 814 (sources vary);[72] the New Royalty in Dean Street, Soho, held 722; the Cabinet, 360; the Gallery of Illustration, 362.[73] More intimate surroundings enabled actors to reintroduce subtlety and nuance into their performances, though all acting was now done behind the proscenium arch. Despite latter-day modifications, throughout the century the fundamental characteristic of acting remained as controlled overstatement in the service of clarity and theatrical effectiveness.[74] Another prime indicator was the gradual disappearance of the old wing-and-shutter system of scenic representation in favour of a single setting or only a few settings, each an extensively realized environment. Yet, despite advances in verisimilitude, the advent of more 'realistic' acting can easily be exaggerated. A photograph of a climactic moment in a St James's drama of 1907 (Alfred Sutro's *John Glayde's Honour*) presents a highly realistic setting, but within it the actress expresses great, melodramatic distress, still speaking the prototypical 'language of the passions' depicted a century before in Siddons's *Illustrations of Rhetorical Gesture and Action* (1807).

Large-scale demographic change helps to explain the important developments occurring in theatres and audiences in the last half of the century, when London's metropolitan population reached 5,650,000.[75] More specific social and theatrical factors were simultaneously in evidence. No more obvious indicator of change in the composition of the late nineteenth-century audience can be found than the supplanting of the old, familiar format of an evening's entertainment, consisting of mainpiece and farce, or afterpiece, perhaps even

---

[71] Donohue and Ellis, *Handbook for Compilers*, 'Chronological chart'; Howard, *London Theatres and Music Halls*; *Report from the Select Committee on Theatres and Places of Entertainment* (1892), appendix 2, 368–86.

[72] Barrett, *T. W. Robertson*, 59–60.

[73] *Report from the Select Committee on Theatrical Licences and Regulations* (1866), appendix 1, 295.

[74] Downer, 'Players and painted stage'; Matthews, ed., *Papers on Acting*; Donohue, 'Actors and acting'.

[75] Cook and Cook, *London and Environs*, 5.

more than two such pieces, plus incidental entertainment, with a new format consisting of a mainpiece (the term itself was falling into disuse) preceded by a brief play quickly dubbed a 'curtain-raiser'. This latter phenomenon, usually light-hearted or frivolous like its predecessor the afterpiece and running perhaps twenty or thirty minutes, allowed play-goers of a certain class to linger over dinner and arrive, 'fashionably late', in time for the main attraction. At the St James's Theatre on 14 February 1895, Langdon Mitchell's *In the Season*, a charming comic drama for three characters, was performed at 8.20, before the opening night performance of *The Importance of Being Earnest* began at 8.45. This new practice would persist well into the twentieth century. Yet, as early as the 1860s, at the rehabilitated Prince of Wales's Theatre, Squire Bancroft and Marie Bancroft were presenting only one play, a full-length piece – a complete turn-around from the double, triple or quadruple bill of old.

In earlier times, the long run had remained an infrequent departure from the standard nightly alternation of mainpiece and afterpiece, as in the case of *The Beggar's Opera* and, a century later, *Tom and Jerry; or, Life in London*, which ran at the Adelphi for ninety-four performances beginning 26 November 1821, with never more than one other piece on the bill.[76] Well into the nineteenth century the most familiar example of the long run remained the Christmas pantomime, but in later years the long run started to catch on, independent of holiday fare, sustained by a burgeoning audience. As in London, provincial urban centres were attracting ever greater audiences. Given the heterogeneous tastes of masses of paying customers, the almost inevitable next phase in the evolution of theatres and audiences was the development of the specialty house, where a single attraction of a certain genre could be found on view night after night.

The specialty house had, nevertheless, a long ancestry, as in the cases of Astley's and the Surrey, whose location across the Thames and predominantly local clientèle dictated the specific range of their offerings. Ironically, when in his 1819 essay on the decline of the drama Walter Scott called for the replacement of the two cavernous patent theatres with several venues of moderate size, such houses were already in existence, though legally unable to offer 'legitimate' drama.[77] North and south of the river, certain venues made a specialty of particular genres or even subgenres, such as nautical melodrama, the major attraction at the Surrey. The single most famous instance of the form is Douglas Jerrold's *Black Ey'd Susan; or, All in the Downs* (1829), graced by

---

[76] Nelson and Cross, eds., *Sans Pareil Theatre, Adelphi Theatre*, 30.
[77] Scott, 'Essay on the Drama'.

Plate 26. Thomas Potter Cooke and Jane Scott as William and Susan in Douglas Jerrold's hugely successful nautical melodrama of 1829, *Black Ey'd Susan; or, All in the Downs*. Engraving dated 1 September 1829 by Richard Sawyer, from an original drawing by Robert Cruickshanks.

the incomparable T. P. Cooke as William, the sailor-hero. London audiences turned out in great numbers at theatres with distinct generic specialties, as for the many burlesques by H. J. Byron, F. C. Burnand and other indefatigable comic rhymers and resolute punsters produced at the Strand. During the decade of the 1860s the prolific Burnand turned out twenty-one burlesques for the Strand, the Royalty, the Olympic and a few other venues. Byron virtually lived at the Strand between 1857 and 1864, at which point he moved house to the Bancrofts' Prince of Wales's; by that time he had seen forty-three of his burlesques and extravaganzas, along with several farces and pantomimes, produced at the Strand or elsewhere.[78] Parodies of more serious works, burlesques often opened during the run of their intended target, their knowing mockery relished by the same audiences who enjoyed the originals. To cite an example from the operatic repertory, Burnand's burlesque *L'Africaine; or, The Queen of the Cannibal Islands* went up at the Strand on 18 November 1865, four months after Meyerbeer's opera *L'Africaine* had its London première in Italian at Covent Garden on 22 July, but only a scant month after the opera's first performance there in English, on 21 October. Given the English penchant for poking fun at the ponderous and solemn, it is unsurprising that specialty houses could not contain all that ingenuity could devise. In the case of Byron's send-up of Mozart's opera, *Little Don Giovanni; or, Leporello and the Stone Statue* (1865), the venue was not the Strand, the Gaiety or the Olympic, but the Bancrofts' high-toned Prince of Wales's – marking the presence of sophisticated opera-goers in their audience. By the mid-1880s similar audiences were enjoying three-act farces at the Court Theatre in Sloane Square, among them Pinero's *The Magistrate* (1885), *The School Mistress* (1886), *Dandy Dick* (1887) and *The Cabinet Minister* (1890).[79] Specialty houses thus figured significantly in the development and elaboration of the dramatic genre, reflecting an audience perennially adept at choosing a suitable evening's entertainment. To be sure, the clientèle of theatres large and small had always known what range and variety of plays they could expect. Traditionally, the presentation of a farce of one or two acts after the mainpiece conferred flexibility and opportunity. In the days when major theatres were the sole choice for 'straight' dramatic performance, some play-goers had asserted their preferences by arriving at half-price time, after the third act of the mainpiece, or by departing as the farce commenced. In a later time, the expansion of the farce into a full-length work eliminated this option but catered to audiences preferring (on a given

---

[78] Nicoll, *History of English Drama*, IV: 295–6.
[79] Dawick, *Pinero*; Pinero, *Plays*, ed. Bratton; Schoch, *Not Shakespeare*.

night) farce instead of more serious fare. The clear dominance of the three-act farce in the closing two decades of the century lies implicit in George Alexander's initial refusal to produce Wilde's *The Importance of Being Earnest*, sent to him in November 1894 as a four-act 'farcical comedy' (as the author characterized it).[80] Alexander evidently knew that farces were written in three acts, not four – or one.

The long run had a transformative effect on acting companies and resulted in pervasive changes in the acting profession, including the influential emergence of the actor's agent. Actors still performed characters reflecting traditional lines of business, but the necessity for keeping twenty or more roles ready to perform at short notice was disappearing. Revivals of classic or other familiar plays soon began to follow suit: the production would run until receipts began to fall off, whereupon actors would audition for something else. Irving appears to have perpetuated the old repertory system at the Lyceum, in a modified way; *The Bells*, in which he played the tormented murderer Mathias at frequent intervals for nearly the length of his career, exemplifies the policy. Like other managers, Irving kept his best performers busy in a variety of works, year in and year out, as in the most visible case of Ellen Terry, who continued in a great range of heroines and ingenues when well past the usual age for such roles. Alexander had gotten his start playing supporting roles opposite Irving and Terry. When he took over the management of the St James's Theatre in King Street, St James's, in 1891, the long run was already so firmly entrenched that it was merely instinctual for Alexander to keep plays up for as long as they would draw an audience. Tried and true actors thrived under the new conditions, as under the old, as in the case of Irene Vanbrugh, on view at the St James's over a period of years as the first Gwendolen Fairfax in *The Importance of Being Earnest* (1895) and the first Zoë in Pinero's Edwardian drama *Mid-Channel* (1909). Evidently, if Irving was the exception, not the rule, he was so only in a relative way. His charismatic personality, idiosyncratic style, impeccable standards, scrupulous preparation and eye for sumptuous ensemble gave the Lyceum its unique cachet, but he was not averse to running a successful new play or revival for as long as the traffic would bear. In this new age, the closest the theatrical situation came to old repertory conditions was the special tour: Alexander, J. L. Toole, Irving, Herbert Beerhbohm Tree (Max Beerbohm's half-brother) and other actor-managers took their companies to the suburbs, the provinces, Ireland and Scotland, and even the United States, Canada and Australia, offering a limited repertoire of plays in alternation – a

[80] Wilde, *Complete Letters*, 620.

Plate 27. Cabinet photo (by Window & Grove) of Ellen Terry as Queen Guinevere in a multi-coloured cloak, in J. W. Comyns Carr's *King Arthur*, produced at the Lyceum in January 1895 with Irving in the title role.

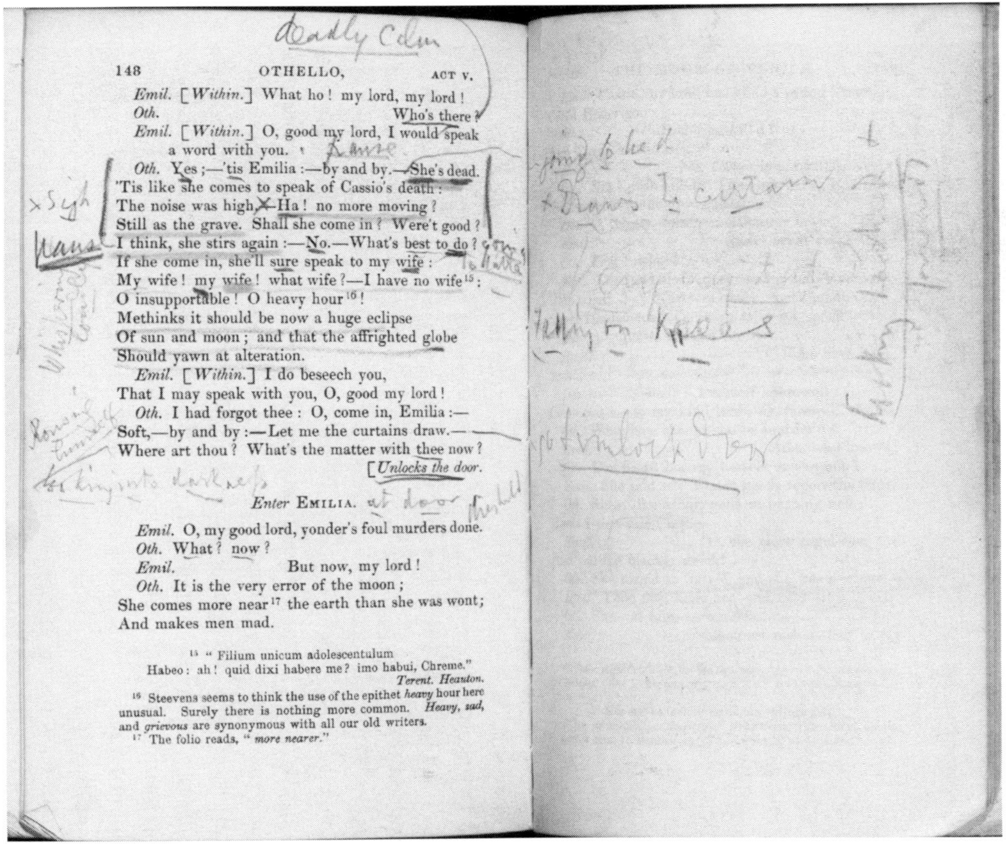

148   OTHELLO,   ACT V.

Emil. [*Within.*] What ho! my lord, my lord!
Oth.   Who's there?
Emil. [*Within.*] O, good my lord, I would speak
   a word with you.
Oth. Yes:—'tis Emilia:—by and by.—She's dead.
'Tis like she comes to speak of Cassio's death.
The noise was high.—Ha! no more moving?
Still as the grave. Shall she come in? Were't good?
I think, she stirs again:—No.—What's best to do?
If she come in, she'll sure speak to my wife:
My wife! my wife! what wife?—I have no wife:
O insupportable! O heavy hour!
Methinks it should be now a huge eclipse
Of sun and moon; and that the affrighted globe
Should yawn at alteration.

Emil. [*Within.*] I do beseech you,
That I may speak with you, O, good my lord!
Oth. I had forgot thee: O, come in, Emilia:—
Soft,—by and by:—Let me the curtains draw.—
Where art thou? What's the matter with thee now?
      [*Unlocks the door.*

Enter EMILIA.

Emil. O, my good lord, yonder's foul murders done.
Oth. What? now?
Emil.   But now, my lord!
Oth. It is the very error of the moon;
She comes more near the earth than she was wont;
And makes men mad.

15 "Filium unicum adolescentulum.
Habeo: ah! quid dixi habere me? imo habui, Chreme."
           Terent. Heauton.
16 Steevens seems to think the use of the epithet *heavy hour* here
unusual. Surely there is nothing more common. *Heavy, sad,*
and *grievous* are synonymous with all our old writers.
17 The folio reads, "*more nearer.*"

Plate 28. Page from the murder scene of Act 5 of *Othello*, Henry Irving's study book for Iago and Othello, dated 2 May 1881, illustrating Irving's precisely detailed analysis of the role.

repertory system in miniature, but one that could not have survived in London itself.

From the actors' perspective, the obvious benefit created by the long run was that, once cast, they had employment night after night. The presence of a play-going cohort of the enormous population of London large enough to keep the long runs running resulted in the virtual abandonment of the old repertory system and its coherent company, constant for an entire season and able to perform the standard repertoire along with an occasional new piece. The security of the old system for actors had now been supplanted by a chronic anxiety fostered by the frequent need to attend auditions, to depend on a persuasive agent and to advertise in trade journals, most importantly the *Era*, the long-lived weekly theatrical periodical which had begun as early as 1838, the year after Victoria's accession to the throne. The long run had the additional effect of promoting a kind of boom-or-bust mentality on the part of actors and producers alike, much to the benefit, on balance, of the theatrical audience.

Important changes in the composition of the theatre audience occur only over time and gradually. In the case of the late nineteenth-century English theatre, however, a clear point of transition has often been cited in the flocking of carriages to the new Prince of Wales's Theatre, above Oxford Street and off the beaten track, in response to the canny initiative of the husband-and-wife team of Squire Bancroft and Marie Bancroft, who in 1865 rehabilitated the dusty old Queen's, a down-at-heels theatre in Charlotte Street, St Pancras, obtained permission to give it a royal name, and opened the doors to a fresh clientèle, a more respectable, even fashionable audience. Despite the out of the way location of the Prince of Wales's, west of Tottenham Court Road and north of the familiar theatre-going precincts of Oxford Street and the Strand, the venture quickly proved an unqualified success. The Bancrofts featured plays by the young, independent-minded T. W. Robertson, whose works emulated a so-called 'cup and saucer' realism – real handles on practicable doors, windows which actually opened and closed, and other accoutrements of an ambitious verisimilitude. Robertson's plays also emphasized a greater three-dimensionality of stage setting and the marked yet unhostile raising of issues of class consciousness, as in *School, Caste, Society* and other plays distinctive for their one-word titles. Robertson's plays constituted an attractive commodity for such audiences. *Caste* is an especially apt example, pointing out the constraining effects of class prejudice while endorsing the status quo of social hierarchy.[81] The story of Robertson's success was in turn fictionalized

---

[81] Barrett, *T. W. Robertson.*

and romanticized in Pinero's charming comedy *Trelawney of the 'Wells'* (Court, 1898). Shaw later downplayed the importance of Robertson's innovations, pronouncing them a 'tiny theatrical revolution';[82] but Shaw had an axe to grind. The less Robertson could be said to have done to revolutionize an allegedly moribund theatre, the more credit Shaw could claim for having done just that – a claim he made for his first commercial success, *Arms and the Man* (Avenue, 1894). Considerable as the Bancrofts' innovation was, it did not by itself initiate an irreversible trend. Indeed, the opening of the splendid new Covent Garden Theatre in 1858 as the London home of grand opera and ballet set a precedent for the widespread return to theatre-going of more polite elements of the population. Even before this event, an economic upturn at mid-century, spurred by the great Crystal Palace exhibition in 1851, helped create a larger segment of the population with sufficient leisure and discretionary funds to make play-going more viable than before.

A survey of typical plays over the century would by implication describe the changing face of the theatre-going audience. To take just two examples of a prominent theme, Knowles's *Virginius* (Covent Garden, 1820), a play with a classical setting, resonates with Victorian anxieties over virtue at risk and demonstrates the immense cost of protecting it: Virginius is forced to kill his beloved daughter Virginia to save her from a fate worse than death. Three-quarters of a century later Pinero's *The Second Mrs Tanqueray* (1893) fascinated St James's audiences with its portrait of a demi-mondaine, Paula, who hopes to bury her questionable past by marrying an upper-class widower, Aubrey Tanqueray, who gallantly burns her confessional letter unread but does not count on the appearance, in his country house, of Paula's former lover. Paula's despairful suicide forms a striking parallel with the death of Virginius's virginal daughter. In each case sexual purity is extolled as the pre-eminent social value, but by Pinero's day audiences can tolerate the titillating representation of a sexually impure woman as the heroine of the piece – until society becomes inconvenienced by her presence. Yet both audiences are invited to endorse a felt necessity for female virtue in domestic life and to ponder the catastrophic consequences of its loss.[83]

The ubiquitous presence of melodrama over the century, with its distressed but sometimes resourceful heroines, implies a continuous endorsement of the same kind, though the settings would change from country to city in the course of time. Such early rural locales as the Bohemia of Isaac Pocock's *The Miller and*

---

[82] Shaw, 'Robertson redivivus', *Our Theatres in the Nineties*, III, 167.
[83] See Shaw's illuminating review, 'An old new play', *Our Theatres*, I, 44–8.

His Men (Covent Garden, 1813) underscore the appeal of fantasy and romance to contemporary audiences. Later, such realistic urban locales as the promenade of the Empire Theatre of Varieties in Leicester Square, one of the settings of Henry Pettitt and Augustus Harris's *A Life of Pleasure* (Drury Lane, 1893), mark a shift in audiences' tastes to a preference for more exact, and sensational, representations of their own lives. Tom Taylor's memorable *The Ticket-of-Leave Man* (Olympic, 1863) captured the trend, with its scenes in the Bellevue Tea Gardens, May Edwards's modest rented rooms in Mrs Willoughby's house, Mr Gibson's bill-broking office in the City, the Bridgewater Arms public house, a city street at night and the churchyard of St Nicholas 'with tombstones and neglected trees', along with its title character, Bob Brierly, a Lancashire lad and felon on parole, and the resourceful police detective Hawkshaw, who became an archetypal figure.[84] The appearance of *A Life of Pleasure* in the same year as Pinero's *Mrs Tanqueray* exemplifies the presence, in the drama of the age, of fantastic ideals constantly at risk in a world of hostile forces: the very stuff of a persistent melodramatic dramaturgy.

One of the most salient indicators of the emergence of a new audience in the last quarter of the century, side by side with continued worry over the impropriety of theatre-going, was the development of houses for quasi-dramatic musical entertainments aimed at persons whose sensibilities rendered them unlikely play-goers or even opera-goers. Prominent among such enterprises was the euphemistically named Gallery of Illustration in Regent Street, first licensed in 1856, where Mr and Mrs German Reed drew audiences for over a decade, beginning in 1860, with such delightful, innocuous pieces as W. S. Gilbert's *Our Island Home* (1870), one of five such works he provided for the Reeds.

Thus a major career in the theatre was launched. As a briefless barrister Gilbert amused himself with writing nonsense rhymes, later collected as *Bab Ballads*; they capture the taste for satiric barbs disguised as harmless silliness which would characterize all he would write in this vein. The habit proved congenial, and he soon became a dramatist.[85] Gilbert's plays run the gamut of dramatic genres from melodrama to musical comedietta, burlesque and satirical farce, his most successful attempt in this last form being *Engaged* (Haymarket, 1877). Excellent of their kind, they have largely been eclipsed by the splendid comic operas on which he collaborated with the composer Arthur Sullivan. Beginning in the mid-1870s with *Trial by Jury* (Royalty, 1875) and *The*

---

[84] Taylor, *Ticket of Leave Man.*
[85] Gilbert, *Bab Ballads*; Stedman, *W. S. Gilbert.*

Sorcerer (Opera Comique, 1877), the collaboration afforded broad opportunities for a laughingly satirical approach to major subjects and issues of the day, such as the army (*Patience*), the navy (*HMS Pinafore*), the peerage (*Iolanthe*) and the melodramatic stage (*Ruddigore*). Despite their stormy relationship, Sullivan and Gilbert produced extremely successful comic operas in the English vein – arias and other songs interspersed with spoken dialogue, with a near total absence of recitative. Richly appreciated by a knowing audience, these operas found an agreeable home in Richard D'Oyly Carte's new, all-electric Savoy Theatre beginning in 1881, simultaneously exposing the flaws of society and complimenting audiences on their sophistication in getting the inside jokes. Over a century later, despite major losses of topicality, the wit and humour of these delightful *jeux d'esprit* remains intact.

As advances in theatre building and changes in audience and plays continued over the closing years of the century, a new theatrical scene began to emerge in other ways as well. The Meiningen Company, a troupe formed in Germany in the 1860s by George II, Duke of Saxe-Meiningen, and directed by him, arrived in London on tour in 1881. The approach to *mise-en-scène* of the Meiningen had been inspired partly by the examples set around mid-century and before by Macready, Phelps and Charles Kean, whose productions the duke had seen. The Meiningen Company's individualized handling of crowds, giving each member a rudimentary identity, dividing them into groups headed by well-drilled actors and dispersing them over several levels, was the most obvious of the company's innovations. Other fresh aspects of their performances (all in German) at Drury Lane of Shakespeare's *Julius Caesar*, *Twelfth Night* and *The Winter's Tale*, particularly the achievement of an atmospheric ensemble heightened by three-dimensional scenery instead of the traditional wing-and-shutter arrangement, recommended them to English-speaking audiences. The duke's approach reflected much earlier efforts in these directions by John Philip Kemble (who had assigned a fictional name to every supernumerary in processions[86]), Charles Kean and Gilbert, but he went much further in the direction of establishing a single, guiding intelligence responsible for the enterprise.[87]

Meanwhile, in the new drama of the late 1880s and early 1890s, Robertson's old subject – how class differences issue in unfortunate incompatibilities of social life – took on new gravity as dramatists began to explore women with dubious pasts, as in Wilde's *Lady Windermere's Fan* (1892) and Pinero's *The*

---

[86] Shattuck, ed., *Kemble Promptbooks*.
[87] Osborne, *Naturalist Drama in Germany*.

Notorious Mrs Ebbsmith (1895), or women tempted to indiscretion, as in Jones's *The Case of Rebellious Susan* (1894), demonstrating the consequences of sexual sin before audiences now more willing to view irremediable moral turpitude on stage. Melodramatic solutions to such problems were still viable in such typical plays as Pettitt and Harris's *A Life of Pleasure*, which trades on crude conventions and a rigid ethos. Meanwhile, other, more sophisticated dramatists were engaging more worldly-wise audiences fascinated with the heavy consequences of transgressive behaviour, set out in a complex, if ultimately reassuring, dramatic intrigue.

Workaday managers and dramatists such as Augustus Harris, along with actor-managers such as Alexander, Herbert Tree, Frank Benson, Lewis Waller and Johnston Forbes-Robertson, were an important but by no means preeminent part of the broad, heterogeneous theatre scene now current in London and beyond.[88] A great range of theatrical and quasi-theatrical entertainment was available well before the closing decade in venues north, south, east and west. Among the options, melodrama, which for some time had been featuring sensation scenes with runaway locomotives, exploding ships, bursting dams and other spectacular catastrophes, remained ubiquitous.[89] Urban settings of course reflect the presence of a large cohort of play-goers eager to see themselves and their circumstances represented on stage, as in Jones and Henry Herman's great hit *The Silver King* (1882). From here through Galsworthy's Edwardian *The Silver Box* (1906) and beyond, the melodramatic ethos persisted unalloyed. 'Oh, God, put back Thy universe and give me yesterday!' cries Denver, the much put upon hero of *The Silver King*, whose progress towards redemption is nonetheless as sure as his just deserts can effect. Produced at the Princess's Theatre, in the perimeter of the West End, Jones and Herman's saga of a broken family adrift in a shadowy world of crime and treachery was one which play-goers in East End and transpontine houses, where change was slower in coming, would have had no difficulty understanding.[90]

For seekers after an evening's entertainment who had access to local or metropolitan music halls, the choices were even more various, especially at the high-toned variety houses of the West End, pre-eminently the Alhambra and the Empire Theatre of Varieties. The career of the brilliant entrepreneur George Edwardes offers a pre-eminent instance of how significant such

[88] Wearing's invaluable *The London Stage 1890–1899* provides exhaustive coverage of some thirty theatres in the West End but omits the greater London theatrical scene.
[89] Booth, *Victorian Spectacular Theatre*.
[90] Davis and Emeljanow, *Reflecting the Audience*; Holder, 'The "lady playwrights"'.

competition with the 'legitimate' theatre was proving to be. After gaining experience under Richard D'Oyly Carte at the Savoy, Edwardes became manager of the Gaiety in 1886 and then of the Prince of Wales's in 1892 and Daly's, in Cranbourne Street, Leicester Square, in 1895, meanwhile having taken over the most fashionable theatre of varieties in London, the Empire, at the top of the Square. The winning combination of variety acts and spectacular ballet at the Empire could be found only there and at the Alhambra, its chief competitor, a stone's throw away on the east side of the Square, while at his three other theatres dramatic offerings prevailed. There, Edwardes pursued a strategy of mounting long-running hits, aiming at producing no more than two plays a year at a given venue. One of the best examples, *A Gaiety Girl*, an amazingly successful musical comedy, opened at the Prince of Wales's late in 1893 and then, almost a year later, transferred to Daly's, where by the end of 1894 it had run for some 397 performances.[91] Edwardes's singular entrepreneurial success, coupled with his effective invention of the new genre of musical comedy, assures him a significant place in the history of the theatre and popular culture of the time.[92]

The emergence of ballet in these newer venues out of opera houses from Vienna and St Petersburg to Paris and London forms a prominent part of the history of nineteenth-century classical dance, and of popular theatre as well. The influence of the European tradition was evident in the work of Katti Lanner, ballet mistress at the Empire, a Viennese prima ballerina who settled in London after an international career and launched a ballet school which soon became a nursery for the Empire, enabling the theatre to develop native talent for the *corps de ballet* while continuing to import continental stars. There she collaborated with Edwardes on complementing the traditional romantic ballet with a second kind of ensemble, the so-called 'ballet divertissement', driven less by plot than by panoramic approaches to up-to-date topics. Between the two balletic offerings at the Empire a range of turns familiar to music hall audiences, from Parisian chanteuses and seriocomic acts to tumbling acrobats and performing dogs, held sway, while pseudo-high-class women of the town provided a more intimate diversion in the five-shilling promenade. The confluence of ballet and variety at the Empire and the Alhambra signals the blithe mingling of ostensibly heterogeneous audiences in a vibrant theatrical setting. The same variety was to be observed in the overall theatrical

[91] Wearing, *London Stage 1890–1899*, 352–3.
[92] Bailey, *Popular Culture and Performance*; Bailey, 'Naughty but nice'.

scene, as evidenced by the remarkable spate of theatre building in the period and the emergent preference for smaller, specialized houses with improved acoustics and the greater comfort provided by stalls seats in place of the old pit benches.

A similar upgrading was observable in the text of the play itself. As the nineteenth century progressed, the publication of inexpensive, paper-bound acting editions had become a veritable industry. Cumberland's British Drama, Dicks', Lacy's and French's (the longest lived of all such publishers), all in fierce competition, were among the foremost. Acting editions offer a mine of information about theatrical practice, comprising one of the most reliable indicators of how broadly and deeply the culture of plays and play-going, and of professional and amateur production, had diffused itself throughout Victorian Britain. The texts of acting editions also demonstrate their distance from the literary version of a work intended for reading. Shaw and other dramatists rebelled against such texts, interlarded with distracting stage directions incomprehensible to the average reader, such as 'Enter L. 2E.' (meaning 'Enter at stage left, second entrance', that is, 'above the second set of wings'). Shaw wanted to restore the act of reading plays as a *literary* experience, and contemporaries such as Pinero and Jones began providing completely finished texts, privately printed and bound in soft covers, for rehearsal, an important sign of the authority such playwrights enjoyed and their confidence in what they had written. Parallel tendencies were observable on the Continent. Henrik Ibsen was intimately familiar with the conventions of the acting edition and began to take issue with them, feeling the same impulse as did Shaw towards providing a clean, literary text. Ibsen's later plays, published chiefly for the Christmas book trade, had stage directions written from the audience's, not the actor's, point of view.

The advent of Ibsen in England signalled the emergence of a troubling, subversive presence, of the kind represented a century before by Kotzebue. To some, including the journalist Clement Scott, reactionary champion of middle-class morality, Ibsen constituted a seditious, morally dubious, foreign influence. When *Ghosts* was produced in London by J. T. Grein's Independent Theatre Society in 1891, Scott, the reviewer for the conservative *Daily Telegraph* and the *Illustrated London News*, pronounced the play immoral and 'suburban' – a term intended to indict Ibsen's apparent concentration on the sordid trivialities of life outside cosmopolitan limits. Following the lead of the first translators of Ibsen's plays, Edmond Gosse and William Archer, Shaw became a champion of Ibsen, and both Shaw and Wilde encouraged actresses such as Elizabeth Robins to sidestep the obstacles of commercial theatrical enterprise and pursue the prospect of an alternative theatre.[93] The result was a series of London productions of *A Doll's House*, *Hedda Gabler* and *Rosmersholm*.

Ibsen's notoriety was considerable, but productions of his plays were few and remained almost anomalous in the thriving commercial theatre of the early 1890s. After a false start as a 'blue book' playwright, Shaw gave up writing plays like *Widowers' Houses*, his first attempt, co-authored with Archer, a trenchant analysis of the evils perpetrated by slum landlords – a play that could not be licensed because of its unsavoury subject. Instead, spurred by Florence Farr's attempt, financed by the tea heiress A. E. F. Horniman, to mount new plays, he wrote *Arms and the Man*, produced at the Avenue Theatre in 1894. It rescued the foundering enterprise, and Shaw became a visible comic force in the last years of the century. Wilde's career followed a roughly parallel course. Invited by George Alexander to write a comedy of modern life instead of poetic tragedies on the order of *The Duchess of Padua*, Wilde responded with *Lady Windermere's Fan*, produced with great success at the St James's in 1892. Intent on widening the horizons of the theatre, Wilde had persuaded Sarah Bernhardt to take on the title role of his symbolist drama *Salome*, written in French, that same year, but the play was denied a licence, achieving production only in 1896 in Paris by the Théâtre de l'Œuvre, while Wilde languished in prison. Wilde had gone on to achieve a series of successes with *A Woman of No Importance* and *An Ideal Husband*, culminating with *The Importance of Being Earnest* in February 1895 at the St James's. For a while, before his ill-fated suit against the Marquess of Queensberry, the father of his lover Lord Alfred Douglas, ultimately landed him in prison in May of that year, serving a two-year sentence for 'gross indecency', Wilde was the unchallenged toast of the London theatre, with two successful comedies playing simultaneously in West End theatres.

Wilde's distinctive gifts for dramatic language, along with his talent for dramaturgical innovations on old, familiar forms, have insured the perennial presence of his plays in the English-speaking theatre. His distinction as a literary critic and dramatic theorist has recently come to be recognized as more modern than late Victorian. But all that was for the future. Wilde's downfall in 1895 had wide repercussions, causing a deep change of mood. A tone of reaction set in. And yet the continuity with the previous ninety-five years would remain high. Despite all the changes which seemed to militate against the effectiveness of actors and their favourable relationship with audiences, the bond between actor and public remained an intimate one. To be sure, the

---

[93] Shaw, *Shaw and Ibsen*; Postlewait, *Prophet of the New Drama*; Powell, *Women and the Victorian Theatre*.

theatre auditorium continued to be divided into discrete sectors representative of social class, profession or occupation and of relative affluence and prevailing taste. Such physical divisions would remain throughout the twentieth century and into our own day, given the remarkable number of nineteenth- and early twentieth-century theatres that have managed to avoid conflagration or the wrecker's ball. To go to the theatre in London, as in most other cities in the West, in the course of the twentieth century was to experience the same broad architectural divisions representative of social structure that audiences encountered when those theatres opened their doors. Drury Lane, the Haymarket, the Adelphi, the Lyceum, the Old Vic, Wyndham's, the Garrick and dozens of other venues built over the long period from King Charles's Restoration to the end of Victoria's reign are emblematic, singly and collectively, of a society still deeply committed to a sense of order, continuity, propriety and (on balance) civility, notwithstanding the sometimes tyrannical behaviour of audiences and perennial threats, inside and outside the theatre, to the preservation of social values and even to life and limb. Shaw was not mistaken when he characterized the theatre as the only institution more conservative than the church.

Yet Shaw, like so many others, realized he was living in a new age, when the perennial vitality of the theatre might be channelled into the service of a more serious, even at times experimental, artistic enterprise. Perhaps the single most noticeable change, for constant play-goers, was that they now began to view plays in a darkened auditorium. The introduction of all-electrified theatres in the 1880s, coupled with the use of the rheostat, or dimmer, made possible the efficient darkening of the auditorium, with profound long-term effects. The application of these technologies to both stage lighting and auditorium illumination set the conditions for a new way of representing the world on the stage and simultaneously a new means of enabling the audience to relate to it. The result was that a new emphasis on theatre art as *art* now became possible. The play of light and shadow was greatly enhanced, even as it had been three generations before through the introduction of gas lighting, augmented by limelight.

At the end of this long period in the history of British theatre from 1660 to 1895, the beginnings of modernism were emerging, but evidence in London and in Britain overall was still rather scant. The Paris production of *Salome* in 1896 formed part of an increasingly visible avant-garde European theatre movement. The American dancer Loïe Fuller, who had already arrived in Paris in 1892, her voluminous scarfs whirling about her as she danced, had found herself praised by Wilde as the 'idol of the Symbolists'. Other signs of change were in evidence. The year 1894 was the date of Debussy's *Prélude à l'après-midi d'un faune* – the moment, according to Pierre Boulez, when modern music, inspired by symbolism, truly began.[94] In 1895 Maurice Maeterlinck's *Pelléas et Mélisande*, which premièred in Paris in 1893, was performed in London at the Opera Comique under the combined auspices of Grein's Independent Theatre and Lugné-Poe's Théâtre de l'Oeuvre – in French, to be sure. Three years later an English translation would appear for a series of matinées with foremost London stars in key roles: Johnston Forbes-Robertson as Golaud, John Martin Harvey as Pelléas and Mrs Patrick Campbell as Mélisande.[95]

As the century drew to a close, other indications of modernism and its off-shoots would surface intermittently. Gordon Craig, Ellen Terry's son with the architect E. W. Godwin, who had acted with Irving, would set the theoretical world of the theatre aflame with his brilliant, outlandish ideas about acting and *mise-en-scène*. Harley Granville Barker, who began as an actor, would become both a skilful dramatist in a sombre new vein and a brilliant theatrical producer who would refashion realistic stage production into a much more subjective, symbolic vehicle for new ideas and insights into art and society. Trends of this kind become all the more conspicuous, and auspicious as well, when set in the long shadow of the re-establishment of the English theatre by Davenant and Killigrew, in the days after Charles's restoration to the throne, comprising the fountainhead of enormous changes from which issued the theatre of the twentieth century and, in turn, the vastly different theatre world of our own time.

[94] Boston Symphony Orchestra, programme, 6–8 January 2000, 37ff.
[95] Wearing, *London Stage 1890–1899*, 95, 92, 98, 115.

Presence, personality and physicality: actors and their repertoires, 1776–1895

JIM DAVIS

He danced, he did not merely walk – he sang, he by no means merely spoke. He was essentially artificial in distinction to being merely natural . . . From the first to the last moment that Irving stood upon the stage each moment was significant . . . [E]very sound, each movement, was intentional – clear-cut, measured dance: nothing real – all massively artificial – yet all flashing with the light and pulse of nature.[1]

In defending Henry Irving against William Archer's criticism that he neither spoke nor moved naturally on stage, Edward Gordon Craig forges a critical language which encourages us to reformulate our perceptions of what mattered in late eighteenth- and nineteenth-century acting. His words provide a fitting epithet for those actors whose physicality, presence and fire enlivened a stage increasingly under pressure to follow a potentially reductive route towards realism and restraint. For Craig, the artificial and the natural were in opposition, yet strangely complementary. Indeed, from the late eighteenth century onwards discussions of acting were often conducted in binaries: the real *versus* the ideal; art *versus* nature; inspiration *versus* study; passion *versus* mannerism; imagination *versus* observation. Behind such debates lies the influence of Diderot, whose *Paradox of Acting*, in which he argued that consistently good acting depended on intellect rather than sensibility, engendered the heart-*versus*-head debate. They find more sophisticated expression in the dramatic criticism of James Leigh Hunt, William Hazlitt and G. H. Lewes,[2] while they are subsequently formulated in the Coquelin–Irving–Boucicault discussions

---

[1] Craig, *Henry Irving*, 74–8.

[2] Of particular value are Hunt, *Critical Essays on the Performers of the London Stage*; Hunt, *Autobiography*; Hunt, *Dramatic Criticism*, ed. Archer and Lowe; *Leigh Hunt's Dramatic Criticism*, ed. Houtchens and Houtchens; Hazlitt, *Complete Works*, ed. Howe; Hazlitt, *View of the English Stage*; Hazlitt, *Dramatic Criticism*, ed. Archer and Lowe; Forster and Lewes, *Dramatic Essays*; Lewes, *On Actors and the Art of Acting*.

of acting in the second half of the nineteenth century and in William Archer's *Masks or Faces?*[3]

Many recent publications have reminded us of the significance that the sculptural and pictorial have in any analysis of this period, as well as an awareness of the philosophical, aesthetic and scientific debates that contributed to the discourse on acting.[4] A crucial factor in any discussion of acting in this period must also be its physical aspect. Actors continually demonstrated their physical skills in melodrama and pantomime through fencing, acrobatics, dancing, the depiction of silent characters and the negotiation of large stages. A sense of the pictorial, the use of rhetorical gesture and an appreciation of the external symbolic forms of their art were all important. Nineteenth-century theatre was physical theatre, just as the nineteenth-century actor was often a personality performer in his or her own right. Many actors followed a specific line of business, whether as tragedians, low comedians, old men or walking gentlemen. As a result, they seem to have absorbed their roles into themselves rather than submerged themselves in the roles. When Hazlitt wrote of actors in 1817, 'Their life is a voluntary dream; a studied madness. The height of their ambition is to be *beside themselves*. Today Kings, to-morrow beggars, it is only when they are themselves that they are nothing',[5] his romantic view of the actor as a sort of inspired lunatic represented a desire rather than a fulfilment. In fact, players during this period, far from being 'beside themselves', were very much themselves in performance and relied on art more than inspiration to create the illusion of nature. Thus, when they represented the 'passions', they consciously used codified gestures and postures to enhance the 'accuracy' of the emotions they depicted. Nevertheless, the contrast between Hazlitt's idealization of the actor and the practice of acting itself recalls the contradictions inherent in the relationship between actor and role, tradition and innovation, absorption and theatricality. Such contradictions have determined much of our response to British acting between 1776, the year in which David Garrick quit the stage, and 1895, when Irving was in the ascendant at the Lyceum.

Within a decade of Garrick's retirement John Philip Kemble and his sister Sarah Siddons had established themselves as the leading tragic performers on

3 Archer, *Masks or Faces?* The Coquelin–Irving–Boucicault debate can be found in Matthews, ed., *Papers on Acting*.
4 Useful studies include Donohue, *Dramatic Character in the English Romantic Age*; Marshall, *Actresses on the Victorian Stage*; Meisel, *Realizations*; Roach, *Player's Passion*; West, *Image of the Actor*. More general surveys or discussions of acting in the period may be found in Donohue, *Theatre in the Age of Kean*; Downer, 'Players and painted stage'; Marker and Marker, 'Actors and their repertory'; Taylor, *Players and Performances in the Victorian Theatre*.
5 Hazlitt, *Examiner*, 5 January 1817.

the English stage. Initially associated with Drury Lane Theatre, the Kembles moved to Covent Garden in 1802. Sarah Siddons was well-nigh perfect, in the opinion of her contemporaries. Believable in every character she played, she made her initial impact in non-Shakespearean roles. She was particularly strong as suffering women like Calista in *The Fair Penitent* and Queen Katharine in *Henry VIII* and in maternal and domestic roles. The pictorial quality of her performances is reflected in James Boaden's view that her attitudes on stage were 'fit models for the painter and sculptor alike'.[6] She studied the role she was to play before every performance and considered the character not in isolation but in relationship to the other roles in the play. Yet, despite such careful study, whatever she did on stage appeared natural and unforced. Renowned for his Coriolanus and Cato, John Philip Kemble was outstanding for his *intensity* in characters dominated by one solitary passion. He was not an intuitive actor: according to Hazlitt, his performances had 'all the regularity of art'[7] and he was 'the only one of the moderns who, both in figure and action, approaches the beauty and grandeur of the antique'.[8] Kemble's classical style was also defended by his supporters as realistic – not in a simple, imitative way, but because it was selective and because it heightened the real world in which it was based. William Robson felt Kemble *was* Coriolanus – 'his voice, his own private manner, his very rigidity, completed the identity – it was Coriolanus moving before you, in all his patrician pride, courage and obduracy'.[9] Yet, for Leigh Hunt, Kemble made a very good 'ideal' but not a very 'real' Coriolanus. Hunt was equally unconvinced by his performance as the reclusive Penruddock, in *The Wheel of Fortune*,[10] although both Hazlitt[11] and Boaden felt he had absorbed the character into himself, as if it were part of his own personal history.[12] In some roles Kemble was outshone by his contemporary George Frederick Cooke. Leigh Hunt, who praised Cooke's Richard III and Iago,[13] made it clear that he preferred Cooke in comedy, although recalling that he 'had no idealism, no affections, no verse'. Compared to Cooke, says Hunt, Kemble was a god 'as far as the ideal was concerned', but he was still 'too artificial, too formal, too critically and deliberately conscious'.[14] It was in

---

[6] Boaden, *Memoirs of the Life of John Philip Kemble*, I: 31.
[7] *The Times*, 25 June 1817.
[8] *Examiner*, 27 October 1816.
[9] Robson, *Old Playgoer*, 34.
[10] Forster and Lewes, *Dramatic Essays*, xxiii, quoting Hunt's *Autobiography*.
[11] *Champion*, 20 November 1814.
[12] Boaden, *Life of Mrs Jordan*, I: 284.
[13] Forster and Lewes, *Dramatic Essays*, 102.
[14] Ibid., 242.

Edmund Kean that Hazlitt, Hunt and their contemporaries were to seek the 'ideal' they so craved.

Eighteenth- and nineteenth-century acting may have aspired to the 'ideal', but whereas this was achieved almost methodically by Kemble, Kean, who made his London début as Shylock at Drury Lane in 1814, seemed to fulfil Hazlitt's desire for its more intuitive embodiment. Yet even Hazlitt's enthusiastic second review of Kean's Richard III at Drury Lane was tempered by his awareness that Kean's effects were achieved through study, which inevitably undermined any appearance of impulse or identification. On reviewing Kean's Richard again later that year, Hazlitt was perturbed by changes in his performance. Not only did he require the actor and character to be inseparable, he also expected the interpretation to remain fixed.[15] Thus, he was delighted to find that Kean's Shylock in 1828 did not differ materially from that which he witnessed in 1814. Despite his desire for inspirational acting, he had by now accepted technique as the only means by which consistency might be maintained: 'Mr Kean's style of acting is not in the least of the unpremeditated, *improvisatori* kind; it is throughout elaborate and systematic, instead of being loose, off-hand and accidental.'[16] G. H. Lewes draws particular attention to this aspect of Kean's technique:

> He was an artist, and in all art effects are regulated . . . Kean patiently and vigilantly rehearsed every detail, trying the tones until his ear was satisfied, practising looks and gestures until his artistic sense was satisfied; and having once regulated these he never changed them.[17]

Lewes's appreciation of Kean anticipates many of the premises in his essay 'On Natural Acting'. In an age of pictorial acting, of realizations, of rhetorical gesture, the semiotics of the actor were an essential part of the process of conveying meaning and significance:

> The supreme difficulty of an actor is to represent ideal character with such truthfulness that it shall affect us as real . . . His art is one of representation, not of illusion . . . The actor has to select. He must be typical. His expressions must be those which, while they belong to the recognised symbols of our common nature, have also the peculiar individual impress of the character represented.[18]

---

[15] See *Morning Chronicle*, 21 February 1814; *Champion*, 9 October 1814.
[16] *Examiner*, 16 March 1828.
[17] Lewes, *On Actors and the Art of Acting*, 18.
[18] Ibid., 111–12.

In Lewes's view, to appear 'natural' on stage is the result of study and selection, not of impulse and intuition. This, in his view, was Kean's achievement. It may also have had its drawbacks, as when Hazlitt refers to the 'succession of striking pictures'[19] that Kean presented as Shylock and Richard, the disjointed (or even inebriated) impact of which is summed up in Coleridge's comment that watching Kean act was like reading Shakespeare by flashes of lightning.[20] Kean was a physical actor, whose small stature led to an active style of performance, in which movement was as significant as speech. In agitated scenes Kean's limbs were always in motion; he performed Shakespeare, wrote one disgruntled critic, as Andrew Ducrow (the great equestrian gymnast and acrobat) would. Yet, even his physical action was based on study and observation.

After Kean's premature death in 1833 William Charles Macready, who had made his London début at Covent Garden in 1816, became the dominant tragedian on the English stage. Not all admirers of Kemble or Kean warmed to him, but he was championed by a new generation of theatre-goers and critics. Macready excelled in the complete and harmonious development of character and in grasping the central idea of the part. He was particularly noted for his ability to introduce touches of tenderness and domesticity into his roles and for the 'sudden, yet natural, infusion into his more heroic vein of some homely touch of truth, which gave reality to the scene'.[21] These qualities were particularly apparent in such roles as Virginius, Richelieu and Werner. For Lewes, Macready was better at demonstrating the domestic rather than the ideal, but in all parts 'strove to introduce as much familiarity of detail as was consistent with ideal presentation'.[22] Lewes found Macready a symbolic or representational actor, as did Westland Marston, who praised his 'psychological insight and his artistic power of translating his emotions into strikingly appropriate – often absolutely symbolic – forms of expression', citing his Macbeth immediately after the dagger scene:

> The crouching form and stealthy, felon-like step of the self-abased murderer, as he quitted the scene, made, however, a picture not to be forgotten. In contrast with the erect, martial figure that entered in the first act, this change was the moral of the play made visible.[23]

---

[19] *Morning Chronicle*, 27 January 1814.
[20] Tracy Davis has argued that Coleridge implies the colloquial usage of the phrase 'flashes of lightning', meaning glasses of gin. '"Reading Shakespeare by flashes of lightning"'.
[21] Marston, *Our Recent Actors*, I: 35.
[22] Lewes, *On Actors and the Art of Acting*, 43.
[23] Marston, *Our Recent Actors*, I: 99.

Whilst there was something 'mannered' about Macready's delivery and the need to make 'points', the move towards the conversational and the domestic implied a reformulation of Shakespearean acting and the beginnings of a style equally appropriate for domestic melodrama.

Macready's leading lady, Helen Faucit, who made her début at Covent Garden in 1836, also brought a touch of domestication to tragic roles, while rendering them graceful and picturesque. Yet she could also convey a sense of spontaneity and nature in the roles she played. The *Art Journal* (January 1867) considered that 'like all true artists, this lady manifestly works from within outwards. Whatever character she assumes has a truth and unity which could be produced in no other way'. Nevertheless, if her impersonations were 'nature' itself, they were 'nature as it appears to the poet's eye – nature in its finest and most beautiful aspects'.[24] Praising her Rosalind, the *Art Journal* acknowledges that 'art the most exquisite must go to produce such results . . . but it is not of the art we think while she is before us, but of the perfect picture of an ideal woman'. As it was for many of Faucit's successors, the relationship between the natural and the ideal appears to be grounded in aesthetics. Yet Henry Morley was ambivalent about her Imogen, precisely because she was too careful, sometimes, 'to make every gesture an embodiment of thought'.[25]

Performing picturesquely was also important in melodrama. In the early nineteenth century many actors specialized in the genre, demonstrating extraordinary physical and acrobatic agility. The large theatres of the period necessitated large-scale performances in which clear visual signs and highly rhetorical language were quite appropriate. A strong sense of timing – inevitable within a form so dependent on music – was also important. The significance of pantomime and dumbshow is emphasized by Doran, who writes of Charles Farley's performance in *A Tale of Mystery* at Covent Garden in 1802 that he 'was great without speaking, and his dumb Francisco . . . was as eloquent and touching as though he had had a thousand tongues'.[26] Thérèse de Camp was much praised, in *The Blind Boy* and *Deaf and Dumb*, for her pantomimic representation in melodrama, 'where face, frame and limbs have all to be eloquent, and tell tales of passion beyond the power of mere airy words'.[27] The initial impact of Madame Celeste later in the century was also enhanced by her performance of mute roles in melodrama.

---

[24] *Dublin University Magazine*, 146, quoted in Russell, *Representative Actors*, 411.
[25] Morley, *Journal of a London Playgoer*, 2nd edn, 286.
[26] *Notes and Queries*, 1859.
[27] *Blackwood's Magazine*, 1832, quoted in Russell, *Representative Actors*, 310. Thérèse de Camp was the wife of Charles Kemble and mother of Fanny Kemble.

Thomas Potter Cooke was one of the most outstanding melodramatic actors. His physical and intellectual skills enabled him to achieve an extraordinary impersonation of Frankenstein's Monster, while his former career as a sailor enabled him to make William in *Black-Ey'd Susan* at the Surrey Theatre (1829) a prototype for many subsequent nautical characters. Particularly impressive was the Monster:

> The thing is a creation of his own brain . . . it contains no trait of the theatre – no shade of anything that has been done before – he comes to our view, a mass of moving matter, without stimulus or intellect – he seems to have eyesight without vision – he moves as if unconscious that he is moving . . . What can be more harassing than the respiration which supplies the place of speech – a feature in this performance as novel as it was natural . . . The creature, raised from the particles of human remains gathered from the charnel-house, is brought before you in the green, ghastly hue of putrescent flesh. It is indeed the realisation of a walking corpse.[28]

This originality also emerged in his Long Tom Coffin in *The Pilot*, in which he gave the sailor character 'a new feature of thoughtfulness and mystery, and a tinge of the romantic'.[29] Whereas sailors had often been depicted as drunk or pugnacious, Cooke successfully reversed this image.

If melodrama required physical skills, so did the Christmas and Easter pantomimes. The most famous pantomime performer of this period was Joseph Grimaldi, who as Clown made a specific 'hit' in the Covent Garden pantomime *Harlequin and Mother Goose* in 1806. Through his satirical attacks on social, political and economic features of Regency life, he turned the Clown into the focal character in early nineteenth-century English pantomime. His large, sparkling eyes and mobile countenance; 'the self-approving chuckles, and the contemptuous look, half pity, half derision, that he gave to the dupe of his artifice';[30] his skill as a dancer and an acrobat; his extraordinary sense of timing all contributed to his reputation. Later in the century George Conquest also became renowned, at the Grecian and Surrey theatres, for his acrobatic and gymnastic skills in pantomime, whether it was the ease with which he disappeared through one trap and reappeared out of another, his feats on the trapeze and on stilts, or his impersonations of monkeys, spiders, octopuses and oysters.

---

[28] *Oxberry's Dramatic Biography and Histrionic Anecdotes*, n.s., vol. 1.
[29] *The Stage or Theatrical Inquisitor*, February 1829.
[30] Hunt, quoted in Findlater, *Joe Grimaldi*, 162. For further confirmation of Grimaldi's significance see Mayer, *Harlequin in his Element*.

Whilst pantomime and melodrama gave scope to physical acting, legitimate acting also flourished in the mid-nineteenth century. After Macready's farewell at Drury Lane in 1851 a number of actors attempted to maintain his innovations, most significantly Samuel Phelps, who at Sadler's Wells from 1844 to 1862 was to present successfully many of Shakespeare's plays. In these he demonstrated talent in both tragic and comic parts while subordinating his performance and that of his actors to the needs of the play. Some found him mannered, but with Charles Kean, who together with his wife Ellen put on a series of spectacular productions of Shakespeare at the Princess's Theatre in the 1850s, he shared the mantle of leading tragedian in this period. Another actor who attempted major tragic roles was Charles Fechter, who broke with tradition at the Princess's in 1861 by performing Hamlet in a blond wig and through the introduction of more detailed business. His performance was highly acclaimed, although to Marston it was 'a Hamlet who might have trodden Pall Mall or the Boulevards in our own day'.[31] His Othello in 1862 repelled Lewes, who felt the role reduced to 'an excitable creole of our own day'. 'It is not consistent with the nature of tragedy', said Lewes, 'to obtrude the details of everyday life'.[32] Fechter could manage the familiar and the colloquial (he was a much better Iago than Othello) but was less effective in moments of passion.

As the century progressed the separation between melodramatic and tragic acting declined. Charles Kean and Charles Fechter were regarded by many as more accomplished in melodramatic roles than in Shakespeare. Lewes felt that Kean was bad in 'any part requiring the expression of intellect or emotion – in any part demanding some sympathy with things poetical', but that he was unrivalled for his restraint in such gentlemanly melodramas as *The Corsican Brothers*.[33] He had a similar view of Fechter, who brought to melodrama a restraint already in existence in the French theatre. This need for restraint was also a reflection of an age in which repression – particularly of the emotions – was so significant. Thus Alfred Wigan, a contemporary of Charles Kean, was praised because 'in delineating the keen, though suppressed emotions, that may actuate thorough-bred gentlemen of the nineteenth century, he cannot be surpassed'.[34] Yet Marston found Fechter wanting precisely because he was deficient in the passions, in keeping with 'the restraint of modern habits', which 'tends to their repression, rather than to their representation'.[35]

---

[31] Marston, *Our Recent Actors*, II: 195.
[32] Lewes, *On Actors and the Art of Acting*, 129.
[33] Forster and Lewes, *Dramatic Essays*, 188.
[34] *Saturday Review* II (23 February 1861): 194.
[35] Marston, *Our Recent Actors*, II: 194.

Despite a growing obsession with realism, the virtuoso aspects of melodramatic acting still surfaced in Dion Boucicault's 'header' – his dive head-first into gauze waters to rescue Eily O'Connor in *The Colleen Bawn* (1860), Charles Warner's delirium tremens scene in Charles Reade's *Drink* (1879) and Henry Irving's exquisite (if repressed) performance as Mathias in *The Bells* (1871). Indeed, A. B. Walkley wrote of Irving, 'Man cannot live by Shakespeare alone, least of all this man. His most persistent triumph has been in melodrama.'[36] Irving dominated the British stage during the late nineteenth century, especially through his management of the Lyceum Theatre from 1878. His presence as an actor was unmistakable, his personality possibly obtrusive, at least to critics like Shaw, for whom 'he had only one part; and that was the part of Irving'.[37] Of his Shylock, Shaw wrote: 'There was no question then of a bad Shylock or a good Shylock; he was simply not Shylock at all; and when his own creation came into conflict with Shakespeare's . . . he . . . positively acted Shakespeare off the stage.'[38] Yet Irving was no different from his predecessors or his contemporaries in his dependence upon personality, and if, like Kean, his range was limited, he excelled in roles such as Iago, Iachimo, Shylock, Benedick, Wolsey, Mephistopheles and Beckett.

When Irving crossed swords with the French actor Coquelin in the Diderot-inspired debate over the actor's reliance on head or heart, he took the side of nature and inspiration. Yet his own practices and speeches imply that the actor should rely on art rather than inspiration. In many ways he endorsed Lewes's notion of the symbolic actor, maintaining that the actor must 'before all things form a definite conception of what he wishes to convey'. In Irving's view the resulting representation was aesthetic, for the ultimate aim of acting was beauty. 'It is most important that an actor should learn that he is a figure in a picture, and that the least exaggeration destroys the harmony of the composition'.[39] For Irving, then, the ideal lay in the pictorial, in something that was heightened and contrived. He was lucky to find in his leading lady, Ellen Terry, exactly those qualities which he so admired. Whatever her shortcomings, Ellen Terry's aesthetic appeal – through her own beauty, through facial expression and through every movement, pose and gesture – was undeniable. Yet she essentially played herself on stage, adapting her parts to her own personality:

---

[36] A. B. Walkley, *Playhouse Impressions* (London, 1892), quoted in Rowell, ed., *Victorian Dramatic Criticism*, 137.
[37] Wilson, ed., *Shaw on Shakespeare*, 262.
[38] *Saturday Review*, 26 September 1896.
[39] Irving, *The Stage As It Is*, 63–4.

she saw her task as learning 'how to translate the character into herself, how to make its thoughts her thoughts, its words her words'.[40]

The history of nineteenth-century acting, however, does not conclude with Irving and Terry any more than it opens with Siddons and Kemble. As with the tragic actors, so with the comic: issues of the real and the ideal, art and nature, exaggeration and restraint, contrivance and spontaneity frequently arise. Moreover, the stage personality of the comic performer, the ways in which he maintained 'his own triumphantly comic self' despite the role performed, combined presence, physicality and careful study to achieve its effects. This was certainly true in the late eighteenth century of William Parsons, who proved so successful as old men, a line hitherto considered unimportant, that authors started to write parts especially for him. He combined English humour with Italian gesticulation and French 'locomotion' in a way that physicalized his roles into something quite original. As Corbaccio in *Volpone* not only was his face expressive, but 'every passion circulated in him to his extremities, and spoke in the motion of his feet, or the more striking intelligence of his hands: the latter became the claws of a harpy, when they crawled over the parchment which blasted all his hopes'.[41] Such performances were probably the result of careful study, for he 'possessed a greater portion of art than nature; but in his art he displayed such consummate judgement that he never failed in extorting true applause'.[42] Parsons seemed to know just what was appropriate to a role, how much restraint or exaggeration was required, and could adapt himself accordingly.

Parsons was an intellectual actor whose effects were based on close observation. When he played drunken characters, 'it appeared as if the observation of his whole life had been of drunks'.[43] Conversely, his contemporary, Richard Suett, reputedly never played a drunken part without being drunk himself first. A popular actor, Suett was extremely tall and thin, with a vacant countenance, an engaging laugh and a croaking voice. 'Shakespeare foresaw him', wrote Charles Lamb, 'when he framed his fools and jesters. They all have the true Suett stamp, a loose and shambling gait, a slippery tongue'.[44] Such a comment implies that, for Lamb, Suett fulfils an ideal, a preconception. Yet, like most comedians, Suett's major achievement lay in his creation of original characters,

[40] Booth, 'Ellen Terry', Stokes, Booth and Bassnett, *Bernhardt, Terry, Duse*, 88.
[41] Boaden, *Memoirs of the Life of John Philip Kemble*, 1: 62.
[42] *Thespian Dictionary* [unpaginated].
[43] Bellamy, 'Life of William Parsons', 58.
[44] Quoted in Russell, *Representative Actors*, 253–4.

such as Dicky Gossip in *My Grandmother*. Another of Lamb's favourites, Joseph Munden, was also renowned for his original roles, especially Old Dornton in *The Road to Ruin*, in which he proved that a low comedian need not resort to broad effects or grimace, but could effectively combine comedy with pathos. Although some accused him of grimacing too much, his facial mobility was enhanced by an ability to throw 'a preternatural interest over the commonest daily life objects' – 'a tub of butter, contemplated by him, becomes a platonic idea'.[45] His pronunciation of specific words further accentuated this trait. Some critics found him too caricatured, although Joseph Cowell believed that Munden 'endeavoured to alter his pure and natural style to suit the declining taste of his auditors, and compete with the caricaturists by whom he was surrounded'.[46] The *Mirror of the Stage* (13 January 1823) very sensibly suggested that insofar as a stage persona is 'a *concave* mirror to nature', then it was necessary for Munden to heighten the colouring of the portrayal he presented and that this was a matter for his own discrimination. In other words, even the low comedian might strive for the 'ideal' rather than the 'real'.

Eulogized by Hazlitt much as Munden was by Lamb, John Liston, who made his London début in 1805, eventually eclipsed Munden in popularity:

> Mr Liston has more comic humour, more power of face . . . than any other actor we remember . . . Munden . . . is a caricaturist in the comparison. He distorts his features to the utmost stretch of grimace, and trolls his voice about with his tongue in the most extraordinary manner, but he does all this with an evident view to the audience; whereas Liston's style of acting is the unconscious and involuntary.[47]

If Liston concealed technique whereas Munden displayed it, the likely results were probably not very different. Liston was particularly strong in provincial coxcombs and cockneys, such as Apollo Belvi in *Killing No Murder* and Lubin Log in *Love, Law and Physic*. His most famous role, the name part in *Paul Pry* (Haymarket Theatre, 1825), demonstrated the importance of posture, costume and props in creating a comic character. Liston's image as Paul Pry was emblazoned throughout London in pastry shops, on public transport, in print shops and pottery warehouses. Some accused Liston of mere buffoonery, but much of his impact was due to careful study. Many accounts refer to Liston's repose and restraint, to his ability to create a character out of almost nothing and to his naturalness. Such claims were no doubt bolstered by his effortlessness,

---

[45] Lamb, 'On the acting of Munden', *London Magazine*, October 1822.
[46] Cowell, *Thirty Years among the Players of England and America*, I: 21.
[47] Hazlitt, *London Magazine*, January 1820.

helped by an appearance already exaggerated by nature itself. Like Parsons, Liston probably knew how far to take each character and found a style to match that of the farce or comedy in which he was playing.

Liston's movement towards a more natural style of acting anticipates the career of his contemporary, William Farren. 'Crusty old bachelors, jealous old husbands, stormy fathers, worrying uncles, or ancient fops with ghastly pretensions to amiability – such were the types which he usually presented to the public . . . He had', said Lewes, 'a marvellous eye for costume, and a quick appreciation of all the little details of manner'.[48] Farren retained a somewhat artificial manner in his representation of established roles, but adopted a more colloquial style in contemporary parts. Reviewing his performance in the title role in Mark Lemon's *Grandfather Whitehead* in 1842, the *Times* claimed 'a sort of turn' had been taken 'in modern English acting . . . We found a comedian really studying character and setting it forth. Shades were discriminated, details were observed, minute touches were delicately given; in a word, abstraction was abandoned, and an individual personage was presented.'[49] Yet, even if Farren represents the transition from the old comedy to the new, from the broad farce and artificial comedy of the past to the domestic comedy of the mid- and late nineteenth century, many earlier low comedians had been equally praised for detailed and careful characterization. Particularly oustanding was John Emery, who played country roles at Covent Garden from 1805 to 1822 and who was responsible for a shift in their origins through his use of the Yorkshire dialect and garments. His jealous scene as Fixture in *A Roland for an Oliver* was highly acclaimed, as was his villainous Tyke, a man torn by conflicting emotions, in *The School for Reform*, a performance which Hazlitt called 'the sublime of tragedy in low life'.[50] Emery was also noted for his 'cameo' performances as Williams in *Henry V* and Barnardine in *Measure for Measure*. The fact that he must have 'Nature to copy from' rather than 'study and reflection' in order to evolve a part was apparent in his performance of Caliban, which he played as a Yorkshire rustic, which rather upset Hazlitt in his perennial quest for the idealized. Emery, wrote Hazlitt, 'is indeed, in his way, the most perfect actor on the stage. His representations of common rustic life have an absolute identity with the thing represented. But the power of mind is evidently that of imitation, not that of creation. He has nothing romantic, grotesque or imaginary about him . . . Mr Emery had nothing of Caliban but his gaberdine,

[48] Lewes, *On Actors and the Art of Acting*, 55–6.
[49] Quoted in Rinear, 'From the artificial towards the real', 21, 26.
[50] *London Magazine*, January 1820.

which did not become him'.[51] For many other critics a Yorkshire accent and a poetic conception were incompatible, but not for Leigh Hunt, who considered Emery's blending of the coarse and poetic aspects of the monster 'one of the best pieces of acting' he had ever seen.

Contemporary with Liston, Farren, Emery and Munden was the elder Charles Mathews. Some found him inadequate as a successor to Parsons or Suett, but his volatile style when paired with an actor like Liston was very effective. He was also very successful in his 'At Home's' – one-man shows in which he depicted a gallery of grotesque and eccentric characters, with all sorts of peculiarities of gesture and diction. Charles Dickens recounts how, as a young man, he always tried to attend the theatre when Mathews was performing and that, if he had become an actor, Mathews was the model he would have followed. Much has been made of the influence of Mathews on Dickens as a writer, sometimes to the detriment of a proper consideration of the comic stage as a whole. Mathews was unique in his time: his strength lay in mimicry and imitation, but one suspects that there was little poetry or pathos about him.

Up until the 1830s the most successful low comedians had been associated with Covent Garden or Drury Lane in the winter and with the Haymarket in the summer. From the 1830s onwards they were just as likely to be found at the Lyceum, Olympic, Adelphi or whichever theatre offered them the best terms. Among the most representative low comedians in the mid-nineteenth century were John Harley, Robert Keeley and John Baldwin Buckstone. Harley, according to Hazlitt, was 'always in the best possible humour with himself and the audience'.[52] The obtrusion of self was tantamount: 'if one never expected Harley to lose himself in his part, one was tolerably content that the part should be lost in Harley'.[53] Like Harley, Keeley 'to a great extent . . . was always Keeley',[54] yet within those limitations he was capable of variety and was particularly good as the passive victim of catastrophe or disaster. In Lewes's view, he achieved the 'ideal' in his representations of comic passion, especially 'in moments of abject terror'.[55] Keeley was the opposite of J. B. Buckstone, for whom characterization was subordinate to mirth and the need to call attention to his humour. Often Buckstone, who was also a playwright and theatre manager, rewrote the roles he performed in the plays of others to suit

---

[51] Hazlitt, *Examiner*, 3 July 1815.
[52] Hazlitt, *Examiner*, 28 January 1816.
[53] Marston, *Our Recent Actors*, II: 293–4.
[54] Ibid., II: 102.
[55] Lewes, *On Actors and the Art of Acting*, 78.

his on-stage personality. An active, demonstrative comedian, through his facial expressions and vocal delivery he attained a complicity with his audience 'by a sort of advertising look, which seemed to say, "Attention! Something droll is about to happen!"'[56] His physicality and on-stage presence clearly indicated the low comedian:

> His voice is in perfect keeping with his person: it suggests a distillation; it seems to lazily flow from a mind charged with fat thoughts and unctuous conceits. He has the true low-comedy air in his walk and gesture; his face looks dry and red with long roasting before the footlights.[57]

Buckstone played traditional parts such as Scrub, Bob Acres and Tony Lumpkin as well as many original roles, while in *Keeley Worried by Buckstone* the stage idiosyncrasies of both performers were put to account when they represented themselves.

J. L. Toole, whose career spanned the second half of the century, was the last in a long line of nineteenth-century English low comedians and was much praised for the combination of pathos and humour he displayed in roles such as Caleb Plummer in *Dot* and Michael Garner in H. J. Byron's *Dearer than Life*. He was at his best in original parts, such as Tom Cranky in Hollingshead's *The Birthplace of Podgers*, Mr Sleek in *The Serious Family* and the title roles in two plays by the Merivales, *The Butler* and *The Don*. Toole's reputation, like that of many of his predecessors, depended in part on the presentation of a consistent stage personality, a characteristic which Joseph Knight, in discussing Toole, succinctly describes:

> The fact is that the art of the low comedy actor is seldom purely histrionic, and sometimes is not art at all. Instead of assuming the personality of another man, and fitting his soul as it were and his whole being into another individuality, he obtains ordinarily his most comic effects from the obtrusion, through a fictitious character, of his own triumphantly comic self.[58]

In other words, the low comedian will normally present the 'real' rather than the 'ideal', although Munden, Emery and Keeley, in their different ways, aspired to a sort of low comedy 'ideal'.

During this period self-consciousness was a feature of low comedy acting, even if what was created was something of the actor's rather than the author's. Once again the 'presence' of the performer proved a significant factor

---

[56] Marston, *Our Recent Actors*, ii: 90.
[57] Russell, *Representative Actors*, 386.
[58] Knight, 'Toole', *Theatre* n.s. (January 1880), 25–6.

in nineteenth-century theatrical experience. If the so-called 'reforms' of the nineteenth-century stage constrained and eventually removed the low comedian from the legitimate theatre, the utopian pursuit of the 'real' rather than the 'theatrical', the 'bland' rather than the 'eccentric', the 'domestic' rather than the 'fantastic', may be partly to blame. Yet, as Michael Booth suggests, comedy acting is subject to social change: just as the genteel comedy of the eighteenth century gave way to a more bourgeois (and grotesque) form in the early nineteenth century,[59] so the class-conscious innovations of the Bancrofts and others gradually led to the ousting of the old low comedian.

The comic actress also embodied many of these contradictions, although in Boaden's view it was more difficult for women to shine in comedy. 'The low comedian may resort, if he chooses, to the buffoonery of the fair', he said, but 'the actress has nothing beyond the mere words she utters, but what is drawn from her own hilarity, and the expression of features, which never submit to exaggeration'.[60] However, Boaden had no qualms about Dorothy Jordan, who made her London début at Drury Lane in 1785. Her exuberance on stage, plaintiveness in roles such as Viola and Rosalind and effective representation of country girls he described as 'heart in action'.[61] Her popularity was the result of her personality: 'It was not as an actress, but as herself, that she charmed everyone', wrote Hazlitt. 'Her face, her tones, her manner were irresistible; her smile had the effect of sunshine, and her laugh did one good to hear it; her voice was eloquence itself – it seemed as if her heart was always at her mouth.'[62] Although Dorothy Jordan gained a reputation in breeches parts, Leigh Hunt felt that male impersonation had limited her range, since he believed it was impossible to erase the 'maleness' acquired by actresses who frequently played in male attire.[63] Boaden complained in 1786 that Mrs Edwards's début as Macheath in The Beggar's Opera and Mrs Webb's performance as Falstaff in the first part of Henry IV at the Haymarket Theatre were vile, beastly and indecent.[64] Yet Boaden certainly had no problems with Dorothy Jordan's

---

[59] Booth, 'Acting of early nineteenth-century comedy', English Plays of the Nineteenth Century, III: 153.

[60] Boaden, Life of Mrs Jordan, I: 71.

[61] Ibid., I: iii.

[62] Hazlitt, Examiner, 22 October 1815.

[63] Hunt, Dramatic Essays, 82–3.

[64] Boaden, Memoirs of the Life of John Philip Kemble, I: 334. By the same token, when Mrs Glover impersonated Paul Pry for her benefit in the early nineteenth century, it was referred to as 'a disgusting exhibition' by the Theatrical Observer (9 October 1834). Yet Donaldson, Recollections of an Actor, 137–8, says of that actress's Hamlet at the Lyceum in 1822 that 'her noble figure, handsome and expressive face, rich and powerful voice, all contributed to rivet the attention of the élite assembled on this occasion', while at the

male impersonations: Viola, he says, enabled her 'to indulge the town with a steadier gaze at her male figure', while in *Cymbeline* it was 'only in the male habit that Mrs Jordan seemed to be the true and perfect Imogen'.[65] Recalling her performances as William in *Rosina* at the York Theatre, he commented: 'The neatness of her figure in the male attire was for years remarkable; but the attraction after all is purely feminine, and the display of female, not male, perfections. Did the lady really look like a man the coarse *androgynous* would be hooted from the stage.'[66]

Leigh Hunt claims that Mrs Jordan's legs had been used as the model for statuary.[67] Not many years after, the legs of Madame Vestris could be purchased in plaster replicas. Vestris was an enormous success in the title role of *Giovanni in London*, which she first played at Drury Lane in 1820. When she played Macheath in *The Beggar's Opera*, the *Examiner* (30 July 1820) expostulated:

> If Madame Vestris goes on in this manner, we really must insist . . . upon her putting on her petticoats. The more we are pleased with her in trousers and boots, the more we long to see her out of them. She so divests Macheath of his blackguardism – renders him so unlike himself and his sex, – in short, makes him such a gentlemanly sort of man, that he and his wives seem like three females playing a frolic in masquerade.

Vestris's impersonations contained a strange mixture of decorum, ambiguity and eroticism. According to the *British Stage* (January 1821), 'the town ran in crowds to see Madame Vestris's legs, though they had been somewhat luke-warm about her singing . . . and . . . discovered that her proportions were most captivating when set off to advantage by a tight pair of elastic pantaloons'. Her confidential, coquettish manner bewitched her audiences and, even though Marston found her incapable of passion or pathos, he acknowledged her as an actress 'who was probably more fascinating than any of her time'.[68]

Whereas Boaden had suggested androgyny would make female impersonation unacceptable to the public in the late eighteenth and early nineteenth centuries, it seems that by the middle of the century it was precisely androgyny that made the practice acceptable to the prurient Victorians. When asked to judge whether Ada Isaacs Menken's costume as Mazeppa was indecent, when

East End Britannia Theatre Sophie Miles played Hamlet in 1867, Marie Henderson in 1869, Julia Seaman in 1871 and Miss M. Bellair in 1873 without eliciting complaints. All were benefit performances.

[65] Boaden, *Life of Mrs Jordan*, I: 76, 80.
[66] Ibid., I: 46.
[67] Hunt, *Dramatic Criticism*, 82.
[68] Marston, *Our Recent Actors*, II: 143, 149.

she appeared at Astley's at mid-century, W. B. Donne, the Examiner of Plays, considered that it was perfectly acceptable, in part because Menken's appearance was androgynous, even masculine. Mary Keeley, whose roles included Smike, Jack Sheppard and Oliver Twist, provided as Bob Nettles in *To Parents and Guardians* 'the only representation of a masculine character by a woman' that had fully satisfied Lewes: 'She was the school-boy in every look and gesture.'[69] Charles Dickens, in 1858, had enthused about Marie Wilton's Pippo in a burlesque of *The Maid and the Magpie*, writing that 'while it is so astonishingly impudent . . . it is so stupendously like a boy, and unlike a woman, that it is perfectly free from offence'.[70] Marie Wilton herself was far from happy playing boys: her preference was for roles like Polly Eccles, the soubrette part in Tom Robertson's *Caste*. Yet if, for Wilton, her liberation from breeches was an ascent up the ladder towards respectability, there were others who were less fazed by such roles. Sarah Lane, the East End counterpart of Madame Vestris and Marie Wilton (and like them the 'manageress' of her own theatre), was still donning male attire into her eighties and her male impersonations were a regular feature of melodramas, pantomimes and burlesques at the Britannia Theatre. That breeches roles were significant in melodrama was also demonstrated by Thérèse de Camp and Madame Celeste, whose character in *The French Spy*, for instance, disguises as both a French spy and an Arab boy. Thus, whilst it would give a false impression to overemphasize male impersonation, it was a significant feature of nineteenth-century British theatre and one that raises many issues in relation to gender politics, gender representation, sexuality and power in performance. It draws attention to the actor's body, to her presence, to the physical nature of performance once again and to ambiguities in the actor–spectator relationship.

In any discussion of comic performance, the light comedian raises issues connected not so much with personality and physical performance as with the distinctions between the natural and the artificial. From William Lewis at the end of the eighteenth century through Richard Jones to Charles Mathews the younger, the airy, mercurial light comedian provided a contrast to the low comedian and, in the case of Mathews, boasted a technique that made this line of business seem much more natural. Mathews stated that he did not 'pretend to be a physical farce actor. My only claim is to be agreeable and natural'.[71] From his first appearance at Vestris's Olympic Theatre in 1835 he won acclaim for his relaxed, effortless style. For Lewes, Mathews was a

---

[69] Lewes, *On Actors and the Art of Acting*, 79–80.
[70] Quoted in Squire and Marie Bancroft, *Mr & Mrs Bancroft On and Off the Stage*, 38.
[71] Quoted in Booth, *English Plays of the Nineteenth Century*, IV: 145.

'natural' actor because he understood the manner appropriate to representing the characters he played in the drama of 'ideal' life:

> If we once understand that naturalness in acting means truthful representa-
> tion of the character indicated by the author, and not the foisting of common-
> place manner on the stage, there will be a ready recognition of each artist's
> skill, whether he represent the naturalness of a Falstaff, or the naturalness
> of Sir Peter Teazle, or the naturalness of a Hamlet, or the naturalness of
> Coriolanus . . . Naturalness being truthfulness, it is obvious that a coat-and-
> waistcoat realism demands a manner, delivery and gesture wholly unlike the
> poetic realism of tragedy and comedy; and it has been the great mistake of
> actors that they have too often brought with them into the drama of ordinary
> life the style they have been accustomed to in ideal life.[72]

Mathews, whose particular talents were shown off to advantage in smaller theatres, often appeared as if he had stepped straight out of the drawing-room and onto the stage. Yet his conviction was the product of a heightened and selective representation of life; he may have appeared 'realistic' on stage, but his 'natural' demeanour owed more to art than to accident.

By the 1870s there was a feeling that the influence of French acting and drama had resulted in a more natural – and for some critics, less exciting – style of acting. Both Madame Vestris's management of the Olympic in the 1830s and Marie Wilton's at the Prince of Wales's from 1865 had encouraged greater restraint in setting and acting and drawn fashionable audiences to their respective theatres. Yet their reforms, however commendable, sounded the death knell for the *theatre theatrical* in England. Ever greater emphasis on the natural and the restrained turned an actor's theatre into a dramatist's theatre and acting itself into a shallow imitation of what it once had been. As early as 1845 a comment from the *Spectator* framed the issue:

> The aim of the French comedian is to impress and delight by representing
> finished pictures of characters in real life, studied carefully from nature; and
> his success is complete in proportion to the degree of perfection with which
> he conceals his art in this living portraiture . . . In effect English acting, in the
> mass, is an affair of personal display and stage-trick; the means are mistaken
> for the end.   (February 1845)

Of course, it all depends on what one sees as the 'end' of acting. The Vic-
torian obsession with the familiar, so explicit in contemporary painting and leading towards photographic realism, inevitably intruded upon the theatre. A restrained, more natural style of acting combined with an infinitely more

---

[72] Lewes, *On Actors and the Art of Acting*, 104–5.

realistic stage setting and more detailed stage business could give credibility both to the comedies Tom Robertson wrote for the Prince of Wales's and to the most sensational of formulaic melodramas. The tendency to push the actor back behind the proscenium arch further accentuated a separation from the audience, which the darkening of the auditorium beginning in the 1880s only increased. In a lit space actor and audience share an experience; actors are more storytellers who represent characters than the thing itself. The darkened auditorium forces a more illusionistic impression along with a tendency to reject theatricality. Such change was a diminution of the actor's physicality and presence: it turned a living body into a talking head.

These developments illustrate the dangers inherent in any survey of acting over such a vast period. It is tempting to embrace an 'all roads lead to Rome' approach to acting in this period, by which the growth of domesticity and detail in performance, abetted by the influence of French acting, ultimately prepares the way for the plays of Ibsen and Shaw. It is equally possible to construct a history of British acting largely as an account of the delineation of major Shakespearean roles, which immediately excludes consideration of all but a handful of actors and actresses. Whilst it is possible to discern patterns, congruencies, traditions and influences through the years, it might also be worth noting the accidental nature of the history we are pursuing. There is equally a danger of periodization, of defining segments of time as the age of Kean or of Irving, and thereby imposing a false heterogeneity upon them. Moreover, we might ask ourselves whose history we are actually telling. The majority of nineteenth-century actors were not 'stars', but rather ordinary workaday professionals who laboured hard for low wages under appalling conditions. Despite the social elevation enjoyed by the West End luminaries of the profession in the late nineteenth century, much remained the same for their brethren.[73] Therefore, the way in which we analyse actors of the past should ideally take into account their social and workplace conditions, the conventions through which their biographies and autobiographies have been mediated and the assumptions governing critical writing on their performances.

It is impossible, when writing about this period, to ignore the accounts of Hazlitt, Leigh Hunt, Lewes and Marston, through which so many actors can be vividly recovered. Yet, even though Lewes praised the restrained and more natural modes of acting that developed in the mid-nineteenth century, he still

[73] See, in particular, Tracy Davis, *Actresses as Working Women*; Jim Davis, ed., *Britannia Diaries 1863–1875*; 'Corin', *Truth about the Stage*. Booth's chapter on acting in *Theatre in the Victorian Age*, 99–140, provides a good survey of the working conditions of the nineteenth-century actor.

remained true to his perception of the 'ideal' in the 'symbolic' or 'representational' actor. Indeed, at the end of the century the acknowledged leaders of the profession were not those actors who transferred everyday behaviour to the stage, but Irving (who was always Irving, but who 'danced' his roles in the stylized manner recalled by Craig), Toole (always his 'own triumphantly comic self') and the picturesque Ellen Terry. In reconsidering Craig's description of Irving, we might do well to remember that Craig, perhaps more than Shaw and Archer, is a vital link between the theatre past and present and that it is in his equating of the natural with the artificial that the 'ideal' was so often achieved in late eighteenth- and nineteenth-century British acting.

13

Theatres, their architecture and their audiences

JOSEPH DONOHUE

On 8 November 1755, at Drury Lane, Garrick introduced a French company performing Jean Georges Noverre's ballet *The Chinese Festival* – to the mounting displeasure of a xenophobic audience, hissing, clapping and crying 'No french Dancers'.[1] By the fifth night a riot was underway, and the sixth night proved to be the last. A contemporary print depicts several members of the audience, one wielding a club, moving through the orchestra pit and up onto the stage. At either side of the forestage appears an ornamental barrier, and the stage boxes, just below the proscenium doors, are outlined by rows of spikes – largely symbolic, to judge from the ease with which they are being breached. The audience's agitation is highlighted by the five chandeliers above the scene, four in parallel and another in the centre. Candles in pairs, four sets at either side of the downstage area, also record the artist's attempt to indicate the full illumination of forestage and auditorium.

The illustration epitomizes a widely held view of the eighteenth-century theatre audience as an unruly mob, an image captured here for posterity on one of those occasions when an ordinarily vociferous audience became indignant over some perceived insult or other failure to defer to their tastes and preferences, and reacted accordingly. Over against such images should be placed depictions of other moments in which that same autocratic audience expressed its pleasure in universal laughter or applause, as in Hogarth's robust representation of a London theatre audience in 1733.[2] Both images are true, and equally characteristic of that open-hearted (if not open-minded) cohort of citizens from various walks of life who attended the theatre as often as they could and who insisted on being well entertained.

Further scrutiny of the *Chinese Festival* print reminds us that another reason why these audiences were so insistent was that, because auditorium light stayed

---

[1] Drury Lane prompter Cross's diary, quoted in Stone, ed., *London Stage 1660–1800*, vol. IV, entry for 8 November 1755. See Troubridge, 'Theatre riots in London', 91–2.

[2] 'The Laughing Audience', reproduced in Thomas and Hare, eds., *Theatre in Europe*, 178.

constant throughout the performance, audience members remained aware of themselves as a live, responsive and often audible presence. Conversely, actors could see their auditors and so had the same conscious awareness of them. Especially in the early years after King Charles II's restoration, the substantial thrust of the forestage resulted in actors being surrounded on three sides by that visible audience. Despite substantial differences in interior configuration from the theatres of Shakespeare's time, the forestage continued to link the actor with the theatre audience as a palpable presence, to be acknowledged, addressed or acquiesced to, as occasion required.

Viewed in this frame of reference, the physical configuration of a theatre becomes simultaneously an architectural and a social and cultural phenomenon. Although Richard Leacroft's authoritative survey of theatre buildings, *The Development of the English Playhouse* (1973), and James J. Lynch's classic study of the eighteenth-century audience, *Box Pit and Gallery* (1953), emphasize one aspect or the other, both works assume that the structural features of the theatre auditorium and stage are best understood by considering what happens when an audience fills the auditorium and actors begin to speak and to move about the stage. To consider both aspects – the theatre building and the theatre audience – together, we need a vantage point from which this dual phenomenon may be viewed.

The single most famous observation on the interconnection between players and audiences must surely be that of Samuel Johnson, who at Garrick's invitation composed a prologue for the reopening of Drury Lane Theatre in 1747 under Garrick's management. 'The drama's laws the drama's patrons give', Johnson wrote, 'For we that live to please, must please to live.' 'The stage but echoes back the publick voice', Johnson added – and this from a critic who would later praise Shakespeare as the inventor of a new, 'mingled' form of drama, comic and tragic, which was 'the mirrour of life'.[3] We may well ask which way the echo really travelled, which way the influence was exerted and felt. Does the dramatist lead the audience into new realms of experience, or are the dramatist and all who contribute to the fictional realization on stage responding to felt preferences and exigencies generated by those who fill the auditorium? Is Johnson implying that the theatre is so conservative and yet so sensitive and intuitive an institution that shifts in social consciousness and attitude, mores and taste, or even short-term fashions and trends, are what determine the nature of plays? By extension, can it also be true that the very

---

[3] Johnson, *Poems*, ed. McAdam, *Yale Edition of the Works of Samuel Johnson*, VI: 89; preface to Johnson's edition of Shakespeare, *Johnson on Shakespeare*, ed. Sherbo, *Yale Edition of the Works of Samuel Johnson*, VII: 66, 65.

shape of the stage on which those plays appear, and even the configuration of the auditorium itself, are determined in much the same way? An overview of theatre building and theatre audiences from the Restoration to the end of the nineteenth century will enable us to test the validity of what might be called 'the Johnsonian premise'.

First, two basic principles: (1) in the theatre *light* is primary, and vital; and (2) the size, shape and orientation of the stage determine everything else of importance about the physical theatre. In the outdoor theatres of the Elizabethan age plays were performed in daylight, in the afternoon; but at indoor theatres like the Blackfriars, plays were performed by candlelight, even in the daytime, and windows were clapped shut, perhaps to enhance the lighting of the stage area and to render auditorium lighting more uniform.[4] Ever since, indoor stages and auditoriums, like the great halls they at first resembled, have been lighted artificially. By the late nineteenth century, when gas and then electricity made possible intensely concentrated light from multiple sources, the closest thing to natural light were the self-venting chandeliers in the ceilings, called 'sun-burners' or 'sunlights' – a nostalgic term reminiscent of the halcyon days of outdoor theatres. Artificial light, however closely it resembled the natural, had long since become the universal means of illuminating stage and auditorium alike.

In the long period down to 1881, when Richard D'Oyly Carte's Savoy Theatre, the first to be lighted entirely by electricity, was built in the Strand and the rheostat (invented in the 1840s) began to be used to dim the house lights, auditoriums had remained illuminated throughout the performance.[5] From Elizabethan until late Victorian times, the mutual visibility of audience members as the performance progressed made the experience of theatre-going fundamentally different, socially, from what it would become by the twentieth century, when the auditorium was darkened and the only light emanated from the stage. The sense of anonymity – and passivity – conferred on later play-goers when the lights went down would have been incomprehensible to earlier audiences, always aware of their identity as a community-in-little and likely to register immediate approval or disapproval, not just at the final curtain. Prologues and epilogues, a staple of traditional performance, would become impracticable without an audience which could be looked in the eye by an actor – or *player*, a more appropriate term for the performer considered in relation to that audience.

---

[4] Smith, *Shakespeare's Blackfriars Playhouse*, 301–3.
[5] Rees, *Theatre Lighting in the Age of Gas*, 187–8.

Whatever its composition, the audience, a coherent community representative of the larger one from which it derived, was always more than an undifferentiated group of enthusiasts. As long as theatres have existed as purpose-built structures, even from ancient times, partitionings of the auditorium have served both for crowd control and as a way of encouraging various classes to attend. From the earliest days of the professional theatre, in the sixteenth century, audiences had been segregated by means of an ascending scale of prices for various sections of the auditorium, affording correlatively greater visual advantage and proximity to the stage. So it was at Burbage's Globe (1599), Davenant's Lincoln's Inn Fields (1661), Robert Adam's Drury Lane (1775), Astley's Olympic (1806), Wilton's Prince of Wales's (1865) and Phipps's Shaftesbury (1888). A broader clientèle served to generate greater profits and effectively identified distinct social groups, preferred, acceptable or merely tolerated (as in the case of prostitutes). After the Restoration, as theatres were adapted from other structures such as tennis courts or were newly constructed or rebuilt, the separation of the auditorium into box, pit and gallery became a normative idea, whatever the size of the actual structure.

And so, in this way as well, the theatre of the age echoed back the public voice – the symbolic if sometimes all too audible speech of a society itself made up of well-defined hierarchical divisions. From an early point in architectural development, theatres would be built with several entrances (eventually including a private entrance for the monarch), relieving upper-class patrons of the distasteful inconvenience of mingling with the middle or lower classes or with prostitutes imitating the respectability of their 'betters'. (At Drury Lane in 1842, Macready limited access for women of the town by allowing them only in the gallery, reached by 'a separate pay-office, and by passing through a dismantled lobby'.[6]) Multiple entrances efficiently shunted lower-class audiences to the gallery door at the side of the theatre. Relegated to the dizzying heights of the sixpenny or one-shilling 'heavens' by their inability or disinclination to pay the higher prices for box, pit or first gallery, these audiences frequently retaliated by making their presence impossible to ignore, by actors and the rest of the audience alike.

Such divisions became even more significant as they underwent reconfiguration in response to a changing cohort of theatre-goers. As early as 1815, at His Majesty's, eight rows of 'stalls', individual upholstered seats, were placed at the front of the pit, traditionally comprised of backless benches set out in rows.[7] The novelty caught on. By 1858 two hundred persons could be seated

[6] Letter to *The Times*, 15 January 1842, quoted in Downer, *Eminent Tragedian*, 208–9.
[7] Leacroft, *English Playhouse*, 170.

in the stalls of the rebuilt Britannia – an eloquent and surprising reminder of the diversity of the East End audience.[8] In late Victorian theatres the return of a more polite and affluent class, after years of disdainful absence, influenced the greater enlargement of the stalls, which like boxes could be booked in advance (at the *box office*, a term still in use), unlike the pit, now relegated well to the rear, behind an imposing physical barrier. Pushing the pit benches (by mid-century, fitted with backs) and their occupants to the rear of the auditorium under the overhang of the first gallery, now designated the dress circle and requiring evening dress of its occupants, constituted explicit acknowledgment by management of the increasingly genteel character of theatre-going.[9] This preferential welcoming of a fresh segment of desirable play-goers suggests that the public voice was reverberating upon theatrical entrepreneurs as well as on 'the stage'. A potent sign of recognition of these more polite persons was Marie Wilton's famous addition of white lace antimacassars to the tops of stalls seats at the rehabilitated Prince of Wales's Theatre in 1865, replicating protective measures taken against overabundant hair oil in the homes of the respectable classes. Given these trends, it was only a question of time before the pit would be eliminated altogether, as it was by Squire Bancroft at the Haymarket Theatre in 1880 (causing a riot).[10] C. J. Phipps, the pre-eminent theatre architect of the period, reconstructed the Haymarket 'to meet the demands of the class of performance given at this house', the architect A. E. Woodrow observed, 'and the class of people frequenting it'.[11] By the early 1890s, at the St James's Theatre in King Street, George Alexander was printing a notice in the programme assuring patrons of the stalls that any usher seen accepting a gratuity would be instantly dismissed, so protecting fashionable play-goers against an importunate employee. These are a few examples of effective legislation by 'the drama's patrons', who had been exerting their formative influence ever since Davenant and Killigrew had had bestowed upon them King Charles's patents allowing the mounting of plays and the establishment of theatres in which to perform them.

The question may still be asked how that law-giving influence was exerted on the emergent configurations of auditorium and stage in the age of the second Charles, and after. The theatres that appeared after the Restoration were, in some cases, survivors from the earlier part of the century, such as the Cockpit in Drury Lane, the Red Bull and Salisbury Court, or in other instances,

---

[8] Davis and Emeljanow, *Reflecting the Audience*, 77.
[9] Booth, *Theatre in the Victorian Age*, 63–4.
[10] Mander and Mitchenson, *Theatres of London*, 99.
[11] Woodrow, 'Some recent developments in theatre planning', 427.

like Gibbons's Tennis Court, were existing structures pressed into theatrical use.[12] A carry-over of another, extremely important kind was an Italianate scenic theatre, which had first emerged through the inspiration of the early seventeenth-century designer Inigo Jones, who had mounted a series of private theatricals, 'masques', devised by Ben Jonson and other dramatists, for James I and his court. Later, in 1635, following Jones's designs, his able apprentice John Webb drew up architectural plans for the great hall at Whitehall for a performance of a French pastoral, *Florimène*, featuring a horizon and vanishing point 'pitched at the same level as the King's eye as he sat enthroned in his state at the further end of the orchestra'.[13] The great halls in which these lavish, costly entertainments were performed had much in common with the theatres that grew up or were rehabilitated later in the century. The seeds of far-reaching change were planted early.

The pattern set by the theatres erected or converted from other structures after Charles's restoration featured a candle-lighted auditorium and a steeply raked stage jutting well out into the audience space, the steep angle being necessary to articulate the audience's perspective on the vanishing point of the scene.[14] Framing the stage was a proscenium arch or 'frontispiece', into which permanent doors (sometimes two sets of them) were introduced to serve as the actors' principal means of entrance and egress. The thrust stage, illuminated by abundant overhead lighting, favoured a frank, audience-oriented style of playing, well down stage (the terms 'upstage' and 'downstage' are literal ones in this age), a style characterized by actors' continued contact and engagement with play-goers who were, on average, as close to the performance as were their Elizabethan and Jacobean predecessors.

This frankly presentational approach to performance maintained a genuinely intimate relationship between player and audience, from prologue through play and entr'acte entertainment to epilogue. And yet, placed in the context of the developing architectural character of the English theatre, this extended moment of close contact with a lively and responsive audience marks a significant point of departure. For, even before the eighteenth century had begun, a tendency had emerged towards creating an ever greater distance between audience and performers, along with a correlative if gradual retreat of the actors back towards the proscenium arch and, ultimately, behind it. This tendency signalled an important change in the relationship between audience

---

[12] Hotson, *Commonwealth and Restoration Stage*, chap. 2, *passim*.
[13] Orrell, *Theatres of Inigo Jones and John Webb*, 128, 146.
[14] Orrell, *Human Stage*, 211.

and player, a distancing effected in the physical theatre itself by slow but measurable changes in the configuration of stage, forestage and auditorium.

A passage in that indispensable memoir, *Apology for the Life of Colley Cibber, Comedian, and Late Patentee of the Theatre Royal* (1740), captures this regressive movement in its early development. Describing the alterations made in the 1674 Drury Lane Theatre by Christopher Rich shortly before the end of the century, Cibber explains that the earlier forestage had extended four feet farther out from the proscenium and that stage boxes now occupied the space where, formerly, doors were fixed between pilasters. Overall, the reconfiguration of the acting space was such that the earlier placement of the actors in almost every scene was 'at least ten Foot nearer to the Audience, than they now can be'. In that favourable situation 'the Voice was then more in the Centre of the House', Cibber ruefully recalled, and so even the most distant spectator could hear 'what fell from the weakest Utterance'.[15] Over two centuries and more, from the emergence of the theatres of the Restoration to the considerable spate of building in the later years of Victoria's reign, the history of the physical theatre remains to an important extent the history of a relentlessly receding forestage, until the main acting space has been withdrawn completely behind the proscenium arch (proscenium doors themselves having long since vanished[16]), leaving only a shallow forestage area, the 'apron' – a term betraying its diminished, after-the-fact status.

Given audiences' increasing appreciation for realistic illusion, the trend proved irreversible. A reviewer describing a moonlit scene in a production of *Don Giovanni* in 1817, at the King's opera house in the Haymarket, noted how much the 'dramatic effect' was enhanced by the elimination of 'side wings, doors, pillars, or picture frames'; the result was that stage and auditorium were completely contiguous and that 'the spectators actually sit in the moonlight, so perfect is the illusion'.[17] To be sure, Italian opera singers were largely unaffected by the preferences asserted by English actors, who for years resisted attempts by architects and managers to eliminate proscenium doors and any other changes that would distance them farther from the drama's patrons.

Over the same period a significant correlative development occurred. Spearheaded by Garrick's own innovations in stage illumination, brighter and more extensive lighting was introduced, especially upstage, where by the end of the eighteenth century climactic moments of spectacular action could be

---

[15] Cibber, *Apology*, ed. Lowe, ii: 85.
[16] Lawrence, 'Proscenium doors'.
[17] *Freeman's Journal*, 23 April 1817, quoted in Lawrence, 'Proscenium doors', 182.

effectively mounted, as in the daring rescue by John Philip Kemble's Rolla of an infant boy in Sheridan's *Pizarro* (1799).[18] A century later, even more extensive and complex spectacles would be realized entirely within a grand, ornate picture-frame stage, for the delectation of an audience held captive in near total darkness. A prominent example of the trend, Henry Irving's 'historically correct' production of Goethe's *Faust* in 1885 featured eleven vivid scenes devised by the adapter W. G. Wills and realized by Hawes Craven and William Telbin's painting, capturing in pictorial perfection the love of Faust and Margaret.[19]

And so, from 1660 onwards, enormous changes took place in the physical features of English theatres, both before and behind the proscenium arch. At the same time, audiences underwent progressive change as urban, suburban and provincial populations swelled, theatres multiplied, and, especially in the 1790s, dramatic genres began to mutate in response to the altering tastes and interests of play-goers. Examination of three documents originating from the early, middle and later years of the long period down to 1895 provides a way of setting these architectural and social changes in perspective. The first of these documents comprises a group of scene designs by John Webb, based on a concept of changeable scenic representation radically different from that employed in early seventeenth-century English theatres. The second and third documents, both printed books, reflect the persistence of changeable scenery, from which, it would seem, everything else of importance followed. In 1790 the architect George Saunders self-published his landmark study, *A Treatise on Theatres*. Almost exactly a century later, in 1888, the architect J. G. Buckle brought out his comprehensive technical handbook, *Theatre Construction and Maintenance*. With these three documents at hand, the history of theatre architecture, the actor's situation, and the composition and behaviour of audiences over the two and one-third centuries beginning in 1660 may all be efficiently, if briefly, traced and described.

A few years before Charles reclaimed the throne, Davenant presented for private entertainment at Rutland House, his London residence, a spectacular opera entitled *The Siege of Rhodes*, featuring a type of moveable wing-and-shutter scenery previously unknown to the English public stage. The surviving designs, by Webb, signal the emergence of a way of representing dramatic locale on stage which quickly became the uncontested standard until well into the nineteenth century, when the so-called box set (a three-sided, joined

---

[18] See Donohue, *Dramatic Character in the English Romantic Age*, pl. 21, after p. 130.
[19] Booth, *Victorian Spectacular Theatre*, 99–100.

configuration of scenery) became the norm.[20] Early designs by Jones for a theatre, possibly the rebuilt Phoenix in Drury Lane in 1636, presented the fascinating dual possibility of a performance space adaptable as a thrust stage surrounded on three sides by the audience or as a perspectival scenic theatre – characteristics combined in the major features of post-Restoration theatres.[21] Webb's connection with Jones had put him in an advantageous position for restating the Jonesian concept of scenic theatre. Davenant's brilliant effort at Rutland House was based on Webb's realization of a kind of thematic scenery, within which the action could be appropriately conducted. Study of the subsequent mounting of *The Siege of Rhodes* at the Cockpit in 1658–59 has shown that Webb's scenes for the opera presented at Rutland House were effectively a 'mock-up' on the exact same scale required for use at the Cockpit before a public audience.[22]

Webb's revolutionary approach to mounting a theatre piece effects the advent of Italianate perspective scenery on the professional English stage. As in the staging of *Florimène*, Webb adapted Jones's concept of a theatre in which scenic elements were laid out as parallel sets of wings terminating in a back shutter or backcloth and oriented so that the vanishing point occurred on the King's sightline, the central axis of the auditorium.[23] Webb's sketches present a series of three pairs of parallel fixed wings, generally representational, on a raked floor, enclosed inside a frontispiece and supported by posts projecting vertically up through the stage floor behind them. Above them, on a flat floor, stood grooves for three pairs of shutters arranged in such a manner that the shutters could be instantly changed at the beginning or conclusion of a scene, in concert, on cue, in sight of the audience. Beyond them were two scenes of relieve and, still further, a permanent backscene. Arranged in parallel along implicit receding lines describing a perspective view, the wings, shutters, relieves and backscene ranged back behind a fixed, ornate frontispiece, affording a King's-eye view of the whole terminating upstage at the vanishing point. Davenant and Webb had jointly ushered in a long period during which illusionistic stage settings, as they may in principle be termed, reigned supreme.[24]

[20] Webb's ground plans for *The Siege of Rhodes* are now in the Lansdowne Collection, British Library. See Keith, 'Designs for the first movable scenery', 29–39, 85–98; Keith, 'John Webb and the court theatre of Charles II'.

[21] Mackintosh, *Architecture, Actors and Audience*, 14. Jones's designs are now in Worcester College, Oxford.

[22] Orrell, *Theatres of Jones and Webb*, 71–3.

[23] Ibid., 127, 146. See also Lawrence, 'Royal box', 145–6.

[24] See Southern, *Changeable Scenery*, 109–23; Leacroft, *Development of the English Playhouse*, 78–9.

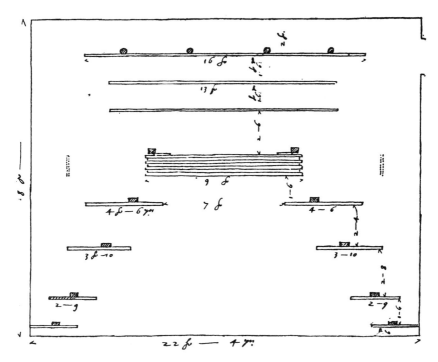

Plate 29. John Webb's ground plan for moveable wing-and-shutter scenery for Davenant's production of *The Siege of Rhodes* at Rutland House in 1656.

Describing scenery as establishing an *illusion* admittedly raises additional questions. Webb's exteriors and interiors are appropriate to the indicated settings of Davenant's opera, but they depict only a generalized, atmospheric background, not a specific locale. As the theatre became a fixture of urban life, the perspectival scenic stage established a mode and idiom notable for spectacular tendencies but, for the most part, untouched by the kind of detailed verisimilitude which would become the norm only in the high Victorian age. Meanwhile, as Richard Flecknoe observed as early as 1664, present-day stages 'for cost and ornament are arrived to the height of magnificence' – as in the five scenes of Settle's *The Empress of Morocco*, produced at Dorset Garden in 1673, which featured a rich, ornate scenic area above the forestage.[25] For many years, the novelty and variety of scenic display, not the accuracy and completeness of the illusion it fostered, were the thing.

[25] Flecknoe, *A Short Discourse of the English Stage* (1664), quoted in Thomas and Hare, *Restoration and Georgian England*, 93, 69, 95–9.

A second question concerns the extent to which Restoration audiences had a 'voice' in the kind of scenic display found on the stages of this new age. An earlier, royal and aristocratic audience at the court of James I had called for scenes more appropriate to the elaborate, spectacular masques in which they themselves participated. This new method of scenic representation had later been imposed upon Restoration audiences as a *fait accompli*, but the royal pedigree it bore was not lost upon the new audiences of the Cockpit and other public theatres, for they could now share monarchical privileges that had previously been denied. At the same time, they could identify vicariously with the King, who enjoyed the ideal perspective on the scene from his vantage point in the royal box, just above the raked pit, fixed on a central axis with respect to the scenery, and so they could, as it were, see the scene through his eyes. The presence of the King, surrounded by his subjects, witnessing a play enacted within the symmetrical embrace of perspective scenery had become emblematic of a well-grounded hierarchical society, of which the theatre auditorium and even the stage itself were a potent extension. Even though the central royal box went out with the Stuarts, later monarchs' presence in a side box close to the proscenium arch would carry the same symbolic weight.

Well over a century later, in 1790, on the eve of the most formative changes in theatre architecture since the Restoration, the architect George Saunders codified his unorthodox views in a plan for an ideal theatre. Entitled simply *A Treatise on Theatres*, Saunders's work presented a pithy account of what was wrong with almost all existing theatres and explained what could be done, through new building or reconstruction, to put things right. Saunders brings to his subject a broad knowledge of contemporary theatre architecture and a sharply critical view of its quality, as in his critique of Michael Novosielski's reconstruction of the King's Theatre in the Haymarket in 1782 as having arrested the progress of sound at every point.[26] Saunders believed in the fundamental importance of sound in the design of theatres, though he knew no more than his contemporaries about the dynamics of the phenomenon. Analysing the way the human voice registers in various parts of the house, Saunders described an ideal theatre based on the premise that nothing is dependable beyond 'the direct force of the voice' (23–4). Consequently, every aspect of the size, scale and configuration of the auditorium and stage follows from an accurate assessment of the impact of that force on box, pit and gallery.

Advocating a theatre of moderate size while reinterpreting the traditional model of auditorium design, Saunders restored the King's box to a central

[26] Saunders, *Treatise on Theatres*, 80–1. All further references will be given within the main text.

point, at the front of the first tier above the pit, accomplishing simultaneously the social goal of the monarch's visibility to almost all the spectators and the aesthetic requirement of his perfect enjoyment of the performance 'at a point which unites the illusion of the scenery with the advantage of hearing' (88). The circular design of Saunders's auditorium, in contrast to the fan-shaped configuration typical of contemporary theatres, reflects his reliance on the direct force of the voice as guiding principle by imitating 'the exact form in which the voice expands' (85). However promising in theory, Saunders's idea is compromised by his a priori conviction that the optimal position for the actor is a point 2 feet back from the inner edge of the proscenium. This, for Saunders, is what placing the actor entirely within the scenic illusion turns out to mean: the actor's body will intercept the perspectival line from the optimal vantage point of the monarch to the vanishing point of the scenery, while at the same time the actor will be close enough to the monarch to be distinctly heard. As for the rest of the spectators, given the circular design, they also will hear clearly, and from a 'moderate distance' (86), though they will view the actor at some angle from the optimal point. Unfortunately, should the actor move to the side or farther upstage, the audience, along with the monarch, will begin to see and hear less distinctly – a point Saunders, though an aficionado of matters acoustical, somehow failed to consider.

Cibber found the steadily receding forestage cause for regret over the loss of opportunity for nuanced performance and easy engagement with the spectator. Despite his brief for the primacy of an audible actor, however, Saunders will have nothing to do with a thrust stage, which he considers inimical to acting and 'too absurd' ever to be considered again (37–8, 36–7n). On the contrary, he insists that the edge of the stage should be on a line with the proscenium arch, which itself should always promote illusion and never be painted in a way that detracts from it (84). Saunders offers two reasons, practical and aesthetic, for this view. The failure to differentiate stage and auditorium into mutually exclusive areas results, he argues, in the subverting of 'good order and prudent regulation'. In addition, citing Count Algarotti's book on opera in performance,[27] Saunders maintains that placing the actor entirely within the scene should be done *for the sake of maintaining the illusion* (37n). Presumably, the predilection of the age for more lifelike mounting of dramatic action was more decisive for the design of contemporary theatres than the technical considerations, acoustical and architectural, to which Saunders devotes so much attention.

[27] Algarotti, *Essay on the Opera*.

And so Saunders's model theatre unintentionally demonstrates that 'illusion' is culturally determined, dependent more on unexamined assumptions about the tastes and desires of a theatre audience than on the physical centrality of the actor and the application of the fledgling science of acoustics. Ultimately, the shallow though well-framed situation of Saunders's hypothetical actor is emblematic of an audience's susceptibility to forces beyond that of the actor's voice, predisposing that audience towards viewing the human presence in the midst of an illusionistic scene – be it rural landscape, royal palace or domestic interior – rather than on a bare platform thrust well out into the auditorium, beyond the embrace of any scenic surround.

An approximately contemporary engraving of a command performance captures some of the complexities of the cultural moment in which Saunders's treatise appeared. The artist depicts a crowded theatre on the occasion of King George III's attendance at a performance of Sheridan's *Pizarro* in 1804.[28] The feeling of intimacy conferred by earlier, smaller theatres has evidently been lost. The theatre in question is Henry Holland's reconstructed Covent Garden of 1792, whose capacity of 3,013 made it of even greater size than in its previous enlargement, in 1782, to a capacity of 2,170.[29] The trend, in blithe disregard of Saunders's recommendations, and as subsequent renovations and rebuildings would indicate, was towards the accommodation of ever larger audiences, as in Covent Garden's major-theatre counterpart in Drury Lane, rebuilt by Holland in 1791–4, featuring a stage 83 feet wide, 92 feet long and 108 feet high and an auditorium boasting a capacity of over 3,600 persons.[30] Edward Dayes's watercolour drawing of 1795 captures both its elegance and its immensity.[31]

Finally, the only common ground shared by Holland's two greatly enlarged theatres and the hypothetical model devised by Saunders only one or two years before is the assumption that theatre architecture and human society are correlative and interdependent entities – an assumption which, in Holland's case, has more to do with accommodating a burgeoning cohort of play-goers and exploiting greater opportunities for scenic illusion than with the problematic audibility of performers in a cavernous auditorium. To be sure, Saunders no less than Holland had honoured the goal of theatre proprietors, time out of mind, of inserting the greatest possible number of paying persons into the available space. As early as the Blackfriars, that motive had resulted in allowing

[28] See Donohue, *Dramatic Character,* pl. 21, after p. 130.
[29] Donaldson, 'New papers of Henry Holland and R. B. Sheridan', 92; *Survey of London,* xxxv: 90.
[30] *Survey of London,* xxxv: 49–52; Donaldson, 'New papers of Henry Holland and R. B. Sheridan', 92.
[31] Reproduced as the frontispiece to *Survey of London,* xxxv.

aristocratic patrons the privilege of sitting on the stage itself – a phenomenon captured, for a later age, in Hogarth's frequently reproduced painting of Act 3 of *The Beggar's Opera*.[32] Garrick had done away with this distracting practice, but in so doing had initiated a move towards ever greater physical separation of the audience from the stage, a trend clearly reflected in Saunders's plan. In most theatres, Saunders had observed, audiences must choose between hearing well and seeing well (91). The century following his futile gesture towards moderation and regularity in public theatre design exacerbated that choice, bringing pervasive change along with unprecedented proliferation to theatre construction and entailing significant alteration in acting style and vocal delivery.

Indeed, over the fifty years before Victoria's coronation in 1837, a pervasive transformation of the London theatre scene was occurring, bringing with it increasingly successful challenges to the dominance of the patent theatres. By 1810 upwards of fourteen places of theatrical entertainment were in operation in greater London, including Drury Lane, Covent Garden, the Little Theatre in the Haymarket and the Haymarket Opera House, along with other carry-overs from the previous century.[33] Audiences were growing and shifting noticeably, as major and minor theatres vied for the shillings and pence of a fresh community of seekers after entertainment.[34] Even before the legal stranglehold of the major theatres on legitimate drama had been officially removed by the Theatre Regulation Act of 1843, new theatre buildings continued to spring up. By 1850, close to sixty places of theatrical or quasi-theatrical entertainment were active in London, including about twenty-five theatres.[35] Similar growth was observable throughout the rest of the country. By this same time the music hall was emerging in earnest out of saloons and song-and-supper clubs, setting a trend of great social as well as theatrical significance and leading to the construction of scores of purpose-built houses aimed at a new clientèle which preferred song and variety acts to other, more traditional types of theatrical performance. Change was constant. For example, in 1856 Covent Garden, having been consumed once again by fire, was rebuilt, opening in 1858 as the opera house it had already become after alterations carried out in 1847.[36] Well-to-do play-goers who out of distaste for lower-class audiences (and for other reasons as well) had abandoned the theatre some decades before began

---

[32] Orrell, *Human Stage*, 89–90.
[33] Donohue and Ellis, *Handbook for Compilers*, chronological chart.
[34] Moody, *Illegitimate Theatre in London, 1770–1840*, 30–1, *passim*.
[35] Donohue and Ellis, *Handbook for Compilers*, chronological chart.
[36] Mander and Mitchenson, *Theatres of London*, 57; Howard, *London Theatres and Music Halls 1850–1950*.

to return. An increasingly large audience was filling houses nightly, from the West End, where a spreading panoply of dramatic genres was on view, to the East End, where melodrama continued to hold sway, though by no means exclusively.[37] The swelling mid-century audience eventually, perhaps inevitably, caused another spate of theatre building in the 1870s (seven new theatres) and 1880s (thirteen new theatres), resulting in a remarkable clustering of houses in the West End, along Charing Cross Road, Shaftesbury Avenue and the Strand, landmarked by Leicester Square, Trafalgar Square and Piccadilly Circus and bordered by the Haymarket and St James's, along with new houses in other districts, such as the Court in Sloane Square.[38]

In this vastly altered theatrical climate prevailing towards the end of the century, the London architect James George Buckle described the 'mutifarious requirements of a modern theatre' in a practical manual published in 1888 and called simply *Theatre Construction and Maintenance*. Notwithstanding its workaday title, Buckle, like Saunders, proffers an idea for a model theatre, though its fundamental principle arises not from acoustics but from the exigencies of fire prevention. Citing appalling statistics of catastrophic conflagrations over a century and more, Buckle identifies the elements of theatre design which would, if invoked pre-emptively, in advance of construction instead of in renovation after the fact, result in a virtually fireproof theatre: 'A Safety Theatre', as he calls it. Although Buckle does not neglect the size and configuration of stage and auditorium or slight acoustical considerations, his approach is descriptive, not prescriptive: he identifies predominant practice and then offers a searching critique of its shortcomings. Nor do aesthetic values intrude at any point. All the same, for Buckle, as for Saunders, there is a critical determining measurement – in this case, the vertical distance above ground level of the highest gallery in the theatre. Even a theatre whose pit lies at street level is gravely endangered in the event of fire, Buckle points out, because the boxes and galleries above it can be reached only with difficulty, if at all, by a stream of water from the hose of a fire apparatus. The fundamental principle of design, for Buckle, is therefore the placement of the gallery entrance at street level; all else follows from this expedient. The only theatre in London that has observed this basic precept of safety is the recently constructed and 'much abused' Criterion, in Piccadilly Circus, whose entire auditorium lies below the level of the street (135).

Buckle's authority on theatre conflagrations is no other than the erstwhile captain of the London Fire Brigade, Eyre Shaw, whose book *Fires in Theatres*

---

[37] Davis and Emeljanow, *Reflecting the Audience, passim*.
[38] Donohue and Ellis, *Handbook for Compilers*, chronological chart.

(1876) had advanced two principles, both endorsed by Buckle. First, since the safety of a building is affected by the structures around it, any building in which large numbers of persons assemble 'should under no circumstances be surrounded by other buildings', since entrance and egress are safe only if directly from and to the street. The second principle is that a full fire wall must be erected between the stage and the auditorium, commencing in the basement and continuing clear to the roof, with a 'metal curtain' behind the proscenium arch which can be lowered at a moment's notice (a precautionary measure provided by Holland for the 1791–94 Drury Lane, but inoperative by the time of the disastrous fire of 1809). Citing the multiple horrors of five fires in the Paris Opera House between 1763 and 1873, as well as his long table of theatres destroyed by fire between 1672 and 1875, Shaw drives home his lesson: 'if a theatre be properly constructed, properly divided, and properly protected, these frightful risks and losses may be avoided' (43). A sampling of a single decade from Shaw's list, from 1839 to 1849, identifies three London theatres and seven in other parts of Britain lost to fire (44–5). Buckle's sobering observation that the average life of such structures is twenty-one years (101) may remind the student of theatre architecture and audiences of how very much the history of theatre building in Britain (and elsewhere) is a history of recovery from fire: of reclamation and innovation embarked upon out of felt necessity – and irrepressible optimism.

By 1892, in a paper delivered to members of the Royal Society of British Architects, A. E. Woodrow could confidently report that standards of safety had undergone considerable improvement. In the London theatre of today, he points out, there are now entrances to pit and gallery on either side, leading directly to the street, and grand staircases are for the most part a thing of the past, obviated by sinking the pit below ground and situating the dress circle at street level, as in the case of the recently opened Royal English Opera House.[39] All the same, new theatres, whether of large or, increasingly in this period, of smaller size, were still a comparative novelty. Whether old or new, Drury Lane, Covent Garden, Her Majesty's and the splendid theatre of varieties at the top of Leicester Square, the Empire (built as late as 1884), still featured grand staircases and the 'spacious vestibule and crush rooms' contiguous to them (428). Even with the stricter regulations imposed by the London County Council beginning in the 1880s, existing theatres constructed on principles fundamentally unsafe could not rectify their shortcomings overnight. It would be years before the precepts and desiderata of the Shaws and Buckles of the

---

[39] Woodrow, 'Some recent developments in theatre planning', 428.

community became common, if not universal, practice. Even so, today only the exceptional new theatre building is not contiguous, or nearly so, to some other building. Prime city real estate is too costly to permit the consumption of so many square yards to implement the basic safety measure of clear space all around the building advocated by architects before the fact, and by historians after it.

Facts of this kind underscore the inherently conservative nature of the theatre as an institution. Finally, the remarkable continuity of theatres and the distinctiveness and variety of their fare combine to attract an audience over the long term, despite the annoyances of poor sightlines and imperfect audibility and the dangers of fire and riot. Viewed from this commonsensical vantage point, the material particularities of stage, scenery and auditorium take second place to the vital presence of the drama's patrons, in all their rough and tumble immediacy. Sheridan's Mr Dangle in *The Critic* (1779) defends the stage in terms that complement Dr Johnson's and echo Hamlet's: 'I say the stage is "the Mirror of Nature", and the actors are "the Abstract, and brief Chronicles of the time": and pray what can a man of sense study better?'[40] We may conclude that Johnson's seemingly cynical reduction of theatrical and dramatic art to a mere simulacrum of public desire and intent was, more likely, a way of characterizing the continued presence and engagement of those patrons in the most intimate and honest way. Certainly, Garrick would have felt no denigration of his art in the prologue written for him to speak by his old Lichfield friend and teacher. Nor, for that matter, should we.

[40] Sheridan, *The Critic, Sheridan: Plays*, ed. Price, 341.

14

Stage design from Loutherbourg to Poel

CHRISTOPHER BAUGH

On 21 February 1896, in the Great Hall of the Polytechnic Institution at 309 Regent Street, London, the first cinema audience in Britain saw a moving picture show – the *Cinématographe* – of the films of August and Louis Lumière. The show, lasting approximately seventeen minutes, was projected onto a screen 6 feet by 4 feet 6 inches and showed some ten 'actualities', including scenes of a landing stage, boating, bathing in the Mediterranean, a collapsing wall and the arrival of a train in a railway station.[1] In some ways, this event might be seen as the achievement of a project begun some 125 years beforehand by Philippe Jacques de Loutherbourg (1740–1812) at Drury Lane. However, Michael Booth cautions that the arrival of film 'was not at all the culmination of a teleological process in which the theatre struggled clumsily towards the divine glory of cinematic realism, but simply one of the many responses of an increasingly sophisticated entertainment technology to the demand for pictorial realism'.[2] Loutherbourg's project was to present 'realistic' and pictorial images of places and events that his audience would recognize as authentic and topographically accurate. In doing so, he considerably expanded scenographic subject matter to include scenes of significant and noteworthy landscapes, scenes of current events and scenes which presented exotic and far-away places that few in the audience had seen and that were the result of his considerable study and research. This had the effect of endowing theatre and scenography with a sense of purpose and authority that was quite new in the eighteenth century. Since much of this material seemed suited to the travelogue, his project began to make the theatre a 'window on the world'. An additional effect was that, although the technology was not available during the eighteenth century, theatre would become a place where spectators might be rendered passive and

---

[1] Hunningher, 'Première on Regent Street'.
[2] Booth, *Victorian Spectacular Theatre*, 14.

quiescent in darkened anonymity as they were presented with authoritative images on the stage.

Furthermore, this project was to mark the decline of actor-dominated performance rhetoric and the birth of the stage picture as a coherent, harmoniously conceived whole. Landscape and topography (both current and historical) were to become objects of art and of the stage. However, the scenic methods employed were not especially new, and it might be argued that in practical terms Loutherbourg achieved very little. The formal technique of deconstructing the real world into two-dimensional, sequentially placed surfaces and their reconstruction into a three-dimensional entity in the mind of the audience had been in use since the Renaissance – especially as formulated in the work of Inigo Jones at the Stuart court and of John Webb at the Restoration. What *was* new was the overall management of all aspects of the visual experience of theatre and their coordination in the hands of an artist who would control all aspects of their production. In this way, atmosphere and aerial perspective, the disposition of stage lighting, properties and costume and every aspect of the visible stage became the palette of the scenographer.

Unfortunately, Loutherbourg said very little about his ideas and approach. He wrote two letters to David Garrick in 1772 – effectively letters of self-advertisement seeking work at Drury Lane - that stressed the totality of his approach. He required change in the methods of both stage lighting and of scene changing, and he focused particularly upon the relationship between designer and scenic artists. He wrote: 'I must make a small model of the settings and everything which is required, to scale, painted and detailed so as to put the working painters and machinists and others on the right track by being able to faithfully copy my models.'[3]

The changes Loutherbourg was proposing were subtle, but they established the terms of the pictorialism that dominated scenography throughout the nineteenth century. Writing in the 1880s, Percy Fitzgerald in many ways confirmed this view, but observed profound change *within* the century itself and therefore cautions us against the neat simplicity of *ex post facto* historical analysis. He suggested that the old system of generalized scenes – 'a street', 'a garden' or 'a forest' – had the merit of subordinating scenery to drama, whereas contemporary fashion offered arbitrarily selected realistic details. He believed that the 'understanding of a leg of mutton in its quiddity is the rule

[3] In Baugh, *Garrick and Loutherbourg*, 123. The letter, in the Harvard Theatre Collection, is undated, but the address suggests a date after February 1772, when Garrick moved into the Adelphi Terrace.

to apply to stage scenery,' and concluded that scenery should offer 'a logical generalisation of the leading features' and no more.[4]

The speed and totality with which Loutherbourg's project was implemented should therefore not be overestimated. The 'quiddity' of a scenic street, garden, forest or farmhouse kitchen used in theatres throughout the nineteenth century would, notwithstanding the size of theatres and extent of their illumination, have been easily recognized as speaking the same scenic language as that of the majority of eighteenth-century scenes. Additionally, whilst the potential for detailed research and 'authority' is well illustrated in the managerial approaches of Kemble, Macready, Kean, Phelps and Irving, the enormously varied fare and general popularity of the nineteenth-century stage, and the establishment of 'minor' theatre traditions that continued after the 1843 Theatre Regulation Act, ensured in many theatres an audience who were anything but passive and anonymous. It should also be remembered that Garrick employed Loutherbourg primarily to collaborate in 'entertainments' – a combination of pantomime and topical review – such as *A Christmas Tale* (1773) and *The Maid of Oaks* (1774) and to add spectacular scenes to existing works. The standard repertoire of comedies, afterpieces and Shakespeare felt very little of Loutherbourg's harmonizing visual impact.

Loutherbourg worked for only a short time in the theatre, from 1772 to 1781 at Drury Lane and for one engagement at Covent Garden, where he collaborated with John O'Keeffe to create *Omai; or, A Trip Round the World* in 1785. It was later generations of scenic artists who realized more thoroughly in the theatre what he had achieved only for special pieces. His model theatre, the *Eidophusikon* (1782, literally translatable as 'same as nature machine', with a stage some 8 feet by 6 feet), which displayed scenes from Milton, views of London from Greenwich Hill and topical shipwrecks, served as a scenic exemplar. It formed a veritable catalogue of ideas and technical solutions for later generations of scenic artists and carpenters and, perhaps, did more to extend Loutherbourg's pictorial values than his work at Drury Lane or Covent Garden.

During the period 1794–1809 London theatre architecture underwent radical revision. The intimate auditorium of the eighteenth century was replaced by the many-galleried *spectatory* of the large new theatres. The forestage continued to exist until the middle of the nineteenth century, but its importance diminished along with its size. It became absurd to see the carefully costumed actor as a harmonious element within the pictured world whilst performing in

---

[4] Fitzgerald, *World Behind the Scenes*, 6.

Plate 30. Philippe Jacques de Loutherbourg, incomplete scenic model for 'Peak's Hole', from *The Wonders of Derbyshire*, Drury Lane Theatre, 1779.

front of the picture and sharing the same architectonic space and illumination as the audience. The progress of the actor towards becoming a unified part of the pictorial scene was slow but, with the increased illumination effected by gas lighting (*c.* 1819), limelight (*c.* 1837) and focusable electric arc lamps (*c.* 1858), inevitable.

Loutherbourg used sophisticated suspended scenery (such as cut-out cloths, in place of wings and headers, for *The Wonders of Derbyshire* in 1779) and ground rows to enable the design of the floor surface of the stage. Ground rows placed towards the rear of the stage were also an important and logical way of interfacing the reality of the actor in the foreground with the scene painted on the backcloth. Questions of scale and perspective were frequently addressed by locating the scene on a terrace, plateau or garden separated from its background by a hedge, balustrade or rocky edge. Such practices encouraged the stage house to extend itself to create a fly tower and to organize the stage floor into the complex of grooves, sloats[5] and below-stage traps that dominated nineteenth-century theatre technology. This process, towards the end of the nineteenth century, culminated in creating the 'window on the world' as a physical reality. Fitzgerald applauds its completion and refers to C. J. Phipps's reconstruction of the Haymarket in 1880, where a 'rich and elaborate gold border, about two feet broad, after the pattern of a picture frame, is continued all round the proscenium, and carried even below the actors' feet'. The result is increased illusion, since 'the actors seem cut off from the domain of prose; there is no borderland or platform in front; and, stranger still, the whole has the air of a picture projected on a surface'.[6] Although magic lantern images in the theatre were familiar, this was written fifteen years before moving images were publicly projected in London.

But the pursuit of pictorialism in the theatre was driven by more than scenographic and architectural forces alone. In all ages, scenic change and theatre architecture are the physical expression and fulfilment of wider aesthetic and cultural imperatives. The demographic case presented by George Rowell, reflecting the changes in the social mix of the audience, is significant, but takes a limited view:

> Into the gap left by the withdrawal of the upper classes there rushed the masses of a capital whose population almost trebled between 1811 and 1851. To accommodate them the theatres multiplied their numbers and trebled their size. To penetrate these vast spaces the actors broadened their style . . . To fix their attention the artist and machinist contrived ever-greater wonders.[7]

Forces governing scenic change may also be discerned in wider aesthetic and cultural concerns and social contexts. Aesthetic critiques of theatre practice by Algarotti and Noverre; the concern for visual rhetoric in acting; illustrated discourses and practical handbooks on attitude and gesture; the romantic and holistic concern for the relationship between the human and the environment exemplified by Rousseau's ideas and by Georg Benda's experiments with mélo-drame in Ariadne and Medea in the late 1770s; the artistic control suggested by the Adam brothers' approach to designing both the interior and exterior of a building; the interest in landscape as a subject of painting; the developing sense of the past, especially the Gothic sensitivity to ruins and an

---

[5] Sloats were long thin slots set within the stage, parallel to the stage front, through which two-dimensional scenes could rise.

[6] Fitzgerald, World Behind the Scenes, 20–1.

[7] Rowell, Victorian Theatre 1792–1914, 2nd edn, 1.

accompanying awareness of historical styles of architecture and dress – all these factors have direct reference to theatrical change and the development of nineteenth-century scenographic style. Increasingly, all of these essentially pictorial pursuits came to be expressed with ease through the pictorial press. The commercial development of steel engraving during the 1820s and of electrotype by the 1840s produced the first illustrated journals and newspapers. The *Illustrated London News* (1842) and its successors did much to create a pictorial literacy that was reflected in and satisfied by the forms and content of the stage picture. The mid-century Examiner of Plays, William Bodham Donne, summarized the totality and effects of this concern with the visual: 'To touch our emotions', he explained, 'we need not the imaginatively true, but the physically real. Everything must be embodied for us in palpable form [and] all must be made palpable to sight, no less than to feeling.' He concluded that the spectators' lack of imagination 'affects equally both those who enact and those who construct the scene'.[8]

The work of William Capon (1757–1827), illustrative of several of these themes, not only expanded on the work of Loutherbourg but also developed the foundation on which nineteenth-century managers were to build their image of a carefully studied, educational and respectable theatre. Where Loutherbourg offered mountains, waterfalls, seascapes and crumbling rocks, Capon contributed meticulously researched architectural scenes undertaken for John Kemble at Drury Lane and, later, at Covent Garden. His work corresponds closely to that of fashionable antiquarian painters, the novels of Walter Scott and the general romantic enthusiasm for England's medieval, Tudor and 'Gothic' past. It is significant that Capon's work coincided with the beginnings of antiquarian and literary scholarship, especially that of Edmund Malone, into the nature and historicity of Shakespeare's plays. The scenic artist's approach parallels the growing desire to conceive of the plays as being firmly bound within a period context illustrated by significant visual and architectural styles.

It is clear that the detailed historicism and purported accuracy of Capon's scenes were timely and well-received innovations. The rebuilding of the patent houses in the 1790s, and again in 1808 and 1809, necessitated the restocking of their scene stores, and Capon provided Gothic streets, chambers and Tudor halls that, at Covent Garden, were still regularly in use in 1828. These were 'generic' scenes for use in any of the increasingly popular 'old English plays' in the repertoire. Size, variety and the quantity of scenery become important features, as does the fact that Capon continued Loutherbourg's practice of

---

[8] Donne, *Essays on the Drama*, 206.

breaking up the regularity of purely two-dimensional painted shutters and backscenes and began to introduce quantities of larger, three-dimensional scenery. There were drawbacks to this approach, and these have beset the theatre and its designers ever since. For example, the twelve scenes prepared for Kemble's *Macbeth* (1794) required the use of a scene drop to hide the lengthy changes, a device a testy critic referred to as the 'perpetual *curtain*'.[9] George Colman the younger complains in the preface to the published edition of *The Iron Chest* (1796) that he was required to transpose two scenes since 'there was not time for the carpenters to place the lumbering framework on which an abbey was painted, behind the representations of a Library, without a chasm of ten minutes in the action of the Play'.

But this play and Joanna Baillie's *De Monfort* (1800) and Matthew Gregory Lewis's *Adelmorn the Outlaw* (1801) as well might also be termed 'modern' in the sense that they are all rather trivial works, made stageworthy primarily on account of the opportunities they offered for spectacular scenic effect. The *European Magazine* (May 1801) reported that the audience of Baillie's play 'rapturously applauded the Composer and the Scene Painter' but 'hissed the dialogue almost from beginning to end', while the *Gentleman's Magazine* (May 1801) admiringly pointed out that painstaking emulation of fifteenth-century architectural style allowed the spectator to 'indulge his imagination to believe he was in some religious pile'. The tension between the claims of literary coherence and scenic transport would continue throughout the century.

It is important to note that, in spite of his knowledge of antiquarian architecture, Capon's image of the past is frequently as 'constructed' as that found in Scott's novels. Nonetheless, his work represents the impetus of authority and research that was to become an important feature of the role of the scenic artist throughout the nineteenth century. Capon's influence upon artists such as Alexander Nasmyth (1758–1840), John Henderson Grieve (1770–1845), Clarkson Stanfield (1793–1867), Grieve's sons Thomas (1799–1882) and William (1800–44), Frederick Lloyds (1818–94) and William Telbin (1813–73) was considerable.[10] His work also confirms the potential of scenery for becoming the leading performer and protagonist in the theatre. The relationship with the 'past' was clearly a significant theme throughout the entire period. David Newsome suggests that this 'thirst' for the past, awakened by Walter Scott,

---

[9] *Oracle and Public Advertiser*, 22 April 1794. For a detailed analysis of the scenes in this production and the seven painters responsible for them, see Donohue, 'Kemble's production of *Macbeth* (1794)'.

[10] Norris, 'Directory of Victorian scene-painters', is an invaluable source of biographical and production information.

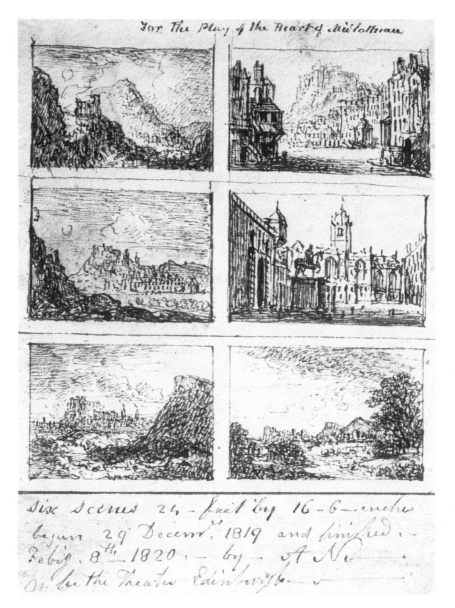

Plate 31. Alexander Nasmyth, six scenes for Walter Scott's *Heart of Midlothian*, Theatre Royal, Edinburgh, 1820.

'supplied exactly the spiritual nourishment for which so many of his contemporaries were craving – evocations of past ages of sanctity, a sense of mystery heightened by . . . recondite imagery'.[11]

For the Victorians, looking backwards to affirm national identity but also seeking to underpin the idea of forward progress, the works of Shakespeare served as essential theatrical vehicles. Macready claimed that it was his ambition to 'illustrate' Shakespeare. We may shudder and think that the potency of Shakespeare's visual poetry is more than sufficient to conjure 'the vasty fields of France' for *Henry V*, without adding the panoramic view of Agincourt that Stanfield designed for Macready's production at Covent Garden in 1839. Nevertheless, seen in the spirit of nineteenth-century progress and the development and unification of the arts through scenography, Macready's ambition is utterly logical and unassailable. Given the rapidity of progress – the enormous achievements of art and the growing commitment to Shakespearean textual scholarship – the time must surely come, the age thought, when, alongside the poetry, beautifully and intelligently spoken, there would be presented an equally beautiful and intelligent physical *realization* of Shakespeare's text.

Garrick, Kemble and, to a lesser extent, Edmund Kean had all experimented with antiquarianism in staging. J. R. Planché had designed *King John* (Covent Garden, 1823) and published the designs in his *Costumes of Shakespeare's Historical Tragedy of 'King John'* (1823). The playbill made clear his intentions: 'Every Character will appear in the precise HABIT OF THE PERIOD, the whole of the Dresses and Decorations being executed from indisputable Authorities'. But it was Macready and his scenic artists Stanfield and Telbin who created the Victorian attitude and mode of spectacular Shakespeare. For example, Macready's production of *King Lear* in 1838 was firmly set in Saxon times, with Druid stone circles, round-helmeted soldiers, semi-circular arches and all the elaborate detail of 'historicist' settings. Additionally, as Jacky Bratton observes, 'Macready, not unlike some of his successors in politically and socially orientated companies today, hoped to justify the theatre by making it a living lesson, in this case a lesson in national poetry and national history brought tellingly to life.'[12] Theatrical art, like other aspects of life, would inexorably progress, therefore, towards perfectibility; it would find a better painter or sculptor, dress the picture with more supernumeraries, invent a brighter lamp or a better effect. Writing in the *Examiner* on 29 October 1842, John Forster asserted that there had been 'nothing so great as the revival of *King John*' and 'no celebration of

[11] Newsome, *Victorian World Picture*, 183.
[12] Bratton, 'Lear of private life', 129.

English history and English poetry so worthy of a national theatre'. However, Alan Downer points out that 'Macready was neither a pedant nor a show-man; he used his scholarly habit of mind and his inherited sense of theatrical effect to serve the ends of the poet' and 'never neglected dramatic propriety.'[13] Echoing criticism of Capon, Macready noted the fine scenic balance that he felt he and Stanfield had achieved, in observing Charles Kean's approach at the Princess's Theatre that 'the text allowed to be spoken was more like a running commentary upon the spectacles exhibited, than the scenic arrangements an illustration of the text'.[14]

Often expressed in theatre reviews, in actors' diaries and, from the 1860s onwards, in the increasing number of books and manuals depicting 'life behind the scenes', the theme of technical and artistic progress towards perfectible realization runs like a leitmotif through nineteenth-century theatrical pro-duction.[15] Inspired, in part, by the easel achievements of painters such as Loutherbourg, Constable and Turner, which attempted to transfix the atmo-sphere and phenomena of nature upon canvas, scenic artists tried to realize the scale and transience of nature on the finite stage through painting and, increasingly, through lighting effects. The pictorial realism of the age aimed to replicate and sublimate the world by picturing it. It offered a vision – through the proscenium arch – into other completely ordered and finished (and fre-quently pre-industrial) worlds. Paradoxically, the urge was, on the one hand, for greater reality, yet at the same time it was a reality composed and structured as pictorial art. From the spectator's point of view it offered absorption, trans-port, loss of self and contemplation of the 'other'. Everything was capable of material and physical creation, although the literal realization of poetic images frequently disappointed and produced absurdity or banality. Developments in gas lighting, along with the more sophisticated and extensive application of iron and steel technologies and of the by-products of the chemical industry that benefited the scene-painter's palette, led the theatre manager to believe that perfection was ultimately achievable.

So fundamental to the century was the practice of historical realization within all of its representational pursuits that, until the time of William Poel and Edward Gordon Craig, it was inconceivable to the artist that perhaps the pictorial route was wrongly planned or inappropriate for the theatre. But

---

[13] Downer, *Eminent Tragedian*, 229.
[14] Macready, *William Charles Macready*, ed. Pollock, II: 446.
[15] This important aspect of the century's approach to making theatre is finely explored in Meisel, *Realizations*.

Plate 32. William Telbin's design for Charles Kean's *The Merchant of Venice*, Princess's Theatre, 1853.

to Macready in the 1830s and 1840s, and especially to Charles Kean in his management of the Princess's from 1851 to 1859, the solution was to apply more 'archaeological' and historical research, employ more scenic artists and to lavish more money and detailed management upon productions. Kean assembled a fine team of scenic artists to support these ambitions: William Telbin, Thomas Grieve and William Gordon (1801–74) specialized in landscape scenes, while Frederick Lloyds and Henry Cuthbert (1810–88) prepared scenes where architecture and archaeological research were needed. The research of this team (frequently summarized on the Princess's playbills) and the resulting authenticity of historical detail were the source of constant comment. In addition, Kean trusted this diligence and hard work to achieve the respectability that he hoped would lead to the establishment of a national theatre to parallel the National Gallery of Art (established in 1824). Queen Victoria was a frequent visitor to the Princess's and, but for Prince Albert's death in 1861, Kean's national theatre might have been formally established. Victoria's comment in her diary on Kean's *A Winter's Tale* in April 1856 summarizes the audience response to his scenography:

319

Though the performance lasted from shortly after 8 to a quarter past 12, we hardly noticed the length of time, for the interest never flagged one minute, and one was led from one more splendid scene to another . . . Albert was in ecstasies, for really the *mise-en-scène*, the beautiful and numerous changes of scenery, the splendid and strictly correct antique costumes, all taken from the best works and models, the excellent grouping of every scene, the care with which every trifle was attended to, make a unique performance.[16]

Kean's playbill note on Act 2, scene 1 reads:

[The] Court of the Gynaeconitis, or Women's Apartments . . . Among the Greeks and their Sicilian cousins it used to be the custom for the females to have rooms of their own, apart from the rooms of the men. The scene represents the court or principal hall of Hermione's apartments. In the centre of the hall, surrounded by four rows of columns, is the Peristyle or open court, one of the principal features in ancient Grecian or Roman architecture, and which we see revived in the beautiful Pompeian House in the Crystal Palace.

In this way, the stage became an animated exhibit and extended Albert's ambitions for the Crystal Palace exhibition of 1851.[17] Whilst sharing some concerns for the dramatic implications of transliterating Shakespeare's stage directions, concerns that became the bedrock of Poel's revolutionary thinking in the 1880s, Henry Morley's newspaper reviews acknowledge the achievement but never query the principal scenographic method: 'Four plays were produced, all mounted not only in the most costly way, but so mounted as to create out of the theatre a brilliant museum for the student.' Antiquity was presented, he asserts, 'not as dusty broken relics, but as living truths'.[18] Shakespeare had become 'a haze of poetry' through which scholarly and beautifully reconstructed ancient art and architecture might be appreciated. Morley's concerns exposed the method clearly. His review of *A Midsummer Night's Dream* (25 October 1856) reads, in part:

Shakespeare's direction for the opening scene of the *Midsummer Night's Dream* is: 'Athens, a Room in the Palace of Theseus'. For this, is read at the PRINCESS'S THEATRE: 'A Terrace adjoining the Palace of Theseus, overlooking the City of Athens'; and there is presented an elaborate and undoubtedly most beautiful bird's-eye view of Athens as it was in the time of Pericles. A great scenic effect is obtained, but it is, as far as it goes, damaging to the poem. Shakespeare took for

[16] Queen Victoria, *Journal*, 28 April 1856, Royal Archive, Windsor Castle, cited in Rowell, *Queen Victoria Goes to the Theatre*, 56.

[17] Richard Foulkes pursues this theme and the extent of Kean's research in 'Charles Kean's *King Richard II*'.

[18] Morley, *Journal of a London Playgoer*, 163.

his mortals people of heroic times, Duke Theseus and Hippolyta, and it suited his romance to call them Athenians; but the feeling of the play is marred when out of this suggestion of the antique mingled with the fairy world the scene-painter finds opportunity to bring into hard and jarring contrast the Athens of Pericles and our own world of Robin Goodfellow and all the woodland elves.

In the second act, Morley is alarmed by the lack of scenic logic in Kean's presentation of the moving wood:

> Oberon stands before the scene waving his wand, as if he were the exhibitor of the diorama, or a fairy conjurer causing the rocks and trees to move. Nobody, I believe, ever attributed to fairies any power of that sort. Oberon should either be off the stage or on it still as death, and it should be left for the spectators to feel the dreamy influence of the wood and water slipping by their eyes unhindered and undistracted.

In the same way, 'Titania's Shadow Dance' contradicted the whole notion of fairies who should have danced in a light so managed as to cast no shadow, in order to give them the true spiritual attribute.[19]

Frederick Lloyds's *Practical Guide to Scene Painting and Painting in Distemper* (undated, *c.* 1875) illustrates a probable version of 'A Terrace adjoining the Palace of Theseus, overlooking the City of Athens' by presenting the front view of a set-scene and a reverse view showing its technical construction. Lloyds's use of ground rows gives the effect of the land falling away from the terrace, only to rise on the distant view shown on the back-cloth, and so helps to retain the balance between foreground perspective reality and painted distance. It is clear, however, that in spite of Shakespeare's language scenography is rapidly becoming established as the performance *text* of theatre. The longevity and ubiquity of this approach become apparent when, writing in 1913, Poel ridicules the process by offering mock advice to theatre management to send their scenic artists to research the country where the play is set and to 'accurately reproduce the colouring of the sky, of the foliage, of the evening shadows, of the moonlight, of the men's hair and women's eyes; for all these details are important to the proper understanding of Shakespeare's play'. This information about a country of which Shakespeare perhaps knew nothing must then be placed on stage so as to 'justify the rearrangement of the play, the crowding of your stage with supernumeraries, the addition of incidental songs and glees, to say nothing of inappropriateness of costume and misconception of character'.[20]

[19] Ibid., 132–4.
[20] Poel, *Shakespeare in the Theatre*, 120–1.

Samuel Phelps and his scenic artist Frederick Fenton (1817–98) at Sadler's Wells followed, in essence, a similar method, but to our sense with greater imagination and subtlety. Their production of *A Midsummer Night's Dream* (1853) also indicates the synergy that was needed between the painted scene and its effective lighting. Fenton employed what he called 'blue nett' without seams to simulate a stage mist, and went on to use it for much of the entire performance. Other gauzes were used here and there, to deepen the effect. All the gauzes were flown out on the exit of Oberon and Titania from the wood after the first scene of Act 4. Fenton describes the next effect:

> When [Theseus, Hippolyta, and their train] retired, servants came in and put out the lights, and simultaneously the [upstage] curtains opened. The fluted columns of the hall were partly 'made out' and covered with waxed linen; inside the columns were lengths of gas jets, kept turned down till the curtains opened and the moonlight streamed into the hall; then the gas within the columns was turned up, and the columns appeared as if illuminated by moonlight.[21]

To all intents and purposes, in his tenure at the Lyceum Theatre (1878–1902) Henry Irving perpetuated Kean's approach to the presentation of both melodrama and Shakespeare. As in the case of Macready, however, Irving's theatrical sensibilities ensured that the pictorial and dramatic effect of the scene predominated over the claims of absolute historical accuracy. In this way, as Richard Schoch puts it, 'the past was thus refigured more as an object for contemplation at a distance – across a darkened auditorium and through a picture-frame proscenium arch – and less as a tangible physical presence'.[22] This visionary quality was enhanced by the increasing work, during the last decades of the century, of the easel artist in the theatre. Earlier generations of scene-painters had left the theatre in pursuit of academic respectability, but Irving's reputation and the growing respectability of the theatre encouraged Lawrence Alma-Tadema to prepare designs for his *Cymbeline* (1896) and *Coriolanus* (1901). Edward Burne-Jones designed his *King Arthur* (1895), and Ford Madox Brown served as scenic adviser to his *King Lear* (1892). These designs were then painted by Hawes Craven (1837–1910), Irving's principal scenic artist, and Joseph Harker (1855–1927).

The claims of scenic spectacle for its own sake were ever-present. Garrick's 'entertainments', with their presentations of topography, boat races, military

---

[21] Quoted Rees, *Theatre Lighting in the Age of Gas*, 139.
[22] Schoch, *Shakespeare's Victorian Stage*, 4.

camps and naval reviews, form a potent precursor to the 'para-theatrical' dioramas, panoramas and designed exhibitions of the nineteenth century. As with
Loutherbourg's *Eidophusikon*, the scenic artist was a consistent partner in these
activities. Stanfield and David Roberts (1796–1864) achieved much of their reputations during the 1820s as painters of panoramas and dioramas, both outside
the theatre building and within, as (usually) a travelogue interlude within the
pantomime. The plot was tortured and twisted to permit the inclusion of these
spectacular and topical scenes. During the early 1830s, when the fashion for
panoramas and dioramas at the patent theatres was at its height, *panorama*
was the term used at Covent Garden, while *diorama* was preferred at Drury
Lane, but there seems to have been little distinction between the two. Both
involved extensive back-cloths, unrolling and travelling horizontally across the
field of view, interspersed with occasional true dioramic effects. Such effects
consisted of sections of heavily sized 'union' cloth or thin linen, painted with
transparent pigment on the front surface and opaque distemper behind. A
cross-fade of lighting from front to back could bring about a change of scene –
usually from sunset to nightfall, or from a peaceful, sunlit scene to one of
storm and avalanche.

Stanfield and Roberts are frequently credited with bringing about something of a revolution in scene-painting.[23] They were extremely fine painters,
and both left the theatre during the late 1830s to achieve considerable success
as easel artists, although Stanfield took several important return engagements
with Macready. Supporting their success was the remarkable increase in the
quantity and quality of pigments available to them, resulting from an expansion of mineral mining and the developing chemical industry. Colours hitherto
obtainable only in the small quantities needed by the easel artist were, by the
1830s, now available in amounts required by the scene-painter, and at a price
the theatre could afford. A comparison of Loutherbourg's likely colour palette
with what Stanfield and Roberts could command at the height of their theatrical careers shows a considerable increase in the brilliance, transparency
and range of colour. The *Times* (27 December 1828) summarizes Stanfield's
achievement in its review of his diorama 'Spithead to Gibraltar' for the Drury
Lane pantomime *Queen Bee* (1828):

> When our memory glances back a few years and we compare in 'the mind's
> eye', the dingy, filthy scenery which was exhibited there – trees, like inverted
> mops, of a brick-dust hue – buildings generally at war with perspective – water

---

[23] There is an extremely useful discussion of this point in van der Merwe's catalogue introduction to *The Spectacular Career of Clarkson Stanfield*, 23–9.

as opaque as the surrounding rocks, and clouds not a bit more transparent – when we compare these things with what we now see, the alteration strikes us as nearly miraculous.

Less reliance by the painter upon opaque earth colours, such as the umbers, *terre verte*, yellow ochre and the 'brick-dust' red ochres, and more upon mineral, lead and other metallic pigments permitted a degree of transparency that more easily enabled the aerial effects of watercolour to be transferred to the stage. Most importantly, the availability of cleaner whites – such as zinc white – meant that, although the chalky carbonate whiting and flake (lead) white (a pigment that degraded and blackened in the fumes of gas lighting) would still be used, the lighter, more transparent white could enable effects of water and clouds to be more powerfully created.[24] The more thoroughgoing and consistent use of gas jets as the dominant form of stage lighting during the 1820s and 1830s permitted these colours to be shown to considerable advantage.

By the middle years of the century, and especially through the efforts of Madame Vestris and her partner Charles James Mathews, England developed the pantomime (with influence from France) into the fairy play or *féerie*. Booth rightly asserts that Victorian pantomime was the most spectacular form of theatre in English stage history and that, in it, 'spectacle existed for its own sake more than in any other sort of theatre, feeding upon itself, growing bigger and bigger'.[25] Spectacular scene followed spectacular scene, calling upon the fullest range of artistic and technological resources. Costumes were miraculously transformed on stage using trick trap-work, and the invention and development of aniline dyes during the period 1830–45 produced sharp 'acid' colours, especially purples, lemon yellows and apple greens, which responded well to gas illumination. Palaces erupted in flames; heroines were saved from perdition by knights errant afloat on stormy seas; or the scene changed to represent a lake from whose depths there magically emerged a host of watery fairies of the deep.[26] Many costumes and scenes also benefited from the development of metallic foils and 'Dutch' metals as cheap alternatives to real metallic leaf, which could give an 'edge' and a lustre to materials and paint by reflecting

[24] A discussion of some of the issues raised here can be found in Wolcott, 'Scene painter's palette'. For dates of mass production of individual pigments, see Wehlte, *Materials and Techniques of Painting*.
[25] Booth, *Victorian Spectacular Theatre*, 92.
[26] See especially Moynet, *L'Envers du théâtre*. Chap. 17, 'Représentation d'une pièce à grand spectacle vue du théâtre', presents a detailed and highly evocative account of the performance of a *féerie* play at the Opéra Comique in Paris. More generally, the book is the memoir of an important practising scenic artist. It covers the middle years of the century very well and gives a precise account of the technology and scenic resources of a well-equipped metropolitan theatre.

the increasingly focusable light from gas batten 'lengths' and oxy-hydrogen limelight. Competition for licences before 1843, and subsequently within the commercial environment of metropolitan theatre, ensured that scenic innovation introduced in pantomime at 'minor' theatres quickly flourished on the 'major' stages also and thereby unified the visual language. Drury Lane's *Aladdin* and Irving's *Faust* opened within a week of each other in 1885, but Booth suggests that, although 'the two productions and the point of view of the two managers were worlds apart',[27] they shared the same scenic attitudes and employed the same production techniques.

By the 1860s the genre of sensation melodrama was established. In the forefront may be considered the plays of Dion Boucicault – especially *The Colleen Bawn*, *The Shaugraun* and *The Streets of London*. The scenery of *The Streets of London* was toured, but the title of the piece reflected the location of performance – *The Streets of Liverpool*, . . . *of New York*, . . . *of Manchester* and so on – and it featured a thrilling and spectacular blazing tenement building. Such scenes of spectacle were interspersed with scenes of narrative 'transition'. These, often termed 'carpenters' scenes', were played in front of a downstage drop or, earlier, closed shutters and were just long enough to permit the fuller stage depth to be set with the wings, cloths, lights and, increasingly, three-dimensional units, or *practicables*, required for the next scene. The ingenuity of the scenic artist and new technologies were exploited both to reduce the number of carpenters' scenes and to increase the spectacle. This was desirable not only for the quantity of spectacular effect desired, but also because one of the driving forces of such theatre consisted in the fullest possible exploration of humanity's confrontation with the disasters and other phenomena of nature. Scenic expression became the protagonist to the dramatic action of the play. The culmination of this scenographic form is well illustrated in Drury Lane melodramas from the 1880s onwards,[28] many of which were designed, and effectively scripted, by Bruce 'Sensation' Smith.[29] They provided the solid dramatic fare either just following or immediately preceding the equally spectacular Christmas pantomimes until the outbreak of World War One.

The demands on the technology and architecture of theatre are obvious. By the late 1850s the development of iron and steel girders, for example, made possible sophisticated suspension arrangements in the flies. An ever-expanding

[27] Booth, *Victorian Spectacular Theatre*, 92.
[28] A detailed description of these melodramas and pantomime spectacles may be found in ibid., 60–92.
[29] An anecdotal but important account of Bruce Smith's career is to be found in Castle, *Sensation Smith of Drury Lane*.

Plate 33. *Sealed Orders*, Act 3, scene 3, Drury Lane Theatre, 1913.

system of below-stage traps required steel to be used as the basis for rising and flown constructions that could support numerous actors. Sophisticated iron-ware brackets, hinges and other hardware made possible the folding, opening and revolving scenery required by special effects. Although the motive power for scenic arrangement still depended upon well-drilled machinists, gas engineers and stage hands employing well-established methods of single- and double-purchase counterweight flying systems, some trial was made of steam power, and by the 1870s hydraulic power was experimented with in Paris. Battery-powered arc lamps were used for special, short-term effects, such as a sunrise, and Moynet describes the extent and sophistication of such a battery installation at the Opéra in Paris.[30] Girders and supporting iron pillars appeared in the auditorium, where cantilevered galleries, each with far more rows of seats than were possible in the traditional Italianate horseshoe auditorium, began to divide the audience into more class-bound divisions.

The advent of mains-generated electricity as the principal source of stage illumination, beginning at the newly constructed Savoy Theatre in December 1881,[31] contributed significantly to the collapse of this scenographic language. Painted scenery requires an even, frontal wash of light, while the scenic artist formulates shading and shadows with paint. Supportive and sensitive artistry

---

[30] See especially Moynet, *L'Envers du théâtre*, 109.
[31] Rees, *Theatre Lighting in the Age of Gas*, 169–76.

was needed to ensure that stage lighting enhanced the painting, maintaining an appropriate foreground–background relationship, but did not run counter to its formal two-dimensional nature. Unfortunately, no scene-painter could paint a shadow that was as dark as that created when bright, focused light glanced off the edge of scenery or moulded details. The scenic artist's typical response to this increase in illumination was to design more three-dimensionally, using practical built units, and to extend the use of surface-mounted, sculpted detail. Such scenery, of course, ran counter to the technology of grooves, shutters and flown and rising pieces placed parallel to the stage front and predicated upon the support of two-dimensional structures. Accordingly, the time allocated for changes had to be extended in order to set and remove scenes, the sequences of scenes in Shakespeare's plays were reordered to simplify changes and more text was excised to render the evening manageable in length.

And so, in various ways, the principles and aesthetic syntax of stage scenery from the period of Loutherbourg onwards were mortally threatened by three-dimensional detail and bright lighting. Fitzgerald identified this threat in 1881, just as the large-scale effects of incandescent electricity were beginning to be realized:

> The mistake in modern scenery is the attempt to combine the hostile elements of pictorial and artificial distance, shadows, &c., with *real* effects of distance . . . A real chair will make a painted chair look flat and poor, while the painted chair will make the real one look dull and prosy. To imitate real objects by the agency of colours and painting requires a flat surface; therefore, constructed set pieces, retiring at right or acute angles to the footlights, are false in principle.[32]

Fitzgerald's 'solution' – clearly unacceptable in the face of technological progress – was nostalgic and backward-looking to an age that balanced the real with the painted by gentle and low-level stage lighting.

The scenographic system that Loutherbourg consolidated operated in a way analogous to eighteenth-century musical forms such as the sonata, toccata or chaconne. These were structured, codified forms of accepted artistic expression whose terms of reference (and willingly acknowledged limitations) were clearly understood by both artists and audiences. The timber-framed stage, in its way as formally structured as the eighteenth-century orchestra, perfectly and elegantly matched the two-dimensional planes of painting that it supported and transformed. To this, the nineteenth century added a theatrical infrastructure of management that could support generations of talented

---

[32] Fitzgerald, *World Behind the Scenes*, 8.

scenic artists, sophisticated improvements in the pigments available to them, and the controlled, even and soft illumination of gas jets in battens required to light their work. But by the last decades of the century, heralded by Charles Kean in the 1850s, focused stage lighting and an overpowering desire to see the 'real' on stage exposed the form and its limitations in ways that became quite unacceptable to Poel and Craig. The language and its syntax became so apparent that no amount of counteractive three-dimensionality and 'reality' on stage could render the scene acceptable.

Nevertheless, the influence of 'prose and real life' was endemic in the theatre of the 1880s – whether it was within the dramaturgy of the 'new drama' of Tom Robertson and Henry Arthur Jones, the 'cup-and-saucer' dramas of the Bancrofts, the Shakespearean productions of Irving and Beerbohm Tree or the sensation scenes of melodrama. Late nineteenth-century scenic artists such as Craven, Harker and William Lewis Telbin (1846–1931) therefore found little alternative other than to add more realistic and 'carpentered' detail and to organize more careful scenic planning. Dramatic absurdities were apparent, leaving Bernard Shaw to comment on Tree's *A Midsummer Night's Dream* (Her Majesty's, 1900), which introduced real rabbits to give greater verisimilitude to the forest, 'You can't see the Shakespeare woods for the Beerbohm Trees'. Additionally, of course, other 'new' dramas were emerging with naturalist agendas that required, for very different reasons, a similar verisimilitude and truth to life. Strindberg's preface to *Miss Julie* (1888) makes the demands clear:

> Even if the walls have to be canvas, it is surely time to stop painting them with shelves and utensils. We have so many other stage conventions in which we are expected to believe that we may as well avoid overstraining our imagination by asking it to believe in painted saucepans.[33]

Representation of the medieval, Tudor and 'Gothic' past was a distinct feature in the theatre throughout the period. It was, as Schoch puts it, 'a time when the desire to know and possess the past rivaled science as the dominant system of cognition'.[34] During the final decades of the century, medievalism had a variety of manifestations that not only supported the last great flowering of this theatre, but also threatened its scenic art. For example, Pre-Raphaelitism advocated a studied emulation of the vivid colour and sharpness of detail that had been the glory of pre-Renaissance Italian art. But in the theatre, it required a well-referenced clarity that stifled the drama within

[33] Strindberg, *Miss Julie*, trans. Meyer, 101–2.
[34] Schoch, *Shakespeare's Victorian Stage*, 1.

Plate 34. Scene by William Lewis Telbin for *Much Ado about Nothing*, St James's Theatre, 1895.

its over-detailed scenic expression. Furthermore, the less optimistic and economically depressed period 1870–99 gave a more urgent political edge to such meditation upon the past. Both Ruskin and William Morris deplored a manufacturing system in which workers were deprived of their pride in using craft skills to produce what they knew to be worthwhile. A similar loss of imaginative control is evident in a theatre tied to producing more detail and greater verisimilitude within an increasingly rigid hierarchy of artistic management. Dismay over contemporary scenography is reflected in Poel's study of early English staging and in Craig's desire for a theatre created by means of the skills of the theatre artist. Poel's dedication to Shakespeare assumes the primacy of the actor and the purpose of the theatre as that of interpretation. The past should be approached with the humility to learn from it, rather than with the colonial instinct of plundering its aesthetics in order to reconstruct them on stage. Craig went further, rejecting interpretation as the mode of theatre and seeking to empower, through his plans for theatre training, artists as well versed in their crafts as those of the past, in order to create new theatre art.

Towards the close of the century, scenographic language was therefore being threatened from more than one direction. From within, the pursuit of historical accuracy and realistic 'archaeological' detail bogged the performance down with scene changes that could not be effectively managed within the constraints of traditional stage architecture. Play texts were therefore doctored and rearranged to accommodate scenic exigencies. Increased levels of illumination led to more physical stage construction and served to expose the formality and intrinsic artificiality of painted scenery. 'Friends' of this theatre, such as Fitzgerald, cautioned against such excess and urged a return to the stage of a more recent past where the majority of scenic elements remained two-dimensional and were lit by soft frontal gas lighting, a stage that offered a speedy, elegant and effective way of supporting, changing and storing scenery. From without, the 'new drama' and the forces of naturalism fostered a more general and thorough dissatisfaction with staging, while simultaneously exacerbating the realistic scenic dilemma. Early film could not yet compare with the rich spectacle of the 'well-upholstered' scenic stage, but it was a force for the future. Others, however – true revolutionaries such as Poel and Craig – urged the complete abandonment of this scenography. They proposed alternatives that involved the careful study and restoration of past techniques of staging, or were in line with millennial modernist thinking that involved a radical revaluation, not only of scenography, but of the theatre and the very nature of live performance itself.

15

Theatre and mid-Victorian society, 1851–1870

RICHARD W. SCHOCH

In a formation that has rapidly become canonical in British historiography, the mid-Victorian years – from 1851 to 1870 – were an 'age of equipoise': a collective sigh of relief at having safely negotiated the landmines of electoral reform, Chartist agitation and revolutionary phobia.[1] As the historian Thomas Babington Macaulay wildly and, as it turned out, accurately prophesied, 1851 – the year in which the Great Exhibition opened at the iron and glass Crystal Palace in London's Hyde Park – would 'long be remembered as a singularly happy year of peace, plenty, good feeling, innocent pleasure and national glory'.[2] Although the mid-Victorian period lacked the sharp social and political contrasts of the 1840s and 1880s, it was nonetheless a crucial period in British history, because it provided a moment of respite in which the nation could pause to consolidate and savour its economic prosperity, technological modernity and political serenity. From the new perspective of the Crystal Palace, a dream of social order founded on respectability at last seemed possible. And leisure pursuits, one of the prized benefits of economic prosperity, were a prime area for achieving and advancing social harmony and intellectual enlightenment.

This chapter explores how the theatre made a bid for respectability, that most cherished of nineteenth-century virtues. Yet the exploration is not straightforward. Indeed, my central claim is that the mid-Victorian theatre both embraced *and* resisted the dominant middle-class goal of respectability – for the theatre as a cultural institution, for the acting profession and even for the social standing of theatre audiences. Just what the mid-Victorians meant by 'respectability' was always a bit unclear, even to them. But a few social attributes have figured in nearly all accounts of respectable behaviour: cleanliness, hard work, self-sufficiency, thrift, piety, deference to authority and even correct speech.

---

[1] The phrase comes from the title of Walter Burn's landmark study, *The Age of Equipoise*.
[2] Quoted in Arnstein, *Britain Yesterday and Today*, 73.

Whilst the cult of respectability belonged principally to the middle classes (and especially to a lower middle class anxious to distinguish itself from the labouring class), it nonetheless migrated both up and down social and economic hierarchies. This chapter employs a topical approach in examining tensions between respectability and vulgarity from a variety of theatrical perspectives: Shakespearean revivals, acting styles, genres of dramatic literature, West End gentrification, pictorialism, royal patronage, middle-class attempts at social control, East End theatre, parliamentary interventions, sensation melodramas and changes in audience taste and composition. And since this chapter is explicitly about theatre and society, what happened *off* stage, whether in the pit, the press or Parliament, is just as significant as what happened on stage.

As might be expected, London's leading tragedians were among the first members of the theatrical profession to renew their commitment to legitimate drama and thereby to reinvent themselves as gentleman proprietors of respectable public establishments. Whilst a devotion to Shakespeare foretold the financial ruin of actor-managers throughout the nineteenth century, that devotion was nonetheless a 'respectable humbug' without which no legitimate theatre could establish a solid reputation. Indeed, a theatre's 'illegitimate', but vastly more popular offerings effectively subsidized its moral obligation to produce Shakespeare: the 'despised melodrama' and the 'tight-rope dancing of the Devil Antonio' compensate for the 'loss and vexation incurred' in performing the Bard.[3] To imagine a Victorian theatre without Shakespeare, however fiscally prudent that would have been, is to imagine a theatre no longer English.

During his brief managerial career at Covent Garden (1837–39) and Drury Lane (1841–3), William Charles Macready, perhaps impelled by disdain for his chosen profession, was renowned for a noble, if failed effort to establish a respectable theatre where the national drama would be produced with appropriate reverence. Achieving that worthy distinction entailed not only restoring the integrity of Shakespeare's texts, but also staging his plays with increased attention to historical accuracy in sets and costumes, attracting royal patronage and expelling prostitutes from the theatre. Within a decade of the passage of the Theatres Regulation Act of 1843, which abolished the long-standing monopoly of London's patent theatres, Samuel Phelps at Sadler's Wells and Charles Kean at the Princess's Theatre embarked upon their famed series of Shakespearean revivals. During his lengthy managerial tenure (1844–62), Phelps was lauded for endearing a local audience to legitimate drama, ensemble acting, textual

[3] *Westminster Review* 18 (1833): 35.

restoration, ambition in performing nearly the entire Shakespearean canon and ingenuity in making do with a paucity of stage resources. 'To that remote suburb of Islington', Macready noted approvingly, 'we must look for the drama if we really wish to find it'.[4] Whether because of the financial constraints imposed by managing a theatre with modest box office potential, the supposedly less refined tastes of a north London audience, or even because of his own uncompromising allegiance to textual purity, Phelps was content to leave spectacular and antiquarian *mise-en-scène* to his West End counterpart, Charles Kean.

In only nine seasons as manager of the Princess's Theatre (1850–59), Kean recreated not merely the medieval and Tudor England of Shakespeare's history plays, but also Assyria (Byron's *Sardanapalus*), Peru (Sheridan's *Pizarro*), Renaissance Italy (*The Merchant of Venice*), medieval France (Dion Boucicault's *Louis XI*) and Periclean Athens (*A Midsummer Night's Dream*). Charles Kean, the actor turned antiquary, 'rummaged out old books', 'turned over old prints' and 'brushed the dirt off old music'[5] in preparing historically correct revivals of Shakespeare. His antiquarian spectacles were celebrated – and censured – for their sets, costumes and properties of unprecedented historical precision, their adherence to the descriptions and illustrations set forth in the works of prominent historians, their re-enactment of events not dramatized by Shakespeare (e.g., the return of Henry V to London after the Battle of Agincourt), their interpolation of dialogue and music of presumed authenticity (e.g., the 'Hymn to Apollo' played in the banquet scene of *The Winter's Tale*), for the historical essays in the playbills, and for the publication of quasi-academic editions of the plays. So fastidious was Kean in his insistence upon authentic stage accessories that his detractors at *Punch* dubbed him not the 'Upholder' of Shakespeare, but the 'Upholsterer'.

To Kean's relatively modest playhouse on Oxford Street, in the heart of the commercial West End, came some of the leading figures of the mid-nineteenth century: not just Victoria and Albert, but also Dickens, Palmerston, Gladstone, Hans Christian Andersen, Lewis Carroll, the Duke of Saxe-Meiningen and even the famous French actress Rachel, who promptly kissed the reserved actor-manager on her visit backstage after a performance of *Macbeth*. The distinguished patrons of Kean's series of grand Shakespearean revivals, and his 1857 election to the Society of Antiquaries, indicate the value which mid-Victorian culture placed not so much upon the theatre itself, as upon the theatre as an agent of historical instruction. Indeed, the theatre's commitment to historical

---

[4] Quoted in the *Athenaeum* 16 (November 1878).
[5] Review of *Henry VIII*, Princess's Theatre, London, *The Times*, 16 May 1855.

representation was the very sign of its modernity. To prefer anachronistic performances of Shakespeare, as Charles Dunphy of the *Morning Post* argued, was
to prefer 'the semaphor to the electric telegraph' and 'the stage-coach to the
locomotive'.[6]

Theatrical modernism was by no means limited to the pervasive use of
archaeologically correct stage décor. Even acting styles, when viewed as cultural practices and not just as techniques, were part of the mid-Victorian theatre's self-conscious emulation of the cult of the gentleman. Both Macready
and Charles Kean received favourable notices for performances not of stature
and magnificence, but of physical and vocal restraint: stage 'business' rather
than declamatory gestures, penetrating looks rather than 'attitudes' or old-
fashioned acting 'points' and an understated gravity of speech rather than thunderous orations. Compared to the volcanic temperament of Edmund Kean or
the patrician grandeur of John Philip Kemble, earlier in the century, mid-
Victorian tragedians favoured a more repressed and constrained physicality.
Indeed, Macready's performances in contemporary dramas – Bulwer-Lytton's
Richelieu and Sheridan Knowles's *Virginius* – were rated more successful than
his Shakespearean roles. In Knowles's play, which Joseph Donohue rightly characterizes as a 'high tragedy freshly cast in the mould of an ideal domesticity',[7]
the Victorians found an emotionally powerful expression of family honour –
epitomized in the drama by Virginius's noble sacrifice of his daughter to save
her reputation. Charles Kean, never widely praised as a classical tragedian, was
regarded as highly effective in 'gentlemanly' melodramas. When Kean played
the title role in Boucicault's adaptation of *Louis XI*, even the usually judgemen-
tal Westland Marston concurred that the actor successfully 'combined the
quaintest realism of detail, sometimes embracing the minutest peculiarities of
a character, with all the heart of passion'.[8] To be sure, this diminution of tragic
dignity was not uniformly welcome. Marston criticized Macready for being
too studied in his performance, and William Bodham Donne lamented that
tragedians had become 'homely' and 'utterly devoid of heroic proportion'.

Performances as Hamlet and Othello in the 1860s by the Anglo-French
actor Charles Fechter provide yet a further instance of how an easy-going
demeanour became suitable even for Shakespeare's tragic heroes. G. H. Lewes
admired Fechter because his characterizations were 'picturesque and graceful',
without succumbing to the temptations of melodramatic 'effect'.[9] Yet Lewes

---

[6] Letter to Charles Kean, 17 March 1857, Fol. Y.c. 830 (2), Folger Shakespeare Library.
[7] Donohue, *Theatre in the Age of Kean*, 138.
[8] Marston, *Our Recent Actors*, I, 190.
[9] Lewes, 'Shakespeare and his latest stage interpreters', 776.

also complained that Fechter had gone too far in rejecting the stale conventions of his predecessors, and ended up 'dragg[ing] the play [*Hamlet*] somewhat too much down into common life' (776). The tone of his performance was 'too colloquial' and the physical contact between the characters was both excessive and inappropriately informal. Lewes was not the only critic to decry Fechter's descent into the vernacular. For *Dublin University Magazine*, the unfortunate display of 'vulgar realism' in *Othello* was only part of the general artistic fashion to 'look at all things from the level of ordinary life'.[10] 'We are nothing if we are not familiar', the journal acknowledged, in a snide allusion to Iago's own claim to be 'nothing if not critical'.

Whilst exaggerated heroism was no longer a model for dignified bourgeois tragedians, nineteenth-century performance styles did not succumb to mass gentrification. The great comic genres of the Victorian theatre – burlesque, pantomime, extravaganza and farce – never respected the decorum and etiquette of tragedy. Indeed, J. R. Planché's extravaganza *The Camp at the Olympic* (1853), to cite one example, ridiculed the histrionic refinement of London's major theatres. The comedian Frederick Robson, playing the energetic spirit of Burlesque, merrily taunted the spirit of Tragedy by singing that 'Burlesque is up! up! up! / And Tragedy down! down! down!'[11] Even Tom Robertson's 'cup-and-saucer comedies', heralded as the dawn of naturalism in evolutionary accounts of modern drama, rely on well-established traditions of melodramatic pictorialism and self-conscious theatricality. What is missing from his domestic comedies are the bold 'effect' of Boucicault's sensation melodramas and the comic mania that Robson could induce among his audiences at the Olympic merely by singing the ditty 'Vilikins and his Dinah' in a cockney accent.

Let us pause to look more closely at how domestic comedies of the 1860s did not reject, but rather modified contemporary dramatic and theatrical conventions – amounting to what George Bernard Shaw, in 1897, referred to as the 'tiny' theatrical revolution brought about by Tom Robertson.[12] The intimacy of the 800-seat Prince of Wales's Theatre, where Robertson's major comedies – *Society* (1865), *Ours* (1866), *Caste* (1867), *Play* (1868), *School* (1869) and *MP* (1870) – were produced under the management of Marie Wilton and Squire Bancroft, made possible an intimate and conversational performance style in which actors engaged in familiar, everyday behaviour – drinking tea, reading newspapers and playing the piano. Henry James dismissed these 'infantile' plays

[10] 'Shakespeare travestied', 174.
[11] Planché, *The Camp at the Olympic*, in *Plays by James Robinson Planché*, ed. Roy, 176.
[12] Shaw, 'Robertson redivivus', *Dramatic Opinions and Essays*, II: 288.

Plate 35. James Rogers as the heroine in H. J. Byron's burlesque *Miss Eily* (1861).

for dealing with such 'little' things as 'carpets, curtains, and knick-knacks'.[13] Robertson's plays, like Pre-Raphaelite paintings and W. M. Thackeray's novels, sought to 'tone down' melodramatic sensation, effect and situation, much as the acting styles of Macready and Kean retreated from the extravagant performance styles of earlier generations.[14] Scenes crucial to the plots of Robertson's

---

[13] 'The London theatres', *Scribner's Monthly* 21 (Jan. 1881): 363, quoted in Booth, *Theatre in the Victorian Age*, 53.
[14] See Meisel, *Realizations*, 358ff.

comedies frequently rely on indirection and understatement. In *Caste*, George D'Alroy's surprise return home after his supposed death in India is almost ludicrously underplayed: he enters carrying a milk-can left hanging on the railings outside the house. The play's one extraordinary event – the old melodramatic *coup de théâtre* of a return from the dead – becomes all too ordinary.

Yet alongside the seeming realism of Robertson's stage action is a pronounced theatricality which reminds spectators that everything they observe is still a performance, however carefully orchestrated to appear otherwise. Robertson never relinquished his fondness for 'strong' end-of-act curtains, in which characters engage in dumbshow and then form a concluding tableau. Unlike the improbable and catastrophic events frequently depicted in sensation melodramas, Robertson's tableaux portrayed ordinary, even quaint behaviour. The final stage picture from Act I of *Ours*, for example, centres on a wet umbrella. Their conventionality notwithstanding, Robertson's tableaux still acknowledged the presence of spectators. Even within scenes, a feeling for the theatrical is pervasive. As the *Athenaeum* observed in its review of *Play*, the love duet sung by the characters Frank Price and Rosie Fanquehere 'won the applause of the house' and was given an encore – patterns of response which have more to do with music hall and saloon entertainment than with the aesthetics of naturalism.[15] The character Polly Eccles, in *Caste*, sings, dances and pantomimes her way through the entire performance, even imitating a soldier on horseback from an equestrian drama at Astley's Amphitheatre, a popular theatre-cum-circus in south London. The play becomes meta-theatrical at a climactic moment, when Polly stage-manages George's unexpected reunion with his wife Esther as a performance of the ballet *Jeanne la Folle; or, The Return of the Soldier*. Marie Wilton, the original Polly, doubtlessly relied on her consummate skills as a burlesque soubrette to pull off these entertaining 'turns'. As much as Robertson's dramatic world pretends to be entirely undramatic, it nonetheless privileges the reality of self-conscious 'performing' – for both characters within scenes and for the audience itself.

Yet what are the social implications of reproducing on stage the trivialities of daily life? For the respectability of Robertson's dramatized worlds surely cannot be separated from the social function of the theatrical establishment which produced those dramas. In 1865, when Marie Wilton assumed management of the unfashionable Queen's Theatre (shortly thereafter renamed the Prince of Wales's) in Tottenham Street, she began a twenty-year managerial career that

---

[15] 22 February 1868.

not only transformed the repertoires of West End theatres, but also irrevocably allied nineteenth-century theatre managers, performers and spectators with the cult of middle-class respectability. Unlike Charles Kean at the Princess's, the Bancrofts did not aspire to attract a socially diverse audience, and unlike Samuel Phelps at Sadler's Wells, they were not committed to cultivating a mainly local audience. What appealed to the Bancrofts was exclusivity – an audience composed principally of the aspiring middle classes, both urban and suburban (the latter of which could easily commute to London on an ever-expanding railway service). Together with her husband, the actor Squire Bancroft, she made a successful bid for the 'carriage trade' by offering her patrons plays which mirrored their own lives, an acting ensemble increasingly drawn from the middle class itself, and a comfortable auditorium with carpeted floors, curtains, chintz upholstery and even lace antimacassars on the stalls seats.

As part of their managerial reforms, the Bancrofts started their performances at 8 o'clock and restricted the bill to the performance of a single play, thus ending the custom of offering half-price admission at 9 o'clock. In consequence, the working class (accustomed to paying the lowest possible price), morally dubious 'men about town' (fond of turning up halfway through the evening) and prostitutes (in search of morally dubious men) were all discouraged from attending performances at the Prince of Wales's. More astonishingly still, the Bancrofts were the first nineteenth-century managers to increase substantially the cost of attending a play. Even as their own production costs declined, due to the combination of falling prices and the cost efficiency of 'long runs', the Bancrofts raised the price of a seat in the stalls to an 'aristocratic' ten shillings – an increase of 600 per cent.[16] In 1880, at the Haymarket, they eliminated the pit entirely by converting it into yet more stalls. The Bancrofts themselves realized previously unfathomable profits, retiring in 1885 with a fortune of £180,000.

Thus far our inquiry into the respectability of the mid-Victorian stage has looked chiefly at the traditional 'internal' factors of performance history: *mise-en-scène*, acting and theatre management. Let us now widen our focus and examine the stage in relation to the society that created it. The diverse composition, tastes and expectations of theatre audiences provide us with the necessary bridge between the on-stage and off-stage worlds. Whilst retaining a focus on the audience, we may now profitably turn to such 'external' aspects of performance events as royal patronage, the middle-class promotion of 'rational

---

[16] *Illustrated London News*, 15 April 1865.

amusement' and the first calls to establish a national theatre. Let us begin at the top, with the alliance between the stage and the throne.

In the summer of 1848, as a paralyzing fear of revolution gripped even her own realm, Queen Victoria sought to align the monarchy more closely with the people. She looked first to the theatre, moving quickly and decisively to establish herself as the nation's leading patron of the drama. She and Prince Albert radically curtailed their visits to performances of French and Italian opera at Covent Garden and Her Majesty's Theatre (for which she had been heavily censured by xenophobic theatrical critics), and in early July made high-profile visits to benefit performances for Macready at Drury Lane (*Henry VIII*) and for Charles and Ellen Kean at the Haymarket (Bulwer-Lytton's *Money* and Centlivre's *The Wonder*). The 'appearance of the Sovereign in the popular act of acknowledging the greetings of her subjects', affirmed the *Spectator* in its account of these two command performances, was an indisputably genuine 'display of loyalty'.[17]

Six months later, in January 1849, Victoria revealed to the King of Prussia that she and her husband had commenced a series of private theatricals at Windsor Castle to 'revive and elevate the English drama'.[18] The Queen selected Charles Kean to superintend the court performances, a role he undertook for nine years. The plays performed before a select audience of royalty, courtiers and politicians were a conventional mix of Shakespeare, classic comedies such as *The School for Scandal*, Tom Taylor's *Still Waters Run Deep* and other favoured contemporary dramas and long-forgotten minor comedies, such as *Hush Money*. Whilst the court theatricals, held in January and early February, were intended to elevate the national drama, the principal beneficiaries of this new form of royal patronage were not playwrights but actor-managers. The productions were typically 'imports' from London's main theatres – the Princess's, the Haymarket, Sadler's Wells and even the Olympic – each of which would close for the evening when its company performed at Windsor. Charles Kean frequently 'previewed' his forthcoming Shakespearean revivals at the court theatricals, thus enabling him to advertise his productions 'as performed before Her Majesty at Windsor Castle'.

During the 1850s the Princess's Theatre was Victoria's favourite playhouse, where she enjoyed Charles Kean's staging of both Shakespeare and melo-drama. She commissioned E. H. Corbould to paint scenes from Kean's 1852 revival of *King John*, but in her own journal she drew a sketch of the closing

---

[17] 15 July 1848.
[18] H. Bolitho, ed., *Further Letters of Queen Victoria* (1938), 15, quoted in Rowell, *Queen Victoria Goes to the Theatre*, 47.

tableau from Act I of the ghostly melodrama *The Corsican Brothers*. Not exclusive in her patronage, the Queen also attended performances not only at major theatres like the Haymarket, but also at such specialty houses as the Adelphi (for melodrama) and the Olympic (for comedy). At the Haymarket she delighted in Planché's topical extravaganza *Mr Buckstone's Voyage 'Round the Globe (in Leicester Square)*, inspired by Wyld's Great Globe, a scale model of the earth then on display in Leicester Square. At the Olympic, the little theatre in Wych Street, she watched in admiration as Robson, playing the elf Jam Bogie, danced a Lancashire clog hornpipe in Planché's *The Yellow Dwarf*. Her last appearance at a public playhouse, in March 1861, was at the Adelphi, in the Strand, to watch Boucicault's sensation melodrama *The Colleen Bawn*. Victoria's eclectic theatrical taste was both genuine and long-standing. Before her accession to the throne, in 1837, she attended the circus at Astley's Amphitheatre; in 1839 she saw Isaac Van Amburgh's lions seven times in six weeks in a Drury Lane panto, examined the animals at close range during a backstage visit and even confided to her diary that she imagined herself as a lion-tamer.[19]

The Queen's passion for the theatre, although at first criticized as a sign of youthful frivolity, became by mid-century the national example of the proper regard for rational amusement. The royal family, unpopular in the waning years of the Hanoverians, shrewdly refashioned itself in the mid-nineteenth century as the model for English family life. And so we ought not to underestimate the degree to which Victoria's unabated devotion to the drama precipitated the expansion of the theatre-going public. When she took her children to see Kean's productions, and her daughter, the Princess Royal, drew sketches of the productions, anti-theatrical moralists could no longer denounce the licentiousness of the playhouse, since it was now good enough for the monarch's children. The high-profile visits of Victoria and Albert to the Princess's Theatre throughout the 1850s sounded a reassuring and encouraging 'all's clear' to those previously unwilling to set foot in a playhouse.

When Victoria successfully recast herself as an exemplary theatrical benefactress, she acted within a resolutely public and politically charged institution. Her sharp and sudden increase in play-going did not make the theatre political. Quite the opposite. The nineteenth-century stage, the 'pulse of the public',[20] was already political, and Victoria strove to turn that politicization to her advantage. Such political efficacy rested, in turn, upon the large and socially diverse audience that a popular London theatre could command. Indeed, what

---

[19] Rowell, *Queen Victoria Goes to the Theatre*, 24–5.
[20] Charles Kean, July 1858, Fol. Y.c. 393 (169 a–c), Folger Shakespeare Library.

qualified the mid-Victorian theatre as a consequential site of national debate was precisely its 'publicity', its *lack* of social uniformity. However frequently invoked in Victorian theatrical writing, 'the people' is not a unitary social subject, but a 'battleground of intersecting fields', as Loren Kruger observes, 'on which the legitimacy of national popular representation is publicly contested'.[21] In other words, people fight over just what 'the people' means. Social diversity does not imply consensus – usually it implies the opposite – and the changing face of the Victorian theatre audience occasioned, as we shall see later, the fervent defence of middle-class interests against the incursions of both fashionable coteries and the working-class 'million'.

Of course the middle class was itself never a single social category, for it comprised 'diverse social groupings split among economic, social, political, and religious lines'.[22] At mid-century, most of the urban middle classes did not have an education, write letters to the newspapers, read literary and scientific journals, own property or belong to learned societies. They were, in F. M. L. Thompson's description, the 'small shopkeepers, traders, and dealers' who lived in Clerkenwell and Islington; they were of lower professional standing than the lawyers and bankers who controlled most middle-class political and reform activity.[23] Who belonged to the middle class was, moreover, a question not simply of demographics but also of ethics. As Dror Wahrman has argued, the Victorian middle class, as a moral force, was principally an 'imagined constituency', a mythologized vision of how members of society should conduct their private lives.[24] To think of the middle class as having a precise social referent would thus be to diminish the pervasive influence of its moral precepts.

The variety of experiences, actual or imagined, which might all be termed *middle class* suggests that we cannot expect *any* class-based reception of theatrical productions to have been either uniform or predictable. In London, particularly, a city of rapidly expanding population, diversity is perhaps the chief characteristic of theatres and theatre audiences. Whether '[h]igh or low, rich or poor', *Blackwood's Magazine* attested, Londoners could take their pick of 'theatres for the east, and theatres for the west; theatres for this side [north] of the river, and theatres for that; theatres for performances equestrian and aquatic; theatres legitimate and illegitimate'.[25] Each of these particular theatres, in

---

[21] Kruger, *National Stage*, 6.
[22] Joyce, *Democratic Subjects*, 164.
[23] Thompson, *Rise of Respectable Society*, 19.
[24] Wahrman, *Imagining the Middle Class*, 263.
[25] *Blackwood's Magazine* 51 (1842): 427.

turn, 'minister[ed] to a distinct class of spectators'.[26] The type of audience that patronized a given theatre depended upon such theatrical and extra-theatrical factors as location, ticket prices, repertoire, production styles, 'star' or ensemble performers, availability of public and private transportation and even the starting and running times of a performance. Without attempting to impose any arbitrary order on the changing demographics of nineteenth-century theatre audiences, it is crucial to note the mid-century *goal* of social integration at respectable West End playhouses (a goal, as we have seen, repudiated by the Bancrofts). We do know that, to a considerable extent, this goal was achieved in some London theatres. As opposed to the opera house or the music hall, sites dominated respectively by the aristocratic *beau monde* and the great unwashed, the West End theatre of the 1850s possessed a nationalistic force because its audience, actual or mythologized, was unique in regarding itself as the nation in microcosm.

Charles Kean's tenure at the Princess's Theatre is a classic example. During his nine years as lessee, from 1850 to 1859, Kean attracted an audience notable not only for the presence of 'John Bull' in the gallery, but also of the respectable middle-class family, the clergy, the aristocracy and the sovereign herself. For the first time since the late eighteenth century, a London theatre audience achieved something resembling social integration, and its audience was truthfully described by a contemporary critic as extending from 'the Queen in the Royal Box to the artisan in the gallery', when only a generation earlier parents had 'dreaded taking their families to a play'.[27] And in a grudging tribute to the diversity of Kean's audience, even a 'Theatrical Squib' was compelled to admit, in the otherwise excoriating poem 'The Celebrated Eton Boy', that at the Princess's Theatre 'Royalty sat in curtained state; / The Noble and the Gentle came (early or late), / The general Public thronged the Pit, / The Clergy of course in *Stalls* would sit'.[28]

The nineteenth-century theatre was important to social reformers because, as Marc Baer persuasively argues, it offered one of the few unregulated opportunities where a 'variety of social orders could learn together how to be English'.[29] In other words, the mid-Victorian theatre's capacity to offer 'virtue' *and* 'cakes and ale' to a mass popular audience explains its centrality in the promotion of rational recreation.[30] Indeed, the inclusive appeal of a respectable and

---

[26] *National Review* (Jan.–Apr. 1856): 422.
[27] *Mr Charles Kean* (*c.* 1859), 321, unattributed monograph in the Folger Shakespeare Library.
[28] *The Celebrated Eton Boy* (London, 1859).
[29] Baer, *Theatre and Disorder in Late Georgian London*, 195.
[30] 'Our amusement', *Blackwood's Magazine* 100 (1866): 698.

educational theatre was the basis for the earliest calls to establish a national theatre. The match between reformist desires to educate the lower middle and working classes and the theatre's self-appointed mission to educate precisely these segments of its diverse audience base made pleas for a national theatre sound, if not entirely convincing, then at least no longer outlandish. The idea was serious enough that Gladstone would spend an afternoon in 1857 backstage at the Princess's Theatre, where Charles Kean engaged him, as the future prime minister recorded in his diary, in a 'long conversation on the question of Government subvention to the Drama'.[31] Yet as Gladstone's twentieth-century editor glosses the passage, 'nothing came of this'.

Like every totalizing historical narrative, the story of the Victorian theatre's long-standing quest for respectability has its own counter-narrative. One such narrative is geographical. For alongside the legitimate West End theatre there continued to flourish a range of 'illegitimate' productions at theatres in the East End (the Royal Effingham, the Britannia, the Pavilion, the Standard and the Grecian) and south London (the Victoria and the Surrey). These playhouses, whose repertoire strongly favoured melodrama, targeted working-class audiences drawn principally, but by no means exclusively, from the surrounding neighbourhoods. Working-class residents of east and south London also formed a regular part of the West End gallery audience, particularly at minor theatres such as the Adelphi and the Strand, and thus witnessed a wider range of performances than any other segment of nineteenth-century theatre audiences. Theatrical migration did not generally flow in the opposite direction, and only infrequently did West End audiences travel to the many East End or 'transpontine' theatres in Lambeth and Southwark. In fact, middle-class critics and spectators who patronized London's principal theatres, as revealed in the 1892 parliamentary report on theatres and places of entertainment, knew little about the offerings and audiences of East End theatres and music halls. 'I have not', the critic William Archer blithely confessed to Parliament, 'frequented low-class theatres very much.'[32] But Archer's lack of experience did not prevent him from speculating that entertainments offered at 'low-class' theatres were 'distinctly more or less indecent, [and] indelicate'. Although most histories of the Victorian stage have focused on London's principal legitimate theatres, the so-called 'illegitimate' playhouses, the kinds of places that William Archer rarely visited, accounted for just over one-third of the city's nightly theatre audiences – *excluding* music halls, penny gaffs and saloon theatres.[33]

---

[31] Entry for 12 May 1857, Gladstone, *Diaries*, ed. Matthew, v: 222.

[32] *Report from the Select Committee on Theatres and Places of Entertainment* (1892), 265.

[33] *Report from the Select Committee on Theatrical Licences and Regulations* (1866), 295.

But numbers alone do not tell the whole story. For it is equally true that East End theatres (but not music halls) began to close by the late 1860s. And on the subsequent history of British theatre East End performances exercised only a minimal influence. Nor, moreover, should we presume that performances outside London's cultural and geographical centre were necessarily activist or oppositional. More probably, any impulse towards a genuinely proletarian theatre was held in check by its own repertoire. In the melodramas performed before working-class audiences, social injustice was personified in the individual villain and not depicted as the dark underside of capitalism itself. In consequence, these plays resolved problems of crime and exploitation by eliminating individual perpetrators, thereby preserving intact the prevailing social and economic structures. In G. F. Taylor's *The Factory Strike* (1836), for example, personal animosity, rather than worker solidarity, is the prime motivator. Like the entertainments of late-Victorian music halls, these immensely popular plays were not conducive to radical social change or protest.

Perhaps the most trenchant challenges to the ascendancy of middle-class respectability came, ironically enough, from within the legitimate theatre itself. Each of the movements towards theatrical respectability that we have noted so far – antiquarian revivals of Shakespeare, cup and-saucer domestic comedy, 'rational' amusement, social integration, royal patronage and the call for a state-subsidized theatre – met with criticism and resistance from some quarters of the theatrical establishment. In other words, the reforming spirit which strove to bring respectability to the mid-Victorian theatre (at least to its professional élite) was neither invariably welcome nor wholly successful, even within London's principal playhouses. Let us review, in turn, these various 'internal' constraints on theatrical respectability.

Charles Kean's antiquarian revivals of Shakespeare, as much as they enjoyed fashionable patronage in the 1850s, were vigorously attacked by journalists and theatrical contemporaries. Whilst some critics focused on Kean's willingness to sacrifice the Bard's poetry for the sake of stage carpentry, others lodged a more mundane complaint: that antiquarian Shakespeare, however edifying, was boring. '[P]rovided we are true to history', lamented the comic actor-manager Charles Mathews, 'we have free permission to be dull and tiresome.'[34] A more ingenious form of meta-theatrical criticism was the mid-century resurgence of Shakespeare burlesques and travesties that satirized contemporary productions. Francis Talfourd's *Macbeth Somewhat Removed from the Text of Shakespeare* (Olympic, 1853), starring Frederick Robson, directly parodied Charles Kean's

---

[34] Quoted by Dallas, 'Drama', 219.

Macbeth, which had just opened at the Princess's Theatre. 'We have been done to death with burlesques', the *Spectator* pleaded in 1853, the year in which a record-setting six Shakespeare travesties were performed in London theatres (30 April 1853). Comic playwrights such as F. C. Burnand and the Brough brothers claimed, for their part, that Shakespeare's dignity was imperilled not by burlesques, but rather by mediocre performers and sensationalizing actor-managers. In that inverted critical perspective they were joined by the austere critic G. H. Lewes, who maintained that Kean, in his spectacular Shakespearean revivals, 'has touched nothing that he has not burlesqued'.[35] At least for Lewes, writing pseudonymously as 'Vivian', legitimate Shakespeare was the true burlesque.

Just as antiquarian Shakespeare was a dominant symbol of theatrical respectability for the 1850s, Tom Robertson's genteel comedies, as we have seen, provided a different model of respectability for the 1860s; not historical instruction, but a mirror of middle-class manners and decorum. Yet the immensely popular sensation melodramas, whose most famous expositor was Dion Boucicault, successfully competed with dramas of quaint bourgeois familiarity. Like the sensation novels of Wilkie Collins, the melodramas centred on the enactment of such disasters and catastrophes as train wrecks, sinking ships and avalanches. The popular dramatist, as *Fraser's Magazine* instructed, must 'thrill [the audience's] nerves with some strong effect, just short of absolute horror . . . and work them up into a fever of physical excitement'.[36] Indeed, the same audiences that smiled knowingly at the picnic spoiled by rain in the opening scene of Robertson's *Ours* also succumbed to the excitement of a man diving into a rock pool in Boucicault's *The Colleen Bawn* (1861) and the house on fire in *The Streets of London* (1864). '[S]ensation pieces', as Lewes reluctantly conceded, although 'appealing to the lowest faculties, do appeal to them effectively.'[37]

For all their obvious contrivances, sensation melodramas had one vital link to Robertson's cup-and-saucer domestic comedies: a commitment to realism. In Robertson's plays, realism consisted in ordinary behaviour. In sensation melodramas, realism went to the opposite extreme: the vivid and life-like representation not of little things, but of affecting and extraordinary events. Also in the 1860s, sensation melodrama joined with the allied subgenre of city melodrama to theatricalize urban and professional life in all its grandeur, danger and vitality. In these melodramatic performances, public life mattered

---

[35] Lewes, *Leader*, 30 July 1853.
[36] *Fraser's Magazine* 64 (Dec. 1861): 772.
[37] Lewes, 'Foreign actors and the English drama', 172.

more than home life. Andrew Halliday's *The Great City* (1867) showed a hansom cab crossing Waterloo Bridge. And Boucicault's *The Streets of London* featured a scene of Trafalgar Square on a snowy winter's night. The audience welcomed that view with 'boisterous applause', the *Spectator* noted, precisely because they had just seen it outside.[38] From the 'hot-pie man' to street tumblers, from a policeman to a beggar woman, all the actors in the scene were 'as real as if just hired out of the streets, as is very likely the case'. Obviously the artificial realism of this scene – the reproduction of recognizable locales for sensational effect – had little to do with an aesthetics of naturalism, let alone with the social consciousness of a Brechtian street scene. Yet for audiences of the mid-Victorian era, the blend of sensation and city melodramas, however much they appealed to the lowest faculties, nonetheless captured both the heady pleasures and lurking dangers of urban life.

Among the most fervent admirers of melodrama, before the death of the Prince Consort in 1861 ended her visits to public theatres, was Victoria herself. Resting insecurely within the cult of middle-class respectability, Victoria's theatre-going was accepted and even honoured, provided that the monarch attended the right sort of play (i.e., Shakespearean) and, moreover, was never actually seen to enjoy herself. When, in a pitch of melodramatic fervour, she clutched the curtains inside the royal box at the Princess's Theatre during John Oxenford's *Pauline*, the Queen openly advertised her taste for undiluted sensational pleasures.[39] The London press reproached her for this public performance of moral failing. Similarly, the *Theatrical Journal* scolded her for attending *The Corsican Brothers*, 'this vulgar Victorian trash', four times in only two months (19 May 1852). As the *Westminster Review* elaborated, the 'extraordinary success' of the play, which 'royalty itself has patronized by repeated visits', only confirms the 'degradation of the stage' (1 January 1853).

Just what was so degrading about this ghostly melodrama which took London by storm when it premièred at the Princess's Theatre in 1852, inspired numerous burlesque imitations and was revived by Henry Irving in 1880? Perhaps it was the play's winning combination of two guilty pleasures of the stage: old-fashioned ghosts and new-fangled technology. The most stunning moment in *The Corsican Brothers* came at the end of the first act with Fabien dei Franchi's premonition that Louis, his twin brother (both roles originally played by Charles Kean), is in danger in Paris. As Fabien hastily writes to his brother seeking reassurance that all is well, the blood-stained spectre of the murdered

---

[38] 'Theatrical realism', 1182.
[39] Baker, *History of the London Stage*, 484.

twin rises from the stage floor. To the haunting strains of violins, Louis's ghost 'glides across the stage – ascending gradually at the same time'.[40] That scene, which gave its name to the stock 'Corsican trap', introduced the novelty of a ghost moving across the stage in a slow incline rather than merely floating upward and out of sight. (In Mark Lemon's burlesque *O Gemini! or, Brothers of Co(u)rse*, commissioned for the Haymarket by J. B. Buckstone, the ghost was inanimate – a turnip jack-o-lantern placed atop a flowing white sheet.[41]) The spectre then reveals to Fabien and his mother a tableau of the painting *The Duel*, depicting his own death at the hands of the villain Château-Renaud. The effect was overpowering. Queen Victoria found the ghost's sudden appearance to be 'quite alarming', and she described the concluding tableau of the duel as both 'unearthly' and 'creepy'.[42] Even G. H. Lewes, a critic hardly prone to puffery, confessed that the scene was 'more real and terrifying' than anything he could remember.[43]

And yet the thrill of sensation, ghosts and new technology was tempered by the play's tone of moral sobriety, which contrasted the pride and honour of the Corsican dei Franchi family with Parisian immorality and decadence. Charles Kean's acting style, moreover, was itself a model of decorum and restraint – modes of behaviour not customarily associated with melodrama. Whilst Lewes complained that Kean 'detonated' his way through Shakespeare (*The Corsican Brothers* alternated with his revival of *Macbeth*), he warmly praised the actor's 'gentlemanly demeanour and drawing-room manner' as the brothers Fabien and Louis (*Leader*, 28 February 1852). Thus, even in a play which catered to the popular taste for sensation and the supernatural, an underlying moral code of traditional virtues still prevailed.

Quite apart from the content of the plays themselves, royal and aristocratic patronage of the theatre was for the Victorian middle class at once both exemplary and suspect. As much as Charles Kean profited from Victoria's repeated visits to the Princess's and from the aristocracy's return to the London stage, he was criticized for being over-fond of the nobility by 'pittites' who remained strong and vocal enough to publicize themselves as the theatre's true and ideal audience. The *Theatrical Journal* demanded that Kean 'cater for the public and not for individuals' – that is, the Queen – and remember that the stage was 'public property' (19 October 1853). Henry Morley openly advised theatre managers to 'take for a standard of the people [they] would please, an honest

---

[40] Boucicault, *Corsican Brothers*, 20.
[41] Review of Lemon's *O Gemini!*
[42] Quoted Rowell, *Queen Victoria Goes to the Theatre*, 58.
[43] Lewes, *Leader*, 28 February 1852.

Englishman of the educated middle class'.[44] Social antagonism, predictably, was directed downwards as well, with *Fraser's Magazine* disdainfully remarking that theatrical managers attend only to the 'convenience and taste of the million'.[45] Yet the 'million' still had their defenders in the theatrical press. In 1855, when the Olympic Theatre, under Alfred Wigan's socially aspiring management, converted a portion of its pit into stalls and then separated the two seating areas with a spiked barrier, the *Theatrical Journal* warned that 'managers of late are getting despotic, and forget that it is the pit and gallery payers who make up the majority of their audience' despite their 'purse-inferior position in life' (27 June 1855). Previously, the same journal had affirmed that a 'sensible, hard-working mechanic is the true patron of the drama – a patron who is uninfluenced by either fashion or prejudice' (9 March 1853).

Polemical statements about the theatre issued by a middle class jealous of its own moral fitness, statements that resist the communitarian ethos propounded by social reformers, testify only too well to middle-class anxiety at having to share the public sphere with both 'sickly and effeminate' aristocrats (*Theatrical Journal*, 9 March 1853) and the vulgar 'million'. Middle-class apprehensions over social mixing were intensified, moreover, by the lingering fear that popular culture, despite well-intentioned efforts to make it rational, was still deviant, still an illicit pleasure for which no atonement could ever suffice. Fearful of being caught in the act of moral imposture, the middle classes 'were acutely concerned to *reinforce*, not reduce social distance', Peter Bailey contends, precisely because aggressive reformers proposed to 'alleviate the tensions and degeneration in society through the fraternal association of all classes in leisure'.[46] This counter-desire for social segregation, as I have shown, characterized not only the enforced exclusivity of the Bancrofts' tenure at the Prince of Wales's Theatre and the Haymarket, but also the subsequent history of the late Victorian and Edwardian theatre.

Middle-class disdain for the 'million' exposes, moreover, a fundamental hypocrisy in its commitment to the social utility of leisure: only the labouring classes, it seemed, required 'rational' amusement; those better off could indulge in less improving pleasures – such as the display of 'pectoral and femoral muscles' by the scantily clad ladies of the *corps de ballet* at the Strand and Gaiety theatres.[47] Whilst many mid-Victorian social reformers were only too eager to insist on instruction above amusement in leisure pursuits, this appeal to

---

[44] Morley, *Journal of a London Playgoer*, 25.
[45] *Fraser's Magazine* 41 (1850): 70.
[46] Bailey, *Leisure and Class in Victorian England*, 115, emphasis mine.
[47] Sala, 'On stage costume', 101.

rational amusement did not fully correspond to the actuality of middle-class experiences. In 1851 William Bodham Donne observed that the oft-repeated maxim that 'the stage is a great moral engine for the education of the people' was an empty platitude.[48] A play is an 'entertainment', asserted the future Examiner of Plays, and 'if it is not entertaining, it is nothing'. Almost twenty years later, *Blackwood's Magazine* similarly affirmed that the 'great majority of people live hard and fast in our day . . . They like the senses rather than the intellect to be gratified'.[49] The same journal had earlier declared, even more forcefully, that whether plays were entertaining or instructive did not matter, since the theatre exercises 'little or no influence' upon the 'great majority of the British people, and especially of the middle classes'.[50]

Among the places where social reformers felt that the stage *should* exercise its moral authority were the East End and the Surrey side of the Thames. Indeed, intellectual amusement survived only in the East End, as E. S. Dallas argued in his description of Sir Thomas Noon Talfourd's *Ion*, performed at the Standard Theatre in Shoreditch – a play which he rightly claimed would no longer be welcome in the West End because of its tedious formality. Unlike middle-class audiences, who had grown weary of 'intellectual amusement' through over-exposure, spectators in the East End had not yet earned the right to 'farce and frivolity, bubble and ballet'.[51] Rather, because East Enders labour physically during the day they must labour intellectually at night. For surely no twenty-four hours may pass without some morally profitable activity. Compounding the missionary zeal of respectable reformers was the commonly held prejudice that the working-class audiences drawn to melodrama were not just uneducated, but potentially criminal. T. W. Erle described the Victoria's audience, drawn principally from the surrounding south London borough of Lambeth, as 'largely graced by the presence of embryo and mature convicts'[52] – just the sort of people who needed to learn the principles of virtue and justice that melodramas taught. And it is precisely this philanthropic interest, sincere or patronizing, in the welfare of the labouring class that explains the occasional foray of middle-class Victorian theatrical observers into the remote eastern regions of the metropolis.

The 1869 performance of a temperance 'ballet' (the code word for a melo-drama in dumbshow) at an East End music hall, as recounted in the stylish

---

[48] Donne, 'Poets and players', 512.
[49] 'Stage morality and the ballet', 356.
[50] *Blackwood's* 79 (Feb. 1856): 228.
[51] Dallas, 'Popular literature – the periodical press', 112.
[52] T. W. Erle, *Letters from a Theatrical Scene Painter* (1880), 101, quoted in Booth, *Theatre in the Victorian Age*, 163.

magazine *Belgravia*, is a case in point. Since a *temperance* music hall was a contradiction in terms – the principle attraction of music halls being the freedom to drink while watching a performance – the critic F. W. Robinson resolved to discover whether temperance, 'allied to a "new Easter ballet" and comic vocalists', could survive in this 'industrious quarter of our city'.[53] In other words, just who would patronize a venue universally associated with drinking to watch a performance on the evils of drink? The capacity audience of 1,500 for each of the twice-daily performances was, as it turned out, composed mostly of poor and 'ragged' children, the 'untaught offscourings of the streets' (519). As for the efficacy of the performance itself (an adaptation of T. P. Taylor's *The Bottle*), Robinson optimistically concluded that despite the rowdy inattention of the juvenile spectators, and despite the performance's 'clumsy efforts to teach a moral', this 'herding together of hundreds of poor children was an advantage to society' (523). Outside the East End, of course, the didacticism of temperance melodrama would have been only too unwelcome. For as all middle-class reformers presumed, only the labouring classes, with their pubs and gin palaces crowding every corner, were susceptible to the vices of alcohol.

Parliament resisted the pressure from temperance societies to regulate the production and consumption of alcohol until 1872, when it passed a fairly minor piece of restrictive legislation. If mid-Victorian government could not muster the political resolve to combat alcoholism and public drunkenness, what possible interest could it be expected to take in the running of theatres? Parliament understood perfectly well the educational potential of popular culture but did not feel obliged to mandate, or worse, to subsidize, rational amusement. 'Free trade' in the drama had already been won with the dissolution of the patent monopoly in 1843, and it was simply counter-intuitive to urge state funding for the theatre little more than a decade after the profession had been deregulated at its own behest. Indeed, establishing a national theatre could hardly have been of commanding interest to mid-century politicians, as their chief concern in domestic affairs lay in eradicating such intolerable social conditions as illiteracy and disease. Gentlemanly advocates of a national theatre, like the scientist Sir William Snow Harris, who quietly lobbied their friends in Parliament, certainly traded on reformist desires to educate the urban working class under the guise of leisure. But even this persistent yoking of education and leisure was not sufficiently compelling. Had it ever been proposed, legislation to form a state theatre would unquestionably have failed to meet even the modestly interventionist social agenda of mid-Victorian parliaments.

[53] Robinson, 'An East End entertainment', 522.

Of course, by the 1870s the commercial West End hardly needed to be subsidized. After generations of financial loss, theatre managers and speculators such as the Bancrofts were able to realize immense profits. A thriving theatre contributed, in turn, to the prosperity of related service industries such as hospitality and transportation. On the north-west corner of Russell Square, in central London, stands a lodge for cabmen originally built in 1901. Still in use, the lodge has provided West End cabbies with a warm and dry refuge for over a century. Those few passers-by curious enough to stop and read the inscription on the door will learn that the lodge was built with funds donated by a celebrity of the day. His name was Sir Squire Bancroft. Like many philanthropists, then and now, Bancroft's generosity was aimed at people he was unlikely to encounter professionally. The closest that London's cabmen ever got to a West End theatre, in the year of Victoria's death, was probably the pavement in front. Cabmen were an indispensable part of the new theatrical economy – swiftly transporting audience members, in comfort and privacy, to and from restaurants, train stations and theatres – but they were most likely not among its targeted audience. As Bancroft's act of *noblesse oblige* suggests, the newly prosperous West End establishment, caring little for what is now called 'audience outreach', preferred instead to reinforce social and occupational distinctions – giving London's cabbies, not a seat in the stalls, but a nice 'cuppa' once they had seen theatre audiences safely home.

16

Gendering Victorian theatre

KERRY POWELL

The theatre was uniquely alluring to women of the Victorian period. It was one of few professions accessible to women, holding out the prospect of a career that would be active, disciplined and – at least for a lucky few – remunerative. Life in the theatre also gave women a voice, for on stage they could speak while others sat waiting in suspense for their next word – including men, who in most other settings compelled women to silence. This control over audiences, over men in particular, often proved intoxicating to Victorian actresses. On the other side of the footlights, stunned Victorian men often became infatuated with women of the stage even as, paradoxically, they felt imperilled by them.

This fascination with the stage could be experienced powerfully and enviously by women who had no connection with the theatre at all. Florence Nightingale, for example, expresses it in *Cassandra* when she calls the opportunity of being a professional the supreme attraction of the life of an actress, much more than the opportunity to achieve fame or wealth. Amateurism was the fate of most women, however talented, singing or drawing 'as an amusement (a *pass*-time as it is called)', denying themselves a vocation to sacrifice their lives to the needs of a husband and children. But the actress was different:

> in the morning she studies, in the evening she embodies those studies: she has the means of testing and correcting them by practice, and of resuming her studies in the morning, to improve the weak parts, remedy the failures, and in the evening try the corrections again.[1]

As Nightingale points out, an actress was not compelled to 'annihilate herself' by becoming merely the 'complement' to her husband.[2] She had autonomy because she had a vocation of her own. If women could assert themselves this way in the theatre, then why not off stage as well? The theatre

---

[1] Nightingale, *Cassandra*, 40–1. The points that I make in this chapter have been developed in a different and more expansive form in my book *Women and Victorian Theatre*.
[2] Nightingale, *Cassandra*, 40.

provided a framework within which Victorians could imagine, on occasion, a world that would be very differently gendered from the one they inhabited, a world in which women who were not literally actresses could claim some of the prerogatives of life on the stage. For example, a character in Mary Elizabeth Braddon's *Aurora Floyd* (1863), although not on the stage any longer, is no less aggressive, and indeed no less performative, in her new role as a wife in the country than she was as a professional actress. 'How should she be abashed on entering the drawing-rooms of these Kentish mansions', writes Braddon, 'when for nine years she had walked nightly on a stage to be the focus of every eye, and to entertain her guests the evening through. Was it likely she was to be overawed . . .?'[3]

If the theatre provided a model for women to lead their lives with more virtuosity, it also provided, as actress Madge Kendal emphasized, a way to make money – and economic independence was a precondition for independence of other kinds. Actresses with financial means of their own could afford to refuse to surrender mind, body or possessions to a man. As one actress reminds her covetous husband in George Moore's *A Mummer's Wife* (1885), 'I earned the money myself, and if you think to rob me of what I earn you're mistaken. You shan't.'[4] In a forgotten theatre novel called *Connie, the Actress* (1902) the heroine is even bolder, leaving her husband with the explanation that she will no longer behave as a 'mere domesticated animal' or 'pussy-cat in the house'.[5] But the prosperity which helped make such an announcement imaginable was comparatively rare among Victorian actresses. Tracy C. Davis has shown that for women more than men, acting was a competitive and underpaid profession in which subsistence wages of £1 or £2 a week, if that much, were the rule rather than the exception even by the 1890s.[6] A pound went further then, of course, as Mrs Patrick Campbell recalls: 'you could get a nice room and board for 18s a week; and many actresses lived on £1 a week'.[7] On the other hand, a leading lady could earn good money, sometimes more than the man who headed the bill with her. Ellaline Terriss writes of earning £25 a week at the Gaiety Theatre while her husband Seymour Hicks, who wrote as well as starred in Gaiety productions, earned only £15. In the theatre, she says, 'it is the woman who usually gets paid the most'.[8]

[3] Braddon, *Aurora Floyd*, 14.
[4] Moore, *A Mummer's Wife*, 326.
[5] Winter, *Connie, the Actress*, 108.
[6] Davis, *Actresses as Working Women*, 34.
[7] Mrs Campbell, *My Life and Some Letters*, 60.
[8] Terriss, *Just a Little Bit of String*, 92.

The professional advantages of acting were obvious to women, whether they were actresses or not. Victorian men, however, tended for the most part to view actresses from a different perspective conditioned by their masculinity. In Oscar Wilde's novel *The Picture of Dorian Gray*, the title character emphasizes the 'glamour' and 'mystery' of the actress Sybil Vane, her erotic and aesthetic appeal to him, a man. What the actress can do for the male spectator becomes, therefore, the distinguishing and most important quality of the performing woman.[9] This masculinist analysis leaves out of account what made acting seem particularly attractive to Victorian women as various as Florence Nightingale and Madge Kendal. What mattered to them was less the 'mystery' and 'glamour' that seduce a masculine spectator than the independence, professionalism and hard work that made up the career of an actress, and her power to subjugate large audiences of men and women alike by the sound of her voice and her physical presence.

These were precisely the qualities that made many Victorian men uneasy. Under the influence of a charismatic actress they sensed danger to themselves and an apprehension that social codes of gender were being challenged before their eyes. With a mixture of fear and admiration they observed the performing woman free herself from the constraints of her gender, becoming almost like a man. For example, the American critic William Winter describes Charlotte Cushman's 'innate grandeur of authority' on the stage, acknowledging that it may make some observers uncomfortable. 'You might resent her dominance, and shrink from it, calling it "masculine"', Winter says, but 'you could not doubt her massive reality nor escape the spell of her imperial power'.[10] Even from his perspective of sympathy with Cushman's acting, Winter must confront the social threat represented by a woman performer's 'authority' and 'power'. Not all actresses produced these effects, of course. Winter was less impressed by the comparatively understated acting of Eleonora Duse, who would 'wander to the back drop and whisper to the scenery' in a manner 'supposedly inspired'.[11] But male reactions varied where actresses were concerned. Max Beerbohm, for example, was made uneasy by Duse's relatively quiet power: 'My prevailing impression is of a great egoistic force . . . In a man I should admire this tremendous egoism very much indeed. In a woman it only makes me uncomfortable. I dislike it. I resent it. In the name of art, I protest against it.'[12]

---

[9] Wilde, *The Picture of Dorian Gray*, ed. Murray, 51.
[10] Winter, *Other Days*, 154.
[11] Ibid., 157.
[12] Beerbohm, *Around Theatres*, 102.

Sarah Bernhardt, perhaps more than any actress of the Victorian era, inspired such feelings of unease. The poet and theatre critic Arthur Symons, for example, felt in her presence 'almost a kind of obscure sensation of peril'. Bernhardt 'tears the words with her teeth, and spits them out of her mouth, like a wild beast ravening upon prey', or so it seemed to Symons. He declares that watching Bernhardt act makes the spectator's pulse 'beat feverishly', yet 'mesmerised one, awakening the senses and sending the intelligence to sleep'.[13] Similarly, Réjane, whom Symons admired almost as much as Bernhardt, 'skins emotions alive', and even in mediocre plays inspired 'an actual physical sensation; the woman took me by the throat'. But Olga Nethersole, a less brilliant and more subdued actress, merely 'forced me to admire her, to accept her; I felt that she was very real, and, as I felt it, I said to myself: "She is acting splendidly."'[14] Even actresses of the second rank compel men to behave in a certain way – she 'forced me', as Symons expresses it.

Because an actress deformed real femininity as understood by most Victorians, they found it difficult to reconcile her with the traditional roles of a woman as wife and mother. Therefore the success of a woman in theatrical work could plausibly be attributed to her being single or her supposedly undomestic nature. When she married, however, the actress was expected to look back without regret, even with disgust, upon her life on stage. In Robert Buchanan's novel *The Martyrdom of Madeline*, for example, the husband of a former actress suggests hesitantly that she might like to go back to acting, her profession before she knew him. 'It is impossible', she exclaims. 'I hate the stage. Rather than return to it I would die.'[15] In real life this was precisely the choice of Mary Anderson, who writes in her memoirs of the relief she felt upon leaving the stage to be married. 'I have never had a single wish', she declares, 'to walk its boards again.' Thus the private lives of domestic women were made to seem irreconcilable with the independence and power associated, if not always accurately, with actresses. As Mary Anderson expresses it after having already married and retired from the stage: 'I have always thought that no woman can serve two masters: public and domestic life.'[16] But no one expressed this duality with greater force than Gordon Craig, the son of Ellen Terry, who believed himself to be a hapless victim of it. For Craig, 'Mother'

---

[13] Symons, *Plays, Acting, and Music*, 27–30.
[14] Ibid., 128.
[15] These same words – 'I hate the stage' – are uttered in *The Picture of Dorian Gray* by Sybil Vane, whom Wilde leaves, as Madeline is left in Buchanan's novel, choosing death over being an actress.
[16] Anderson, *A Few More Memories*, 17, 21.

was a nurturing and indispensable part of his life, yet separate and at war with the famous actress Ellen Terry:

> E. T. was always getting in the way of my mother . . . I continue to speak of them as two, because although one and the same person, they were leagues apart and agreed to differ on almost every subject . . . E. T. was the 'strongest' of the two, but Mother was more cunning, and the dearest – no woman could possibly have been a better mother, a truer wife, a more faithful, unswerving guardian and guide . . . had it not been for E. T. – that public person who came between us.

Ellen Terry seems to have recognized this duality in herself, and regretted it – 'so imperfect', Craig quotes her as having said, 'unable to be one thing or another . . . never entirely one'.[17]

This otherness of the stage world, its alienation from what Victorians thought of as real life, was marked forcefully by theatrical conventions such as the darkened auditorium, a spotlit performing space, the proscenium stage framed like a painting and the stage curtain itself – all of them barriers dividing audience from actors. In this 'world which is independent of ours', as George Eliot described it, an actress might transcend a fixed domestic identity, live 'myriad lives' and exercise a power and independence that was inaccessible to most wives and mothers.[18] Not only were actresses allowed some of the prerogatives of men – they were remarkable in the Victorian period for enacting the roles of men as well. 'There are few leading actresses who have not played or aspired to play masculine roles', as the popular Victorian male impersonator Vesta Tilley writes in her memoir.[19] For Victorians who conceived of identity as fixed and indissolubly linked to transcendent categories of gender, the 'myriad lives' and unconventional gendering of actresses could only be alarming, even frightening, but all the same strangely alluring for male spectators in particular. When actresses played men's roles, their tights, cinched waists and ornately trimmed knickers called attention to their femininity and transcribed their assumed masculinity into the realm of male desire. At the same time, as Tracy Davis has pointed out, the roles of men provided actresses with stronger parts than did the predictable women's roles of ingenue, shrew and adventuress.[20]

---

[17] Craig, *Ellen Terry and her Secret Self*, 52, 57, 63, 65–6.
[18] Eliot, *Daniel Deronda*, 583–6.
[19] Tilley, *Recollections of Vesta Tilley*, 208. Good recent analyses of Victorian actresses playing male roles include Senelick, 'Evolution of the male impersonator', and Tracy C. Davis, *Actresses as Working Women*, especially 114–15.
[20] Tracy C. Davis, *Actresses as Working Women*, 114.

But when Max Beerbohm reviewed Sarah Bernhardt's performance as Hamlet in 1899, he could only dimly imagine what would account for her wanting to play the part:

> Gentleness and a lack of executive ability are feminine qualities, and they were both strong in Hamlet. This, I take it, would be Sarah's own excuse for having essayed the part. She would not, of course, attempt to play Othello – at least I risk the assumption that she would not, dangerous though it is to assume what she might *not* do . . . But in point of fact she is just as well qualified to play Othello as she is to play Hamlet. Hamlet is none the less a man because he is not consistently manly . . . Sarah ought not to have supposed that Hamlet's weakness set him in any possible relation to her own feminine mind and body.

What troubles Beerbohm, then, is the destruction on stage of barriers dividing masculine from feminine. *Hamlet* becomes for him an accidental comedy in the hands of this eminent actress. Performing as Hamlet, Sarah Bernhardt is an 'aberration' and 'painful', words drawn from the same lexicon that the eminent theatre critic William Archer had used to characterize an all-female production of *As You Like It*. For Beerbohm, moreover, the gravest sin of this female Hamlet lies in her usurping the sacred text of Shakespeare. As Hamlet, Beerbohm insists, Bernhardt did not really portray the title character at all, but had, preposterously, become her own playwright. Sarah Bernhardt had egotistically substituted herself for Shakespeare's hero and made Hamlet 'from first to last, *très grande dame*'.[21]

Bernhardt's performance was a serious attempt to impersonate a man, and as such it departed from the burlesque tradition of cross-dressing in the theatre. Cross-dressing like Bernhardt's, because it dispensed with the erotic element, was seen to be in hopeless conflict with her own femininity and even humanity. The theatrical newspaper the *Era*, for example, declared that 'it is only the unsexed woman, the woman who . . . approaches nearly to the masculine – the monstrosity in short – who can deceive us as to her gender on the stage'.[22] Women seriously impersonating a man and wearing authentic male costume – as opposed to the sexy tights and knickers of traditional female cross-dressing – suggested a range of feminine subjectivity that alarmed even progressive men such as William Archer and Max Beerbohm.

Beautiful perhaps, but dangerous, the actress added to her borderless sexuality the additional terrors of her professionalism and her inhabiting a public space. As a character in Geraldine Jewsbury's novel *The Half-Sisters* puts it:

---

[21] Beerbohm, *Around Theatres*, 48–9.
[22] *Era*, 17 June 1899, 13.

I have got a real horror of all professional women. A woman who makes her mind public, or exhibits herself in any way, no matter how it may be dignified by the title of art, seems to me little better than a woman of a nameless class. I am more jealous of the mind than of the body; and, to me, there is something revolting in the notion of a woman who professes to love and belong to you alone going and printing the secrets of her inmost heart, the most sacred working of her soul, for the benefit of all who can pay for them.

The trouble with actresses, from this Victorian point of view, is that they cannot 'belong' absolutely to one man, being commodities in a free market of men at large. Their bodies have become texts for a mass audience to 'read', and they themselves writers and printers, 'publishing both mind and body too'. As a published text, therefore, the actress is available to anyone who can afford her, like a prostitute.[23]

Prostitutes solicited openly in theatres at the beginning of the period, but this 'scandal to public decency' was halted, or at least greatly diminished, through the efforts of vigilant early Victorian theatre managers such as W. C. Macready and Madame Vestris.[24] Nevertheless, the distinction between playhouse and whorehouse remained problematic even at the end of the nineteenth century. In 1892 the official censor, E. F. S. Pigott, invoked 'order and decency' when he told a parliamentary committee that his duty was to prevent 'turning theatres into disorderly houses, if not houses of ill fame'.[25] The Examiner of Plays – the censor's official title – thus saw himself as being responsible for enforcing the relatively newly drawn boundaries between houses of prostitution and theatres. He believed that interventions on his part were necessary to ensure that playhouses would never again become a site for the buying and selling of women's bodies.

This conflation of acting with prostitution was compounded by a common assumption that the rigours of performance made women of the stage uniquely susceptible to madness. Adelaide Ristori, in her autobiography, reflects on the connections between her work as an actress, her volatile temperament and mental illness:

Sometimes I fell victim to an inexplicable melancholy, which weighed on my heart like lead, and filled my mind with dark thoughts. I believe that this strange inequality of temperament might be entirely attributed to the excessive emotion I experienced in performing my most impassioned parts. For I so entirely identified myself with the characters I represented that, in the

---

[23] Jewsbury, *The Half-Sisters*, II: 18–19.
[24] Archer, 'Drama', II: 569.
[25] *Select Committee on Theatres and Places of Entertainment* (1892), question nos. 5179, 5183.

end, my health began to suffer, and one evening, when I had been acting in *Adrienne Lecouvreur*, the curtain had scarcely fallen after the last act, when the great tension of nerves and mind and body I had undergone during that final scene of passion and delirium brought on a kind of nervous attack, and an affection of the brain which deprived me of consciousness for a good quarter of an hour.[26]

This account by Ristori resembles a scene in actress Anna Cora Mowatt's novel *A Mimic Life* in which a woman playing Ophelia succumbs to the madness of her character – the implication being that the strenuous emotionality of performing might well overwhelm an actress's reason.[27] Ellen Terry, whose own spirits rose and fell between exhilaration and deep depression, visited insane asylums in search of inspiration for the parts she enacted on stage. These forays into madhouses and hospitals, and the self-identification with madness and disease expressed by actresses, suggests that the social formulations linking theatrical women with derangement was being incorporated into the consciousness of individual actresses. In their own outbreaks of 'brain fever', their yearnings and affinities for sickness, actresses sometimes internalized the dominant view that women of the stage represented an irrational or even insane distortion of authentic femininity.

The rhetorical practice that depicted actresses as prostitutes, madwomen and deformed specimens of femininity was contradicted by another discourse, emanating largely from the theatre itself, which brought women of the stage under the auspices of domesticity instead of emphasizing their remoteness from it. Representing the actress as being in harmony with Victorian ideals, refined and respectable, might seem to have worked against the rhetoric of disease and death which also framed performing women throughout the period. In reality, however, these contrasting rhetorics combined as one force to monitor and constrain women of the stage while reinforcing traditional assumptions of male privilege that the very existence of actresses called into question. In the cup-and-saucer comedies of Tom Robertson at the Prince of Wales's Theatre beginning in the 1860s, Marie Bancroft made herself into the young woman of the Victorian home as well as an actress. Playing her signature roles as Naomi Tighe in *School* and Polly Eccles in *Caste*, Bancroft helped to define and sustain femininity as most Victorians came to understand it. Her performances were crucial elements in what Michel Foucault has described as a discourse of power, an activity of regulation through public

---

[26] Ristori, *Studies and Memories*, 12.
[27] Mowatt, *A Mimic Life*, 27, 185.

discussion. Whilst actresses like Bancroft defined gender through their performances, the stage itself was being regulated by a middle-class influence on the
other side of the footlights. Respectable young women were in the audience,
but rarely 'unaccompanied', even late in the century, as Virginia Woolf recol-
lects.[28] Playwrights found themselves writing for chaperoned girls and their
watchful guardians – for middle-class families – thus closing all the more the
gap between the theatre and domestic life.[29]

In such an environment it was tempting for the actress to demonstrate her
solidarity with the audience, charming it into laughter or tears by dramatizing its most cherished ideals. By this scenario the audience overpowered the
actress, rather than, as had been the case with Sarah Siddons, the other way
round. 'Power was seated on her brow', William Hazlitt had written of Siddons,
who dominated the stage with her flashing eyes and clarion voice, spellbinding
her audience and rendering other actors mute when they were supposed to
speak.[30] Power such as this is what Gordon Craig missed in his famous mother
Ellen Terry, the most popular of late Victorian actresses. 'Rather than carry the
public along, or fight it', he complains, 'she would side with the cow-like animal and begin to imitate its face and to drop tears all over the place.' Siddons,
by contrast, 'refused to be dominated' by her audience, refused to be 'made
tearful by it when she was about to scorch and brand it'.[31] From her son's point
of view, Ellen Terry was overcome by the prejudices of an audience she had
the genius, but not the will, to master.

Terry was one of many actresses who, whether consciously or not, performed and thus helped to fashion and reinforce the dominant Victorian ideologies of gender. In the case of Helen Faucit, Macready's leading lady at
Covent Garden Theatre, it was clearly a conscious strategy. For Faucit, the job
of the actress was to help make the stage a moral influence by dramatizing
for audiences 'the types of noble womanly nature as they have been revealed
by our best dramatic poets, and especially by Shakespeare'.[32] She was lauded
by Mrs C. Baron Wilson in *Our Actresses* (1844) for representing 'a feminine
grace and delicacy that deserved the highest applause'.[33] Faucit's husband,
Sir Theodore Martin, writes approvingly that 'people saw in her not only a
great actress, they felt themselves in the presence of one who was herself the

---

[28] Vicinus, *Independent Women*, 146.
[29] William Archer develops this argument in *English Dramatists of To-Day*.
[30] Macqueen-Pope, *Ladies First*, 327–9.
[31] Craig, *Ellen Terry and her Secret Self*, 157.
[32] Martin, *Helen Faucit*, 166.
[33] Wilson, *Our Actresses*, II: 13.

ideal woman of whom poets had written'.[34] The acting style of Helen Faucit was praised as being 'deeply pathetic', emphasizing sympathy, gentleness and tears – the epitome of Victorian womanhood.[35] This 'pathetic' style, even when she was playing Lady Macbeth – dropping tears 'all over the place' – would later define what was termed the 'womanliness' of Ellen Terry on stage and elicit the disgust of her son Gordon Craig, who knew his mother could rise above this type of performance if she would but allow herself to do so.[36]

But Ellen Terry knew what she was doing, and did it purposefully. She 'made them cry as much as I would, and as much as I could', nor was she the only actress to do so. Madge Kendal worried that 'I cry so much that I perhaps do not do my author justice', but reassured herself with the reflection that an actress's job was to dramatize 'sympathy' as a complement to the 'intelligence' supplied by male performers. Kendal, therefore, like Helen Faucit, Ellen Terry and other Victorian star actresses, wanted her acting to exemplify authentic womanliness.[37] Although Florence Nightingale had seen the stage as providing women with an escape from the narrow confines of Victorian femininity, these highly successful actresses actually reinforced the constraints that made other women yearn for the 'freedom' of theatrical life.

Furthermore, it was *only* as actresses that Victorian women could realistically hope to succeed in the theatre. A few women became managers of theatres in spite of the odds against them, and a few wrote plays, especially in the last two decades of the nineteenth century when the number of theatres increased significantly. But women who wanted to be playwrights did not always realize how greatly the odds were stacked against them. Even at the close of the Victorian period Cicely Hamilton wanted more than anything else 'to write a good play', but learned from a male theatre manager that it would be 'advisable to conceal the sex of its author until after the notices were out, as plays which were known to be written by women were apt to get a bad press'.[38] The heroine of a play called *Our Flat* (1889) is an aspiring woman playwright

---

[34] Martin, *Helen Faucit*, 294, 301, 306, 341, 394. Thus the actress becomes involved in what Teresa de Lauretis has called a 'technology of gender' – representing gender in a particular fashion, absorbing that representation subjectively, and disseminating it as a measure of social control (*Technologies of Gender*). The force behind this representation of the female, as Laura Mulvey points out in relation to cinematic narrative, is ultimately masculine, whether in the form of a monitory protagonist, director, spectator, etc., whose 'gaze' determines the shape of the story ('Visual pleasure and narrative cinema').

[35] Mrs Wilson, *Our Actresses*, II: 20.

[36] Craig, *Ellen Terry and her Secret Self*, 157.

[37] Kendal, *Dramatic Opinions*, 78–9, 82.

[38] Hamilton, *Life Errant*, 60.

who signs her first play as a man, hoping to conceal her sex until a contract is signed.[39] A few years after *Our Flat* was staged, Florence Bell and Elizabeth Robins disguised their authorship of *Alan's Wife* from the influential theatre manager Beerbohm Tree, who they hoped would produce it, being well aware of his view that 'women can't write'.[40] The rarity of women playwrights was noted in the popular magazine *All the Year Round*, which drew attention to the fact that two plays by women had been staged at major London theatres in 1894. 'Though we can count women novelists by the score', the anonymous critic observed, 'the number of women dramatists is extremely limited, and can easily be told off on the fingers'.

Although Victorians themselves probably did not recognize it, they actually defined playwriting in such a way as to mark it as distinctively a masculine activity. For example, Frank Archer's practical handbook on playwriting, *How to Write a Good Play* (1892), compares the writing of plays to other endeavours that were, and still are, male-dominated. 'Play-making may not be one of the exact sciences', the author says, 'but it is more nearly allied to them than appears at first sight. It can fairly be described as a sort of *sympathy in mathematics*.' The playwright is, therefore, a kind of architect whose 'constructive ability' arises out of an analytical mind that the Victorians rarely associated with women.[41] This masculinist perspective also finds expression in a story by Henry James, *Nona Vincent*, in which a male playwright discovers that his craft relies upon qualities of 'line and law' that Victorians deemed to be masculine. The 'dramatic form', says James's imaginary dramatist, 'had the high dignity of the exact sciences, it was mathematical and architectural. It was full of the refreshment of calculation and construction.' Women are needed for the 'vulgar' necessity of performance, but in James's world only a man can write a good play.[42] If ever a woman wrote a good play, the fact could be explained from the Victorian point of view by the woman playwright's 'masculine' style. The progressive critic William Archer liked Constance Fletcher's play *Mrs Lessingham* (1894) very much, but wrote, 'it would be a very keen critic who should detect a feminine hand in the workmanship'. In the same fashion the author of an essay entitled 'Women as dramatists' (1894) explains

---

[39] Mrs Musgrave, *Our Flat: Farcical Comedy in Three Acts*, is quoted from the unpaginated licensing ms. in the Lord Chamberlain's Collection. The play was first performed in London at the Prince of Wales's Theatre and was apparently never published.
[40] Letter from Bell to Robins, possibly from November or December 1892, in the Fales Library, New York University.
[41] Archer, *How to Write a Good Play*, 71.
[42] James, 'Nona Vincent', VIII: 157.

the success of Joanna Baillie's writing for the earlier nineteenth-century stage on the basis of the supposed 'masculine' strength and vigour of her prose.[43]

Typical of the Victorians, the anonymous but surely male author of 'Women as dramatists' explains the lack of women playwrights by a constitutional defect that he has observed in women generally. Their use of language is undisciplined, he argues, and their personalities lack the comic sense that most plays require:

> Chiefly, perhaps, because most women are devoid of deep and mirthful humour, and on account of their prolixity of diction and their tendency to introduce an abundance of small irresponsible details into their writings, as witness the lady novelist and her methods, female dramatists have been few and far between, though quite a large number of authoresses have essayed to write for the stage.[44]

Somewhat surprisingly, the success of women in writing novels, the dominant genre of Victorian literature, is offered as the reason for their failure as playwrights. The Victorians had marked the novel as a feminine genre because of its preoccupation with domestic experience and private feeling and its production and consumption in a home setting.[45] But plays which were conspicuously domestic risked not being received as plays at all. Even *A Doll's House* was dismissed by one critic because 'it is as though someone has dramatised the cooking of a Sunday dinner'.[46] There was also the argument that the leisurely pace and undisciplined verbiage of novels allowed their writers to camouflage 'what is so often wanting in the novelist' – namely, knowledge of the world and experience of life.[47]

Except for those occasions – probably numerous – when their dramas were passed off as the work of men, Victorian women who wrote plays competed against male dramatists on an equal basis on only two occasions. Both occasions were open playwriting competitions sponsored by theatre managers in response to charges that in choosing certain dramas for production, they had at the same time consigned to oblivion many excellent unacted plays. Untried women playwrights won both of these open playwriting competitions, one held near the beginning of the Victorian period, the other at the end. Ben Webster – the Haymarket Theatre manager best known for producing plays by himself and men such as Dion Boucicault and John Westland

---

[43] 'Women as dramatists', 300.
[44] 'Female dramatists of the past', 18.
[45] Gail Finney, among others, makes this point; see *Women in Modern Drama*, 17–18.
[46] *Illustrated Sporting and Dramatic News*, 29 June 1889.
[47] *The Stage of 1871*, 15.

Marston – presented a £500 prize in 1844 to Catherine Gore for her play *Quid Pro Quo: or, The Day of Dupes*, which won out over ninety-six other plays sent in anonymously and judged by a special committee.[48] In 1902 the Playgoers' Club staged another open playwriting contest in response to grumblings that the cosy association of actor-managers and 'certain well-known dramatists' made it difficult for new playwrights to get a fair hearing. The most prominent theatre managers of the day, George Alexander and Beerbohm Tree, associated themselves with the playwriting contest and promised to produce the winning play. 'Many hundreds of manuscript plays came pouring by every post into the club letter-box', according to one drama critic, and a special committee was appointed to sit in judgement. In the end the winning play was *The Finding of Nancy* by Netta Syrett, a novelist who was, like most professional women writers, 'absolutely ignorant of the stage'.[49] *The Finding of Nancy* was presented at the St James's Theatre, where it failed miserably, just as Catherine Gore's prize play had done at the Haymarket almost sixty years earlier.

Trying to explain the hostile reception given her play in 1844, Catherine Gore singled out drama critics. Most of them were men and playwrights themselves and, Gore was convinced, would not allow a woman to succeed in playwriting and thus influenced popular opinion against her. A similar fate, after all, had thwarted women dramatists before the Victorian era. Gore pointed out that before the outbreak of resentment against her own play, the theatrical establishment had 'succeeded in condemning the very superior plays of Joanna Baillie, Lady Dacree, and Lady Emmeline Wortley, [and] could scarcely fail to crush any attempt of mine'. Noting that the male critics who condemned her play *Quid Pro Quo* were also, 'almost without exception, rival dramatists', Gore concluded that an outsider, and especially a woman, would not be allowed to succeed as a playwright. Although *Quid Pro Quo* enjoyed some success on stage later on, this development did nothing to change Gore's mind about the formidable obstacles any woman playwright had to overcome.[50]

A few, but very few, plays by women in the Victorian period were popular successes with audiences and critics alike. Perhaps the most successful was *A Mother of Three* (1896), written by a woman who, as the *Times* reported in its obituary of Clo Graves, 'quite early . . . adopted an almost masculine appearance and dress'.[51] This witty farce is most memorable for its representation of a strong mother who claims as her own the rights and responsibilities of

---

[48] This is the account given by Catherine Gore in the preface to *Quid Pro Quo*, iii.
[49] *The Times*, 9 May 1902, 8; Syrett, *Sheltering Tree*, 118.
[50] Gore, preface to *Quid Pro Quo*, v.
[51] 'Miss Clo Graves', 17.

Victorian fatherhood when her husband disappears for a period of years. The scenes which drew the loudest laughter were those in which Fanny Brough disguised herself in a wig and trousers to pass as the father of her three marriageable daughters, thereby providing them a 'certificate of respectability'. The real father returns finally and is awakened to his own 'neglected responsibilities'. Resolving to assist his wife 'in the discharge of her domestic duties', the long-absent father effectively feminizes himself just as his wife had already put on the clothing as well as the responsibilities of a man. Clo Graves's comedy thus concludes with a coordination of masculine and feminine, figured in the masculinized dress and behaviour of her 'mother of three' and the feminization of her neglectful husband.[52] Graves's play could not be contained by what she called, tongue-in-cheek, 'Woman's true sphere', yet press reviews were enthusiastic. Large crowds packed the Comedy Theatre nightly to see the funniest and most popular play ever written by a Victorian woman dramatist, a play long since and unjustly forgotten today.[53]

Another notable but forgotten disruption of business-as-usual in the theatre occurred at the close of the Victorian period with the production of the play by Netta Syrett which won the contest sponsored by the Playgoers' Club, thus duplicating the result of the national playwriting competition of more than a half-century earlier. Just as Catherine Gore had never attempted to write a play before she authored the prize play of 1844, Netta Syrett was an experienced novelist who had never written for the stage. Syrett's play, like Gore's before it, was staged by an all-star cast in a prestigious theatre – the St James's this time – but with results that were dismaying to the playwright. Her play, *The Finding of Nancy* (1902), concerns the cramped life of a lonely single woman who works as a secretary in a business office. 'Or do we and thousands of women like us live at all?' asks the title character Nancy Thistleton. Wanting to live, the title character becomes involved with a married man who is separated from his alcoholic wife. 'I haven't kept the rules of the game', says Nancy Thistleton at the final curtain, but she ends up happily anyway in the arms of her lover.[54]

The play was met with a firestorm of criticism. Clement Scott of the London *Daily Telegraph* called the play immoral and was responsible, according to Netta Syrett herself, for her being fired from her job as a teacher. The *Times* attacked on another front, pointing out with disdain that 'the play is written not only by a lady – Miss Netta Syrett – but for ladies'. The reviewer was astonished

---

[52] Graves, *A Mother of Three*, 18, 63, 65.
[53] *Sketch*, 15 August 1896.
[54] Syrett, *The Finding of Nancy*, never published, is quoted from the licensing manuscript in the Lord Chamberlain's Collection of the British Library, 7, 8, 54.

that Syrett could ever imagine an audience would be interested in the subject matter of her play, or that 'the thing we want most to hear about, and that we go the play to see, is the career of woman'. The *Times* admitted that it is natural – 'perhaps almost inevitable' – that a woman writer should take this outlook, 'but it is a mistake nevertheless'. To the *Era*, on the other hand, *The Finding of Nancy* demonstrated that actor-managers were after all the best judges of what was good drama and what was not. Their motives in selecting plays for production might be self-interested, but if *The Finding of Nancy* was any indication, it seemed unlikely that there were any unacted masterpieces that the actor-managers had overlooked. Overwhelmed by this hostile reaction, Syrett returned to the writing of novels with the conviction that a woman could not make her way in the theatre as a playwright.[55]

Despite the institutional prejudice that barred most women of the theatre from writing or producing plays, there was a critical moment in the 1890s when masculine control of the theatre seemed to be endangered. Elizabeth Robins, an actress born in Ohio, was the key figure in this struggle for control of the London stage. Starting a new career for herself in London in the late 1880s, Robins realized in her own experience the obstacles that Victorian women encountered whenever they performed on stage, wrote plays or tried to become 'actress-manageresses'. Out of her disappointments arose Robins's vision of a radical 'Theatre of the Future' in which gender discrimination would be set aside. Women would be free to realize their potential in the theatre, and this new standard of equality would raise the level of English drama as a whole and increase its value to society. These reforming ideas had an impact in the early to middle 1890s, so much so that Robins and like-minded women seemed for a while in a position to challenge the male-dominated theatrical establishment. Bernard Shaw recognized clearly enough what was happening: 'we are on the verge of something like a struggle between the sexes for the dominion of the London theatres', he wrote in 1895, suggesting that women like Robins, Florence Farr, Janet Achurch and others represented the tide of the future.[56]

Towards their revolutionary goal, Robins and another transplanted American actress, Marion Lea, formed what they called the 'Joint Management' for mounting their own productions. It was meant to be a first step towards the visionary theatre that Robins had in mind – one with independent management and high artistic standards, cooperative rather than competitive, and freed from

---

[55] Syrett, *Sheltering Tree*, 119, 126.
[56] Shaw, preface to Archer's *Theatrical 'World' of 1894*.

the economy of self-interest which regulated the theatres and national life as a whole. The first English-language production of Ibsen's *Hedda Gabler* was the Joint Management's most notable achievement. But any hope that the impact of *Hedda Gabler* would transform the theatre world was soon defeated. Despite the notoriety that she had earned in her brilliant acting of the title role and as the producer of *Hedda Gabler*, Robins was dismayed not only to find the theatre as resistant as ever to significant change, but also to discover that although she and Marion Lea were receiving offers to perform, they were 'not such parts as we had in mind – but pretty little dears however much they were called heroines or "leading parts"'.[57] At the end of the manuscript of her memoir *Whither and How*, Robins added these frustrated comments in the margins:

> Marion Lea and I had started out to do something that hadn't ever been tried before, never realising the peril of this, a peril the more should the first steps show marked success . . . Offers of engagements under regular managers began to flow in. The first on record I refused to go further with, because I knew to what a blind alley it would lead. All the theatres then were either frankly commercial like the Adelphi, or commercial in disguise, & without exception were under the management of men . . . Men who wrote plays for women had long been seeing that they simply had little or no chance of being acted.[58]

With that recognition, Robins writes, 'a helplessness and depression fell upon me, for I saw what I was facing'. The 'rational Theatre' of her hopes was no nearer now than before, notwithstanding the success of *Hedda Gabler*.

Finding few or no 'plays for women', or by women either, Robins determined to write them herself. With her friend Florence Bell she wrote *Alan's Wife* (1893), the story of a working-class woman who justifies and even celebrates her murder of her sick child as the kindest, strongest and most courageous action of her life. Even Bernard Shaw was made uncomfortable by the central character of the play, so unlike the drawing-room heroines who populated his own early reformist dramas. Beerbohm Tree, to whom Robins once read the play in the hope he would produce it at the Haymarket Theatre, told her that 'it would be too horrible, too gruesome' for him to think of staging.[59] Only J. T. Grein's Independent Theatre would agree to produce *Alan's Wife*, and even under Grein's progressive, non-commercial management it closed prematurely after only two matinées.[60]

---

[57] Robins, 'Heights and depths', ms., Fales Library, New York University.
[58] Robins, 'Odd bits'.
[59] Letter from Bell to Robins (1892), ms., Fales Library, New York University.
[60] *Alan's Wife* was published with an introduction by William Archer (1893).

Another remarkable play by Robins, *The Mirkwater*, was turned down by George Alexander and several other leading actor-managers and was never produced or published despite Robins's high hopes for it. The heroine has assisted in the suicide of her incurably ill sister, a victim of breast cancer. She is arrested for murder at the final curtain, but despite her 'crime' has earned the sympathy of the audience – or would have, if the play had ever had an audience. Another daring play for its time, *The Silver Lotus*, was written by Robins in the mid-1890s and met with the same fate as its predecessor, *The Mirkwater*. It concerns a young mother driven to alcoholism by the death of her children and the indifference of her husband. Rejecting the usual theatrical depictions of women as ingenues or shrews, Robins's doomed plays brought forward complex women who had other things than men on their minds. They struggled with alcoholism and breast cancer, with suicide and sickness, and in moments of crisis these transgressive women were strong enough to kill. These plays remain virtually unproduced and mostly unpublished – monuments to the difficulties that overwhelmed women playwrights when they wrote unconventional heroines into their works. The theatre as it was in the Victorian period, even at the end of the period, had no place for them.

Robins was perhaps the most important of several women revolutionaries of the theatre – including Eleanor Calhoun, Florence Farr and Janet Achurch – but by the mid 1890s she had grown weary of 'battering at the door' of an institution which resisted her best efforts at reform. It had been different earlier in that crucial decade when she was planning with Marion Lea the 'wild projects' of their Joint Management in a confident assault on the economic and gender injustices of the Victorian theatre. Her feminist critique of the institution pointed towards a new kind of theatre, one in which profit would not be a motive, or even a concern – a theatre in which actresses and plays would be regarded from a perspective that valued aesthetic and social worth rather than their economic use to a small number of powerful men who ran the existing playhouses. She could foresee 'a Theatre we can worship' springing up from the ashes of an unjust and exhausted 'Theatre as it is.'[61] But for Robins and her sister revolutionaries of the theatre that day of reckoning would never be realized. It would remain an unfulfilled dream, and indeed to a large extent remains one today.

[61] Robins, 'Whither and how', chap. 2, 9.

17

Popular entertainment, 1776–1895

DAVE RUSSELL

'Popular entertainment' is used in this chapter as a convenient label for the music hall, circus, fairground amusements and other performance-centred spectacles which, while often overlapping and cross-fertilizing with the 'legitimate theatre', essentially ran parallel to it and were broadly distinguishable as separate entities by contemporary observers. The chapter is concerned with the growth, increasing specialization and impact of commercial amusements in general and the music hall, the most dynamic and influential element of the nineteenth-century popular stage, in particular. It begins, however, with two cautionary notes.

The focus on commercial entertainment results only from spatial constraint. Particularly from about 1850 and most noticeably in smaller towns and villages, Britain possessed a rich and dense amateur cultural life enabling thousands of performers from a wide variety of social backgrounds to amuse their communities in settings from parlour to concert hall. This cultural voluntarism vastly increased the opportunities available to contemporary audiences and indeed, for some genres, provided the major source of supply. Notwithstanding the efforts of D'Oyly Carte, Gilbert and Sullivan operetta owed much of its popularity to amateur performance, as in Hanley, Staffordshire, where a series of amateur productions attracted 15,000 people during a six-day run in 1896.[1] Amateur activities also produced 'casual labour' for the professional stage, as exemplified by the use of children in pantomime-ballets and spectacles, and acted as a training ground for future professionals and the thousands of semi-professionals so crucial to the entertainment industry; Harry Lauder was only the best-known music hall star to receive a stage education in amateur concert parties. Overall, an amateur tradition embracing music, drama, the toy theatre, blackface minstrelsy and much else besides made a varied and vital

---

[1] *Musical Herald* (August 1896).

contribution to nineteenth-century cultural life. Its exclusion here should not deter others from giving it the serious consideration it still generally lacks.

The second point flows from Hugh Cunningham's shrewd assessment of popular leisure in the period 1780–1840:

> Historians with an apparently insatiable compulsion to compartmentalise have seen these different forms of entertainment in isolation one from the other – there are histories of sport, of drama, of the pantomime, and of the circus. Yet what is most striking is the connections between these different forms of entertainment, connections so strong that one can speak of this world of entertainment as part of one close-knit popular culture.[2]

The urge to compartmentalize is, of course, an understandable and necessary element of the theatre historian's project, while real divisions, sometimes fiercely defended, did exist. For these reasons, and for the less honourable one of organizational simplicity, this chapter often treats popular entertainments as discrete forms. However, there is much to be gained in emphasizing the essential unity of the field of popular entertainment, particularly before 1840 but, in many senses, right through to 1914 and beyond.

The mutability of the boundaries between cultural forms certainly allowed remarkable flexibility between various performance types. Between 1848 and 1853, for example, brothers George and John Sanger ran in swift succession a booth featuring conjuring tricks and performing birds and mice, a magic lantern show, a penny gaff and, finally, a very small circus.[3] Later, performers crossed into the music hall from every imaginable location. For circus artists, such as juggler Paul Cinquevalli, or acrobats such as the Brothers Griffith, the move involved little more than a relocation of skills, but, for those such as Albert Chevalier, James Fawn, Charles Godfrey and Marie Kendall who moved from the 'legitimate' stage to become music hall singers, it necessitated a more thorough reorientation. Those who in various ways serviced popular entertainment had to show equal opportunism. In a career covering the second half of the century, Bradford-born musician John Dodsworth conducted in music halls and theatres, conducted and composed for brass bands and played in concert orchestras, enjoying a brief spell with the prestigious Manchester-based Hallé in the late 1860s. The rather better-known Charles Morton, founder of the Canterbury and Oxford Music Halls, was at various times also a publican, a theatre owner and manager, the proprietor

---

[2] Cunningham, *Leisure in the Industrial Revolution*, 35.
[3] Speaight, *A History of the Circus*, 50.

of a pleasure garden and manager of a light opera company.[4] Performers also had to be flexible in terms of venue. Punch and Judy men, for example, had largely moved from the fairground to the street in the early nineteenth century, but the growth of the children's Christmas party, the seaside holiday and the music hall from the mid-nineteenth century gave new opportunities for the more highly capitalized.[5] Such easy movement represents only one aspect of popular entertainment's coalescence. Performers from different sectors often socialized together, particular pubs becoming popular haunts for 'theatricals' of all description, and shared elements of the trade press and other professional services. They were often bound together, too, by shared social stigma and opposition to their calling. When, in 1851, a correspondent for a provincial paper criticized early music hall for its 'representations of a debasing and lust-serving order', he pointedly extended his strictures to the theatre and circus.[6] Whilst one sector was often quietly pleased at the embarrassment of another, common enemies gave unity of a sort.

Popular entertainment: range and growth

In the late eighteenth century commercial popular entertainment was most accessible to the 30 per cent of the population that lived in towns, London, housing 8 per cent of Britain's population in 1801, offering the greatest riches. Larger population centres obviously proved attractive to proprietors, and the theatre, concert hall, fairground, pleasure garden, public house, perhaps the circus and certainly street entertainment would have been familiar in most large towns. Urban Britain was certainly more likely to enjoy regular and varied fare than its rural counterpart, which generally enjoyed a more episodic pattern of cultural consumption, built around annual fairs and feasts. Although some of the labouring classes, especially young men in skilled trades, could afford regular access to a range of amusements, and many others made it their business to enjoy feasts and holidays, not all of these activities were widely available. It was those slightly higher in the social scale who were undoubtedly the major beneficiaries of the commercialization of leisure that was such a feature of the period from the later seventeenth century.

---

[4] *Bradford Weekly Telegraph*, 2 September 1910; Morton and Newton, *Sixty Years' Stage Service*.
[5] Byrom, *Punch and Judy*; Leach, *Punch and Judy Show*.
[6] *Leeds Mercury*, 10 January 1852. The resources available to students of popular entertainment can also provide a certain satisfying unity. The National Fairground Archive at the University of Sheffield is exceptionally rich in this regard.

In terms of basic content, there was considerable continuity between this popular entertainment of the later eighteenth century and its late Victorian equivalent. The Urma Acrobatic Trio, the juggler Marvello, the skipping rope-dancer Rose Finette, female tumblers Letta and Minnie and the Bostons theatrical troupe, all visitors to one provincial hall in 1895, would have held no major surprises for audiences of a century (or even several centuries) earlier who visited pleasure grounds, watched the 'outside shows' which tempted people into the travelling theatre booth or patronized fairground stalls.[7] Even the comic singer, the definitive product of the nineteenth-century music hall, was prefigured in earlier decades. Similarly, until the 1860s and indeed beyond, there was also a considerable degree of continuity in terms of the venues in which entertainments were consumed. Crucial in this context was the continued importance of the street and other public spaces. Street performers proffered a full range of entertainment from acrobatics to Shakespearean rendition and from blackface minstrelsy to the German band. They were a vital source of entertainment for the poor and remained so well into the twentieth century, although better-off neighbourhoods were also visited: mathematician Charles Babbage, a virulent enemy of street music, claimed to have been visited on 165 occasions in a ten-month period in 1860–61.[8]

What, then, had changed? In terms of the scale of popular amusements, four interrelated processes, especially powerful from about the 1840s, can be identified: a massive increase in the amount of entertainment available; a much enlarged audience and a widening of its social base; a far greater regularity of attendance; and an expansion in the number of permanent venues. In Newcastle, for example, the period 1840–70 alone saw the emergence of four music halls, a second theatre to rival the Theatre Royal and the establishment of much enlarged circus and concert seasons.[9] Obviously, the exact nature, chronology and extent of increased patronage varied substantially according to geographical location. London's distinctive role as entertainment centre allowed for the development of highly specialized venues, such as Bullock's Museum and Exhibition Hall, opened in 1812 and which, under a variety of names, became the key centre for entertainments by magicians such as David Devant. Perhaps the most dramatic metropolitan venture was Olympia, the giant exhibition hall and grounds opened in 1884. When Buffalo Bill's 'Wild West Show' appeared

---

[7] *Bradford Daily Telegraph*, 5 February to 12 March 1895.
[8] Cohen and Greenwood, *Buskers*, 151.
[9] Barker, 'Performing arts in Newcastle upon Tyne', 64–7.

in 1887, viewing space was available for 40,000.[10] Similarly, individual types of, and venues for, popular amusement enjoyed very different life cycles. Some simply declined over the period. The fair was undermined from a number of different directions in the nineteenth century, and, for all its impressive urban resilience, numbers certainly fell in the rural south. Many showpeople, therefore, had to find new outlets or cease work altogether. This process only added to the problems of the travelling theatre which, although still a feature in some rural areas well into the twentieth century, was proving harder to sustain from the 1850s and 1860s as permanent venues began to attract audiences. The pleasure garden, one of the most dynamic features of the London recreational environment in the late eighteenth and early nineteenth centuries, was in terminal decline by the 1850s. Although some provincial gardens prospered, notably the sixty-acre site at Belle Vue, Manchester, famed for its spectacular pyrodramas, a combination of moral reform and the demand for building land proved disastrous: none of the sixty or more London gardens survived beyond the 1870s.[11] Overarching all these various separate histories, however, is the central fact of expansion.

Perhaps the most striking aspect of popular entertainment, itself a function of this great growth, was the increasing degree of specialization. For all the overlaps noted before, the period saw increasingly distinctive entertainment types emerge from the eclectic offerings of the eighteenth-century fairground, public house and pleasure garden. The first was the circus, usually seen as the creation of ex-army horse-breaker Philip Astley who, with his wife, began displays of trick-riding in a roped off enclosure on the south bank of the Thames in 1768, before opening Astley's Amphitheatre as a permanent site in 1769. Astley's contribution was to marry well-established equestrian display with other acts, including rope-walkers, dancing monkeys and a 'learned pig', to create a new and distinctive blend.[12] By the early nineteenth century a network of permanent and semi-permanent circus buildings existed in the major urban centres, with capacities as high as 3,000; over the course of the century London had nineteen such buildings, with three still in existence in 1890, while Liverpool had fifteen and Bristol ten. From about the early 1840s, the 'big top' became a feature of the travelling companies. The circus's exhibition of human skill and exotic animal life gave it a quasi-educational air, which promoters were quick to emphasize. Royal patronage – Queen Victoria saw

---

[10] Mander and Mitchenson, *Victorian and Edwardian Entertainment*, illustration 101; *Illustrated London News*, 16 April 1887.
[11] Mayer, 'World on fire'; Wroth, *London Pleasure Gardens*, xi–xiv, 11.
[12] Speaight, *History of the Circus*, 24–8, 31–47.

the American lion tamer Isaac Van Amburgh seven times during his London visit of 1838 – provided a valuable social cachet, and the circus was able to attract socially mixed audiences across the century.[13] By the late century, by which time it had a large enough pool of artists to allow individual circuses, like music halls, to change acts regularly, it had matured into an important sector of the entertainment industry and one increasingly dominated by large companies capable of generating substantial profits.[14]

A second emergent form was the circus's close relative, the touring menagerie or 'wild beast show'. Such shows had existed on a small scale from the early eighteenth century, but really came of age in 1805 when Soho bootmaker George Wombwell began the first major travelling company. At his death in 1850 Wombwell had three touring shows, the largest of which comprised some forty vans, and several rival companies, including Bostock's, Chipperfield's and Hilton's, also worked on a grand scale.[15] Like the circus, the menagerie was generally deemed respectable and improving, and on Womb-well's death the *Times* claimed that 'no one probably did more to bring forward the study of natural history among the masses'. His educational reputation was further enhanced by the exceptionally high quality of the bands he, and indeed some other circus and menagerie proprietors, used to advertise their shows; one provincial paper noted enthusiastically 'the splendid selection of sacred and operatic music played by Wombwell's band' during a visit in 1851. The mantle of rational recreation helped protect him at odd moments of controversy, as when one of his baboons escaped in Glasgow and caused con-sternation by visiting a church and then a pub or, more seriously, when, in 1825, public opinion turned against him for allowing a lion to be baited by fighting dogs.[16]

Whilst many entrepreneurs claimed (sometimes justifiably) an educational dimension for their products, rational recreation itself did actually provide yet another distinctive set of new popular amusements. Some were overtly commercial in organization. The diorama show, featuring the unfurling of an elaborately painted back-cloth depicting scenes drawn from historical, geo-graphical or contemporary political situations, was important here. The most important element, however, was the public lecture. Although never conceived as commercial ventures by the mechanics institutes, working men's improve-ment societies and other educational entities that made such use of them,

---

[13] Ibid., 189–96, 41, 81–2.
[14] Cunningham, *Leisure in the Industrial Revolution*, 173; Speaight, *History of the Circus*, 50–1.
[15] Beaver, *Spice of Life*, 36–8.
[16] Ritvo, *Animal Estate*, p. 215; *Leeds Intelligencer*, 6 December 1851; Ritvo, *Animal Estate*, 225.

speakers were often paid fees, entrance charges were sometimes made and, crucially, audiences clearly sought enjoyment alongside elucidation. In 1850 a lecture entitled 'Astronomy and Natural Philosophy' at the Bradford Mechanics Institute was so well attended that the audience's breath condensed on the lecturer's slides and rendered some of them illegible. The local press, although delighted with the attendance, criticized some of the audience for showing approval by whistling and raising 'clouds of dust by useless stamping . . . and in a variety of other ways to annoy quiet and well-behaved people, by making them feel as if they were in the purlieus of a beer-garden, or the tap-room of a public house'.[17]

Concert life, the final area of new growth to be considered, was remarkably diverse. The concert was a well-established part of élite culture by the end of the eighteenth century, but in various forms it came to pervade British social life.[18] The 1840s and 1850s were especially important, witnessing the growth of concerts with minimum admission prices of between 3d and 1s, according to location and quality. Unsurprisingly, London offered the biggest choice of events, while Manchester, at the centre of a particularly well-populated hinterland and blessed from 1858 with the presence of Charles Hallé's symphony orchestra, was probably the leading provincial concert centre. In just one month of 1891, for example, during the late century peak of concert activity, the local press recorded eighteen events involving professional musicians, many of them coming under the umbrella of one of the five fortnightly concert series then operating in the city. Amateur orchestras and choirs, of course, filled the gap in many places. Whatever the source, the public performance of music was at the core of popular entertainment.

Numerous factors facilitated these related processes of growth and specialization. The simple facts of population growth and increased urbanization were certainly central in expanding the potential audience base. Between 1801 and 1891 the population of Great Britain (excluding Ireland) rose from 10.7 million to 33.1 million and the percentage of (English and Welsh) town-dwellers increased from 33 per cent to 75 per cent, with 48 per cent living in towns with populations of over 50,000 by 1891.[19] Given the largely working-class nature of this latent public, however, significant changes in the supply of both spare time and disposable income were necessary if it was to translate into a real one. It is dangerous to make generalizations about these issues across a period too long and too complex to characterize neatly. Suffice it to say that, gradually

---

[17] *Bradford Observer*, 17 October 1850.
[18] Russell, *Popular Music in England*.
[19] Mathias, *First Industrial Nation*, 415.

from the 1850s and more rapidly from the early 1870s, increasingly large sections of the working class enjoyed a (reduced) 54- to 56-hour working week, with the new hours of leisure increasingly concentrated into clear blocks on Saturday afternoons and, crucially, in the evenings. Alongside this, it has been suggested that between 1850 and 1900 real wages rose by about 80 per cent, with perhaps 40 per cent of that increase coming in the 1890s. This proved a crucial, perhaps the crucial, stimulus to the entertainment industry.[20] The 'communications revolution' of the nineteenth century in the form of the great expansion of the press and improvements in transport, represents a further significant contextual factor. It is indeed difficult to envisage the emergence of a national popular entertainment industry, so often dependent on the rapid movement of performers around the country, without the railway network. Cultural change also played a part alongside this raft of economic factors. Perhaps most important, and for the 'legitimate theatre' as much as the wider field of popular entertainment, was the emergence of a more liberal theology in the final decades of the century, placing rather less emphasis on hell and damnation and allowing for the possibility of pleasure being seen as an acceptable, even necessary and valuable experience.[21] Freed from the tight restraints imposed by high Victorian religious sensibilities, the younger generation in particular could contemplate popular amusements more sympathetically.

All of these various 'demand side' factors, however, only identify a context in which ever larger numbers could become potential consumers of popular entertainment; the decision to cross the threshold of the music hall, circus or other form of entertainment depended on the nature of the product supplied. Here, the inventiveness, open-mindedness and resilience of the amusement entrepreneur, ultimately the final arbiter in the making, holding and expanding of audiences, was utterly crucial. It is in the history of the music hall that the processes of entrepreneurial initiative are most visible and instructive.

Music hall

The music hall was both the most significant of the new specialized entertainment forms of the nineteenth century, a fertile source of new performance genres and styles that penetrated deep into the wider Victorian popular culture, and the junction point of virtually all previous genres of popular amusement. The crucial figure in its emergence was the publican. Musical entertainment,

---

[20] Cunningham, 'Leisure and culture'.
[21] McCleod, *Religion and Class in a Late Victorian City*, 246.

whether provided by customers performing in turn in a 'free and easy', or by itinerant musicians, had long been part of public house culture. From the early 1830s, under commercial pressure from the newly created beerhouses on the one hand and the emergent temperance movement on the other, some licensees offered more formal entertainment provided (usually) by professional or semi-professional entertainers and often located in a separate room. There was no single originator of music hall; it was, rather, the collective product of publican-entrepreneurs working along similar lines in major urban centres all over Britain and shaping the entertainment to fit local need.[22] One of the first ventures was undertaken by Thomas Sharples in Bolton, Lancashire, who opened a concert-room at the Millstone Inn in 1832. In 1840 the venue was moved to the Star Inn and eventually had a capacity of 1,000; a picture gallery, a museum and menagerie were swiftly added to its attractions. By the end of the decade a number of towns in the north and the Midlands had strong concert-room traditions, one survey of Liverpool listing thirty-two public houses offering such entertainment and providing employment for over two hundred people.[23] London was inevitably a major centre, and, in the British Saloon, opened next to the Bunch of Grapes on Southwark Bridge Road in 1840, it possibly had the first concert-room built separately from public house premises.[24]

The early halls went under a variety of names, including 'singing saloon' and 'casino', but by the late 1850s 'music hall', a suitably refined designation then more normally associated with the art music tradition, seems to have become the norm. It is at this point that large-scale halls such as Wilton's (1856), the London Pavilion and the Oxford (both 1861) begin to appear in London's West End and in the centres of many major provincial cities, aiming not merely at a relatively well-defined local clientèle but also at a wider audience. By 1866 it was estimated that London possessed thirty-three halls with an average capacity of 1,500.[25] Noting the complete halt of theatre building in London between 1843 and 1866, Michael Booth has suggested that the 'reasons for this cessation are to be found outside the theatre, in the depressed economy and the preponderance of slumps over booms'. However, the spurt of music hall building suggests other possibilities, not least the announcement of its first major challenge to the theatre as a centre of popular entertainment. The

---

[22] Bailey, 'Making sense of music hall', viii–xxiii; Kift, *Victorian Music Hall*; Russell, *Popular Music in England*, 83–167; Stuart and Park, *Variety Stage*.

[23] Poole, *Popular Leisure and the Music Hall*, 51–61; Kift, *Victorian Music Hall*, 80–7; Razzell and Wainwright, eds., *Victorian Working Class*, 280–2.

[24] Earl, 'Music hall at the Grape Tavern'.

[25] *Select Committee on Theatres and Places of Entertainment*, 1866, appendix 3.

same period also saw music hall beginning to acquire the trappings of an emergent industry in the form of a trade press, professional bodies such as the London Music Hall Proprietors' Protection Society and a service sector; the first booking agency, for example, was founded in 1858.[26]

Most important of all, music hall began to produce the first stars and the first products which defined it as a distinctive cultural force and not merely an amalgam of pre-existing forms and styles. Most of its artists in the 1840s and 1850s, whether they were singers or circus-style performers, were known to audiences from other venues and performed familiar material and routines. Indeed, the fare at early halls was probably indistinguishable from much on offer at many pleasure gardens, saloon theatres and the so-called 'penny gaffs', the cheap, usually unlicensed theatres that were such a feature of the East End of London and major provincial locations.[27] Although the Theatre Regulation Act of 1843 attempted to draw a clear line between legitimate theatre and other popular entertainment by banning smoking and the drinking of alcohol in the auditorium during theatrical performances, its impact on the content of programmes was only gradual and partial. In the mid-1860s, however, with the advent of the so-called 'swell songs' and their exponent, the 'lion comique', the halls had their first distinctive stars. The most notable were George Leybourne, famed for 'Champagne Charlie' (1866), the Great Vance, Harry Rickards and Arthur Lloyd. Fashionably attired, they sang songs that were part celebration of upper-class male lifestyle, part satire on the pretensions of the working- and lower-middle-class 'counterfeit' swells in their audience. They set, in Peter Bailey's words, 'a new standard of comic realism' and did so to tunes written by a new generation of songwriters which made skilful use of polka and waltz rhythms, particularly in the now crucially important chorus, to create an increasingly recognizable music hall style.[28] As the century progressed, male impersonators, 'eccentric' comedians, coster serenaders, imperial balladeers and a range of other characters emerged to give the halls an ever clearer and distinctive feel.

Whilst singers (and not exclusively comic singers) probably comprised about half of a typical music hall programme until the late 1890s, the halls also gave room to every conceivable style of the circus-type entertainment – performing animals, strongmen, acrobats – that were to become ever more important in its *fin de siècle* and Edwardian variety phase. Music hall always offered some art

---

[26] Booth, *Theatre in the Victorian Age*, 7; Cunningham, *Leisure in the Industrial Revolution*, 169–70.
[27] Springhall, *Youth, Popular Culture and Moral Panics*, 11–37.
[28] Bailey, 'Champagne Charlie'; Bennett, 'Music in the halls'.

music in the form of popular classical selections and overtures at the beginning of the evening and also provided a home for ballet, doing much to keep the art alive in Britain following its loss of favour in the theatre and opera house from the late 1840s. In London, where the marketplace was substantial enough to allow for the emergence of specialized music halls, the Alhambra (1860) and the Empire, Leicester Square (1884), made ballet their central feature. It was the supposed link between the dress of the dancers, the consequently aroused sexual desire of male patrons and the presence of prostitutes along the theatre's promenade that made the Empire the focus of a famed attack by purity campaigners in 1894.[29]

The sketch, a short playlet of anywhere between ten and forty minutes in length, provided a final and increasingly important element. Although various types of dramatic entertainment were offered from the very beginning, the sketch became an established part of the programme from the late 1870s onwards, its new importance probably representing an attempt to elevate music hall's status during one of the periodic attacks on its moral tone.[30] The sketch was the source of a controversy that bedevilled music hall from the 1850s up until just before the First World War and which produced the period's most intense conflict between the legitimate theatre and the popular stage. As noted, the theatrical legislation of 1843 prohibited dramatic performance in a place where drink was served during the performance, but the nascent music hall industry, especially in the capital, challenged this almost from the outset. Although provincial halls were sometimes pulled into this controversy, from as early as the 1860s many of the more adventurous owners successfully obtained dramatic licences from local magistrates – often against much opposition from theatrical interests – which allowed sketches to be performed legally. Some halls even chose to offer different types of entertainment at different times; Pullan's in Bradford, for example, offered music hall and melodrama on alternate weeks in the late 1870s. In London, however, the sheer scale of theatrical enterprise and the consequent competitive edge between theatre and music hall made such accommodation impossible and legal action a likelihood. Charles Morton found himself the (willing) defendant in a series of high-profile court cases brought by theatre managers between 1856 and 1865.[31] The 1866 Parliamentary Select Committee on Theatrical Licensing was called largely to address this issue, and it heard the two sides present essentially straightforward

[29] Guest, *Ballet in Leicester Square*; Tracy C. Davis, 'Moral sense of the majorities', 45.
[30] *Report from the Select Committee on Theatres and Places of Entertainment* (1892), evidence of James Graydon [2898].
[31] Morton and Newton, *Sixty Years' Stage Service*, 48–51; Kift, *Victorian Music Hall*, 140–3.

economic arguments about the impact of 'free trade' in the theatre with skilfully constructed if sometimes overwrought moral rationalization. Whilst
music hall's advocates, which included Dion Boucicault, asked permission to
educate its audience through the performance of dramatic interludes, theatre
managers stressed the industry's lack of respectability and dismissed the possibility of 'the elevation of the public by music halls'. 'It is degrading', Adelphi
theatre manager Ben Webster asserted, 'to act before such a class of people as
prefer drinking and smoking to the intellectual amusement of the drama'.[32]
Although the committee found for the halls, no legislative action followed,
nor did it after another committee reached broadly similar conclusions in 1892.
An uneasy truce was reached in 1896, when theatrical managers agreed not to
prosecute their rival managers, provided that only one sketch of a maximum
of thirty minutes and with a maximum cast of six was performed per night,
but there were regular transgressions, which were periodically drawn to the
magistracy's attention.[33] It was not until 1912 that the issue was finally settled,
when the Lord Chamberlain's Office announced that stage play licences would
be given to music halls in his jurisdiction under the broad terms of the 1896
agreement.[34]

In terms of both style and content, many sketches were barely distinguishable from the melodramas that were a staple of the nineteenth-century theatre.
An ever-growing number, however, were comic in nature and effectively gave
birth, if not to a new genre of stage entertainment then to one that blended
the techniques and conventions of pantomime, farce and music hall comedy
to create an interesting hybrid.[35] They had their greatest impact in terms of
the influence wrought on early film comedy. Interestingly, although a small
number of sketches were sent to the Lord Chamberlain for licensing, the tendency of music hall to avoid problems by not looking for them, together with
the Lord Chamberlain's shortage of staff, meant that most were not. As late
as 1909, George Redford, the Examiner of Plays since 1895, could cheerfully
claim that 'the music halls ignore us, and we ignore them'.[36]

The growth of music hall was by no means uncontested. Apart from anxious
theatrical managers, the industry was faced from the beginning with recreational reformers convinced that it was 'dangerous to the habits and morals of
the people'.[37] Its close links with the drink trade and its attraction of prostitutes,

---

[32] Report from the Select Committee on Theatrical Licences and Regulations (1866), [2953].
[33] Report from the Joint Select Committee on Stage Plays (1909), xv–xvi.
[34] Era, 13 January 1912.
[35] Rutherford, '"Harmless nonsense"'.
[36] Joint Select Committee on Stage Plays (1909), [463].
[37] Leeds Intelligencer, 20 December 1851.

the perceived lewdness of some of its performers and its popularity with large numbers of young and boisterous members of the working class were the major sources of grievance. As Dagmar Kift has shown in an exemplary study of provincial music hall, the exact make-up of the opposition groupings and the extent to which these general concerns translated into effective action against the halls varied considerably according to local circumstance.[38] Individual halls were closed, and as the century progressed life certainly became ever harder for the smaller public house halls; a number of these fell easy prey to the newly established London County Council, the licensing agency for London under the 1888 Local Government Act, between 1889 and 1891.[39]

Overall, however, it is the music hall's capacity for survival and expansion that impresses. Magistrates and senior police officials were not always convinced that the supposed level of moral degeneration was large enough to warrant an attack on property rights, while many believed the halls to be at best well run or, at worst, a useful focal point where potential and actual troublemakers could be corralled and kept under the law's gaze. Most important of all to the halls' survival, however, were the changes made within the industry. Early proprietors often wrapped their product in the language of rational recreation, arguing that music hall reduced drunkenness, minimized opportunities for political discussion amongst working men, allowed husbands and wives to take their recreation together and much else. These were not empty claims: many reasonably dispassionate middle-class observers supported them in varying degree. However, if the industry was to expand it had to reach new audiences, unattracted by the halls in their existing form. The initial audience for music hall obviously varied to some extent according to location.[40] In London, there were sufficient venues to allow for some halls to develop a distinctive social tone, whereas in the provinces, social differentiation tended to accord with seat prices within a single venue or small number of halls. Generally, however, the music hall audience can be characterized as largely young, particularly in the gallery, which tended to be dominated by those between about 14 and 21 years of age; predominantly male, although young unmarried or recently married working-class women did attend quite frequently; and working-class, although its poorest sections were probably largely excluded on economic grounds. Other social groups were certainly represented, from 'bohemian' army officers, medical students and city gentlemen to shopkeepers, tradesmen and their wives, who took up some of the better seats in halls

---

[38] Kift, *Victorian Music Hall*, 77–134.
[39] Summerfield, 'Effingham Arms and the Empire', 216–18; Kift, *Victorian Music Hall*, 161–71.
[40] Kift, *Victorian Music Hall*, 62–74.

all over the country. However, the key to profit maximization lay in attracting that large body of 'respectable' society spanning the upper working class to the middle reaches of the middle class, which had previously largely eschewed the halls.

Managements took up this challenge from the 1880s, building luxurious and often exotically decorated 'theatres of variety', policing the moral tone of the entertainments, increasing the number of sketches, 'circus' and novelty acts at the expense of the comic singer and seeking to contain the more vociferous aspects of audience behaviour. Women, a sizeable potential audience and also one which would confer respectability on proceedings, were targeted with especial enthusiasm. The main thrust for these changes came from younger owner-managers such as Edward Moss, Oswald Stoll, Thomas Barrasford and Frank Macnaghten, who had learnt their trade in the provinces and in Scotland and Wales, and who appreciated that profitable mass entertainment demanded a product which gave the minimum offence to the maximum number. Although still utilizing the language of rational recreation, they played a key role in legitimating what Peter Bailey has called 'a more overt and unconditional hedonism . . . [a] reconception of leisure in more modern terms as a consumer's entitlement rather than a worker's reward'.[41] In all these ways, they engineered the process that saw 'music hall' evolve into 'variety' and become an embracing national institution increasingly able to cross class boundaries and to construct a shared comic lingua franca. This process only reached full fruition in the Edwardian period, at the same moment when a variety theatre building boom increased the industry's reach still further.[42] Nevertheless, by the 1890s, because of the pace of change in the industry, as important a decade on the popular stage as in legitimate theatre, variety was clearly established as the nation's first mass entertainment industry, London's thirty-five major halls alone attracting 14 million admissions annually.[43]

It was not, however, simply a matter of numbers. Even before its new successes in the late Victorian and Edwardian period, music hall, as a broad field of entertainment if not necessarily as an institution, imposed itself upon the national culture to an impressive degree. By the late nineteenth century music hall song clearly pervaded most forms of working-class entertainment. The working men's club represented such a major source of employment for music hall acts that complaints about it being dominated by the 'mill-horse

---

[41] Bailey, 'Theatres of entertainment/spaces of modernity', 10.
[42] Russell, 'Varieties of life'.
[43] *Report from the Select Committee on Theatres and Places of Entertainment* (1892), evidence of James Graydon [3004].

round of tenth-rate music-hall business' became frequent in its official press.[44] Again, the smoking concerts and similar functions beloved by sports clubs and the like were often dominated by music hall material. Crucially, from at least the 1860s music hall songs also began to penetrate the drawing-rooms of middle-class Britain. Precisely how far up the social scale they went is hard to judge. One late century claim that the songs of Albert Chevalier and Gus Elen 'are as familiar in the drawing-rooms of Belgravia as in the humbler parlours of the East End' sounds a little exaggerated, but the skilfully illustrated song sheets usually sold for between two and four shillings, suggestive of a substantial market beyond the working class.[45] Again, almost from the outset, music hall artists toured British concert halls, the Great Vance, for example, appearing on the same programme as the Halifax Glee and Madrigal Society at Bradford in 1871. In this way, audiences that found music hall morally problematic could enjoy its product and meet its representatives in a less threatening environment and pave the way for an eventual acceptance of the institution. The celebrity recitals of coster singer Albert Chevalier in the 1890s are especially important here.[46] Clearly, not all doubters could be drawn in even at a safe distance, and the halls, by a process of negative stimulus, were partially responsible for the emergence from the 1850s of highly refined 'society' entertainers. Mr and Mrs Paul and Mr and Mrs German Reed – the emphasis on marital harmony is revealing – were probably the best known, although others, such as Henry Russell, with descriptive pieces such as 'Woodman spare that tree', and many blackface minstrel troupes filled a similar space with greater or lesser degrees of self-consciousness. Some music hall singers skilfully reinvented themselves for this market. By 1881 Harry Liston, once a 'lion comique', was touring with his show 'Merry Moments', advertised as 'chaste, novel and amusing'.[47]

Arguably the greatest success, however, came through what Chevalier later termed the 'music-hallisation of the theatre'.[48] This was perhaps most advanced in pantomime, a genre increasingly dominated by music hall performers, especially comic singers, from the late 1870s. Apart from their intrinsic box office appeal, music hall performers were well suited to the needs of the pantomime, as the 'speaking opening', ever lengthier and increasingly comic in nature, gradually marginalized the harlequinade from the 1830s. They were also adept at the front-of-curtain routines that allowed for spectacular scene

---

[44] Taylor, *From Self-Help to Glamour*, 57.
[45] Stuart and Park, *Variety Stage*, 220; Traies, 'Jones and the working girl'.
[46] Russell, *Popular Music in England*, 95.
[47] Mander and Mitchenson, *Victorian and Edwardian Entertainment*, illustrations 57 and 58; Lee, *Music of the People*, 95–6; *Yorkshire Post*, 22 December 1881.
[48] Bailey, 'Theatres of entertainment', 11.

shifts behind. Augustus 'Druriolanus' Harris, manager of Drury Lane from 1879, who made the lavish and much altered pantomime the theatre's most distinctive product, undoubtedly played a major role here. However, Harris is perhaps best seen as an accelerator rather than as the instigator of this process. James Fawn, for example, appeared at the Adelphi in *The Children of the Wood* as early as 1874, where he launched the song 'Tommy make room for your uncle', later a major music hall success. Similar patterns emerged in the provinces. In 1881 the Leeds Grand Theatre's 'Red Riding Hood', starring music hall's Jenny Hill and Harry Rickards, was described as 'of the music halls music-hally; but it is what the music in a pantomime should be – jolly and catching'.[49] The music hall invasion certainly had its critics, with the *Times* referring scathingly to the consequent 'corruption of Boxing-Day morals'.[50] The trend was irreversible, however, and it enriched both forms of entertainment. While music hall stars such as Dan Leno took the role of the pantomime dame to new heights, they in turn found a new audience, some of which eventually followed them to the halls. At the very end of the period, musical comedy, one of the most significant new genres of the late Victorian stage, provided further proof of the potent influence of music hall. Not only did it frequently recruit some music hall artists, its lavish productions, emphasis on the modern day and certain aspects of its musical and dramatic language led some critics to see it as 'little more than another form of variety show'.[51] It was, in fact, rather more than this, but the similarities were clear and indicative of music hall's successful trajectory from the 1840s onwards.

Popular entertainment and the theatre

In the late eighteenth and early nineteenth centuries the theatre, from London patent house to modest travelling booth, was obviously the central performance-based form of popular entertainment. Gradually at first, but with ever greater speed from mid-century, it faced increasing and determined competition. Michael Booth is surely right to argue that it met this challenge extremely successfully: 'That the theatre succeeded in doing this, in appealing to all classes of society, and becoming solidly established and generally profitable, is no small measure of its achievement. The sheer popularity of Victorian theatre is a lesson of a kind to the theatre of our day.'[52] It did so

[49] *Yorkshire Post*, 24 December 1881.
[50] Quoted in Beaver, *Spice of Life*, 23.
[51] Bailey, 'Theatres of entertainment', 11.
[52] Booth, *Theatre in the Victorian Age*, 26.

partly because the products of the 'legitimate stage' met audience needs, partly because it fed intelligently from its adjacent forms – the use of animals, the borrowing of music hall stars and so forth – but also because audiences appear to have shown considerable flexibility. Whilst the two largest sectors, theatre and music hall, undoubtedly had distinct audiences to some extent, they shared a considerably sized one as well. Many theatre personnel claimed otherwise, but their arguments often suggest a straining for moral and artistic superiority. It is more likely that, as one witness stated in 1866, 'the pit and the gallery audiences at theatres probably attend the music halls too: they are the same class of people'. By 1892 the manager of Middlesex Hall could note that some people (probably not gallery or pit dwellers in this case) attended both forms on the same night, explaining that he often featured a leading turn at the end of the show to satisfy those dropping in from the West End theatres.[53] There was, for much of the period, certainly little to choose between music hall and theatre in terms of behaviour and atmosphere. A study of popular theatre in Birmingham between 1840 and 1870 suggests a level of boisterousness and (in appropriate moments) audience participation that would not have looked out of place in the halls.[54] Similarly, the distinctions relating to the consumption of tobacco and alcohol introduced by the legislation of 1843 were interpreted or altered in ways which minimized the difference between the two. The consumption of alcohol, either purchased at the bar or brought in from outside, was extremely common in Victorian theatres, while smoking sometimes took place despite managerial injunctions to the contrary. In 1879 Bradford magistrates actually allowed local theatres to permit smoking, although 'notwithstanding the threats of those who insist on their rights', the management of the Theatre Royal refused to take advantage of their offer. (To confuse matters still further, some music halls did not allow drinking or smoking to take place during the performance.[55]) The extensive eating of oranges, nuts and chocolate was another shared feature.

It is probable that the theatre lost audiences to the halls from the very end of the nineteenth century. A representative of the London suburban theatres

---

[53] For an example of the 'separation' argument, see the evidence of William Fladgate, a solicitor acting for theatrical managers, *Report from the Select Committee on Theatres and Places of Entertainment* (1892), [864–865]; *Report from the Select Committee on Theatrical Licences and Regulations* (1866), 7; evidence of James Graydon, *Report from the Select Committee on Theatres and Places of Entertainment* (1892), [2888–2891].

[54] Reid, 'Popular theatre in Birmingham', 65–89.

[55] On drinking in the theatre, see *Report from the Select Committee on Theatrical Licences and Regulations* (1866), 3, and Jackson, ed., *Victorian Theatre*, 27–8; *Yorkshireman*, 27 April 1879. On smoking, Jackson, ed., *Victorian Theatre*, 44; *Bradford Observer*, 29 May and 16 June 1879.

claimed that between 1900 and 1909 their number had fallen from thirty-six to seventeen, while the number of halls had risen from about twenty to sixty; as he put it, 'these are eloquent figures'. Even then, the traffic was not all one way. Music halls lost out to the theatre during the pantomime season, and in some provincial locations theatre arguably maintained premier position. Jeremy Crump, for example, argues that in Leicester, music hall 'came to rival, but did not displace, popular legitimate theatre' in the period up to 1914.[56] That judgement may be typical of the situation in many provincial settings: only much needed local research will tell. Ultimately, of course, over the course of the twentieth century the theatre survived while variety died a lingering death.

This chapter has concentrated largely on institutional rather than ideological concerns, and it is useful to end by remedying this to a small degree. At its most basic, popular entertainment must be seen simply as a rich source of pleasure, spectacle and excitement; no wonder Hartlepool enjoyed a public holiday to allow its inhabitants to watch Van Amburgh's circus enter the town in 1843.[57] The enjoyment gained in witnessing a chosen event was often matched or even exceeded by the pleasures of expectation and retrospection:

> Tommy Hurd was the leading comedian. Never did he speak without setting the house in a roar. What Tommy had said and Tommy had done in the farce on Monday lasted me and my companions for delightful conversation for the whole of the week afterwards.

W. E. Adams's memories of his youthful trips to Tommy Hurd's booth theatre in Cheltenham can stand for endless similar pleasures in innumerable locations.[58]

Entertainment was never just entertainment, however. Activities which took up so much of the time, money and emotional commitment of so many people can never have been ideologically neutral. It is difficult, perhaps unwise, to define the impact that popular entertainment in general had upon popular political mentalities and social identities: the field of study (and the period under study) is enormous, and specific forms and genres may well have impacted in distinctive and particular ways. Common elements can be identified, however, most notably in the popular imperialism that surfaced

[56] Evidence of J. B. Mulholland, *Joint Select Committee on Stage Plays* (1909), [4081–4082]; evidence of Henry Tozer, *Joint Select Committee on Stage Plays* (1909), [4884–4886]; Crump, 'Provincial music hall', 69.

[57] Cunningham, *Industrial Revolution*, 35.

[58] W. E. Adams, *Memoirs of a Social Atom* (1903), quoted in Jackson, *Victorian Theatre*, 24.

in so many areas of entertainment, especially in the late nineteenth century. The music hall and pantomime were often overt sites for such expression, but it could be found in more subtle ways, as in the symbolic importance of the animals collected in circuses and menageries, impressive illustration 'of British domination both of vast tributary territories and of the natural world'.[59] Further common ground is provided by what Bailey refers to as a 'sexualised consumerism', with music hall and circus, in particular, prone to present relatively sexually explicit performances by women artists under the guise of art.[60]

Scholars hunting for meaning have a wide range of theoretical models against which to test their findings. Interpretations of popular entertainment can be placed all along a continuum defining it, at one extreme, as a powerful agent for the construction and reinforcement of the social and political status quo or, at the other, as a space in which subordinate social classes and social groups can resist and contest dominant ideologies and engender utopian visions of the world as it should be. My own view places it rather closer to the first position than to the second. Popular entertainment was, above all, a commercial venture, and the pursuit of profit provided little space for radical agendas. Others will disagree, and all the better for that. What is important is that the still remarkably underexplored territory of popular entertainment continues to draw students to its riches.

[59] Russell, *Popular Music in Britain*, 145–67; Ritvo, *Animal Estate*, 243.
[60] Bailey, 'Parasexuality and glamour'.

18

The Bells: a case study
A 'bare-ribbed skeleton' in a chest

DAVID MAYER

That a play of no great merit, carried almost entirely by one actor in the leading role, should have a chapter to itself in what is otherwise a broad examination of the nineteenth-century stage is not altogether remarkable. *The Bells* invites consideration as a stand-alone 'exhibit' or 'case study' because it is one of the few nineteenth-century plays where so many elements of its production and reception by the public in Britain and abroad survive. In addition, this play is an index to the career of a remarkable actor. *The Bells* was a play in which Henry Irving, its leading actor, passed in the space of a few days from comparative obscurity to celebrity and fame, enabling him to establish himself as Britain's leading interpreter of serious and classical roles. Beginning with the role of Mathias, Irving became known as an actor in possession of a singular gift for enacting characters, intellectually superior and somewhat aloof, who are secretly tormented by suppurating guilt for hideous hidden crimes, by anguish, regret and remorse.[1] In his lifetime and for years beyond, Irving's performance in *The Bells* was so well known that his voice and mannerisms were imitated by numerous variety artistes.

Between 1871 and 1905 *The Bells* was seen by audiences in Britain and North America, receiving critical reviews by a range of British, American and Canadian journalists. Their press notices, supplemented by eye-witness accounts from a range of spectators, provide valuable insights into the drama's appearance on the stage and offer valuable information about Irving's approach to his role and its popular and critical reception.[2] Photographs – albeit studio

---

[1] Irving's own acting script exists in a modern playable text. A full orchestral score, band parts and a piano reduction of the incidental music costumes are available. Pictures of scenic elements and key scenes survive and are published in this edition. See Mayer, ed., *Henry Irving and* The Bells.

[2] Especially useful are Saintsbury and Palmer, eds., *We Saw Him Act*, and Gielgud, *A Victorian Playgoer.*

photographs rather than stage photos – also survive of Henry Irving posed in-role. Moreover, *The Bells* is a play which enjoyed continued popularity from its first performance in 1871 to the death of its principal actor in 1905, then to be revived and enjoyed again in replica performances as Henry Irving's son toured the English provinces from 1909 for a further decade. Even beyond Irving's death *The Bells'* history continues: after the early death of Irving's eldest son H. B. 'Harry' Irving, Henry Irving's own script and band parts passed to the actors John Martin-Harvey and Henry Banton and were in use as further productions of *The Bells* toured Britain, North America and the British Empire. *The Bells* was one of the earliest full-length stage melodramas to be adapted as a film, first in 1913 and again in 1914. It is still revived, albeit with limited success, in modern times as a stage play, and has been adapted both for television and radio. In all, *The Bells* was performed 151 times in its first Lyceum season; it was toured by the Lyceum company throughout Britain and North America, and stayed in Irving's repertoire – receiving in excess of 800 performances – for the full thirty-four years in which he remained with the Lyceum company. Only a night before his death in October 1905, and against the advice of colleagues and his physicians, Irving performed the physically and emotionally taxing role of Mathias.

Again *The Bells* merits particular scrutiny because, not untypical of successful English stage plays, it was adapted from a foreign source, and indeed is one of several versions of the same Paris hit to be placed in competition on the London stage within a few crowded weeks. The numerous attractions of Parisian theatres, hitherto isolated by the Germans' encircling siege of that city, suddenly became available in the autumn of 1871 as the Franco-Prussian war ended. London theatre managers, their eyes on the Paris stage for new attractions, raced to adapt the Théâtre Cluny's popular *Le Juif polonais* by Emile Erckmann and Pierre-Alexandre Chatrian for English audiences. At the Royal Alfred Theatre in Marylebone, another adaptation of the Polish Jew's drama, *Paul Zegers; or, The Dream of Retribution*, was first to be seen.

The sudden, overwhelming success of *The Bells* and Henry Irving's new fame were unexpected, but the production and its development were carefully planned and thoroughly calculated. Exactly what happened at the Lyceum Theatre, where Irving was in residence as a young comic character actor, is unclear. In the aftermath of *The Bells'* success, the Lyceum's lessee, the American impresario-manager H. L. Bateman, was inclined to take credit for his foresight in commissioning an effective translation and adaptation of the Paris hit from the alcoholic, unpredictable Leopold Lewis, but there were also conflicting claims that Lewis had sufficient prescience to have made his own translation and was attempting to persuade Bateman to stage it.[3] Lewis and Irving – often against Bateman's directives – collaborated to develop and bring this drama to the Lyceum stage. And once *The Bells* was in preparation, Bateman had the wisdom to purchase or to lease the score for the considerable incidental music for *Le Juif polonais* by the composer Etienne Singla from the Théâtre Cluny management and to engage the Cluny's *chef d'orchestre*, M. LaRochelle, installing him as conductor in the pit. It is also likely, however, given his appreciation of the power of effective customized incidental music, that Irving abridged and reshaped the music to his own needs, possibly even reducing the melodic line of the first violin part because his own voice in the leading role was to provide the 'music'.[4] Although full of misgivings and grudging every penny spent on the production, Bateman also commissioned new sets and costumes from Hawes Craven and other Lyceum scenic artists.

Much of this chapter will attempt to account for the success of *The Bells*, querying its intimate association with Henry Irving, asking whether any Victorian actor but Irving might have enjoyed comparable success in the role of Mathias and examining the cultural and social ethos of the nineteenth century for the long success of the play and Irving's parallel triumph in different but significantly related roles.

On 25 November 1871 *The Bells* was performed at the somewhat shabby and down-at-heels Lyceum Theatre. In the pit stalls to review the drama was the influential critic Clement Scott. Scott's enthusiastic review appeared in the *Observer*, other critics were similarly effusive in their praise and the Lyceum's fortunes changed abruptly. A middle-class clientèle was drawn to the theatre and would support Lyceum productions for the duration of Irving's association with it, initially as an employee, from 1878 until 1895 as the lessee, and from 1899 until his death again as an employee. Within months the play had attracted its comic parodies, with such titles as *The Bells-Bellesqued and the Polish Jew Polished-off; or, Mathias, the Muffin, the Mystery, the Maiden, and the Masher.* As his fame grew, Irving's idiosyncratic acting was imitated in music hall turns and in 1877 was venemously attacked in a pamphlet by a trio of young Scottish critics.[5]

---

[3] One of the witnesses to the first night of *The Bells* who was privy to the gossip surrounding its production was the journalist-balladeer-dramatist George R. Sims. In 1871, Sims was still an apprentice in a London textile house and had yet to make his mark as a writer. His account of the première is found in Sims, *Glances Back*, 52–66.

[4] Burgin, 'Lyceum rehearsals'.

[5] The pamphlet *The Fashionable Tragedian, A Criticism, with Ten Illustrations* (1877), was published anonymously, but the authors were subsequently identified as Robert Lowe, George Halkett and William Archer. See Laurence Irving, *Henry Irving, the Actor and his World*, 291–2.

Irving threatened legal action and won an apology and retraction before the case came to court. All of these events further secured success and enduring popularity for the Lyceum's drama and its leading actor.

The Bells enacts the terminal hours of a seemingly honest and upright man, Mathias (pronouced by Irving and the Lyceum Theatre's cast as 'Mátt-e-us', the German pronunciation, not 'Math-í-us'), who, fifteen years earlier, had secretly murdered and robbed a passing traveller, a Polish Jew, who sought refuge from a snowstorm in his inn. Concealing his crime and investing the money gained in the robbery of the Jewish seed merchant, Mathias has prospered and become mayor of his small Alsatian village, and now, to forestall detection and prosecution, he has encouraged the engagement of his daughter to a young officer in the rural constabulary. Thus the police, Mathias imagines, will now unwittingly shield the criminal. Mathias's final hours – the three acts of this brief drama – are filled with unutterable guilt which gradually reveals itself in small incriminating gestures, uneasy glances and averted eyes succeeded by terrifying hallucinatory visions, imagined sounds and incriminating confessional dreams. As memories of his crime accumulate, Mathias responds with dismay and disgust at blood-contaminated gold coins from the Jew's money belt which lie next to his daughter's dowry and with frantic displacement activity such as drinking too freely and dancing strenuously. The spectacle of Mathias slowly breaking under emotional stress invites comparison with a rare old porcelain vase visibly disintegrating under pressure: first small flaws appear, the barely apparent lines then gradually widening to visible cracks and enlarging leaky fissures. Finally and suddenly – but no longer unexpectedly – the whole breaks apart, losing form and spilling contents.

The Bells takes its title, first, from the recollected and imagined sound of sleigh bells and, later, from the tolling of an executioner's bell and church bells which announce Sunday and Mathias's daughter Annette's marriage. Sleigh bells attached to the horse's harness fifteen years ago signalled the arrival of the Polish Jew at Mathias's inn. Now, as the play begins, Mathias returns in a blizzard from a visit to a nearby town where, at a fair, he has witnessed a showman's remarkable performance ballasted with scientific and moral authority: a mesmerist, a popular hypnotist who, with a few passes of his arms, has put local people into trances and then caused them to reveal their innermost thoughts and to blurt out their hidden secrets. As the snowstorm swirls about his inn and as his fireside cronies remark how this blizzard is like the one which brought the mysterious – and since vanished – Polish Jew to their village, Mathias, wrought to a high pitch of anxiety by the memory of the mesmerist, imagines that he can hear the faint sound of 'bells! Sleigh bells on the road!' Inaudible to his family and friends, but clearly audible to himself and, significantly, to the audience, who empathically share his anxiety and who increasingly guess at the reasons for his fear, the tinkling of the recalled and imagined bells continues to torment Mathias further. When the guests have gone for the night and his family have retired, Mathias's horrors increase. The jangling of harness bells grows louder. The walls of the inn appear to melt away, and Mathias sees a vision of his younger self, hatchet in hand, as he stalks and ambushes a horse-drawn sled carrying the Jewish merchant away from his inn. The reproachful bitter eyes of the Jew alight on Mathias, and he collapses in terror as the first act ends.

The second act establishes Mathias as a devoted family man, enjoying the company of his wife, Catherine, who is altogether innocent of any knowledge of the source of Mathias's wealth, and his daughter Annette, she for whose benefit the murder and robbery were committed. Annette is adored and plied with gifts. Alone, Mathias counts out her dowry, separating any remaining coins from the Jew's money belt from new gold earned since the murder. Again, as the stacks of gold cross his desk, Mathias hears the imagined bells and moves to speed the marriage, exacting from his prospective son-in-law a promise to protect him against all adversaries. The betrothal party continues with feasting, drinking, singing and dancing. Again the Jew's sleigh bells, inaudible to the innocent party-goers, are heard by Mathias and the audience. To drown out their sound, Mathias seizes Catherine and, shouting, whirls her in a frantic waltz to end the second act.

The third and final act is set in Mathias's bedroom. Helped into his bed by an anxious Catherine, Annette, his son-in-law-to-be and friends who fear that Mathias has drunk too much and overtaxed himself, he falls into a deep, dream-disturbed sleep. As his dream begins, his bedroom metamorphoses into a spectral, hazy, high-ceilinged law court where three judges and a prosecutor sit barely visible in soft-edged shafts of limelight. To this court of justice Mathias is summoned and charged with the Jew's murder. Declaring his innocence, Mathias defies his accusers until the prosecutor demands that the defendant submit to the questioning of the very mesmerist whom Mathias had seen at the fair the previous day. Protesting, Mathias is forced into a chair, and the Mesmerist stands above and behind him. Beginning his hypnotic passes, the Mesmerist causes Mathias to fall into a second sleep from which he is awakened to explain his crime. Now in a deep trance, Mathias both narrates and enacts the Jew's arrival at his inn, Annette's sick cries, the sight of the Jew's gold. He relates how he follows the Jew, tracking him through the snow to the bridge where he must cross a frozen river. Finally, as the sound of sleigh bells grows louder, he acts out the murder, smashing the Jew with blows of his axe, robbing his corpse and disposing of the body in a nearby burning lime kiln. The bells cease. Exhausted, he pauses, awaiting the court's verdict. The judge's voice is implacable and insistent: Mathias is to hang for his crime. Suddenly church bells and daylight break into the dream, cutting across the tolling of the executioner's bell. The court fades behind gauzes. Mathias's family comes to his bedside to awaken him for church. Parting the bed curtains and still in the throes of his dream, Mathias clutches at the grasp of an imagined executioner's rope around his throat. 'Take the rope from my neck – take', he gasps, 'the – rope – from – neck'. Mathias struggles briefly, then succumbs to a fatal heart attack as his family and friends gather uncomprehendingly in grief.

The Bells' limited success in modern revivals makes a point: a strong leading actor in the role of Mathias is essential to carrying the play. No matter how competent or brilliant the supporting actors may be, they cannot compensate for a weak lead. This phenomenon is evidence of Irving's power as an actor, someone capable of transmuting a modest adaptation into an astounding personal success and rising above a mediocre script to become identified in the public mind with the role. It is therefore essential to outline Henry Irving's stage career, and to identify the roles which brought him acclaim. We will find that in these roles, although consistently varied in nationality, age, ruling passions and obsessions, there is a constant thread that helps us to understand Irving's choice of parts and, likewise, his appeal to theatre audiences.

Henry Irving, born Henry Brodribb in 1838, was reared in a rural Methodist family which eschewed the stage, dancing and other social frivolities as wicked and ungodly. Enjoyment of such worldly vanities could not be admitted and was the cause for self-reproach, shame and quiet remorse. Moving to London, Brodribb was educated for commercial employment and, as a young adolescent, obtained a clerkship in the City where, away from the censorious eye of his mother, he began to attend plays. He also enrolled for evening elocution and drama classes in a 'spouting academy' where stage-struck men (such academies were too disreputable for respectable young women) were taught rudimentary acting skills by 'resting' professional actors. It was the practice of such academies to prepare plays for public performance and to offer evenings of platform recitations.

Brodribb was soon persuaded to appear at such an evening and chose as his recitation piece a narrative poem, 'The Uncle', by Henry Glasford Bell. The narrator of 'The Uncle' is an adult who recalls his orphaned childhood in his uncle's home. The uncle is secretive, morose and withdrawn, inclined to gaze longingly at a woman's portrait and to guard a locked chest. One day the uncle explains to the child that the portrait is that of his late sister-in-law, the boy's mother. Then carried away by memories, the uncle reveals his jealousy of his brother, the boy's father. The father had disappeared and the uncle had hoped to marry his brother's widow, but she would not have him and died of grief. Displaying the chest to the boy, the uncle undoes the lock and raises the lid. Within is 'a bare-ribbed skeleton' of the boy's murdered father. His guilty secret out in the open, the uncle dies in a delirious frenzy.[6]

So macabre and disturbing was this poem that the academy's proprietors dissuaded Brodbribb from performing it. He chose and performed instead a political speech, but he was also attracted to Thomas Hood's ballad 'The Dream of Eugene Aram', another tale of secret envy – here, for wealth – murder, concealment guilt and apprehension of the guilty protagonist. On tour and relaxing after performances, Irving would recite Hood's poem in private readings.[7] These poetic recitations, both of which remained in Irving's repertoire of short platform pieces throughout his life, and both of which were regularly performed at benefits for actors and other charitable causes, are an index to the roles which Irving would develop and for which he would receive acclaim from a shocked, frightened, morally and emotionally disturbed public. The thread, beginning with 'The Uncle' and 'The Dream of Eugene Aram', is of crime arising from envy, sexual jealousy or desire for wealth and power, hidden beneath an intelligent, humorous, charming and affable public persona. But concealment brings the protagonist inner pain, suffering, remorse and festering guilt which cannot be contained forever. His better nature divides from its wicked self. The two selves struggling for dominance force knowledge of crime and guilt into the open, and neither self survives.

Bodribb's brief success with the spouters persuaded him to attempt a stage career. Adopting the surname of Irving in 1856, he began working as a provincial actor, appearing in companies in Dublin, Glasgow, Sunderland, Edinburgh, Manchester, Oxford and Liverpool. By 1866 he was established in London and in the autumn of 1871 was engaged by the Lyceum Theatre's manager, H. L. Bateman, to play supporting roles. It was in these circumstances that Irving met Leopold Lewis.

Lewis's association with the theatre rests chiefly on his adaptation of *The Bells*. Little is known of him today, but he was well enough known to his

---

[6] H. G. Bell's 'The Uncle', together with Sir Julius Benedict's piano score, which Irving commissioned from the composer in the 1880s, is published in Hayes and Nikolopoulou, eds., *Melodrama*, 268–75. For an account of this and other recitation pieces, see Mayer, 'Parlour and platform melodrama'.

[7] Belford, *Bram Stoker*, 72–4.

colleagues and contemporaries to have been caricatured by the artist Alfred Bryant for a weekly theatrical journal. Three other plays by him were performed at London theatres, but none of these was ever published in actors' or readers' editions, and none would have brought him much remuneration. He survived as a journalist and translator, and was observed, red-faced with drink, sitting alone in theatre stalls and in cafés. He may have been the first to note the Paris success of *Le Juif polonais* and was reported to have been seen at the Lyceum trying to sell his translation to Bateman. It is likely, but not altogether certain, that Irving read the initial translation, saw a chance for himself as Mathias, worked with Lewis to reshape the play, and persuaded Bateman to lease performing rights to the play from Lewis. Lewis retained rights to the script of *The Bells*, subsequently selling them to Samuel French. French's published version, however, differs in some details from Irving's own script – notably in descriptions of set arrangements – and may reflect the development of the script in the first weeks of public performance. Lewis certainly may have worked with Irving to make further changes to *The Bells* after opening night. Catherine was removed from the vision scene at the close of the first act. Mathias's gift to Annette was changed from a hat to a gold necklace, perhaps to emphasize Mathias's criminally acquired wealth, perhaps to introduce a property which fits noose-like about the throat and transfers guilt from father to daughter or makes her inadvertently complicitous. Finally, the opening moments of the third act were altered to ease the transition from Mathias's bedroom to the courtroom dream scene.[8]

The immediate successes of *The Bells* and Irving's Mathias were sufficient to bring changes to the Lyceum. By 1878 Irving had succeeded Bateman as lessee of that theatre, beginning with this act a tenancy as resident actor-manager which was to last until 1899, when severe financial difficulties forced the 61-year-old Irving to relinquish the lease to a management committee of trustees and to concentrate his resources on leading the acting company. By that later date he had built the Lyceum into a commercial concern employing as many as 350 performers – actors, dancers, singers, orchestral musicians (although this number was, for most productions, closer to fifty) – a permanent administrative staff of forty-eight and 230 regularly employed on production tasks.[9] As much to the point, Irving had found a model or general outline for stage roles – and was able to encourage dramatic writers and to commission

---

[8] Much of this information is hearsay associated with the passing of the script and incidental music from H. B. Irving to John Martin Harvey and Henry Baynton and thence to Eric Jones-Evans. See Mayer, *Henry Irving and* The Bells, 9–13.

[9] Alan Hughes, 'Lyceum staff'.

scripts – which were to suit his unique talents and to meet the unconscious predilections of his London and more distant audiences.

This is not to say that Irving turned away from the established repertoire of the English stage. His Shakespearean roles included Hamlet (1874 and 1878), Shylock (1879), Othello, alternating with Iago (1881), Benedick (1882 and 1891), Romeo (1882) and Lear (1892).[10] His Malvolio (1884) was a failure, chiefly because audiences and critics objected to the bawdy humour of *Twelfth Night*. But the parts which drew comment and supported a public following were Eugene Aram in W. G. Wills's version of *Eugene Aram*, which Bateman and Irving commissioned as a companion piece to *The Bells*, Sir Edward Mortimer in George Colman the younger's *The Iron Chest* (1879), Richard III (1877), the title role in Dion Boucicault's adaptation of Casimir Delvigne's *Louis XI* (1878), Iago (1881), Synorix in Alfred Tennyson's *The Cup* (1881), Mephistopheles in Wills's *Faust* (1885, 1887 and 1895), Macbeth (1888), Robert Landry in Watts Phillips's *The Dead Heart* (1889), Iachimo (1896), and the double roles of Lesurques and Dubosq in Charles Reade's *The Lyons Mail* (1877) and Louis and Fabien in the Lyceum's revival of Boucicault's 1852 adaptation of *The Corsican Brothers* (1880). All but the final pair of Corsican Brothers, Lesurques in *The Lyons Mail* and Robert Landry are transgressors: murderers or conspirators to murder or defraud, would-be seducers, usurpers, instigators of others' vile acts. They are manipulative. All are devious, cynical and ironically humorous, and deeply untruthful. Most have appealing, winning public faces. All have a hidden, secret side that only rarely is perceived – apart from the audience – by others. Landry is a good man whose better self has been deadened by years of imprisonment and who places revenge above social and affectionate relationships. Landry must revive this better self. Dubosq is thoroughly bad, but is also mirrored by his absolute double, the good and virtuous Lesurques. So identical in appearance are these two that no one, not even close family members, can immediately distinguish between Dubosq and Lesurques, and the state is ready to guillotine the innocent one for the villain's crimes. Louis and Fabien dei Franchi are both innocent of crime but, although two distinct people, are so alike that they feel and emote as one.

Mathias is the first of such complex transgressive roles for Irving and the Lyceum company, establishing a precedent, not merely of compelling, two-faced characters, but for a significant change within a theatrical genre. *The Bells*, we should note, operates within the climate and expectations of the

---

[10] For a full discussion and analysis of Irving's Shakespearean roles see Hughes, *Henry Irving, Shakespearean*.

prevailing nineteenth-century theatrical form, melodrama. Thus, there are certain givens expected of this genre that ought to be met but which, in this drama and in others associated by the Lyceum, fail to be observed. The omission or alteration of these givens, far from being a liability, brought new and warmly appreciative audiences to Irving's performances.

Melodrama as largely, but not exclusively, practised before Irving's control of the Lyceum was villain-driven in an environment where evil put goodness at risk. Here the villain, a clearly defined and recognizable stage character, whether for motives of avarice or lust or desire for power or for other dangerous and unsocial motives, schemed and acted to threaten or destroy the lives of other characters. What distinguished these other characters from the villain was moral goodness: enacted dramatically as loyalty, innocence, guilelessness, sexual honesty or naïveté, altruism, truthfulness and bravery. The action of melodrama hitherto obliged the good characters – hero and heroine – to reclaim the lives and peace of mind disturbed by villainy, to identify the villain, punishing or expelling him from society and resuming the placid equanimity of their previous lives.

Irving disrupts this previous pattern, although this is not immediately apparent. The continual presence of music, even with the Théâtre Cluny's score abridged, retains the emotional intensity of earlier melodrama and prompts the audience's moral and psychological responses throughout the performance. Irving will use incidental music in all of his Lyceum plays. The disruption occurs in his characters: his villains are heroes turned inside-out. They are disturbingly appealing, partly because of the humour and irony that infuse their speech and actions. Readers familiar with Anthony Hopkins's performance as Hannibal Lecter in *The Silence of the Lambs* will recognize and understand this phenomenon. Beneath the humour, sarcasm and cynicism are depths of awareness and pain. Audiences see apparent good nature and ebullience laminated with secret obsession, selfish cruelty and bitter remorse. In close proximity to such company, the good characters of his plays are comparatively bloodless, uninteresting and in danger of being too insipid to be appealing. Although there is incidental music to instruct the audience's interpretation of characters and action, the moral clarity or 'legibility'[11] that characterizes the inhabitants of earlier melodrama is no longer as sharply outlined. Indeed, their moral legibility is deliberately blurred and confused by the protagonist's contradictory acts. Further, although spectators are concerned that justice be done and that virtue be rewarded, they do, albeit often against their wishes and

[11] Brooks, *Melodramatic Imagination*, 5–80.

inclinations, have understanding of and empathize with the villain-protagonist. Emotions and moral values collide and rebound, taking unpredictable trajectories throughout the auditorium. Under the wickedness are deep strata of guilt and, if not remorse, then acute awareness of crime and moral transgression. Sorrow, regret, longing for forgiveness are hinted at, if not made explicit. Villainy has become far more ambiguous and, because a troubled, unassuageable conscience is involved, not altogether antithetical to goodness. In this respect villainy is far more interesting and understandable to theatre audiences than virtue, which can turn to unappealing priggishness.

Also, and perhaps far more significantly, Irving's Lyceum melodramas with their melancholy, pained, ultimately self-destructive hero-villains edge closer to what we understand as tragedy. This is not the high tragedy of great men fallen, but it contains elements of overreaching and suffering and a protagonist who procures and witnesses his own downfall. Tragedy, or at least the illusion of tragedy, and seriousness blended with spectacle and fine acting had qualities which critics were fast to commend to the new Lyceum audiences. Irving and his various house dramatists were to cultivate and to exploit these possibilities as his theatrical career developed.

To what extent Irving and his authors were conscious of working this vein is unknown and probably unknowable. What we can recognize is that *The Bells*, other dramas in the Lyceum repertoire and Irving's roles are part of a larger literary, theatrical and scientific phenomenon visible in the final quarter of the nineteenth century, identifying and depicting the 'double-self'. Although Freud's lectures and writings on the unconscious do not appear until 1902 (Irving was to die only three years later), interest in the nature and workings of the mind had begun more than a full century earlier. Franz Anton Mesmer's experiments with the curative uses of hypnotism in the last decades of the eighteenth century had created an awareness that individuals were not in full control of their actions. Behind the faces presented to the world were secret thoughts and impulses which others, versed in the skills of hypnotism, might awaken. From Mesmer, both revered and stigmatized, interest in the behaviour of the inner mind divided, some practitioners working as the showman Mathias encounters at the fair in Ribeauville, others – Charcot, Adler, Freud – attempting to diagnose and treat madness or aberrant behaviour. Members of the Lyceum audience were more likely to know the showman or the middle-class neighbour who practised mesmerism as a parlour entertainment. The showman and the scientist were there to demonstrate that within the mind lay another hidden identity, a twin of the outer self that might be liberated. The scientist foresaw healing properties in liberating this twin;

showmen and artists – people of a vivid and theatrical imagination – saw the liberated twin as a danger. Another Victorian scientific development, photography, showed the world its unadorned face, but photography also led to experiments to prove evidence of a second, secret world of the supernatural, to 'spirit photographs' and revelations of fairies, just as a new fashion for seances and the calling up of supernatural spirits had partly persuaded Victorians that the material, visible world masked a second, occult world which could be revealed only through intervention and spirit manipulation.

In this climate of partly recognizing, partly fearing both the power and vulnerability of the unconscious mind, novelists and dramatists explored the appeals of the *Doppelgänger*, or double self, and the terror of the mind controlled by another. The earliest literary appearance of the *Doppelgänger* may have been James Hogg's Scottish novelette *The Private Memoirs and Confessions of a Justified Sinner* (1824), in which the narrator, returning from a night of debauchery, meets the Devil – his own self – on the edge of an Edinburgh forest. Robert Louis Stevenson, in *The Strange Case of Dr Jekyll and Mr Hyde* (1886), creates in Dr Jekyll a scientific enquirer who, Faustus-like and overreaching, seeks to know too much and tests a dangerous chemical potion on his own body. The effect is to fracture and divide his identity, generating a second self, a Mr Hyde, who is as dangerous, murderous and corrupt as Dr Jekyll is benign, harmless and good. The popularity of this novelette assured that it would be translated to the stage; it was adapted for the American actor Richard Mansfield by T. Russell Sullivan. Mansfield chose, significantly, to introduce *Dr Jekyll and Mr Hyde* (1888) to British audiences at the Lyceum. Oscar Wilde similarly explored the double outer and inner self in *The Picture of Dorian Gray* (1891), and George Du Maurier's novel *Trilby* (1891) told of a talentless artists' model, Trilby O'Ferrall, who is transformed into an astoundingly accomplished singer – a second identity – when under the driving hypnotic spell of the charlatan Svengali, but who, again talentless and voiceless, collapses and dies when Svengali's mesmeric influence is withheld. The rights to *Trilby* (1895), initially adapted for the New York stage by Paul Potter, were acquired by the actor-manager Herbert Beerbohm Tree, who made Svengali attractive and dangerously repulsive, creative and destructive, intelligent and brutish in equal measure. As Mathias and Mephistopheles and Dubosq–Lesurques were to Irving, so Svengali was to Tree, a complex stage role that both fascinated and repelled, yet drawing large audiences and acclamation.

Theatre is a medium that lends itself to the enactment of multiple layers in character and to fissures and slippages in identity. The split self specified by Lewis's text was realized on the Lyceum stage, which deployed its full technical resources to fragment and dissolve and to make Mathias's seemingly solid environment become visibly unstable – a spectacular metaphor for mental meltdown. The dramatic text is the first site investigated in seeking verbal self-betrayal or acts which contradict words or which qualify or otherwise undermine previous acts or gestures. The Leopold Lewis Lyceum text is rich in both verbal and enacted revelations, allowing Mathias numerous opportunities in 'visions' where he narrates past events, in soliloquies and asides, and in revealing acts that expose his two conflicted selves. Thus the audience see Mathias as, equally and ambiguously, the good father and the murderous criminal. As Mathias, alone in his study, counts out his daughter's dowry, separating gold obtained in the robbery from new coins, his two selves, the father and the criminal, speak by turns, the criminal Mathias addressing the paternal, respectable Mathias as if the latter were a fool whose mistakes might entrap them both. Each time the Jew's remembered sleigh bells are heard, we, as spectators, are drawn into Mathias's inner world where calendar and clock turn back a full fifteen years, yet, for the most part, we are with Mathias in the present. Even the travelling Polish Jew is a part of this ambiguity, too. He is the 'other': a stranger, a non-Christian (Annette's fiancé and Mathias's future son-in-law is named Christian), but the Jew is also a guest in Mathias's inn and, therefore, especially deserving of hospitality and protection. When Mathias is compelled by the Mesmerist to re-enact his crime, his accompanying narrative informs that the Jew's ambush was planned and committed as the infant Annette lay ill and close to death. Money obtained in the robbery has saved her life. Mathias had therefore acted, supposedly, in her interest, but this act, undertaken for the noblest of motives – protecting little Annette – was also the basest of crimes. Annette's physical presence on the stage underlines the ambivalent character of his rationalizing: the healthy young woman, whose wedding the audience has no reason to oppose, is consequently both a triumphant justification for murder and robbery and a living reminder of a 15-year-old sin. Such contradictions are, for us and for Mathias, emotionally difficult because they are both morally simple and morally difficult.

However, if the script, in its stage directions or dialogue, does not altogether specify action or business or provide words which turn certainty into ambiguity, the inspired actor may find seams in the dialogue which can be unpicked and, with even small gestures, opened to disturbing revelations of duality. Irving was noted for an early moment in *The Bells* when, ostensibly preoccupied in replacing his snow-covered boots with comfortable shoes, Mathias hears one of his friends refer to the Ribeauville mesmerist's ability to make people 'tell everything that weighs upon their conscience'. According to Gordon Craig, Irving froze in mid-gesture:

> By the time the speaker had got this slowly out – and it was dragged purposely – Irving was buckling his second shoe, leaning over it with his two long hands stretched down over the buckles. We suddenly saw these fingers stop their work; the crown of the head suddenly seemed to glitter and become frozen – and then, at the pace of the slowest and most terrified snail, the two hands, still motionless and frozen, were seen to be coming up the side of the leg . . . the whole torso of the man, almost seeming frozen, was gradually and by an almost imperceptible movement, seen to be drawing up and back, as it would straighten a little, and to lean a little against the back of the chair on which he was seated. Once in that position – motionless – eyes fixed ahead of him and fixed on us all – there he sat for the space of ten or twelve seconds, which, I can assure you, seemed to us like a lifetime, and then said in a voice deep and overwhelmingly beautiful: 'Oh, you were talking about that – were you?'[12]

Another witness to this moment recalls: 'but his hands crept up. He was buckling his right shoe and paused. And in that pause Irving used his face. You saw his face registering stark terror, anticipating his words of agreement, and with that thought his body slumped.'[13] So directly did Irving gaze into his audiences' faces and share Mathias's self-revealing momentary terror with them that women, now suddenly complicit in his guilty secret, screamed and fainted.[14]

Scenic effects also play a role in creating two concurrently visible worlds, the present concrete environment of Mathias's Alsatian inn and the frightening – usually suppressed – world of memory and hallucinatory dreaming. Snow – falling outside the inn and tracked in on Mathias's and visitors' clothing – functions as a visible metaphor for covering up and concealing. The 'vision scene' that closes the first act allows the spectator to travel with Mathias's memory as the upstage wall of the inn dissolves to reveal, not only the site of the murder but also a *tableau vivant* of the instant immediately before the crime. The elder Mathias, still on stage, terrified by the imagined sleigh bells and wracked with the memory of his crime, views his younger self, axe in hand, approaching his victim. For the moment the two worlds intersect: the double selves meet as the gauze between them seems to dissolve, but they do not yet interact. Another act, separating vision and dream, will bring the two selves dangerously closer.

[12] Craig, *Henry Irving*, 59.
[13] Eric Jones-Evans in Mayer, *Henry Irving and* The Bells, 82.
[14] Sir Donald Sinden, speaking of his grandmother's attendance at *The Bells*, to the author, 27 October 1999.

In the third act's dream episode, the Mesmerist, who has gained access to forbidden areas of Mathias's unconscious mind, compels Irving as Mathias to enact both his selves. In this dream Mathias now wears the clothing worn as he tracked the Jew fifteen years earlier and, under hypnosis, progressively shifts from distancing narrative to vivid physical playing, ending his account of the murder with savage re-enactments of the killing, the theft of gold from the Jew's money belt and the cruel disposal of the traveller's corpse in the limekiln – 'Go into the fire, Jew! Go into the fire' – before collapsing in hysteria as he imagines the Jew's eyes glaring from the furnace. Brought out of his hypnotic state, Mathias is dazed and unable to recall how his earlier self has been compelled to appear before the court, but it is this final rejoining of the two interacting selves under the Mesmerist's hypnosis that causes Mathias's death.

Music, too, is a vital part of this effective deployment of theatrical resources. Etienne Singla's potent score works to establish a physically tangible world of provincial life: town bands and wedding festivities, Sunday church and a scouring wind. But the music also establishes a dimension of mental and emotional terror issuing from Mathias's tormented mind, supporting with tremolos and minor passages the convoluted devious reasonings, the unanswerable anxieties and the terrible predisposition to murderous violence that characterize the aging *burgomaster*.

Although *The Bells* requires both a vision and a dream episode, and although the walls of the Alsatian inn must vanish as vision and dream take hold on Mathias's tormented unconscious, there is little remarkable in the stage technology required for *The Bell*'s illusions. Yet rarely has theatre technology been so effectively or appropriately employed to dramatize someone's fraught mental state and ultimate breakdown. The 'vision' is dependent on standard Victorian stage scenery: the gauze which appears opaque until light falls on objects and people upstage of it, and 'sink-and-rise' scenic units which divide, some lowering into and beneath the stage floor on 'sloats' or 'bridges', some hauled upwards into the flies. The back wall of the inn was made of such sink-and-rise pieces and broke apart to fly and descend. Behind the wall – upstage – was a gauze and, upstage of the gauze, a small tableau of a snow scene with the young Mathias stalking the Jew in his horse-drawn sleigh. Farthest upstage was a painted drop of a forest and a snow-covered stone bridge. The dream of the Court of Justice was even less complicated: Mathias's canopied and curtained bed was downstage right. A few stools were the only bedroom furniture. Irving simply climbed into the curtained 'bed' and exited into the wings as the curtains closed. He then stood upstage of the back wall of the bedroom, again a gauze, and was lit so as to be visible. The Judges, Prosecutor, and Mesmerist, all products of Mathias's troubled conscience, were faintly lit with low-intensity limelights, each with a 'frosted' lens to remove the sharp-edged beams normally produced by limes. This was the only illumination. In the dim light behind a fogging gauze, with only Mathias and, for a brief time, the Mesmerist clearly visible, attention was focused on Irving and his appalling re-enactment of the old crime.

The only technical innovation was to be found in the second act, set in Mathias's parlour. The room is comfortably furnished with chairs, desk and a tiled stove. Here, Mathias has a conversation with his future son-in-law, Christian, presumably to discuss marriage with Annette and to secure Christian's promise to protect his father-in-law. But Christian, curious about the unsolved disappearance of the Jew, has reopened investigations. He announces this fact as Mathias picks up fire-tongs to put coal into the stove. Within the stove was a small red-tinted electric lamp, one of the first electric lights used on the London stage, aimed and focused to cast its beam directly on Mathias's face. This technology was a part of what became another admired moment of Irving's stage business: the shock of Christian's announcement again inspired sudden fear, causing Mathias to drop the tongs with a loud clatter and to pause, his face – fully visible and diabolical in the red light of the open stove door – slowly losing its terror and becoming guileful.

To turn again to Irving's popular roles, it becomes apparent how many of them express or expose the duality of the self, the open and the hidden, the apparently honest and virtuous life spoilt and forever contaminated by unacknowledged criminal acts. Taken in company with changes to the form of melodrama and the inquiry into the macabre and occult, these emphases amount to substantial theatrical innovations which would not have occurred and received the sanction of public approval had audiences resisted such change. The question thus arises: in what ways is the Lyceum audience complicit in redirecting the vectors of melodrama and encouraging plays which explore hidden guilt and the hidden or partly revealed second self? Or to phrase the question another way: what pleasure is derived from witnessing Mathias, Mortimer, Synorix, King Louis and Eugene Aram suffer, and who are the beneficiaries of this pleasure?

The answer may lie in what we have learned to recognize as the Victorians' double standard of morality and sexual mores, at least insofar as theatrical suffering from guilt aroused by the great crimes of murder and usurpation permitted audiences to suffer and be punished – vicariously, of course – for lesser crimes of adultery, other domestic disloyalties and social *gaffes*. This is hardly to insist that the majority of the Lyceum audience were adulterers, but it does speak to the Victorian preoccupation with appearances and concealment, particularly with appearances of rectitude, virtue and respectability and concealment of behaviour that acknowledged sexual urges or acts. We know from literature and published sermons that the Victorians were bedevilled by the need to assure themselves and others of their respectability. Their diaries frequently report misgivings and inabilities to assure themselves that they are truly successful in their efforts. To be a Lyceum spectator witnessing Mathias suffer secretly and alone, unable to acknowledge and atone for an act committed fifteen years in the past, and finally to see Mathias punished for his crime and die still blameless in the eyes of his family and community, is to experience – by proxy – suffering, punishment and expiation and, eventually, to return home from the theatre with a still unblemished reputation. What the spectator hid and repressed is still concealed, but the burden of repression is easier to bear, for someone else has taken the blame and been condemned for it. Meanwhile, the spectator has had the pleasure of seeing an actor of remarkable skill, intelligence and emotional range in one of the great stage roles, if not one of the better plays, of the nineteenth century.

19

The new drama and the old theatre

PETER THOMSON

Good work is knocking at the stage doors! Why isn't it admitted? Why does
the actor put the banalities on? When he is his own manager, why not produce
things that are worthy of him?[1]

The speaker of these words is Alma King, the actress whom Royce Oliphant –
the title character of Leonard Merrick's theatrical novel *The Actor-Manager*
(1898) – loves but does not marry. Merrick knew the London theatre world
from the inside. He, like Oliphant at the novel's opening, had been a jobbing
actor with literary aspirations, and he writes feelingly of the mutual loneliness
of two young actors who hoped for more when they entered the profession.
Out of work and penniless, Alma has recently understudied the role of Hilde
Wangel in Ibsen's *The Master Builder* for the Independent Theatre Society. Her
vision of a literary drama chimes with Oliphant's, and the novel as a whole tests
that vision against the realities of the late nineteenth-century theatre. Alma
vanishes from the story for a prolonged period, touring to South Africa with
a second-rate company and a repertoire of pot-boilers. Oliphant, by contrast,
rises meteorically when he takes over the leading role in his own play (based on
the notorious case of the Tichborne claimant), marries the beautiful Blanche
Ellerton and becomes an actor-manager. 'Only no *Brand*, Royce', Blanche
cautions, 'if you're going to open the campaign with *Brand* because you want
to play the part, we shall be doomed' (240). Not yet bold enough to stage Ibsen,
Oliphant opts for a poetic play from a French author (Maurice Maeterlinck in
the disguise of Sylvain Lacour) 'laid on an imaginary island, and the period
was described simply as "The Past"' (243). It is a *succès d'estime*, which Blanche,
with her eye on the empty stalls, considers the French for a failure. Oliphant's
next choice is an English play of ideas by 'a dramatist with a literary reputation'
(263):

[1] Merrick, *Actor-Manager*, 7.

> *The Average Man* was eulogised by those organs which embody the views of
> the critical for the delectation of the cultured; it was received with respect by
> the entire Press; it was even commented on by the public. It did not, of course,
> excite the interest aroused by a football match, but its thesis was mentioned;
> there were a great many people in London who said 'Fancy!'   (266)

With his young enterprise on the financial rocks, Oliphant is forced to accept his
wife's choice of the next play, from the fertile pen of Félix Reybaud (Victorien
Sardou in disguise), 'a playwright who was sincere in nothing but his desire to
tickle the public taste' (273). It plays to full houses.

Merrick's bleak novel is an informed commentary on the theatre he knew.
The conventional wisdom of hindsight, especially when orchestrated by
George Bernard Shaw, tends to blame the leaders of the late Victorian stage for
blocking the access of socially and artistically alert 'new' plays. That is to say
that there is a general acceptance of Shaw's view that 'one of the worst priva-
tions of life in London for persons of serious intellectual and artistic interests
is the want of a suitable playhouse'.[2] It is, of course, true that a commercial
theatre, operating entirely without subsidy, was inclined to play safe, but it
would be a mistake to suppose that the British theatre shunned anything 'new'
during the second half of the nineteenth century. On the contrary, as Martin
Meisel noted in a seminal book, '[s]ince the middle of the century it had been
changing rapidly from a theater of flamboyant make-believe to a theater of
sophisticated verisimilitude'.[3] The ground rules of the new drama had been
confirmed in the 1860s by the success of Tom Robertson's sequence of starkly
titled comedies at the Prince of Wales's theatre in London – *Society* (1865), *Ours*
(1866), *Caste* (1867), *Play* (1868), *School* (1869) and *M.P.* (1870) – but the historical
focus on London has encouraged theatre historians to overlook the fact that
the first two of these were premièred in Liverpool, that the companion piece
Birth (1870) was first staged in Bristol, and that ten days after Robertson's premature death on 3 February 1871, *Policy* opened in Glasgow. Dramatic novelty
was cherished nationwide.

Robertson's stage directions were much more innovatory than his plots,
but what they served to promote was a significant shift in the predominant
style of acting. Audiences flocked to see performances that were no longer
larger than life, but lifesize. The new excitement was that of knowing people
who looked and behaved 'just like that' in familiar rooms and amid furniture
'just like ours'. Even the best of Robertson's plays are conventional at the

---

[2] Preface to *Plays Unpleasant* (1898), in Shaw, *Prefaces*, 718.
[3] Meisel, *Shaw and the Nineteenth-Century Theater*, 65.

core. Brought up in the ambience of his father's theatrical stock company, he constructed his comedies out of the collision of stock characters, all shaped to suit traditional 'lines of business' – juvenile leads, heavies, Irish, low comedy, old men, light/gentlemanly comedy, chambermaids and so on.[4] His innovation was to set his unreal people the task of doing 'real' things – drinking cups of tea, making puddings – and the inherent contradiction carried into the audience a conviction of novelty.

Different perceptions of the new have confused theatre-goers in every decade. In 1995 the latest Alan Ayckbourn play, *Communicating Doors*, was still relatively 'new' when Sarah Kane's *Blasted* was staged at the Royal Court's Theatre Upstairs. Reviews of *Communicating Doors* were lukewarm, but *Blasted* turned the stomachs of many drama critics. The moral outrage of the *Daily Mail's* headline, 'This Disgusting Feast of Filth', revives memories of critical reactions to Ibsen's *Ghosts* a century earlier. There is a sense in which an Ayckbourn play is old before he has written it, whereas Kane's play had the arresting effect of the incontestably new. A similar contrast is implicit in Shaw's reactions to the plays of Pinero on the one hand and Ibsen on the other; yet Shaw's attitudes did not coincide with those of the majority of theatre-goers, and certainly not with those of the actor-managers.

Actor-managers: the old theatre or the new drama?

As the century drew to its close by no means all of London's theatres were managed by actors, but many of the most prominent were. Henry Irving (Sir Henry from 1895) had been running the Lyceum since 1879. Playhouse and player were household names, but the repertoire was not copied anywhere else. Lavishly pictorial revivals of Shakespeare set the tone of what was essentially a celebrity house, and the new plays Irving staged successfully were those he could most readily camouflage as old ones. The Lyceum maintained an inimitably splendid isolation so long as Irving governed it. Most people assumed it was as prosperous a business as its stage sets and quantity of employees suggested. But it is essential to our understanding of the management of the theatres of the period to recognize that Irving depended on touring (across Britain and especially North America) for his profits.[5] He was one of the pioneers of whole-company touring, itself an offshoot of the development of a coherent railway network, and this kind of touring was one of the two most

---

[4] The impact of 'lines of business' on playwriting during the first half of the nineteenth century is neatly described in Cross, *Next Week* – East Lynne, 47–54.

[5] See Tracy C. Davis, *Economics of the British Stage*, 219–25.

significant factors in the decay of the traditional stock companies. The other was the institution of the long run. H. J. Byron's *Our Boys* (opened 1875) at the Vaudeville held the record, with 1,362 performances, until displaced by Brandon Thomas's *Charley's Aunt* (opened 1892), initially at the Royalty and subsequently at the Globe, with 1,466. Within a year of its London opening, *Charley's Aunt* was being toured around Britain by four companies, around Germany by seven and around North America by nine.[6] A long run supplemented by national tours might make any shrewd manager as rich as it made Charles Wyndham (1837–1919).

It was with some justification that Wyndham thought of himself as a promoter of the new drama, though history, with equal justification, has cast him as a prop of the old. His acting career had begun in the newly united America in the aftermath of the Civil War, introducing Tom Robertson to sometimes bemused audiences under the banner of Wyndham's Comedy Company, and it was partly to gratify the local taste for more full-blooded fare that he added Bronson Howard's *Saratoga* to his repertoire. It was as Bob Sackett in *Brighton*, the Anglicized version of Howard's original (plays were even more pliable then than they are now) that Wyndham made his 1875 début at the Criterion, the theatre in which he maintained a managerial interest for the remaining forty-four years of his life. His full control of the Criterion began in the same year as Irving's of the Lyceum – 1879. Together with his leading lady and eventual second wife, Mary Moore, Wyndham turned his basement playhouse into a suite of comfortable receiving rooms for theatrical visitors. For the first time, coffee was available in the intervals and programmes were on sale in the foyer.[7] Wyndham was a social success far more readily than the introspective Irving; but what is more significant here is his introduction to London audiences of a new dramatic genre, the full-length farce. Precedence belongs to *Pink Dominos* (1877), bowdlerized for English ears from a French source by James Albery, Mary Moore's husband. Wyndham's gentlemanly handling of risqué material enabled him to sail close to the wind without causing offence, but it was his own squeamishness that diminished the effect of what might otherwise have been a second significant innovation – a play that resisted the outright condemnation of a wife's adultery. If Henry Arthur Jones's *The Case of Rebellious Susan* (Criterion, 1894) reads tamely now, that should not blind us to its historical daring. It was, after all, at Wyndham's insistence that Jones left ambiguous just what it was that happened between Lady Susan Harabin and

---

[6] See Brandon-Thomas, *Charley's Aunt's Father*, 188.
[7] For a succinct account of Wyndham's career, see George Rowell, 'Charles Wyndham'.

Lucien Edensor on a particular Sunday in Cairo. Lady Susan, it is as well to remember, had left her adulterous husband with the resonant exit line, 'I am going to find a little romance, and introduce it to our married life.'[8]

Although *The Case of Rebellious Susan* ends with the estranged couple reconciled, it does so without endorsing the necessary inequality of women in matters of sex. Jones's play of 1894 was bracketed by two notorious explorations of the 'woman question', Pinero's *The Second Mrs Tanqueray* (1893), which had recently completed its run at the St James's when *Rebellious Susan* opened, and Grant Allen's shocking novel *The Woman Who Did* (1895), in both of which the peccant heroines were driven to suicide. In effect, Allen openly and Pinero silently endorse the 'prime antithesis' – 'the male, active and aggressive; the female, sedentary, passive, and receptive'.[9] Jones rejects the antithesis, without the socio-political subtlety of Shaw's contemporary *Mrs Warren's Profession*, but with characteristic combativeness. A. E. W. Mason knew Jones well:

> He was a man of large ideas violently expressed. Critics like Bernard Shaw and Max Beerbohm expected his work with eagerness and criticised it with care. Most of the others were repelled by an uncouthness in his style and the untempered vigour of his convictions. He was the most positive man you could meet in a twelvemonth. Causes were tonics to him and he drank of them greedily.[10]

Wyndham's support for Jones's interventions into the woman question (he would later stage two more of Jones's best plays, *The Liars* in 1897 and *Mrs Dane's Defence* in 1900) benefited both men, as well as giving what was then felt as a cutting edge to the new drama. It is clear in retrospect that Jones was too much a man of his time to provide a lasting radical impulse to the English drama, but there are signs that, in the mid-1890s, before a crusty seam of reactionariness was exposed in him, he apprehended the cultural shift that has subsequently been defined as modernism. In a dedicatory letter to the published version of *Rebellious Susan* he addresses Mrs Grundy, 'the august and austere effigy of our national taste and respectability', reassuring her that 'there is not the slightest necessity for disturbing our cherished national belief that immorality is confined to the Continent, and especially to France'. The sting is in the postscript: 'My comedy isn't a comedy at all. It's a tragedy dressed up as a comedy.'[11] The insight that recognized an association between

---

[8] Jones, *Representative Plays*, 300.
[9] Allen, *The Woman Who Did*, 64.
[10] Mason, *Sir George Alexander & The St James' Theatre*, 92.
[11] The dedicatory letter is reproduced in Jones, *Plays*, ed. Jackson, 105–7.

dramatic genre and human gender is incorporated in a passage of dialogue at the opening of Act 2. Sir Richard Kato, the play's *raisonneur* (Wyndham's role), is probing the worldly-wise widow Inez Quesnel (played by the highly intelligent Gertrude Kingston, later an active supporter of suffragettes):

KATO: Well, now tell me – I'm only asking in the purest spirit of scientific inquiry – are there any depths and treasures which we mere outsiders, men, never suspect?

INEZ: Shall I tell you? Yes, treasures of faithfulness, treasures of devotion, of self-sacrifice, of courage, of comradeship, of loyalty. And above all, treasures of deceit – loving, honourable deceit, and secrecy and treachery.

KATO: I had already suspected there might be an occasional jewel of that sort in the dark unfathomed caves.

INEZ: You're laughing at me. You men never will see anything but a comedy in it. So we have to dress up our tragedy as a comedy just to save ourselves from being ridiculous and boring you. But we women feel it is a tragedy all the same.[12]

This is, in effect, a direct address to the men and women in the audience at the Criterion. English comedy, Jones says, is a patriarchal preserve: if comedy is to develop, it must be opened up to women. A similar perception lies behind Grace Tranfield's despairing comment at the end of Shaw's (as yet unperformed and unpublished in 1894) *The Philanderer*: 'They think this is a happy ending, Julia, these men: our lords and masters.'[13] It should not surprise us that Wyndham's staging of Jones's plays encouraged the old theatre's belief that it was accommodating the new drama.

George Alexander (1858–1918) might equally have claimed that his management of the St James's from 1890 until his death was a forward-looking one. He was, after all, the first to stage many of Pinero's major plays, as well as Oscar Wilde's *Lady Windermere's Fan* (1892) and *The Importance of Being Earnest* (1895). He entered management, after serving an acting apprenticeship with Irving at the Lyceum and on tour, with a determined policy of giving preference to British plays, and invited writers of distinction (Thomas Hardy, Conan Doyle, H. G. Wells) to submit work for his consideration. His staging of Henry James's *Guy Domville* (1895) began as a homage to literature, and its ending as a *fiasco d'estime*[14] was almost as disconcerting to Alexander as it was to James. It necessitated a hasty negotiation with Wyndham, who had the first claim on *The*

---

[12] *Representative Plays*, II: 303–4.
[13] Shaw, *Complete Plays*, 60.
[14] I borrow this term from Peter Ustinov, who used it to describe the reception of Stravinsky's *Rite of Spring*.

Importance of Being Earnest. The 'serious' Alexander was probably better suited than the quick-fire Wyndham to the creation of an appropriately 'straight' Jack Worthing, and a first night at the St James's was always an occasion: 'in those days', wrote Alexander's widow, 'people went to see the St James' plays before ordering a new gown'.[15] Alexander insisted that his stage hands wore white overalls (with cuffs coloured to demarcate their particular duties), cotton gloves and white soft shoes.[16] His theatre was a model of unruffled efficiency, but it became clear as time passed that his business practices were more modern than his repertoire. The 'typical' St James's play became too easy to characterize:

> In a typical St James's play the humorous characters were delightfully playful, the serious characters charmingly sentimental, and the plot savoured of scandal without being objectionably truthful. Adultery was invariably touched on and inevitably touched up; theft was made thrilling, and murder romantic.[17]

This is a late recollection by Hesketh Pearson, who had worked with Alexander, and it records, not the truth, but what came to be believed to be true. In the new century, Alexander would be a justice of the peace, a London county councillor and a Conservative candidate for Parliament. He was by then a representatively conservative middle-class man of property. It may well be that the breaking of the Oscar Wilde scandal when *The Importance of Being Earnest* was less than two months into its run broke his resolve. A. E. W. Mason, his wise biographer, argues that Alexander's removal of Wilde's name from the playbills prolonged the play's run at the St James's – it lasted a month longer than *An Ideal Husband* at the Haymarket, where Wilde's name was retained.[18] It was, nevertheless, a surrender to the power of the old theatre, the one Henry Arthur Jones ascribed to Mrs Grundy, over the new drama. The leadership of a vigorous movement had been in Alexander's hands in 1893, when he had the courage to stage *The Second Mrs Tanqueray*. He was, not surprisingly, nervous of it, to the extent of planning to provide it with the protective underpinning of incidental music. 'I can't see that anything of this sort is required', wrote Pinero; 'Don't you think "incidental" scraping vulgarises a piece that doesn't belong to either "the kettle-on-the-hob" or "the Blood-on-the-Breadknife" order of play?'[19] *Mrs Tanqueray* is strong enough to

---

[15] 'A note by Lady Alexander', in Mason, *Sir George Alexander*, 233.
[16] Duncan, *St James's Theatre*, 219.
[17] Pearson, *Last Actor-Managers*, 23.
[18] Mason, *Sir George Alexander*, 81.
[19] Quoted ibid., 49.

have survived the battering it took at Shaw's hands.[20] And if, on the page, it seems to guide women to accept the application of a double standard in sexual relationships – unlike *The Case of Rebellious Susan* – we should be wary of over-looking the capacity of Mrs Patrick Campbell, in the title role, to subvert on stage the play's overt message. The evidence suggests that her performance, far from feeding the complacency of its audiences, ruffled it. Pinero was, to the end of his life, quite incapable of knowing when he had written a good play. As a result, he wrote several bad ones; but *Mrs Tanqueray*, for all its flaws, is not one of those. It can be fairly argued that, aided by Alexander's discreet stage management and Mrs Patrick Campbell's critical intelligence, it thrust the new drama further towards adulthood, but it must also be regretted that Alexander, in the long run, lacked the courage of Mrs Pat's convictions.

Mason records a telling incident during the rehearsal of his own play, *The Witness for the Defence*, at the St James's. Alexander suddenly stopped in the middle of a dialogue with Ethel Irving, explaining that 'We're in the centre of the stage'.

> I was a little staggered, for I had never thought of actor-managers as people liable to be distressed upon finding themselves in that position. As a rule they drift by some process of magnetism inevitably towards it. But he explained. 'You see, we play to rather sophisticated audiences here, and if I'm in the centre of the stage they'll say, "There of course is the actor-manager", and the illusion of your play's gone.'[21]

Alexander's concern signals a developing stagecraft that had been pioneered by the Bancrofts in the ensemble pieces of Tom Robertson. Bravura actor-managers such as Irving and Beerbohm Tree had no such scruples.

Tree was always a loose cannon on the theatrical battlefield. His repertoire during the ten years of management that preceded his move to Her Majesty's in 1897 included three plays by Shakespeare and three by Henry Arthur Jones, one by W. S. Gilbert, one by Oscar Wilde, one by Maeterlinck and even (briefly) one by Ibsen. But there were also seven scamped adaptations from the French and two from the German, as well as twelve plays that have no hold on history. Tree's greatest success was as a flamboyantly preposterous Svengali in Paul Potter's adaptation of *Trilby* (1895). There, as almost always, he was strangely hard to resist, partly, perhaps, because he was resolutely uncommitted. Whilst the up-market periodical the *Nineteenth Century* opened its pages to a debate

---

[20] See, for example, Shaw, *Our Theatres in the Nineties*, I: 44–8.
[21] Mason, *Sir George Alexander*, 4.

on the merits and demerits of theatrical government by actor-managers, Tree sat energetically on the fence:

> Far be it from me to throw into a peaceful and united camp of criticism the apple of discord or the bone of contention. Yet this army, united as it is in one common cause, its holy crusade against the Actor-Manager, is divided into creeds, the one side championing the divine right, the undying laws of an artistic monarchy, the other leaning towards the republic of untrammelled modernity and artistic emancipation. You are all familiar with the old ballad 'How happy could I be with either, were t'other dear charmer away.' Well, in that attitude of perplexed hesitancy stands the lover of the modern drama.[22]

There is evidence here of what Martin Meisel has called 'the schizophrenic London theater of the nineties'.[23] Tree was capable of staging Ibsen with as little conviction as he played the faithful husband, staged Shakespeare or founded the Royal Academy of Dramatic Art. Acting was his way of concealing unbelief.

The Ibsen question

Late Victorian taste did not easily assimilate art that exposed life in the raw. When Edgar Degas's grim portrait of addiction, *L'Absinthe*, was exhibited in London in 1892, it was greeted with much the same stream of abusive adjectives as greeted Ibsen's *Ghosts*: 'vulgar, boozy, sottish, loathsome, revolting, ugly, besotted, degraded, repulsive'.[24] Despite William Archer's advocacy, and perhaps *because of* Shaw's, no commercial management would countenance staging the work of the gloomy Norwegian, but an unlikely initiative had already been taken by John Hollingshead, manager of the light-hearted Gaiety from 1868 to 1886. It was Hollingshead who established, from 1871, a fashion for experimental matinées that was already on the wane by the 1890s. The Gaiety matinées sometimes featured one-off comebacks by retired stars, more often understudies in rare possession of leading roles. They were generally hastily mounted, played in front of the scenery for the evening's performance – either revealed or blanked off by flats – and scantily attended. As the fashion spread to other theatres – Terry's, the Comedy, the Royalty, the Vaudeville and eventually Tree's Haymarket – it provided managers with an opportunity to test new plays and actors engaged in long runs to earn extra pocket

---

[22] In a lecture of 1891, reprinted in Tree, *Thoughts and After-Thoughts*, 164.
[23] Meisel, *Shaw and the Nineteenth-Century Theatre*, 6.
[24] Quoted in McConkey, *British Impressionism*, 109.

money. Edward Terry, for example, took the opportunity of assessing Frances Hodgson Burnett's dramatization of her popular novel *Little Lord Fauntleroy* in a long series of matinées beginning in May 1888 when Pinero's *Sweet Lavender* was securely bedded in his theatre in the evenings; Brandon Thomas, newly married, was able to augment the £8 per week he received as Pinero's Geoffrey Wedderburn by creating the role of Lord Fauntleroy's solicitor.[25] But it was at the Gaiety, on the afternoon of 15 December 1880, that an Ibsen play in English was first presented on the London stage. The translation was by William Archer, who agreed under protest to accept the title *Quicksands*, with the more familiar (and more accurate) *The Pillars of Society* relegated to the subtitle. The whole venture cost W. H. Vernon, who played Bernick, about £70, which included the cost of renting the theatre and token payments to the actors. After only a week of rehearsals, the production was predictably shambolic, and there was scarcely a ripple in the press. The anonymous critic for the *Times* (18 December 1880) suggested that the play 'conveys the impression of being the work of a man of talent', but Archer failed in his attempt to place his translation with a publisher until 1888, when it appeared alongside his translation of *Ghosts* and Eleanor Marx's of *An Enemy of Society*.

It was Ibsen's champions, more than the plays themselves, that alerted the guardians of British morals, among whom the Examiner of Plays was the appointed wielder of Mrs Grundy's scissors. A version of *A Doll's House*, patched together from a woeful translation and disfigured with a 'happy' ending by Henry Arthur Jones and Henry Herman, was presented as *Breaking a Butterfly* at the Prince's Theatre in 1884, but it had completely lost touch with Ibsen's original text. Not until June 1889, in Archer's translation and in a production largely directed by him, featuring Janet Achurch and her husband Charles Charrington, did *A Doll's House* receive its first London performance. Archer was privately surprised that the play had been licensed, and it may have been its location in the unfashionable Novelty Theatre in Holborn and the brevity of the proposed run that spurred the censor's leniency. If so, he had underrated the prurient buzz of interest in Ibsen. The critics attended in force as the week's run progressed. A. B. Walkley, probably the most intelligent and open-minded of them, detected 'the beginning of a dramatic revolution . . . The great intellectual movement of the day has at last reached the theatre. There is a future for the stage after all.' But admirers of the play were outnumbered by scandalized detractors. 'Of no use – as far as England's stage is concerned', pronounced the *Referee*; 'unnatural, immoral and, in its concluding scene,

---

[25] See Brandon-Thomas, *Charley's Aunt's Father*, 121–37.

undramatic', said the *People*; the *Standard* issued the magisterial summary, 'It would be a misfortune were such a morbid and unwholesome play to gain the favour of the public.'[26] Most damaging of all was the change of heart of the self-important but influential Clement Scott. Having initially praised the production in the *Daily Telegraph*, he turned on Ibsen and the Ibsenites in the July 1889 issue of the *Theatre*, which he edited. That 'so unnatural a creature' as Nora should be 'the ideal woman of the new creed' demonstrated the moral depravity of that creed, whose adherents must, like Ibsen's characters, be 'unlovable, unlovely and detestable'.

There was no chance that the vociferousness of his enemies would keep Ibsen off the London stage. A tame, single-night revival of *A Doll's House* was staged at Terry's theatre in January 1891, and an almost equally tame *Rosmersholm*, with a miscast Frank Benson and a harassed (by Shaw) Florence Farr, was given two matinées at the Vaudeville in February and March. It was not these productions, but that of *Ghosts* at the inauguration of the Independent Theatre in the Royalty on 13 March that marked 1891 as *the* Ibsen year. J. T. Grein, the indomitably optimistic Dutch founder of the Independent Theatre, had chosen Antoine's Parisian Théâtre Libre as his model, though financial constraints meant that, over the brief life of his society (1891–8), he achieved only one-fifth of Antoine's extraordinary 111 plays by eighty-three different authors. As an organization funded by subscription, the Independent Theatre was unaffected by the Lord Chamberlain's ban on *Ghosts*, but for the critics 13 March was a night of the long knives. Clement Scott's leader in the *Daily Telegraph* of 14 March 1891 still has a dubious celebrity. He pronounced *Ghosts* 'an open drain . . . a loathsome sore unbandaged . . . a dirty act done publicly'. Walkley's voice in the *Star* of the same date, was a lone one: 'One wonders whether these hysterical protestants have ever read anything, observed anything, pondered anything. Have they no eyes for what stares them in the face: the plain, simple fact that *Ghosts* is a great spiritual drama?'

Because inherited syphilis is one of the play's themes, *Ghosts* was anathema to middle-class Victorian moralizers. How many of them, one wonders, had relatives who suffered from the contemporary malady of 'general paralysis of the insane', which was tertiary syphilis, or inherited syphilis, by another name. Walkley's rhetorical questions strike at the heart of the English theatre's dilemma. It had to keep its eyes shut. If it opened them, it would experience the pain of growing up. No wonder that the great child-man of the drama, J. M. Barrie, advertised his conversion from the novel by composing a burlesque

---

[26] These quotations from reviews are culled from Whitebrook, *William Archer*, 88.

called *Ibsen's Ghost* for the comedian J. L. Toole at the theatre that bore his name. In his dedication to the published *Peter Pan*, Barrie recalled 'my first little piece . . . a parody of the mightiest craftsman that ever wrote for our kind friends in front'.[27] The first words of *Ibsen's Ghost*, which opened on 30 May 1891, were: 'To run away from my second husband just as I ran away from my first, it feels quite like old times', and the curtain fell just after the whole cast had shot themselves 'beautifully'. It is easy to deduce that Barrie's burlesque conflated *A Doll's House*, *Ghosts* and *Hedda Gabler*. Even Archer thought it 'a piece of genuinely witty fooling which ought not to be missed'.[28]

The production of *Hedda Gabler* which Barrie must have seen was by some way the best presented of the Ibsen year of 1891. Like the Achurch–Charrington *Doll's House*, it was translated and 'directed' ('stage-managed' in the parlance of the time) by William Archer, whose active role in the early stagings of Ibsen has been overlooked because he never claimed it. Since he was in love with his Hedda, the vibrantly sensitive and unflinchingly intelligent American actress Elizabeth Robins, there may well have been an invisible current energizing the performance, sufficient to convert a scheduled run of five matinées at the Vaudeville to ten, and those ten extended to four weeks of evening performances (replacing a flagging revival of Bulwer Lytton's *Money*). It was audiences, not critics, and perhaps Robins rather than Ibsen, who kept *Hedda Gabler* running. Though not as vituperative as they had been about *Ghosts*, reviewers found the thrust of the play distasteful. The *Observer* labelled it 'a contribution to the drama of disease', the *Pictorial World* 'a bad escape of moral sewage-gas', and Clement Scott, speaking on behalf of all manly men, regretted that Robins 'has glorified an unwomanly woman. She has made a heroine out of a sublimated sinner. She has fascinated us with a savage.'[29]

There was more of Ibsen before the year ended. An undistinguished matinée of *The Lady from the Sea* at Terry's theatre in May was followed by yet another indifferent *Doll's House* at Wyndham's Criterion in June, but it was the October publication of Shaw's *The Quintessence of Ibsenism* that moved the debate to another level. If, for Shaw, it was crucial to the progress of English drama that Ibsen's realism, his attack on the folly of inert idealism, be adopted, it became equally crucial for opponents of Shaw's socio-dramatic programme to block Ibsen's access to English writers. In a quite extraordinary way, Ibsen became the supple hinge of a dramatic door that might open either way. Every

---

[27] The dedication is reprinted in *The Plays of J. M. Barrie*, 3–16. This quotation, together with the opening lines of *Ibsen's Ghost*, appears on p. 5.
[28] Quoted in Whitebrook, *William Archer*, 130.
[29] Reviews here are culled from John, *Elizabeth Robins*, 60–1.

production of an Ibsen play during the 1890s – and there were several more to come – became a test case, in which either Ibsen or the English drama was on trial. And it was now that Shaw himself resolved to enter the fray in the guise of a playwright.

Shaw's unpleasant plays

Each of the three plays, his first in prose, that Shaw later published under the collective title of *Plays Unpleasant* (1898) was intended to advance the Ibsenite cause. *Widowers' Houses* had its origins, indeed, in a collaboration between Shaw and the chief priest of Ibsenism, William Archer, with Archer supplying the plot and Shaw the dialogue. For all his modernist leanings, Archer was unable to free himself from the bonds of the 'old' drama. The play he sketched out was a conventional romantic comedy of love's triumph over misalliance. A well-born young man is shocked to discover that the woman he loves is the daughter of an unscrupulous slum-landlord, but love conquers all, and the play would end with our hero 'throwing the tainted treasure of his father-in-law, metaphorically speaking, into the Rhine'.[30] Only a trace of Archer's plot remains in Shaw's play, but the characters, as Martin Meisel observed, fall readily within the stereotypes of nineteenth-century drama: Sartorius is a 'heavy father', Cokane a 'stage swell', Lickcheese a 'low comedian' and Trench and Blanche Sartorius are 'romantic leads'. 'It was on the broad back of the nineteenth-century lines, casts and stereotypes that Shaw built his drama of ideas.'[31] It was part of Shaw's mischief to deploy the techniques of the 'old' drama in order to pollute them into newness. *Widowers' Houses* was hurriedly rebuilt on the foundations of the Archer–Shaw *Rhinegold* in response to J. T. Grein's appeal for a British play, and the Independent Theatre duly staged it for two ramshackle performances at the Royalty in December 1892. Shaw should have been gratified by the outraged response of the London reviewers. It meant that his attempt to implicate the respectable middle classes in the social crime of the city slums had, at least in part, succeeded. But *Widowers' Houses* owes to Ibsen nothing more than its concern to open the eyes of its audiences to realities that they would prefer to ignore. *Mrs Warren's Profession*, the third of the 'unpleasant' plays, does the same thing much better.

In *Widowers' Houses* Sartorius had risen from poverty by exploiting the poor, and he used his wealth to enhance the life of his daughter. Mrs Warren has

---

[30] From Archer's review of the Independent Theatre production in *The World*, 14 December 1892.

[31] Meisel, *Shaw and the Nineteenth-Century Theatre*, 37.

risen from poverty by exploiting the comparatively prosperous frequenters of prostitutes, and she uses her wealth to enhance the life of her daughter. Shaw's Fabian understanding of Marx recognized exploitation as the lifeblood of capitalism, and in *Mrs Warren's Profession* organized prostitution is a metaphor for capitalism. A defence of the 'profession', however ironic, was unacceptable in the British theatre, where it was customary for prostitutes to die. The second Mrs Tanqueray had done the decent thing by killing herself in Pinero's play – the major sensation of the 1893 theatrical season – and she, though 'loose', was scarcely a prostitute. Shaw knowingly undertook *Mrs Warren's Profession* as a counter to *The Second Mrs Tanqueray* (Brecht, who celebrated the 'terrorist' in Shaw, would label his own counter-plays *Gegenstücke*), but knew, as he wrote it, that there was no chance of its being staged. He waited over four years – until March 1898 – before submitting it to the Lord Chamberlain's Office, and then only because its publication in *Plays Unpleasant* was imminent, and a public reading was required in order to secure his copyright. George Redford, the Examiner of Plays, returned it with a whole act cut and the nature of Mrs Warren's profession scrupulously unspecified.[32] In the next century Shaw would amuse himself by regularly resubmitting the full text to the Lord Chamberlain's Office, and was surprised when a licence was finally granted in 1926.[33] The nineteenth-century stage, then, was denied access to a play that had the wit and insight to place women fully into the network of economics, about which they were conventionally encouraged not to bother their pretty little heads.

It is the second and flimsiest of the unpleasant plays, *The Philanderer*, that openly features Ibsen. Act 2 is set in a fictional Ibsen Club whose membership is closed only to manly men and womanly women, and Jo Cuthbertson, whose life has been passed 'in witnessing scenes of suffering nobly endured and sacrifice willingly rendered by womanly women and manly men' (*Complete Plays*, 36), is a caricature of Clement Scott – a drama critic whose life has been passed in witnessing nineteenth-century plays. Leonard Charteris, the philanderer of the title, is Shaw's wry self-portrait. Hesketh Pearson, a sometimes wayward biographer, plausibly summarizes Shaw's attitude to women:

> The fact that they were not of primary importance in his life is balanced by the fact that he often made them of primary importance in his art, the explanation of which is that they always appealed far more to his imagination than to his bodily needs.[34]

---

[32] In that form, the play was duly read at the Victoria Hall, Bayswater.
[33] The story is amusingly told in Nicholson, *Censorship of British Drama*, 106–9.
[34] Pearson, *Bernard Shaw*, 111.

Charteris, like Shaw in 1893, having flirted with any number of women, has managed to avoid both marriage and any significant change in the tenor of his life. Neither author nor character can quite understand what all the fuss is about. *The Philanderer* is Shaw's feeble contribution to the late Victorian debate about marriage that had its seminal theatrical source in *A Doll's House* and *Hedda Gabler*, but his distance from Ibsen on the subject of women is one of the many reasons why, for all his propagandizing, Shaw could never have written plays like Ibsen's.

The Philanderer was written for the Independent Theatre, but not produced. Shaw's explanation takes us back to the world of the actor-managers:

> even before I finished it, it was apparent that its demands on the most expert and delicate sort of high comedy acting went beyond the resources then at the disposal of Mr Grein. I had written a part which nobody but Charles Wyndham could act, in a play which was impossible at his theatre.[35]

The Philanderer lacks the dramatic stamina for the sort of long run the actor-managers depended on, but Shaw is here confessing to an interdependence between his 'new' drama and the 'old' theatre. No other actor could play dispassionate volatility in so assured/a-Shawed a way as Wyndham. If Shaw was to see himself portrayed on stage, he wanted it done in style. The reference to the Criterion and its actor-manager stands awkwardly against a rhetorical flourish earlier in the same preface:

> The New Theatre would never have come into existence but for the plays of Ibsen . . . Every attempt to extend the repertory proved that it is the drama that makes the theatre and not the theatre the drama. Not that this needed fresh proof, since the whole difficulty had arisen through the drama of the day being written for the theatres instead of from its own necessity.[36]

This is a convenient and shapely argument, but theatrical history is rarely convenient and often shapeless. *The Philanderer*, by Shaw's confession, has a foot in each of two camps: the *play* is with the new drama, the ideal *player* with the old theatre.

Towards a new theatre

The prosperity of British theatres in the late nineteenth century made them resistant to any change that was more than cosmetic. In the fashionable West

---

[35] Shaw, *Prefaces*, 720.
[36] Ibid., 718.

End of London, in fact, a cosmetic theatre was in vogue: so much so that Shaw found himself preferring the bleak staging of a matinée at the Court Theatre in February 1897 to the sort of play which featured 'a tailor's advertisement making sentimental remarks to a milliner's advertisement in the middle of an upholsterer's and decorator's advertisement'.[37] But actor-managers who mounted such plays could make a lot of money (Wyndham left £200,000 to his widow). It is difficult to envisage any company in Britain, however 'independent', mounting in 1896 anything so extravagantly experimental as Jarry's *Ubu roi*. That sort of thing was best left to the French. But conservatism was not confined to the theatre: it was a middle-class mode that spread over other arts. The doyen of Victorian painters, William Frith, reacted to the mildly revisionist New English Arts Club on its foundation in 1886 much as Clement Scott reacted to Ibsen. Minds capable of receiving such 'impressions' must, he thundered, be 'in a state of disease'.[38] William Rothenstein, one of the new guard, was, by contrast, inspired by Degas's diseased *L'Absinthe* to 'paint' Ibsen in a canvas that he called *The Doll's House*, and A. B. Walkley went so far as to link Ibsen – and himself – with the art of the French Impressionists.[39] The condition of the drama in England was as much debated as the condition of painting and music, and London's tendency to quarantine itself in order to avoid infection from the Continent was as often deplored as it was celebrated.

Great play has sometimes been made of the impact on the English stage of the visit of the Meiningen Company to Drury Lane in 1881. Their controlled and individualized stage crowds and the discipline of their playing certainly impressed Irving and had their effect on subsequent Lyceum productions. The conduct of their theatres by the best actor-managers had its precedent in the Meininger, but the detection of a profound influence outside the Lyceum is probably the product of generalizing overstatement. The same is true of the visit to the Royalty by André Antoine's Théâtre Libre in 1889. J. T. Grein was certainly inspired by it, and it gave impetus to the proliferation of earnest little theatres outside as well as inside London, but the major theatres continued on their way, unruffled by the antics of a company that could not afford cosmetic aids. Antoine's impact on the mainstream was no greater than that of William Poel.[40] It was not until the next century, above all in the theatre work of Granville Barker and the visionary theorizing of Edward Gordon Craig, that the radical potential of a new theatre would be realized in Britain. But the

---

[37] Shaw, *Our Theatres in the Nineties*, III: 58.
[38] Quoted in McConkey, *British Impressionism*, 56.
[39] See John Stokes, *Resistible Theatres*, 155–6.
[40] For Poel's Elizabethan revivals, see Joel Kaplan's chapter in this volume.

talents of both Barker and Craig were nursed in the nineteenth-century theatre (Barker's by Poel, Craig's by Irving), a theatre that often fulfilled supremely well the tasks it set itself.

That the theatre and the drama are to some extent opposed is common knowledge to all playwrights. Copyright remained a vexed issue, despite the various attempts made through the century to sharpen the teeth of the 1833 Dramatic Copyright Act. The legal status of copyright readings like the one Shaw arranged for *Mrs Warren's Profession* was, for example, uncertain, and any kind of international control had to await the Berne Convention of 1886. But it was easier to apply the Berne Convention (and any kind of copyright, for that matter) to published than to performed work. It is not surprising under the circumstances that successful playwrights increasingly sought to publish their plays in a form more substantial than French's acting editions. Henry Arthur Jones in particular amassed a small fortune through the industrious courting of publishers. For actor-managers and for most of the playwrights who served them, the test of a play was its performance. For men like Antoine and Grein, the quality of a new play was assured *before* its performance, was the *reason* for the performance and would *survive* however shoddy the performance. On the one hand a commodity, on the other a work of art. The opposition is neatly encapsulated in an exchange that A. E. W. Mason ascribes to the eve of the première of *The Importance of Being Earnest*. Asked by a reporter whether he thought the play would be a success, Wilde allegedly replied, 'My dear fellow, you have got it wrong. The play *is* a success. The only question is whether the first night's audience will be one.'[41]

[41] Mason, *Sir George Alexander*, 78.

20

1895
A critical year in perspective

JOEL KAPLAN

The theatrical year 1895 would, no doubt, have been characterized by Lady Bracknell, its most enduring contribution, as crowded with both incident and premature experience. Its greatest sensation was, to be sure, the meteoric fall of Lady Bracknell's creator. In mid-February Oscar Wilde had two highly successful works playing opposite one another at two of the West End's principal playhouses. *An Ideal Husband* had opened at the Haymarket in early January, with matinée idol Lewis Waller in the role of Sir Robert Chiltern. It was still performing to packed houses when, the following month, George Alexander opened *The Importance of Being Earnest* to enthusiastic notices at the St James's. Wilde, now at the peak of his powers, was applauded alike by actor-managers, play-goers and progressive critics who counted him among the reformers of the British stage. Weeks later his career lay in ruins. The libel charges he had pressed against the Marquess of Queensberry triggered the succession of trials that in a matter of months brought him to Reading Gaol, convicted of 'gross indecency'. Wilde's name disappeared from programmes and playbills, and by late spring both works had been taken off by their respective managements. Clement Scott, doyen of London's critical fraternity, responded in predictable (and personal) fashion: 'Open the windows! Let in the fresh air!' An exasperated William Archer, translator and general champion of Ibsen in England, read the event as a serious blow for the development of a home-grown avant-garde: 'Really the luck is against the poor British drama.'[1]

If in 1895 Wilde was on the way down, others were on the way up. On 25 May, the very day of Wilde's imprisonment, Queen Victoria conferred a knighthood upon the 57-year-old Henry Irving. The honour, the first bestowed upon an actor, was in recognition of a quarter-century of service to the theatre. Irving's achievements as both performer and theatre manager had been the subject of much debate through the previous decades. If, for many, Wilde was

---

[1] Whitebrook, *William Archer*, 175.

an idiosyncratic recruit to a socially committed 'new' theatre, Irving's string of Lyceum successes – his appearances in *The Bells*, *The Corsican Brothers* and *Richelieu*, as well as his sumptuous stagings of Shakespeare – placed him clearly in the camp of the 'old'. As early as 1883 Archer had tried to alert British play-goers to the melodramatic theatricality of Irving's Lyceum, and nothing that followed was likely to change the minds of Irving's opponents – certainly not his Mephistopheles of 1885, his Lear of 1892 or his appearance, in 1895, in the title role of Comyns Carr's *King Arthur*. Irving's knighthood was, in fact, an ambiguous achievement. On the one hand it signalled the arrival of a social respectability and aesthetic seriousness that the acting profession had been lobbying for since the previous century. On the other, it seemed to endorse a safe, comfortable, rather old-fashioned concept of theatre-going in which spectacular entertainment was preferred to thought-provoking texts or truly troubling performances.

This same tension between the old drama and the new is bodied forth in the London repertoire for 1895. Among the West End's most conspicuous successes were *The Shop Girl*, the latest of George Edwardes's long-running Gaiety musicals; Hall Caine's brooding melodrama *The Manxman* (Shaftesbury); Pinero's *The Notorious Mrs Ebbsmith* (Garrick), featuring in its title role the equally notorious Mrs Patrick Campbell, and Beerbohm Tree's lavish adaptation of George Du Maurier's *Trilby* (Haymarket), with Tree himself giving the performance of his career as the mesmerist Svengali. These were the commercial blockbusters of the season. On the alternative 'little theatre' front matters were more variable. A setback appeared in J. T. Grein's resignation from a financially beggared Independent Theatre. But 1895 also saw William Poel's founding of the Elizabethan Stage Society, a company that would have an immediate and lasting impact on the manner in which Shakespeare's texts were spoken and staged. The complacency of London's theatre establishment was also challenged in 1895 by the arrival of some of the Continent's most notable performers and troupes. In June of that year Sarah Bernhardt and Eleonora Duse competed with one another, in identical roles as it turned out, at Daly's and Drury Lane. The occasion provided play-goers and critics with the opportunity to assess the state of English acting, comparing Bernhardt and Duse not only with one another but also with the very best home-grown talent. London audiences were also exposed to a brief season of Ibsen – which went some way to making up for a paucity of English productions – and Maeterlinck when Aurélien Lugné-Poe's avant-garde Théâtre de l'Oeuvre visited the city in March.

All of the above are significant and will be considered in due course. But if a single event had to be selected as the most important and influential theatre occurrence of 1895, it would have to be the appointment of Bernard Shaw as drama critic of the *Saturday Review*. In December 1894 Shaw, a noted music reviewer but unsuccessful playwright, was offered the post on Frank Harris's reorganized weekly. He promptly accepted, at the rate of £6 a week, and on New Year's Day 1895 found himself at the Garrick Theatre, for the first time assuming the terrifying persona of 'GBS'.

Two things need to be said at the outset about Shaw as critic. First, he was determined that wearing both playwright's and reviewer's caps would not compromise his integrity. And, second, he was prepared to push a social and aesthetic agenda in which he passionately believed, regardless of whether he was 'fair' to individual plays, playwrights or performers. Shaw admits as much in his 1906 preface to *Our Theatres in the Nineties*. His comments of the previous decade, he cautions us,

> must be construed in the light of the fact that all through I was accusing my opponents of failure because they were not doing what I wanted, whereas they were often succeeding very brilliantly in doing what they themselves wanted. I postulated as desirable a certain kind of play in which I was destined ten years later to make my mark . . . and I brought everybody: authors, actors, managers and all, to the one test: were they coming my way or staying in the old grooves?[2]

Shaw's push was for an informed and politically committed drama, one that would redeploy the language of the stage to do battle with the conventions of Victorian popular theatre as well as the social and economic assumptions embodied in such work. Shaw's blind spots were enormous. They included a flat refusal to see any merit whatsoever in the work of Arthur Pinero, perceived by supporters and detractors alike as the most weighty of London's serious dramatists. Nor was Shaw able to appreciate the unique genius of *The Importance of Being Earnest*. He alone among London critics dismissed the play as a rewarmed bit of Gilbertism. Yet Shaw's insistence on a larger, overarching context for the discussion of drama effectively changed the nature and terms of critical discourse. For Shaw, Archer's contest between 'old' and 'new' playmaking and Scott's moral crusade against Ibsen and Ibsenism, as well as the critic's day-to-day task of assessing individual performances and styles of presentation, all took their place as parts of a greater argument about the nature and use of the arts and their relationship to social, political and economic matters. Within six months, drama, theatre and the larger issues of performance

---

[2] Shaw, *Our Theatres in the Nineties*, I: v. Subsequent references will use the abbreviation *OTN*, followed by volume and page number.

had been made a subject for serious and sustained debate. If we are careful to note the nature of Shaw's prejudices – what in 1895 he would not or could not see, as well as what he did – a useful account of the theatrical year can be provided by shadowing the critic to a selection of those pieces, both sombre and frivolous, which he attended during his first season in harness.

That said, I would like to begin by considering a work Shaw did not himself review. Shaw's taste, or at least his sense of critical responsibility, was eclectic enough to have taken him to the Gaiety Theatre some time in 1895. He did, after all, attend the circus, the music hall and the opera as well as the 'legitimate' theatre. But *The Shop Girl*, the most recent of George Edwardes's musicals, had opened the previous November and was, therefore, old news when Shaw took up his critical post. *The Shop Girl*, however, which would play through 1895 and well into 1896 – some 546 performances in all – is a striking and important representative of the year, with far-reaching social and aesthetic implications. The genre to which it belonged was itself a relatively recent innovation. In 1892 impresario George Edwardes – a manager quite as central to the London scene as Tree, Alexander or Charles Wyndham – staged *In Town* at the Prince of Wales's. A popular compound of book, song and dance presented in familiar but stylized London surroundings, the piece proved profitable enough for Edwardes to commission a more elaborate successor. The result was *A Gaiety Girl*, the first entertainment to call itself 'musical comedy', and a piece which in turn inspired a succession of similar works – *The Sunshine Girl, The Shop Girl, The Girl Behind the Counter, The Girl from Kays, The Earl and the Girl* – most of them presented at Edwardes's two playhouses, Daly's and the Gaiety. Each of these works evidences what historian Peter Bailey has called the 'brokered sexuality' of the late Victorians, as romantic narratives tracing the upward mobility of London shop girls became larger, uncritical celebrations of the period's commodity culture.[3] The fact that so many were set in recognizable department stores – the great halls of Whiteley's, Harrod's and Army & Navy were all represented in recognizable detail – suggests how complete the collusion actually was. *The Shop Girl* of 1894–6 was composed, we are told, in response to the public's taste for the 'local and real'. It helped to introduce the two-part, broken-backed structure that was to become at once the form and meaning of the genre. The play's first two acts, set in 'the Mantle Department of the Royal Stores', allow shop girl Bessie Brant, a young heiress masquerading as a worker, to assert her independence. By mid-evening, however, the play shifts to a sumptuous fancy-dress bazaar in South Kensington, at

---

[3] Bailey, '"Naughty but nice"', 36–55.

which Bessie herself becomes a commodity. Here, to the cheers of Edwardes's on-stage and off-stage spectators, Bessie is transformed from worker to glittering society object. At the play's close she is whisked away by a well-born suitor to 'the finest obtainable House in Mayfair'. Such trajectories were central to the form, as the sumptuous replication of consumer goods became in the end an endorsement of the economic status quo. Surveying the complexities of the genre, democratic but intensely class-conscious, exploiting the figure of the liberated woman while infantilizing her as a 'girl', celebrating a (female) work ethic in need of firm (male) managerial control, Archer wondered, with a shudder of recognition, whether this, rather than Ibsen or Wilde, might be the period's 'real new drama'.[4]

It is as well to keep in mind the spectre of *The Shop Girl* playing invisibly through what Shaw presents in the pages of the *Saturday Review* as the theatrical year 1895. For Shaw, however, the year proper began at the Garrick in early January with Sydney Grundy's *Slaves of the Ring*, a 'new and original play' in three acts, loosely based upon Wagner's music dramas. The work itself need not detain us long. Shaw's review, however, published on 5 January – 'it is not a work of art at all: it is a mere contrivance for filling a theatre bill' – allows GBS to identify in his first column two targets that would preoccupy him throughout the coming year. The first was the 'plutocracy' of much West End theatre, a lavish and opulent reproduction of the surfaces of society life that seemed to anaesthetize judgement. The second was the deference shown by English playwrights to the practices and values of the well-made play. The first of these offences was one of production, the second of dramaturgy. Both were rife in the theatre of the 1890s and they often went hand in hand. But for Shaw the second was by far the more dangerous. Indeed, it sets up one of the central polarities – the contest between 'constructed' and 'organic' drama – that for Shaw defined what was at stake in the theatre of 1895, and helps us to understand Shaw's later characterization of his columns as 'a siege laid to the theatre of the nineteenth century by an author who had to cut his own way into it at the point of the pen, and throw some of its defenders into the moat' (*OTN*, 1: v).

The defender most in need of a good dunking, as far as Shaw was concerned, was not Grundy but rather Arthur Wing Pinero (after 1909 Sir Arthur), the most considerable English playwright of the decade. Shaw's appraisal of Pinero was unique in the period. Critics, from the liberal Archer to the reactionary Scott, had identified Pinero as the face of English Ibsenism, praising or damning him

---

[4] Archer, *Theatrical World of 1894*, 245.

accordingly. Shaw's position was that Pinero was a sham, a poseur whose erotically charged problem plays were impeding the arrival of truly progressive drama. Shaw had not been reviewing when Pinero's *The Second Mrs Tanqueray* was first staged in 1892. But he used the play's publication in February 1895 as an excuse to damn the work three years after the fact. His principal complaint, that it was too 'constructed' and irresponsibly lavish, was the same that he had registered against *Slaves of the Ring*. Pinero, however, was a more formidable opponent, and in the stage presentation of *The Second Mrs Tanqueray* had found himself an accomplished ally in the hitherto unknown actress Mrs Patrick Campbell. Between them, Shaw complained, playwright and performer had helped to create the phenomenon he dubbed 'pineroticism,' a cheap attempt to capitalize on Ibsen's notoriety by accommodating him to Mayfair sensibilities: 'It seemed to them that most of Ibsen's heroines were naughty ladies. And they tried to produce Ibsen plays by making their heroines naughty. But they took great care to make them pretty and expensively dressed.' *Mrs Tanqueray* was accordingly dismissed out of hand. Its 'naïve' stage machinery was, Shaw proclaimed, contemptible, as was its representation of a protagonist critics had three years earlier hailed as the English Hedda Gabler: 'There is no cheaper subject for the character draughtsman', Shaw grumbled, 'than the ill-tempered sensual woman seen from the point of view of the conventional man' (*OTN*, 1: 45).

In March 1895 matters were brought to a head by Mrs Patrick Campbell's appearance in Pinero's second 'sex problem play', *The Notorious Mrs Ebbsmith*. If Mrs Tanqueray irritated Shaw, Mrs Ebbsmith made his blood boil. To begin with, Pinero's new heroine was drawn from a world Shaw knew, and one that he claimed Pinero did not. A defiant platform orator and free-thinking social-ist living openly with a married MP, Agnes Ebbsmith might have contained a promising idea for a heroine of a distinctly Shavian bent. In Pinero's hands, however, she was manoeuvred into abandoning thought altogether. Suspecting that her hold over her lover is entirely sexual, Pinero's Mrs Ebbsmith stages a strong Act 2 close in which she appears fashionably turned out in a spectacularly low-cut evening gown. This image of an independent woman dwindling into what looked like a conventionally provocative society object was exacerbated, for Shaw, when at the close of the following act Mrs Ebbsmith (in an action borrowed from Hedda Gabler) threw a Bible into a wood-burning stove. Its immediate retrieval brought down Pinero's curtain to thunderous applause. Shaw's disgust was complete: 'I disliked the play so much that nothing would induce me to say anything good of it' (*OTN*, 1: 65). Praising Mrs Pat's performance but distancing it from the text itself – 'Mrs Patrick Campbell . . . pulls her author through by playing him clean off the stage' – Shaw proceeded to attack as shallow, ignorant and ill-advised Pinero's attempt to put on stage a political world of which he knew nothing. Women who take a wider view of the world are not a 'special variety of the human species', nor do they 'Trafalgar Square' visitors in their own drawing-rooms. The Bible burning is, in turn, dismissed as 'a piece of claptrap so gross' that it absolved him 'from all obligations to treat Mr Pinero's art as anything higher than the barest art of theatrical sensation' (*OTN*, 1: 63). The pattern, Shaw claimed, was familiar but depressing. A not untalented playwright had succeeded by pandering to his audiences, giving them melodrama of a familiar cut, while convincing them that they were being courageous, discerning and intellectually acute. It mattered little that Pinero's Ibsen was not Shaw's, or that to Pinero Shaw's new drama might seem as 'bloodless' as Pinero's seemed 'thoughtless' to Shaw. Pinero was one of the dramatic rivals Shaw would later grant had been 'succeeding very brilliantly in doing what they themselves wanted'. In 1895, however, such success was for Shaw a very real threat.

Although Oscar Wilde shared with Pinero a common society audience and although their plays were presented by the same upmarket managements – both *The Second Mrs Tanqueray* and *Lady Windermere's Fan* made their débuts in 1892 at George Alexander's St James's Theatre, with Alexander himself in the male leads – Wilde, on the whole, escaped condemnation. Wilde's virtue was the Irish 'otherness' he shared with Shaw, conferring upon each an alien's eye for subversive observation. Wilde's way, to be sure, was not Shaw's. But this did not stop the two from referring to their stage plays, only partly in jest, as joint shots fired in the cause of a new Celtic drama. In January 1895 the most recent specimen was Wilde's *An Ideal Husband*, presented by actor-manager Lewis Waller to inaugurate his management of the Haymarket. First-night audiences were enthusiastic, and it was clear that the work would settle into a profitable long run. Shaw, however, was impatient with fellow-reviewers who failed to appreciate the originality of Wilde's wit – or its political implications. In his 12 January column, after lamenting the failure of Henry James's *Guy Domville* at the St James's, Shaw turned his attention to Wilde's Haymarket reception. The critics of *An Ideal Husband*, Shaw notes, 'protest that . . . [Wilde's] epigrams can be turned out by the score by any one light-minded enough to condescend to such frivolity'. Observing that Wilde's plays, 'though apparently lucrative, remain unique', he commends Wilde's critics for their pecuniary self-denial. The point is well taken and is used to launch an oft-reprinted assessment of Wilde as 'our only thorough playwright: He plays with everything; with wit, with philosophy, with drama, with actors and audience, with the whole theatre'. In context, however, the passage is linked to Wilde's 'otherness' and the critical purchase this allows him (and Shaw) in their representations of England and Englishness: 'Such a feat scandalizes the Englishman, who can no more play with wit than he can with a football or cricket bat. He works at both . . . and is shocked, too, at the dangers to the foundations of society when seriousness is publicly laughed at' (*OTN*, 1: 9–10). What follows is a lynx-eyed identification of the play's 'modern note' in Wilde's defence of Robert Chiltern's courageous wrongdoing 'against the mechanical idealism of his stupidly good wife'. The exchange, Shaw concludes, was worthy of Ibsen or Shaw himself.

Shaw's faculties, however, seemed to desert him when *The Importance of Being Earnest* opened at the St James's the following month. A full-length farcical comedy, *Earnest* represented a departure from Wilde's previous work. Initially intended for comedian Charles Wyndham, it was passed on to Alexander after the failure of *Guy Domville*. Alexander immediately cut Wilde's four-act text to three, giving it the expected shape of a late Victorian farce. The play, no doubt, gained from such compression, but managed in turn to raise questions among its first audiences about tone, form and purpose. Wilde's epigrams were still in place, as was his acute observation of contemporary English manners. But the sober and sometimes sentimental melodrama that had characterized *An Ideal Husband* and its predecessors had been transformed into an absurdity designed to guy both theatrical conventions and the broader social practices upon which they were built. Passages such as Miss Prism's determined but displaced identification of her handbag or Jack's equally 'off-centred' act of forgiveness ('Cannot repentance wipe out an act of folly? Why should there be one law for men, and another for women? Mother, I forgive you') had their darker counterparts, not only in Pinero's works but also in Wilde's own plays of modern life. Here, however, the very geniality that led Archer to characterize the play as 'a sort of *rondo capriccioso*, in which the artist's fingers run with crisp irresponsibility up and down the keyboard of life' (*World*, 20 February 1895) and *Spectator* critic A. B. Walkley to pronounce it 'absolutely free from bitter afterthought' (23 February 1895), threw audiences off their guard. They laughed throughout. Indeed, the response to Jack's long Act 2 entrance in formal mourning, complete with black cane and black-bordered handkerchief, was so explosive and prolonged that it threatened to stop the show in its tracks. Wilde's transformation of up-market melodrama into absurdist farce managed to entertain while burying the play's critique of Victorian values (sobriety, idealism, duty) deep in the collective subconscious. Only Shaw seemed immune. His review of 23 February damns the piece by applying to it the most dismissive epithet in the arsenal of a progressive critic – 'old'. For Shaw, *Earnest* was literally bottom-drawer, a work of, perhaps, the 1870s, dressed up by Wilde in his mid-1890s style. Locating antecedents in the farces of W. S. Gilbert and H. J. Byron, Shaw blames himself for laughing at a piece so mechanical and heartless. Whether he genuinely missed the joke is, at this distance, difficult to say. A reference, however, to *Arms and the Man* midway through the review makes one wonder if Wilde's shift of tactics was, for Shaw, a bit close to the bone. He need not have worried. *Earnest* would, in the end, prove to be both the pinnacle and close of Wilde's playwriting career.

If Wilde's fall, as Archer suspected, was a blow for the cause of new drama in London's West End, the future of England's little theatre movement was in 1895 beginning to look equally grim. J. T. Grein's trail-blazing Independent Theatre, which in 1891–92 had presented play-goers with English premières of Ibsen's *Ghosts* and Shaw's *Widowers' Houses*, was experiencing major financial difficulties. In May 1894 the company had managed to produce Ibsen's *The Wild Duck*, with Winnifred Fraser in the role of Hedwig and Lawrence Irving, son of Sir Henry, as Dr Relling. The play was deemed an artistic success, but it effectively depleted what was left of the Society's budget. As a result Grein had to cancel the group's 1895 season, scheduled to include the English première of Ibsen's *The Lady from the Sea* as well as a new play by Shaw himself. The enterprise was instead reorganized as a limited liability company, with Grein and Dorothy Leighton as managing directors. The reformed group did manage to mount two plays at the Opera Comique, as well as Leighton's own *Thyrza Fleming* at Terry's. Shaw was, however, unimpressed. In a column entitled 'The Independent Theatre Repents', he made a pointed contrast between the Society's glory days and the 'wretched respectability' it now seemed to seek out. Mrs Oscar Beringer's *Salve*, seized upon by Shaw as an instance of the Independent Theatre's new timidity, was derided as a piece that might 'merit high praise at the Pavillion or Marylebone theatres'. 'What in the name of all that's Independent', Shaw went on to ask, 'has it to do with the aims of Mr Grein's society?' (*OTN*, 1: 69). Indeed, the group's principal achievement in 1895 seems to have been its sponsorship that March of Aurélien Lugné-Poe's Théâtre de l'Oeuvre at the Opera Comique. The avant-garde troupe, which in 1896 would stage the world première of Wilde's *Salome* in Paris, offered London play-goers a brief season (in French) of Ibsen (*Rosmersholm* and *The Master Builder*) and Maeterlinck (*L'Intruse* and *Pelléas et Mélisande*). With a nod to Grein for 'services rendered to English art', Shaw pronounced himself delighted with the 'vigilant artistic conscience' of the enterprise and excessively short-tempered with fellow-critics so distracted by the petty details of theatrical representation that they seemed incapable of judging the performance:

> when I find players speaking with such skill and delicacy that they can deliver M. Maeterlinck's fragile word-music throughout five acts without one harsh or strained note, and with remarkable subtlety and conviction of expression; and when I see these artists, simply because their wigs are not up to Mr Clarkson's English standard . . . denounced as 'amateurs' by gentlemen who go into obedient raptures [over] M. Mounet Sully . . . shall I violate the sacredness of professional etiquette, and confess to a foreigner that the distinction some of our critics make between the amateur and the expert is really a distinction between a rich enterprise and a poor one? (OTN, I: 77)

Although the collapse of Grein's Independent Theatre proved a setback for opponents of the theatrical status quo, relief appeared in an unlikely quarter. In both June and December of 1895, William Poel, a former building contractor turned actor and theatrical antiquarian, offered the first productions of his newly formed Elizabethan Stage Society. Poel's experiments with period drama stretched back to the 1880s, when he staged *Hamlet* on a platform in St George's Hall for members of the New Shakespeare Society. The early nineties had seen similar revivals of *The Duchess of Malfi* (Opera Comique) and *Measure for Measure* (Royalty), the latter in a partial reproduction of the old Fortune playhouse. The Elizabethan Stage Society of 1895 was an attempt to formalize Poel's belief in open staging and the swift, musical diction he associated with it. In a pamphlet issued the following year, Poel argued his case for 'a theatre specially built on the plans of the sixteenth century . . . which could be used as a school-house for instruction in the poetic drama as well as for performances of Shakespeare's plays in accordance with his original design'.[5] It was a minimalist approach that flew directly in the face of Victorian spectacular theatre. The Shakespeare of Irving, and later Tree, had been a sumptuous, upholstered affair that revelled in both the magical and realistic. Augustin Daly's *A Midsummer Night's Dream* (Daly's Theatre) and Forbes Robertson's *Romeo and Juliet* (Lyceum), both produced in 1895, were cases in point. The former sported troupes of fairies fitted up 'with portable batteries and incandescent lights', the latter a representation of the *Veneto* so painterly that Shaw attacked what he considered its essential wrong-headedness by parodying the language of art criticism: 'The sky is too cold, and the cypresses too pale: better have painted them with dabs of warm brown on an actually gold sky . . . than have risked that Constablesque suggestion, faint as it is, of English raininess and

---

[5] Woodfield, *English Theatre in Transition*, 142.

chill' (*OTN*, 1: 199). As a response to such sumptuosity, Poel's manifesto and his practical embodiment of his beliefs in a non-profit, subscription society – one that would stage thirty-six productions over the next two decades – was a threat to the old drama and the old theatre as potent as any posed by Wilde, Ibsen or Maeterlinck.

Shaw's reviews of 20 July and 14 December take us, accordingly, to Burlington Hall and Gray's Inn, where Poel's productions of *Twelfth Night* and *The Comedy of Errors* allowed the critic to compare the relative merits of Victorian and Elizabethan stage management. In the process he was able to revisit the problematic distinction between 'amateur' and 'professional' performance that had occupied him on the occasion of Lugné's May tour. At Burlington Hall Shaw extolled 'the immense advantage of the platform stage' as opposed to a pictorial theatre. Indeed, the intimacy with audiences enjoyed by players no longer obliged to act 'across the footlights' caused him to speculate on whether Burbage, faced with the prospect of performing in Irving's Lyceum, might have recoiled, 'beaten the moment he realised that he was to be looked at as part of an optical illusion through a huge hole in the wall, instead of being practically in the middle of the theatre' (*OTN*, 1: 190). Five months later, when Poel's players reappeared in *The Comedy of Errors* at Gray's Inn, their ignorance of stock company technique seemed to Shaw a distinct advantage. Clinging now to the concept of the 'amateur' as 'the saviour of theatrical art', Shaw dismissed the 'professional' of his day as a hopeless incompetent mired in 'stage business' copied from outmoded London premières. What chance, he asked, had such actors in coming to terms with the 'old' intimacy of Shakespeare or Marlowe, let alone the 'new' intimacy of Ibsen, Maeterlinck – or Shaw himself? The prescience of Shaw's observation that Poel's 'amateurism' might provide, in the end, not only a radical technique for Elizabethan performance but also a training ground for a drama yet to come was underscored, four years later, when the Elizabethan Stage Society cast as its lead in *Richard II* a promising but unknown young actor named Harley Granville Barker.

Encouragement was also forthcoming from the Continent. In addition to Lugné's Théâtre de l'Oeuvre, 1895 had brought to the English stage two of Europe's most accomplished and influential actresses. In June both Sarah Bernhardt and Eleonora Duse had come to London's West End to compete with one another in, as it turned out, identical roles. Seeing each appear, in turn, as the protagonists of Dumas's *La Dame aux camélias* and Sudermann's *Heimat* allowed critics the opportunity for pointed comparison as well as a reassessment of English talent and technique. There was no mistaking Shaw's position. Bernhardt, he was willing to concede, was magnificent, but her energetic, self-conscious theatricality was built on the same kind of personal 'fascination' he had already identified in the performances of Henry Irving, Ellen Terry and Mrs Patrick Campbell. All were skilled practitioners who enthralled play-goers, Shaw maintained, not by entering into the parts they played, but by substituting their personalities for those parts. The same point made about Mrs Pat in *The Notorious Mrs Ebbsmith* was now registered about the Camille and Magda of Madame Bernhardt. In each case, audiences were transfixed by a development of the old 'points' system – a sequence of identifiable 'explosions' filtered through a particularly forceful personality. Duse, however, was another matter entirely. Praising her performances as 'without qualification . . . the best modern acting I have ever seen', Shaw proceeded to anatomize a technique that seemed the actorly equivalent of what Ibsen and Wagner had wrought as dramatic craftsmen. Duse's peculiarly modern genius lay in her ability to integrate the various 'points' that marked the progress of her parts into continuous, seamless illusions of character, effacing herself entirely in the integrity of her roles. The technique, illustrated by a telling analysis of Duse's tying up a bunch of flowers in the third act of *Camille*, seemed to Shaw the complete antithesis of the high-energy celebrity performances of Bernhardt and her English imitators. As a result, Shaw found in this 'plain little woman' who 'without her genius would be . . . of no use to any manager' the true heir to Ristori, Salvini and Coquelin, the 'first actress whom we have seen applying the method of the great school to characteristically modern parts or to characteristically modern conceptions of old parts'. The final proviso was important, for it allowed a freshly approached Shakespeare or Molière to stand side by side with the founders of the new drama. Duse, like Poel, was for Shaw a radical in the most literal sense.

The old drama, however, was not ready to pack its bags just yet. If there was any doubt on this point, Shaw found himself disabused at the year's close when, on 2 November, actor-manager Herbert Beerbohm Tree opened a stage adaptation of George Du Maurier's novel *Trilby* at the Haymarket. In Tree's version the tale's misalliance between art student Billy Bagot and model Trilby O'Ferrall is pushed to one side to allow greater scope for the work's villain, the sinister mesmerist Svengali, played of course by Tree himself. The popular press likened Tree's villainy to that of Lucifer and Mephistopheles – 'what authority there is in his magic, what intensity in his rage, his agony, his ambition!'[6] – as it recoiled in horrified fascination from his influence over the luckless Trilby. It was a role that allowed tremendous scope to an actor whose

---

[6] Taylor, *Players and Performers in the Victorian Theatre*, 167.

stage performances were built on passion and spontaneity rather than on any consistent or systematic technique. Taking its place in a gallery of larger than life stage rogues, Tree's Svengali kept *Trilby* running well into the following summer. Shaw, not surprisingly, was underwhelmed. His assessment of the challenges posed and met by the work is neatly summed up: 'Trilby is the very thing for the English stage at present. No need to act or create character: nothing to do but make up after Mr du Maurier's familiar and largely popular drawings, and be applauded before uttering a word as dear old Taffy, or the Laird, or darling Trilby, or horrid Svengali.' As 'horrid' Svengali Tree outdid himself, obliterating behind outlandish whiskers and a more outlandish stage accent the little subtlety Du Maurier had managed to build into his original. 'Imagine', Shaw warned his readers, 'Svengali taken seriously at his own foolish valuation, blazed upon with limelights, spreading himself intolerably over the whole play with nothing fresh to add to the first five minutes of him – Svengali defying heaven, declaring that henceforth he is his own God, and then tumbling down in a paroxysm of heart disease.' The fault, however, lay less with Tree than with a public that had 'done its silly best to teach him that it want[ed] none of his repeated and honourable attempts to cater for people with some brains' (*OTN*, I: 241). Tree, two years earlier, had been the driving force behind major productions of both Ibsen's *An Enemy of the People* and Wilde's *A Woman of No Importance*. In the new century he would invite Poel's Elizabethan Stage Society to perform at His Majesty's, travel to Russia to see the Moscow Art Theatre and create the role of Henry Higgins in the English première of *Pygmalion*. But Tree was a bit of a weather vane. And as the theatrical year 1895 drew to a close – in spite of the collective example set by Duse, Poel, Grein, Lugné-Poe, Ibsen, Maeterlinck and Wilde – Shaw could only shake his head at the direction in which he seemed to be pointing.

Central to Shaw's critique of the theatre in 1895 was the accusation that London's commercial stage was unwilling or unable to deal with issues of enduring importance. In part this was the legacy of a curious but effective system of censorship that placed in the hands of an Examiner of Plays absolute power over what English audiences could or could not see. Grein and Poel had found a way out by embracing the fiction that the Independent Theatre and Elizabethan Stage Society were private clubs playing to members only. The West End's commercial playhouses, however, were directly subject to the Examiner's dictates. Indeed, many of London's leading actor-managers willingly embraced the practice, as it absolved them of the legal responsibility for distinguishing between acceptable and unacceptable work. When, in

February 1895, E. F. Smyth Pigott, the current Examiner of Plays, died after some twenty years of service, Shaw used the occasion to denounce him as 'a walking compendium of vulgar insular prejudice' – underscoring his broader point by noting in the process that Smyth Pigott was 'declared on all hands to have been the best reader of plays we have ever had' (*OTN*, II: 49). Shaw's column of 2 March, however, was not so much an attack upon the man as upon the office – an office that had confined English drama in brackish backwaters during one of the most exciting decades in the history of western theatre. It had kept London play-goers from an early acquaintance with Ibsen, while preventing local authors from dealing critically with crucial questions of sex, money and religion. *Mrs Warren's Profession*, Shaw's own play on the economics of prostitution, was too dangerous for even Grein to touch, while entertainments that used sex primarily to titillate were legally played to large, enthusiastic crowds. There is, no doubt, an element of special pleading in such analysis, especially in Shaw's readiness to lump together George Edwardes and Arthur Pinero. But the point is well taken, as is Shaw's lament that censorship itself would not 'be abolished before the appointment of a successor to Mr Pigott creates a fresh vested interest in one of the most mischievous of our institutions'.

On one front, however, progressive critics might be forgiven for seeing at the close of 1895 at least a glimmer of hope. The final weeks of our theatrical year saw two vastly different works being readied for West End commercial stages, each purporting to deal seriously with the forbidden subject of faith. The first was Wilson Barrett's *The Sign of the Cross*, a panoramic tale of conflicting ideologies set among the pagans and Christians of ancient Rome. Barrett, who had both written and produced the piece, appeared himself in the role of Marcus Superbus, a prefect won to Christianity and martyrdom in the arena by the Christian maiden Mercia. The most influential of the period's 'toga' dramas, the piece was planned by Barrett as a reply to what he termed Pinero's 'divorce court plays'. Melodramatic in its alignment of sympathy – 'My heroine is emblematic of Christianity; my hero stands for the worn out paganism of decadent Rome'[7] – the piece, by its close, posed awkward questions about spirituality and empire. Uneasy analogies between Nero's Rome and late Victorian Britain were not lost on audiences who, for the duration of the piece, were themselves asked, in the terms of Edwin Long's painting of 1889, to choose between Christ and Diana. The intensity of response demanded

---

[7] Mayer, *Playing out the Empire*, 108.

transformed the piece into a cultural phenomenon. Credited with drawing church-goers and clergy to the theatre in record numbers, *The Sign of the Cross* had, by the time of Barrett's death, enjoyed more than 10,000 performances worldwide. Indeed, attendance was seen as something akin to worship, with bishops granting Lenten dispensations for those minded to attend. Souvenirs were hawked, from crucifixes to piano reductions of Edward Jones's hymn for the Christians, in what became a merchandizing revolution. In the midst of all this Barrett took to the lectern to defend his 'purification' of the stage. The answer to the era's corrosive cynicism, he maintained, was a spiritual redemption that turned its back, ironically, on some of the same values Wilde had mocked earlier that year in *The Importance of Being Earnest*. Shaw, only half-ironically, granted the modernity of the piece. Suggesting that its appeal for many lay in 'the strange, perverted voluptuousness of its Christians, with their shuddering exaltations of longing for the whip, the rack, the stake and the lions', he impishly found much to praise in the 'straightforward sensuality' of the unreconstructed Marcus. The play was, Shaw declared, not biblical at all, but a sly instance of getting Ibsen in by the back door. Even Marcus's condemnation of 'crimes committed under the cloak of duty!' was seen to strike an authentically 'Norwegian keynote'.

The second of the season's asymmetrically matched plays of church and state was Henry Arthur Jones's *Michael and his Lost Angel*. In spite of the tendency of contemporaries to bracket Jones together with Pinero as a producer of *fin de siècle* problem plays, for Shaw a gulf separated the two. Pinero was, as we have seen, damned alongside Scribe, Sardou and poor Sydney Grundy as a 'constructor' of theatrical contrivances. Jones's plays, in sharp distinction, seemed to 'grow' rather than being 'cut out of paper and stuck together' (*OTN*, II: 14). *Michael and His Lost Angel* was Jones's attempt to portray the dilemma of a well-meaning but weak-willed clergyman battling the dictates of a strict and austere religion. The play opens with the right-minded but naïve Reverend Michael Feversham condemning a 'fallen' girl to the humiliations of public confession. In the acts that follow Michael himself becomes involved with a married woman and, after a panicked attempt to conceal his transgression, submits himself to the same ordeal. It was a subject that, in 1895, had the power to scandalize London play-goers. Some objected to the character of its hero, others to the representation of religious paraphernalia and a church service in a theatrical context. The close of Jones's fourth act drew particular fire. Here Jones's audience became, in effect, Michael's congregation, as Michael from the altar steps of the Church of Saint Decuman accused himself of having 'broken the sanctity of the marriage vow'. The detailed presentation of 'the

Chancel of the Minster church', complete with altar, reredos and 'a long vista of columns, arches, roof, and stained glass windows', together with the depiction of a church service including a reconsecration and the singing of a processional hymn, led many to complain that Jones was toying with sacred things for their entertainment value. Matters were not helped, moreover, by the notoriety that had gathered about the play before its opening. Sir Henry Irving, it was rumoured, had turned down the part of Michael Feversham, and Mrs Patrick Campbell, who had initially accepted the role of Jones's temptress, expressed misgivings about the propriety of the piece and walked out of rehearsals. Indeed, by the time the play opened at the Lyceum on 15 January 1896, with Forbes Robertson and Marion Terry in the leads, a small but powerful moral opposition had already formed. In the event, *Michael and His Lost Angel* was taken off by the Lyceum management after ten performances. Sympathizers, however, could take comfort in the fact that, whatever pressure may have been exerted, box office receipts were healthy throughout. Indeed, they were actually on the increase when the play was withdrawn. Also encouraging was the reception of the piece by progressive critics. The *Daily Graphic* pronounced it 'a great play', finding it 'difficult to imagine treatment more masterly or more effective', while Archer, writing for the *World*, spoke of Jones as having 'enriched, not our theatre only, but our literature'.[8]

For Shaw, all of this was beside the point. In the second of two *Saturday Review* columns (25 January 1896) devoted to the controversy it generated, he handily demolishes the play's popular opposition by pointing out that Goethe set the prologue of *Faust* not in a West Country church but in heaven itself, introducing both God and Satan as dramatis personae. It is, however, in his column of 18 January that Shaw deals most directly with the issues posed by the play and its production. He begins by noting the 'organic' qualities of Jones's craft, but moves logically from this to an attack on the assumptions that underlie the work: 'Mr Jones's technical skill is taken as a matter of course. Nobody ever dreams of complimenting him about it: we proceed direct to abusing his ideas without delay.' In *Michael and His Lost Angel*, as far as Shaw is concerned, the idea most in need of abuse is the necessity of Michael's repentance:

> As to the first two acts, I ask nothing better; but at the beginning of the third comes the parting of our ways; and I can point out the exact place where the roads fork. In the first act, Michael, a clergyman, compels a girl who has committed what he believes to be a deadly sin to confess it publicly in church.

[8] Foulkes, *Church and Stage in Victorian England*, 203–4.

In the second act he commits that sin himself. At the beginning of the third he meets the lady who has been his accomplice, and the following words pass between them:

AUDREY. You're sorry?
MICHAEL. No. And you?
AUDREY. No. (*OTN*, II: 15–16)

Shaw's point is that in spite of this dialogue – and, he might have added, two similar exchanges later in the play – Jones's clergyman behaves as if he were sorry. He tears his hair, thumps his chest, and finally, as we have seen, accuses himself before his congregation. From Shaw's point of view all this is melodramatic posturing, imposed on the story for the sake of its effect. The same holds true of the fifth-act demise of Michael's partner in crime, who dies, Shaw observes, 'of nothing but the need for making the audience cry'. Throughout the column Shaw pays Jones the courtesy of distinguishing between the playwright's point of view and that of the reviewer – a courtesy never extended to Pinero – alerting readers to the different expectations implied by each. Shaw, however, not only argues the merits of his reading but, in a key passage, offers to 'rewrite the last three acts', producing an alternative text in which Michael's refusal to feel guilt is thundered heroically to his 'shocked and shamed parishioners'.

Shaw's offer to recompose Jones's play, taken together with his sly 'Ibsenite' reading of *The Sign of the Cross*, neatly sums up from the point of view of an advanced but interested party the gains and losses of the theatrical year 1895. Chances were at last being taken by a handful of playwrights and performers anxious to bring the late Victorian stage into alignment with the contemporary world. Such gestures, however, were too timid to satisfy a critic already exasperated by what he regarded as the self-serving compromises of a Pinero or Grundy. Against them, moreover, Shaw had to set the fall of Wilde, the collapse of the Independent Theatre and, perhaps above all, the dispiriting fate of Tree, who had, within a period of two years, turned his back upon Ibsen and Wilde in order to impersonate a bewhiskered mesmerist. For Shaw himself the answer was clear. His campaign for a new drama needed to open a second front. Indeed, by May of our year Shaw had already presided over the copyright reading at the Theatre Royal, South Shields, of *Candida*, his own play about a Victorian clergyman wrestling with the demands of conscience and sensuality. His allies, moreover, would be a weakened but still credible avant-garde and a handful of practitioners praised by Shaw – but scorned by reactionary colleagues – as either amateurs or élitists. Among the first was Poel and the Elizabethan Stage Society, whose modest accomplish-ments in 1895 hardly indicated the scope or nature of the revolution that had taken place; among the second, Duse, whose notions of inhabiting a character were quietly dismantling a century of actor training, and the notorious Wilde, whose *Salome*, still under the Examiner's ban, would become, within a decade, a flagship of continental modernism.

Bibliography

Ainger, Michael. *Gilbert and Sullivan: A Dual Biography*. Oxford University Press, 2002.

Algarotti, Francesco. *An Essay on the Opera*. London: L. Davis and C. Reymers, 1767.

Allen, Grant. *The Woman Who Did*. 1895. Oxford University Press, 1995.

Allen, Shirley S. *Samuel Phelps and Sadler's Wells Theatre*. Middletown, CT: Wesleyan University Press, 1971.

Altick, Richard. *The English Common Reader: A Social History of the Mass Reading Public, 1800–1900*. University of Chicago Press, 1957.

Anderson, Mary, *A Few More Memories*. London: Hutchinson, 1936.

Anthony, Sister Rose. *The Jeremy Collier Stage Controversy, 1698–1726*. Milwaukee: Marquette University Press, 1937.

Appleton, William W. *Charles Macklin: An Actor's Life*. Cambridge, MA: Harvard University Press, 1960.

Appleton, William W. *Madame Vestris and the London Stage*. New York: Columbia University Press, 1974.

Archer, Frank. *How to Write a Good Play*. London: French, 1892.

Archer, William. 'The Drama'. In *The Reign of Queen Victoria: A Survey of Fifty Years of Progress*. Ed. Thomas H. Ward. London: Smith, Elder, 1887.

Archer, William. *English Dramatists of To-Day*. London: Sampson, Low, 1882.

Archer, William. *Masks or Faces?* London: Longman's, 1888.

Archer, William. *The Theatrical 'World' of 1894*. London: Walter Scott, 1895.

Armstrong, Norma. 'The Edinburgh Stage 1715–1820: A Bibliography.' Unpublished Library Association Fellowship thesis, 1968.

Arnot, Hugo. *The History of Edinburgh from the Earliest Accounts to the Year 1780*. Edinburgh: Turnbull, 1816.

Arnott, James Fullarton, and John William Robinson. *English Theatrical Literature, 1559–1900: A Bibliography*. London: Society for Theatre Research, 1970.

Arnstein, Walter. *Britain Yesterday and Today*. Lexington, MA: D. C. Heath, 1992.

Austin, Revd Gilbert. *Chironomia; or a treatise on rhetorical delivery*. London: T. Cadell and W. Davies, 1806.

Avery, Emmett L. *The London Stage 1700–1729: A Critical Introduction*. Carbondale: Southern Illinois University Press, 1968.

Avery, Emmett L. 'The Restoration audience'. *Philological Quarterly* 45 (1966): 54–61.

Avery, Emmet L., and Arthur H. Scouten. *The London Stage 1660–1700: A Critical Introduction*. Carbondale: Southern Illinois University Press, 1968.

Backscheider, Paula. *Daniel Defoe his Life*. Baltimore: Johns Hopkins University Press, 1989.

Baer, Marc. *Theatre and Disorder in Late Georgian London*. Oxford: Clarendon Press, 1992.

Bailey, Peter. 'Champagne Charlie: performance and ideology in the music hall song'. In Bratton, ed., *Music Hall*, 48–69.

Bailey, Peter. *Leisure and Class in Victorian England*. 2nd edn. London: Methuen, 1978.

Bailey, Peter. 'Making sense of music hall'. In *Music Hall: The Business of Pleasure*. Ed. Peter Bailey. Milton Keynes: Open University Press, 1986, viii–xxiii.

Bailey, Peter. '"Naughty but nice": musical comedy and the rhetoric of the girl, 1892–1914'. In Booth and Kaplan, eds., *Edwardian Theatre*, 36–60.

Bailey, Peter. 'Parasexuality and glamour: the Victorian barmaid as cultural prototype'. *Gender and History* 2 (1990): 148–72.

Bailey, Peter. *Popular Culture and Performance in the Victorian City*. Cambridge University Press, 1998.

Bailey, Peter. 'Theatres of entertainment / spaces of modernity: rethinking the British popular stage, 1890–1914'. *Nineteenth Century Theatre* 26 (1998): 5–24.

Baker, H. Barton. *History of the London Stage and its Famous Players*. London: George Routledge & Sons, 1904.

Baker, Herschel. *John Philip Kemble: The Actor in his Theatre*. Cambridge, MA: Harvard University Press, 1942.

Bancroft, Squire, and Marie Bancroft. *Mr & Mrs Bancroft On and Off the Stage*. 2 vols. London: Richard Bentley & Son, 1888.

Barish, Jonas A. *The Antitheatrical Prejudice*. Berkeley: University of California Press, 1981.

Barker, Kathleen. 'The performing arts in Newcastle upon Tyne, 1840–1870'. In *Leisure in Britain, 1780–1939*. Ed. John K. Walton and James Walvin. Manchester University Press, 1983, 53–71.

Barker, Kathleen. *The Theatre Royal Bristol 1766–1966: Two Centuries of Stage History*. London: Society for Theatre Research, 1974.

Barnett, Dene. *The Art of Gesture: The Practices and Principles of Eighteenth-Century Acting*. Heidelberg: Carl Winter, 1987.

Barrett, Daniel. *T. W. Robertson and the Prince of Wales's Theatre*. New York: Peter Lang, 1995.

Barrie, J. M. *The Plays of J. M. Barrie*. London: Hodder & Stoughton, 1928.

Bate, Jonathan. *Shakespearean Constitutions: Politics, Theatre, Criticism, 1730–1830*. Oxford: Clarendon Press, 1989.

Baugh, Christopher. *Garrick and Loutherbourg*. Cambridge: Chadwyck-Healey, 1990.

Bawcutt, N. W. *The Control and Censorship of Caroline Drama: The Records of Sir Henry Herbert, Master of the Revels 1623–73*. Oxford: Clarendon Press, 1996.

Beaver, Patrick. *The Spice of Life: Pleasures of the Victorian Age*. London: Elm Tree Books, 1979.

Beerbohm, Max. *Around Theatres*. New York: Alfred A. Knopf, 1930.

Behn, Aphra. *The Works of Aphra Behn*. Ed. Janet Todd. Vol. v. Columbus: Ohio State University Press, 1996.

Belford, Barbara. *Bram Stoker, A Biography of the Author of Dracula*. New York: Alfred A. Knopf, 1996.

Bell, H. G. 'The uncle'. In Hayes and Nikolopoulou, eds. *Melodrama*, 268–75.

Bellamy, Thomas. 'The life of William Parsons, comedian'. *Miscellanies: In Prose and Verse*. Vol. ii. London, [1796].

Bennett, A. 'Music in the halls'. In Bratton, ed., *Music Hall*, 1–22.

Bentley, Gerald Eades. *The Jacobean and Caroline Stage.* 7 vols. Oxford: Clarendon Press, 1941–68.

Bevis, Richard W. *The Laughing Tradition: Stage Comedy in Garrick's Day.* Athens: University of Georgia Press, 1980.

Black, Jeremy, ed. *Culture and Society in Britain 1660–1800.* Manchester University Press, 1997.

Blitzstein, Marc. 'The Threepenny Opera'. Unpublished libretto. Copyright copy. Library of Congress. ML50/.W42D82/1954/Cage.

Boaden, James. *The Life of Mrs Jordan.* 2 vols. London: Edward Bull, 1831.

Boaden, James. *Memoirs of the Life of John Philip Kemble.* 2 vols. London: Longman, Hurst, Rees, Orme, Brown & Green, 1825.

Boaden, James, ed. *The Private Correspondence of David Garrick.* London: H. Colburn and R. Bentley, 1831–2.

Booth, Michael R. *English Plays of the Nineteenth Century.* 5 vols. Oxford: Clarendon Press, 1969–76.

Booth, Michael R. *Theatre in the Victorian Age.* Cambridge University Press, 1991.

Booth, Michael R. *Victorian Spectacular Theatre 1850–1910.* London: Routledge & Kegan Paul, 1981.

Booth, Michael R., and Joel H. Kaplan, eds. *The Edwardian Theatre: Essays on Performance and the Stage.* Cambridge University Press, 1996.

Boswell, Eleanore. *The Restoration Court Stage (1660–1702).* London: George Allen & Unwin, 1932.

Botica, Alan Richard. 'Audience, playhouse and play in Restoration theatre, 1660–1710'. D.Phil. thesis. Oxford University, 1985.

Boucicault, Dion. *The Corsican Brothers.* New York: Samuel French, n.d.

[Boyl]E, [Rober]T. *Some Considerations about the Reconcileableness of Reason and Religion.* London, 1675.

Braddon, Mary Elizabeth. *Aurora Floyd, A Novel.* New York: Coryell, 1885.

Brandon-Thomas, Jevan. *Charley's Aunt's Father.* London: Douglas Saunders, 1955.

Bratton, J. S. 'The Lear of private life: interpretations of *King Lear* in the nineteenth century'. In Foulkes, ed., *Shakespeare and the Victorian Stage,* 124–37.

Bratton, J. S., ed. *Music Hall: Performance and Style.* Milton Keynes: Open University Press, 1986.

Bratton, Jacky. 'Jane Scott the writer-manager'. In Davis and Donkin, eds., *Women and Playwriting,* 77–98.

Brecht, Bertolt. *Collected Plays: Two.* Ed. John Willett and Ralph Manheim. London: Methuen, 1994.

Brewer, John. *The Pleasures of the Imagination: English Culture in the Eighteenth Century.* New York: Farrar, Straus & Giroux, 1997.

Brooks, Peter. *The Melodramatic Imagination: Balzac, Henry James, Melodrama, and the Mode of Excess.* New Haven: Yale University Press, 1984.

Brownsmith, John. *The Dramatic Time-Piece.* London, 1767.

Bull, John. *Vanbrugh and Farquhar.* London: Macmillan, 1998.

Bulwer, Edward Lytton. *England and the English.* Ed. Standish Meacham. University of Chicago Press, 1970.

Burgin, G. B. 'The Lyceum rehearsals'. *The Idler* (London, 1893): 122–41.

Burn, Walter. *The Age of Equipoise: A Study of the Mid-Victorian Generation.* London: Allen & Unwin, 1964.

Burnim, Kalman A. *David Garrick: Director.* Carbondale: Southern Illinois University Press, 1961.

Byrom, Michael. *Punch and Judy: Its Origin and Evolution.* Aberdeen: Shiva Publications, 1972.

Campbell, Lily Bess. *Scenes and Machines on the English Stage During the Renaissance: A Classical Revival.* Cambridge University Press, 1923.

Campbell, Mrs Patrick. *My Life and Some Letters.* New York: Dodd, Mead, 1922.

Cannan, Paul D. 'New directions in serious drama on the London stage, 1675–1678'. *Philological Quarterly* 73 (1994): 219–42.

Carlisle, Carol Jones. *Helen Faucit: Fire and Ice on the Victorian Stage.* London: Society for Theatre Research, 2000.

Castle, Dennis. *Sensation Smith of Drury Lane.* London: Charles Skilton, 1984.

Cibber, Colley. *An Apology for the Life of Mr Colley Cibber Written by Himself.* Ed. Robert W. Lowe. 2 vols. London: John C. Nimmo, 1889.

Cibber, Colley. *Love Makes a Man.* London: Richard Parker and others, 1701.

Clark, William. *The Early Irish Stage: The Beginning to 1720.* Oxford: Clarendon Press, 1955.

Cohen, David, and Ben Greenwood. *The Buskers.* Newton Abbot: David & Charles, 1981.

Colman, George. *Random Records.* 2 vols. London, 1830.

Comparison Between the Two Stages, A. London, 1702.

Conolly, L. W. *The Censorship of English Drama, 1737–1824.* San Marino: Huntington Library, 1976.

Cook, Emily Constance, and E. T. Cook. *London and Environs.* 2 vols. Llangollen: Darlington, 1897–8.

Cordner, Michael. 'Marriage comedy after the 1688 revolution: Southerne to Vanbrugh'. *Modern Language Review* 85 (1990): 273–89.

'Corin'. *The Truth about the Stage.* London: Wyman & Sons, 1885.

Cotton, Nancy. *Women Playwrights in England, c. 1363–1750.* Lewisburgh, PA: Bucknell University Press; London: Associated University Presses, 1980.

Cowell, Joseph. *Thirty Years among the Players of England and America.* New York, 1846.

Craig, Edward Gordon. *Ellen Terry and her Secret Self.* New York: Dutton, 1932.

Craig, Edward Gordon. *Henry Irving.* London: J. M. Dent & Sons, 1930.

Crean, P. J. 'The Stage Licensing Act of 1737'. *Modern Philology* 35 (1938): 239–55.

Cross, Gilbert B. *Next Week – East Lynne.* Lewisburg: Bucknell University Press, 1977.

Crump, Jeremy. 'Provincial music hall: promoters and public in Leicester, 1863–1929'. In Bailey, ed., *Business of Pleasure*, 53–72.

Cumberland, Richard. *Supplement to the Memoirs of Richard Cumberland.* London, 1807.

Cunningham, Hugh. 'Leisure and culture'. In *The Cambridge Social History of Britain.* Ed. F. M. L. Thompson. Vol. II. Cambridge University Press, 1990, 279–339.

Cunningham, Hugh. *Leisure in the Industrial Revolution.* London: Croom Helm, 1980.

Cunningham, J. E. *Theatre Royal: The History of the Theatre Royal Birmingham.* Oxford: George Ronald, 1950.

Dallas, E. S. 'The Drama'. *Blackwood's Magazine* 79 (Feb. 1856): 219.

Dallas, E. S. 'Popular literature – the periodical press'. *Blackwood's Magazine* 85 (Jan. 1859): P. 112.

Danchin, Pierre. *The Prologues and Epilogues of the Restoration, 1660–1700*. 4 parts 7 vols. Publications Université Nancy II, 1981–8.

Davenant, William. *The Siege of Rhodes: Made a representation by the art of prospective in scenes and the story sung in recitative music*. London: Henry Herringman, 1656.

Davies, Thomas. *Memoirs of the Life of David Garrick, Esq.* 2 vols. London, 1780.

Davis, Jim, ed. *The Britannia Diaries 1863–1875: Selections from the Diaries of Frederick C. Wilton*. London: Society for Theatre Research, 1992.

Davis, Jim, and Victor Emeljanow. *Reflecting the Audience: London Theatregoing, 1840–1880*. Iowa City: University of Iowa Press, 2001.

Davis, Tracy C. *Actresses as Working Women: Their Social Identity in Victorian Culture*. London: Routledge, 1991.

Davis, Tracy C. *The Economics of the British Stage, 1800–1914*. Cambridge University Press, 2000.

Davis, Tracy C. 'The moral sense of the majorities: indecency and vigilance in late-Victorian music halls'. *Popular Music* 10.1 (1991): 39–52.

Davis, Tracy C. '"Reading Shakespeare by flashes of lightning": challenging the foundations of Romantic acting theory'. *ELH: A Journal of English Literary History* (1995): 933–54.

Davis, Tracy C., and Ellen Donkin, eds. *Women and Playwriting in Nineteenth-Century Britain*. Cambridge University Press, 1999.

Dawick, John. *Pinero: A Theatrical Life*. Niwot: University Press of Colorado, 1993.

Deelman, Christian. *The Great Shakespeare Jubilee*. London: Michael Joseph, 1964.

De Lauretis, Teresa. *Technologies of Gender: Essays on Theory, Film, and Fiction*. Bloomington: Indiana University Press, 1987.

Dennis, John. *The Critical Works of John Dennis*. Ed. Edward N. Hooker. 2 vols. Baltimore: Johns Hopkins University Press, 1939–43.

Dibdin, Charles. *A Complete History of the English Stage*. 5 vols. London, 1797–1800.

Dobson, Michael. *The Making of the National Poet: Shakespeare, Adaptation, and Authorship, 1660–1769*. Oxford: Clarendon Press, 1992.

Donaldson, Ian. 'New papers of Henry Holland and R. B. Sheridan: (I) Holland's Drury Lane, 1794'. *Theatre Notebook* 16 (1962): 90–6.

Donaldson, Walter. *Recollections of an Actor*. London, 1865.

Donkin, Ellen. *Getting into the Act: Women Playwrights in London 1776–1829*. London: Routledge, 1995.

Donne, William Bodham. *Essays on the Drama*. London, 1858.

Donne, William Bodham. 'Poets and players'. *Fraser's Magazine* 44 (Nov. 1851): 512.

Donohue, Joseph. 'Actors and acting'. *Cambridge Companion to Victorian and Edwardian Theatre*. Cambridge University Press, 2003.

Donohue, Joseph. 'Burletta and the early nineteenth-century English theatre'. *Nineteenth Century Theatre Research* 1 (spring 1973): 29–51.

Donohue, Joseph. *Dramatic Character in the English Romantic Age*. Princeton University Press, 1970.

Donohue, Joseph. 'Kemble's production of *Macbeth* (1794): some notes on scene painters, scenery, special effects, and costumes'. *Theatre Notebook* 21 (1966–7): 63–74.

Donohue, Joseph. 'The London theatre at the end of the eighteenth century'. In Hume, ed., *London Theatre World*, 337–70.

Donohue, Joseph. *Theatre in the Age of Kean*. Oxford: Basil Blackwell, 1975.

Donohue, Joseph, and James Ellis. *A Handbook for Compilers: The London Stage 1800–1900. A Calendar of Performances*. Amherst, MA: privately printed, 1976.

Downer, Alan S. *The Eminent Tragedian: William Charles Macready*. Cambridge, MA: Harvard University Press, 1966.

Downer, Alan S. 'Nature to advantage dress'd: eighteenth century acting'. *PMLA* 58 (1943): 1002–37.

Downer, Alan S. 'Players and painted stage: nineteenth century acting'. *PMLA* 61 (1946): 522–76.

Downer, Alan S., ed. *Oxberry's 1822 Edition of King Richard III*. London: Society for Theatre Research, 1959.

Downes, John. *Roscius Anglicanus or an Historical Review of the Stage*. Ed. Judith Milhous and Robert D. Hume. London: Society for Theatre Research, 1987.

Dryden, John. *The Letters of John Dryden*. Ed. Charles E. Ward. Durham: Duke University Press, 1942.

Dugaw, Diane. *Deep Play: John Gay and the Invention of Modernity*. Newark: University of Delaware Press, 2001.

Dunbar, Janet. *Peg Woffington and her World*. London: Heineman, 1968.

Duncan, Barry. *The St James's Theatre: Its Strange and Complete History 1835–1957*. London: Barrie & Rockliff, 1964.

Dunton, John. *The Dublin Scuffle*. Dublin, 1699.

Earl, J. 'The music hall at the Grape Tavern, 1846–1882'. *Theatre Notebook* 53 (1999): 62–73.

Eliot, George. *Daniel Deronda*. Oxford: Clarendon, 1984.

Ellington, Edward Kennedy 'Duke'. Duke Ellington Collection, series 4: scripts and transcripts. Smithsonian Archives. Washington, DC.

English Drama of the Nineteenth Century: An Index and Finding Guide. Ed. James Ellis, assisted by Joseph Donohue, with Louise Allen Zak. New Canaan, CT: Readex Books, 1985.

Eshelman, Dorothy H. *The Committee Books of the Theatre Royal, Norwich 1768–1825*. London: Society for Theatre Research, 1970.

Evans, Bertrand. *Gothic Drama from Walpole to Shelley*. Berkeley: University of California Press, 1947.

Farquhar, George. *The Works of George Farquhar*. Ed. Shirley Strum Kenny. 2 vols. Oxford: Clarendon Press, 1988.

'Female dramatists of the past'. *Era* (23 May 1896): 18.

Findlater, Richard. *Joe Grimaldi: His Life and Theatre*. Cambridge University Press, 1978.

Finney, Gail. *Women in Modern Drama*. Ithaca: Cornell University Press, 1989.

Fiske, Roger. *English Theatre Music in the Eighteenth Century*. Oxford University Press, 1973; 2nd edn, 1986.

Fitzgerald, Percy. *The World Behind the Scenes*. London: Chatto & Windus, 1881.

FitzSimons, Raymund. *Edmund Kean: Fire from Heaven*. New York: Dial Press, 1976.

Forster, John, and George Henry Lewes. *Dramatic Essays*. Ed. William Archer and R. W. Lowe. London, 1895.

Foulkes, Richard. 'Charles Kean's *King Richard II*: a Pre-Raphaelite drama'. In Foulkes, ed., *Shakespeare and the Victorian Stage*, 39–55.

Foulkes, Richard. *Church and Stage in Victorian England*. Cambridge University Press, 1997.

Foulkes, Richard, ed. *Shakespeare and the Victorian Stage*. Cambridge University Press, 1986.

Fuegi, John. *Brecht and Company*. New York: Grove Press, 1994.

Furnas, J. C. *Fanny Kemble: Leading Lady of the Nineteenth-Century Stage*. New York: Dial Press, 1982.

Ganzel, Dewey. 'Patent wrongs and patent theatres: drama and the law in the early nineteenth century'. *PMLA* 76 (1961): 384–96.

Garlick, Görel. 'George Saunders and the Birmingham New Street Theatre: a conjectural reconstruction'. *Theatre Notebook* 52 (1998): 131–2.

Garrick, David. *Letters*. Ed. David M. Little and George M. Kahrl. 3 vols. Cambridge, MA: Belknap Press of Harvard University Press, 1963.

Garrick, David. *The Plays of David Garrick*. Ed. Harry William Pedicord and Fredrick Louis Bergmann. 7 vols. Carbondale: Southern Illinois University Press, 1980–2.

Gay, John. *John Gay: Dramatic Works*. Ed. John Fuller. 2 vols. Oxford: Clarendon Press, 1983.

Gay, John. *The Letters of John Gay*. Ed. C. F. Burgess. Oxford: Clarendon Press, 1966.

Gielgud, Kate Terry. *A Victorian Playgoer*. Ed. Muriel St Claire Byrne. London: Heinemann, 1980.

Gilbert, W. S. *The Bab Ballads*. Ed. James Ellis. Cambridge, MA: Belknap Press of Harvard University Press, 1970.

Gladstone, W. E. *The Gladstone Diaries*. Vol. v, *1855–1860*. Ed. H. C. G. Matthew. Oxford: Clarendon Press, 1978.

Goldsmith, Oliver. 'An essay on the theatre; or, a comparison between laughing and sentimental comedy'. *Westminster Magazine* 1 (1773): 4–6.

Gore, Catherine. *Quid Pro Quo; or, the Day of Dupes*. London: National Acting Drama Office, n.d.

Graves, Clotilde. *A Mother of Three: An Original Farce in Three Acts*. London: French, n.d.

Gray, Charles Harold. *Theatrical Criticism in London to 1795*. 1931. Rpt. New York: B. Blom, 1964.

Greene, John C, and Gladys L. H. Clark. *The Dublin Stage 1720–1745: A Calendar of Plays, Entertainments, Afterpieces*. Bethlehem, PA: Lehigh University Press, 1993.

Guest, Ivor. *Ballet in Leicester Square: The Alhambra and the Empire 1860–1915*. London: Dance Books, 1992.

Hamilton, Cicely. *Life Errant*. London: J. M. Dent, 1935.

Harbage, Alfred. *Cavalier Drama*. New York: Modern Language Association, 1936.

Hare, Arnold, ed. *Theatre Royal, Bath: A Calendar of Performances at the Orchard Street Theatre, 1750–1805*. Bath: Kingsmead, 1977.

Hasse, John Edward. *Beyond Category*. New York: Simon & Schuster, 1993.

Havel, Vaclav. *The Beggar's Opera*. Trans. Paul Wilson. Ithaca: Cornell University Press, 2001.

Hayes, Michael, and Anastasia Nikolopoulou, eds. *Melodrama: The Cultural Emergence of a Genre*. New York: St Martin's Press, 1996.

Hazlitt, William. *Complete Works of William Hazlitt*. Ed. P. P. Howe. Vol. v. London: J. M. Dent & Sons, 1930.

Hazlitt, William. *Dramatic Criticism*. Ed. William Archer and R. W. Lowe. London, 1895.

Hazlitt, William. *A View of the English Stage*. London, 1818.

Highfill, Philip H., Jr, Kalman A. Burnim and Edward A. Langhans. *A Biographical Dictionary of Actors, Actresses, Musicians, Dancers, Managers and Other Stage Personnel in London, 1660–1800*. 16 vols. Carbondale: Southern Illinois University Press, 1973–93.

Hillebrand, H. N. *Edmund Kean*. 1933. Rpt. New York: AMS Press, 1966.

Hitchcock, Robert. *An Historical View of the Irish Stage*. 2 vols. Dublin: Marchbank, 1788–94.

Hodgkinson, J. L., and Rex Pogson. *The Early Manchester Theatre*. London: Society for Theatre Research, 1960.

Hogan, Charles Beecher. *Shakespeare in the Theatre, 1701–1800*. 2 vols. Oxford: Clarendon Press, 1952–7.

Holder, Heidi J. 'The "lady playwrights" and the "wild tribes of the East": female dramatists in the East End theatres, 1860–1880'. In Davis and Donkin, eds., *Women and Playwriting*, 174–92.

Holland, Peter. *The Ornament of Action: Text and Performance in Restoration Comedy*. Cambridge University Press, 1979.

Home, John. *Douglas: Pamphlets*. Edinburgh, 1757.

Hotson, Leslie. *The Commonwealth and Restoration Stage*. Cambridge, MA: Harvard University Press, 1928.

Howard, Diana. *London Theatres and Music Halls 1850–1950*. London: Library Association, 1970.

Howe, Elizabeth. *The First English Actresses: Women and Drama 1660–1700*. Cambridge University Press, 1992.

Howell, Mark. 'The "regular theatre" at Jacob's Well, Bristol 1729–69'. In *Scenes from Provincial Stages*. Ed. Richard Foulkes. London: Society for Theatre Research, 1994.

Hughes, Alan. *Henry Irving, Shakespearean*. Cambridge University Press, 1981.

Hughes, Alan. 'The Lyceum staff: a Victorian theatrical organisation'. *Theatre Notebook* 27.1 (1974): 11–17.

Hughes, Derek. *English Drama 1660–1700*. Oxford: Clarendon Press, 1996.

Hughes, Derek. 'Who counts in Farquhar?' In *A Subtler Music: Essays on the Drama and Opera of Enlightenment Europe*. Ed. Luis Gámez. Stamford: Paul Watkins, 1997.

Hughes, Leo. *The Drama's Patrons: A Study of the Eighteenth-Century London Audience*. Austin: University of Texas Press, 1971.

Hume, Robert D. '"Before the Bard": Shakespeare in early eighteenth-century London', *ELH: A Journal of English Literary History* 64 (1997): 41–75.

Hume, Robert D. '"The change in comedy": cynical versus exemplary comedy on the London stage, 1678–1693'. *Essays in Theatre* 1 (1982–3): 101–18.

Hume, Robert D. *The Development of English Drama in the Late Seventeenth Century*. Oxford: Clarendon Press, 1976.

Hume, Robert D. *Henry Fielding and the London Theatre, 1728–1737*. Oxford: Clarendon Press, 1988.

Hume, Robert D. 'Jeremy Collier and the future of the London theater in 1698'. *Studies in Philology* 96 (1999): 480–511.

Hume, Robert D. 'The London theatre from *The Beggar's Opera* to the Licensing Act'. In *The Rakish Stage*, ed. Hume, chap. 1.

Hume, Robert D. 'Marital discord in English comedy from Dryden to Fielding'. *Modern Philology* 74 (1976–7): 248–72; rpt. in Hume, ed., *Rakish Stage*, 176–213.

Hume, Robert D. 'The multifarious forms of eighteenth-century comedy'. In *The Stage and the Page: London's 'Whole Show' in the Eighteenth-Century Theatre*. Ed. George Winchester Stone, Jr. Berkeley: University of California Press, 1988, 3–32. Reprinted in Hume, ed., *Rakish Stage*, 214–44.

Hume, Robert D. 'Securing a repertory: plays on the London stage 1660–5'. In *Poetry and Drama 1570–1700: Essays in Honour of Harold F. Brooks*. Ed. Antony Coleman and Antony Hammond. London: Methuen, 1981, 156–72.

Hume, Robert D., ed. *The London Theatre World, 1660–1800*. Carbondale: Southern Illinois University Press, 1980.

Hume, Robert D., ed. *The Rakish Stage*. Carbondale: Southern Illinois University Press, 1983.

Hunningher, Joost. 'Première on Regent Street'. In *Cinema: The Beginnings and the Future*. Ed. Christopher Williams. London: University of Westminster Press, 1996, 41–53.

Hunt, Leigh. *Autobiography*. Ed. J. E. Morpurgo. London: P. Cresset, 1948.

Hunt, Leigh. *Critical Essays on the Performers of the London Stage*. London, 1807.

Hunt, Leigh. *Dramatic Criticism*. Ed. William Archer and R. W. Lowe. London, 1894.

Hunt, Leigh. *Leigh Hunt's Dramatic Criticism*. Ed. Lawrence Huston Houtchens and Carolyn Washburn Houtchens. New York: Columbia University Press, 1949.

Inchbald, Elizabeth. *The Plays of Elizabeth Inchbald*. Ed. Paula Backscheider. 2 vols. New York: Garland, 1980.

Irving, Henry. *The Stage As It Is*. Reprinted in *The Drama Addresses*. London: William Heinemann, 1893.

Irving, Laurence. *Henry Irving, the Actor and his World*. London: Faber & Faber, 1951.

Jackson, John. *The History of the Scottish Stage*. Edinburgh: Peter Hill, 1793.

Jackson, Russell, ed. *Victorian Theatre*. London: A. & C. Black, 1989.

James, Henry. 'Nona Vincent'. In *The Complete Tales of Henry James*. Ed. Leon Edel. Vol. VIII. London: Rupert Hart-Davis, 1963, 153–87.

Jewsbury, Geraldine. *The Half-Sisters: A Tale*. 2 vols. London: Chapman & Hall, 1848.

John, Angela V. *Elizabeth Robins: Staging a Life*. London: Routledge, 1995.

Johnson, Samuel. *Johnson on Shakespeare*. Ed. Arthur Sherbo. *Yale Edition of the Works of Samuel Johnson*. Vol. VII. New Haven: Yale University Press, 1968.

Johnson, Samuel. *Poems*. Ed. E. L. McAdam, Jr. *Yale Edition of the Works of Samuel Johnson*. Vol. VI. New Haven: Yale University Press, 1964.

Johnson, Samuel. *The Poems of Samuel Johnson*. Ed. David Nichol Smith and Edward L. McAdam. 2nd edn. Oxford: Clarendon Press, 1974.

Johnson, Samuel. 'Preface'. In *Samuel Johnson on Shakespeare*. Ed. W. K. Wimsatt, Jr. New York: Hill & Wang, 1960.

Jones, Henry Arthur. *Plays by Henry Arthur Jones*. Ed. Russell Jackson. Cambridge University Press, 1982.

Jones, Henry Arthur. *Representative Plays*. 4 vols. Boston: Little, Brown & Co., 1925.

Joyce, Patrick. *Democratic Subjects*. Cambridge University Press, 1994.

Keith, William Grant. 'The designs for the first movable scenery on the English public stage'. *Burlington Magazine for Connoisseurs* 25 (1914): 29–39, 85–98.

Keith, William Grant. 'John Webb and the court theatre of Charles II'. *Architectural Review* 57 (1925): 49–55.

Kemble, Fanny. *Fanny Kemble's Journals*. Ed. Catherine Clinton. Cambridge, MA: Harvard University Press, 2000.

Kendal, Madge. *Dramatic Opinions*. London: John Murray, 1890.

Kenny, Shirley Strum. 'Humane comedy'. *Modern Philology* 75 (1977): 29–43.

Kenny, Shirley Strum, ed. *British Theatre and the Other Arts, 1660–1800*. Washington: Folger Books, 1984.

Kewes, Paulina. *Authorship and Appropriation: Writing for the Stage in England, 1660–1710*. Oxford: Clarendon Press, 1998.

Kewes, Paulina. '"[A] Play, which I presume to call *original*": appropriation, creative genius, and eighteenth-century playwriting'. *Studies in the Literary Imagination* 34.1 (2001): 17–47.

Kift, Dagmar. *The Victorian Music Hall: Culture, Class and Conflict*. Cambridge University Press, 1996.

Kinservik, Matthew J. *Disciplining Satire: The Censorship of Satiric Comedy on the Eighteenth-Century London Stage*. Lewisburgh, PA: Bucknell University Press, 2002.

Knapp, Mary E. *Prologues and Epilogues of the Eighteenth Century*. New Haven: Yale University Press, 1961.

Knight, Joseph. 'J. L. Toole'. *Theatre* n.s. (January 1880): 24–9.

Kruger, Loren. *The National Stage*. University of Chicago Press, 1992.

Krutch, Joseph Wood. *Comedy and Conscience after the Restoration*. Revised edn. New York: Columbia University Press, 1949.

Lafler, Joanne. *The Celebrated Mrs Oldfield: The Life and Art of an Augustan Actress*. Carbondale: Southern Illinois University Press, 1989.

Lamb, Charles. 'Munden's farewell'. *London Magazine* (July 1824).

Lamb, Charles. 'On the acting of Munden'. *London Magazine* (October 1822).

Langford, Paul. *A Polite and Commercial People: England 1727–1783*. Oxford University Press, 1992.

Langhans, Edward A. *Restoration Promptbooks*. Carbondale: Southern Illinois University Press, 1981.

Langhans, Edward A. 'Staging practices in the Restoration theatres 1660–1682'. Ph.D. thesis. Yale University, 1955.

Langhans, Edward A. 'The theatres'. In Hume, ed., *London Theatre World*, 35–65.

Langhans, Edward A. 'Tough actresses to follow'. In Schofield and Macheski, eds., *Curtain Calls*.

Lawrence, W. J. 'Proscenium doors: an Elizabethan heritage'. In W. J. Lawrence, *The Elizabethan Playhouse and Other Studies*. Stratford-upon-Avon: Shakespeare Head Press, 1912, 157–89.

Lawrence, W. J. 'The royal box'. In *Old Theatre Days and Ways*. 1935. Rpt. New York: Benjamin Blom, 1968, 143–51.

Leach, Joseph. *Bright Particular Star: The Life and Times of Charlotte Cushman*. New Haven: Yale University Press, 1970.

Leach, Robert. *The Punch and Judy Show: History, Tradition and Meaning*. London: Batsford, 1985.

Leacroft, Richard. *The Development of the English Playhouse*. London: Eyre Methuen, 1973.

Lee, Edward. *Music of the People: A Study of Popular Music in Great Britain*. London: Barrie & Jenkins, 1970.

Lewes, George Henry. 'Foreign actors and the English drama'. *Cornhill Magazine* 8 (August 1863): 172.

Lewes, George Henry. *On Actors and the Art of Acting*. London, 1875. New York: Grove Press, 1957.

Lewes, George Henry. 'Shakespeare and his latest stage interpreters'. *Fraser's Magazine* 64 (December 1861): 776.

Liesenfeld, Vincent J. *The Licensing Act of 1737*. Madison: University of Wisconsin Press, 1984.

Lock, F. P. *Susanna Centlivre*. New York: Twayne, 1979.

Loftis, John. *Comedy and Society from Congreve to Fielding*. Stanford University Press, 1959.

Loftis, John, 'Political and social thought in the Drama'. In Hume, ed., *London Theatre World*, 253–85.

Loftis, John. *The Politics of Drama in Augustan England*. Oxford: Clarendon Press, 1963.

Loftis, John. *Sheridan and the Drama of Georgian England*. Cambridge, MA: Harvard University Press, 1977.

Loftis, John. *Steele at Drury Lane*. Berkeley: University of California Press, 1962.

Loftis, John, ed. *Restoration Drama: Modern Essays in Criticism*. Oxford University Press, 1966.

Love, Harold. 'Who were the Restoration audience?' *Yearbook of English Studies* 10 (1980): 21–44.

[Lowe, Robert, George Halkett and William Archer.] *The Fashionable Tragedian, A Criticism, with Ten Illustrations*. 1877.

Lynch, James J. *Box Pit and Gallery*. Berkeley: University of California Press, 1953.

Mackesy, Piers. *The War for America*. Cambridge, MA: Harvard University Press, 1964.

Mackintosh, Iain. *Architecture, Actors and Audience*. London: Routledge, 1993.

MacMillan, Dougald. *Catalogue of the Larpent Plays in the Huntington Library*. San Marino: Huntington Library, 1939.

Macqueen-Pope, Walter James. *Carriages at Eleven: The Story of the Edwardian Theatre*. London: Hutchinson, 1947.

Macqueen-Pope, Walter James. *Ladies First: The Story of Women's Conquest of the British Stage*. London: Allen, 1952.

Macready, William Charles. *William Charles Macready: Reminiscences and Selections from his Diary and Letters*. Ed. F. Pollock. 2 vols. London, 1875.

Mander, Raymond, and Joe Mitchenson. *The Theatres of London*. London: Rupert Hart-Davis, 1963.

Mander, Raymond, and Joe Mitchenson. *Victorian and Edwardian Entertainment from Old Photographs*. London: Batsford, 1978.

Mann, David D., and Susan Garland Mann, eds. *Women Playwrights in England, Ireland, and Scotland 1660–1823*. Bloomington: Indiana University Press, 1996.

Marker, Frederick, and Lise-Lone Marker. 'Actors and their repertory'. *Revels History of Drama in English*, vol. VI, 95–141.

Marsden, Jean I. 'Rape, voyeurism, and the Restoration stage'. In *Broken Boundaries: Women and Feminism in Restoration Drama*. Ed. Katherine M. Quinsey. Lexington: University of Kentucky Press, 1996.

Marshall, Gail. *Actresses on the Victorian Stage: Feminine Performance and the Galatea Myth*. Cambridge University Press, 1998.

Marston, Westland. *Our Recent Actors*. 2 vols. London: Sampson, Low, 1888.

Martin, Sir Theodore. *Helen Faucit (Lady Martin)*. Edinburgh: Blackwood, 1900.

Mason, A. E. W. *Sir George Alexander & the St James' Theatre*. London: Macmillan, 1935.

Mathias, Peter. *The First Industrial Nation*. 2nd edn. London: Methuen, 1983.

Matthews, Brander, ed. *Papers on Acting*. 1915. New York: Hill & Wang, 1958.

Mayer, David. *Harlequin in his Element: The English Pantomime, 1806–1836*. Cambridge, MA: Harvard University Press, 1969.

Mayer, David. 'Parlour and platform melodrama'. In Hayes and Nikolopoulou, eds., *Melodrama*, 210–34.

Mayer, David. *Playing out the Empire: 'Ben-Hur' and other Toga Plays and Films, 1888–1903*. Oxford: Clarendon Press, 1994.

Mayer, David. 'The world on fire . . . pyrodramas at Belle Vue Gardens, Manchester, c. 1850–1950'. In *Popular Imperialism and the Military, 1850–1950*. Ed. John M. MacKenzie. Manchester University Press, 1992, 179–97.

Mayer, David, ed. *Henry Irving and* The Bells. Manchester University Press, 1980.

McCleod, D. Hugh. *Class and Religion in the Late Victorian City*. London: Croom Helm, 1974.

McConkey, Kenneth. *British Impressionism*. London: Phaidon, 1989.

Meisel, Martin. *Realizations: Narrative, Pictorial, and Theatrical Arts in Nineteenth-Century England*. Princeton University Press, 1983.

Meisel, Martin. *Shaw and the Nineteenth-Century Theater*. Princeton University Press, 1963.

Merrick, Leonard. *The Actor-Manager*. London: Hodder & Stoughton, n.d.

Milhous, Judith. 'Company management'. In Hume, ed., *London Theatre World*, 1–34.

Milhous, Judith. 'The multimedia spectacular on the Restoration stage'. In Kenny, ed., *British Theatre*, 41–66.

Milhous, Judith. *Thomas Betterton and the Management of Lincoln's Inn Fields, 1695–1708*. Carbondale: Southern Illinois University Press, 1979.

Milhous, Judith. 'United Company finances, 1682–1692'. *Theatre Research International* 7 (winter 1981/2): 37–53.

Milhous, Judith, and Robert D. Hume. 'Dating play premières from publication data, 1660–1700'. *Harvard Library Bulletin* 22 (1974): 374–405.

Milhous, Judith, and Robert D. Hume. 'A Drury Lane account book for 1745–46'. *Theatre History Studies* 10 (1990), 67–104.

Milhous, Judith, and Robert D. Hume. 'The Drury Lane actors' rebellion of 1743'. *Theatre Journal* 42 (1990): 57–80.

Milhous, Judith, and Robert D. Hume. 'The London theatre cartel of the 1720s'. *Theatre Survey* 26 (1985): 21–37.

Milhous, Judith, and Robert D. Hume. 'New light on English acting companies in 1646, 1648, and 1660'. *Review of English Studies* n.s. 42 (1991): 487–509.

Milhous, Judith, and Robert D. Hume. 'Playwrights' remuneration in eighteenth-century London'. *Harvard Library Bulletin* n.s. 10 (1999): 3–90.

Milhous, Judith, and Robert D. Hume. 'Profits at Drury Lane, 1713–1716'. *Theatre Research International* 14 (1989), 241–55.

Milhous, Judith, and Robert D. Hume. 'Receipts at Drury Lane: Richard Cross's diary for 1746–47'. *Theatre Notebook* 49 (1995): 12–26, 69–90.

Milhous, Judith, and Robert D. Hume. *A Register of English Theatrical Documents, 1660–1737*. 2 vols. Carbondale: Southern Illinois University Press, 1991.

Milhous, Judith, and Robert D. Hume. 'The silencing of Drury Lane in 1709'. *Theatre Journal* 32 (1980): 427–47.

Milhous, Judith, and Robert D. Hume. *Vice Chamberlain Coke's Theatrical Papers, 1706–1715*. Carbondale: Southern Illinois University Press, 1982.

'Miss Clo Graves, novelist and dramatist'. *The Times* (5 December 1932): 17.

Moncrieff, William Thomas. *The Cataract of the Ganges!; or, The Rajah's Daughter*. [Drury Lane, 27 October 1823.] London: Simpkin & Marshall, 1823.

Moody, Jane. *Illegitimate Theatre in London, 1770–1840*. Cambridge University Press, 2000.

Moore, George. *A Mummer's Wife*. New York: Boni & Liveright, 1922.

Morgann, Maurice. *Essay on the Dramatic Character of Falstaff*. 1777.

Morley, Henry. *The Journal of a London Playgoer from 1851 to 1866*. 2nd edn. London: George Routledge & Sons, 1891.

Morton, William H., and Henry Chance Newton. *Sixty Years' Stage Service, Being a Record of the Life of Charles Morton, 'The Father of the Halls'*. London: Gale & Polden, 1905.

Mowatt, Anna Cora. *A Mimic Life*. Boston: Ticknor & Fields, 1856.

Moynet, Jean-Pierre. *L'Envers du théâtre: machines et décorations*. Paris, 1873.

Mulvey, Laura. 'Visual pleasure and narrative cinema'. *Screen* 16 (1975): 6–18.

Murphy, Arthur. *The Life of David Garrick*. 1801. 2 vols. in 1. Rpt. New York: Benjamin Blom, 1969.

Musgrave, Mrs H. *Our Flat: Farcical Comedy in Three Acts*. Unpublished ms. Lord Chamberlain's Plays. British Library.

Nalbach, Daniel. *The King's Theatre 1704–1867: London's First Italian Opera House*. London: Society for Theatre Research, 1972.

Nash, Mary. *The Provoked Wife: The Life and Times of Susannah Cibber*. London: Hutchinson, 1977.

Nelson, Alfred L., and Gilbert B. Cross, eds. *Sans Pareil Theatre, Adelphi Theatre: A Chronology and Index, 1806–1850*. Westport, CT: Greenwood Press, 1988.

Nethercot, Arthur H. *Sir William D'Avenant, Poet Laureate and Playwright-Manager*. University of Chicago Press, 1938.

Newsome, David. *The Victorian World Picture: Perceptions and Introspections in an Age of Change*. London: Fontana, 1998; John Murray, 1997.

Nicholson, Steve. *The Censorship of British Drama, 1900–1968*. Vol. I. University of Exeter Press, 2003.

Nicholson, Watson. *The Struggle for a Free Stage in London*. London: Constable, 1906.

Nicoll, Allardyce. *A History of English Drama 1660–1900*. Vol. I: *Restoration Drama*, 4th edn, 1965; vol. II: *Early Eighteenth-Century Drama*, 3rd edn, 1965; vol. III: *Late Eighteenth-Century Drama 1750–1800*, 2nd edn, 1952; vol. IV: *Early Nineteenth-Century Drama, 1800–1850*, 2nd edn, 1963; vol. V: *Late Nineteenth-Century Drama*, Cambridge University Press, 1962.

Nightingale, Florence. *Cassandra: An Essay*. Old Westbury, NY: Feminist Press, 1979.

Noble, Yvonne. '*The Beggar's Opera* in its own time'. In *Twentieth Century Interpretations of* The Beggar's Opera. Ed. Yvonne Noble. Englewood Cliffs, NJ: Prentice-Hall, 1975.

Noble, Yvonne. 'Charles Coffey and John Mottley: an odd couple in Grub Street'. Unpublished article.

Norris, Hilary. 'A directory of Victorian scene-painters'. *Theatrephile* 1.2 (March 1984): 38–52.

Orrell, John. *The Human Stage: English Theatre Design, 1567–1640*. Cambridge University Press, 1988.

Orrell, John. *The Theatres of Inigo Jones and John Webb*. Cambridge University Press, 1985.

Osborne, John. *The Naturalist Drama in Germany*. Manchester University Press, 1971.

O'Toole, Fintan. *A Traitor's Kiss: The Life of Richard Brinsley Sheridan, 1751–1816*. New York: Farrar, Straus & Giroux, 1997.

Owen, Susan J. *Restoration Theatre and Crisis*. Oxford: Clarendon Press, 1996.

Oxberry's Dramatic Biography and Histrionic Anecdotes. N.s. 1. London, 1826.

Paulson, Ronald. *Hogarth: His Life, Art, and Times*. New Haven: Yale University Press, 1974.

Payne, Deborah C. 'Reified object or emergent professional? Retheorizing the Restoration actress'. In *Cultural Readings of Restoration and Eighteenth-Century English Theatre*. Ed. J. Douglas Canfield and Deborah C. Payne. Athens: University of Georgia Press, 1995.

Pearson, Hesketh. *Bernard Shaw*. London: Collins, 1942.

Pearson, Hesketh. *The Last Actor-Managers*. London: White Lion, 1950.

Pearson, Jacqueline. *The Prostituted Muse: Images of Women and Women Dramatists 1642–1737*. New York: St Martin's Press, 1988.

Pedicord, Harry William. *The Theatrical Public in the Time of Garrick*. Carbondale: Southern Illinois University Press, 1954.

Penley, Belville S. *The Bath Stage*. London: Lewis, 1892.

Peters, Julie Stone. *Congreve, the Drama, and the Printed Word*. Stanford University Press, 1990.

Pinero, Arthur Wing. Trelawney of the 'Wells' *and Other Plays*. Ed. J. S. Bratton. Oxford: Clarendon Press, 1995.

Pix, Mary. *The Plays of Mary Pix*. Ed. Edna Steeves. New York: Garland, 1982.

Planché, James Robinson. *The Extravaganzas of J. R. Planché (Somerset Herald), 1825–1871*. Ed. T. F. Croker and Stephen Tucker. 5 vols. London: French, 1879.

Planché, James Robinson. *Plays by James Robinson Planché*. Ed. Donald Roy. Cambridge University Press, 1986.

Planché, James Robinson. *The Recollections and Reflections of J. R. Planché*. 2 vols. London: Tinsley, 1872.

Poel, William. *Shakespeare in the Theatre*. London: Sidgwick & Jackson, 1913.

Poole, Robert. *Popular Leisure and the Music Hall in Nineteenth-Century Bolton*. University of Lancaster Press, 1982.

Pope, Alexander. *The Correspondence of Alexander Pope*. Ed. George Sherburn. 5 vols. Oxford: Clarendon Press, 1956.

Porter, Roy. *London: A Social History*. Cambridge, MA: Harvard University Press, 1994.

Postlewait, Thomas. *Prophet of the New Drama: William Archer and the Ibsen Campaign*. Westport, CT: Greenwood Press, 1986.

Powell, Kerry. *Women and the Victorian Theatre*. Cambridge University Press, 1997.

Price, Cecil. *Theatre in the Age of Garrick*. Oxford: Basil Blackwell, 1973.

Razzell, P. E., and R. Wainwright, eds. *The Victorian Working Class: Selections from Letters to the* Morning Chronicle. London: Frank Cass, 1973.

Rees, Terence. *Theatre Lighting in the Age of Gas*. London: Society for Theatre Research, 1978.

Reid, D. 'Popular theatre in Birmingham'. In *Performance and Politics in Popular Drama*. Ed. David Bradby, Louis James and Bernard Sharratt. Cambridge University Press, 1980.

Report from the Joint Select Committee of the House of Lords and the House of Commons on the Stage Plays (Censorship). London: The Stage, [1910].

Report from the Select Committee on Dramatic Literature: with the Minutes of Evidence. 2 August 1832. Rpt. Shannon: Irish University Press, 1968.

Report from the Select Committee on Theatres and Places of Entertainment. London: House of Commons, 1892. Rpt. Shannon: Irish University Press, 1970.

Report from the Select Committee on Theatrical Licences and Regulations. 1866. Rpt. Shannon: Irish University Press, 1970.

Revels History of Drama in English, The. Vol. v. *1660–1750*. Ed. John Loftis. London: Methuen, 1976.

Revels History of Drama in English, The. Vol. vi. *1750–1880*. Ed. Michael R. Booth. London: Methuen, 1975.

Richards, Kenneth. 'Samuel Phelps's production of *All's Well that Ends Well*'. In Richards and Thomson, eds., *Nineteenth-Century British Theatre*, 179–95.

Richards, Kenneth, and Peter Thomson, eds. *Essays on Nineteenth-Century British Theatre*. London: Methuen, 1971.

Rinear, David L. 'From the artificial towards the real: the acting of William Farren'. *Theatre Notebook* 31 (1977): 21–8.

Ristori, Adelaide. *Studies and Memories: An Autobiography*. Boston: Roberts, 1888.

Ritvo, Harriet. *Animal Estate: The English and other Creatures in the Victorian Age*. Cambridge, MA: Harvard University Press, 1987.

Roach, Joseph R. *The Player's Passion: Studies in the Science of Acting*. Newark: University of Delaware Press, 1985.

Roberts, David. *The Ladies: Female Patronage of Restoration Drama, 1660–1700*. Oxford: Clarendon Press, 1989.

Robins, Elizabeth. 'Heights and depths'. Ms. Fales Library, New York University.

Robins, Elizabeth. 'Odd bits'. Handwritten and typed notes at end of 'Whither and how'. Ms. Fales Library, New York University.

Robins, Elizabeth, and Florence Bell. *Alan's Wife*. London: Henry, 1893.

Robinson, F. W. 'An East End entertainment'. *Belgravia* 9 (1869): 522.

Robson, William. *The Old Playgoer*. London, 1846.

Rosenfeld, Sybil. *Georgian Scene Painters and Scene Painting*. Cambridge University Press, 1981.

Rosenfeld, Sybil. *A Short History of Scene Design in Great Britain*. Oxford: Basil Blackwell, 1973.

Rosenfeld, Sybil. *Strolling Players and Drama in the Provinces 1660–1765*. Cambridge University Press, 1939.

Rosenfeld, Sybil. *The York Theatre*. London: Society for Theatre Research, 2001.

Rosenthal, Laura J. *Playwrights and Plagiarists in Early Modern England: Gender, Authorship, Literary Property*. Ithaca: Cornell University Press, 1996.

Rowell, George. 'Charles Wyndham'. In *The Theatrical Manager in England and America*. Ed. Joseph Donohue. Princeton University Press, 1971, 189–213.

Rowell, George. *Queen Victoria Goes to the Theatre*. London: Paul Elek, 1978.

Rowell, George. *The Victorian Theatre 1792–1914*. 2nd edn. Cambridge University Press, 1978.

Rowell, George. *William Terris and Richard Prince: Two Players in an Adelphi Melodrama*. London: Society for Theatre Research, 1987.

Rowell, George, ed. *Victorian Dramatic Criticism*. London: Methuen, 1971.

Royalty Theatre 1800–28. Scrapbook of clippings. Harvard Theatre Collection.

Russell, Dave. *Popular Music in England, 1840–1914: A Social History*. 2nd edn. Manchester University Press, 1997.

Russell, Dave. 'Varieties of life: the making of the Edwardian music hall'. In Booth and Kaplan., eds., *Edwardian Theatre*, 61–85.

Russell, W. Clark. *Representative Actors*. London: Frederick Warne, 1872.

Rutherford, L. '"Harmless nonsense": the comic sketch and the development of music-hall entertainment'. In Bratton, ed., *Music Hall*, 131–51.

Saintsbury, H. A., and Cecil Palmer, eds. *We Saw Him Act: A Symposium on the Art of Sir Henry Irving, Litt D. Cambridge and Dublin; LL.D., Glasgow*. New York: Benjamin Blom, 1939.

Sala, G. A. 'On stage costume'. *Belgravia* 8 (1869): 101.

Saunders, George. *A Treatise on Theatres*. Printed for the author, 1790.

Saxon, A. H. *Enter Foot and Horse: A History of Hippodrama in England and France*. New Haven: Yale University Press, 1968.

Schoch, Richard W. *Not Shakespeare: Bardolatry and Burlesque in the Nineteenth Century*. Cambridge University Press, 2002.

Schoch, Richard W. *Shakespeare's Victorian Stage: Performing History in the Theatre of Charles Kean*. Cambridge University Press, 1998.

Schofield, Mary Anne, and Cecilia Macheski, eds. *Curtain Calls: British and American Women and Theater 1660–1820*. Athens: Ohio University Press, 1991.

Scott, Sir Walter. 'Essay on the Drama'. In *Miscellaneous Prose Works of Sir Walter Scott, Bart*. Edinburgh: Robert Cadell, 1850, Vol. I.

Scouten, Arthur H. *The London Stage 1729–1747: A Critical Introduction*. Carbondale: Southern Illinois University Press, 1968.

Scouten, Arthur H. 'Notes toward a history of Restoration comedy'. *Philological Quarterly* 45 (1966): 62–70.

Scouten, Arthur H., and Robert D. Hume. 'Restoration comedy and its audiences, 1660–1776'. *Yearbook of English Studies* 10 (1980): 45–69.

Scullion, Adrienne. 'The eighteenth century'. In *A History of Scottish Theatre*. Ed. Bill Findlay. Edinburgh: Polygon, 1998.

Senelick, Laurence. 'The evolution of the male impersonator on the nineteenth-century popular stage'. *Essays in Theatre* 1 (1982): 29–44.

'Shakespeare travestied'. *Dublin University Magazine* 59 (Feb. 1862): 174.

Shapiro, Michael. 'The introduction of actresses in England: delay or defensiveness?' In *Enacting Gender on the English Renaissance Stage*. Ed. Viviana Comensoli and Anne Russell. Urbana: University of Illinois Press, 1999.

Shattuck, Charles H. *The Shakespeare Promptbooks: A Descriptive Catalogue*. Urbana: University of Illinois Press, 1965.

Shattuck, Charles H., ed. *Bulwer and Macready: A Chronicle of the Early Victorian Theatre*. Urbana: University of Illinois Press, 1958.

Shattuck, Charles H., ed. *John Philip Kemble Promptbooks*. 11 vols. Charlottesville: University Press of Virginia for the Folger Shakespeare Library, 1974.

Shattuck, Charles H., ed. *William Charles Macready's* King John: *A Facsimile Prompt-Book*. Urbana: University of Illinois Press, 1962.

Shaw, George Bernard. *The Complete Plays of Bernard Shaw*. London: Odhams Press, 1931.

Shaw, George Bernard. *Dramatic Opinions and Essays*. 2 vols. New York: Brentanos', 1928.

Shaw, George Bernard. *Our Theatres in the Nineties*. 3 vols. London: Constable, 1932.

Shaw, George Bernard. 'Preface'. In William Archer, *The Theatrical 'World' of 1894*. London: Walter Scott, 1895.

Shaw, George Bernard. *Prefaces by Bernard Shaw*. London: Odhams Press, 1938.

Shaw, George Bernard. *Shaw and Ibsen: Bernard Shaw's* The Quintessence of Ibsenism *and Related Writings*. Ed. J. L. Wisenthal. University of Toronto Press, 1979.

Sheldon, Esther K. *Thomas Sheridan of Smock-Alley*. Princeton University Press, 1967.

Shepherd, Simon, and Peter Womack. *English Drama: A Cultural History*. Oxford: Blackwell, 1996.

Sheridan, Richard Brinsley. *The Critic. Sheridan: Plays*. Ed. Cecil Price. Oxford University Press, 1975.

Siddons, Henry. *Practical illustrations of rhetorical gesture and action, adapted to the English drama*. London: Richard Phillips, 1807.

Sims, George R. *Glances Back*. London: Jarrolds, 1917.

Smith, Irwin. *Shakespeare's Blackfriars Playhouse: Its History and its Design*. New York University Press, 1964.

Smith, John Harrington. *The Gay Couple in Restoration Comedy*. Cambridge, MA: Harvard University Press, 1948.

Sorelius, Gunnar. *'The Giant Race Before the Flood': Pre-Restoration Drama on the Stage and in the Criticism of the Restoration*. Studia Anglistica Upsaliensia 4. Uppsala: Almqvist & Wiksell, 1966.

Southern, Richard. *Changeable Scenery: Its Origin and Development in the British Theatre*. London: Faber & Faber, 1952.

Speaight, George. *A History of the Circus*. London: Tantivy Press, 1980.

Speaight, George. *The History of the English Puppet Theatre*. 2nd edn. Carbondale: Southern Illinois University Press, 1990.

Spence, Joseph. *Observations, Anecdotes, and Characters of Books and Men*. Ed. James M. Osborn. 2 vols. Oxford: Clarendon Press, 1966.

Sprague, Arthur Colby. *Shakespeare and the Actors: The Stage Business in his Plays (1660–1905)*. Cambridge, MA: Harvard University Press, 1944.

Sprague, Arthur Colby. *Shakespearian Players and Performances*. Cambridge, MA: Harvard University Press, 1953.

Springhall, John. *Youth, Popular Culture and Moral Panics: Penny Gaffs to Gangsta Rap, 1830–1996*. London: Macmillan, 1998.

'Stage morality and the ballet'. *Blackwood's Magazine* 105 (March 1869): 356.

The Stage of 1871. N.p.: n.p., n.d.

Staves, Susan. *Players' Scepters: Fictions of Authority in the Restoration*. Lincoln: University of Nebraska Press, 1979.

Staves, Susan. 'Why was Dryden's *Mr Limberham* banned?: a problem in Restoration theatre history'. *Restoration and Eighteenth-Century Theatre Research* 13.1 (1974): 1–11.

Stedman, Jane W. *W. S. Gilbert: A Classic Victorian and his Theatre*. Oxford University Press, 1996.

Steele, Richard. *The Plays of Richard Steele*. Ed. Shirley Strum Kenny. Oxford: Clarendon Press, 1971.

Steele, Richard. *Richard Steele's* The Theatre. Ed. John Loftis. Oxford: Clarendon Press, 1962.

Stockwell, La Tourette. *Dublin Theatres and Theatre Customs 1637–1820*. 1938. Rpt. New York: Benjamin Blom, 1968.

Stokes, John. *Resistible Theatres*. London: Paul Elek, 1972.

Stokes, John, Michael R. Booth and Susan Bassnett. *Bernhardt, Terry, Duse*. Cambridge University Press, 1988.

Stone, George Winchester, Jr, and George M. Kahrl. *David Garrick: A Critical Biography*. Carbondale: Southern Illinois University Press, 1979.

Stratman, Carl J. *Britain's Theatrical Periodicals 1720–1967*. New York: New York Public Library, 1972.

Strindberg, August. *Miss Julie*. Trans. Michael Meyer. London: Eyre Methuen, 1976.

Stuart, Charles Douglas, and A. J. Park. *The Variety Stage: A History of the Music Halls from the Earliest Period to the Present Times*. London: Unwin, 1895.

Summerfield, Penny. 'The Effingham Arms and the Empire: deliberate selection in the evolution of music hall in London'. In *Popular Culture and Class Conflict, 1590–1914*. Ed. Eileen Yeo and Stephen Yeo. Brighton: Harvester Wheatsheaf, 1981, 216–18.

Survey of London. Vol. xxxv. *The Theatre Royal Drury Lane and the Royal Opera House Covent Garden*. Ed. F. H. W. Sheppard. London: Athlone Press, 1970.

Swift, Jonathan. *Irish Tracts, 1728–1733*. Ed. Herbert Davis. Oxford: Basil Blackwell, 1955.

Symons, Arthur. *Plays, Acting, and Music*. New York: Dutton, [1903].

Syrett, Netta. *The Finding of Nancy*. Unpublished ms. Lord Chamberlain's Plays. British Library.

Syrett, Netta. *The Sheltering Tree*. London: Bles, 1939.

Tave, Stuart M. *The Amiable Humorist: A Study in the Comic Theory and Criticism of the Eighteenth and Early Nineteenth Centuries*. University of Chicago Press, 1960.

Taylor, Aline McKenzie. *Next to Shakespeare: Otway's* Venice Preserv'd, *and* The Orphan, *and their History on the London Stage*. Durham: Duke University Press, 1950.

Taylor, George. *Players and Performances in the Victorian Theatre*. Manchester University Press, 1989.

Taylor, John. *From Self-Help to Glamour: The Working Men's Club, 1860–1972*. Oxford: History Workshop Pamphlet, 1972.

Taylor, Tom. *The Ticket of Leave Man*. In *Plays by Tom Taylor*. Ed. Martin Banham. Cambridge University Press, 1985, 164–222.

Terriss, Ellaline. *Just a Little Bit of String*. London: Hutchinson, 1955.

Terry, Ellen. *Ellen Terry's Memoirs*. Ed. Edith Craig and Christopher St John. New York: Putnam's Sons, 1932.

'Theatrical realism'. *Spectator* 37 (15 Oct. 1864).

Thespian Dictionary; or, Dramatic Biography of the Present Age, The. 1805.

Thomas, David, and Arnold Hare, eds. *Restoration and Georgian England, 1660–1788*. Cambridge University Press, 1989.

Thompson, F. M. L. *The Rise of Respectable Society*. Cambridge, MA: Harvard University Press, 1988.

Tilley, Vesta (Matilda Alice [Powles], Lady de Freece). *The Recollections of Vesta Tilley*. London: Hutchinson, 1934.

Tomalin, Claire. *Mrs. Jordan's Profession: The Actress and the Prince*. New York: Alfred A. Knopf, 1995.

Traies, J. 'Jones and the working girl: class marginality in music-hall song, 1860–1914'. In Bratton, ed., *Music Hall*, 23–48.

Tree, Herbert Beerbohm. *Thoughts and After-Thoughts*. London: Cassell, 1913.

Troubridge, St Vincent. *The Benefit System in the British Theatre*. London: Society for Theatre Research, 1967.

Troubridge, St Vincent. 'Theatre riots in London'. In *Studies in English Theatre History in Memory of Gabrielle Enthoven*. London: Society for Theatre Research, 1952, 84–97.

Trussler, Simon. *The Cambridge History of British Theatre*. Cambridge University Press, 1994.

Vanbrugh, Sir John. *Sir John Vanbrugh: Four Comedies*. Ed. Michael Cordner. Harmondsworth: Penguin, 1989.

Van der Merwe, Pieter. *The Spectacular Career of Clarkson Stanfield, RA, 1793–1867*. Sunderland: Tyne and Wear County Council Museums, 1979.

Van Lennep, William, *et al. The London Stage 1660–1800: A Calendar of Plays, Entertainments & Afterpieces Together with Casts, Box-Office Receipts and Contemporary Comment Compiled from the Playbills, Newspapers and Theatrical Diaries of the Period*. 11 vols. Carbondale: Southern Illinois University Press, 1960–8.

Vicinus, Martha. *Independent Women: Work and Community for Single Women, 1850–1920*. University of Chicago Press, 1985.

Victor, Benjamin. *The History of the Theatres of London and Dublin from the Year 1730 to the Present Time*. 3 vols. London: T. Davies, 1761–71.

Wahrman, Dror. *Imagining the Middle Class*. Cambridge University Press, 1995.

Walpole, Horace. *Horace Walpole's Correspondence*. Ed. W. S. Lewis *et al*. 48 vols. New Haven: Yale University Press, 1937–83.

Wearing, J. P. *The London Stage 1890–1899: A Calendar of Plays and Players*. 2 vols. Metuchen, NJ: Scarecrow Press, 1976.

Wehlte, Kurt. *The Materials and Techniques of Painting*. London: Van Nostrand Reinhold, 1975.

West, Shearer. *The Image of the Actor: Verbal and Visual Representation in the Age of Garrick and Kemble*. London: Pinter Publishers, 1991.

West, Shearer. 'The public and private roles of Sarah Siddons'. In *Sarah Siddons and her Portraitists: A Passion for Performance*. Ed. Robyn Asleson. Los Angeles: J. Paul Getty Museum, 1999.

White, Arthur F. 'The office of revels and dramatic censorship during the Restoration period'. *Western Reserve University Bulletin* n.s. 34.13 (1931): 5–45.

Whitebrook, Peter. *William Archer*. London: Methuen, 1993.

Wilde, Oscar. *The Complete Letters of Oscar Wilde*. Ed. Merlin Holland and Rupert Hart-Davis. London: Fourth Estate, 2000.

Wilde, Oscar. *The Picture of Dorian Gray*. Ed. Isobel Murray. Oxford University Press, 1981.

Wilkinson, Tate. *Memoirs of his Own Life*. 4 vols. York: printed for the author, 1790.

Wilkinson, Tate. *The Wandering Patentee; or, A History of the Yorkshire Theatres, from 1770 to the Present Time*. 4 vols. York: printed for the author, 1795.

Williams, Gary Jay. *Our Moonlight Revels: A Midsummer Night's Dream in the Theatre*. Iowa City: University of Iowa Press, 1997.

Williams, Simon. 'European actors and the star system in the American theatre, 1752–1870'. *Cambridge History of American Theatre*. Vol. I, *Beginnings to 1870*. Ed. Don B. Wilmeth and Christopher Bigsby. Cambridge University Press, 1998.

Williamson, Jane. *Charles Kemble, Man of the Theatre*. Lincoln: University of Nebraska Press, 1970.

Wilmeth, Don B. *George Frederick Cooke: Machiavel of the Stage*. Westport, CT: Greenwood Press, 1980.

Wilson, Mrs C. Baron. *Our Actresses; or, Glances at Stage Favourites, Past and Present*. 2 vols. London: Smith, Elder, 1844.

Wilson, Edwin, ed. *Shaw on Shakespeare*. New York: Dutton, 1971.

Wilson, John. *John Wilson's* The Cheats. Ed. Milton C. Nahm. Oxford: Basil Blackwell, 1935.

Wilson, John Harold. *All the King's Ladies: Actresses of the Restoration*. University of Chicago Press, 1958.

Wilson, M. Glen. 'The career of Charles Kean: a financial report'. In Richards and Thomson, eds. *Nineteenth-Century British Theatre*, 39–50.

Winston, James. *The Theatric Tourist*. London: T. Woodfall, 1805.

Winter, John Strange. *Connie, the Actress: A Novel*. London: White, 1902.

Winter, William. *Other Days; Being Chronicles and Memories of the Stage*. New York: Moffat, Yard, 1908.

Winton, Calhoun. 'Dramatic censorship'. In Hume, ed., *London Theatre World*, 286–308.

Winton, Calhoun. *John Gay and the London Theatre*. Lexington: University Press of Kentucky, 1993.

Winton, Calhoun. 'John Gay's *Beggar's Opera* and Vaclav Havel's'. In *Augustan Subjects: Essays in Honor of Martin C. Battestin*. Ed. Albert J. Rivero. Newark: University of Delaware Press, 1997.

Wolcott, John R. 'The scene painter's palette: 1750–1835'. *Theatre Journal* 33.4 (1981): 477–88.

'Women as dramatists'. *All the Year Round* (29 Sept. 1894): 299–301.

Wood, John. *A Description of Bath*. London: Bathoe, 1765.

Woodfield, Ian. *Opera and Drama in Eighteenth-Century London: The King's Theatre, Garrick and the Business of Performance*. Cambridge University Press, 2001.

Woodfield, James. *English Theatre in Transition: 1881–1914*. London: Croom Helm, 1984.

Woodrow, A. E. 'Some recent developments in theatre planning'. *Building News* (25 March 1892): 427–30.

Works in Architecture of Robert and James Adam, The. Rpt. London: Alec Tiranti, 1959.

Wroth, Warwick. *The London Pleasure Gardens of the Eighteenth Century*. London: Macmillan, 1896.

Index

Note: Italicized page numbers refer to illustrations.